A History of Silicon Valley

Almost a 3rd Edition/ 2016 Update

Piero Scaruffi

2016

Scaruffi, Piero
A History of Silicon Valley. Almost a 3rd Edition
All Rights Reserved © 2016 Piero Scaruffi

Printed and published in the United States

ISBN-13: 978-1508758730
ISBN-10: 1508758735

(In the USA only one company is authorized to sell ISBNs: Bowker. And Bowker sells them at an outrageous price when other nations issue ISBNs for free. I consider this as, de facto, one of the most blatant scams in any industry. To protest against this government-sanctioned Bowker ISBN monopoly rip-off, I opted to obtain a free ISBN from Amazon CreateSpace, which will then appear as the publisher of this book, and I encourage all authors and publishers to do the same)

Photo credits: Piero Scaruffi
Due to Bruce Damer for pictures of machines in his Digibarn.
Some pictures were also taken at the Intel Museum and at the Computer History Museum.

Table of Contents

A History Of This History of Silicon Valley

The idea for this book came to Arun Rao. At first I thought it was a stupid idea: who would want to read a history of Silicon Valley and why would it matter anyway? In Silicon Valley people are only interested in the latest release of whatever is popular and in the future (not in the past). The rest of the world probably doesn't even know where Silicon Valley is.

Luckily, at the same time I was researching the great moments and places in history when science and art boomed at the same time: Athens, Florence, Paris, etc. Those are big mysteries. Nobody in Egypt would have guessed that the next hub of creativity would have been located in the arid, boring, uncivilized land of Greece. Nobody in medieval Europe would have guessed that the next hub of creativity would have been located in Italy, a region split into dozens of tiny states, decimated by the plague, torn by endemic warfare, ruled by barbaric dynasties (and no less barbaric popes) and half occupied by foreign powers. And who would have guessed the artistic and scientific boom of France at the turn of the 19th century, after France had lost one war after the other and had gone through a civil war? These are veritable paradoxes. The history of creativity appears to be a history of paradoxes.

I started wondering which is the place in my own age that nobody would have guessed would become the hub of creativity in the 21st century. And suddenly I realized that I was living in the middle of it. Who a century ago would have bet on this area as the future of technology? Why did it happen here instead of so many more advanced regions of the East Coast and of Western Europe? The traditional explanations did not make sense. One Stanford professor encouraged his students to start businesses? Countless German professors had done so. One inventor from Bell Labs opened a small lab in Palo Alto? Countless inventors had opened laboratories on the East Coast. The nice weather? I am from Italy and the regions of Italy with splendid weather have invented very little (other than the mafia and the pizza) over the last few centuries. There was a lot more money, brains and know-how on the East Coast and in Western Europe.

Yet, here we are: the Bay Area has become the world's most spectacular show of creativity. And rather than slowing down it seems to be accelerating. As I write, Silicon Valley is the home of the #1 company in semiconductors, of the #1 company in personal computers, of the #1 company in databases, of the #1 company in Internet technology, of the #1 company in social media, and of the most valued company in the world. Fifty years ago there was no #1 here.

Why did it happen here?

To answer that question, we wrote the "red book", the first edition of our "A History of Silicon Valley" (2011). I researched the chronology, Arun, who works in the financial world, wrote analyses of the most influential events. The next question was whether anyone could be interested in reading it. We reprinted the book three times and each time sold all copies within weeks. Note: no literary agent had been interested in the book (we submitted it to more than 50), so we had given up trying to find a publisher and had self-published it with poor editing.

Arun was unhappy with the many typos and I already had a boatload of updates. When he found the time, Arun curated a new edition, the "blue book". This time he only published it as an ebook. You can purchase it on Amazon.

Needless to say, progress (or, at least, change) is endemic around here. Arun had hardly finished his massive proof-editing, revising, polishing and updating job that I already had accumulated more than 30 pages of updates. James Yan was curating the Chinese translation (Note: finding a Chinese publisher was much easier than finding a US publisher). After that was completed, I started thinking about a third edition. This time it was my turn to work while Arun was busy with his job. This "green book" is limited to my chapters but is updated to 2016 and contains dozens of little additions to the early chapters. I have become fascinated with the very early days of California. The answer to the paradox probably lies in the early history of the colonization. Furthermore, I have become intrigued by all the failed attempts to replicate Silicon Valley in other countries, and, at the same time, by the explosive success of East Asia (although a success of a different kind). Those are, in a nutshell, the novel contents of this "green book".

Piero Scaruffi
www.scaruffi.com
Silicon Valley

Introduction

This book is a history of the high-tech industry in the San Francisco Bay Area.

I have read many books on Silicon Valley. The best ones are listed in the bibliography. Most of them are (explicitly or implicitly) collections of essays. Those are easy to write. We're all good at analyzing the world. I could not find a book that is a detailed chronological history of Silicon Valley, which is, of course, much more difficult to write. I also felt that I disagreed with most of the conclusions of those books: those "essays" only partially represented Silicon Valley, and were based on a small sample of biographies and case studies. I felt that they pretty much missed the point, propagating a handful of very popular myths while missing too much of the real story. I cannot help thinking that there is a correlation between the two facts: because those authors did not study the detailed chronology of Silicon Valley, they formed a very partial vision of it. So I set out to write a detailed chronicle, densely packed with facts. I know that a detailed chronicle is not an easy book to read compared with an eloquent analysis, but that in my opinion is the book that was missing. In a sense, I wanted to see the data before drawing the conclusions. After all, my background is in the empirical sciences.

Needless to say, this also means that my history is not fictionalized and not sensationalistic. I stick to the facts. If you want to read Hollywood-style anecdotes, you are reading the wrong book.

As you read through this preface, you will find my bias to my history of Silicon Valley. It matured as I wrote. The more details I added to my chronicle, the more apparent some threads became. They may sound quite controversial to those who only heard the myths (and, obviously, to those who fabricated those myths). I just beg the reader to believe that the bias came after analyzing the data, not before.

It is difficult to write a history of Silicon Valley without mentioning what else was going on in computers around the world. Therefore this book is also a minor history of computing (and biotechnology) in disguise.

A meta-theme of this book concerns how one industry led to the next one in an apparently endless cascade of continuous reinvention: gold led to railways that led to shipping operations that led to ports that had two side effects: ports created coastal cities that needed electrical power that required high-voltage power transmission that established the region as a leader in electrical engineering; and ports needed radio communications that needed electronics that created the semiconductor industry that led to the microprocessor that led to the personal computer that created the software industry that benefited from the Internet that created huge fortunes that were invested in biotech and greentech. That's, in a nutshell, the history of the Bay Area during the 20th century. The question is how.

Silicon Valley does not exist in a vacuum. Its history cannot be divorced from the history of the Bay Area's economy and society at large. Even more importantly, its ascent cannot be dissociated from the artistic and cultural renaissance that took place in the region. The great centers of technological progress often boasted artistic creativity at the same time: Athens, Italy during the Renaissance, Belle-Epoque Paris, and Berlin at the turn of the century. Silicon Valley was part of a region in which creativity was treasured, along with a provocative, subversive and irreverent attitude. Alternative lifestyles and a utopian counterculture seem to have always been in the genes of the Bay Area, starting with the early poets and visual artists and then continuing with the hippie generation. Scholarly books tend to discuss too many abstract models and ignore the most important of all factors: creativity. Silicon Valley has consistently boasted a very high degree of creativity. It is also a unique form of creativity built around the three pillars of "freedom", "cooperation" and "play", precisely the pillars of the Bay Area counterculture over the decades. One could argue that everything else is a footnote.

It is difficult to explain where the spirit of Silicon Valley came from, unless you are familiar with the spirit of the counterculture of the Bay Area. Historians who have written mostly about the established worlds of technology and finance will find wildly different explanations for the phenomenon than a historian who has written a 1,000 page book on rock music (me).

Somewhat related is a mindset of independence and individualism that predates Silicon Valley and that led to the "do it yourself" philosophy of the hobbyists who started Silicon Valley. Traditionally, the emphasis on Silicon Valley's development has been on technology transfer from universities, in particular commercialization via startup company creation. While that certainly played an important role, the hobbyist (whether a university alumnus or not) played an equally important role. The hobbyists represent the passion to toy and tinker with novel technology. It was part of the US psyche, but in the Far West it had the additional advantage of being far enough from all the industrial colossi.

That attitude might explain Silicon Valley better than any economic theory. We tend to take for granted that Silicon Valley is an economy of high-tech companies and we think it is natural that they were started by engineers, not businessmen. But maybe we should instead look at Silicon Valley businesses from the opposite direction: because this was a place where engineers rather than businessmen started companies, then it was inevitable that their companies would be high-tech companies.

There now seems to be agreement among scholars that Silicon Valley started in the early years of the 20th century, meaning that behaviors normally associated with Silicon Valley were pioneered back then. I feel that one should go even further back. As one analyzes how the various waves of business got started, one realizes that the one thing they have in common is a spirit of the Wild West. The Wild West's eccentric and independent character is the predecessor to all the inventors and gurus of Silicon Valley. The prominent attitude towards risk-taking may also derive from the pioneers of the Wild West.

Each and every mass-consumed product has changed society, from Coca Cola's soda to McDonald's burgers, from Levi's blue jeans to Hollywood's movies. However, Silicon Valley has specialized in products that cause much bigger social change of a more endemic kind. There are, in fact, places in the world where much more sophisticated technology is created, from nuclear power plants to airplanes. But personal computers, web services and smart phones (and, in the near future, biotechnology and greentech) have changed our lives in a more invasive and pervasive manner. Somehow these are the technologies in which Silicon Valley excels. It is not about the complexity and sophistication of the technology, but about the impact it will have on human society. In a sense, Silicon Valley "loves" socially destabilizing technologies. Could it be that this happens because Silicon Valley arose from what used to be a very unstable quasi-anarchic society?

Much has been written about the "knowledge economy" of Silicon Valley, mostly by people who worked at very high levels (or did not work at all in Silicon Valley). The knowledge that the average engineer has is usually limited to her/his field. In fact, it is hyper-specialized. The anecdotal histories of Silicon Valley are full of self-made multimillionaires but they rarely talk about the thousands of engineers who retired early because their hyper-specialized skills became useless and it was just too difficult for them to retrain. Those specialists actually had very limited knowledge which was often worthless outside their cubicle. By definition, labs that are full of specialists are designed to produce incremental improvements on existing technology, not groundbreaking innovation. Most of the innovation came from elsewhere.

At the same time, though, the great innovators of Silicon Valley (Fairchild, HP Labs, Intel, Xerox PARC, Apple, Google, Facebook) built companies not so much around a technology as around their people. They hired the best and nurtured highly creative environments. The way companies cared for creating superior "firepower" inside their labs (rather than for a "return on investment") may have more to do with innovation than any other myth of Silicon Valley. And, again, a big chunk of innovation came from the independent eccentric hobbyist (whether inside or outside the academia), who did have a lot of "knowledge" about the technology and the industry, but not because of the famed networks of venture capitalists and entrepreneurs. Hobbyists invest all their spare time into their hobby, absorbing knowledge from magazines, blogs and party chats.

Many have written about the importance of venture capitalists in the development of Silicon Valley. However, we need to give credit to the biggest venture capitalist of all: the government. The history of high-tech in the Bay Area constitutes a prime example of the benefits of technologies that move from military to civilian use, and of government intervention in general. The initial impulse to radio engineering and electronics came from the two world wars, and was largely funded by the armed forces. It was governments (US and British) that funded the development of the computer, and NASA (a US government agency) was the main customer of the first integrated circuits. The ARPA (another US government agency) created the Internet. The World-Wide Web was created at CERN, a center funded by multiple European governments (the worst possible nightmare for those who hate government bureaucracies).

Much has been made of the way Silicon Valley attracts and spawns businesses, trying to explain it in terms of academic and financial factors. However, this model would not work in Siberia or the Congo, and not even in most of Western Europe and Japan. In fact, there were very few places where it could have worked, and there are still very few places where it can work today. The Bay Area managed to attract brains from all over the world thanks to its image as a sunny, "cool," advanced and cosmopolitan region, a dreamland for the highly educated youth of the East Coast, Europe and Asia. Because the Bay Area was underpopulated, those national and international immigrants came to represent not an isolated minority but almost a majority, a fact that encouraged them to behave like first-class citizens and not just as hired mercenaries. And I believe that the wave of college-level immigration got started in the 1960s, before the boom of Silicon Valley, and for reasons that are more related to the "summer of love" than to microprocessors.

The biggest of all myths must be dismissed at the onset: we must recognize that Silicon Valley invented very little. Computers were not invented in Silicon Valley. Robots were not invented here either. Silicon Valley did not invent the transistor, the integrated circuit, the personal computer, the Internet, the World-Wide Web, the browser, the search engine, social networking, nor the smart phone. Neither biotech nor greentech are from Silicon Valley. Silicon Valley was instrumental in making them go "viral." Silicon Valley has a unique (almost evil) knack for understanding the socially destabilizing potential of an invention and then making lots of money out of it; Schumpeter's "creative destruction" turned into destructive creativity. That's, ultimately, what people mean when they talk about Silicon Valley as a factory of innovation.

The eccentric independent is truly the protagonist of this story. People, especially Europeans, wonder why Silicon Valley happened where it happened. One simple answer is that the US in general is friendlier than Europe towards the eccentric independent, and California in particular is the friendliest. The suit and tie is my favorite metaphor. In Europe you can't possibly be a successful employee if you don't wear a suit and tie. Therefore the employees who rise in the hierarchy tend to be the ones who are better at dressing up, and not necessarily the ones who are more knowledgeable, competent and creative. In California even billionaires wear blue jeans and t-shirts.

Another reason why it could not happen in Europe is the risk-averse mindset that I can summarize in an autobiographical anecdote. I worked for a decade at a European multinational. Every time one of us had an idea for a new product line, the management would ask us a trick question: "Has anybody else done it yet?" If we answered "yes," the management would conclude: "Then we are too late." If we answered "no," the management would conclude: "Then there is no need for it." A case in which we could work on something new just did not exist. Silicon Valley, instead, amplified the passion of the US for risk-taking. Silicon Valley has cultivated a philosophy of risk-taking and turned it into a science.

Another key difference between Silicon Valley and most of the world, particularly Europe, is the mindset of faculty at universities. European universities are static, feudal bureaucracies in which a professor is the equivalent of a baron (granting favors to assistants) and is, in turn, the vassal of a department head. For life. On the contrary, the Bay Area's universities and colleges encourage their faculty to start their own companies.

One can finally wonder why it happened on the West Coast and not on the East Coast, which was more educated, wealthy and cosmopolitan. I think the answer is the same one as the answer to the question why the hippies were born in San Francisco, or why the Free Speech Movement was born in Berkeley: a unique strand of anti-establishment sentiment and a firm belief in changing the world.

I also felt that too little is written about the "failures" of Silicon Valley, i.e. the many industries that had a strong base here, including massive research programs at the local universities, but never made it big: robotics, laser, virtual reality, etc. Hence I also chronicle those less exciting fields.

There were a number of financial stimuli to the development of Silicon Valley. Once fortunes were created, though, Silicon Valley benefited from the generosity of its own millionaires. Philanthropy and "angel" investing provided a secondary boost to the creation of creativity. "Be creative when you are not yet rich, and support creativity when you get rich:" that could be the motto of Silicon Valley's entrepreneurs. The lifestyle of the Bay Area creates social pressure to "be different" and social pressure to "be good." Rich, self-made people who meet at a party don't just boast of how they made their money: they also boast of how they are spending it to help worthy causes or to help fledging startups. In a sense, here self-made multimillionaires feel a sense of gratitude towards the system that allowed them to become self-made multimillionaires. It's a phenomenon that has been part of the fabric of US society, and here may find its most sublime expression.

Therefore a major theme is that Silicon Valley was a sociological and economic experiment before it was a technological and financial experiment. Silicon Valley fostered a marriage of advanced technology and unbridled capitalism via a triangular relationship with utopian collectivism: Silicon Valley wed utopian collectivism and advanced technology (the sociological experiment), and, at the same time, Silicon Valley wed utopian collectivism and unbridled capitalism (the economic experiment).

Piero Scaruffi's Biography

Piero Scaruffi received a degree in mathematics (summa cum laude) in 1982 from the University of Turin, Italy, where he did work in the general theory of relativity. In 1983 he relocated to Silicon Valley to work at Olivetti's Advanced Technology Center, where he was employed first to port the Unix e-mail program to Olivetti's version of Unix and then to implement the first object-oriented system (Smalltalk) for a Wintel personal computer. In 1985 he started and managed Olivetti's Artificial Intelligence Center, leading a number of joint projects with universities in the US and Europe. After a visiting scholarship at Stanford University to conduct research on cognitive science, in 1999 he joined Intellicorp. There he continued to work on artificial intelligence-based business solutions.

Since 2003 he has been a free-lance consultant for Silicon Valley and European companies. He has lectured in three continents on "Theories of Mind" and "History of Knowledge," most recently at UC Berkeley. He has published a number of books on artificial intelligence and cognitive science, the latest ones being "The Nature of Consciousness" (2006) and "Demystifying Machine Intelligence" (2013). Meanwhile, he pioneered Internet-based journalism with thousands of articles on music, science, cinema, literature, and history. In 1985 he started his first e-zine, distributed by e-mail over the Internet. Between 1986 and 1990 he created an online database, downloadable via FTP. That database mutated into his own website Scaruffi.com in 1995. In 2006 the New York Times ran an interview with him titled "The Greatest Website of All Time."

Meanwhile, Piero has continued writing poetry both in Italian, for which he was awarded several prizes in the 1980s, and in English. His book "Synthesis" (2009) collected poems and meditations. In parallel, Piero has become a controversial music critic. His latest books on music are: "A History of Jazz Music" (2007), and "A History of Rock and Dance Music" (2009). He has organized several interdisciplinary cultural events in the Bay Area, notably the monthly "Leonardo Art Science Evening Rendezvous" (LASERs) held at Stanford, UC Berkeley and USF since 2008. He has also published an ebook "A Visual History of the Visual Arts". In 2014 he also founded the L.A.S.T. (Life Art Science Technology) festival, arguably the largest such event ever held in the Bay Area.

An avid traveler who spends months on the road, he has visited more than 150 countries of the world as of 2014.

Pioneers: Stanford University, Radio Engineering, the Melting Pot, and an Artistic Genesis (1900-25)

After the Gold Rush

Just over twenty thousand people lived in San Jose in 1900 compared with San Francisco's 342 thousand, one of the top 10 cities of the USA. There is a good reason to argue that the San Francisco counterculture was founded in 1859 by Joshua Norton, an English Jew raised in South Africa who had emigrated to San Francisco at the time of the Gold Rush but ended up dealing with rice instead of gold, and who in that year declared himself Emperor of the United States. He wore Napoleonic clothes and issued his own currency. Not only was he respected by the citizens of San Francisco, but a huge crowd showed up at his funeral.

When James Lick died in 1876, he was the wealthiest man in California. His "high-tech" occupation had been piano manufacturing. He had in fact accumulated a little fortune by building and selling pianos in South America. In Peru he had met Domingo Ghirardelli, a maker of chocolate. When Lick moved to California, he invited Ghirardelli to set up shop in San Francisco, an advice that turned out to be golden: one year later gold was discovered near Sacramento, and both immigrants benefited by the economic boom. Lick was smart enough to buy land all around the Bay Area, while living in the small village of San Jose.

Lick was planning to use his fortune to build himself the largest pyramid on Earth, but somehow the California Academy of Sciences convinced him to fund the Lick Observatory, the world's first permanently occupied mountain-top observatory, to be equipped with the most powerful telescope on Earth. That observatory, erected in 1887 on nearby Mt Hamilton, was pretty much the only notable event in the early history of San Jose.

Stanford University

Until 1919, the only road connecting San Jose to San Francisco was the old "El Camino Real," a dusty country road (at the time known as US 101) that snaked its way through orchards and barren hills. The only way to travely quickly was the Southern Pacific Railroad. It had been acquired by the railway empire of Leland Stanford, the president of the company charged with the western section of the first transcontinental railroad. Stanford was a former California governor and a US senator. The

Stanfords donated land and money to start a university near their farm after their only son, Leland Junior, died. They had a station built on the Southern Pacific route, the station of University Park, later renamed Palo Alto.

Stanford University opened in 1891. It was not the first university of the Bay Area: the Berkeley campus of the University of California had opened in 1873 at the other end of the bay. However, Leland was a man with a plan: his express goal was to create the Harvard of the West, something like New York State's Cornell University. At the time, despite the huge sums of money offered to them by Leland, neither the President of the Massachusetts Institute of Technology (MIT) in Boston, nor the President of Cornell were willing to move to such a primitive place as the Bay Area from their comfortable East Coast cities; so Leland had to content himself with a humbler choice: a relatively young Cornell graduate, David Starr Jordan. In 1892 he hired Albert Pruden Carmen from the College of New Jersey (later renamed Princeton University) to teach electricity (at the time still a new discipline) within the Physics Department. The following year, another Princeton graduate, Fred Perrine, became the first professor of electrical engineering within a department furnished with equipment donated by local electrical firms.

Stanford's Quadrangle (2010)

The light bulb (Edison) and the alternating current motor (Tesla) had been invented on the East Coast, but California pioneered their domestic use. In 1860s Horatio Livermore's Natoma Water and Mining Company, based in Folsom, had built an extensive network of dams to supply water to the miners of the Gold Rush on the American River. Leveraging that investment, in July 1895 his company opened a 35 km hydroelectric power line to bring electricity from Folsom to Sacramento, with water powering four colossal electrical generators (dynamos), the first time that high-voltage alternating current had been successfully conducted over a long distance. In September 1895 Sacramento celebrated the coming of electricity with a Grand Electrical Carnival, and very soon the streets of the state's capital were roamed by electric streetcars. Unlike on the East Coast, where electricity mainly served the industry, in the Bay Area and in Los Angeles electricity first came to the cities for public and domestic use. That also explains why electric consumer goods (such as the washing machine) would spread more rapidly in California, creating a myth of high-tech living.

Santa Clara Valley

The Santa Clara Valley (the valley between Palo Alto and San Jose) was known as the "Valley of Heart's Delight" because it was an endless expanse of orchards. Its agriculture was growing rapidly and, thanks to the invention of the refrigerated railroad car, it soon became the largest fruit production and packing region in the world. At one point there were 39 canneries in the valley, notably the San Jose Fruit Packing Company. At the peak, Chinese workers represented 48% of agricultural labor in the Santa Clara Valley. In 1863 the second railroad of California (after the pioneering Sacramento-Folsom of 1855) connected San Francisco to Mayfield (now Churhill Avenue in Palo Alto), a rough town popular with loggers (and later with students), and then to San Jose (in 1864) with a daily ride that took three and a half hours. The Menlo Park depot (built in 1867) was the major station on that route until Palo Alto began to grow.

The first transcontinental railroad was finally completed in 1869, linking the East Coast with Oakland (and then by ferry to San Francisco).

Perhaps the first "high tech" of the Bay Area came in the form of the aerial tramway invented in 1867 by the British-born Andrew Hallidie, a former gold miner and a bridge builder. Installed on high towers that frequently overlooked incredibly steep slopes, it was used across the Sierra Nevada to transport ore, supplies and miners. In 1873 Hallidie, using a similar design with help from German-born engineer William Ep, inaugurated the Clay Street Hill Railroad in San Francisco, the world's first cable-car system.

At the time the Bay Area also had its flirt with oil, in fact predating the celebrated Edward Doheny well of 1892 that started the oil rush in Los Angeles. In 1879 a San Francisco banker and politician, Charles Felton, founded the Pacific Coast Oil Company (PCO). Within a few months the new company discovered large oil deposits on Moody Gulch, a few kms west of San Jose in the south bay. In 1880 PCO opened a refinery in the island Alameda, located near Oakland by the bay, i.e. with good access to the railroad terminal and the port. In 1902 Rockefeller's Standard Oil, that two years earlier had acquired PCO, built a new refinery further north, in what is now Richmond, one of the largest and most advanced refineries in the world. In 1907 this refinery invented Zerolene, one of the most successful Standard Oil products.

The agricultural boom increased the demand for firewood and lumber, which made the fortune of the Santa Clara Valley Mill & Lumber Company of Felton. (But mostly the boom made the fortune of the "railroad barons", who provided the main form of transportation for goods and people. In fact, Santa Clara county confronted the arrogant railroad empires in a case that became famous in and had consequences for the whole nation: in 1886 the Supreme Court of the USA decreed that corporations should have the same rights as persons, and therefore the Southern Pacific Railroad Company was entitled to deduct mortgage from its taxable income just like any household). And, of course, ports dotted the bay, notably Redwood City's port that shipped lumber to San Francisco. Redwood City was located in the "Peninsula," i.e. the stretch of land between San Francisco and Palo Alto.

Most of the Peninsula belonged to San Mateo County and was underpopulated. The county road from San Francisco to Belmont (north of Redwood City) served the wealthy San Franciscan who had bought a mansion in the countryside, typically for the summer, when San Francisco was blanketed by its famous fog. These mansions usually controlled a large tract of land and constituted self-sufficient agricultural units. The First World War (1917) helped populate one town, Menlo Park, just north of Palo Alto, where the Army established Camp Fremont to train tens of thousands of soldiers.

The Bay Area became one in the early years of the 20th century. In the 1880s Frank Smith, who had made his fortune with his borax mines in Nevada and Death Valley, settled in Oakland and began to create a network of railways that eventually (1903) would become the Key System, connecting San Francisco, Oakland and San Jose.

Not much else was going on in the sleepy bay accidentally discovered in 1769 by Spanish explorer Gaspar de Portola.

A lot was going in the rest of the US. The nation was booming with innovative ideas revolutionizing agriculture, industry, mining and transportation. Since there were more and more numbers to crunch, it is not surprising that in those years inventors devised several computing machines. The most influential were William Burroughs' adding machine of 1885 and Hermann Hollerith 's tabulator of 1890 (chosen for the national census). However, the new sensation at the turn of the century was electricity, which was enabling a whole new spectrum of appliances, from the light bulb to the phonograph.

Electrical Engineering

The railway brought people to the Bay Area, and created the first fortunes. But then, the Bay Area needed electricity. California had plenty of water, coming down from its mighty Sierra Nevada mountain range. Entrepreneurs understood that dams (hydroelectric plants) could provide the electrical power needed by the coastal cities, and engineers were working on solving the problem of how to distribute that power. The East Coast had not faced the problem of carrying high-tension voltage over long-distances, but that was precisely the problem to be solved on the West Coast. Stanford professors and students, under the leadership of the new head of the Electrical Engineering Department, Harris Ryan, another Cornell alumnus who had arrived in 1905, helped solve the problem. They inaugurated a cooperative model between university and industry. The Bay Area's electrical power companies used the Stanford High Voltage Laboratory (as well as the one at UC Berkeley) for the development of long-distance electric power transmission. That cooperation, in addition, raised a generation of electrical engineers that could match the know-how of the East Coast.

Radio Engineering

At the same time, San Francisco's inhabitants showed a voracious interest in the radio technology invented in Europe at the turn of the century. The Italian inventor Guglielmo Marconi, then in Britain, had galvanized the sector with his long-distance radio transmissions, beginning in 1897 and culminating with the radio message from the US President Theodore Roosevelt to the British king Edward VII of 1903. Marconi's company set up radio stations on both sides of the Atlantic to communicate with ships at sea. However, it was not yet trivial how to create a wireless communication system.

In 1906 an independent with a degree from Yale, Lee DeForest, had built a vacuum tube in New York without quite understanding its potential as a signal amplifier. In fact his invention, the "audion", was useful to amplify electrical signals, and therefore to wireless transmissions. (In 1904 the British chemist John-Ambrose Fleming had invented the two-element amplifier, or "diode", and a few months before DeForest the Austrian physicist Robert von Lieben had already built a three-element amplifier, or "triode"). In 1910 DeForest moved to San Francisco and got into radio broadcasting, a business that he had pioneered in January when he had broadcasted from New York when he had broadcasted from New York a live performance by legendary Italian tenor Enrico Caruso. In fact, DeForest is the one who started using the term "radio" to refer to wireless transmission when he formed his DeForest Radio Telephone Company in 1907. However, his early broadcasts did not use the audion yet. Interest in radio broadcasting was high in the Bay Area, even if there were no mass-produced radios yet. A year earlier, in 1909, Charles Herrold in San Jose had started the first radio station in the US with regularly scheduled programming, including songs, using an arc transmitter of his own design. Charles Herrold had been one of Stanford's earliest students and founded his own College of Wireless and Engineering in San Jose.

The Bay Area stumbled into electronics almost by accident. In 1909 another Stanford alumnus, Cyril Elwell, had founded the Poulsen Wireless Telephone and Telegraph Company in Palo Alto, later renamed the Federal Telegraph Corporation (FTC), to commercialize a new European invention. In 1903 the Danish engineer Valdemar Poulsen invented an arc transmitter for radio transmission, but no European company was doing anything with it. Elwell understood its potential was not only technological but also legal: it allowed him to create radio products without violating Marconi's patents. Elwell acquired the US rights for the Poulsen arc. His radio technology, adequately funded by a group of San Francisco investors led by Beach Thompson, blew away the competition of the East Coast. In 1912, he won a contract with the Navy, which was by far the biggest consumer of radio communications. Thus commercial radiotelegraphy developed first in the US. The "startup" was initially funded by Stanford's own President, David Starr Jordan, and employed Stanford students, notably Edwin Pridham. Jordan had just inaugurated venture-capital investment in the region.

In need of better receiver amplifiers for the arc transmissions, FTC hired Lee DeForest, who by 1912 had finally realized that his audion could be used as an amplifier. The problem with long-distance telephone and radio transmissions was that the signal was lost en route as it became too faint. DeForest's vacuum tube enabled the construction of repeaters that restored the signal at intermediate points. The audion could dramatically reduce the cost of long-distance wireless communications. FTC began applying the audion to develop a geographically distributed radiotelegraphy system. The first tower they had built, in July 1910, was on a San Francisco beach and it was 90 meters tall. Yet the most impressive of all was inaugurated in 1912 at Point San Bruno (just south of the city), a large complex boasting the tallest antenna in the world (130 meters).

By the end of 1912 FTC had grown; it had stations in Texas, Hawaii, Arizona, Missouri and Washington besides California. However, the Poulsen arc remained the main technology for radiotelephony (voice transmission) and, ironically, FTC was no longer in that business. Improvements to the design by recent Cornell graduate Leonard Fuller (mostly during World War I, when the radio industry was nationalized to produce transmitters for the Navy) that allowed the audion to amplify a signal a million times eventually led FTC to create the first global wireless communication system. The audion was still used only for receivers, while most transmitters were arc-based. It was only in 1915 that DeForest realized that a feedback loop of audions could be used to build transmitters as well. DeForest had already (in 1913) sold the patent for his audion to Graham Bell's AT&T in New York, and AT&T had already used it to set up the first coast-to-coast telephone line (January 1915), just in time for the Panama-Pacific International Exposition. Meanwhile, DeForest had moved to New York. There, in 1916, he shocked the nation by broadcasting the results of the presidential elections with music and commentary from New York to stations within a range of 300 kilometers, and this time using an audion transmitter. Radiotelephony would switch from the Poulsen arc to his audion during the 1920s. In due time Leo Fuller took Elwell's place as chief engineer of FTC, in 1920 Navy engineer and former Marconi engineer Haraden Pratt was hired to launch commercial wireless telegraph service, and sugar magnate Rudolph Spreckels bought control of FTC.

The wireless industry was booming throughout the US, aided by sensational articles in the mainstream press. Earle Ennis had opened a company (Western Wireless Equipment Company) to sell wireless equipment for ships. He also ran a radio broadcast to deliver news to ships at sea. In 1910 he organized the first air-to-ground radio message, thus showing that the same technology could be used by the nascent airline industry.

Because of its maritime business, the Bay Area became one of the largest centers for amateur radio. The Bay Counties Wireless Telegraph Association was founded in 1907 by (then) amateurs such as Haraden Pratt, Ellery Stone and Lewis Clement. Among the amateurs of the second decade were Charlie Litton, an eleven-year old prodigy who operated an amateur station in Redwood City in 1915, and Frederick Terman, a teenager who operated an amateur station in Palo Alto in 1917. Some of those amateurs went on to create small companies. Little did they know that their hobby would in time of war constitute a strategic industry for the Air Force, Navy and Army: during World War I (in 1918) Elwell's technology would be a pillar of naval communications for the US. The Navy had set up radio stations all over the place. In January 1918 the President of the US, Woodrow Wilson, proudly spoke live to Europe, the Far East and Latin America.

Magnavox Corp. was founded in 1910 in Napa (north of the bay). It was the brainchild of Peter Jensen (one of the Danish engineers imported by FTC to commercialize the Poulsen arc) and Edwin Pridham (a Stanford graduate who also worked at FTC). In 1917 they introduced a new type of electrical loudspeaker.

Alas, after World War I it became obvious that radio technology was strategic, and it couldn't be left in the hands of West-Coast independents.

The US government basically forced a large East-Coast company, General Electric, to buy the US business of Marconi. The US government also helped the new company to acquire the most important radio patents. Thus a new giant, RCA, was born and soon became the dominant player in consumer electronics, as the number of radios grew from 5,000 in 1920 to 25 million in 1924. Hence FTC was doomed and other Bay Area-based radio companies had to live with only military applications.

Radio engineering created two worlds in the Bay Area that would greatly influence its future: a high-tech industry and a community of high-tech amateurs.

Culture and Society

In the 1890s most of California was still unexplored. A vast area of the state, the Sierra Nevada, was virtually inaccessible. The fascination for finding out what lay inside drew men from all backgrounds but especially scientists. In 1860 (just a few years after becoming a state of the USA) California had created the Office of State Geologist and had hired Josiah Whitney, professor of geology at Harvard University, to lead it. Between 1863 and 1864 Whitney had led expeditions that had included botanists, zoologists, paleontologists and topographers to explore the High Sierra, discovering" what today are known as Yosemite and King's Canyon national parks. Another geologist, Clarence King, who had traveled overland to California in 1863 from Yale, had become the first white man to spot Mount Whitney, the highest mountain in the USA outside of Alaska. The mountains were largely explored by the least documented of all explorers: the European shepherds, who probably created many of the trails used today by mountaineers. The High Sierra was an ideal terrain for sheep, thanks to its many meadows and relatively mild climate. One such shepherd was John Muir, originally from Scotland, a nomadic sawyer who had reached San Francisco in 1868, having traveled by steamship from Florida via Cuba and Panama. He settled in Yosemite for a few years and eventually became influential enough to convince the USA to create Yosemite and Sequoia National Parks in 1890, but never actually hiked what is today North America's most famous trail, the John Muir Trail from Yosemite to Mt Whitney. The idea for that trail must be credited to Theodore Solomons, born and raised in San Francisco, who in 1892 set out to independently explore regions of the Sierra Nevada that no white man had seen before. The 1890s were the golden age of Sierra exploration.

San Francisco was still living with the legacy of the "Gold Rush" of 1849. The "Barbary Coast," as the red-light district was known, was a haven for brothels and nightclubs. The thousands of Chinese immigrants who had been lured to California to build railways, mine gold and grow food had fathered a new generation that settled in "Chinatown," the largest Chinese community outside Asia. The port served steamers bound for the coast or Asia as well as ferry traffic to the bay and the Sacramento River, and supported a large community of teamsters and longshoremen that also made it the most unionized city in the US.

Dubious characters still roamed the landscape: the career of despised media tycoon William Randolph Hearst got its start in 1887 when his father handed him the San Francisco Examiner. But there were also honest enterprising men, such as Amadeo Giannini, who founded the Bank of Italy in 1904 to serve the agricultural economy of the Santa Clara Valley (it was later renamed Bank of America). At the turn of the century one could already sense San Francisco's predisposition towards rebellion: John Muir's Sierra Club (formed in 1892) led the first environmental protest when the state planned a dam in Yosemite; the American Anti-Imperialist League (formed in 1898) organized the first anti-war movement when the US went to war against Spain (a war largely architected by Hearst to sell more copies of his newspapers); and the Union Labor Party (formed in 1901) became the first pseudo-socialist party to win a mayoral election in a US city. In 1871 Susan Mills and her husband Cyrus founded Mills College in Oakland, the first women's college in the western states.

Most of this was irrelevant to the rest of the nation. San Francisco made the national news in 1906 because of the earthquake and fire that leveled most of it.

California was also blessed with some of the most reformist governors in the country, notably Hiram Johnson (1911-1917), who democratized California and reduced the power of the political barons, and William Stephens (1917-1923), who did something similar to curb the political power of unions. Their policies focused on raising the living standards of the middle class, and therefore of the suburbs.

Immigration made San Francisco a cosmopolitan city. There had already been Italians when California was still under Mexican rule. They were fishermen and farmers. By the turn of the century, old and new Italians had created an Italian quarter in North Beach. Then came the Japanese, who replaced the Chinese in agriculture. At the beginning of the century San Francisco boasted two Japanese-language newspapers: "The New World" and the "Japanese American." Mexicans immigrated from 1910 to 1930, following the Mexican revolution and the construction of a railway.

San Francisco was also becoming friendly toward the arts. In 1902, the California Society of Artists was founded by a cosmopolitan group that included the Mexican-born painter Xavier Martinez and the Swiss-born painter and muralist Gottardo Piazzoni. At the California School of Design, many students were influenced by muralist and painter Arthur Mathews, one of the founders of the American Arts and Crafts Movement that tried to reconcile craftsmanship with industrial consumerism (a major national trend after the success of Boston's 1897 American Arts and Crafts

Exhibition). A symbolic event took place after the 1906 earthquake when Mathews opened his own shop (both as a craftsman and a painter) and started publishing one of the earliest art magazines in town, the Philopolis. Another by-product of the American Arts and Crafts Movement was Oakland's California College of the Arts and Crafts founded in 1907 by one of the movement's protagonists, Frederick Meyer.

More and more artists were moving to San Francisco. They created the equivalent of Paris' Montmartre artistic quarter at the four-story building called "Montgomery Block" (also nicknamed "Monkey Block"), the epicenter of San Francisco's bohemian life. Another art colony was born in the coastal city of Carmel, about two hours south of San Francisco. Armin Hansen opened his studio there in 1913. Percy Gray located there in 1922 and impressionist master William Merritt Chase taught there in 1914.

Architects were in high demand both because of the fortunes created by the railway and because of the reconstruction of San Francisco after the earthquake (for example, Willis Polk). Mary Colter studied in San Francisco before venturing into her vernacular architecture for the Southwest's desert landscape. The Panama-Pacific International Exposition of 1915, held in San Francisco, for which Bernard Maybeck built the exquisite Palace of Fine Arts, symbolized the transformation that had taken place in the area: from emperors and gold diggers to inventors and investors (and, soon, defense contractors). A major sculptor was Ralph Stackpole, who in 1913 founded the California Society of Etchers and in 1915 provided sculptures for the Panama-Pacific International Exposition, notably the Palace of Varied Industries (demolished after the exposition). Influenced by the Panama-Pacific International Exposition, during the 1920s Maynard Dixon created an original Western style of painting. Last but not least, in 1921 Ansel Adams began to publish his photographs of Yosemite. It was another small contribution to changing the reputation of that part of California and the birth of one of the most vibrant schools of photography in the world. Literature, on the other hand, lagged behind, represented by Frank Pixley's literary magazine the "Argonaut," located at Montgomery Block.

Classical music was represented by its own school of iconoclasts. From 1912 to 1916, Charles Seeger taught unorthodox techniques such as dissonant counterpoint at UC Berkeley. Starting with "The Tides of Manaunaun" (1912), pianist Henry Cowell, a pupil of Seeger, began exploring the tone-cluster technique. That piece was based on poems by John Osborne Varian, the father of Russell and Sigurd Varian, who had moved to Halcyon, a utopian community founded in 1903 halfway between San Francisco and Los Angeles by the theosophists William Dower and Francia LaDue. Varian's sons Russell and Sigurd later became friends with Ansel Adams through their mutual affiliation with the Sierra Club.

The Prehistory of Office Automation

Elsewhere (mainly in New York and Detroit) the frantic growth in statistical and bookkeeping activities, bootstrapped by the Census Bureau of the US government, was fueling a new industry: calculating machines. In 1924 Hollerith's Tabulating Machine Company of New York changed its name to International Business Machines (IBM). Other inventors created useful business machines too. In 1922 National Cash Register (NCR) of Ohio sold more than two million electrical cash registers (about 90% of the market). In 1925 Burroughs of Detroit introduced a portable adding machine (still weighing quite a bit but "portable" by a strong man).

The Bay Area had its share of glory during the boom of office calculators. In 1911 Rodney and Alfred Marchant of Oakland began selling one of the many clones of the Odhner arithmometer, and in 1918 their chief engineer, the Swedish-born Carl Friden, built an original model that established the company as one of the most innovative in calculators. In 1934 Friden would start building his own electromechanical calculators, some of the most sophisticated and most expensive on the market.

Scouts: Electrical Engineering, Nuclear Engineering, the Navy, and a Culture of Innovation (1925-40)

Stanford and Electrical Engineering

A pivotal event in the history of the Bay Area's high-tech industry took place in 1925: Harris Ryan's student, Frederick Terman (a ham radio fan who had also studied at MIT in Boston with Vannevar Bush, joined Stanford University to work at Ryan's pioneering radio-communications laboratory. Terman was the son of a Stanford professor, so he represented a highly educated generation that had been raised in the Bay Area, a step forward from the immigrants of previous decades. Within two years, the young apprentice became a visionary on his own, fostering a new science on the border between wireless communications and vacuum-tube electronics. Terman didn't just perfect the art of radio engineering. The Bay Area offered precious few opportunities for employment, and during the Great Depression that started in 1929 virtually none. Terman encouraged his students to start their own businesses rather than wait for jobs to be offered to them. After all, Stanford had perfected a number of engineering technologies that could potentially be of general interest (one being the resistance-capacity oscillator built by Bill Hewlett in 1935). Many of those students were coming from the East Coast. He encouraged them to start businesses in the Bay Area. He viewed the university as an incubator of business plans. It was a step up from Harris Ryan's philosophy of encouraging cooperation between academia and industry.

A vibrant industry was taking hold around Stanford University by the time Ryan retired in 1931 and Cyril Elwell's Federal Telegraph Corporation (FTC) moved east. Several startups were spin-offs of the early radio companies.

Stanford's student Ralph Heintz, a former radio amateur and employee of Earle Ennis, had started a business to install short-wave radios on ships and airplanes. In 1926 he founded Heintz & Kaufmann in San Francisco; but soon had to start manufacturing their own vacuum tubes to compete with RCA, for which they hired radio hobbyists Bill Eitel and Jack McCullough.

Litton Engineering Laboratories had been founded in 1932 by ham-radio hobbyist, Stanford student, and FTC manager Charlie Litton at his parents' Redwood City home to manufacture tools for vacuum tube manufacturers (the same job he had at FTC). Eitel-McCullough (later Eimac) was formed in 1934 in San Bruno by Heintz's employees Bill Eitel and Jack McCullough to develop better vacuum tubes for the amateur or ham radio market (which would become the Armed Forces' favorite tubes during the war). Another FTC employee, German-born Gerhard Fisher invented the metal detector in 1928, and founded Fisher Research Laboratories in 1931 in his home's garage in Palo Alto. Many of these independents who scouted the market for radio communications and electronics had started out as ham radio amateurs, some of them at a very early age.

Stanford's "Engineering Corner" (2010)

The local tradition of radio engineering led an immigrant to settle in San Francisco to conduct his experiments. In 1927, Philo Farnsworth, a stereotypical amateur who had been discovered in Utah by San Francisco venture capitalists Leslie Gorrell and George Everson, carried out the first all-electronic television broadcast. It was based on a theory that he had conceived as a teenager. Farnsworth's team included the young Russ Varian and Ralph Heintz. In 1931 the investors decided to cash in. They sold the company to the Philadelphia Storage Battery Company (later renamed Philco). At the time, Philco was the main maker of home radios in the US and therefore in a much better position to mass-manufacture television sets. The power of RCA, however, was such that the Russian-born scientist Vladimir Zworkyn of their New Jersey laboratories was credited by the media with inventing television. Farnsworth's reputation was saved by his good San Francisco friend, Donald Lippincott, formerly a Magnavox engineer and now an attorney, who in 1930 defended the young inventor's intellectual property against RCA. Lippincott exemplified a tradition of heavy intellectual-property litigation in the Bay Area that would be crucial to the development of the high-tech industry run by young inventors.

Berkeley and Nuclear Engineering

Meanwhile, another industry came to the Bay Area because of just one creative scientist and his groundbreaking invention. UC Berkeley had opened LeConte Hall in 1924 to enlarge its Department of Physics. It had gone on a hiring spree to fill it with young talent. In January 1931, one of these young physicists, Ernest Lawrence, hired in 1928 from Yale University, designed the first successful cyclotron (a particle accelerator). It was theoretically known that nuclear particles undergo transformations as they travel faster, but no lab had devised a machine yet that could accelerate particles to the point that this phenomenon would be observable. It was called "cyclotron" because its principle was to send particles in a loop through the same accelerating field, thus increasing their speed with each cycle. A former FTC executive, Leonard Fuller, had become the head of the Electrical Engineering Department at the University of California and had managed to obtain from FTC a 1000-kilowatt generator that Lawrence used to build his monster (actually quite small, just 66 centimeters in diameter). The Radiation Laboratory that Lawrence opened that year in August right halfway between LeConte Hall and the campus' bell tower (and later moved up the hill and renamed Lawrence Berkeley Lab) became one of the most celebrated research centers for atomic energy and would bring several of the world's most promising scientists to Berkeley. Another nuclear physicist, Robert Oppenheimer, had joined UC Berkeley in 1929, one year after Lawrence. He was important in shaping the intellectual mood of the campus with his passion for Eastern philosophy and his donations to socialist causes. During the 1930s, several of his friends, relatives (including the woman he married in 1940) and students were affiliated with the Communist Party. Lawrence and Oppenheimer created in Berkeley a school of nuclear physicists that would eventually take the leadership away from Western Europe.

The relevance of atomic energy became more and more self-evident as the 1930s progressed, and not only for particle physics. John Lawrence, brother of the Lawrence Berkeley Labs' founder, realized that it could be useful in another field too: in 1936 he founded the Donner Laboratory to conduct research in nuclear medicine. In 1939 Ernest Lawrence was awarded the Nobel Prize in Physics, the first time the prize came to the Bay Area. As important as Lawrence's engineering/scientific achievements was his concept of "big science:" he created a large interdisciplinary team of engineers and scientists to focus on a practical project. It didn't come just out of good will, but also out of necessity: the construction of his increasingly bigger cyclotrons required an increasingly large number of specialists in different disciplines. Lawrence's team would include four future Nobel Prize winners (Edwin McMillan, Luis Alvarez, Glenn Seaborg and Emilio Segre) plus mechanical engineers such as William Brobeck, as well as the physicians who followed his brother John.

Last but not least, Lawrence was skilled at obtaining donations from philanthropists, a difficult task in the middle of the Great Depression.

The Stanford counterpart to Lawrence was Swiss physicist Felix Bloch, who fled the Nazis in 1934. He and Oppenheimer organized a joint Berkeley-Stanford seminar on theoretical physics that brought European science to the West Coast. Bloch would become Stanford's first Nobel Laureate. Meanwhile, young graduate Bill Hansen imported know-how about Lawrence's accelerator and set out to find a way to use high-frequency waves to accelerate electrons to high energy.

Lawrence Berkeley Labs Overlooking UC Berkeley (2010)

NACA

The military was creating cities from empty land. The vast activity in radio engineering convinced the Navy in 1933 to open a base between Palo Alto and San Jose called Naval Air Station Sunnyvale (later renamed

Moffett Field). The contacts that had existed between the Bay Area's engineering companies and the military bureaucracy found a major outlet.

In 1915 the US government established the National Advisory Committee for Aeronautics (NACA) to help the aviation industry. In 1920 NACA created its first laboratory, the Langley Aeronautical Laboratory in Virginia. NACA was particularly influential in pioneering the use of the wind tunnel (an energy intensive facility) to improve aircraft aerodynamics. In 1939 NACA added the Ames Aeronautical Laboratory at Moffett Field, also with its own wind tunnel. Charles Lindbergh selected this area (that didn't have powerful political sponsors) because of the facilities at the naval air base (including an adequate supply of electricity for the wind tunnels). The wind tunnel was designed, like the one in Virginia, by a Stanford alumnus, Russell Robinson. The aviation industry was in Los Angeles, but the Bay Area produced many of the components for this industry. In 1958 NACA would be absorbed into the newly created NASA (National Aeronautics and Space Administration) at Moffett Field. The area to the north would develop into the town of Mountain View, and the area to the south would develop into Sunnyvale (originally the two were part of just one huge Mexican ranch).

NASA Ames at Moffett Field

Culture and Society

Meanwhile, San Francisco was changing. It had become one of the financial capitals of the US. In 1930, its Ferry Building was the second busiest transportation terminal in the world after Manhattan. The Bayshore

Highway opened in 1932 to Palo Alto and in 1937 reached San Jose. In 1964 it would be renamed US I-101, previously the number for El Camino Real. The rapidly spreading urban area required the building of the Oakland Bay Bridge and of the Golden Gate Bridge, completed respectively in 1936 and 1937. The latter was the longest bridge yet built in the world. Rich patrons allowed the city to open its own Museum of Art (1935) and to found the first professional ballet company in the US (1933), the San Francisco Opera Ballet, whose protagonists were three brothers, William, Harold and Lew Christensen, who had cut their teeth in the vaudeville. William Christensen on Christmas Eve of 1944 premiered Pyotr Tchaikovsky's "Nutcracker" in the USA, turning that ballet into an enduring nation-wide Christmas tradition.

Capitalizing on the pioneers of the previous generation, the arts flourished. Among the new talents were: the surrealist sculptor Adaline Kent, one of Ralph Stackpole's students at the California School of Fine Arts; the Japanese-born painter Chiura Obata, famous for his 1927 paintings of the Sierra Nevada, who founded the East-West Art Society; and the bizarrely reclusive Achilles Rizzoli, who between 1935 to 1944 created intricate visionary architectural drawings in the "Art Nouveau" style. German-born Abstract Expressionist painter Hans Hofmann moved to UC Berkeley in 1930 and became the most influential teacher of the Bay Area, pushing for curricula that were heavy on modern art. It turned the Bay Area into one of the US's friendliest regions for experimental artists.

The Bay Area was probably the only place in the world where the dominant fine art was photography (perhaps as a reaction to Los Angeles' movie industry). After Ansel Adams, the Bay Area produced Dorothea Lange, famous for her work on the homeless of the Great Depression, Imogen Cunningham, famous for her industrial landscapes of the late 1920s, and James Weston, based in Carmel, famous for his still lifes and nudes of the late 1920s. Seven Bay Area-based photographers (including Adams, Cunningham, Weston and Weston's apprentices Willard Van Dyke and Sonya Noskowiak) founded Group f/64 in opposition to Alfred Stieglitz's pictorialism that had dominated photography in the first decades of the century. The group held their first (highly publicized) exhibition in 1932.

Another art that was relatively unique to San Francisco (as far as the US goes) was wall painting, heavily influenced by Diego Rivera's work in Mexico. In 1936 muralist Edith Hamlin painted the Western-themed murals for the Mission High School. Whereas the dominant art in Los Angeles generated colossal revenues and the arts on the East Coast created world-famous movements, San Francisco artists were mostly independents and eccentrics, just like the hobbyists of radio engineering.

In 1935 art historian Grace Morley founded the San Francisco Museum of Art, the second museum in the US devoted exclusively to modern art. Again, San Francisco had its own idea of what "modern art" was. In 1946 Morley hired filmmaker Frank Stauffacher to start the "Art in Cinema" series, that inspired the California School of the Arts to assign a film course to Sidney Peterson. Peterson, who had been a painter and sculptor in France at the time of Dada, directed the manifesto of the San Francisco avantgarde with poet James Broughton: "The Potted Psalm" (1946).

In 1939 San Francisco celebrated its status as a vibrant center of innovation with a World's Fair (the "Golden Gate International Exposition") that was held on an artificial island in the middle of the bay, Treasure Island. Its highlight was Ralph Stackpole 's 24-meter tall colossus "Pacifica" (dynamited in 1942 to make room for a naval base). In the years that it lasted, 16 million visitors came to visit.

In 1911 James Phelan had a villa built in the south bay, precisely in the hills of Saratoga overlooking Santa Clara Valley. He had made his fortune during the Gold Rush as a trader and a banker and had then become the mayor of San Francisco and was soon to become a US Senator from California. Phelan had bequeathed this villa (named "Montalvo" in honor of the 16th century Spanish writer who coined the name "California") to the state so that it could be turned into a cultural center to support promising artists, writers, musicians and architects. It took a while, but in 1939, Villa Montalvo opened the doors to an artist residency program, the first one in the Western United States.

The great musical innovator of the Bay Area (and perhaps of the whole country) was Henry Cowell, a bisexual who spent four years in prison for that "crime." In 1930 he commissioned the Russian instrument builder Leon Theremin to create the first electronic rhythm machine (the "Rhythmicon"). Cowell later taught the influential course "Music of the Peoples of the World" at UC San Francisco (already tested in 1933 at the New School for Social Research in New York) promoting atonality, non-Western modes, percussion ensembles, and even chance composition. He also was probably the first classical composer to live a parallel life as a successful pop songwriter. In San Francisco his pupil Lou Harrison took advantage of the Bay Area's ethnic Babel and incorporated Chinese opera, Native-American folk, jazz, and later the gamelan music of Indonesia into Western classical music. In New York, his other pupil John Cage became famous by expanding on several of his master's intuitions.

Rich patrons also funded San Francisco's legendary nightlife, a legacy of "Barbary Coast" that religious groups tried in vain to suppress. In 1936 Joe Finocchio opened the gay bar "Finocchio's" on Broadway. Those were the years of the Great Depression, which had started with the financial collapse of 1929. However, not a single bank failed in San Francisco. The

Bay Area was certainly affected by the crisis, but it fared a lot better than the rest of California and of the US. In fact, it was during the Great Depression that San Francisco leapfrogged to the higher ranks of metropolitan areas, despite remaining a relatively small city in itself. After growing rapidly since the earthquake (416,000 people in 1910), the population stabilized at 634,000 during the 1930s. Residential growth was now spreading to the north, east and south.

At the time San Francisco was famous around the country for its ethnic diversity, but little else. At the end of the 1930s San Francisco was still a relatively lawless place. A popular joke was that the organized crime of Chicago and New York had no chance to infiltrate San Francisco because the entire city was just one big racket.

Stanford and US Industry

Stanford University was becoming a major center of innovation, and its doctrine of encouraging entrepreneurship was beginning to pay off. In 1937 Fred Terman's students William Hewlett and David Packard started working on an audio-oscillator. In January 1939 they founded a company called Hewlett-Packard in a Palo Alto garage. Their first customer was Walt Disney: the Hollywood animation company purchased their oscillator in 1939 for the animation film "Fantasia." Also in 1937 Stanford University's Professor William Hansen teamed up with two hobbyists who had a brilliant idea: brothers Sigurd Varian (an airplane pilot) and Russ Varian (a Stanford dropout who had roomed with Hansen, and a former engineer in Philo Farnsworth's television laboratory). They were refining an electronic device that worked as an amplifier for generating electromagnetic waves at higher frequencies than radio frequency (microwaves). Working with Hansen at Stanford they developed the klystron tube, the first generator of microwaves. This invention revolutionized and greatly improved radar technology (and, in fact, enabled airborne radars, Sigurd Varian's original motivation) on the eve of World War II. The radar dish broadcasts pulses of microwaves, which bounce back whenever they hit an object in a time interval that reveals the distance of the object.

These pioneers knew each other well via Stanford: in 1938 Terman organized a research team around Russ Varian, with Charles Litton reporting to him and Dave Packard reporting to Litton.

In 1940 the cash-rich Sperry Corporation of New York, which specialized in aircraft navigation equipment, basically "bought" Hansen and the klystron from Stanford. It rewarded Stanford with a huge investment in its electrical engineering lab, allowing the lab to grow even more rapidly. Stanford already had a national reputation in high-voltage power transmission. It had now found the money to expand in electronics too. The Varian story was a further refinement of the FTC story:

interaction between industry and university led to an advanced technology whose first customer was the government and whose first application was warfare.

The house where Bill Hewlett and Dave Packard started HP – the garage to the left

Progress in Electronic Computation

Computers were being invented very far from the Bay Area. In 1931 Vannevar Bush (the Professor of Electrical Engineering at MIT in Boston who had graduated Terman in 1924) constructed the most sophisticated of mechanical analog computers, the "differential analyzer", installed in 1935 at the Moore School of the University of Pennsylvania. In 1936 the British mathematician Alan Turing described a machine capable of performing logical reasoning by manipulating symbols (like a mathematician does), the "Turing machine." He then described a "universal Turing Machine," capable of simulating any Turing machine by reading a symbolic description of the machine to be simulated.

High-tech Construction

The New Deal and World War II sent huge government investments to the West Coast. Henry Kaiser, who had paved roads in Cuba, was one of the contractors for the colossal concrete Hoover Dam (inaugurated in

1936), then built the first integrated steel mill in the Pacific states (at Fontana, near Los Angeles, in 1942). During World War II his shipyards built thousands of cargo ships (Richmond alone in the north Bay built 727) employing the latest technology (inherited from the prefabrication techniques of dam building) that allowed him to shorten the shipbuilding process from one year to 48 days. Those shipyards alone caused a population boom. Kaiser was getting immensely rich but his conglomerate was actually known for treating the workers humanely. In the 1940s Kaiser's corporate welfare programs was among the most generous in the USA. After two more giant dams (the Bonneville and Grand Coulee Dams), Kaiser then ventured into aluminum, steel, real estate, broadcasting and many other businesses.

The Hoover Dam also created the fortune of another Bay Area construction and engineering company, the one that would become number one in the country. Started by a railroad worker, Warren Bechtel, it remained (and still remains) privately held within the family. Bechtel also built San Francisco's Bay Bridge (1936). In 1937 John McCone created Bechtel-McCone-Parsons (BMP) to build oil refineries, starting with one in Richmond. In 1940 Bechtel began expanding abroad with a project in Venezuela. In 1942 it built Marin City, north of the Golden Gate Bridge, for guest worker housing during the wartime boom of shipyards. It then ventured into power plants and chemical plants all over the world.

The Aerospace Industry in Los Angeles

The Bay Area was also home to early aviation (after all, John Joseph Montgomery of Santa Clara College had built one of the earliest airplanes in the 1880s, two decades before the Wright brothers),, although not much came out of it: Allan Loughead started out in San Francisco with his Alco Hydro-Aeroplane Company in 1912 before founding Lockheed in Los Angeles a decade later.

The history of aviation in the Los Angeles area well illustrates how California developed via the interaction between defense spending, university and industry. Aviation was, after all, the first high-tech industry to spread globally from California.

In 1921 Donald Douglas founded an aircraft-building company in Los Angeles to commercialize his "Cloudster", the first airplane to lift a load exceeding its own weight, and in 1925 Claude Ryan founded a company in San Diego to build the Ryan M1 (Charles Lindbergh's "Spirit of St Luis" that flew from New York to Paris in 1927 was a Ryan plane). In 1926 Allan Loughead, Jack Northrop and Kenneth Jay founded yet another company to build aircrafts, Lockheed. Both Douglas and Lockheed soon came to rely on lucrative contracts from the military (e.g., the World

Cruisers of 1924, the T2D-1 torpedo bomber of 1927, the flying boat Sinbad of 1930).

Using a donation by philanthropist Daniel Guggenheim, the California Institute of Technology (formerly Throop Polytechnic Institute) opened the Guggenheim Aeronautical Laboratory (GALCIT) in 1928. The lab featured a state-of-the-art wind tunnel and teachers such as Harry Bateman (a British mathematician), Todor Karman (a Hungarian physicist) and Douglas' chief engineer Arthur Raymond. This group pioneered the collaboration among university research, industrial labs and government agencies that would become common in the Bay Area. That collaboration changed a world that was still dominated by railroads.

Meanwhile an important decision was taken by the government. The Post Office had launched air mail in 1918 using old British planes built by Geoffrey de Havilland at the Aircraft Manufacturing Company (Airco), then the largest aircraft manufacturer in the world. Transcontinental air mail had begun in 1924 but the complexity of manning the equipment required for safe long-distance air travel had prompted the government to subcontract mail delivery to commercial airlines. A scandal led in 1934 to a law ordering the dissolution of holding companies mixing airlines and aircraft manufacturers, thus boosting competition in the field.

One year after its DC-1 had set a new record for coast-to-coast flight (11 hours from Los Angeles to New York in April 1935), Douglas struck gold with the 21-passenger DC3 (first delivered to American Airlines in June 1936) that did for air travel what the Ford Model T did for car travel. Its transcontinental record, meanwhile, was beaten repeatedly by Howard Hughes' H-1 Racer planes, down to 7 hours in 1937. By 1939 Southern California was home to most of the aircraft industry of the USA and Douglas airplanes were carrying more than 90% of civilian air passengers.

Meanwhile at GALCIT the self-taught Jack Parsons experimented with solid-fuel rockets (the JATO of 1942), Karman's student Frank Malina with liquid fuel (the WAC Corporal of 1945, built jointly by Douglas and GALCIT), and the Chinese-born Qian Xuesen, aka Hsue-shen Tsien, even speculated about nuclear-powered rockets. In 1942 these university researchers (Karman, Malina, Parsons) founded a company, Aerojet Engineering, thus pioneering the model of the start-up. In 1944 Karman, Parsons and Malina founded the Jet Propulsion Laboratory (JPL) to work on rockets, ostensibly a joint project between the army and the university, and in 1945 Karman was drafted by the military to start Project RAND at Douglas, the prototype of the "think tank", later turned into the self-standing RAND Corporation (1948).

World War II made the fortune of several other aircraft builders: Northrop, who founded his own company in 1939 in Los Angeles, Jim McDonnell, who established his firm in St Louis (Missouri) also in 1939, and, of course, Boeing (founded in 1916 in Seattle by William Boeing, that reached its wartime apogee with the B-29 of 1944, the first intercontinental bomber). In the Los Angeles area the other big ones (besides Douglas, Lockheed and Northrop) were Vultee (originally founded by Jerry Vultee and Vance Breese as the Airplane Development Corporation in 1932 to sell six-passenger V-1 passenger planes to American Airlines) and Dutch Kindelberger's North American Aviation, another huge beneficiary of military contracts. Lockheed became a darling of the Air Force when its Lockheed Advanced Development Projects (LADP), aka "Skunk Works", located on the northern side of the San Gabriel mountains, established in late 1943 under Kelly Johnson, designed the first jet fighter of the USA, the P-80 Shooting Star, later followed by other strategic projects like the spy plane U-2 (1957) and the F-104 Starfighter (1958). By 1943 the industry had already built 100,000 warplanes. By the end of the war industrial production in the Los Angeles area was second only to the Detroit area. Uniquely in history, Los Angeles had been industrialized in a brief period of time (the war) and largely by government intervention, creating a third massive industrial region (after the Northeast and the Midwest). In other words, World War II had the side effect of revolutionizing the economy of California and of integrating California with the national industrial complex. World War II accelerated western migration, California's population growing from 7 million in 1940 to 10.5 in 1950, until in 1962 California passed New York state as became the most populous state. If California had been one of the three top beneficiaries of military spending during the World War, it would become the number one in 1958 during the Cold War.

Weird people already abounded in those days. For example, architect Julia Morgan was designing a castle on the coast for newspaper magnate William Randolph Hearst (eventually completed in 1947). But rocket science went beyond the extravagant. The esoteric cult Ordo Templi Orientis, founded in Germany by Theodor Reuss, had spread to Britain, where it fell under the sell of magician Aleister Crowley, who had turned it into his own personal cult, known as "Thelema" from the manifesto published by Crowley as "The Book of the Law" (1904). By the end of World War II only the California chapter survived, surprisingly led by one of the most distinguished rocket scientists, Jack Parsons.

Moles: The Military Boom, Artistic Boom, and Economic Boom (1941-48)

The Bay Area as a Strategic Weapon

The Japanese attack on Pearl Harbor dragged the US into World War II. It had an enormous impact on Bay Area scientists since they had the most advanced radio technology in the nation..

In 1940 the US government sponsored a new laboratory at the MIT, the Radiation Laboratory (or "Rad Lab"), for the purpose of developing defense systems. The MIT Rad Lab became the birthplace of cybernetics thanks to the work of Norbert Wiener and others. The Rad Lab (as well as its successor, the Research Laboratory of Electronics) applied Ernest Lawrence's concept of "big science": large interdisciplinary teams working together to solve mission-critical problems.

In June 1941, the US government established a new agency (the Office of Scientific Research and Development) to coordinate nation-wide scientific research for the US military, and put Vannevar Bush in charge of it. Traditionally the US government (like every other government) had relied on top-secret military labs (or their private contractors) to develop military technology. Bush, instead, directed funding to and influenced the direction of research programs at universities. Bush's approach created a new template for interaction between science and government, as well as between science and war.

Fred Terman had graduated from the MIT in 1924 with a thesis supervised by Bush, and the Rad Lab summoned Terman from Stanford to direct the Radio Research Laboratory, that in 1942 was being relocated to Harvard University. Terman was basically in charge of electronic warfare, a new kind of warfare that was fought in labs instead of tanks, ships or planes.

Berkeley was no less strategic, thanks to its know-how in nuclear physics. In 1942, the US government launched the "Manhattan Project" to build a nuclear bomb, and appointed UC Berkeley Professor Robert Oppenheimer in charge of it. Oppenheimer applied Lawrence's concept of "big science" and assembled a large team of physicists to design the weapon. The project soon exceeded the capacity of the Berkeley campus and was moved to Los Alamos in New Mexico. It was Lawrence himself who designed an electromagnetic process to separate the explosive U-235 isotope from the U-238 isotope of uranium that led to the building of the facility at Oak Ridge in Tennessee. In parallel Edwin McMillan and Glenn Seaborg at the Radiation Lab in Berkeley used the cyclotron to discover a new element, plutonium, and immediately realized that it was even better than U-235 at sustaining an explosive chain reaction. The government rushed to build another plant, this time to produce plutonium, at Hanford in the state of Washington. The "Trinity" bomb that was detonated in July 1945 in the desert of New Mexico used plutonium. The bomb dropped on Hiroshima one month later used U-235, the one dropped on Nagasaki used plutonium.

The Cyclotron

Business was mainly affected by World War II in terms of providing high-tech components to the booming defense industry. This was a lucrative business that turned several small companies into giants.

Companies also benefited from the war by cultivating new technologies. The Dalmo Manufacturing Company, based in San Carlos since 1944, had evolved from the shop that Tim Moseley had opened in 1921 in San Francisco to manufacture simple electrical appliances. During World War II it developed the first airborne radar antenna, which was crucial for the air force to win the war. The invention was largely the work of the Russian-born engineer Alexander Poniatoff, who had joined the company in 1934. Moseley's company (now a joint venture with Westinghouse renamed Dalmo-Victor and based in nearby Belmont) was becoming a major defense contractor. Meanwhile, in 1944 Moseley himself invested in Alexander Poniatoff's new company Ampex, located in San Carlos, to manufacture electrical parts for radar that were hard to find. Poniatoff, however, moved into a new field, the tape recorder, a novelty that a US soldier, Jack Mullin, had brought back from occupied Germany. It was one of Germany's fields of excellence: the magnetic tape had been invented by Fritz Pfleumer in 1927. The first tape recorder (later dubbed Magnetophon) had been introduced by AEG in 1935 and perfected into a high-fidelity system in 1941. AEG used tape made by IG Farben, a manufacturer of the lethal gas used in Nazi extermination camps. In 1947, Ampex delivered its own tape recorder, which had been requested by pop-star Bing Crosby and soon became a favorite among pop and movie stars.

The First Computers

Again, the computer was being invented far from the Bay Area. Konrad Zuse built the first program-controlled computer in 1941 in Germany. The British had built a series of machines, all of them dubbed Colossus, to help decipher encrypted German messages, notably in 1943 the Colossus Mark 1, an electronic computer (it used vacuum tubes, not relays). The closest thing in the US was the "Harvard Mark I," designed by Howard Aiken of the Harvard Computation Lab and completed in February 1944 in collaboration with IBM.

In 1946 the ENIAC, or "Electronic Numerical Integrator and Computer," was unveiled by John Mauchly and his student Presper Eckert at the Moore School. But the Moore School scientists and the Hungarian-born mathematician John Von Neumann at Princeton University had already shown theoretically how it would be more efficient to build a computing machine that holds both its data and its instructions, the "stored-program architecture."

In 1943 MIT mathematician Norbert Wiener pioneered Cybernetics (later refined through a series of ten Macy Conferences from 1946 until 1953), a science devoted to the study of control and communication. In 1945 Vannevar Bush at MIT envisioned the Memex, an electromechanical device capable of accessing archives of microfilms, of creating paths of navigation by linking pages, and of combining microfilms with annotations. In 1947 John Von Neumann at Princeton University advanced the notion of self-reproducing automata. In 1948 Claude Shannon at AT&T's Bell Labs jumpstarted information theory.

In 1947, at AT&T Bell Labs in New Jersey, three scientists (John Bardeen, William Shockley and Walter Brattain) demonstrated the first transistor. The first transistor was truly made by Bardeen and Brattain, using germanium, but Shockley was the one who immediately realized the potential of the transistor: it was a better amplifier than the vacuum tube and it was easier to mass manufacture.

The main centers for research on electronic computing were Cambridge and Manchester (in Britain), Boston (Harvard and MIT),

Philadelphia (UPenn's Moore School of Electrical Engineering, BRL), New York (IBM) and New Jersey (Bell Labs, Princeton, RCA Labs). The media started publicizing the notion of the "giant brains", although only a handful of people had actually seen one and even fewer were capable of using them. In 1950 Turing (still in Britain) half-jokingly proposed a test to determine whether a machine could be considered intelligent or not.

The first programmable electronic computer was finally built in 1951 at Manchester, commercialized as the Ferranti Mark 1 (1951), the first programmable electronic computer.

The effect of WWII was that the government could assemble the best brains in computer science and electronic engineering to solve big problems instead of having them scatter among competing corporations. Once the military secrets were lifted, these scientists were free to spread the know-how at will: there were no patents and no industrial secrets.

All of this was happening far away from the Bay Area, that at the time had neither the universities nor the industry to match the East Coast and Western Europe.

The Bay Area and the Cold War

The Bay Area finally got involved in computers via a newly created offshoot of Stanford University. In 1946 Stanford spun off the Stanford Research Institute (SRI). Its purpose was to create an industrial research center that would leverage Stanford's high-tech know-how for commercial products. After six months, SRI moved off campus (to Menlo Park, which had swollen after the government had run a large military hospital there between 1943 and 1946) and began to relax its ties with the university. One of its very first projects was to improve the ENIAC: SRI replaced some key components with the latest electronic novelties and obtained a smaller machine. The original ENIAC was a 30-ton monster that covered 167 square meters of floor space and contained 17,468 vacuum tubes, 70,000 resistors, 10,000 capacitors and 1,500 relays.

SRI was a first consulting firm embedded in an academic world but serving the military and large corporations, a concept later adopted by many think tanks around the world.

At the same time Fred Terman returned to Stanford University as the dean of the engineering school, and used his connections with the US military (notably the recently instituted Office of Naval Research) to found and fund a new Electronics Research Lab (ERL). The Korean War (1950) brought another huge infusion of money from the Office of Naval Research to carry out research in electronics, which Terman used to open an Applied Electronics Laboratory (AEL). After the Soviet launch of the first artificial satellite, Sputnik, the US government rapidly increased funding for research, and the beneficiaries were mainly MIT on the East Coast and Stanford University on the West Coast.

After the invention of the klystron, Bill Hansen continued his research into accelerating electrons and in 1947 inaugurated his first linear accelerator.

Meanwhile, his former assistants, the Varian brothers, opened their own business in San Carlos in April 1948 to work on radio, radar and television. The ties with Stanford were still strong: Ed Ginzton, an alumnus of the klystron project, was both a director at Varian Associates and a Stanford professor. The Varian brothers chose San Carlos because that city north of Palo Alto was becoming an electronic industrial center. San Carlos was a mini-urban experiment: it had been built *ex-novo* between 1917 and 1925 just north of Redwood City by the Mercantile Trust Company following the arrival of the Southern Pacific railway. San Carlos was still a very tiny village in 1930, but then Charles Litton (1930s), Dalmo (1944) and Eitel-McCullough (1945) opened offices there. Around them other companies were created to serve the electronics industry.

The San Francisco Renaissance and the Economic Boom

It was during World War II that the foundations for the "San Francisco Renaissance" were laid down. San Francisco had previously lacked a literary scene that could match its visual arts. The poets Kenneth Rexroth and Madeline Gleason started it. In 1954, Gleason founded the Poetry Center at San Francisco State University and, in April 1947 organized the first "Festival of Modern Poetry." Rexroth and Gleason helped Berkeley poet Robert Duncan, one of the first openly gay intellectuals who wrote "The Homosexual in Society" in 1944. Rexroth also befriended poets William Everson, a former Catholic monk, Muriel Rukeyser, a Jewish feminist, and Philip Lamantia. In the 1940s San Francisco also witnessed a dramatic increase in black immigrants. Most of them settled around Fillmore Street, the "Harlem of the West." That street became the epicenter of nightlife and of live music.

The end of the war was unleashing the industrial potential of the US. Industrial production rose by almost 50% in the ten years after the war. The civilian economy, busy engineering the lifestyle of the winners, was an avid consumer of new appliances. The defense economy, busy countering the moves of the Soviet Union in the "Cold War," was an avid consumer of new weapons. In 1946 a new entity joined the US government in funding technological innovation: the venture capital firms. Three big firms debuted in 1946. First was Boston's American Research and Development Corporation (ARD), led by the French-born former Harvard Business School's Professor Georges Doriot with assistance from MIT's President Karl Compton and Federal Reserve Bank of Boston's

President Ralph Flanders, which was the first publicly owned venture-capital firm (that would fund spin-offs of MIT and Harvard). Second was New York's J.H. Whitney & Company, led by Jock Whitney (his partner Benno Schmidt coined the term "venture capital"). Third came New York's Rockefeller Brothers, led by Laurance Rockefeller (later renamed Venrock). They were often attracted by the potential of commercializing technologies invented during the war. The exuberance of private investors spread to California, where at least two such ventures were incorporated in 1946: Industrial Capital, founded by San Francisco's stock broker and "angel" investor Edward Heller, and Pacific Coast Enterprise.

The US was beginning one of the longest and fastest periods of economic expansion in history. The population of California had been less that 100,000 people in 1850 and 1.5 million people in 1900. During World War II, it rose from seven million to over nine million in just four years.

Engineers: Stanford Industrial Park, Inventions, Discoveries, and Rebellion at the Dawn of the Computer Age (1949-61)

Commercial Computers

The first usable computers came out of academia: the Moore School's EDVAC (1949), Cambridge University's EDSAC (1949), Alan Turing's Pilot ACE (1950), etc; but IBM was actively involved with Harvard's computers, and in 1950 the Remington Rand Corporation of New York purchased Mauchly's and Eckert's computer business, quickly renamed Univac and first delivered in 1952. IBM's first electronic computer too came out in 1952. The era of commercial computers had begun with a race between Univac and IBM. Their customers were agencies of the military establishment. IBM probably won out (in the long term) because of its involvement in the Semi-Automatic Ground Environment (SAGE) project, the biggest computer project of the era, funded by the military at the MIT.

The transition from the early task-specific computers to the general-purpose IBM and Univac computers was largely enabled by the development of Random Access Memory (RAM), mainly by the Chinese-born physicist An Wang at Harvard and by Jay Forrester at MIT. Wang can also be credited for introducing the idea of outsourcing hardware manufacturing to the Far East, as magnetic-core memories were probably the first computer component whose price declined rapidly thanks to cheap labor in the Far East.

Within a few years all the big firms of office automation (Remington Rand, IBM, NCR, Burroughs) and all of the big electrical corporations (General Electric, RCA, AT&T, and Western Electric) entered the market. They were all located very far from the Bay Area. In fact, the Whirlwind and the SAGE projects at the MIT gave Boston a huge lead in computer science over the rest of the country.

The Birth of the Semiconductor Industry

The transistor had been invented at AT&T's Bell Labs, and, when AT&T started licensing the technology to others, the beneficiaries were all on the East Coast and the Midwest: Sylvania (Massachusetts), Motorola (Arizona), Texas Instruments (Texas), etc. Transistors were not necessarily made of silicon at the time, but in 1954 Gordon Teal's team at Texas Instruments discovered a cheap way to make transistors out of silicon. The "transistor" became a household name when Regency introduced the first portable radio, the TR-1 (1954), which used Texas Instruments' transistors. A few companies introduced transistorized computer, but the first commercial model was the IBM 7070 in 1960.

The Computer Industry on the West Coast

On the West Coast the computer industry was limited to serve the needs of the booming aviation industry of Los Angeles, namely Northrop, Douglas and Hughes.

These projects too were mostly funded by government agencies. They financed the Standards Western Automatic Computer (SWAC) at UCLA, designed by Harry Huskey, who in 1947 had been a member of Turing's ACE team. RAND Corporation, selected in 1955 to write the code for SAGE, created a new System Development Division that in 1957 was spun off as System Development Corporation (SDC).

The first startups were also spinoffs of aviation projects. Northrop's computer lab was eventually sold to Bendix, a maker of appliances and radios based in Indiana. In 1956 Bendix introduced their first digital computer, the Bendix G-15, designed by the same Harry Huskey. In 1957 some of the former Northrop engineers led by Max Palevsky quit Bendix and joined Packard Bell (a Los Angeles-based maker of consumer radios) to open their computer labs. Finally, there were at least two spin-offs from the California Institute of Technology (CalTech): the Librascope division of General Precision; and the ElectroData division of Consolidated Electrodynamics Corporation (CEC). The Los Angeles startups focused on building "small" computers ("small" compared with the giants marketed by IBM and Univac). All of them were funded, directly or indirectly, by military projects.

The Stanford Industrial Park

In the Bay Area, the Terman doctrine of close interaction between academia and industry was further implemented in 1951 when Stanford University, prodded by the rapidly growing Varian that needed more space, created the Stanford Industrial Park. Located along Page Mill Road, the southern border of the campus, the park was meant to be an area for companies interested in high-tech innovation. Stanford had meant to lease the unused land to companies, and Terman simply proposed that land be leased "only" to high-tech companies. There had been industrial parks before, but none so oriented towards technological innovation. Its first tenant (in 1953) was going to be Varian, then Hewlett-Packard, General Electric (1954), Eastman Kodak, Zenith (1956), Lockheed (1956), and many others.

Incidentally, it wasn't the only scheme devised to increase Stanford's revenues. In September 1955 the Stanford Shopping Center opened its doors to the first tenant: this part of Stanford was reserved for retailers and would become a celebrated open-air shopping mall.

The founders of Hewlett-Packard created a unique corporate culture. Their management style had little to do with the cold, opportunistic style of the East Coast. Instead of focusing only on profits, HP focused on its human resources. Employees were treated like family members. Hewlett-Packard probably introduced the custom of addressing even the owners of a large company by their first names. Hewlett-Packard pioneered the idea that the workers of a company are co-owners of it, giving them stock options. While most companies hired specialists whose value depended on how long their specialization was valuable, HP pioneered the practice of retraining employees for different functions in the company, thus avoiding the career pitfall of hyper specialization. Lay-offs were anathema, no matter how well or badly the company was doing. HP was also one of the first companies to promote women to higher management positions. Hewlett-Packard invested first not on technology or customers but on its own workforce. Before it created products, it created a sense of community. The company had done well during the war, providing high-quality electronic equipment, and it was rapidly expanding. Revenues grew from $5.5 million in 1951 (215 employees) to $88 million in 1961 (5,040 employees).

Varian (whose revenues had increased more than tenfold during the Korean War) went public in 1956, Hewlett-Packard in 1957, and Ampex in 1958. The IPO (Initial Public Offering) meant that the region was becoming less dependent on the big conglomerates of the East Coast. These three companies had raised the money they needed without having to sell bits to the incompetent East Coast electronics companies. These IPOs also marked the beginning of a partnership between Silicon Valley and Wall Street.

The Valley was finding other places to apply computer technology. In 1950 the Stanford Research Institute was hired by Bank of America to design a computer for the automation of check processing. In September 1955, the prototype of the ERMA (Electronic Recording Machine Accounting) was ready and the following year the machine was manufactured by General Electric and NRC. It was the first successful use of a computer for a banking application, and even pioneered optical character recognition.

HP Labs (2010)

The Culture of Invention

The Bay Area was becoming an ever more attractive location for business. The inventions continued to flow. Notably, in 1956 Charles Ginsburg at Ampex Corporation, heading a team that included a young Ray Dolby, built the first practical videotape recorder, a device that changed the way television programming worked (previously, all programs had been broadcast live, and, obviously, at the same time in all time zones). In 1961 Laurence Spitters, a Wall Street investment banker who had moved to San Francisco and joined Ampex in 1958, founded Memorex in Santa Clara taking three Ampex engineers with him to work on computer magnetic tape .

UC Berkeley had its own stored-program computer project, CALDIC (California Digital Computer), completed in 1954 by Professor Paul Morton who employed former ENIAC staff from Pennsylvania and local students (including a young Doug Engelbart). This team (notably Albert Hoagland) emphasized magnetic data storage.

Friden was still the leading manufacturer of high-end calculators. In 1949 it had introduced a fully-automatic calculator, the Model STW. In 1957 Friden acquired the Commercial Controls Corporation, manufacturer of the tape-driven Flexowriter electric typewriter that had been used as the output device (the "teleprinter") of the Harvard Mark I and could be attached as well to Friden calculators to produce invoices automatically. In

1963 Friden introduced the first fully-transistorized calculator, the model EC-130 designed by Bob Ragen. In 1965 Friden was acquired by Singer.

The number of engineers produced by Stanford and UC Berkeley was beginning to draw the attention of East-Coast companies. In 1952 IBM opened its first West-Coast laboratory in San Jose. In September 1956 this lab unveiled the Random Access Method of Accounting and Control (RAMAC) 305, another vacuum-tube computer and the first to use magnetic-disk storage, invented by Jacob Rabinow at the National Bureau of Standards in 1954. Its RAMAC 350 hard-disk drive had a capacity of five megabytes. This computer shipped with a processing unit, a card-punch machine, a console (card feed, typewriter, keyboard), a printer and the 350 hard-disk drive.

The Original Location of IBM's Western Labs (2010)

The Defense Industry

The defense industry was still the main employer of the Bay Area. In 1956 sales in the US of electronic equipment exceeded $3 billion, and half of that went to the military. During the Korean War (1950-53), California finally overtook New York as the state receiving the largest share of military contracts (26% of all contracts). The majority of the money went to the aircraft industry based near Los Angeles, but next was the Bay Area. Afraid that the Soviet Union was leapfrogging their missile technology, in 1953 the Army, thanks to Terman, commissioned Sylvania to create a missile detection system. Sylvania set up an Electronic Defense Lab (EDL) in Mountain View, near Moffett Field, not the first defense contractor to get involved in military projects at this location. This project, directed by Stanford alumnus Bill Perry, lasted several years and eventually led to Sylvania's Ballistic Missile Early Warning System (BMEWS). In 1958 IBM shipped its first transistorized 709 (originally built with vacuum tubes) specifically for this project, before that machine was renamed IBM 7090. In 1959 Sylvania was bought by General Telephone to form General Telephone and Electronics, or GT&E. By then Sylvania's EDL had become one of Santa Clara Valley's largest companies, with over 1,000 employees, and already spawned the first start-ups in the field of microwave devices for military applications, such as Microwave Engineering Laboratories in 1956. In fact, in 1952 General Electric had already dispatched one of its top researchers, Barney Oldfield, to set up a new Microwave Laboratory at Stanford, one of the very earliest examples of industry-government-university collaborations (radars and missile defense systems).

In 1954, Charlie Litton sold his glorious San Carlos-based vacuum-tube operations to Litton Industries. Despite its name, Litton was based in Los Angeles and owned by Tex Thornton, a former vice-president at Hughes Aircraft with strong ties to the Defense Department (he had started Electro Dynamics Corporation in 1953). Litton's original business in San Carlos became the Electron Devices Division of Thornton's Litton Industries. Thornton was one of the businessmen who understood that the Cold War would require increasingly sophisticated weapons. By 1959 he could count on sales of $120 million, of which about 50% came from the government. By 1963 sales would top half a billion dollars. Meanwhile, in 1954 General Electric opened its Electric Microwave Lab at the Stanford Industrial Park to manufacture electronic devices for radars and missile defense systems.

When the Department of Defense awarded Lockheed a contract to work on the project for a submarine-launched ballistic missile (the Polaris), Lockheed relocated its electronics research group to the Stanford Industrial Park (1956) and built a factory for its Lockheed Missiles Division near Moffett Field in Sunnyvale. That same year the US decided to invest in satellites to spy on the Soviet Union (a project code-named "Corona") and that division of Lockheed got the contract and opened another factory, the Advanced Projects division. Within ten years it would become the main employer of the region. For the record, the Corona satellite, first launched in June 1959, was the world's first reconnaissance satellite program, capable of taking pictures of the Soviet Union from the sky. The project was carried out by Itek (the camera), Kodak (the film), General Electric and Lockheed Missiles Division in Sunnyvale. The Corona project was then assigned to a new entity, initially called Air Force Satellite Test Center (later renamed many times and eventually Onizuka Air Force Station) based in the "Blue Cube" (or Lockheed "Building

100"), built in 1960 between Sunnyvale and Milpitas, not far from Moffett Field.

In 1957 Paul Cook opened Raychem in Redwood City to manufacture wires and cables for the military and aerospace industries.

The Valley's companies were still small by the standards of the East-Coast conglomerates. In 1956 both General Electric and RCA had revenues of over $700 million, while Varian (the largest of the native Bay Area companies) barely reached $25 million. HP had more employees (901) but less in revenues ($20.3 million).

Lockheed's Palo Alto Research Laboratories (2010)

The Culture of Discovery

In those years the scientific reputation of Stanford and UC Berkeley grew rapidly. In 1952, Felix Bloch of Stanford University was awarded the Nobel Prize in Physics, the first for Stanford. Berkeley had already accumulated more Nobel Prizes than any other university in the five years since the end of the war: John Northrop and Wendell Stanley (1946), William Giauque (1949), Glenn Seaborg and Edwin McMillan (1951).

At the end of the war Robert Oppenheimer realized that the future would need a new kind of weapons laboratory, one that wouln't just build them but also improve them. He helped conceive Sandia National Laboratories, established near Los Alamos and assigned to the University of California. Later, President Truman decided to transfer its management to AT&T.

When the US decided to develop a "hydrogen" bomb to stay ahead of the Soviet Union (that had detonation its first atomic bomb in August 1949), in 1952 the Atomic Energy Commission established a branch of the Lawrence's Radiation Laboratory (later renamed Lawrence Berkeley Lab) in the town of Livermore (on the underdeveloped east side of the bay), soon to become known as the Lawrence Livermore Laboratory. The lab in Livermore was charged with military projects, while the lab in Berkeley was free to conduct theoretical research. In 1954 the lab in Berkeley, which had relocated up the hill from the UC Berkeley campus, installed a 10,000-ton synchrotron (nicknamed "Bevatron") that could accelerate protons to 6.2 BeV (one billion electronvolts), enough to create antimatter on Earth: the first antiproton was detected in October 1955.

The lab in Livermore, instead, became one of the sites for the top-secret Project Sherwood with Princeton and Oak Ridge to produce a "controlled" nuclear fusion reaction. Fusion is the kind of nuclear reaction that takes place in the sun and generates enormous amounts of energy out of hydrogen. The goal of Project Sherwood was to turn hydrogen (the most available element on Earth) into energy for industrial and domestic purposes. Unfortunately, fusion seems to happen only at very high temperatures. The project was started in 1951 under British physicist James Tuck of Los Alamos, who had worked on fusion for nuclear weapons within the Manhattan Project, but in 1953 Berkeley alumnus Amasa Bishop was appointed the new director.

In August 1955 Homi Bhabha chaired the United Nations' Conference on the Peaceful Uses of Atomic Energy and said: "I venture to predict that a method will be found for liberating fusion energy in a controlled manner within the next two decades. When that happens the energy problem of the world will truly have been solved forever for the fuel will be as plentiful as the heavy hydrogen in the oceans."

Culture and Society

The Californian governors of the post-war era helped modernize the state. Earl Warren (1943-1953), a charismatic politician, unified the state behind him and launched an ambitious program of public works, basically continuing the New Deal. He built state universities and community colleges as well as a vast network of freeways. Goodwin Knight (1953-1959) and Pat Brown (1959-1967), a San Francisco lawyer, continued these policies. The political climate was so united that at one point Warren was nominated by all three main parties and Pat Brown switched from one party to another. These governors invested heavily in the infrastructure of the state while wisely managing its finances. Thanks to the prosperity created by their policies, immigrants flocked to the "Golden State" from all over the country.

Meanwhile, San Jose experienced a population boom in the 1950s due to the soldiers who relocated there after World War II. They could find affordable suburban housing and well-paid jobs. In 1955 a new fast road connected San Jose to San Francisco, the I-280 freeway.

World War II had two parallel effects on the distribution of the Bay Area. On one hand the massive defense build-up around San Francisco transferred valuable technological know-how to an area that had very little of its own (there were virtually no electronics firms). At the same time, massive black migration to the shipyards of the East Bay resulted in white families fleeing south, where the government was building freeways and subsidizing suburban mortgages for single-family detached homes. Rural areas such as the Santa Clara Valley gained a more urbanized middle-class population. Silicon Valley's urban development covered about 50 square kms (US Geological Survey, 1940); by 1960 it covered 290 square kms.

The cultural life of San Francisco was beginning to take off too, although in a rather bizarre manner. In 1951 Zen apostle Alan Watts moved from Britain to San Francisco, where he became a major influence on the assimilation of Eastern philosophy into Western lifestyle. He started a radio program in 1953 at Berkeley's KPFA station.

India had become fashionable in California since at least 1948 when Indra Devi, born Eugenie Peterson in Latvia but relocated in 1927 to India where she had learned yoga from Tirumalai Krishnamacharya, had opened a studio in Hollywood and become an evangelist of yoga among the rich and fashionable.

Meanwhile, Peter Martin can be credited as the man who imported the spirit of New York's intelligentsia into San Francisco. In 1952 he began publishing a literary magazine titled "City Lights." The following year, Lawrence Ferlinghetti was convinced by Ken Rexroth to move to San Francisco. He opened a bookstore, "City Lights," which was an experiment in itself: the first all-paperback bookstore in the nation. The bookstore soon became the headquarters of alternative writers.

In October 1955, Allen Ginsberg 's recitation of his poem "Howl," organized by Rexroth at the Six Gallery, transplanted the "Beat" aesthetic to San Francisco. Other writers came to inspire the local "Beat Generation." Jack Kerouac moved to San Francisco in 1956 and Robert Creeley moved to San Francisco in 1957. Among the local talents who embraced the new style were Michael McClure and Jack Spicer (part of Robert Duncan 's Berkeley circle). The most lasting influence was perhaps that of two poets who had studied in Oregon at Reed College. Gary Snyder and Philip Whalen, because they adopted Zen Buddhism, started a trend that would make California an international center of Zen and would make Zen a staple of the counterculture. Snyder, in particular, delved into

Chinese and Japanese poetry, bringing to California the passion for exotic cultures (instead of contempt for their poor emigrants).

Seymour Locks, a Stanford graduate, began teaching at San Francisco State College in 1947 and was influential in creating two different cultures. First of all, he practiced as a sculptor using found objects, i.e. junk, as his raw material. Secondly, in 1952 he started experimenting with light shows. Locks influenced Elias Romero, whose light shows began in 1956.

At the same time, San Francisco still maintained its old sexually permissive atmosphere. In 1955 the police staged a coordinated campaign of persecution against homosexuals, but its outcome was to cement solidarity within that community, and, for example, in the same year the "Daughters of Bilitis" was founded in San Francisco, the first exclusively lesbian organization in the US. In 1959 Stanford University hired Austrian-born chemist Carl Djerassi, who four years earlier at Syntex of Mexico City had invented synthetic progesterone, which accidentally turned out to be "the birth-control pill." Syntex was run by Uruguayan-born Alejandro Zaffaroni and manufactured synthetic steroid hormones.

A notable event in the artistic life of the Bay Area was the 1945 establishment of the Photography Department at the California School of Fine Arts (later renamed the San Francisco Art Institute), thanks to Ansel Adams. It recognized photography as a fine art in a way that no other academic institution had yet done. In 1946, Adams convinced other distinguished photographers to accept positions at the school: Minor White, a former student of Alfred Stieglitz in New York, Berkeley's Dorothea Lange, and San Francisco's Imogen Cunningham.

Another notable event was the birth of the art movement later dubbed "Bay Area Figurative Painting." The founder was David Park, who moved to San Francisco in 1943 to teach at the California School of Fine Arts and later exhibited the first abstract paintings with figurative elements. He influenced Elmer Bischoff, who started teaching at the School of Fine Arts in 1946, and Richard Diebenkorn, who began teaching at Oakland's California College of Arts and Crafts in 1955. In 1947 and 1949 New York's abstract expressionist Mark Rothko taught at the same school. The Contemporary Bay Area Figurative Painting Exhibition at the Oakland Art Museum of September 1957 featured Park's, Bischoff's and Diebenkorn's student Henry Villierme, the leader of the second generation. Oakland's California College of Arts and Crafts instead raised Nathan Oliveira (class of 1952) and Bruce McGaw (class of 1955). Paul Wonner graduated in 1955 from U.C. Berkeley.In 1949 the Austrian-Mexican surrealist Wolfgang Paalen moved to San Francisco after pioneering abstract expressionism in New York. Together with Lee Mullican and Gordon Onslow-Ford he formed the group Dynaton, that debuted in 1951.

Starting in 1952, Wally Hedrick began constructing collages of metal objects that he scavenged in junkyards (cans, lamps, radios, appliances).

Jess Collins in 1952 founded the King Ubu Gallery, which in 1954 Hedrick renamed Six Gallery and turned into an artist-run cooperative. Around it revolved artists such as Manuel Neri and Mary-Joan "Jay" DeFeo, a UC Berkeley alumna who had absorbed influences from Native-American, African and prehistoric art. Most of them were also grouped in Bruce Conner 's Rat Bastard Protective Association (an non-existent association, just a term coined in 1959). They represented the counterpart to the Beat movement in the visual arts. Bruce Conner, who had arrived in 1957 in the city, upped the ante of the movement with his chaotic sculptures of junk wrapped in sexy nylon stockings.

San Francisco's avantgarde cinema scene came to life thanks to Frank Stauffacher 's "Art in Cinema," held in the San Francisco Museum of Modern Art since 1946. It marked the first time in the US that an art museum presented a series of experimental films. Despite the focus on avantgarde films, the events often drew a sold-out crowd. The San Francisco International Film Festival debuted in 1957 (and eventually became the longest-running film festival in the Americas).

Very little of this fervor reached the south bay. In 1955 peace activist Roy Kepler opened a bookstore in Menlo Park to sell paperbacks (which at the time were shunned by most high-brow bookstores), and his Kepler's remained an outpost of alternative culture in the Peninsula.

A bizarre contribution to the cultural life of the Bay Area came from the Central Intelligence Agency (CIA). In 1953 the CIA launched a secret project, "MK-Ultra," to develop a truth drug that would control the mind of its victims. This was in response to reports that the Communists in North Korea had brainwashed US prisoners of war. The CIA administered Lysergic Acid Diethylamide (LSD) to the volunteers of the program. One of these volunteers (in 1959) was a Stanford student named Ken Kesey. In 1960 Ampex's electrical engineer Myron Stolaroff, having been introduced to LSD by Canadian inventor Alfred Hubbard (perhaps the first person to view LSD as a tool to achieve higher dimensions of thought), founded the International Federation for Advanced Studies in Menlo Park recruiting scientists such as Willis Harman of Stanford University.

Up until the 1950s the Bay Area was mainly known (outside California) as a haven for unorthodox artists and writers. Very few engineers dreamed of moving from imperial Europe (who cities and universities still dominated the world) to provincial California, and very few engineers dreamed of moving from the political and industrial hubs of the East Coast and the Midwest to the picturesque but isolated Bay Area. It was mainly the artists who found that distant western outpost fascinating.

Electronic Brains

The computer industry was still largely absent from the Bay Area. In the rest of the nation it was however progressing rapidly. In 1956 there were 800 computers in operation in the USA. By 1959 there were about 6,000. There was excitement about the potential applications of "electronic brains". In 1952 a "Conference on Mechanical Translation" was organized at MIT by Yehoshua Bar-Hillel. In 1954 George Devol designed the first industrial robot, Unimate, finally delivered to General Motors in 1961. In 1956 John McCarthy of MIT organized the first conference on Artificial Intelligence at Dartmouth College. Allen Newell at RAND Corporation in Los Angeles and Carnegie Mellon University's Herbert Simon in Pittsburgh unveiled the "Logic Theorists" in 1956 and in 1957 the "General Problem Solver," a computer program that represented another step in abstracting a Turing machine. Also in 1957 Frank Rosenblatt conceived the "Perceptron," the first neural network. In 1959 McCarthy and Marvin Minsky, who had joined MIT in 1958, founded the Artificial Intelligence Lab.

Software was considered such a negligible part of computing that it didn't even have a name. The first practical programming language was introduced in 1957 (John Backus' FORTRAN). Both manufacturers and customers were beginning to realize that computers were powerful hardware but their usefulness depended on their software applications.

Most computers at this point were still the size of entire rooms, but in 1957 a former MIT scientist and SAGE engineer, Ken Olsen, founded the Digital Equipment Corporation (DEC). Its "mini-computer" PDP-1 (Program Data Processor) was introduced in 1960. It changed the history of both hardware and software. For example, in 1962 the designers of the first Computer-Aided Design (CAD) system, Digigraphics, used a PDP-1. DEC minicomputers were also instrumental in automating the factory.

Semiconductors in the Bay Area

A series of events in the second half of the 1950s led the Bay Area into the nascent computer industry. The defense industry was still driving a big chunk of the Valley's economy. It was so prevalent that in 1955 Stanford University merged the Applied Electronics Laboratory and the Electronics Research Laboratory into the Systems Engineering Laboratory under the direction of Fred Terman to focus on electronic warfare. The Cold War was proving to be a gold mine for electronics. NASA too opened a research center at Moffett Field in Mountain View (1958). New ideas for defense-related business were floating around. It was not easy, though, to start a new company. In 1955 private investors or "angels," including John Bryan, Bill Edwards and Reid Dennis (an employee of the Fireman's Fund in San Francisco), established "The Group" to invest together in promising electronics companies of the Bay Area. They invested their own money.

The timing could not have been more auspicious for semiconductors. William Shockley, inventor of the transistor, had joined Beckman Instruments, a company based in Los Angeles that was willing to open an entire research center for transistors. In 1956, Beckman opened its Shockley Semiconductor Laboratory division in Mountain View to work on semiconductor-based transistors that would replace vacuum tubes. The early transistors were made of germanium. It was only in 1954 that Morris Tanenbaum's team at Bell Labs and Gordon Teal's team at Texas Instruments both produced silicon transistors. The one made by Texas Instruments was the first silicon transistor to be commercially available. Silicon is easily found in nature (in sand all over the world), unlike germanium. Shockley knew it was the right direction. He tried in vain to convince former coworkers at Bell Labs to follow him west. Eventually he settled on hiring young engineers, all of them still in their 20s. Among them were Philco's physicist Robert Noyce (an MIT graduate) from Philadelphia, Johns Hopkins University chemist Gordon Moore (a Caltech graduate) from Maryland(but actually the only one born and raised in the Bay Area), Austrian-born Western Electric industrial engineer Eugene Kleiner (a New York University graduate) from New Jersey, Swiss-born Caltech physicist Jean Hoerni (who had studied philosophy at Cambridge University) from Los Angeles, Dow Chemical's metallurgist Sheldon Roberts (another MIT graduate) from Michigan, Western Electric's mechanical engineer Julius Blank from New Jersey, MIT physicist Jay Last (who had just graduated) from Boston, and Stanford Research Institute's physicist Victor Grinich (the only Stanford graduate). At the time the Bay Area was not a particularly suitable place for young engineers, but Shockley attracted talents because of his prestige, reinforced by the Nobel prize.

The reason transistors were so important in those days was the Cold War: had a nuclear war broken out, the USA would have fought it with weapons guided by vacuum tubes. The military needed something more reliable and smaller. Shockley was very good at assembling teams, as he had demonstrated at Bell Labs. Unfortunately for him, just one year later, in October 1957, these eight engineers quit his firm to form Fairchild Semiconductor in Mountain View. They obtained funding from Sherman Fairchild's New York-based Fairchild Camera and Instrument thanks to the help of a young investment banker, Arthur Rock. It was the first venture-funded "startup" company in the Bay Area. Note that 33 companies turned down the "eight traitors" before Fairchild decided to give them a chance.

Yet again, a series of coincidences made it happen. Eugene Kleiner's father approached his New York brokerage firm, Hayden Stone, about loaning money to the new venture. The case was assigned to one of their employees, Arthur Rock, who flew to California and liked the idea. Nobody was willing to invest in a separate company, but an existing company offered to fund them and keep them under its umbrella as an independent unit based in California, Fairchild Semiconductor. Rock had accidentally met Sherman Fairchild, an inventor and a very rich man. Sherman's father George had been a partner of Tom Watson, basically the co-founders of the modern IBM, except that Watson had four children and George Sherman only one. Hence Sherman Fairchild had inherited the largest share of IBM stock. Noyce was actually the last one to join the "traitors."

Fairchild's main selling point was that transistors could be made with a cheap and ubiquitous material like silicon instead of the germanium that the industry had been using. Shockley called them traitors, and maybe they were. Yet they legitimized the practice of quitting a company and starting a competing company, thus betraying their employer but also advancing the state of technology.

The rupture was made possible by the realization that the semiconductor industry did not require a huge capital investment: silicon can be found everywhere and it is cheap. Unlike the old economy of big, complex, and expensive products, in the semiconductor industry starting a competitor in competition against one's own employer was relatively easy. The new company focused on making silicon transistors, just what Shockley had wanted to do initially. The problem was other competitors: Texas Instruments in Dallas, Motorola in Phoenix, Transitron and Raytheon in Boston, plus RCA and Philco.

Shockley's Old Laboratory Building (2010)

The Beginnings of Venture Capital

There were still few groundbreaking ideas coming out from the Bay Area electronics sector, but somehow there was an interest in funding ideas. In 1957 Dean Watkins of Stanford's ERL (where he had supervised the project for traveling-wave tubes or TWTs, tubes that allowed the amplification of radio signals to very high power) started Watkins-Johnson to manufacture components for electronic intelligence systems. It was one of the first venture-capital funded companies in the Santa Clara Valley (it would also prove to be one of the most successful of its generation, with sales decupling in four years). Its main investor was Tommy Davis, a realtor in southern California.

At the same time, spurred by the Cold War and by the need to boost the post-war economy, the US enacted a law to help start new companies: the Small Business Investment Company Act of 1958. The government pledged to invest three dollars for every dollar that a financial institution would invest in a startup (up to a limit). In the next ten years, this program would provide the vast majority of all venture funding in the US. The Bay Area was a major beneficiary.

Numerous venture firms sprung up. In 1958 Draper, Gaither and Anderson was founded in Palo Alto by Rowan Gaither (founder of the RAND Corporation), William Draper, and Fred Anderson. It was the first limited-partnership venture-capital firm in California, although short-lived. A limited partnership made it easier to compensate partners with carried interest and reduced investors' risk. One year later, Frank Chambers established the venture-capital company Continental Capital in San Francisco. In 1961 Tommy Davis and Arthur Rock (an investment banker who had been a student of Georges Doriot at Harvard and who had just relocated from New York after facilitating the Fairchild deal) founded the limited-partnership company Davis & Rock in San Francisco. They mainly raised money on the East Coast for investment in the Bay Area. In 1962 Bill Draper and Franklin Johnson formed Draper & Johnson. In 1961 the Venture Capital Journal started being published in San Francisco.

The Integrated Circuit

The major jump for computers came with the invention of the integrated circuit. It was Jack Kilby at Texas Instruments who (in 1958) invented the integrated circuit, a tiny silicon device containing a large number of electronic switches. With Kilby's technique, multiple transistors could be integrated on a single layer of semiconductor material. Previously, transistors had to be individually carved out of silicon or germanium and then wired together with the other components of the circuit. This was a difficult, time-consuming and error-prone task that was mostly done manually. Putting all the electrical components of a circuit on a silicon or germanium "wafer" the size of a fingernail greatly simplified the process. It heralded the era of mass production. The first customers of integrated circuits were the Air Force and NASA, followed by Lockheed and Boeing for the Polaris (1961) and Minutemen (1962) missile systems.

The golden team at Fairchild Semiconductor merely improved the idea. In 1959, Jean Hoerni invented the planar process that enabled great precision in silicon components, and Robert Noyce designed a planar integrated circuit. Hoerni's planar process, in particular, enabled the mass production of chips and can be credited with inventing the semiconductors industry as it came to be. Fairchild introduced the 2N1613 planar transistor commercially in April 1960, and the first commercial single-chip integrated circuit in 1961 (the Fairchild 900), a few months after the Texas Instruments' SN502.

The motivation to package multiple transistors into the same chip arose due to the fact that the wiring had become the real cost. Both Fairchild and Texas Instruments had improved the process of printing the electronic chips, but each chip contained only one transistor and the wiring ran outside the chip. Progress in the wiring was not keeping pace with progress in printing, and therefore the wiring was becoming the real cost. The integrated circuit was saving money. For the record, this wasn't really "silicon" valley yet: almost all the transistors made in the world were still made of germanium, and this would still be true throughout the early 1960s.

Meanwhile, Fairchild continued to harness talent, such as Don Farina (from Sperry Gyroscope), James Nall (from the National Bureau of Standards), Bob Norman (from Sperry Gyroscope), Don Valentine (from Raytheon, their Los Angeles sales manager), and Charles Sporck (from General Eletric, their production manager), all hired in 1959. Later hires were Jerry Sanders (1961, sales, from Motorola), Pierre Lamond (1962, from Transitron), Jack Gifford (1963, just graduated from UCLA, and in 1966 product marketing in Mountain View), Mike Markkula (1966, from Hughes, also in marketing). However, Fairchild Semiconductor made a big mistake when it did not focus on integrated circuits. A number of engineers who disagreed (led by David Allison) left Fairchild to start Signetics in 1961. Signetics benefited from the decision in 1963 taken by the Department of Defense to push for architectures based on integrated circuits. Throughout 1964, Signetics dwarfed Fairchild in the manufacturing of integrated circuits, until in 1965 Fairchild began to invest seriously.

Fairchild is important in the history of Silicon Valley's semiconductor industry not only for the technology it patented but also for the people it hired and trained. In fact, its contribution might be bigger as a creator of talent than as an innovator. Fairchild represented a corporate culture that treasured human resources: it hired the best of the best, and then it trained them to become even better. To use a physics metaphor, the potential energy at Fairchild was probably bigger than all the kinetic energy it ever produced. Since the early days Robert Noyce introduced an unorthodox management style at Fairchild Semiconductor, treating team members as family members, disposing of the suit-and-tie dress code, and inaugurating a more casual and egalitarian work environment.

An early supporter of the Bay Area's semiconductor industry was Seymour Cray, the chief engineer at the Minneapolis-based Control Data Corporation (CDC). Cray sponsored research at Fairchild that resulted (in July 1961) in a transistor made of silicon that was faster than any transistor ever made of germanium. Cray's new "super-computer," the CDC 6600 (first delivered in 1964 to the Lawrence Livermore Lab), would employ 600,000 transistors made by Fairchild. At the time when General Electric, RCA and Texas Instruments still made germanium-based products, Fairchild became the first silicon-only company.

The Bay Area was beginning to get into computer hardware, but it was still largely software illiterate. The most propitious omen for the region was that in 1961 George Forsythe at Stanford started an influential "Division of Computer Science" within the Department of Mathematics.

The Old Offices of Fairchild Semiconductor (2010)

The Advent of DNA

Meanwhile, the great scientific news of the decade came from Europe. In April 1953, Francis Crick and US-born James Watson, two molecular biologists working in Britain at the Cavendish Laboratory (the Department of Physics of Cambridge University), discovered the double helical structure of DNA. The code of life looked amazingly similar to a computer program. The always alert Fred Terman (now Stanford's provost) foresaw the potentiality of biotechnology, and decided to invest in Stanford's chemistry department.

Hippies: Fairchild, the Spin-offs, the Minicomputer, Artistic Creativity, and Social Revolution (1961-68)

The Era of Large Computer Projects

IBM giant computers dominated the market: in 1960 IBM owned more than 81% of the computer market. Its domination further increased in 1964 when it introduced the System/360, designed by Gene Amdahl. It was difficult to compete with IBM and the other "mainframe" manufacturers. A group of computer engineers including Max Palevsky from Packard formed Scientific Data Systems (SDS) in 1961 in Los Angeles and introduced their first model in 1962. It was basically a mini-computer, meant to challenge IBM and the other mainframe manufacturers. Their first customer was NASA. Scientific Data Systems' SDS 940 was built in 1966 for the time-sharing system at UC Berkeley, funded by DARPA's Project Genie.

Progress kept coming from the East Coast: in 1961 Fernando Corbato at MIT created the first working time-sharing system, CTSS (Compatible Time Sharing System), that evolved into MULTICS (Multiplexed Information and Computing Service); Charles Bachman at General Electric in New York developed the first database management system, Integrated Data Store or IDS (1961); AT&T introduced the first commercial modem (1962); Steve Russell and others at MIT implemented the computer game "Spacewar" on a PDP-1 (1962); in 1963 MIT student Ivan Sutherland demonstrated "Sketchpad," the first computer program ever with a Graphical User Interface (GUI); etc.

The seeds were also being planted for connecting computers through a network. In 1962 Paul Baran at the RAND Corporation proposed that a distributed network of computers was the form of communication least vulnerable to a nuclear strike, a highly sensitive topic during the Cold War. At the same time Joseph Licklider, a former MIT professor of psychology who had become vice-president at Boston's consulting firm Bolt Beranek and Newman (BBN), was preaching about the power of computer networks. In 1965 Harvard student Ted Nelson coined the word "hypertext" to refer to nonsequential navigation of a document.

 Ted Nelson

The Department of Defense had established the Advanced Research Projects Agency (ARPA) in 1958. Within a few years, this agency provided the highest proportion of funding for computer engineering research. In 1962, ARPA created a specific office devoted to computers, the Information Processing Techniques Office (IPTO) and hired the visionary Licklider to be its first director. Licklider sponsored the pioneering time-sharing system Project MAC (Machine Aided Cognition) at MIT, established in 1963 by Robert Fano. Licklider also dispatched money to the budding research centers in the Bay Area: Stanford University, UC Berkeley (neither of which had a graduate program in computer science yet), and especially Douglas Engelbart's team at SRI. Licklider's funds established a West-coast counterpart to Project MAC, called Project Genie. It started in 1964 at UC Berkeley and its main achievement was a public-domain time-sharing system. Several team members (notably Charles Thacker) started a company, Berkeley Computer Corporation (BBC), to market it.

Another benefactor of Engelbart was NASA's Office of Advanced Research and Technology in the person of Bob Taylor. He had joined NASA in 1961 after working for Maryland-based defense contractor Martin Marietta. NASA was interested in using computers for flight control and flight simulation, not purely "number crunching." Licklider was succeeded at IPTO in 1963 by Ivan Sutherland, who in 1965 hired Bob Taylor away from NASA. Taylor used ARPA to promote his philosophy: he wanted computers to be more useful than for just rapid large-scale arithmetic, and one way was to connect them in a network. Taylor was a crucial person in the US government, funding key projects in computer science research. In February 1966, Taylor launched an ARPA project to create a computer network, later named ARPAnet (the predecessor to the Internet). Each node was to be connected via a small "gateway" computer. Bolt Beranek and Newman (BBN) won the contract to develop the Interface Message Processor (IMP), basically, the first router.

The SRI Building with Doug Engelbart's Laboratory (2010)

Software and Services

Two major software ventures were created in Texas: Ross Perot founded Electronic Data Systems (EDS) in 1962 (and de facto invented the business of outsourcing) and University Computing Company (later renamed Uccel) was founded in 1963.

The Bay Area didn't contribute much to the nascent software industry, but at least computerized dating originated at Stanford in 1959 with a matchmaking program running on an IBM 650 mainframe computer designed by math students Jim Harvey and Phil Fialer for the Happy Families Planning Service.

The big computers were at Lockheed and NASA, used for military projects and for space projects. That's where advanced software was produced, but usually only for internal use, with at least one notable exception: in 1966 Roger Summit at Lockheed in Palo Alto developed the first version of Dialog on an IBM /360, an online information retrieval system that was first used by nearby NASA Ames via a leased telephone line to search its database of 200,000 article citations. That was the precursor of the "search engine".

As the costs of owning and operating a mainframe were prohibitive for most companies, time-sharing became a lucrative business. In 1966 Tymshare, founded by two General Electric engineers, started one of the most popular time-sharing services out of Los Altos. It was the company that brought the software business to Silicon Valley in earnest. The importance of time-sharing for the spreading of software skills cannot be overstated. Before time-sharing systems, only a small elite had access to computers. Time-sharing allowed students to program all they wanted. It multiplied by an order of magnitude the number of hours of programming around the world. Indirectly, it also enabled the concept that software can be a hobby, just like reading comics or playing the guitar. It helped not only computer lovers in high-tech cities like Boston but also and especially computer buffs in low-tech parts of the world like the Midwest.

Tymshare later created a circuit-switched network, Tymnet, that predated the Internet.

Culture and Society

The culture-makers of San Francisco couldn't care less about computers. Cultural life was, in fact, moving in the opposite direction, towards primitive, grotesque and provocative forms of expression. The assault to the senses was global. In 1959 dancer and mime Ron Davis had founded the R.G. Davis Mime Studio and Troupe, better known as the San Francisco Mime Troupe, specializing in silent anti-establishment mimed comedies inspired by the Italian "commedia dell'arte." And, incidentally, San Francisco's most famous dancer was Carol Doda, who became famous because, at the age of 26 in 1964, she performed topless in a bar, the Condor Club, creating a whole new profession.

In 1961 Bruce Baillie and Mildred "Chick" Strands founded the San Francisco Cinematheque to show experimental films and videos. At the same time, Bruce Baillie started the artist-run cooperative Canyon Cinema that also distributed the films (one year before Jonas Mekas started the more famous Film-Makers Cooperative in New York).

In 1962 composers Morton Subotnick and Ramon Sender established the San Francisco Tape Music Center to foster avantgarde music. Pauline Oliveros' dadaistic chamber music and Terry Riley's repetitive patterns had little to do with classical music. Subotnick indulged in chaotic live electronic music, thanks to Berkeley-based hobbyist Don Buchla, who built his first electronic synthesizer in 1963.

The experimental music of the Bay Area was, again, representative of an alternative lifestyle and an anti-conformist approach to innovation.

The first technical director of the Tape Music Center, Michael Callahan, was still a teenager when he helped poet Gerd Stern create the multimedia show "Verbal American Landscape". The duo then moved to New York where in 1964 they helped Steve Durkee form USCO, whose first mentor was a luminary like Marshall McLuhan at the University of Rochester. Their multimedia performance "Who R U" shocked San Francisco in 1964. In 1966 their show "Shrine" at New York's Riverside Museum coined the term "be-in".

Unlike Europe and the East Coast, where the audience was mainly music specialists, in San Francisco experimental music reached a broad and diverse audience. It was, yet again, the spirit of the eccentric independent, indifferent to the rules and the traditions of the genre.

Tony Martin also injected the light show (pioneered by Seymour Locks and Elias Romero) into the artistic mix of the Tape Music Center. Locks' improvisational light shows were an early influence on trumpet player Stan Shaff and electrical engineer Doug McEachern. Starting in 1963, they crafted public three-dimensional sound events and in 1967 established the sound theatre Audium, which in 1975 would move to a new location on Bush St and begin offering weekly performances in complete darkness. Bill Ham took Locks' light show into the psychedelic era, "decorating" a 1965 rock concert in Virginia City and organizing a three-week performance of "electric action painting" in San Francisco the following year. Both Martin and Ham had been trained in abstract expressionism as art students. The light show spread to New York (where Danny Williams animated Andy Warhol's "Exploding Plastic Inevitable", that also staged a sensational act in San Francisco in May 1966), to Seattle (notably Don Paulson's Lux Sit & Dance and Ron McComb's Union Light Company, both formed after a November 1966 concert held by community-based radio station KRAB) and to Los Angeles (Single Wing Turquoise Bird in 1968). The other influence on the light show was free jazz. Bill Ham's Light Sound Dimension (LSD) debuted in 1967 at the San Francisco Museum of Modern Art and featured electronic jazz improvisers. In 1968 became a weekly light and sound event at the Light Sound Dimension Theatre.

In 1962 Michael Murphy, a former Stanford student who had spent two years in India to practice meditation, opened the "Esalen Institute" at Big Sur to promote the integration of Eastern and Western philosophy and "spiritual healing." Esalen became the epicenter of the "human-potential movement," named after Aldous Huxley's lectures on the idea that humans are not fully realizing their potential, which could lead to much better lives.

The visual arts found a new haven in the East Bay. Peter Voulkos, who had started the "Funk" movement by applying the aesthetics of abstract expressionism to ceramic sculptures, had moved to UC Berkeley in 1959. UC Davis (between Berkeley and Sacramento), in particular, became a major artistic center. Pop art was pioneered by Wayne Thiebaud (even before Warhol made it famous in New York), who moved to Davis in 1960. Ceramic artist Robert Arneson became the local leader of the funk aesthetics pioneered by Voulkos. William Wiley, who joined Davis in 1963, expanded funk to painting. Roy De Forest joined the faculty in 1965. The most influential of the Davis group was perhaps Wayne Thiebaud's assistant Bruce Nauman, who (after joining the San Francisco Art Institute in 1966) went on to dabble in a variety of media (photography, neon, video, printmaking, sculpture, performance). He established a praxis of interdisciplinary art. Meanwhile, the first public showing of computer art was held at San Jose State University in May 1963, organized by Joan Shogren, who had programmed a computer with "artistic" principles.

There were other symbols of the era. In 1966 Dutch coffee roaster Alfred Peet opened Peet's Coffee & Tea in Berkeley's "gourmet ghetto". Its second location was in downtown Menlo Park, the only coffee house in town. Both stores became the fashionable social hubs of the 1970s outside San Francisco.

Something truly monumental was happening in the Bay Area. In 1964, Mario Savio at UC Berkeley started the "Free Speech Movement," the first major case of student upheaval, peaking with the "Sproul Hall Sit-In" of December in which 768 protesters were arrested. This movement eventually would lead to massive student marches and riots around the nation and Western Europe. The underground political magazine "Berkeley Barb", founded in August 1965 by Max Scherr, became the main organ of anti-establishment propaganda. Meanwhile in 1964 in the South Bay, MkUltra's alumnus Ken Kesey organized the "Merry Pranksters," a group of young freaks who traveled around the country in a "Magic Bus." They lived in a commune in La Honda and experimented with acid.

LSD began to be manufactured in large quantities by Owsley "Bear" Stanley at the UC Berkeley campus. It soon became widely available and relatively cheap. UC Berkeley had hosted an Institute for Personality Assessment and Research since 1949. The CIA was involved from its inception and probably contributed to the diffusion of psychoactive drugs on campus. Incidentally, the most famous of LSD gurus, Timothy Leary, was at the time (late 1950s) the director of the Kaiser Foundation Psychological Research in Oakland and did teach at UC Berkeley. Yet he did not try LSD until 1960, when he had just moved to Harvard. Whatever the original source of hallucinogenic drugs, they became the common denominator of the Bay Area's cultural life, and the symbol of an attack on the "American way of life."

In 1965 the cultural world became even more effervescent. For example, Ron Davis of the San Francisco Mime Troupe published the essay "Guerrilla Theatre." Ben Jacopetti inaugurated the Open Theater as a vehicle devoted to multimedia performances for the Berkeley Experimental Arts Foundation. The Family Dog Production organized the first hippie festival. The authorities had lost control of the situation and a youth culture was taking over the area, headquartered in the Haight-Ashbury district. Word of mouth was spreading throughout the US and young people were attracted to San Francisco's extravagant and tolerant society. By 1966 the media could not ignore the phenomenon anymore. Stewart Brand, who had been a volunteer at Stolaroff's International Federation for Advanced Studies and a member of the Merry Pranksters, organized the "Trips Festival," collating Ken Kesey's "Acid Test," Jacopetti's Open Theater, Sender's Tape Music Center and rock bands. The Jefferson Airplane and the Grateful Dead popularized a new genre of music inspired by psychedelic drugs, acid-rock. Willie Brown formed the Artists Liberation Front at the Mime Troupe's Howard Street loft. The first issue of the San Francisco Oracle, an underground cooperative pamphlet, was published. Emmett Grogan and members of the Mime Troupe founded the "Diggers," a group of improvising actors and activists whose stage was the streets and parks of the Haight-Ashbury district and whose utopia was the creation of a Free City. The first "Summer of Love" of the hippies was going on, including a three-day "Acid Test" with the Grateful Dead performing. Huey Newton, Bobby Seale, Angela Davis and other African-American Oakland-based activists founded the socialist-inspired and black-nationalist "Black Panther Party" (the violent counterpart to the pacifist "flower power" ideology of the hippies).

In June and July of 1966 landscape architect Lawrence Halprin and his wife, dancer Anna Halprin, started a series of cross-disciplinary workshops titled "Experiments in Environment" that involved architects, environmentalists, musicians, filmmakers, choreographers and light shows. They were held at the Sea Ranch (a coastal community envisioned by Al Boeke and designed in 1964 by Lawrence) and on Mt Tamalpais, both located north of San Francisco.

Coming out of the Free Speech Movement, the Free University was inaugurated in 1965, operating out of a trailer at San Francisco State University. Within a few years there would be dozens of Free Universities around the USA, that provided both free college-level education and country-wide networking. Next door to the Free University of Menlo Park in 1966 Dick Raymond founded the Portola Institute to bring computer education to schools and hired Stewart Brand and Bob Albrecht. In 1968 Willis Harman started teaching the influential class "Human Potential" at Stanford University

The gay community, which on New Year's Day of 1965 had staged a widely publicized "Mardi Gras Ball", was indirectly a beneficiary of the hippie phenomenon. Eureka Valley, the area south of the Haight-Ashbury (the headquarters of the hippies), was a conservative middle-class neighborhood that did not quite appreciate the crazy circus going on a few blocks away. Many families decided to emigrate to the suburbs and Eureka Valley became a ghost town. Gay couples, unwelcome elsewhere, were able to snatch up cheap Victorian homes and renovate them. The district soon became known for its main street, Castro Street.

The revolution was widespread and octopus-like.

In retrospect, nothing has undermined the "American way of life" and its traditional moral values as much as California did: the male society of the Gold Rush, the sexual promiscuity of the hippies, the same-sex families of gay couples, the decadent lifestyle of the Hollywood stars, and the eccentric indulgence of the tycoons.

Science in the Bay Area

Stanford University was hyperactive also. Ed Ginzton continued Hansen's work on a particle accelerator propelled by ever more powerful klystron tubes (i.e. microwaves). Ginzton was the co-founder with Russell and Siguard Varian of Varian Associate. He still kept one foot in Stanford and had built by 1952 a one-billion electron-volt (1GeV) particle accelerator, the Mark III. It was the most powerful in the world, and led to Stanford's Microwave Laboratory. In 1951 Pief Panofsky had been hired away from the Berkeley's Radiation Lab, where he had designed the latest proton accelerator. The two joined forces to launch "Project M" for building a more powerful machine. The result was the Stanford Linear Accelerator Center (SLAC), the longest linear accelerator in the world, which started operating in 1962.

Other East-Coast transplants thrived at Stanford. In 1963 John McCarthy, the founding father of artificial intelligence, moved to Stanford from MIT. In 1966 he opened the Stanford Artificial Intelligence Laboratory (SAIL) on the hills a few kilometers away from the campus. It became a West-Coast alternative to Project MAC. Another transplant from the East Coast, Herbert Simon's pupil Ed Feigenbaum, designed the first knowledge-based or "expert" system, Dendral (1965). It was an application of Artificial Intelligence to organic chemistry (a collaboration with Carl Djerassi). It differed from Simon's Logic Theorist because it aimed at a specific domain (organic chemistry). Just as humans tend to be experts only in some areas, the project emphasized the importance of domain heuristics, the "rules of thumb" that experts use to find solutions to problems. Following his former scientist Carl Djerassi, Al Zaffaroni relocated biotech pioneer Syntex from Mexico City to the Stanford Industrial Park in 1963, and the following year the birth-control pill was introduced commercially.

Stanford's inventions even reached into music. In 1967, John Chowning, a graduate in music composition and a pioneer of computer music, was using the computer at the Stanford Artificial Intelligence Lab. He invented "frequency modulation synthesis," a technology that allowed an electronic instrument to simulate the sound of orchestral instruments. Yamaha refined this invention in the 1970s to manufacture electronic keyboards.

At SRI, Douglas Engelbart toyed with the first prototype of a "mouse" (1963), part of a much bigger project funded by NASA to reinvent human-computer interaction. Indirectly McCarthy and Engelbart started two different ways of looking at the power of computers: McCarthy represented the ideology of replacing humans with intelligent machines, whereas Engelbart represented the view of augmenting humans with machines that can make them smarter.

Stanford had become an ebullient scientific environment and it was rapidly expanding beyond the original "Quadrangle." In 1968, Niels Reimers established an office at Stanford University, later renamed Office of Technology Licensing (OTL), to literally market Stanford's inventions to industry. By 2001 Stanford's income would pass the $1 billion mark.

Fairchild's Golden Years

Progress at Fairchild had been rapid, and mainly due to two new employees from the Midwest: Dave Talbert (hired in 1962) and Bob Widlar (hired in 1963). In 1963 Widlar (a wildly eccentric character) produced the first single-chip "op-amp." In 1964 Talbert and Widlar created the first practical analog (or "linear") integrated circuit that opened a whole new world of applications. Over the years their work accounted for the vast majority of linear designs at Fairchild and set the standard for design of semiconductor devices.

Another isolated genius at Fairchild was Frank Wanlass, who worked for Fairchild for less than two years (1962-63). He completely changed the face of the semiconductor industry. In 1963 he invented a new technique to build integrated circuits, Complementary Metal-Oxide Semiconductor (CMOS). A Metal-Oxide Semiconductor (MOS) element consists of three layers: a conducting electrode (metal), an insulating substance (typically, glass), and the semiconducting layer (typically, silicon). Depending on whether the semiconductor has been doped with electrons (n-type) or holes (p-type), the MOS circuit can be nMOS or pMOS. CMOS, by combining both types in appropriate complementary symmetry configurations, greatly reduced current flows. Thanks to CMOS, MOS circuits thus provided low power consumption, low heat and high density, making it possible to squeeze hundreds of transistors on a chip, and eventually to drop semiconductors into digital watches and pocket calculators.

Wanlass quit Fairchild in December 1963 to join General Microelectronics (GMe), where the first MOS product was completed in 1964, a few months ahead of Fairchild. Yet Wanlass quit again after just one year and moved to the East Coast, and then back to his native Utah. The gospel of CMOS spread thanks to Wanlass' job changes and to his willingness to evangelize.

CMOS wasn't the only innovation of the time. In 1963 Sylvania introduced the first commercial TTL integrated circuits, the Universal High-Level Logic family (SUHL), developed by Thomas Longo, who in 1962 had created the first gigahertz transistor, the Sylvania 2N2784.

Initially the main customers of MOS circuits were government agencies (NSA and NASA). Lee Boysel, a young Michigan physicist working at Douglas Aircraft in Santa Monica, met Frank Wanlass of General Microelectronics (GMe) in 1964 and learned about MOS technology. In 1965 Lee Boysel moved to IBM's Alabama laboratories to apply his MOS skills. In 1966 Fairchild hired Boysel from IBM to start a MOS group. Boysel perfected a four-phase clocking technique to create very dense MOS circuits. In 1967, at a time when computer memory made of transistors were still a rarity, Boysel proved that he could build an entire computer with MOS technology.

Finally, there was another independent genius, Federico Faggin, originally hired in Italy. He relocated to Fairchild's Palo Alto labs in 1968. Faggin invented silicon-gated MOS transistors. Silicon control gates are faster, smaller and use less energy than the aluminum control gates that had been commonplace until then. Now that both contacts and gates were made of silicon, the manufacturing process was simpler. It was this invention that allowed for the exponential growth in chip density (the number of transistors that could be packed into a chip). Fairchild introduced the first silicon-gate integrated circuit in October 1968.

On the business side, Fairchild wasn't doing well. Under the casual management of Noyce, it was basically run by the marketing people. The competitors were catching up and the company posted its first loss in 1967.

Federico Faggin of Fairchild Semiconductor (2010)

The Semiconductor Community

Several semiconductor companies dotted the landscape between Stanford and San Jose, and almost all of them could trace their roots back to Fairchild. They were:

- Amelco (a division of Teledyne), co-founded in 1961 by three Fairchild founders including Jean Hoerni. It developed one of the first analog integrated circuits;
- Molectro, founded in 1962 as Molecular Science Corporation by James Nall of Fairchild. In 1965 it hired the two Fairchild geniuses, Bob Widlar and Dave Talbert, and was acquired in 1967 by East-Coast based National Semiconductor (controlled by pioneer high-tech venture capitalist Peter Sprague). National eventually relocated to Santa Clara (in 1968) after "stealing" many more brains from Fairchild (notably Charlie Sporck, Pierre Lamond, Don Valentine, Floyd Kwamie and Regis McKenna);
- General Microelectronics (GMe), founded in 1963 by Fairchild engineers (including Don Farina and Phil Ferguson), that developed the first commercial MOS (Metal-Oxide Semiconductor) integrated circuits in 1965 (for the Victor 3900 calculator), and was eventually (1966) bought by Philadelphia-based Philco (that in turn had been acquired by Ford Motor);
- Applied Materials Technology (AMT), founded in 1967 by Mike McNeilly;
- Electronic Arrays, founded in 1967 by Jim McMullen;
- Intersil, started in 1967 by Jean Hoerni to produce low-power CMOS circuits for electronic watches (funded by a Swiss watchmaker); and
- Monolithic Memories, founded in 1968 by Fairchild engineer Zeev Drori.

- Electronic Arrays, founded in 1967 in Mountain View by Jim McMullen with people from General Microelectronics and Bunker Ramo.

The Semiconductor Spin-offs

Fairchild was generating the same phenomenon of "spin-offs" similar to FTC two generations earlier. Virtually the only semiconductor companies that were not based in the Santa Clara Valley were Texas Instruments, Motorola and RCA. They did not have a genealogical tree like Fairchild's spin-offs. The Bay Area was unique in encouraging engineers to expand their ideas outside their employer and to continuously innovate over already successful businesses.

The vast incestuous network of local spin-offs was creating a self-sustaining manufacturing community. It mixed Darwinian competition and selection with symbiotic inter-dependent cooperation. It was this odd coupling of competition and cooperation that made the rapid pace of technological progress in semiconductors possible. The startups were very jealous of their industrial secrets but at the same time aware of who was working on what, and not shy to band together when advantageous.

As a whole, the system of companies which were easily born and easily "killed" was highly flexible and therefore capable of adapting quickly to changing circumstances. The system "metabolized" a complex technology by way of inter-related specialized technologies. The system exhibited a form of collective learning from the responses to its actions. The network as a whole, in fact, constituted an efficient organism that, just like biological organisms, was capable of adaptation, evolution, reproduction, metabolism and learning. It is not true that Silicon Valley companies shared knowledge (they were actually were jealous of their industrial secrets); but it is true that the network as a whole did so through its dynamics.

In 1965 Gordon Moore predicted that the processing power of computers would double every 12 months (later revised to 18 months; this came to be known as "Moore's law"). The semiconductor industry experienced a rapid acceleration towards increased power, smaller sizes and lower prices.

The Military Sponsors

The military played a fundamental role in fostering this process. The new technologies were too expensive and unstable to be viable for the general market. The military was the only entity that was willing (in fact, eager) to experiment with novel technologies, and it did not bargain on price. The "Cold War" was even more powerful than World War II in motivating the US government to invest in research. Global intelligence and communications were becoming more important than the weapons themselves, which were really used only in Vietnam. And these systems were built out of microwave devices that were the Bay Area's specialty. The US government served as both a munificent venture capitalist that did not expect a return (and not even co-ownership) and an inexpensive testbed.

For communications, the field of digital signal processing was born due to the military. In 1964 the head of Sylvania's Electronic Defense Lab (EDL), Stanford alumnus Bill Perry, took most of his staff and formed Electromagnetic Systems Laboratory (ESL) in Palo Alto. He worked on electronic intelligence systems and communications in collaboration with Stanford and in direct competition with his previous employer. His idea was to embed computers in these systems, something that had become feasible thanks to Fairchild's integrated circuits. By turning signals into digital streams of zeros and ones, ESL pioneered the field of digital signal processing. It was initially for the new satellite reconnaissance systems designed by Bud Wheelon, a former Stanford classmate who in 1962 had been appointed director of the Office of Scientific Intelligence at the CIA.

ESL's innovation was not only technological, but in employee compensation too. Perry's intention was to replicate Hewlett-Packard's corporate culture, and in fact to better it. HP handed out stock only to management, but ESL was the first company to extend the program to every employee. Perry went on to become defense secretary under President Bill Clinton).

An important boost to the industry of integrated circuits came from NASA's Apollo mission to send a man to the moon. NASA had been using analog computers, but for this mission in August 1961 it commissioned MIT's Instrumentation Lab to build a digital computer. The Apollo Guidance Computer (AGC) was the first computer to use integrated circuits. Each unit used more than 4,000 integrated circuits from Fairchild. That number represented a significant share of the worldwide market for integrated circuits. In 1964 NASA switched to Philco's integrated circuits, thus turning Philco into a semiconductor giant and enabling it to buy General Microelectronics.

In 1965 Hewlett-Packard employed about 9,000 people, Fairchild had 10,000, and Lockheed's Missile Division had 28,000 employees. The defense industry was still dominant.

The semiconductor boom also created a fertile ground for hobbyists. Halted Specialties Company would become the first electronics superstore of Silicon Valley. It opened its doors in 1963 in Santa Clara to sell electronic components and instruments.

Few of the companies that had thrived in the age of microwave electronics made a successful transition to the age of the integrated circuit. The protagonists had changed. What had remained was the template of collaboration among university, industry, and the military.

Other Tech Companies beyond Semiconductors

Other tech companies besides semiconductors started to thrive also. In 1961 Laurence Spitters, a Wall Street investment banker who had moved to San Francisco and joined Ampex in 1958, founded Memorex in Santa Clara. He took three Ampex engineers with him to manufacture high-precision magnetic tapes that could also be used as data storage. At the other end of the bay, Berkeley wasn't just the site of student riots and psychoactive drug tests: in 1965 UC Berkeley's Lotfi Zadeh invented Fuzzy Logic. Ray Dolby, a former Ampex employee, founded Dolby Labs in Britain in 1965 and relocated to San Francisco in 1976. Also new investment companies sprouted, notably Sutter Hill Ventures, formed in 1964 by Bill Draper and Paul Wythes.

Towards a More Humane Electronic Brain

Computers were becoming more affordable thanks to integrated circuits, starting with DEC's PDP-8 of 1965. DEC spawned several companies, notably Data General.

Also, unbeknownst to most in the US, in 1965 Italian computer manufacturer Olivetti introduced an affordable programmable electronic desktop computer, the P101.

Crowning this race to miniaturization, in 1967 Jack Kilby at Texas Instruments developed the first hand-held digital calculator.

Hewlett-Packard still concentrated on instrumentation. It got into computers (the HP 2116A in November 1966, its first machine that used integrated circuits) and desk calculators (the 9100A in 1968) and hand-held calculators (the HP-35 in 1972) only because they were the natural evolution of instrumentation. The 2116A was marketed as an "instrumentation computer" and boasted interfaces for more than 20 scientific instruments. It had been designed by engineers from Data Systems, a Detroit company that HP had acquired in 1964. Data Systems already marketed a computer, the DSI 1000. It was nonetheless an engineering achievement, the second 16-bit minicomputer to be available commercially. It used integrated circuits from Fairchild and memory chips from Ampex. However casual and half-hearted, it was the beginning of the computer industry in Silicon Valley.

In 1970 Electronic Arrays introduced its own chipset for calculators and in 1971 its subsidiary International Calculating Machines (ICM) introduced the calculator ICM 816, followed by Sony's ICC-88 (the first time that Sony didn't use a in-house chipset) and by the MITS 816.

Unbeknownst to the masses and to the media, an important experiment was conducted at Stanford for the first time in the world. Two psychology professors, Patrick Suppes and Richard Atkinson, created a computer-based program to teach children from lower-income families, the precursor of e-learning. Later, Suppes became the Terman of e-learning, encouraging local startups in this field.

Lasers

Laser technology was one of the other high-tech industries flowering in Silicon Valley. A Stanford graduate, Ted Maiman, working at Hughes Research Laboratories in Los Angeles had demonstrated the first laser (a ruby laser) in May 1960. He beat the more famous teams of Charles Townes at Columbia University and Arthur Schawlow at Bell Labs, not to mention the very inventor of the laser, Gordon Gould, who had moved to the firm TRG (Technical Research Group) from Columbia. In 1959 Gould had coined the term, which stands for "Light Amplification by Stimulated

Emission of Radiation." Schawlow joined Stanford's Microwave Lab in 1961.

Meanwhile, Eugene Watson and Earl Bell had worked at Varian in the 1950s, where Herb Dwight had led the project to build the first practical helium-neon laser (completed in 1961). To capitalize on that invention, in 1961 Dwight and Bell founded Spectra-Physics in Mountain View, the world's first laser startup. In 1962 they hired Watson as a sales manager. Revenues soared mostly because labs all over the world wanted a taste of the new technology. Watson and Spectra-Physics' young scientist James Hobart then opened Coherent Radiation Laboratories (later Coherent Laser) in May 1966 at the Stanford Industrial Park. They staffed it with Spectra-Physics engineers and commercialized the more powerful lasers invented at Bell Labs (the carbon-dioxide laser) and at Spectra-Physics (the ion laser). Another spin-off of Spectra-Physics would be Chromatix in 1969 in Sunnyvale. Spectra-Physics went on to build in 1974 the first bar-code scanner ever used in a store.

The laser was a formidable invention. No other invention would be integrated so quickly in society and become so pervasive in such a short time (bar-code scanners, compact discs, cutting and welding, holography, precision surgery).

Culture and Society

Ironically, San Francisco was still moving in the opposite direction, away from technology and towards nature and humanity. In January 1967 a "Human Be-In" was held at the Golden Gate Park, and the beach town of Monterey hosted the first major rock festival in June of that year. John Lion started the Magic Theatre in 1967.

In 1968 Stewart Brand of the Portola Institute published the first "Whole Earth Catalog," a sort of alternative yellow pages that listed products targeting the hippie lifestyle and featured articles on all sorts of counterculture topics. Not only did the catalog sell well (in 1971 it would print one million copies): it also introduced the praxis of letting readers review products. The Whole Earth Catalog, just like (on a smaller scale) the flyer-based grass-roots campaigns of the hippies, pioneered the process of "going viral" without the traditional marketing that came from the mainstream media.

In 1968 Chip Lord founded the Ant Farm to promote avantgarde architecture and design.

The news media went berserk reporting from San Francisco about the bizarre youth counterculture. Millions of young people around the world started imitating it. The whole hippie phenomenon paralleled the Bay Area's flare in interest for computer science and the growth of the Bay Area's semiconductor industry. Indian musician Ali Akbar Khan founded the Ali Akbar College of Music in 1967 in Berkeley to teach and spread

Indian classical music, which was becoming increasingly popular among rebellious youth like everything else from India and the Far East.

At the same time, many new residential areas were being created between San Francisco and San Jose. The underpopulated Bay Area fostered a different urban model than the one popularized by Manhattan's skyscrapers. There was plenty of free space south of San Francisco, and therefore no need for high-rise buildings. Earthquakes also helped shape the urban environment as an endless flow of flat buildings with no particular center. The community lay horizontally, reached by walking instead of elevators. The main square had disappeared. Even Main Street and Broadway (the two staples of urban topography in most US towns) were missing (or few knew where they were). San Francisco was called "the city" because the cities of Silicon Valley were not cities.

One of the most important events of 1965 for Silicon Valley had nothing to do with technology per se. The Immigration Act of 1965 greatly increased the quotas of immigrants allowed from various countries. It allowed immigration based on rare skills, such as software or hardware engineering. For example, only 47 scientists migrated to the US from Taiwan in 1965, but in 1967 the number was 1,321. That immigration law started a brain drain of engineers and scientists from Europe and especially the Far East towards Silicon Valley that would have far-reaching consequences.

Geniuses: DRAM, Intel, SRI, PARC, Arpanet, and Utopia (1968-71)

DRAM

The booming sales of smaller computers and the Bay Area's experiments in semiconductors came together in July 1968 when Robert Noyce and Gordon Moore started Intel in Mountain View to build semiconductor memory chips. It was funded with money collected by Arthur Rock. The price of magnetic core memories had been declining steadily for years. The founders of Intel, however, believed that semiconductor computer memory could fit a lot more information (bits) and therefore become a cheaper method to hold large amounts of data.

Intel was not alone in believing in new memory technology. An IBM researcher, Robert Dennard, achieved the first breakthrough in 1966, when he built the first DRAM. His DRAM, or dynamic random access memory, needed only one transistor and one capacitor to hold a bit of information, thus enabling very high densities. It was called "dynamic" because it needed to be refreshed continuously. The combination of Kilby's integrated circuit and Dennard's dynamic RAM was capable of triggering a major revolution in computer engineering, because together the microchip and the micromemory made it possible to build much smaller computers.

Lee Boysel at Fairchild Semiconductor achieved a 256-bit dynamic RAM in 1968. Then he founded Four Phase Systems in 1969 (with other Fairchild employees as well as Frank Wanlass from General Instrument) to build 1024-bit and 2048-bit DRAMs (kilobits of memory on a single chip). Advanced Memory Systems, founded in 1968 not far from Intel by engineers from IBM, Motorola, and Fairchild Semiconductor, introduced one of the first 1K DRAMs in 1969. Intel introduced its own in 1970, the 1103.

Four Phase

Before DRAMs, the semiconductor firms mainly made money by building custom-designed integrated circuits. Like all customized solutions, they did not have a huge market (often just one customer) but were lucrative and safe. DRAMs, instead, were general-purpose and rapidly became a commodity. Their advantage was that they could be sold by the thousands. Their disadvantage was that the semiconductor firms had to learn to live with competition, i.e. with a constant downward pressure on prices. By 1972 Intel had more than 1,000 employees and posted revenues of $23 million. Intel pioneered what would become a well-honored Silicon Valley tradition: all employees were made shareholders through "stock options" from the moment they joined the company.

Intel's First Office Building (2010)

Case Study: Gordon Moore

Gordon Moore's story is emblematic of how Silicon Valley was started, and useful to demystify some legends about what stimulates people to work in Silicon Valley. He was a fifth-generation Californian who studied at San Jose State College and then at UC Berkeley before graduating as a chemist at the California Institute for Technology (Caltech) in Pasadena, where his research was founded by the Office of Naval Research, like many scientific projects of the time: in the 1950s the Cold War was raging. Jobs for scientists were not easy to find in California, so he and his wife (also a Bay Area native) moved to Johns Hopkins University's Applied Physics Laboratory (APL). Shockley, another California-raised man, had moved back to the Bay Area because of his mother, and was looking for talents to jump-start his laboratory (located a few blocks away from his mother's house). Moore intended to move back to the Bay Area for a similar reason: to be near his folks (and in-laws). So two of the founding fathers of Silicon Valley defy the stereotype of the immigrant: they were family men, looking for a stereotypical family life. Shockley offered Moore that opportunity, and he joined his lab; not to change the world or to become a millionaire, but simply to live a normal bourgeois life. Luckily for Moore, none of Shockley's East Coast friends wanted to move to the Bay Area: the East Coast was the high-tech place to be, the Bay Area was, by comparison, a third-world country. So much for the much vaunted appeal of the California weather. When Moore joined Shockley, interest in transistors mainly came from the government, that needed to build more reliable rockets. Again, the Cold War helped Moore get a start. When the eight "traitors" were plotting against Shockley, One man whom Shockley had convinced to move west was Robert Noyce, an engineer of the Philco Corporation in Philadelphia. Shockley had attended a semiconductor symposium on the East Coast specifically to unearth young talents. Noyce got convinced because he loved the prospect of working on state-of-the-art transistor technology, but also because his brother had moved to the Bay Area and housing was much more affordable in the Bay Area than in Philadelphia (he already had a wife and two children). Noyce and Moore led the rebellion of the eight "traitors" that founded Fairchild and then Moore became Fairchild's director of Research and Development. The reason they left Shockley and started Fairchild was not the money: it was the love of science (and Shockley's impossible attitude). Moore, as a teenager, had played with explosives, and he came from a family that had witnessed the explosive growth of the Bay Area; last but not least, he married a sociologist. These factors may account for the fact that, ultimately, the so-called "Moore's Law" describes an exponential growth, and is actually a social meditation on (technological and social) change. Moore was a visionary about the future of electronics working inside that industry, a rarity at the time. In fact, the famous (and very brief) paper of April 1965 titled "Cramming More Components onto Integrated Circuits" (in the anniversary issue of Electronics) had been preceded in 1963 by a longer essay, titled "Semiconductor Integrated Circuits", that appeared in "Microelectronics - Theory, Design, and Fabrication" (McGraw-Hill, 1963). His prediction was actually a bold prediction, based on rather scant data: Fairchild's chip of 1959 had hosted only 1 transistor, whereas Intels' chip of 1965 had 50. He extrapolated and decided that the chip of 1975 would contain 65,000. To some extent this was a self-fulfilling prophecy, because Moore at Intel set out to prove his "law" right, and he did. Moore went on to become the longest-serving CEO of Intel and the richest man in California (in the 2000s).

The DRAM

By then IBM had shot far ahead of the competition. The competition relied on the anti-trust laws to manufacture "clones" of IBM mainframes. They were called the "bunch" from the initials of their names: Burroughs, Univac (that in 1971 bought RCA's computer business), NCR, Control Data Corporation (that had acquired Bendix), and Honeywell (that in 1970 bought General Electric's computing business).

Honeywell had jumped late into computers but had made some bold acquisitions and hired bright engineers. Bill Regitz was one of them, a specialist in core memory systems from the Bell Labs. He became a specialist in MOS (Metal Oxide Semiconductor) technology and came up with an idea for a better DRAM (using only three transistors per bit instead of the four or more used by the previous mass-market DRAM chips). He shared that idea with Intel (and eventually joined Intel) and the result was the Intel i1103, a 1,024-bit DRAM chip, introduced in the fall of 1970. It wasn't the first one, but it was the first one that could be easily used to build computer memories. Hewlett-Packard selected it for its 9800 series, and IBM chose it for its System 370/158. It became the first bestseller in the semiconductor business.

Within two years Intel was dominating the market for DRAMs. By the end of the year not only Intel but the whole Santa Clara Valley had become the place to go and buy semiconductor technology: five of the seven largest US semiconductor manufacturers were based here.

In 1969 Jerry Sanders, the marketing guru of Fairchild Semiconductor, founded Advanced Micro Devices (AMD), a firm that was initially staffed with former Fairchild employees and focused on logic chips, starting with the Am2501 logic chip in 1970, but in 1971 it entered the memory market with the Am3101, a 64-bit static RAM.

However, core memory was still the memory of choice among large computer manufacturers, still accounting for more than 95% of all computers in the mid 1970s.

AMD's "White House" Headquarters (2010)

Bay Area High-Tech Creativity

Besides the semiconductor industry, the Bay Area was now producing all sorts of high-tech ideas. In December 1968, Doug Engelbart of the Stanford Research Institute (SRI) publicly demonstrated the NLS ("oN-

Line System"), one of the most celebrated "demos" of all times. It was a project started in 1962 and financed by NASA and ARPA. NLS featured a graphical user interface and a hypertext system running on the first computer to employ the mouse. Engelbart stood in front of the audience in San Francisco and interacted live with a computer in Menlo Park (at SRI's offices). When the Apollo program ended and ARPA and NASA ended funding to Engelbart's team at the SRI, SRI sold the team and its NLS to Tymshare.

The hippie anti-military ideology indirectly affected SRI. Student protests against SRI's reliance on military projects caused Stanford to spin off SRI as an independent non-profit entity, which later (1977) renamed itself SRI International. In 1969, SRI's Artificial Intelligence group, led by Charlie Rosen, demonstrated "Shakey the Robot," a mobile robot that employed artificial intelligence techniques. In 1970 Stanford University's Ed Feigenbaum, capitalizing on Dendral, launched the Heuristic Programming Project to create "expert systems" that could match the behavior of human experts in specific domains.

Shakey the Robot of SRI (1969)

Xerox PARC

In 1969 the New York-based photocopier giant Xerox decided to get into computers and acquired Scientific Data Systems (SDS) for $900 million. That division went on to produce the Sigma line of 32-bit mainframe computers. Xerox's venture into computers would be so unsuccessful that the division would be closed in 1975.

However, a major corporate center came out of Xerox's foray. In order to support its venture into computers, in 1970 Xerox set up the Palo Alto Research Center (PARC) in the Stanford Research Park to conduct research in computers far away from the company's headquarters. Xerox PARC hired Bob Taylor, the former director of ARPA's IPTO, to lead the Computer Science Laboratory (CSL). A year earlier Xerox's scientist Gary Starkweather had invented the laser printer. The first working laser printing system was developed at PARC.

Among the center's many promising talents was Alan Kay, hired in 1971, a pupil of computer-graphic pioneer Ivan Sutherland in Utah and a lecturer at Stanford's AI Lab (SAIL) in 1970. Kay had the vision of a mobile computer that he named Dynabook, and of "object-oriented" (a term that he coined) educational software. He designed a completely new software environment to develop software applications, Smalltalk. It was inspired by Simula 67, a programming language for simulations that had been defined in Norway by Ole-Johan Dahl and Kristen Nygaard. Kay created a GUI with children in mind (overlapping windows and then the "desktop" metaphor).

Kay had a completely different view of what a computer was and what it should do, and that vision came from his passion for education. In a sense, he envisioned children as the ultimate users of computers, and therefore computers as tools for children. Once framed this way, the problem became one not of faster processing but of better interaction. It was not humans who had to learn the language of computers but computers who had to learn the "language" (or at least the way) of humans. Dan Ingalls developed most of the programming language in 1972. In 1973 Smalltalk was ready for use by children. Patrick Suppes, a philosopher of science at Stanford, had been running the Computer Curriculum Corporation since 1967, a pioneering firm in interactive e-learning. One of his students, Adele Goldberg, joined the PARC team and helped deploy Smalltalk in schools.

Taylor did not hesitate to hire away from SRI the very team that he had helped Engelbart establish, notably Bill English. PARC also hired most of the gurus behind the Berkeley Computer Corporation (BCC) that had tried to commercialize Berkeley's Project Genie, notably Charles Thacker, who in 1972 led the development of a PDP-10 clone called MAXC, that directly competed with Xerox's Sigma 7 (clearly Xerox PARC was not well integrated in Xerox's computer business). PARC also benefited from an "amendment" credited to senator Mike Mansfield 1970 that was meant to reduce funding for pure research by DARPA. This never happened (funding actually increased) but it was enough to convince many computer scientists in academia to join industrial research centers. Such was the case with Taylor, Kay, Thacker, English, Bob Metcalfe (MIT) and Charles Simonyi (UC Bekeley), all of them coming from some of the biggest recipients of DARPA funding.

Perhaps as important as the technology was the work ethic at Xerox PARC, an ethic that basically consisted in not having a work ethic at all. Xerox funded the center, and left the scientists free to do what they wanted with the money. Unlikely as it may sound for someone coming from government agencies, Taylor fostered an environment that was casual, informal and egalitarian, with no dress code and no work hours. Xerox PARC came to symbolize for research centers the equivalent of the alternative lifestyle preached by the hippies (if not a premonition of the punks).

Alas, in 1972 Rolling Stone magazine published an article written by Stewart Brand, titled "Spacewar", that hailed the hippy-like community of hackers at PARC, hardly the style favorite at headquarter

Besides HP, IBM had to face a new competitor that was based in the Bay Area. The chief architect of IBM's mainframes, Gene Amdahl, started his own business in 1970 in Sunnyvale to build IBM-compatible mainframes, less expensive and faster than IBM's models. Amdahl's first machine would come out in 1975.

Meanwhile, the hippy anti-military ideology indirectly affected the SRI: student protests against SRI's reliance on military projects caused Stanford to spin off the SRI as an independent non-profit entity, which later (1977) renamed itself SRI International.

Xerox PARC's Old Building (2010)

The Age of the Minicomputer

Hewlett-Packard was ready to enter the minicomputer market with the 3000, a project begun in 1970 and released in November 1972. HP used a new strategy to design this machine: it employed both hardware and software engineers to write the specifications. The result was that the 3000 was one of the first computers to be completely programmed in a high-level language instead of the prevailing assembly languages, and (from 1974) it came with a database management system (IMAGE), something that in the past only mainframes had been able to offer. The PDP of DEC had introduced a "do-it-yourself" mindset in data centers. By enabling staff with little computing skills to manage strategic data, the HP/3000 pushed that mindset one floor up to the business offices. The success of this machine would transform HP's culture. To start with, HP would use this product to expand from its traditional industrial base into the business world. In a few years revenues from the 3000 would account for almost half of total revenues, propelling HP to the forefront of the minicomputer industry.

Disks

IBM's San Jose laboratories were assigned the task to develop a cheap storage medium to load the 370 mainframe's microcode and replace the cumbersome tape units. Previous IBM mainframes had used non-volatile read-only memory to store the microcode, but the 370 instead used a read and write semiconductor memory that had become affordable and reliable, besides solving many engineering problems. However, semiconductor memory was volatile (it was erased whenever the power was switched off). Therefore IBM had to provide a medium to reload the microcode. In 1971 David Noble came up with a cheap read-only 80-kilobyte diskette: it was nicknamed the "floppy disk." It made it easy to load the control program and to change it whenever needed.

It was originally designed to be written once and read many times, but just one year later a team at Memorex led by Alan Shugart built the first read-write floppy-disk drive, the Memorex 650. It obviously could serve more purposes than just loading control programs into a mainframe.

Even more important, perhaps, was the product introduced in November 1973: the 3040 hard-disk drive, the so-called "Winchester drive", with a total capacity of 60 megabytes. It was developed at the same San Jose laboratories by Kenneth Haughton's team for the low-end System/370 models. This was the drive that truly enabled transactional systems.

IBM had opened another laboratory in the Bay Area, in Palo Alto. Ben Riggins was relocated here after conceiving CICS (Customer Information Control System) in Chicago. Riggins had realized that many corporations (especially utilities) needed a simple way to access information online and in real time. CICS, developed in Palo Alto, was released in 1969. The Winchester hard disk and CICS bootstrapped the market for online transaction systems. CICS would remain one of software's all-time bestsellers, licensed by virtually all of IBM's top customers and used daily (if unconsciously) by millions of people for bank operations, utility payments, credit-card transactions, etc.

The Videogame

People also began to realize that advanced computer technology could be used for purposes totally unrelated to computing. Inspired by Steve Russell's ten-year old but still popular "Spacewar," in 1971 Ampex employees Nolan Bushnell and Ted Dabney quit their jobs and created the first arcade videogame, "Computer Space." It was a free-standing terminal powered by a computer and devoted to an electronic game that anyone could use. When, in May 1972, Magnavox introduced the first videogame console, Ralph Baer 's transistor-based "Odyssey," Bushnell was inspired again, this time by an electronic ping-pong game. He founded Atari in Santa Clara (mainly with Ampex engineers) and asked his engineer Allan Alcorn to create a similar game, which became "Pong" in November 1972, a runaway success.

Atari's Pong Videogame System (1972)

The Financial and Legal Infrastructure

The high-tech industry of the South Bay began attracting serious capital in 1968 when ARD's investment in Digital Equipment Corporation (DEC) was valued at $355 million. It was the first well-publicized case of an investment in a computer company that paid off handsomely. The same model could be replicated on the West Coast. New investment companies were founded: Asset Management by Franklin Johnson (1965); Hambrecht & Quist by William Hambrecht and George Quist in San Francisco (1968); Bryan & Edwards by John Bryan and Bill Edwards (1968); Crosspoint Venture by John Mumford in Woodside (1970); and so on. As their returns beat national stock index averages, New York firms such as Bessemer Securities opened branches in the Bay Area.

At the same time, a law firm located in the Stanford Industrial Park, evolved from a firm that a Redwood City attorney John Wilson had started in 1961. Its customers were Tymshare, ESL and Coherent Laser. Wilson's firm just added two Berkeley graduates (Larry Sonsini in 1966 and Mario Rosati in 1971) and laid the foundations for the typical Silicon Valley law firm, which specialized in setting up startups, writing contracts between founders and venture capitalists, taking startups public through IPOs, and, controversially, accepting equity in its clients as a form of payment.

Wilson Sonsini's Law Offices (2010)

Biotech's First Steps

In 1959 the medical department of the University of the Pacific had moved to Stanford University's campus in a joint venture between the City of Palo Alto and Stanford University. In 1968 this medical center was purchased by Stanford University and renamed as Stanford University Hospital. Coupled with the success of Syntex, this event symbolized the coming of age of the area in pharmaceutical research.

A few early biotech companies were created. Alza was founded in 1968 by former Syntex's President Alejandro Zaffaroni in Palo Alto and rapidly became the most successful of the new pharmaceutical companies.

Cetus, the first biotech company of the Bay Area was founded (in 1971) by Donald Glaser, a Nobel-winning nuclear physicist at UC Berkeley who had switched to molecular biology, to develop methods to process DNA. In those days the composition of DNA was still largely a mystery, and the main business was to devise automated methods to carry out research on DNA.

Arpanet
In October 1969 the Arpanet was inaugurated with four nodes, three of which were in California: UCLA, in the laboratory of Leonard Kleinrock; Stanford Research Institute in Doug Engelbart's Augmentation Research Center; UC Santa Barbara; and the University of Utah.

The Arpanet involuntarily introduced a paradigm shift that would have wide-ranging implications (and not only technological ones): it shifted the emphasis from the privately-owned top-down control of the telephone system and its inflexible switching circuits towards a model of public adaptive bottom-up communication in which there was no center and command was spread throughout a dynamic population of "routers". A few years later that would become the very ideology of the "counterculture", albeit in a completely different context. By accident the Arpanet had just invented the counterculture.

A historical footnote: the Arpanet had been preceded by the Octopus network, implemented in 1968 at the Lawrence Livermore Laboratories by connecting four Control Data 6600 mainframes (the project had begun in 1964).

Then in November 1971 Bell Labs unveiled its Unix operating system, designed by Kenneth Thompson and Dennis Ritchie, and meant as a successor to MULTICS. In 1973 they also rewrote it in a programming language called C, developed by Ritchie the year before. That marked the first time that an operating system was written in a high-level language, and therefore easy to port across computers. Unix spread from one corner of the computer world to the other, and was eventually chosen as the ideal operating system for the Arpanet.

The Unbundling of IBM and the Software Industry
IBM had traditionally "bundled" the software with the computer. In theory the software was free, but its cost was factored into the price of the computer. In 1969 IBM decided to open up its software business to the competition. This historical "unbundling" created a golden opportunity for independent software companies, as the market for mainframe applications

was colossal. Firms such as Informatics (Los Angeles, 1962) and Cullinane (Boston, 1968) introduced software packages addressing big industries. The world of computing was beginning to be called "Information Technology" (IT).

All of this happened far away from the Bay Area. Most software companies were based on the East Coast or in the Midwest, because most computer users were based on the East Coast or in the Midwest. The only major exception was Los Angeles, where the aviation industry was based. The Bay Area had only two major users of computers: Bank of America in San Francisco (that had already installed the ERMA in 1955) and the Lawrence Livermore Laboratories in the East Bay (an early adopter of the PDP-1 in 1961). Not much, however, existed in the Santa Clara Valley.

In 1975, just months before the introduction of the first Apple computer, the whole market for software products in the US was still worth less than $1 billion.

Labor Fluidity

Silicon Valley, however, already exhibited a unique job dynamics that would only accelerate in the age of software. First of all, California was blessed with an almost unstoppable economy, which mostly outperformed the rest of the US. Therefore there were plenty of jobs available. It was an employee's market and not an employer's market. The job of the "head hunter" (an employment broker) was more important than elsewhere since recruiting talented people was not easy. Second, California law forbade any labor contract that limited what an employee could do after quitting. Section 16600 of the California Business and Professions Code, a clause that dated back to the 19th century, was enforced by courts. In the rest of the US, trade secrets were guarded jealously and employees were forbidden to join competitors.

The job market in the Bay Area exhibited high turnover. Silicon Valley engineers exhibited a preference for horizontal instead of vertical mobility, that is, for hopping from job to job instead of following a career of promotion after promotion. Europe and the East Coast had an entrenched concept of vertical mobility (a career within a company). Sometimes, even at the expense of skills, an engineer might be promoted to a role that had nothing to do with engineering simply because it was the only available higher-level position. However Silicon Valley was about horizontal mobility, changing jobs in order to maximize one's skills based on available opportunities across the industry. In fact, it became commonly understood by engineers that staying with the same company for more than a few years did not look "good" on a resume. This created a system that was an odd and involuntary model of cooperation.

Job turnover and no protection for trade secrets were clearly not beneficial to the individual company, but they were to the entire ecosystem because they fostered an endless flow of knowledge throughout the community. No educational institution could spread knowledge as fast and efficiently as this pervasive job mobility did. This resulted in rapid dissemination of knowledge within an industry across companies, as well as in cross-fertilization of ideas across research groups.

Somewhat related to the high-speed job market was the status symbol of being an engineer. Probably no other region in the world held its engineers is such high esteem. The engineers represented a higher social class in Silicon Valley than, say, marketing executives. The status symbol of being an engineer was only second to the status symbol of being an entrepreneur.

Culture and Society

The effervescent cultural scene of San Francisco attracted artists whose eccentric visions were tamed in their native East Coast. In particular, George Kuchar, the prophet of lo-fi cinema, moved from New York to the San Francisco Art Institute in 1971.

The leading art in San Francisco, however, was now an art that mixed fiction and painting: the comic strip. A number of eccentric cartoonists, most of whom had moved west during the "Summer of Love" and lived in the Haight-Ashbury neighborhood, repudiated Walt Disney's poor-heart ethics and adopted mocking tones and a vulgar language: the "underground comix" movement was born. The pioneer had probably been Joel Beck, one of the original contributors to the Berkeley Barb, with the full-length comic book "Lenny of Laredo" (1965; but the movement coalesced in 1968 when publisher Don Donahue opened "Apex Novelties", Robert Crumb penned the comic book "Zap Comix" (1968) for that very publisher, and Gary Arlington opened the first comics-only store in the USA (in the Mission District). Then came Bill Griffith's strip "Young Lust" (1970), that mocked sexual attitudes, Roger Brand's comic magazine "Real Pulp Comics" (1970), that promoted the whole burgeoning scene, Trina Robbins' "It Ain't Me Babe Comix" (1970), the first all-women comic book, Dan O'Neill's collective "Air Pirates" (1971), Gilbert Shelton's "The Fabulous Furry Freak Brothers" (1971), Justin Considine's "Binky Brown Meets the Holy Virgin Mary" (1972).

Meanwhile, Philip Dick marked the convergence of the drug culture and the science fiction culture with his masterpieces "Do Androids Dream of Electric Sheep" (1968) and "Ubik" (1969). He died in extreme poverty before his novels "Blade Runner" (based on "Do Androids..."), "Total Recall" (written in 1966), and "Minority Report" (written in 1956) were turned into Hollywood blockbusters.

The contradictions of the "hippie" era peaked with the election of a conservative governor who seemed to stand for everything that California was not. Ronald Reagan, a former Hollywood actor who was governor from 1967 till 1975, ended an enlightened age in which the state of California was focused on building its infrastructure. Reagan inaugurated an age in which citizens revolted against government and cared more about improving their economic conditions (for example, by lowering taxes) than investing in the future. The dream land of idealistic immigrants was on its way to become a pragmatic state of greedy bourgeois.

The post-hippie era in California also witnessed the rapid political growth of the grass-roots environmentalist movement. It started with the article "Tragedy of the Commons," published in Science in 1968 by Garrett Hardin of UC Santa Barbara. The first victory of the movement came in 1969 when the Sierra Club managed to stop Walt Disney from building a tourist resort in the mountains of a national park. Anti-nuclear sentiment also increased, leading David Brower to split from the Sierra Club and start Friends of the Earth in Berkeley. In the fall the United Nations organized a conference titled "Man and his Environment" in San Francisco. One of the speakers, California-based peace activist John McConnell, the editor of the utopian "Mountain View" magazine, proposed an international holiday. In March 1970, San Francisco allowed him to hold the first "Earth Day." In 1972 the United Nations held its first "Conference on the Environment" in Sweden. One of the people who traveled from the US to attend it was Peter Berg, who in 1973 founded Planet Drum in Berkeley. The influence of the environmentalists would be felt for decades.

At the same time that the Reaganite establishment was curbing public spending on ideological grounds, a rising environmentalist movement pressed to curb the infrastructure boom of the previous decades on almost opposite ideological grounds. The effect of this "double whammy" was to be felt decades later.

In the arts it was notable that in 1971 Judy Chicago and Miriam Schapiro established a "Feminist Art Program" at the California Institute of the Arts specifically to train female artists.

In 1970 the PARC also started an artist-in-residency program. In 1969 the physicist Frank Oppenheimer opened the Exploratorium at the Palace of Fine Arts. Its first show was "Cybernetic Serendipity", an exhibition of computer art that Jasia Reichardt had organized the previous year at the Institute of Contemporary Arts in London.

Hobbyists: The Microprocessor, Computer Kits, Ethernet, Internet, the Alto, and Genetic Engineering (1971-75)

The Microprocessor

A microprocessor is a programmable set of integrated circuits; basically, a computer on a chip. It had been theoretically possible for years to integrate the CPU of a computer on a chip. It was just a matter of perfecting the technology. In 1970 Lee Boysel at Four Phase Systems had already designed the AL1, an 8-bit Central Processing Unit (CPU). It was de facto the first commercial microprocessor. (Gary Boone at Texas Instruments designed the TMX 1795 a few months later, and, more importantly, the first single chip microcontroller, the TMS-0100).

Yet the microprocessor that changed the history of computing was being developed at Intel. Ted Hoff at Intel bet on silicon-gated MOS technology to hold a 4-bit CPU onto a chip. In 1970 he hired Federico Faggin, the inventor of silicon-gated transistors. Faggin implemented Hoff's design in silicon, and in November 1971 Intel unveiled the 4004, a small thumbnail-size electronic device containing 2,300 transistors, spaced by 10,000nm gaps, and capable of processing 92,000 instructions per second. This had started as a custom project for Busicom, a Japanese manufacturer of calculators (that in January had introduced the world's first pocket calculator, the LE-120A Handy). Intel's tiny 4004 chip was as powerful as the ENIAC, but millions of times smaller and ten thousand times cheaper. By August 1972 Intel had ready an 8-bit version of the 4004, the 8008, whose eight-bit word allowed it to represent 256 ASCII characters, including all ten digits, both uppercase and lowercase letters and punctuation marks.

The Intel 4004 Chip (1971)

Intel was not convinced that a microprocessor could be used to build a computer. It was up to Bill Pentz at California State University in Sacramento to prove the concept. In 1972 his team built the Sac State 8008, the first microcomputer, and helped Intel fine-tune the microprocessor for the task of building computers.

Bill Pentz

Intel's initial motivation to make microprocessors was that microprocessors helped sell more memory chips. A few months earlier Intel had introduced another important invention, the EPROM, developed by the Israeli-born engineer Dov Frohman. An EPROM (Erasable Programmable Read Only Memory) is a non-volatile memory made of transistors that can be erased. By making it possible to reprogram the microprocessor at will, it also made it more versatile.

The 4004 and the 8008 had been produced in small quantities (the latter mainly as the basis for DEC's own processors), but in April 1974 Intel unveiled the 8080, designed at the transistor level by Japanese-born Masatoshi Shima. It lowered both the price and the complexity of building a computer while further increasing the power (290,000 instructions per second). It was bound to happen. (In 1968 a reclusive electrical engineer, Gilbert Hyatt, had founded Micro Computer in the Los Angeles region and filed for a patent on what would be known as the microprocessor, but apparently never built one).

Meanwhile, at least 60 semiconductor companies had been founded in the Santa Clara Valley between 1961 and 1972, many by former Fairchild engineers and managers. It was a highly competitive environment, driven by highly-educated engineers.

The center of mass for venture capital had steadily shifted from San Francisco towards Menlo Park. In 1972, the venture capital firm Kleiner Perkins, founded by Austrian-born Eugene Kleiner of Fairchild Semiconductor and former Hewlett-Packard executive Tom Perkins, opened offices on Sand Hill Road. It was followed by Don Valentine of Fairchild Semiconductor who founded Capital Management Services, later renamed Sequoia Capital. That year the Electronic News correspondent Don Hoeffler popularized the term "Silicon Valley," the new nickname of the area between Pale Alto and San Jose, which fell in the Santa Clara Valley. In 1974 Reid Dennis (a member of the "group") and Burton McMurtry (of Palo Alto Investment) founded the investment company Institutional Venture Associates. In 1976 it split into two partnerships, McMurtry's Technology Venture Associates and Dennis' Institutional Venture Partners, while Tommy Davis launched the Mayfield Fund. In 1968 Harvey Wagner and several UC Berkeley professors had founded Teknekron, one of the world's first startup incubators focused on IT.

In 1970 Regis McKenna, a former marketing employee of General Microelectronics (1963) and National Semiconductor (1967), started his own marketing agency, one of the many that were proliferating to help the engineering startups with advertising and public relations (in the days when engineers read magazines such as "Electronic News"). McKenna was one of the people responsible for making New York listen to the West Coast. In those days most magazines had little interest in the West Coast. McKenna and the other marketers managed to get the attention of New York and often the "inventor" would capture the attention of the New York media more than its product. In a sense, the "cult of personality" that would become a staple of Silicon Valley was born back then, when the eccentric personality of founders and engineers was often more easily "sold" to influential magazines than their exotic technologies. Regis McKenna was one of the people who promoted Silicon Valley as an "attitude". This process would culminate in 1982, when Time magazine would put Steven Jobs (then 26) on the front cover.

Regis McKenna

Mail-order Computer Kits

The Intel 8008 was used by companies targeting the electronic hobbyist market, which was huge. These companies were mostly selling kits by mail-order that hobbyists could buy to build exotic machines at home. The first two companies were Scelbi (SCientific, ELectronic and BIological), first advertised in March 1974 by a Connecticut-based company, and Mark-8, developed by Virginia Tech's student Jon Titus and announced in July 1974. However, they were all beaten at the finish line by Vietnamese-born engineer Andre Truong Trong Thi, who used the 8008 to build the Micral in February 1973 for a governmental research center in France (and it was an assembled computer, not just a kit).

Magazines such as "Radio Electronics," "QST" and "Popular Electronics" were responsible for creating excitement about the microprocessor. Basically, the microprocessor reached a wider audience than its inventors had intended because of hobbyist magazines. Otherwise it would have been known only to the few large corporations that were willing to buy microprocessors in bulk. The most creative and visionary users were not working in those corporations.

Networking Computers

Networks of computers did not connect yet millions of people, but they were laying the foundations for one of the most dramatic social revolution of all times. Notably, in 1972 Ray Tomlinson at Boston's consulting firm Bolt, Beranek and Newman (BBN) invented e-mail for sending messages between computer users.

In 1971 computer-science students from UC Berkeley, including Lee Felsenstein (formerly an activist of Berkeley's Free Speech Movement in 1964) formed Resource One, an organization operating out of an abandoned warehouse in San Francisco and aiming to create a public computer network. Lee Felsenstein (the software specialist), Efrem Lipkin (the hardware specialist) and Mark Szpakowski (the user interface specialist) had access to a Scientific Data Systems' time-sharing machine. The first public terminal of what came to be known as the "Community Memory" was set up in 1973 inside Leopold's Records, a record store run by the Student Union of UC Berkeley, and it was later moved to the nearby Whole Earth Access store. This college drop-outs had created the first public computerized bulletin board system.

Groups of computer users were already working together, sharing "notes" on files that were accessible by the whole network. The most popular of these early note-sharing systems (later "groupware") was perhaps PLATO Notes, written in August 1973 by University of Illinois' student David Woolley.

Taylor at Xerox PARC also promoted the idea of the distributed network of computers, except that now the network consisted of small computers rather than the big computers of the Arpanet. In 1973 Bob Metcalfe, a mathematician who had worked on Project MAC at the MIT, coined the term "Ethernet" for a local-area network. PARC wanted all of its computers to be able to print on their one laser printer. Unlike the Internet, which connected remote computers using phone lines, the Ethernet was to connect local computers using special cables and adapters. Unlike the Internet, which was very slow, the Ethernet had to be very fast to match the speed of the laser printer. The first Ethernet was finally operational in 1976. The Ethernet allowed offices to connect personal computers and perform the same work of a mainframe at a fraction of the cost. The industry has long believed that this was false (the "Grosch law" credited to Herb Grosch). The Ethernet created the conditions for a seismic change in the way information-technology budgets were allocated.

Metcalfe instead enunciated "Metcalfe's Law:" the value of a network of devices increases exponentially with the number of connected devices. This was popularly translated in terms of users: the value of a network increases exponentially with the number of the people that it connects.

Meawhile, Radio Frequency Identification (RFID), an evolution of the radar technology used in World War II and perfected at the Los Alamos National Laboratory during the 1970s, was turned into an industrial product by Charles Walton, a former IBM scientist, who had founded Proximity Devices in Sunnyvale in 1970, and in 1973 designed a "portable radio frequency emitting identifier".

The Arpanet had 2,000 users in 1973 (the year when the first international connection was established, to the University College of

London), and Vinton Cerf of Stanford University had nicknamed it the "Internet." A study showed that about 75% of its traffic was e-mail messages: the Internet had become a replacement for telephone and mail communications (not the intended purpose). The following year Cerf and Bob Kahn of DARPA published the Transmission Control Protocol (TCP), which became the backbone of Internet transmission: it enabled Arpanet/Internet computers to communicate with any computer, regardless of its operating system and of its network.

Vint Cerf figured out a 32-bit address space for an estimated 16 million time-sharing machines for each of two networks in 128 countries (TCP/IP would run out of addresses in 2011 and be replaced in 2012 by IPv6).

Built into the Arpanet's engineering principle was actually an implicit political agenda: the "packets" represent an intermediate level between the physical transport layer and the application that reads the content. The packets, in other words, don't know what content they are transporting. All packets are treated equal regardless of whether they are talking about an emergency or about tonight's movie schedule. Each computer in the network picks up a packet and ships it to the next computer without any means to decide which packet is more important. The routing is "neutral". The hidden policy was soon to be called "net neutrality" and later vehemently defended by activists: the Internet was being designed so that participants in the network (later called Internet Service Providers) could not favor one content over the others (e.g. a Hollywood movie over an amateur's Youtube movie).

Vint Cerf

A transformation was taking place in the nature of the Arpanet that was not visible from outside. The Arpanet, a military tool, had been handed (out of necessity, not by design) to Unix hackers. These hackers were imbued with a counterculture that was almost the exact opposite of the military culture. So the Arpanet was increasingly being "hijacked" by a bunch of hackers to become a social tool (although originally only used to chat and play games).

The Hobbyist Market

By that time a large number of young people were children of engineers. They were raised in technology-savvy environments. Many of them picked up electronic kits as teenagers and eventually continued the local tradition of the high-tech hobbyists. In fact, that tradition merged with the mythology of the juvenile delinquent and with the the the hippie ideology in legendary characters like John Draper (better known as Captain Crunch), the most famous "phone phreak" of this age who in 1971 built the "blue boxes" capable of fooling the phone system. Phreaking went viral and in October 1971 Esquire Magazine published an article exposing the underground phenomenon, resulting in Draper's arrest. One of his fans was Steve Wozniak, back then an engineer at the Cupertino public radio station KKUP.

The hobbyist market was growing. The year 1974 ended in December with an advertisement in hobbyist magazines of Ed Roberts' kit to build a personal computer, the Altair 8800, based on Intel's 8080 microprocessor and sold by mail order (for $395). It was the first product marketed as a "personal computer." Roberts' company MITS, which used to make calculators, was based in Albuquerque, New Mexico. Two Harvard University students, Bill Gates and Monte Davidoff, wrote a BASIC interpreter for it, and then founded a company named Micro-soft, initially also based in Albuquerque. MITS sold 2,000 Altair 8800 systems in one year and started the whole personal-computer frenzy, despite offering only 256 Kbytes of memory (static RAM). Additional static RAM and cards, which could be used to connect to input/output units (e.g., a teletype), were not included in the price. Basically, the Altair was meant for hobbyists. Roberts assumed that his customers were technically savvy enough to buy the missing pieces, connect them together and program the box.

One of the most daring architectures built on top of the Intel 8080 came from Information Management Science Associates (IMSAI), a consulting company for mainframe users founded by William Millard in 1972 in San Leandro, in the East Bay. Its engineers realized that a number of microprocessors tightly coupled together could match the processing power of a mainframe at a fraction of the price. In October 1975 they introduced the Hypercube II, which cost $80,000 (the comparable IBM

370 mainframe cost about $4 million). Ironically, they were more successful with IMSAI 8080, a clone of the Atari 8800 that they sold to the hobbyist market starting in December 1975, while only one Hypercube was ever sold (to the Navy).

The IMSAI 8080 (1975)

The Hobbyist Revolution Continued

In 1973 Gary Kildall, who was an instructor at the Naval Postgraduate School in Monterey, developed the first high-level programming language for Intel microprocessors, PL/M (Programming Language /Microprocessor). It was "burned" into the Read Only Memory (ROM) of the microprocessor. Intel marketed it as an add-on that could help sell its microprocessors. However, when in 1975 Kildall released an operating system for Intel's 8080 processor, CP/M (Control Program/Microcomputer), which managed a floppy drive, Intel balked. Intel was not interested in software that allowed users to read and write files to and from the disk; but makers of small computers were.

The 8080 had inspired several companies to create 8080-based kits, notably MITS and IMSAI. Both needed software for the ever more popular floppy disk. MITS offered its own operating system. IMSAI bought Kildall's CP/M. Kildall's CP/M was largely based on concepts of the PDP-10 operating system (VMS). Kildall then rewrote CP/M isolating the interaction with the hardware in a module called BIOS (Basic Input/Output System). This way CP/M became hardware-independent, and he could sell it to any company in need of a disk operating system for a microprocessor.

In 1974 Kildall started his own company, Digital Research, to sell his product on hobbyist magazines. CP/M soon became a standard.

Kildall's operating system was a crucial development in the history of personal computers. It transformed a chip invented for process control (the microprocessor) into a general-purpose computer that could do what minicomputers and mainframes did.

In 1975 Alan Cooper, a pupil of Gary Kildall's at Monterey and a DRI alumnus, started his own software company, Structured Systems Group (SSG) in Oakland to market his General Ledger, a pioneering business software for personal computer, only sold via computer magazines.

Several hobbyists rushed to mimic Altair's concept. In 1972 the Portola Institute had spawned a magazine, the People's Computer Company, run by Bob Albrecht and devoted to computer education, as well as a coworking space, the People's Computer Center (PCC) in Menlo Park, for proto-nerds to play with a minicomputer, one of them being Lee Felsenstein of the "Community Memory". In March 1975 a group of PCC regulars such as Bob Marsh, Lee Felsenstein and Steve Wozniak met in Gordon French's garage to discuss the Altair. This was the first meeting of what would be known as the Homebrew Computer Club and later relocated to the SLAC's auditorium. These were young people who had been mesmerized by the do-it-yourself kits to build computers. Some of them would go on to build much more than amateur computers. For example, Hewlett-Packard engineer Steve Wozniak demonstrated the first prototype of his Apple at the Homebrew Computer Club meeting of December 1976. Bob Marsh and Lee Felsenstein (formerly an activist of Berkeley's Free Speech Movement in 1964) used the Intel 8080 to design the Sol-20 for Processor Technology in Berkeley, which was released in June 1976, and became the first microcomputer to include a built-in video driver, and the archetype for mass-produced personal computers to come.

Another influential member of the Homebrew Computer Club was Li-Chen Wang, who in 1976 signed his Tiny Basic with the motto "Copyleft - All Wrongs Reserved" to mock the standard "Copyright - All Rights Reserved" of proprietary software, an idea that predated Richard Stallman's "GNU Manifesto" (1983).

The Apple I

The Hobbyist Community

The role played by hobbyists should not be underestimated. The computer market was split along the mainframe-minicomputer divide. IBM and the "BUNCH" sold mainframes. DEC, HP, and others sold minicomputers. These large corporations had the know-how, the brains, and the factories to produce desktop computers for the home market. They did not do it.

The market for home computers was largely created by a group of hobbyists. They were highly individualistic home-based entrepreneurs who worked outside the big bureaucracies of corporations, academia, and government. Many of them did not have a higher education. Many of them had no business training. Many of them had no connections whatsoever with universities or government agencies. However, it was a grass roots movement of hobbyists that created what the corporate world had been unable to do. They created their own community (via magazines, stores and clubs) to obviate to the lack of financial, technological, and marketing infrastructure.

One could argue the personal computer was not invented by an individual, by a laboratory, or by a company; it was invented by a community. In fact, its dynamics was not too different from the dynamics of a community that had taken hold a decade earlier in the Bay Area: the community of the counterculture (agit-prop groups, hippie communes, artistic societies). Until then progress in computer technology had been funded by governments, universities and corporations. The next step would be funded by humble hobbyists spread all over the nation.

To serve the growing community of computer hobbyists, in 1975 a Los Angeles hobbyist, Dick Heiser, had the idea to start a computer store,

Arrowhead Computers. It became the first computer retail store in the world. In December 1975 a member of the Homebrew Club, Paul Terrell, opened a store in Silicon Valley, the Byte Shop, which became a reference point for the local hobbyists, and sold the first units of Wozniak's Apple hobbyist computer.

The Byte Shop

In 1976 William Millard of IMSAI 8080 fame opened the "Computer Shack," a store located in Hayward (again in the East Bay) that offered everything a personal computer user needed. That store would soon become a nation-wide chain, Computerland. It sold computers to the public, a proposition that only a few years earlier (when computers were astronomically expensive and impossible to use) that would have been inconceivable. The retail sale of a computer represented a monumental paradigm shift not only for the industry but also for society as a whole.

Journalists and hobbyists were the true visionaries, not corporate executives with their gargantuan staffs of planners and strategists. The journalists relayed news across the country. The hobbyists organized the newsletters, clubs, and conferences that cemented the community. It was the editor of one such magazine (Dr. Dobb's editor Jim Warren) who in April 1977 organized the first personal computer conference in San Francisco, the "West Coast Computer Fair." It was attended by 13,000 people, the largest computer conference ever. Newsletters, clubs (such as the Southern California Computer Society formed in September 1975), and user conferences proliferated in the following years.

This hobbyist network had another role. It compensated for the fact that most of those early microcomputers came with no customer support, very little quality control, and only the most elementary software. The network provided the education and the support that large computer manufacturers provided to their customers. The network even did the marketing and proselytizing. At the same time, the network influenced the manufacturers. The community of users probably helped shape the personal computer market more than any technological roadmap.

Many of the real geniuses of this microcomputer revolution never made money out of it. Often they didn't even get recognition from the ones who did make money. In particular, software was still a strange "good", that the law didn't know how to treat. When it came to software, intellectual property basically did not exist. IBM had officially lost the monopoly of software but de facto still owned most of the business software in the world, and software did not have a perceived value. The pioneers of microcomputers freely exchanged software, or, better, borrowed from each other. No surprise then that some of Bill Pentz's original code ended up in Gary Kildall's CP/M and that Kildall claimed Microsoft had "stolen" some of his code. (Microsoft did not develop DOS, but bought it from Tim Paterson, who had clearly plagiarized some of Kildall's code). And, of course, later on when software became more valuable than hardware, the promiscuous origins of the software industry would cause major controversies. Financial success almost never reflected technical merit. Few people doubt that CP/M was not only the original but also the better operating system, and Kildall had even conceived before Microsoft the low-cost licensing model that would make Microsoft rich.

Microprocessor Wars

Meanwhile, a business decision in Texas involuntarily launched another wave of personal computers. Texas Instruments owned the market for CPUs used in calculators. When in 1975 it decided to increase the price of the CPU to favor its own calculators, the other manufacturers were left scrambling for alternatives. Texas Instruments had realized it was getting difficult to compete with Intel. Intel boasted a full line of state-of-the-art semiconductor products: RAMs, EPROMs and CPUs. Microprocessors (CPUs) drove memory sales which then funded improvements in microprocessors.

The market for calculators collapsed. Out of the ruins, Commodore decided to change its business. Tom Bennett at Motorola in Arizona had created the 8-bit 6800 in 1974, a more advanced microprocessor than anything that Intel had introduced yet. Chuck Peddle, a former employee of Tom Bennett's at Motorola, developed the 8-bit 6502 at MOS Technology (1976) in Norristown (Pennsylvania); it was much cheaper ($25) than the 6800 ($180) or Intel's 8080 ($360). He was hired by

Commodore to build an entire computer, the Commodore PET (Personal Electronic Transactor), first demonstrated in January 1977.

Competition to Intel eventually came from Silicon Valley itself. In 1975 Jerry Sanders' Advanced Micro Devices (AMD) introduced the AMD 8080, a reverse-engineered clone of the Intel 8080 microprocessor, putting further pressure on prices. AMD coined a new business model: reverse engineering other people's products (typically, Intel) and improve over the originals. Far from being mere copycats, the engineers at AMD had to be as skilled as the ones at Intel in order to match and surpass its achievements.

Perhaps even more importantly in 1975 AMD launched the 4-bit 2901 chip for the "bit-slice" method of building microprocessors. This method conceives a microprocessor as a set of modules: a control unit and several arithmetic logic units (ALUs). While the bit-slice method leads to bigger microprocessors (apparently defying the whole point of the microprocessor), at the time it offered a huge cost-saving advantage in creating high-performance microprocessors. Using the big-slide method, a manufacturer was able to create virtually any kind of microprocessor by attaching a series of ALUs horizontally. For example, by joining four 2901s, one obtained a 16-bit microprocessor. By contrast, the Intel 8080 was an 8-bit microprocessor and could only be an 8-bit microprocessor. Furthermore, bipolar chips were faster than MOS chips but generally avoided because of the problem of cooling them down. Splitting them into several ALUs made them feasible again, and bipolar transistors were faster than the unipolar MOS transistors used by Intel. The first bit-sliced microprocessor was made by National Semiconductor in 1973, the IMP-16, a 16-bit architecture that consisted of four identical 4-bit ALUs (the IMP-00A). In 1974 Intel introduced the 2-bit 3002, and Monolithic Memories (MMI), another Fairchild spinoff founded in 1969 by Zeev Drori, introduced the 4-bit 6701. However, it was the AMD 2901 that caused a sensation and became a de-facto standard. After all, at a time when semiconductor companies were founded by physicists, AMD had been founded by marketing experts. One reason of AMD's success was the ability to find "second sources": Motorola (1975), Raytheon (1975), Thomson (1976), National (1977), NEC (1978) and Signetics (1978) all signed up to manufacture the 2901. Computer manufacturers were more likely to invest on a chip made by multiple and reliable sources than on chips made only by the inventor.

Federico Faggin left Intel with coworker Ralph Ungermann right after finishing the 8080, taking Shima with them, and, having convinced Exxon to make a generous investment, started his own company, Zilog. It became a formidable competitor to Intel when in July 1976 it unveiled the 8-bit Z80 microprocessor, which was faster and cheaper than the 8080 (designed at transistor level by the same Shima). National Semiconductor had already introduced PACE in December 1974, the first 16-bit microprocessor.

The new startups invested heavily on microprocessors, forcing competition at the technological level. The established companies used microprocessors as a weapon, forcing competition at the price level.

Relational Databases

On the software front, a new field of databases was born at IBM's San Jose laboratories (later renamed Almaden Research Center). In 1970 Edgar Codd had written an influential paper, "A Relational Model of Data for Large Shared Data Banks," in which he explained how one could describe a database in the language of first-order predicate logic. A Relational Database group was set up in San Jose. In 1974 Donald Chamberlin defined an algebraic language to retrieve and update data in relational database systems, SEQUEL, later renamed SQL (Structured Query Language). It was part of the development of the first relational database management system, code-named System R, begun in 1973 and finally unveiled in 1977 (running on a System 38). However, IBM's flagship database system remained the IMS, originally developed in 1968 for NASA's Apollo program on IBM's mainframe 360. That was the most used database system in the world. Since IBM was not eager to adopt a new technology, it did not keep it secret and the idea spread throughout the Bay Area.

In particular, IBM's work on relational databases triggered interest in a group of UC Berkeley scientists led by Michael Stonebraker, who started the Ingres (INteractive Graphics REtrieval System) project in 1973, a project that would transplant the leadership in the field of databases to the Bay Area and create colossal fortunes.

Meanwhile, computers started sharing data. In 1974 DEC introduced DECnet, a product to connect two PDP-11 minicomputers, one of the earliest peer-to-peer network architectures, which the following year included the ability to access files on other machines (via DEC's Data Access Protocol or DAP).

IBM's Almaden Labs (2010)

User Interfaces

Experiments with new kinds of hardware and software platforms were changing the vision of what a computer was supposed to do. Engelbart's group at SRI had lost funding from ARPA (and was eventually disbanded in 1977). Several of its engineers started moving to PARC, which was a pioneer in graphical user interfaces, optical character recognition, and WYSIWYG applications.

In 1973 Xerox PARC unveiled the Alto, the first workstation with a mouse and a Graphical User Interface (GUI). Inspired by Douglas Engelbart's old On-Line System, and developed by Charles Thacker 's team, it was a summary of all the software research done at PARC and it was far ahead of contemporary computers. More importantly, it wasn't just a number cruncher: it was meant for a broad variety of applications, from office automation to education. It wasn't based on a microprocessor yet, but on a Texas Instruments 74181 chip (it wasn't a full microprocessor). It even allowed users to mix text and graphics on the screen. In 1974 Hungarian-born Charles Simonyi developed Bravo, the word processor that introduced the "what you see is what you get" (WYSIWYG) paradigm in document preparation.

The Xerox Alto Computer (1973)

The State of Computing Jumps Ahead

During the 1950s and 1960s computers had evolved rapidly from the ENIAC. Most of the credit goes to a few companies that devised how to sell computers to corporations and to the government agencies that de facto subsidized those companies with large projects. However, there had only been an evolution and not a revolution. Computers had evolved into faster and cheaper machines that were also easier to program and maintain. They were now employed to perform mission-critical industrial and business applications, not only scientific ones. They had not changed significantly, though. The Arpanet, the Unix operating system and the minicomputer, instead, represented a different kind of progress, one that could be more appropriately termed as a revolution. Each of them changed the way computers were used, what they did, and who used them. In fact, they changed the very meaning of a "computer." The term itself became misleading, as computers were beginning to be used less to "compute" than to perform many other functions.

Again, this revolution had taken place mostly far away from the Bay Area, although centers like the SRI and the Xerox PARC were beginning to put the South Bay on the map. PARC's experiments with graphical user interfaces, desktop computers, and local area networks expanded the computer culture of the Bay Area. PARC also played the role of a venture capitalist investing in new technologies. By hiring Robert Taylor, Xerox transplanted the futuristic vision of ARPA's IPTO into the Bay Area. The IPTO's mission, in turn, represented two decades of computer research in the Boston area. Xerox was transferring Boston's lead in computing to the Bay Area, which also happened to be the world's capital of semiconductor engineering. This was similar to what Shockley had done when he had transferred the East Coast's lead in semiconductors to the world's capital of radio engineering. And, again, the recipient of the transplant was a community imbued with a different spirit than the one of the scientists of the East Coast.

Other Tech-Based Industries

While the semiconductor industry was booming, another Bay Area industry was in its infancy. A local biomedical drug industry had been created by the success of Alza. Silicon Valley soon developed as a center for biomedical technology, the industry of medical devices that draws from both engineering and medicine.

Meanwhile, several groups of biologists were trying to synthesize artificial DNA in a lab, trying to extract a gene from any living or dead organism and insert it into another organism ("recombinant DNA"). In 1972 Paul Berg 's team at Stanford University synthesized the first recombinant DNA molecule. In 1973 Stanford University's medical Professor Stanley Cohen and UCSF's biochemist Herbert Boyer invented a practical technique to produce recombinant DNA. They transferred DNA from one organism to another, creating the first recombinant DNA organism. That experiment virtually launched the discipline of "biotechnology," the industrial creation of DNA that does not exist in nature but can be useful for human purposes. Boyer had just discovered that an enzyme named EcoRI allowed him to slice DNA molecules to produce single strands that could be easily manipulated. Cohen had just devised a way to introduce foreign DNA into a bacterium. They put the two processes together and obtained a way to combine DNA from different sources into a DNA molecule. Cohen decided to continue research in the academia, while Boyer decided to go into business.

The Asilomar Conference on Recombinant DNA, organized by Paul Berg in February 1975 near Monterey, set ethical rules for biotechnology. Meanwhile, the Polish geneticist Waclaw Szybalski coined the term "synthetic biology," opening an even more ambitious frontier: the creation (synthesis) of new genomes (and therefore of biological forms) that don't exist in nature.

That attention to Biology was not coincidental. In 1970 Stanford had set up an interdepartmental Human Biology Program focused on undergraduate students. The founders were all distinguished scholars: Joshua Lederberg, a Nobel laureate who was the head of Genetics at the Medical School, David Hamburg, chair of Psychiatry at the Medical School, Norman Kretchmer, chair of Pediatrics, Donald Kennedy, chair of Biology, Paul Ehrlich, who had jump-started environmental science with his book "The Population Bomb" (1968), Sanford Dornbusch, former chair of Sociology, and Albert Hastorf, former chair of Psychology. This was an impressive cast, and Lederberg and Hamburg were already teaching a pioneering course titled "Man As Organism" since 1968. However, there was little support for this idea from the establishment. The reason that Stanford went ahead was money: the Ford Foundation (not the Stanford establishment) believed in multidisciplinary approaches and its generous funding made the program possible. The class on "Human Sexuality" started in 1971 by Herant Katchadourian attracted a record 1,035 students in its first year. Well into the 21st century the Human Biology Program would still remain the single most successful program at Stanford.

A major oil crisis hit the world in 1973. It was a wake-up call that the US did not control the main material required by its economy: oil. It became the first drive to seriously explore alternative sources of energy, although it would take many more crises and wars before the government would launch a serious plan to get rid of fossil fuels. In 1973 the Lawrence Berkeley Lab founded the Energy and Environment Division, which came to specialize in lithium-ion batteries. The federal government, instead, chose Colorado as the site for the main research center in alternative sources of energy. In 1974 it mandated the establishment of the Solar Energy Research Institute, later expanded to wind and biofuel and renamed National Renewable Energy Laboratory (NREL).

Research on lasers at Stanford University yielded a major discovery in 1976. John Madey invented the "free-electron laser," a laser that differed from previous varieties (ion, carbon-dioxide and semiconductor lasers) because it can work across a broader range of frequencies, from microwaves to (potentially) X-rays.

In 1962 Texas Instruments introduced what would be known as LED (Light-emitting diode) technology, invented by James Biard and Gary Pittman. A few months later Nick Holonyak at General Electric developed the red LED, soon followed by all the other colors. Progress in LED displays was slow. In 1968 Hewlett Packard introduced red LED displays developed by Monsanto, but the technology was still expensive and rudimentary. In the 1970s Thomas Brandt at Fairchild Semiconductor finally used Hoerni's planar process to mass produce LEDs. From this point on progress in LEDs would become exponential. In fact, a Hewlett Packard scientist, Roland Haitz, formulated the Moore's law for LEDs: the efficiency of LEDs was doubling approximately every 36 months.

Culture and Society

The New Games Movement was an offshoot of the participatory spirit of the hippy era. Its practitioners staged public highly-physical games whose goals were therapeutic, creativity-augmentation and community-bonding, not unlike Steve Russell's computer game "Spacewar" (1962) and not unlike Stewart Brand's mock-simulation anti-war game "Soft War" (1966). The most famous prophet of the movement was Bernie De Koven, who in 1971 created the Games Preserve in Pennsylvania, a farm where people could convene a play physical games; but San Francisco had pioneered the idea in the 1960s, new-age writer George Leonard had promoted it, and in 1973 Patricia Farrington created the New Games Foundation with its first "tournament" held in the Marin Headlands north of San Francisco.

The utopian sharing economy of the hippies manifested itself again in Menlo Park in 1974, when Dick Raymond of the Portola Institute, just before he helped to jumpstart the Homebrew Computer Club, founded the Briarpatch society, a community of mutually supporting businesses linked together via a newsletter (edited by Gurney Norman), kept alive by local philanthropists, and spreading thanks to the missionary work of Andy Phillips. By the mid-1970s San Francisco's art scene was shifting towards video, performance art, participatory installations, mixed media, and time-based art, often accompanied with live electronic music. Alternative art spaces popped up in the Mission and South of Mission (SOMA) districts, notably notably Southern Exposure in 1974 (a nonprofit collective that gathered at Project Artaud, a "live and work" artist space), New Langton Arts in 1975 and Gallery Paule Anglim in 1976. "Conceptual" artists Howard Fried and Terry Fox pioneered video art and performance art. Lynn Hershman 's "The Dante Hotel" (1973) pioneered site-specific installations. The ultimate site-specific installation was David Ireland's own house at 500 Capp Street, which the artist began to remodel in 1975 with sculptures made of found objects. Chip Lord 's Ant Farm created one of the most influential installations in 1974 in the desert of Texas, "Cadillac Ranch," using parts of old cars. The Ant Farm also organized multimedia performances such as "Media Burn" (July 1975) during which they burned in public a pyramid of television sets.

In 1970 Tom Marioni founded the Museum of Conceptual Art (MOCA), one of the first alternative art spaces in the nation. There he debuted his "Sound Sculpture As" (1970) which, together with Paul Kos's

"The Sound of Ice Melting" (1970), which recorded the sound of disintegrating ice, pioneered sound sculpture.

The Mission District had a large Mexican and Chicano (descendants of Mexican immigrants) population. In 1972 two Chicanas, Patricia Rodriquez and Graciela Carillo, started painting murals in their neighborhood, soon joined by other women, mostly students of the San Francisco Art Institute. They came to be known as Las Mujeres Muralistas, and specialized in sociopolitical activism, such as the large mural "Panamerica" (1974).

In 1973 British painter Harold Cohen joined Stanford University's Artificial Intelligence Lab to build AARON, a program capable of making art, thus creating an artistic equivalent of the Turing test: can a machine be a good artist if experts appreciate its art? The project would continue for several decades. In 1975 John Chowning founded Stanford's laboratory for computer music, later renamed Center for Computer Research in Music and Acoustics (CCRMA).

The Bay Area stole a bit of Hollywood's limelight in 1971 when film producer George Lucas opened Lucasfilm in San Francisco, a production company that went on to create "American Graffiti" (1973), "Star Wars" (1977) and "Indiana Jones and the Raiders of the Lost Ark" (1981).

The "underground comix" movement continued to prosper, but now the reference point was the magazine "Arcade" (1975-76), started by Bill Griffith (of "Young Lust" fame) and Swedish-born cartoonist Art Spiegelman (later more famous for the character "Maus").

The city's main sociocultural development was the rapid rise of the gay community. The first "Gay Pride Parade" was held in 1970. Around that time gays and lesbians started moving to the "Castro" district in large numbers. It was the first openly gay neighborhood in the US and it would elect the first gay politican (Harvey Milk) in the US later that decade. Arthur Evans formed the "Faery Circle" in San Francisco in 1975. It evolved into the "Radical Faeries" movement at a conference held in Arizona in 1979 and later became a worldwide network of groups that mixed gay issues and new-age spirituality and that staged hippie-style outdoors "gatherings".

Meanwhile, the "Seed Center", which was really just the backroom of DeRay Norton's and Susan Norton's Plowshare Bookstore in downtown Palo Alto, had become a new centre of counterculture by (re)publishing Thaddeus Golas' "The Lazy Man's Guide to Enlightenment" (1971), the Bible of California-style spirituality.

Down in Silicon Valley the entertainment and intellectual scene was far less exciting. On the other hand, credit must be given to hard-drinking establishments like Walker's Wagon Wheel (282 E. Middlefield Road, Mountain View, demolished in 2003) for the "technology transfer" that

Silicon Valley became famous for. There was little else for engineers to do than meet at the Wagon Wheel and talk about technology.

Entrepreneurs: Apple, Oracle, Unix, Biotech, Alternative Music, and Spirituality (1976-80)

The Apple Vision

Apple's hometown, Cupertino, was a young city created only in October 1955. It was Santa Clara County's 13th city, originally known as the "Crossroads" because it developed around the crossroads of Stevens Creek Boulevard and Saratoga-Mountain View Road (later Saratoga-Sunnyvale Road, and then De Anza Boulevard). The area had one large employer, who was also one of the state's richest men: Henry Kaiser. He owned the local rock quarry and cement plant (renamed Kaiser Permanente Cement Plant in 1939). After the war Cupertino's high school, Homestead High School, started a class on electronics under John McCollum, one of the first in the world. One of McCollum's students and assistants was a kid named Steve Wozniak.

In April 1976, Apple Computer was started in Cupertino by the hobbyist Steve Wozniak (now a college dropout and a Hewlett-Packard employee) and the hippie Steve Jobs. Jobs was another college dropout who had joined Atari in 1972 and who had experimented with LSD and Buddhism in the 1960s, and had grown up on Stewart Brand 's "Whole Earth Catalog," and actually knew very little about semiconductors. Wozniak had designed their first microcomputer in his Cupertino apartment and built it in Jobs' garage in nearby Los Altos. Wozniak used MOS Technology's 6502 microprocessor ($20) because he could not afford the more advanced Motorola 6800 or Intel 8080 (both about $170). The user had to provide her/his own monitor but an Apple I could be hooked up to an inexpensive television set. Their friend Paul Terrell of the Byte Shop was the first one to promote an Apple I.

Wozniak was unique in that he designed both the hardware and the software of the Apple I. He was still an HP employee when he did that. He was reluctant to resign and did so only in October 1976. The key difference between the Apple I and its predecessors (such as the famous Altair) was actually in the amount of its memory. Wozniak felt that a computer without a programming language was an oxymoron and strived to build a computer powerful enough to run a real programming language. The main requirement was to install more memory than the first personal computers had. Unfortunately, static RAM was expensive. Therefore he had to turn to cheaper dynamic RAM. A 4K DRAM chip had just been introduced in 1974. It was the first time that RAM (semiconductor memory) was cheaper than magnetic core memory. Being much cheaper than the static RAM used by the Altair, the DRAM allowed Wozniak to pack more of it in the Apple than the Altair. The key design issue was how to continuously refresh the dynamic RAM so that it would not lose its information (the static RAM used by the Altair did not lose its information). Roberts, basically, had merely dressed up an Intel microprocessor in order to create his Altair. Wozniak, instead, dressed up a memory chip in order to create the Apple I.

The 4K computer Wozniak created was capable of running a real programming language. Since there was no language yet for that microprocessor, Wozniak also had to write, in assembly language, the BASIC interpreter for the Apple I. Note that Wozniak's motivation in creating the Apple I was not a business plan but simply the desire to own a computer; a desire constrained by a lack of money. The Apple I was the result of an optimization effort more than anything else: Wozniak had to minimize the parts and simplify the structure.

Wozniak, however, shared the same "business" vision that Roberts had with the Altair. His personal computer was meant for hobbyists, i.e. for technically savvy users who were going to program the computer themselves to solve their problems. Wozniak had simply made it much easier to write a program. He did not envision that the average user of a personal computer would be someone who "buys" the application programs (already written and packaged).

It was, however, the Apple II, still based on a 6502 and released in April 1977, which really took off. Apple was funded by former Fairchild and Intel executive Mike Markkula, who had retired at age 32 thanks to the stock of those two companies. The Apple II desktop computer was fully assembled, requiring almost no technical expertise. It boasted the look and feel of a home appliance. It had a monitor and a keyboard integrated with the motherboard shell, as well as a ROM hosting a BASIC interpreter and a RAM of 4 kilobytes (but no operating system). Part of its success was due to Apple's Disk II (introduced a few months later), the first affordable floppy-disk drive for personal computers, which replaced the cassette as the main data storage medium.

The other factor in its early success was the software: a dialect of BASIC licensed from Microsoft (popularly known as "Floating Point BASIC") and the word-processor EasyWriter, written in 1978 by John Draper while in jail for phone phreaking. (Another factor in the success of the Apple II was New York-based marketing strategist Regis McKenna).

Apple was just one of many companies that used the 6502. Commodore was another one: after the PET (released in October 1977) in 1980 came the VIC-20, the first personal computer to sell one million units. The Atari 800, announced in late 1978 and designed by Jay Miner, was also based on the 6502. British computer manufacturer Acorn, founded in 1978 near Cambridge University by German-born Herman Hauser, also used the 6502 computer for the BBC Micro that was deployed throughout the British educational system. However, most companies used the 6502 for something else. In October 1977, Atari introduced a videogame console, the VCS (Video Computer System, later renamed 2600). Previous generations of videogame machines had used custom logic. The videogame console that pioneered the use of a microprocessor was Fairchild's Video Entertainment System, released in August 1976 and based on Fairchild's own F8 microprocessor.

The other popular low-cost microprocessor was the Zilog Z80, used for example in Tandy/Radio Shack's TRS-80 personal computer, another bestseller of 1977. One of the many startups that preferred the Z80 over the 8080 was Cromemco, started in 1976 by Stanford students Harry Garland and Roger Melen in their dormitory (hence the acronym Crothers Memorial). The companies that missed the opportunity were, surprisingly, the ones that dominated the market for calculators. Texas Instruments' TI 99/4 (December 1979) was based on its own 16-bit TI 9940 processor that was simply too expensive; and the even more expensive Hewlett-Packard's HP-85 (January 1980), based on an HP custom 8-bit processor, was something halfway between a mini and a micro.

The year 1977 was a turning point, as 48,000 personal computers were sold worldwide. The following year more than 150,000 were sold, of which 100,000 were Tandy/ Radio Shack TRS-80s, 25,000 Commodore PETs, 20,000 Apple IIs, 5,000 IMSAIs and 3,000 Altairs.

Steve Jobs' Childhood Home and Garage (2010)

The Value of Software

Steve Jobs' vision was to create a computer that was a home appliance. In reality the Apple II was still a hobbyist novelty, like most small computers based on microprocessors. It never became a home appliance, but it got transformed into something no less pervasive: an office tool. The transformation was not due to a hardware idea but to software. In October 1979 Harvard University's business-school student Dan Bricklin and his friend Bob Frankston shipped VisiCalc, the first spreadsheet program for personal computers. That was the moment when sales of the Apple II truly started to take off.

A software application made the difference between selling thousands of units to hobbyists and selling millions of units to the general public. The Apple II only had 64 kilobytes of memory, and the application could only use a memory space of 48 Kbytes. VisiCalc fit in 32. Apple went public the following year. Its IPO (initial public offering) raised a record $1.3 billion, creating more instant millionaires than any other event in history at that point. Visicalc was ported to the Tandy TRS-80, Commodore PET and the Atari 800, becoming the first major application that was not tied to a computer company.

WordStar, a word-processor developed in 1979 by former IMSAI engineer Rob Barnaby for the CP/M operating system and published by MicroPro, a company founded in 1978 by another former IMSAI employee, Seymour Rubinstein, became the first widely known word-processor for personal computers (and the new best-selling package for this class of machines); and its success propelled MicroPro to become the first major software company of the Bay Area. WordStar and VisiCalc were the two top-selling programs of the early 1980s, each boasting sales of more than half a million copies by 1983.

The company that understood the value of software was Tandy, an old Texas shoe business that in 1963 had converted to electronics buying the Radio Shack chain, and that, thanks to a former Byte Shop employee, Steve Leininger, suddenly found itself at the vanguard of personal computer technology. Its TRS-80 of 1977 boasted an unprecedented library of applications (mostly games, but also word processors and spreadsheets).

The age of Visicalc represented a major shift in the use of computers. Other than for scientific research and military applications, commercial mainframe computers had been useful mainly for business applications such as accounting and minicomputers were mainly employed in factories. The new software for personal computers opened up the market of regular offices that were still mostly based on paper or that were using expensive time-sharing services.

After the Japanese company Epson launched the MX-80 dot-matrix printer in 1979 home printing too became feasible.

Software companies tended not to understand the value of software. Bricklin and Frankston founded Software Arts in Boston to commercialize VisiCalc, which they had originally prototyped on MIT's Multics system and funded with their own money. But their company never sold its product. They gave it to a publisher, Daniel Fylstra 's Personal Software (later renamed VisiCorp), that paid them royalties. Eventually this led to a legal dispute that indirectly allowed the competition to overtake VisiCalc. It never occurred to Bricklin and Frankston to look for venture capital to jumpstart their business.

Of course, not everybody shared Steve Jobs' vision. Just like in the old days, an IBM executive had predicted a very small market for computers, so in 1977 DEC's founder Kenneth Olsen proclaimed that "there is no reason anyone would want a computer in their home."

Apple's Old Building in Cupertino (2010)

The Pace of Progress in Semiconductors

Meanwhile, the war of the microprocessors was still raging. In June 1979 Intel introduced the 16-bit 8088 (containing 29,000 transistors), and in September 1979 Motorola introduced the 16-bit 68000 microprocessor (containing 68,000 transistors). In between the two, Zilog introduced the 16-bit Z8000 (only 17,500 transistors). At the same time, sales of DRAM continued to skyrocket. Intel then assigned the task of designing the 8086 (eventually released in June 1978) to a software engineer, Stephen Morse: it was the first time that a microprocessor was designed from the perspective of software.

Chips got more powerful and foreign manufacturers entered the market. In 1974 the size of the chips had reached 4 kilobytes and in 1975 it was already 16 kilobytes. In 1977 the semiconductor industry of Silicon Valley employed 27,000 people. By 1979 there were 16 companies selling DRAMs of 16 kilobytes. Five of them were based in Japan.

Progress in semiconductor technology was no longer making the headlines, but continued faster than ever. By 1980 integrated circuits (the vast majority of which were manufactured in the US) incorporated 100,000 discrete components. In 1978 George Perlegos at Intel created the Intel 2816, an EEPROM (Electrically Erasable Programmable Read-Only Memory), basically an EPROM that did not need to be removed from the computer in order to be erased.

In 1977 the market for memory chips of all kinds was twice the size of the market for microprocessors. Combined, the two markets had grown from $25 million in 1974 to $550 million in 1979. However, it was not obvious yet that computers were going to be the main market for microprocessors. In 1978 the industry sold 14 million microprocessors, but only 200,000 personal computers were manufactured. The vast majority of microprocessors were going into all sorts of other appliances, calculators, and controllers, with Japanese conglomerates becoming increasingly aggressive.

An impressive phenomenon of the era was the number of hardware spinoffs launched by enterprising Chinese immigrants trained in some of Silicon Valley's most advanced labs: Compression Labs (CLI) by Wen Chen (1976) to make video conferencing and digital television components; Solectron by Roy Kusumoto and Winston Chen (Milpitas, 1977) to make printed circuit boards; Data Technology Corporation (DTC) by David Tsang (Milpitas, 1979) for floppy-disk and hard-disk drives; Lam Research by David Lam (Fremont, 1980) for equipment for chip manufacturing (or "etching"); Integrated Device Technology by Chun Chiu, Tsu-Wei Lee and Fu Huang (San Jose, 1980) for semiconductor components; Weitek by Edmund Sun, Chi-Shin Wang and Godfrey Fong (San Jose, 1981) for chips for high-end computers; fiber-optic pioneer E-Tek Dynamics by Ming Shih (San Jose, 1983); magnetic-disk manufacturer Komag by Tu Chen (Milpitas, 1983); etc.

The Business of Storing Data

Another front was being opened by companies studying how to store data. More computers around meant more data to store. It was intuitive that some day the industry for data storage would be a huge one. Audiocassettes were used for data storage by most microcomputers of the first generation, including the Apple II, the Radio Shack TRS-80 and the Commodore PET. Floppy disks had become increasingly popular, especially after Alan Shugart developed the smaller version (originally in

1976 for Wang). The first "diskettes" were manufactured by Dysan, a storage-media company formed in 1973 in Santa Clara by Norman Dion.

The growing number of applications running on personal computers required a growing number of floppy units. Finis Conner, working for Shugart, had the idea of building a fixed, rigid disk of the same physical size as Dysan's flexible diskette that would provide both high performance and high capacity, equivalent to an entire bunch of floppy drives. Shugart and Conner formed Shugart Technology in December 1979 in Scotts Valley (south of San Jose), later renamed Seagate Technology, with funding from Dysan. In 1980, Seagate introduced the first hard-disk drive for personal computers (capable of 5 Megabytes), and soon hard disks would greatly improve the usability of small machines. That same year Sony introduced the double-sided, double-density 3.5" floppy disk that could hold 875 kilobyte.

Seagate also published the specifications of a computer interface that would allow users to connect different peripherals to the same personal computer, a device-independent "parallel" connection. They named it SASI (Shugart Associates Systems Interface), later renamed SCSI (Small Computer System Interface) when it was adopted as an industry standard. In 1981 the manager of the SASI project, Larry Boucher, quit Seagate to found Adaptec in Milpitas (north of San Jose), taking with him several Seagate engineers in a move that evoked the memory of Shugart's own exodus from IBM of 1969. Adaptec specialized in manufacturing computer cards (at factories in Singapore) to solve the growing problem of input/output bottlenecks in personal computers as the machines had to deal with a higher and higher traffic of data.

Storing data was not enough. It was also important to guarantee that the transactions of those data were reliable. Since computers and their software were prone to crashes, this was not a trivial problem, particularly in the arena of financial transactions. Former HP employee James Treybig convinced a few HP engineers to work at a fault-tolerant machine and started Tandem Computers in Cupertino. In 1976 they delivered the first product, the Tandem 16, based on a CPU derived from the HP3000 and running a proprietary operating system. Many of these CPUs were managed as a team so that if one failed the others could continue its job. Tandem servers were ideal for mission-critical business applications carried out by banks.

They immediately had a competitor in Boston: Stratus, founded in 1980 by Bill Foster from Data General (and a former coworker of the Tandem founders at HP), Gardner Hendrie from Computer Control Company and Bob Freiburghouse, founder in 1974 of Translation Systems, one of the earliest software companies specializing in compilers.

The exponential growth of digital communications led to the rapid expansion of the field of cryptography. The most pressing problem was to secure communications over distances between parties that had never met before, i.e. who could not exchange a secret key in private before beginning their digital communications. This problem was solved in 1976 by combining ideas from Stanford (Whitfield Diffie and Martin Hellman) and UC Berkeley (Ralph Merkle), opening the era of Public-Key Encryption (PKI). The following year the Israeli cryptographer Adi Shamir at the MIT invented the RSA algorithm and added digital signatures to PKI.

Whitfield Diffie

The ever larger amount of data stored on disks created ever bigger databases, which, in turn, required ever more powerful database management systems. Larry Ellison, a college dropout from Chicago who had moved to California in 1966, had been employed at Ampex in Redwood City. He worked as a programmer on a database management system for the Central Intelligence Agency (CIA) codenamed "Oracle," under the management of his boss Bob Miner, the son of Middle-Eastern immigrants. In August 1977 Bob Miner and Ed Oates (also an Ampex alumnus, now at Memorex) founded the Software Development Laboratories to take advantage of a software consulting contract facilitated by Larry Ellison at his new employer, Precision Instruments (also a manufacturer of tape recorders, based in San Carlos, mainly serving NASA and the Navy). The startup used offices in PI's Santa Clara building. When Ellison joined them, he steered them towards developing an SQL relational database management system of the kind that IBM had just unveiled in San Jose but targeting the minicomputer market. Miner and their fourth employee Bruce Scott (another former member of Miner's team at Ampex) wrote most of it in the assembly language of the PDP-11. The company was soon renamed Relational Software and relocated to Menlo Park, and in 1978 the CIA purchased the first prototype. In 1979 Relational officially shipped the first commercial SQL relational database management system, Oracle. In 1982 the company would be renamed one more time and would become Oracle Corporation.

A rival project, Michael Stonebraker 's relational database system Ingres at UC Berkeley, was demonstrated in 1979. For all practical purposes, Ingres looked like a variant of IBM's System R for DEC minicomputers running the Unix operating system. Being open-source software like UC Berkeley's Unix (BSD), within one year Ingres was deployed by many universities around the country as the first available relational database system (IBM's System R was not available outside IBM). In 1980 Stonebraker himself started a company, Relational Technology, later renamed Ingres, to market the system. That same year, Roger Sippl and Laura King, who had implemented an experimental relational database system, started Relational Database Systems in Menlo Park, a company that was later renamed Informix. In 1984 some of Stonebraker's students (notably Mark Hoffman and Bob Epstein) formed Systemware, later renamed Sybase, in Berkeley.

All of these startups had something in common: they did not target the huge market of mainframe computers. They targeted the smaller market of minicomputers, in particular the ones running the Unix operating system. IBM's IMS dominated the database market for mainframe computers, but IBM had failed to capitalize on the experimental System R developed at its San Jose laboratories. IBM eventually released a relational database management system, the DB2, in 1983, but it was running only on its mainframe platform. IBM still showed little interest in smaller computers. This allowed Oracle, Sybase and Informix to seize the market for database systems on minicomputers.

The old practices of "business intelligence" and "decision support" were evolving into "data mining" and "data analytics" as the amount of data increased. The pioneers were Britton Lee, founded in 1979 by David Britton, Geoffrey Lee and Ingres' alumnus Robert Epstein (before he founded Sybase), and Teradata, a Caltech spinoff of 1979 that would acquire Britton Lee in 1990 (one year before being acquired by NCR). Teradata came out of research by Phil Neches and others for a high-performance specialized architecture hardware to run large databases, a database management appliance in the tradition of Tandem's machines, implemented by multiple microprocessors working in parallel. Teradata (whose system first shipped in 1983) and Tandem's NonStop SQL (1984) popularized the "shared nothing architecture" in which each server of the cluster computes its own data, an architecture that would become popular in the age of the Web.

Those database management systems were ok for larger machines but obviously not for the personal computer. In 1980 most personal computers had only 32 Kbytes of RAM and a cassette tape drive. The 120-Kbyte floppy drive was still a rarity but random access to storage was coming. Hard drives did not exist yet for personal computers. The first major database program for this class of machines was Personal Filing System (PFS), written by John Page for the Apple II. This would become part of a suite of software products (or "productivity tools") sold by Software Publishing Corporation, founded in 1980 by three former Hewlett-Packard employees to implement Fred Gibbons' vision: he was one of the first people to view a personal computer as the equivalent of a music player, playing not music but applications. In 1983 the same company would start selling the word-processor PFS:Write, followed by a spreadsheet program, a reporting program and a business graphics program.

The Old Omex/Precision Instruments Building where Oracle Began as Software Development Laboratories (2010)

Early Telecommunications and Networks

The other field still in its infancy was the field of telecommunications. The company that put Silicon Valley on the map of telecommunications was probably ROLM, founded by a group of Stanford students. In 1976 they introduced a digital switch, the CBX (Computerized Branch Exchange), a computer-based PBX (private branch exchange) that competed successfully with the products of Nortel and AT&T. Meanwhile, the Southern Pacific Railroad of Burlingame (south of San Francisco) renamed its Southern Pacific Communications (SPC), which had been selling private phone lines since 1972 during the days of the AT&T monopoly on public telephony, as "Sprint" (Switched PRIvate Network Telecommunications) in 1978 when it was finally allowed by the government to enter the long-distance telephony business. Its Burlingame laboratory was another early source of know-how in telecommunications. Sprint would be later (1982) acquired by GTE and then (1986) by United Telecom of Kansas.

In 1979 Bob Metcalfe, the "inventor" of the Ethernet, left Xerox PARC to found 3Com (Computers, Communication and Compatibility) in Santa Clara. The idea was to provide personal computer manufacturers with Ethernet adaptor cards so that businesses could connect all the small computers in one local-area network. 3Com became the first company to ship a commercial version of TCP/IP (1980). In 1979, Zilog's cofounder Ralph Ungermann and one of his engineers at Zilog, Charlie Bass, formed Ungermann-Bass in Santa Clara to specialize in local-area networks, particularly in the Ethernet technology.

Nestar Systems, started in Palo Alto in 1978 by Harry Saal and Leonard Shustek, introduced a pioneering client-server network of personal computers. That was another Stanford spinoff. Shustek had worked as a student with Forest Baskett at Stanford on a graphics terminal that in 1976 had been licensed to Tektronix.

The main competitor of Ethernet was "token ring", pioneered in Britain after 1974 by the Cambridge Ring developed at Cambridge University by Maurice Wilkes' Polish-born student Andrew Hopper. In 1979 the MIT developed its own token-ring network that was commercialized in 1981 by Howard Salwen's Proteon as the ProNet. Also in 1981 Apollo of Boston introduced their proprietary Apollo Token Ring (ATR), and in 1985 IBM introduced its own token-ring solution, developed in their Zurich laboratories. Also in 1981 Sytek (founded in 1979 in Sunnyvale by Michael Pliner and other former employees of Ford Aerospace of Sunnyvale) introduced LocalNet, a broadband LAN that covered longer distances than Ethernet. The most successful of the proprietary LAN solutions came from Corvus, founded by Michael D'Addio and Mark Hahn in 1979 in San Jose. Ethernet boards were too expensive and too large to fit inside an Apple II. On the other hand, the real problem was that hard drives were expensive and Apple II users wanted to share one. So Corvus developed its own variant of the Ethernet, first Constellation in 1980 and then Omninet in 1981 that allowed multiple Apple II to share the same hard drive.

Meanwhile, in Georgia in 1977 Dennis Hayes, a hobbyist who was employed at National Data Corporation on a project to provide bank customers with modems for electronic money transfers and credit card authorizations, started working on a modem for personal computers. He created a device that converted between analog and digital signals and therefore allowed personal computers to receive and transmit data via telephone lines. He soon founded his own company, Hayes Microcomputers Products, and announced the Micromodem 100 that could transmit at 110 to 300 bits per seconds (bauds). This modem was a lot simpler and cheaper than the ones used by mainframes, and, more importantly, it integrated all the functions that a modem needed to perform. Texas Instruments too introduced a 300-baud modem for its TI 99/4 in 1980. Meanwhile, the Bell Labs deploted the first cellular phone system (in Chicago in 1978).

The mother of all computer networks was still largely unknown, though. In 1980 the Arpanet had 430,000 users, who exchanged almost 100 million e-mail messages a year. That year the Usenet was born, an

Arpanet-based discussion system divided in "newsgroups," originally devised by two Duke University students, Tom Truscott and Jim Ellis. It used a protocol called UUCP (Unix-to-Unix Copy), originally written in 1978 by Mike Lesk at AT&T Bell Laboratories for transferring files, exchanging e-mail and executing remote commands. Despite the fast growing number of users, at the time nobody perceived the Arpanet as a potential business.

In 1977 DARPA, working closely with SRI International, chose the San Francisco Bay Area to set up a "packet" radio network (Prnet) capable of exchanging data with Arpanet nodes. It was the beginning of wireless computer networking. After early experiments by Canadian ham radio amateurs, in December 1980 Hank Magnuski set up in San Francisco a ham radio to broadcast data (the birth certificate of the AmPrnet). The first wireless products for the general market would not appear for a decade, but, not coincidentally, would come from a company based in Canada, Telesystems, and a company based in the Bay Area, Proxim (founded in 1984 in Sunnyvale).

In 1980 CompuServe introduced a chat system, the CB Simulator, that was modeled after Citizen's Band radio (CB radio). This was the most popular form of short-distance two-way radio communications. CB clubs had multiplied all over the world during the 1970s as more and more ham-radio hobbyists had been able to purchase the equipment thanks to a drop in the price of electronics.

On a smaller scale, another influential communications technology was getting started in those days. Radio-frequency identification (RFID) is basically a combination of radio broadcast technology and radar. It is used to have objects talk to each other. The idea, that dates back at least to 1969, when Mario Cardullo sketched it while working at the Communications Satellite Corporation (Comsat) and before starting ComServ in Washington, was tested by pioneering projects like Raytheon's "Raytag" (1973) and Fairchild Semiconductor's "Electronic Identification System" or EIS (1975), but it truly matured at the Los Alamos National Laboratory in the 1970s. Its first mass-scale applications came thanks to two spin-offs from that laboratory: Amtech in New Mexico and Identronix in California (established in 1977 in Santa Cruz and soon managed by Vic Grinich, one of the original "traitorous eight" who had split off from Shockley Labs to start Fairchild Semiconductors). Their work originated the automated toll payment systems that became common on roads, bridges and tunnels around the world after Norway pioneered them in 1987, as well as the remote keyless entry systems.

Video Games

Computers also started making an effect in the gaming/entertainment industry. The Atari 2600 home videogame console, a machine that included paddle and joystick controllers and that could be connected to a tv set, was a runaway success that yielded Atari more than 50% of the market. In 1980 Atari hired Alan Kay from the Xerox PARC to work on computer graphics for its products.

The business of gaming software came to the Bay Area via Broderbund, founded after hobbyist Doug Carlston had written the game "Galactic Empire" for the TRS-80 in 1979. This came one year after Toshihiro Nishikado, a veteran game designer who had developed Japan's first video arcade game in 1973, created the first blockbuster videogame, "Space Invaders." In 1980 it was ported to the Atari 2600, and broke all sales records, creating the demand for videogame consoles that made the video arcade obsolete. "Galactic Empire" thrived in its wake.

Hobbyists were also finding ever-newer uses for microprocessors. For example, in 1977 Dave Smith, a former UC Berkeley student who had started a company to make music synthesizers, built the "Prophet 5," the first microprocessor-based musical instrument, and also the first polyphonic and programmable synthesizer. Dave Smith also had the original idea that led (in 1983) to the MIDI (Musical Instrument Digital Interface), a standard to attach musical instruments to computers. Fundamental for the development of the multimedia world was the introduction in 1978 of Texas Instrument's TMS5100, the first digital signal processor. Daniel Kottke, one of Apple's earliest employees who helped Wozniak assemble the very first Apple computers in Jobs' garage, also assembled a portable Apple to compose and play music for his own use (in 1980).

User Friendliness

Progress was also needed in developing user-friendly computers. The Xerox Alto had been the single major effort in that area. Xerox never sold it commercially but donated it to universities around the world. That helped trigger projects that later yielded results such as the Stanford University Network (SUN) workstation. In 1979 Steve Jobs of Apple had his first demonstration of an Alto at Xerox PARC, and realized that the mouse-driven GUI was the way to go. Xerox eventually introduced in April 1981 the 8010 Star Information System, which integrated a mouse, a GUI (largely designed by Norm Cox), a laser printer, an Ethernet card, an object-oriented environment (Smalltalk), and word-processing and publishing software. The graphical user interface was largely designed by David Canfield-Smith, who had coined the term "icon" in 1975 at Stanford, and made icons a key method of interaction of the new machine.

Programming this computer involved a whole new paradigm, the "Model-View-Controller" approach, first described in 1979 by Trygve Reenskaug. Xerox PARC was also experimenting with portable computers: the NoteTaker, unveiled in 1976 but never sold commercially, was basically a practical implementation of Alan Kay 's Dynabook concept (by a team that included Adele Goldberg). In 1977 Xerox PARC gave a presentation to Xerox's management of all the achievements of the research center, titled "Futures Day." Despite the spectacular display of industrial prototypes, the management decided that Xerox should continue focusing on document processing. This started the exodus of brains from Xerox PARC towards the Silicon Valley startups.

Computer graphics began to be commercialized. In 1979 filmmaker George Lucas hired Ed Catmull to open a laboratory (later renamed Pixar) in San Rafael (far away from Hollywood, on the quiet sparsely populated hills north of San Francisco) devoted to computer animation for his San Francisco firm Lucasfilm. Catmull had studied with Ivan Sutherland at the University of Utah, established the Computer Graphics Laboratory at the New York Institute of Technology in 1975, and helped create a computer animation in a scene of the film "Futureworld" (1976) that was the first ever to use 3D computer graphics.

Ed Catmull

The 1980s also witnessed the birth of the first computer graphics studios. Carl Rosendahl started Pacific Data Images (PDI) in 1980 in his Sunnyvale garage. Richard Chuang and Glenn Entis created a 3D software platform (initially running on a DEC PDP-11) that turned PDI into the first mass producer of computer animation, initially for television networks but later (after Thaddeus Beier and Shawn Neely perfected feature-based morphing on Silicon Graphics' workstations) also for feature films.

These projects were way ahead of their time. The ordinary world of computing was content with the VT100, the "video" display introduced by

Digital (DEC) in 1978, the computer terminal that definitely killed the teletype. Progress in video terminals had been steady, driven by cheaper and more powerful memory. In 1978 it reached the point where a video terminal was cheap enough for virtually every organization to purchase one.

The Bay Area was also the hub for a lively debate on artificial intelligence. In 1950 Alan Turing had asked, "When can the computer be said to have become intelligent?" In 1980 UC Berkeley philosopher John Searle replied, "Never." Searle led the charge of those who attacked the very premises of artificial intelligence. Nonetheless, in the same year Stanford's Ed Feigenbaum and others founded IntelliGenetics (later renamed Intellicorp), an early artificial intelligence and biotech startup, and the first of many to capitalize on the "expert systems" pioneered by Stanford University.

In 1978 Earl Sacerdoti, a scientist at SRI International's AI Center, founded Machine Intelligence Corporation, one of the earliest robotics startups.

French conglomerate Schlumberger acquired in 1979 the whole of Fairchild Camera and Instrument, including Fairchild Semiconductor and the following year hired Peter Hart from the SRI International to establish the Fairchild Laboratory for Artificial Intelligence Research (FLAIR), later renamed the Schlumberger Palo Alto Research (SPAR) Center, a clear reference to Xerox PARC.

John Searle of UC Berkeley (2010)

The Unix Generation

Betting on the Unix operating system was a gamble. The dominant computer company, IBM, had no intention of adopting somebody else's operating system. AT&T (the owner of Bell Labs) had made Unix available to anyone that wanted to use it. No major computer manufacturer was interested in an operating system that all its competitors could use too.

The vast majority of the users of Unix were at Bell Labs and in universities around the world. Universities that received the source code of the operating system began to tinker with it, producing variants and extensions. UC Berkeley had received its copy in 1974. Within three years its version, assembled by former student Bill Joy as the "Berkeley Software Distribution" (BSD), became popular outside Berkeley. The second BSD of 1978 included two pieces of software developed by Joy himself that became even more popular: the "vi" text editor and the "C shell." Berkeley made it very easy for other universities and even companies to adopt BSD. Unix hence became by far the world's most portable operating system. Until then, however, the vast majority of Unix implementations used a PDP-11. Eventually, in 1980, a company, Onyx, started in Silicon Valley by former Harvard Professor Bill Raduchel, had the idea to build a microcomputer running UNIX. The Onyx C8002 was based on a Zilog Z8000, had 256-kilobyte RAM and included a 10-megabyte hard disk for the price of $11,000, a cheaper alternative to the PDP-11. It was followed by Apollo in the same year, then SUN Microsystems in 1981 and Silicon Graphics in 1982.

Consulting and software companies followed until a major Unix backer arose. In 1979 Larry Michels founded the first Unix consulting company, Santa Cruz Operation (SCO), another major act of faith in an operating system that had no major backer in the industry. In 1980 Microsoft announced the Xenix operating system, a version of Unix for the Intel 8086, Zilog Z8000 and Motorola M68000 microprocessors. What was missing was the killer application. Help arrived from the US government. In 1980, when the time came to implement the new protocol TCP/IP for the Arpanet so that many more kinds of computers could be interconnected, DARPA (Defense Advanced Research Projects Agency) decided not to go with DEC (which would have been the obvious choice) but to pick the Unix operating system, specifically because it was a more open platform. Until that day there had been little interaction between the Internet world and the Unix world. After that day the two worlds began to converge. It is interesting that DARPA decided to unify the "nodes" of the network at the operating system level, not at the hardware level.

Membership in the Unix world mainly came through academia. Just about every Unix user had been trained in a university. All software refinements to the Bell Labs code had come from universities. However, the Unix community soon came to exhibit "counterculture" dynamics that mirrored the dynamics of the computer hobbyists who had invented the personal computer.

Unix was another case of a technology ignored by the big computer manufacturers and left in the hands of a community of eccentric independents. They could not avail themselves of the financial, technological and marketing infrastructure of the computer business. The big difference, of course, was that in this case the universities served as local attractors for the community more than magazines, clubs or stores. The Internet played the role that magazines had played in the 1970s, helping to disseminate alternative ideas throughout the nation. Another difference was that the average Unix innovator was a highly educated scientist, not just a garage engineer (hence the widely used expression "Unix guru" instead of the more prosaic "computer hobbyist"). However, just like hobbyists, Unix users came to constitute a counterculture that reenacted the rituals and myths of the counterculture of the 1960s. Both movements were founded on dissent, on an anti-establishment mood. Last but not least, both the personal computer and the Unix account had an appeal on this generation as a medium of individual expression in an age in which the media were castrating individual expression.

Both in the case of the personal computer and of the Internet, it was not a surprise that the invention happened: it was feasible and there was a market for it. The surprise was how long it took. The business "establishment" created a huge inertia that managed to postpone the inevitable. Viewed from the top, government funding from the 1910s till the 1960s had accelerated innovation whereas large computer corporations in the 1970s had connived to stifle innovation (outside their territory).

Evans Hall on the UC Berkeley Campus, where Researchers
Developed the BSD Unix and Invented "vi" (2010)

The Visible Hand of Capital

The amount of money available to venture capitalists greatly increased at the end of the decade because of two important government decisions. First, venture capital became a lot more appealing. In 1978 the US government enacted the "Revenue Act," which reduced the capital gains tax rate from 49.5% to 28%. Second and more importantly, in 1979 the government eased the rules on pension funds, allowing them to engage in high-risk investments.

The investment returns numbers were likely important too. Arthur Rock had invested less than $60,000 in Apple in January 1978 and reaped almost $22 million in December 1980 when Apple went public. For several years Kleiner-Perkins was able to pay a 40% return to the limited partners of its high-tech fund. The base of the Bay Area's venture capital industry started moving from San Francisco to 3000 Sand Hill Road, in Menlo Park, a complex of low-rise wooden buildings a few blocks from the Stanford Research Park. Within a few years several more venture-capital funds were founded and several of the East-Coast funds opened offices here.

3000 Sand Hill Road, Menlo Park (2010)

The Invisible Hand of Government

Government spending also helped in less visible manners. In 1977 the Defense Department hired Bill Perry, the former ESL founder, to head their Research and Engineering Lab. The US had just lost the war in

Vietnam, and one country after the other was signing friendship treaties with the Soviet Union. The US government decided that it was likely to lose a conventional war against the Soviet Union. The only hope to defeat the Soviet Union lay in launching a new generation of weapons that would be driven by computers, a field in which the Soviet Union lagged far behind. In the next four years the budget for the Defense Advanced Research Projects Agency (DARPA) was increased dramatically, leading to a number of high-tech military projects: the B-2 stealth bomber, the Jstars surveillance system, the Global Positioning System (GPS, launched in 1972), the Trident submarine, and the Tomahawk cruise missile. Many of these projects depended on technology developed in Silicon Valley.

The GPS was a by-product of the "space race" of the 1960s. Now that the USA had satellites orbiting around the Earth, it was possible to imagine that a constellation of satellites provided a better way for navigation than the traditional ways. The signals from three satellites over your head are enough to pinpoint your position. If there are enough satellites to cover the entire Earth, the GPS can pinpoint your position anywhere. The GPS project (originally a military project) was started in 1973 by Air Force colonel Bradford Parkinson, a Stanford alumnus (and future Stanford professor). The first satellites were launched in 1978. After 1978 military planes started using the GPS to figure out their position and their route. Until then they had used the ancient systems of navigation. Civilian airplanes continued to use the ancient systems, and they frequently ended up off route: in 1983 the Soviet Union shot down a Korean airliner killing 269 people because it had accidentally entered Soviet air space.

Biotech

The age of biotech started in earnest in the Bay Area with Genentech. It was formed in April 1976 by Herbert Boyer (the co-inventor of recombinant DNA technology or "gene splicing") and by 28-year-old venture capitalist Robert Swanson, who set up offices at Kleiner Perkins' offices in Menlo Park. They subcontracted experiments to the laboratories of UCSF, the City of Hope, and the California Institute of Technology in Pasadena (whose student Richard Scheller became one of their early employees) to genetically engineer new pharmaceutical drugs. Genentech's first success came in 1977 when they produced a human hormone (somatostatin) in bacteria, the first cloning of a protein using a synthetic recombinant gene. In 1978 Genentech and City of Hope produced human insulin using recombinant DNA technology (approved for sale in 1982); a year later Genentech cloned the human growth hormone.

The biotech business had begun with human proteins made in bacteria. The field got another boost in 1977 when Fred Sanger at Cambridge University in Britain developed a method for "sequencing" DNA molecules (genomes), i.e. for deciphering the sequence of the constituents of a DNA molecule, a process not all too different from deciphering the sequence of characters in a computer message. (For the record, the first genome that Sanger sequenced was the genome of the Phi X 174 bacteriophage). Another method was developed by Walter Gilbert 's team at Harvard University. Gilbert joined forces with MIT Professor Phillip Sharp and founded Biogen in Geneva in 1978. In 1979 Walter Goad of the Theoretical Biology and Biophysics Group at Los Alamos National Laboratory established the Los Alamos Sequence Database to collect all known genetic sequences from a variety of organisms and their protein translations (basically, a catalog of genes and their functions), hiring the consulting firm BBN (Bolt Beranek and Newman), the same firm that had set up the Internet.

Thanks to Sanger's method, it was possible to sequence DNA, but it was a cumbersome and expensive process. GenBank (Genetic Sequence Data Bank) was created in 1982 as a successor to Los Alamos' Sequence Database and maintained for a while by IntelliGenetics before 1989 when it was assigned to the newly created National Center for Biology Information, This public database of nucleotide sequences and their protein translations allowed scientists all over the country to share their results. In 1983 John Wilbur and David Lipman created the first "search engine" for DNA, so that a biologist could search the GenBank for sequences. In 1990 Stephen Altschul's team would introduce an even faster algorithm, BLAST (Basic Local Alignment Search Tool), and since then the GenBank would double in size every 18 months, mirroring Moore's Law of electronic chips.

The field of "regenerative medicine" was born in 1981 when, independently, Martin Evans and Martin Kaufman at Cambridge Univ and Gail Martin at UC San Francisco isolated embryonic stem cells of the mouse. Stem cells are the mothers of all the cells of our body. Once they specialize in a specific job, they cannot be used to make cells of a different kind, but, before they specialize, when they are still "pluripotent", they can develop into all cell types. The stem cells of the embryo are pluripotent. The stem cells of your nose are adult stem cells: they can develop into nose cells, not into liver cells. For more than a decade these studies were limited to other animals, but then scientists started studying the human embryonic stem cells. William Haseltine coined the expression "regenerative medicine" in 1992.

More biotech companies surfaced in those years on both coasts of the US. In 1979 Sam Eletr, who had been the manager of a medical instruments team at HP Labs, founded GeneCo in Foster City, near Oracle. It was later renamed Applied Biosystems to build biotech instrumentation: first a protein sequencer and later a DNA synthesizer. Also notable in the Bay Area was Calgene, formed in 1980 by UC Davis scientists. Scientists from UCSF and UC Berkeley formed Chiron in 1981 in Emeryville. Biotech became a "hot" field for venture capitalists.

A decision by the Supreme Court opened the floodgates of biotech startups. In 1980 it ruled that biological materials (as in "life forms") could be patented. Due to these scientific and legal developments, the Bay Area's first biotech company, Cetus, went public in 1981, raising a record $108 million. In 1983 Kary Mullis at Cetus would invent the "polymerase chain reaction," a process capable of amplifying DNA, i.e. of generating many copies of a DNA sequence.

Outside the Bay Area the most successful company in recombinant DNA technology was perhaps Los Angeles-based Applied Molecular Genetics (later abbreviated to Amgen), founded in April 1980 by four venture capitalists (notably William Bowes) who hired a stellar team of scientists from Caltech and UCLA. In 1983, Taiwanese-born physiologist Fu-Kuen Lin cloned the hormone erythropoietin (better known as EPO), later patented as Epogen, into the ovarian cells of hamsters; two years later Larry Souza cloned another hormone, granulocyte colony-stimulating factor (G-CSF), later patented as Neupogen. Revenues passed $1 billion in 1992.

Genentech's Campus (2010)

Culture and Society

The Bay Area's cultural life was booming at the same time that the computer industry was beginning to boom; and it was still rather eccentric by the standards of mainstream culture. The Residents started the new wave of rock music with their bizarre shows and demented studio-processed litanies. In 1976 William Ackerman launched Windham Hill to promote a new genre of instrumental music, "new age" music. It was the soundtrack to a "new age movement" that simply updated Esalen's "human potential movement" and the spiritual element of the hippie generation for the new "yuppies" (young urban professionals), thereby creating an alternative spiritual subculture that promoted Zen-like meditation, astrological investigation, extra-sensorial powers, crystal healing, holistic medicine). A huge influence on the new-age movement, besides the Esalen center, was the "human potential movement" launched by George Leonard's "The Transformation" (1972). At the same time punk-rock reached California where it mutated into a particularly abrasive and vicious form, hardcore, notably with the Dead Kennedys. Meanwhile the gay community patronized disco-music. Punk-rock was headquartered at the Mabuhay Gardens (on Broadway) and disco-music at the The logo of the Dead Kennedys, designed by collage artist Winston Smith, became an international symbol of rebellion. In 1977 rock keyboardist Vale Hamanaka (aka V Vale) started the punk-rock fanzine Search & Destroy, the rare link between the beat and punk cultures because it was originally funded by beat poets Allen Ginsberg and Lawrence Ferlinghetti. In 1980

Vale and Andrea Juno turned it into a much more intellectual magazine, Re/Search, that became one of the most influential publications of the Bay Area counterculture. (Haight-Ashbury).

Non-musicians were doing well too. In 1976 playwright Sam Shepard relocated to San Francisco to work at the Magic Theatre. The Herbst Theatre was established in 1977 on the site of the 1945 signing of the United Nations' charter. In 1977 George Coates founded his multimedia theater group, Performance Works. In 1978 Mark Pauline created the Survival Research Laboratories, which staged performances by custom-built machines. In 1979 Martin Muller opened the art gallery Modernism. In 1980 Sonya Rapoport debuted the interactive audio/visual installation "Objects on my Dresser."

San Francisco, an old port city, was transitioning from a shipping economy to a banking and tourism economy. This was leaving many old buildings empty. The Survival Research Laboratories were the main group taking advantage of those abandoned building for staging unorthodox (and mildly illegal) events, but not the only one. For example, the Suicide Club was founded in 1977 by Adrienne Burk, Gary Warne and Nancy Prussia and staged all sorts of provocative activities: costumed street pranks, sewer walks, a vampyre party in an abandoned funeral home, Nancy Prussia rode naked in a cable car, a treasure hunt that would become a staple of the Chinese New Year parade, pie fights, and especially bridge climbing. Also in 1977 Jack Napier, a member of the Suicide Club, started the Billboard Liberation Front, that coordinated graffiti artists (including the young Shepard Fairey) devoted to "improving" the commercial billboards, an entertaining form of anti-capitalistic warfare. If SRL was about machine exploration, the Suicide Club was about urban exploration. Both had something in common: an unusual degree of intensity (paralleled in music by the local punk-rock scene).

There were already many examples of philanthropy. For example, in 1979 Stanford University's professor and former Syntex scientist Carl Djerassi purchased land in the Santa Cruz Mountains west of Stanford and started the Djerassi Resident Artists Program. The program would attract dozens of world-class artists to create sculptures in the forest. In the mid-1980s John Rosekrans would establish the Runnymede Sculpture Farm on the family's vast estate in Woodside, acquiring over 160 outdoor monolithic sculptures.

The main scientific achievement of those years (not only in California) was the "Inflationary Theory", devised by Alan Guth at the Stanford Linear Accelerator (SLAC) at the end of 1979, a theory that changed the way cosmologists viewed the history of the universe.

The Bay Area was a tolerant but boring place. In 1977, San Francisco's city supervisor Harvey Milk became the first openly gay man to be elected to office in the US. Meanwhile, Silicon Valley was just a place to work. The only major entertainment was represented by the amusement park Great America, which opened in 1976 in Santa Clara. The rest of Silicon Valley was one large set of strip malls and dingy buildings.

Warriors: Personal Computers, Killer Applications, and SUN Microsystems (1980-83)

The Coming of the Personal Computer

In 1980 IBM enjoyed a virtual monopoly in the mainframe-computer market. It then decided to enter the personal computer (PC) market. IBM opened a small Entry Systems Division in Florida under the direction of Donald Estridge, who opted for building a computer from off-the-shelf, widely available components. One reason for this decision was that IBM was still wary of an antitrust lawsuit brought against it by the government in 1969. The best way to avoid accusations of monopolistic practices was to make the specifications available to its competitors. IBM put William Lowe in charge of the top-secret project, code-named "Acorn."

IBM had two key decisions to make about its PC, regarding the processor and the operating system. To start with, IBM chose the Intel 8088 microprocessor instead of a proprietary IBM microprocessor (IBM had already acquired the rights to manufacture Intel chips). IBM did not have an operating system for Intel's processors, so it was necessary to buy one from a third party. When in 1978, Intel had introduced the 8086, a young Seattle programmer, Tim Paterson, had been hired by Seattle Computer Products (SCP) to develop a CP/M-compatible operating system for it. In December 1980 he finished work on his 86-DOS. Asked by IBM to deliver an operating system for the 8086, in 1981 Bill Gates' Microsoft bought the rights on 86-DOS from SCP and hired Paterson to port 86-DOS to the first prototype of the machine provided by IBM. It was renamed MS-DOS, and Microsoft decided to retain the rights on the operating system.

IBM launched its machine as the IBM PC in August 1981. The basic version with 16 kilobytes of RAM and a cassette unit sold for $1,600. Another revolutionary move by IBM was to let outside distributors (initially Sears & Roebucks and Computerland) sell the PC. Previously, the best-selling computer in IBM's product line had sold only 25,000 units over five years. The PC would sell a million units in less than three years.

The IBM PC legitimized the personal computer. No other computer company before IBM had entered the personal-computer market. The PC companies such as Apple, Tandy and Commodore were not considered real computer companies by the corporate world but rather more akin to toy makers.

The business models chosen by IBM and Microsoft would have far-reaching consequences. Because IBM had used off-the-shelf components for their PC, and because Microsoft had retained the rights on MS-DOS, it didn't take long for engineers all over the world to realize that one could build a "clone" of the IBM PC. The only difficult trick was to replicate the BIOS (Basic Input/Output System), the software written to "bootstrap" the computer. Rod Canion and other former Texas Instruments engineers founded Compaq to reverse engineer IBM's BIOS. In January 1983, after licensing MS-DOS from Microsoft, Compaq introduced the 8088-based Portable PC, fully compatible with the IBM PC but even smaller (a premonition of the laptop). It was equipped with 128 kilobytes of RAM and priced at $3,000 (the same configuration cost $3,800 on the IBM PC). Soon there would be an entire PC-clone industry worth more than the entire personal-computer industry of the previous years. Compaq was the most aggressive because it had hired marketing and sales executives from IBM. It was not a garage-style startup but a carefully planned large-scale operation. Compaq's strategy was to sell almost exclusively through retailers and resellers.

The personal-computer industry was already mature before the introduction of the PC-clone. About 1.4 million personal computers were sold in 1981, half of them in the US. However, less than 1% of all households in the US had one. That changed in 1982. Another winner of 1981 (at the low end of the spectrum) was the Commodore VIC20. It sold 800,000 units in 1982. Its successor, the slightly more powerful Commodore 64 introduced in August 1982 with a price tag of only $600, would fare even better. It was the first affordable color computer. It could be directly plugged into a television set, and came with 64 kilobytes of RAM. The technology was only part of the reason for its success: Commodore decided to sell it in retail stores instead of electronics stores, thus addressing a much bigger audience. It went on to sell more than 20 million units (four times the Apple II).

Next to these giants there were the many makers of microcomputers based on the Zilog Z80: Sinclair, Osborne, Sony, Sharp, NCR, Olivetti, Philips and, of course, most models of the popular Tandy Radio Shack TRS-80 series, which was still a best-seller. Notably, in April 1981 Osborne Computer, founded in 1980 in Hayward by British-born hobbyist Adam Osborne (an old member of the Homebrew Computer Club), delivered the Osborne 1. It was a portable computer running the CP/M operating system that weighed only 11 kgs and cost $1,800. Hardware engineer Lee Felsenstein, a fellow member of the Homebrew Computer Club, designed it and basically, it was a commercial version of the Xerox NoteTaker. A few months later, in 1982, Japanese manufacturer Epson introduced an even smaller computer, the HC-20, designed around a Motorola microprocessor dressed up by Hitachi. In April 1982 GRiD

Systems, founded in 1979 by a former Xerox PARC scientist of the Alto team, John Ellenby, and already gone public before it had a product, introduced a portable computer based on the Intel 8086 microprocessor, the 1101. Manuel Fernandez, a refugee from Cuba who had become the CEO of Zilog during the Z80 era, founded Gavilan and in May 1983 introduced the first portable MS-DOS computer marketed as a "laptop" ($4,000).

Finally, there was Apple. In 1982 it became the first personal-computer company to pass the $1 billion mark in revenues. Unlike the IBM PC, which featured an operating system used by many other manufacturers, the Apple II relied on a proprietary Apple operating system that did not encourage independent software companies. Willingly or unwillingly, IBM had established an open software standard, whereas Apple still lived in the era of closed proprietary architectures. It wasn't clear which of the two strategies would be the winning one. That year almost three million personal computers were sold worldwide.

The First IBM PC (1981)

The Coming of Software

A major reason for the skyrocketing sales in personal computers was that they were becoming more useful. And that was due to the software, not the hardware. A number of word-processing and spreadsheet programs could run on the IBM PC. In the next few years a lot of software applications turned the PC into a necessity for any office. They caused the rapid decline of application-specific machines, for example Wang's word-processing machine Office Information System, the wildly successful 1977 descendant of the Wang 1200.

Software application companies sprung from nothing and made highly useful office software. In 1981, Los Angeles-based Context Management Systems introduced Context MBA for Apple computers. It was a software package that integrated spreadsheet, database, charting, word-processing and communication functions. In 1982 they ported it to the PC. In January 1983, the Massachusetts-based Lotus Development Corporation, founded the year before by Mitch Kapor (previously responsible for VisiCalc at VisiCorp) introduced the spreadsheet program "Lotus 1-2-3" for MS-DOS (i.e. the IBM PC). It was developed by MIT alumnus and Lotus' co-founder Jonathan Sachs, who had already developed a spreadsheet for Data General's minicomputer. Visicorp's VisiCalc had been ported to the IBM PC, but it was still limited to Apple II's 8-bit architecture and 48 kilobyte memory space. Lotus 1-2-3, on the other hand, was written specifically for the IBM PC in assembly language, taking advantage of its 16-bit Intel processor and of its 640 kilobyte memory space. It became a bestseller. Lotus instantly became the second largest software company for personal computers after Microsoft, with sales in 1983 of $53 million.

Software Plus, founded in 1980 by George Tate and Hal Lashlee, was a Los Angeles-based distributor and publisher of software for personal computers, a booming business. In 1981 they stumbled into the Vulcan database management system for the CP/M operating system developed at home by Wayne Ratliff, an employee of NASA's Jet Propulsion Labs, modeled after the database system of his lab's Univac mainframe. Software Plus acquired the program, changed its own name to Ashton-Tate, turned Vulcan into a popular product, dBase ($700), and in 1982 ported it to MS-DOS.

Intuit, founded in 1983 by Scott Cook and Tom Proulx in Palo Alto, offered Quicken, a personal finance management tool for the Apple II. Designed by Proulx, it was a personal finance management tool running on the IBM PC and the Apple II. It was originally conceived for the younger people saddled with school debts and struggling to make ends meet at the end of the month, but, recession after recession, tools like this would become popular with an ever broader audience.

Ray Noorda's Novell in Utah in 1982 came up with the idea of a network operating system to allow several personal computers to share the same files and printers. Their NetWare for DOS was the first stepping-stone to enable personal-computer users to work as a team.

A network effect was created between the PC-clones and the software manufacturers. The IBM PC could not run the many applications written for the CP/M operating system, but that rapidly became a non-issue. Thanks to IBM's charisma and to Microsoft's licensing skills, in 1982 fifty companies bought a MS-DOS license. As more computers used MS-DOS, the motivation to make software applications for MS-DOS increased. As more applications were written for MS-DOS, the motivation for hardware manufacturers to buy a MS-DOS license increased. Furthermore, Microsoft invested the money in greatly improving the operating system. In March 1983, release 2.0 of MS-DOS offered features derived from the Unix operating system (such as subdirectories and pipes) that made it much more competitive against CP/M on technical grounds.

An impressive number of software companies were started in 1982 in Silicon Valley, a fact that began to alter the relative proportion between hardware and software. Some notable ones included Autodesk, Symantec, Activision, Electronic Arts, and Adobe.

Autodesk was founded in 1981 in Mill Valley to commercialize Mike Riddle 's Interact, the first Computer-Aided Design (CAD) program for CP/M and MS-DOS personal computers, the first affordable tool for creating detailed technical drawings. Riddle, a user of ComputerVision's CAD system for graphical workstations, teamed up with John Walker 's Marinchip Systems that had built a computer based on a Texas Instrument microprocessor. Both had a second life. Riddle, based in Arizona, was an inventor who had built a successful electric guitar tuner. Walker, a libertarian-leaning intellectual, had designed one of the first Trojan viruses, Animal (1975). Walker renamed Riddle's Interact as AutoCAD, ported it to the Victor 9000, one of the early graphics Intel-based personal computers, and turned it into a novelty hit.

Symantec was founded in March 1982 in Sunnyvale to pursue artificial intelligence-based research, notably in natural-language processing. Gary Hendrix, who had worked at the SRI International with Charlie Rosen, a pioneer of perceptron (neural-network) machines, founded and hired a group of specialists from Stanford University. Symantec went on to specialize in development tools for software engineers, i.e. software to help build other software.

Borland was founded in 1983 in Scotts Valley (between San Jose and Santa Cruz) by three Danish developers (Niels Jensen, Ole Henriksen, and Mogens Glad) and Philippe Kahn, a Frenchman who had cut his teeth on the Micral project. They targeted the growing needs not of the end user but of the software developer.

Activision was founded in October 1979 by music industry executive Jim Levy and a group of Atari game designers. It became the first company focused on game design. Until then the games for a console had been published exclusively by the console manufacturer. Activision introduced the praxis of giving credit and even publicizing the creators. Its first success, "Pitfall" (1982), drove many others to start similar companies.

Apple's marketing manager Trip Hawkins founded Electronic Arts in May 1982 in San Mateo. He aimed to market home computer games, viewed not as mere games but as a form of interactive digital media. Both their business plan and their ethics treated game publishing just like book publishing, and treated videogame production just like a movie studio treated movie production.

Adobe was founded in December 1982 in Mountain View to commercialize printer software made by John Warnock (a former employee of Evans & Sutherland) and Charles Geschke. They had worked at Xerox PARC on the page-description language InterPress, whose purpose was to enable all computers of a network to print on any printer of the network. By then they were both in their 40s. They left Xerox to develop a simpler language, PostScript. PostScript was the first building block for desktop publishing, which still needed a viable computer platform and a suitable software environment (both unsuccessfully pioneered by Xerox's Star). Unlike most startups, Adobe was profitable from its first year.

The first inkjet printer had been built by Rune Elmqvist at Elema in Sweden (later acquired by Siemens) in 1948 (ten years later the same man invented the pacemaker). It had taken almost 30 years for Siemens to introduce a commercial inkjet printer: the PT80 of 1977. Siemens' inkjet products as well as similar products from other competitors were mainly used for medical applications. By then IBM had acquired inkjet technology from Stanford University (Richard Sweet's technology) to make its IBM 4640 printer, but that was another failed product. The winning technology was invented in 1977 by Ichiro Endo at Canon: a new inkjet technology called "thermal inkjet", reinvented independently in 1979 by John Vaught at Hewlett-Packard.

The Argentine-born mathematician Trabb Pardo and Les Earnest (who had previously built the first spelling checker at the MIT in 1961) founded Imagen in 1980 to commercialize a pioneering desktop publishing system used at the Stanford Artificial Intelligence Laboratory.

Visicalc had opened up the market of offices to the computer industry. Electronic Arts understood that the same device could be used by millions of people to play games, and Xerox PARC scientists that computers could be used for education and for publishing.

Generally speaking, an important transition was underway. Computers are formed by two interacting substances: hardware and software. At the beginning the cost of a computer was entirely the cost of its hardware parts and of assembling them. Until the 1970s the hardware still represented most of the cost. However, in the 1980s the falling prices of hardware components had enabled ever more sophisticated software applications and triggered a growing demand for them. This meant that the cost of software was escalating at the same time that the cost of hardware was plunging. This vicious loop also constituted a new powerful motivation for the hardware industry to continue producing more powerful chips in order to support ever-larger software applications. Semiconductor components had become commodities, while software now represented the luxury item. Software was also the place where profit margins could be very high.

One could see the same phenomenon in the world of mainframes, which still accounted for the majority of IT revenues. Computer Associates, was formed in 1976 by two Standard Data employees and Columbia University alumni, Chinese-born Charles Wang and Russell Artzt. It was a joint venture with a company owned by Swiss billionaire Walter Haefner, was initially focused on system utilities for mainframe computers. But in the early 1980s it inaugurated a cynical strategy of growth not through invention but through ruthless acquisitions that would eventually gobble up all the historical software companies of the mainframe world (Uccel in 1987 for a record $830 million, ADR in 1988, Pansophic in 1991, Cullinet in 1989).

Electronic Arts' Offices (2010)

Losers

The growing complexity of computer applications also induced a growing concern for the user experience. User interfaces were still too technical for a machine that aimed at becoming a home appliance used by ordinary people. After Xerox invested in Apple, in November 1979 Steve Jobs of Apple was given a "demo" of the Alto. That demo set the course of Apple for the 1980s. Jef Raskin was put in charge of building a "computer appliance" and hired his former student Bill Atkinson from UC San Diego. In January 1983 Apple introduced the Lisa, the first personal computer with a GUI, the "WIMP" (Window, Icons, Mouse, Pull-down menus) paradigm pioneered by the Xerox Alto. The Lisa, based on a Motorola 68000 microprocessor and equipped with one megabyte of RAM and five megabytes of hard-disk storage, heralded the second building block of desktop publishing. Unfortunately, it was too expensive ($10,000) and too slow to truly capture the imagination (and the wallets) of the masses. In October VisiCorp introduced the equivalent GUI for the IBM PC, VisiOn. Neither application lived up to the expectations of their creators.

The principal victim of the personal-computer boom was the videogame console. In the early 1980s there were many best-sellers: Atari 2600 and 5200, Bally Astrocade, Coleco Vision, Emerson Arcadia 2001, Fairchild Channel F, Magnavox Odyssey, Mattel Intellivision, Sears Tele-Games, etc. However, personal computers were getting cheaper and were beginning to offer graphics and sound. A personal computer could play videogames but also run many other useful applications. In 1983 the US market for videogame consoles crashed.

Indirectly, this crisis dealt a blow to virtual reality. In 1982 Atari opened a Sunnyvale Research Laboratory, modeled after the Xerox PARC, and appointed PARC veteran Alan Kay to head it. The center assembled the best minds in virtual reality (Tom Zimmerman, Scott Fisher, Brenda Laurel, Jaron Lanier) but lasted only two years.

Winners

The semiconductor industry in Silicon Valley was booming, serving a market that ranged from watches to airplanes. The startups continued to multiply:

- Linear Technology, founded in 1981, and Xilinx, a Zilog spin-off formed in 1984, addressed programmable logic (chips that customers could program themselves);
- Maxim, founded in 1983 by former Fairchild's marketing executive and AMDs' co-founder Jack Gifford, perfected the analog integrated circuits that Fairchild pioneered;
- Cypress Semiconductor, an AMD spin-off formed in 1982 by a team of CMOS experts, and Altera, founded in 1983, focused on high-performance integrated circuits.;
- VLSI Technology, a Fairchild spin-off of 1979, and LSI Logic, formed in 1981 by Fairchild's engineer Wilfred Corrigan, specialized in ASICs (Application-Specific Integrated Circuits) for embedded systems.

Meanwhile, voice messaging became a household feature after Octel Communications, founded in 1982 by Robert Cohn and Peter Olson in Milpitas (near San Jose), introduced a voice-mail system. It was smaller and cheaper than the traditional ones because it used Intel and Zilog microprocessors.

Logitech, the first major seller of mouse devices for personal computers, was founded in 1981 in Switzerland but had its roots in Silicon Valley, as Swiss-born Daniel Borel and Italian-born Pierluigi Zappacosta had met there in graduate school and had met there the third founder, Giacomo Marini, an executive at Olivetti's Advanced Technology Center, located next door to Apple.

Intimations of the Future

SRI International's scientist Stan Honey founded Etak in Sunnyvale in 1983 with seed money from Atari's founder Nolan Bushnell. Etak became the first company to digitize maps. In 1985 it introduced the Navigator, a navigation system for cars. It was based on the Intel 8088 and the maps were stored on cassette tapes.

Hewlett-Packard experimented with the touch-screen just invented in Europe with the HP-150 (1983), a personal computer based on the Intel 8088, one of the world's earliest commercial touchscreen computers.

Few people heard of "Elk Cloner," a program that a 15-year-old high-school student, Rich Skrenta, unleashed on an Apple II in 1982. It was the first personal-computer virus. Elk Cloner was capable of spreading from floppy-disk to floppy-disk, and therefore from computer to computer. What this hacker had implicitly realized is that the widespread adoption of personal computers had de facto connected millions of people (even though the "connection" still relied on copying files on floppy-disks).

Expert Systems

A mini-bubble within the bubble of software existed with startups that specialized in "expert systems." These were systems based on artificial intelligence (AI) techniques developed at Stanford and operating in a narrow domain (such as troubleshooting or configuring complex equipment). The novel approach to computing adopted by these systems consisted in emphasizing the knowledge required to solve a problem.

An expert system had two fundamental components: a knowledge base, constructed by eliciting knowledge from a human expert, and an "inference engine," which contained a set of algorithms to perform inference on the knowledge base. This was therefore a nonsequential kind of computing that differed from most software (in which the solution is achieved via a sequence of instructions). Expert systems targeted complex problems for which a traditional program was not feasible. Just like a human expert, an expert system could only provide a "plausible" solution, not necessarily a perfect one. The favorite programming languages for these programs were Prolog and Lisp. In fact, there were also startups specializing in "Lisp machines."

A few startups tried to build expert systems. In 1981, Stanford Professor (and expert-system pioneer) Ed Feigenbaum and others founded Teknowledge, which for a while was the most hyped of the AI startups. In 1983, Intellicorp introduced its flagship object-oriented development environment, KEE (Knowledge Engineering Environment), also running on Lisp Machines. Brian McCune, an alumnus of the Stanford Artificial Intelligence Laboratory (SAIL), was one of the founders in 1980 of Advanced Information and Decision Systems (AIDS) in Mountain View, later renamed Advanced Decision Systems (ADS). It was a consulting firm specializing in AI research for the Department of Defense. He and Richard Tong, a Cambridge University graduate, designed a concept-based text-retrieval system, Rubric, a progenitor of search engines.

Japan was ahead in robotics, but in the early 1980s the USA was home to a few success stories of its own. In 1980 Philippe Villers (cofounder of CAD pioneer Computervision in 1969), Stanford professor Victor Scheinman and others founded Automatix in Boston to make robots with rudimentary machine vision (invented at SRI). In 1982 the American Robot Corporation was founded in Pittsburgh and later renamed American Cimflex before merging with A.I. pioneer Teknowledge of Palo Alto. In 1982 General Motors and Japan's Fanuc (a 1972 Fujitsu spinoff that had introduced its first robot in 1977) established the joint venture GMF Robotics. Finally, Adept was founded in 1983 by Brian Carlisle and Bruce Shimano, two Unimation executives and previously both students of Victor Scheinman at Stanford (later acquired by Japan's Omron).

Workstations

One step up from the personal computer, the world was completely different. The early 1980s were the age of the workstation, similar to a personal computer because it was dedicated to a single user but more powerful (especially in graphics). It was also designed to be connected to a network and to run the Unix operating system. This kind of computer targeted the engineering market. They were usually based on the Motorola 68000 (not on Intel microprocessors) and they usually ran the Unix operating system. The market came to be dominated by Apollo (founded in 1980 in Boston by former NASA scientist William Poduska), SUN (1981), Silicon Graphics (1982) and Hewlett-Packard (1983). They all stole market share from DEC's much more expensive minicomputers. Both SUN and Silicon Graphics originated at Stanford University.

SUN Microsystems was founded in February 1982 in Palo Alto by two foreign Stanford students, German-born Andrea Bechtolsheim of the computer science department and Indian-born Vinod Khosla of the business school. In 1981, Bechtolsheim, while working at the Stanford University Network, had modified a Xerox PARC's Alto into a workstation running Unix and networking software. His goal was simply to have machines for individual researchers that would make it as easy as possible to be connected and share data. Khosla realized that this could become a business. They joined forces with Scott McNealy, a former Stanford graduate and now at Unix startup Onyx, and hired Berkeley graduate Bill Joy of BSD fame. He developed a dialect of Unix, SunOS, based on BSD (Berkeley's version of Unix). Backed by venture capitalists such as Kleiner Perkins, SUN was started to market that concept.

The SUN workstation was an evolution of a display terminal invented in 1971 at the Stanford Artificial Intelligence Laboratory (SAIL) and of the Xerox Alto computer (some units of which Xerox had donated to Stanford University in 1979). The SUN workstation marked a turning point in VLSI (Very Large Scale Integration) hardware technology for integrated circuits, which allowed Bechtolsheim to pack a Motorola 68000 CPU, a memory bank, a parallel port controller and a serial port controller into the main CPU board. The other two boards were a graphics display controller and an Ethernet controller (which was still a laboratory device, no commercial Ethernet controller being available in those days). The SUN workstation had more than one spin-off because Yeager's software for connecting multiple Ethernet controllers would later evolve into Cisco's first router, and the version for high-performance graphics display designed by the young James Clark would become the foundation for Clark's first startup, Silicon Graphics.

The original SUN terminal

Unlike the Apollo workstation, which used custom hardware and a proprietary operating system, the SUN workstation used standard off-the-shelf hardware components and a standard operating system (Unix). Thus, in a sense, it replicated the business model of the IBM PC. Soon, the concept of the SUN workstation was competing with Microsoft. The SUN workstation was basically a more powerful personal computer that also happened to be hooked to a network. It ran Unix instead of Windows. It used a Motorola 68000 processor instead of the Intel x86 processors used by Windows-based computers. Also the SUN corporate culture was to the Microsoft culture what the counterculture was to the mainstream.

Silicon Graphics was started in November 1981 by Jim Clark and Abbey Silverstone of Xerox to manufacture graphic workstations. Previously, Evans & Sutherland's Picture System had pioneered hardware implementations of computer graphics. At Stanford University in 1980, former Evans & Sutherland's employee Jim Clark and his student Marc Hannah developed an improved version (funded by DARPA) called the "Geometry Engine." The original idea was to have Motorola 68000-based workstations connected to a DEC VAX minicomputer that boasted high-performance graphics needed for engineering design. Later those workstations became stand-alone Unix computers. Silicon Graphics benefited from an exodus of HP engineers, including Jim Barton who went on to create a real-time version of Unix (essential for flight simulation) and the first video-on-demand system (Full Service Network for Time Warner)

Workstation developers talked about the RISC (Reduced Instruction Set Computer) architecture, which promised faster CPUs. For three decades, there had been a trend towards implementing more and more complex functions directly in the hardware of a computer. The principle behind the research in RISC architectures was that, while it is nice to be able to perform complex operations, applications mostly execute simple operations. Hence, it might be more efficient to perform those (frequent) simple operations faster than to implement (infrequent) complex operations. So again, many startups were formed:

- Ridge Computers was founded in 1980 in Santa Clara by a group of Hewlett-Packard engineers (including Hugh Martin);
- In 1980 David Patterson and Carlo Sequin launched the RISC project at UC Berkeley;
- The following year, John Hennessy started a RISC project at Stanford University. Hennessy eventually left Stanford, founded a company, MIPS, and in 1985 released the first major RISC processor, the R2000. Silicon Graphics would switch to MIPS processors in 1986 (the IRIS 4D series). MIPS was also adopted by Nintendo in Japan, and by Siemens and Bull in Europe;
- When SUN introduced its SPARC architecture in 1986, it was based on Berkeley's RISC project; and so did Pyramid Technology, formed in 1981 by former HP employees;
- British computer manufacturer Acorn debuted a RISC processor in 1985, the Acorn Risc Machine or ARM, designed by Sophie Wilson. It would become the company's most successful product, causing the birth in 1990 of a spin-off, Advanced RISC Machines (ARM), which in 1991 would introduce its first embeddable RISC chip.

The giant in the field of minicomputers was DEC. In October 1977 it introduced a 32-bit family of computers, the VAX, to progressively replace the various 16-bit PDP-11 models. DEC had designed a proprietary multi-user operating system for the VAXes, the VMS. However, in 1978 Bell Labs had already ported the PDP-11 Unix to the VAX platform. Unix had become "the" operating system for universities and DEC hardware had always been a favorite of universities. Therefore DEC involuntarily had one of the most popular Unix platforms. DEC calculated that in 1985 about 25% of all VAXes was running Unix. The VAX with Unix was also the computer of choice for the Internet, since Unix had become the operating system for the Internet and the PDP-11s had become the preferred minicomputers for the Internet.

SUN's Old Building (2010)

The Great Unix Wars

Unix was important to all software developers. In 1983 Oracle announced that its engineers (basically Bob Miner and Bruce Scott) had rewritten its database management system in the C programming language, the language preferred by all Unix systems. It was an achievement that made Oracle's product easily portable across computer platforms. It was therefore ported to the most popular minicomputers and even to mainframes (that already had C compilers). It was also the first 32-bit relational database management system.

Something important happened in 1983 that had little to do with Unix technology but would have repercussions on Unix computers. The US government decided that AT&T (the company that owned Bell Labs and the Unix operating system) constituted a monopoly violating the anti-trust law. The government ordered the dismemberment of this colossal conglomerate (at the time the largest company in the world). AT&T had been forced since 1958 to make non-telephone technologies available to others. But now, broken up into separate companies, it was free to make money out of the Unix operating system. Before the end of the year AT&T had a commercial version ready, which was renamed Unix System V. That was the beginning of the great Unix wars of the 1980s, pitting System V against BSD, i.e. AT&T's corporate profit-driven world versus the idealistic Bay Area hobbyists (notably SUN, which was rapidly dwarfing the competition).

To further complicate the Unix landscape, in 1983 Richard Stallman at MIT started working on a free clone of Unix that would contain no Unix code, code-named GNU. In 1985, he issued a GNU manifesto and launched the Free Software Foundation that denounced proprietary software.

In theory, the Internet belonged to the US government (via DARPA). In practice, most decisions were taken by the various scientists that cooperated casually in maintaining it. For example, SRI International had always maintained the "directory" of Internet nodes (a text file that returned a physical network address for each node). In 1983 Paul Mockapetris at SRI was assigned the task of developing the Domain Name System, so that each node would be identified by a "domain name" in a hierarchy of domain names. The DNS mapped domain names (such as www.scaruffi.com) into IP addresses, replacing the old text file named HOSTS.TXT that SRI maintained on behalf of the entire Arpanet. The concept was refined (like all other concepts on the Internet) by the community via "Requests for Comments" (RFCs). The following year the first DNS was implemented in Unix by students at UC Berkeley. This process was eventually formalized (in January 1986) in an Internet Engineering Task Force (IETF), which was open to everybody.

The Counterculture and the Computer Culture

Just like the personal computer and the Unix, the Internet too was largely shaped by a community of eccentric independents. From the beginning, Arpanet was run by a powerful government agency. Yet its director, Lawrence Roberts, had relied not on top-down decisions but on a decentralized model that involved the very users of the Internet to submit proposals for future directions. He organized retreats for Arpanet users. It was truly a government-mandated collaborative effort. It was another case in which the consumer was the producer, a community of "prosumers." In a sense, the Arpanet was conceived from the beginning as a project in progress, not as a fully specified project, a concept that is more likely to surface in military projects than in commercial product development. One of the side effects of this approach was that the Arpanet changed mission over time, transforming from a military project to survive a nuclear attack into a system for interpersonal communication and knowledge sharing. It fostered collaboration among geographically remote research labs, which was already not one of the initial goals.

Even more unexpectedly, Arpanet became a popular tool for intranode communications and collaboration, as each node started connecting its multiple computers among themselves. E-mail itself was a user idea, never planned by the Arpanet's bureaucracy. Nobody commissioned it, approved it, or promoted it. A user deployed it and other users started using it. By 1973 it probably accounted for the majority of Arpanet traffic. Again, the pseudo-socialist and anarchic idealism of the counterculture had found another form. The ethics of the Internet, just like the ethics of the Unix world and the ethics of the early personal-computer hobbyists, was not the brutal, heartless ethics of the corporate world nor the brutal, heartless ethics of Wall Street. It was the utopian ethics of the hippie communes transposed into a high-tech environment.

Incidentally, in 1982 Scott Fahlman at Carnegie Mellon introduced the three-character sequence :-) to represent a smile in email messages, the "smiley", the first "emoticon".

The nature of the revolution in personal computers, Unix, and the Internet mirrored more closely the continuous renovation of rock music than anything else. Rock magazines and radio stations were used to hail a "next big thing" every month and got music listeners to expect a new genre every month. Similarly, computer magazines (and later Usenet groups) started talking about a technological "next big thing" every month and thus created the expectation for it in computer users.

However, the parallel between counterculture and the high-tech industry had an obvious limit: neither the personal computer nor Unix nor the Internet had anything to do with San Francisco itself. The headquarters of personal-computer innovation was the Santa Clara Valley, the part of the Bay Area that had witnessed the fewest student riots, hippie be-ins, and rock concerts. Stanford, in particular, had been largely indifferent to the whole counterculture. Unix and the Internet had now strong roots in Berkeley, but it was only in part a phenomenon of the Bay Area. It looked as if the marriage between counterculture and high-tech culture had to take place in neutral territory, close enough to the epicenter but far enough not to be affected by its more extreme manifestations.

Shrink-wrapped Software

Until the dotcom boom of the 1990s Silicon Valley was home to many small software vendors but no major one. The 1980s witnessed a boom of software startups, but most of them remained small throughout the decade, and didn't survive more than a decade. However, the companies in Silicon Valley were among the first to adopt the "shrink-wrapped" model of the software business: selling software programs in boxes by mail order and through retail outlets.

The distribution channels were the visible difference, but behind it there were bigger conceptual differences. First of all, the idea behind "boxed" software was to sell thousands of units, not just a handful. Software had long been an artisan-kind of field, in which software companies customized a package for a customer (typically a very larger company or agency). Once boxed, a program was the same for everybody, larger or small. Secondly, the boxed product had to be priced like a consumer good, no more than the machine on which it would run. And, finally, there was no direct sales force, which made an enormous difference in client relationships. Companies like IBM invested huge amounts of resources in developing and maintaining client relationships (and would continue to do so longer after the era of the mainframe). Companies in the low-price high-volume business could not afford a direct sales force of that nature, and therefore sacrificed client relationship altogether. Silicon Valley would never develop a passion for client relationships even after it became the main software center in the world. Silicon Valley engineers would always perceive custom applications as not as exciting as the application that is being used (without customizations) by thousands or millions of people.

Lasers and Nanotechnology

The personal computer was much larger than all the other sectors, but the early 1980s were also, for example, the era of semiconductor lasers. Startups specializing in these high-power lasers included: Stanford Research Systems (SRS), founded in 1980 in Sunnyvale; Spectra Diode Labs, a 1983 joint venture between Spectra-Physics and Xerox PARC; and Lightwave, founded in 1984 in Mountain View. Despite the immense and rapid success of laser technology in all sorts of applications, the laser industry never took off like the computer industry. There were many parallels with the computer industry: Stanford had one of the best research teams in the world; Ed Ginzton was for lasers what Terman had been for electronics; Ginzton's laboratory at Stanford spun off several startups; and employees fluctuated among those companies and founded new ones. While lasers were similar to computers, this is a significant example of an industry based in Silicon Valley that did not achieve momentum.

Micro-Electro-Mechanical Systems (MEMS) represented the infancy of nanotechnology. These were miniaturized devices made of microsensors, microactuators and microelectronics. In 1982 Kurt Petersen wrote the influential paper "Silicon as a Mechanical Material" and founded Transensory Devices in Fremont (later IC Sensors in Milpitas), a pioneering company in commercializing MEMS devices. Petersen envisioned "a broad range of inexpensive, batch-fabricated, high-performance sensors and transducers easily interfaced with the rapidly proliferating microprocessor."

In 1980 Stanford Electrical Engineering professor John Linvill had the idea for the Center for Integrated Systems, a lab that, working in close interaction with the industry, was to bring together material, hardware and software engineers for the purpose of designing integrated circuits. For example, Gregory Kovacs would design sensor systems that combine detectors on silicon wafers the same way electrical circuits are integrated on computer chips.

Anarchy

The 1980s was the age of the spiritual revival that turned so many former hippies into new-age adepts. Arguing for a return to a more natural way of life, they were fiercely opposed to science and rationalism, and viewed technology as evil. The intellectual zeitgeist of the Bay Area was hardly in sync with its high-tech boom. The dichotomy between luddites and technophiles would remain a distinctive contradiction of the Bay Area, just like materialism and spirituality could coexist in the lifestyle of the same "yuppie" (young urban professional).

An important contribution to these booming industries came from people who were completely immune to the intellectual mood of the Bay Area: immigrants. The 1970s had witnessed the first wave of immigration of engineers from Europe and Asia. In the early 1980s they contributed significantly to the boom of Silicon Valley. For example, Chinese and Indian executives ran 13% of Silicon Valley's high-tech companies founded between 1980 and 1984. Additionally, the Bay Area had been attracting young people from the other states of the US since the 1960s. It was sunny, "cool," advanced, cosmopolitan, and opportunities popped up all the time. It had the mythological appeal of the Far West and the quasi-mystic appeal of the Promised Land. At the same time it had become a nice and wealthy place for living, a dreamland for the highly educated youth of the East Coast and the Midwest. Silicon Valley was quite unique in that it was both a place of great ethnic diversity and a place of high technological saturation.

It was also a place where the boring corporate world was inexistent and despised. In 1980, there were about 3,000 electronics firms in the Bay Area: the vast majority had less than 10 employees, and only 15% of them had more than 100.

Silicon Valley exhibited a propensity towards spawning new firms even when the market was not ready for an avalanche of products. Viewed from above, the creation and destruction of companies was chaotic. The lifespan of startups was getting shorter, not longer. What mattered was not the life expectancy of an individual company but the success of the entire ecosystem. The price to pay for the latter was a short lifespan for most of the individual companies.

High labor mobility was crucial to the implementation of this model of continuous regeneration as well as to sustain the breathtaking growth of successful startups. The mobility of labor was also enabled by an anti-union spirit. This was not trivial. After all, San Francisco was the most unionized city in the country at the beginning of the 20th century, and socialist agit-prop groups were ubiquitous in San Francisco and Berkeley during the 1960s. Perhaps it was precisely a desire not to be identified with the old-fashioned business style of San Francisco that led Silicon Valley to adopt the opposite stance towards unions.

The old computing world (mainly based on the East Coast) was controlled top-down and not at one but two levels. First, the users of a mainframe or mini had to be hired by a company or university, i.e. access was controlled top-down by the owner of the expensive computer. Second, the technology of that mainframe or mini computer was proprietary, i.e. controlled top-down by the computer manufacturer. The personal-computer world, instead, was decentralized and anarchic at both levels.

It was ironic how an invention whose original purpose was purely military and reserved for a tightly-guarded small number of laboratories was rapidly evolving into a ubiquitous data processing and communication device for ordinary offices and even households.

Artists: New Paradigms of User-Computer Interaction, Open Architectures, Cisco, Synthetic Biology, and Cyberculture (1984-87)

The Graphical User Interface

A new era began in January 1984 when Apple introduced the Macintosh, the successor to the Lisa. Based on a 32-bit Motorola 68000 CPU, it still featured a proprietary Apple operating system with the Lisa GUI. It went on sale for $2,000.

The Macintosh created a new industry: desktop publishing. In 1985 Apple also introduced the LaserWriter, the first printer to ship with Adobe's PostScript. Aldus of Seattle, founded in 1984 by Paul Brainerd (who coined the term "desktop publishing") introduced PageMaker, the software application that made it easy to create books on a Mac. In 1987 Adobe followed with Illustrator, a PostScript-based drawing application. All the pages were actually rendered in the printer, which meant that the laser printer contained a more powerful processor (with 1.5 megabytes of RAM) than the Macintosh itself. The "desktop publishing" buzzword was spread by marketing executive John Scull, who pulled together Apple, Adobe, and Aldus and virtually invented the whole industry.

The Macintosh emphasized the user interface over anything else. For example, before the Macintosh each application had its own set of keyboard commands. The Macintosh introduced a standard set of commands: Z for "Undo," X for "Cut," C for "Copy," V for "Paste," W to close a window, etc. Each and every Macintosh application had to comply with this standard.

The Macintosh also introduced a new marketing concept: "Buy me because I'm cool." It was the "look and feel" that mattered. Previously, personal computers had sold well because of their killer applications. All computer manufacturers still thought of software as a means to the end of selling hardware. Apple turned the concept upside down: the hardware was a means to power appealing software. In a sense, fashion had come to the computer industry. Apple became the master of style, the equivalent of Italian fashion designers for digital devices. Nonetheless, the Macintosh was always thought of with the killer application in mind, and that was desktop publishing. However, that per se would not have been enough to justify that the company ignored legacy compatibility (Apple II applications did not run on the Mac).

The Macintosh marked a dramatic change in philosophy for Apple. The Apple II was Wozniak's machine: an open platform for which (given the limits of the technology of the time) anyone could write software and attach hardware extensions. Crucially, Apple refused to license the Mac's operating system, whereas Microsoft's operating system worked on any IBM clone. The Macintosh was Jobs' machine: a closed platform that can only run Apple-sanctioned software and attach to Apple-sanctioned hardware. In a sense Jobs had hijacked Wozniak's vision of an open world of computing and turned it into a walled garden. (By then Wozniak's health had been severely impacted by a 1981 airplane accident that he miraculously survived). Unlike IBM (that spawned an entire generation of clones), Apple did not tolerate any clone. Ironically, the combination of IBM's open platform and Apple's closed platform contributed to turn Microsoft into the world's largest software company (and to make Bill Gates the richest person in the world). Apple had the better product, but Jobs' decision to opt for a closed world handed the victory to the lesser product, the Intel/Microsoft machines.

There was no room for hobbyists in an industry that was trying to turn the personal computer into a commodity. Apple had hired Pepsi's President John Sculley. In 1985 Steve Wozniak and Steve Jobs left Apple (the first saw the writing on the wall, the second had to be fired). At the same time the company, following its first quarterly loss, laid off 20% of its workforce, an action that went against the old culture of the company. The first Apple computer with color graphics, the Macintosh II, debuted in March 1987, priced at $3,900. Its other improvement was a plug-and-play bus architecture that made it easier to add expansion cards. The "Mac" was a critical success. It helped cement the community of Apple fans, but the "open architecture" created by the IBM-Microsoft axis was winning (in the broader market) over Apple's closed, proprietary architecture.

That closed architecture, that didn't allow anyone else to use Apple software, was Steve Jobs' ultimate legacy, built on a culture of carefully guarded, industrial secrets. Apple's executives liked to joke that Apple had created more secrecy than the CIA. That paranoia was perhaps the result of Jobs being raised in the middle of the "phreaking" movement: aware that even the technology of the most powerful company in the world (AT&T) could be "hacked", Jobs had wanted to build the super-secure architecture, and the super-paranoid company.

Competition pressed down against Apple. During 1984 Ashton-Tate announced its Framework for the IBM PC. It integrated word-processing, database management, and business graphics within a windowing environment. VisiCorp's VisiOn had been a flop (in January 1985 VisiCorp went bankrupt), but Digital Research thought that it had the muscle to create a mass-market GUI for the IBM PC and in 1985 it launched GEM (Graphical Environment Manager), a GUI for the CP/M operating system designed by former Xerox PARC's employee Lee Jay Lorenzen.

In November, Microsoft responded with Windows 1.0 for MS-DOS, a rather mediocre imitation of the Lisa GUI. Unlike Apple, which controlled its own hardware, Microsoft had to deal with the hardware delivered by PC manufacturers. But PC manufacturer were only interested in cutting prices to be more competitive, not in tweaking their hardware to run a better GUI. Therefore Microsoft couldn't match the Apple GUI until the hardware of PC clones became adequate. It was no surprise that these operating environments for the PC market stagnated.

Also in August 1984 IBM introduced a multitasking operating system named TopView for its new 80286-based PC AT. It never became popular and eventually lost to Windows. A Bay Area programmer, Nathan Myhrvold, had the idea of cloning TopView for MS-DOS and founded Dynamical Systems Research in Oakland. To be on the safe side, Microsoft bought the company in 1986 and hired Myhrvold. Five years later, he would establish Microsoft Research and eventually become the company's chief technology officer.

Office Automation

Desktop publishing was not new to the users of (more expensive) Unix workstations. Boston-based Interleaf, founded by David Boucher and Harry George (two former associates of Kurzweil Computer), had introduced a document processor that integrated text and graphics editing for the Unix workstation market. Steve Kirsch saw an opportunity in that idea and founded FrameTechnology in 1986 in San Jose to commercialize FrameMaker, a publishing platform invented by British mathematician Nick Corfield. But those were products for the high end of the market.

Both on the software and on the hardware fronts there was a push towards making it easier to produce high-quality documents on a PC. In 1985 Hewlett-Packard introduced its own laser printer for the home market, the LaserJet.

HP had decided to start selling printers for the little handheld scientific calculators and John Vaught's team had been working since 1979 on thermal-inkjet technology. HP launched the ThinkJet in 1984 and Japan's Canon introduced the BubbleJet-80 in 1985. Soon the inkjet printer began to replace the dot-matrix printer in the world of personal computers. Color printing came with HP's PaintJet, introduced in 1987, and evolved out of HP's plotter technology. Inkjet technology began to offer laser-printing quality at a much lower price with the HP Deskjet of 1988. Until then Epson's dot-matrix printers had ruled the market, but now HP was rapidly becoming the leader, challenged only by Canon (whose laser printers would become the standard engine for HP's later printers).

In January 1987 Aldus released PageMaker for Windows.

Office tools such as the spreadsheet, word-processor, and presentation programs represented one of the fastest growing markets. In many cases, they were the real reason to own a PC. In 1987 Microsoft unveiled a spreadsheet program for Windows called Excel. These applications began to make Windows more appealing. The most popular word-processors for MS-DOS were WordStar and WordPerfect. Microsoft's own word-processor, MSWord (adapted from Xerox's Bravo by Charles Simonyi after he joined Microsoft), released in 1983, was not successful until, ironically, Microsoft made it available on the Apple Macintosh in 1985. Only in 1989 would Microsoft release a version of Word for Windows. In 1984 Robert Gaskins and Dennis Austin had developed Presentation, later renamed PowerPoint. It was an application for the Macintosh to create slide presentations. In August 1987, Microsoft bought the whole company and ported the product to Windows. For a while the leader in this sector was Software Publishing, which had acquired Harvard Graphics' 1986 presentation program for Windows.

Graphics

The Macintosh was just one of many events of 1984 that displayed a phenomenal acceleration in using computers as graphic media. In 1984, Wavefront, founded near Los Angeles by Bill Kovacs, who had been creating graphic applications with Evans & Sutherland's Picture System in an architect studio, introduced the first commercial 3D-graphics software, Preview. It ran on a Silicon Graphics workstation.

Commodore and Atari meanwhile started a corporate war. In 1985 Commodore launched the Amiga 1000, a 16-bit home computer with advanced graphics and audio (multimedia). It was designed by former Atari's employee Jay Miner with a GUI by Carl Sassenrath, and running a multitasking operating system. It was Commodore's response to the Macintosh. Atari's entry in this market was the ST. Both used the Motorola 68000 microprocessor. The two companies engaged in a major feud because Commodore's founder Jack Tramiel had been fired and had bought Atari, bringing key engineers with him to the rival company. Neither computer could attract the kind of third-party software that Apple and especially the MS-DOS camp could attract. Therefore both languished regardless of their technological merits.

Software had become the key to sell a computer. In 1986, Berkeley Softworks (later renamed GeoWorks) was a third-party vendor in the Bay Area. It was founded by videogame expert Brian Dougherty, who created GEOS (Graphic Environment Operating System), a GUI for the Commodore 64. It provided the look and feel of the Macintosh even on old 8-bit computers with very limited RAM. It rapidly became the third most popular operating system after MS-DOS and the Mac OS.

Steve Jobs himself had launched a new company, NeXT, to build the next generation of computers with an even more advanced GUI than the Macs. Yet he opted for proprietary hardware and a proprietary operating system, and even a new programming language (the object-oriented Objective-C). These design choices dramatically inflated the investment (the machine would not be released until 1989) and discouraged third-party software developers. Unusual for the time, NeXT also invested in sophisticated audio features, mostly designed by Julius Smith of Stanford's CCRMA from 1986 on. Furthermore, the NeXT computer was the first to implement Adobe's brand new Display PostScript, which "printed" directly on the computer's screen, thus ensuring that the user saw on the screen exactly what he would get from the printer.

Research labs were contributing actively to the progress in computer graphics. In 1984 Nicholas Negroponte, who had conducted research on human-computer interfaces at the MIT's Architecture Machine Group, founded the MIT Media Lab to foster the development of multimedia technologies.

Nobody could yet offer photo-quality images on a computer, but at least in 1987 an international standard for image file format was introduced, the JPEG (Joint Photographic Experts Group). The timing was perfect because in 1986 camera manufacturer Kodak had built the first megapixel sensor, capable of representing a photograph with 1.4 million pixels (a pixel being the fundamental unit of a computer display). The world was getting ready for scanning, storing, manipulating, and transmitting images.

There were two obvious kinds of audience for graphics computers outside the computer industry: artists and film studios. In 1984 Joel Slayton at San Jose State University established the CADRE laboratory ("Computers in Art, Design, Research, and Education") that bridged the artistic and high-tech communities. In 1986 Steve Jobs bought Lucasfilm's division that had worked on computer animation, Pixar, and turned it into an independent film studio run by computer-graphics veteran Ed Catmull. Pixar introduced the Pixar Image Computer, the most advanced graphics computer yet, although a commercial flop.

Clearly, personal computers and workstations were mature enough that now the attention was focused on making them easier to use as well as capable of dealing with images and sound.

Virtual Reality

In 1984, a lab at NASA Ames in Mountain View created the first virtual-reality environment. "Virtual reality" was basically an evolution of the old computer simulation systems, such as the ones pioneered by Evans & Sutherland. The software was interactive, meaning that it recreated the environment based on the user's movements, i.e. the user was able to interact with the computer via body movements.

The history of virtual reality dated back to the 1960s and was associated with military applications. Charles Comeau and James Bryan at Philco built a head-mounted display in 1961 ("Headsight"). Meanwhile, Bell Helicopter designed a head-mounted display for pilots that communicated with a moving camera. Ivan Sutherland at ARPA had speculated about the "Ultimate Display" in 1965. In 1966 he moved to Harvard University where he took Bell Helicopter's head-mounted display and connected it to a computer: the images were generated by the computer rather than by a camera. When he moved to the University of Utah, he created a rudimentary virtual-reality system in 1969 on a PDP-1 attached to a Bell Helicopter's display with funding from the Central Intelligence Agency (CIA), ARPA, the Office of Naval Research and Bell Laboratories.

Thomas Furness at Wright-Patterson Air Force Base in Ohio started work in 1969 on a helmet for pilots that displayed three-dimensional computer graphics (the Visually Coupled Airborne Systems Simulator), first demonstrated in September 1981. He then used it to design a virtual cockpit (the "Super Cockpit"), first announced in 1986. It allowed a pilot to fly a plane through a computer-simulated landscape by moving his head and his hand. Furness went on to establish in 1989 the University of Washington's Human Interface Technology Lab (HITL) in Seattle. In 1995 Pattie Maes at the MIT developed the ALIVE (Artificial Life Interactive Video Environment) system. Meanwhile, in 1979 Eric Howlett in Boston invented an extreme wide-angle stereoscopic photographic technology, LEEP (Large Expanse Extra Perspective).

Other researchers designed virtual reality devices for mapping and exploration. In 1979 Michael Naimark at MIT's Center for Advanced Visual Studies debuted the Aspen Movie Map, a project directed by Andy Lippman that allowed the user to navigate a representation of a city (Aspen) stored on laserdiscs. The "movie map" had been created over two years by wide-angle cameras mounted on top of a car. In 1984 UC Berkeley alumnus Michael McGreevy joined NASA Ames Research Center and started the project for the Virtual Planetary Exploration Workstation, a virtual-reality system for which he built the first low-cost head-mounted display, the Virtual Visual Environment Display system (VIVED). The system was hosted on a DEC PDP-11 interfacing an Evans and Sutherland Picture System 2.

Videogame experts also become involved. In 1985 Scott Fisher, an MIT alumnus who had worked both at the Center for Advanced Visual Studies in 1974-76 and at Negroponte's Architecture Machine Group in 1978-82, moved to the Bay Area. He joined Alan Kay 's research group at Atari and the left for NASA Ames. There he built the VIrtual Environment

Workstation (VIEW), incorporating the first "dataglove." By moving the dataglove the user moved in the virtual world projected into her head-mounted display. In 1985 Jaron Lanier, another self-taught videogame expert, established VPL Research at his house in Palo Alto, the first company to sell Virtual Reality products, notably the "Data Glove" invented by Thomas Zimmerman. VPL developed the data glove for NASA, based on the one designed by Scott Fisher. Timothy Leary, the prophet of LSD, saw VPL's virtual reality as a way to experience alternative realities just like hallucinogenic drugs.

The history of virtual reality also overlaps the history of computer games. A MUD (Multi-User Dungeon) is a computer game played by many users simultaneously on different computers, all of them connected to the same virtual world. There were predecessors but the game that created the term and started the trend on the Internet was MUD. It was created in 1978 in Britain by Essex University student Roy Trubshaw and launched online in 1980. In 1986 Lucasfilm launched "Habitat," a social virtual world created by Randy Farmer and Chip Morningstar. It ran on a Commodore 64 computer connected via dial-up lines. Each user in this virtual world was represented by an "avatar."

New Paradigms of User-Computer Interaction

With new technologies came new paradigms of computer-human interaction. In 1987 a Virginia-based company, Linus Technologies, introduced the first pen-based computer, WriteTop. It allowed the user to write directly on the screen. It was PC-compatible and cost $2,750. Also in 1987 Jerry Kaplan, formerly chief technologist at Lotus and co-founder of Teknowledge, started GO Corporation in Silicon Valley to manufacture similar portable computers with a pen-based user interface. GO never delivered anything of any consequence. Yet it went down in the history of the Valley for the impressive amount of venture capital that it managed to amass: $75 million.

In 1987 Apple demonstrated its HyperCard software, which allowed Macintosh users to create applications using interconnected "cards" that could mix text, images, sound, and video. The cards constituted a hypertext. Designed by Bill Atkinson, it was another idea derived from Xerox PARC, which had built a hypertext system called NoteCards in 1984. NoteCards in turn was based on the old experiments of Ted Nelson and Douglas Engelbart. HyperCard also pioneered the idea of "plug-ins," of external software that is allowed to access the application's internal data in order to extend its functionalities.

An early handheld mobile computer came out. It went largely unnoticed in the US, but in 1984 Psion (established in Britain in 1980 by David Potter as the software arm of local computer manufacturer Sinclair) introduced a hand-held computer. The Psion Organiser was the archetype of a "personal digital assistant."

Bill Atkinson of General Magic (2010)

The Semiconductor Wars

Governments, at least in the US and Japan, quickly realized the strategic importance of semiconductors. The US owed its lead in the Cold War to its semiconductor advantage. Japan owed its lead in all sorts of gadgets to semiconductors. Eventually the ferocious competition between companies was escalated to a governmental level and the outcome indirectly helped Silicon Valley focus on the microprocessor.

Silicon Valley's technological lead was undisputed in the 1980s. In 1985 Intel introduced the 32-bit 80386 that contained 275,000 transistors and was capable of performing three million instructions per second. The first 32-bit microprocessor had been shipped already in 1983 by National Semiconductor (the NS32032) and the second had been Motorola in 1984 (the MC68020). Yet it was the Intel 80386 (abbreviated as 386) that shook the market. It boasted almost 100 times more transistors than the 4004 (275,000) and it could run both MS-DOS and Unix.

However, 1985 was the year of the first crisis of the semiconductor industry, brought about by cheaper Japanese products. The Japanese government, via the Ministry of International Trade and Industry (MITI), had sponsored a project headed by Yoshio Nishi at Toshiba for Very Large-Scale Integration (VLSI). Its primary goal was conquering the DRAM market. In 1984 Japanese firms introduced the 256K DRAM chips. Silicon Valley's companies could not compete with the low prices of those chips.

Silicon Valley had gotten its start by selling customized military systems, not by selling commodities. It relied on a network of local know-how and on intimate relationships with the customer. Commodities, instead, rely on economy of scale. So Japan started to win. In 1981 US manufacturers had enjoyed a 51.4% share of the world's semiconductor market, whereas Japanese companies had 35.5%. In 1986 the situation had been reversed, with Japan's share reaching 51% and US companies reduced to a 36.5% share. Specifically, by 1985 Japanese firms had gained 70% of the DRAM market. Intel, AMD and Fairchild had to exit the DRAM market. It was mainly a Silicon Valley problem, because non-Silicon Valley firms such as Motorola, Texas Instruments and Micron continued to manufacture competitive DRAMs. Thousands of hardware engineers were laid off in Silicon Valley, pushing the region towards software.

What saved Intel was the microprocessor. The "computer on a chip" was too complex and required too big a manufacturing investment to be handled like a commodity. Japanese microprocessor technology was simply licensed from the US. In 1984 the world market for microprocessors was worth $600 million: 63% of those sales went to US companies, 30% to Japanese companies, and 7% to European companies. But the situation was even better for the US: 99% of those microprocessors were designed under license from a US manufacturer.

Government intervention helped the chip manufacturers. In 1984 the US government passed the Semiconductor Chip Protection Act, which made it much more difficult to copy a chip. In 1987 the US government set up Sematech (SEmiconductor MAnufacturing TECHnology), a consortium of US-based semiconductor manufacturers funded by DARPA (basically the antidote to MITI program). The semiconductor industry recovered and Silicon Valley-based companies such as VLSI Technology, Linear Technology, LSI Logic, Cypress Semiconductor, Maxim, Altera, and Xilinx went on to become international juggernauts.

Intel's corporate culture changed dramatically after the crisis that almost sank it. Power shifted from Noyce to Andy Grove, who replaced Noyce's idealistic philosophy and casual management with a brutal philosophy of Darwinian competition and iron discipline. Born in Hungary, Andy Grove (real name Andras Grof) had studied at UC Berkeley and worked at Fairchild; he was Intel's third employee in 1968.

Meanwhile, in 1984 Phil Moorby working in Boston at Prabhu Goel's Automated Integrated Design Systems (later renamed as Gateway Design Automation) wrote AIDS Sim (later renamed Verilog), a programming language similar to C but to design electronic chips. This greatly increased the productivity of hardware designers.

Experimenting with Business Models

In 1985 IBM had shipped its four millionth PC, but the following year IBM made a historical mistake. Determined to stamp out the clones, IBM decided to introduce a new computer based on a proprietary architecture built on top of the old Intel 286 microprocessor. Compaq, which had been growing faster than any other company in the history of the US, did not miss the chance to introduce in September 1986 a faster machine based on the 386. When in April 1987 IBM at last delivered a 386-based machine, the Personal System/2 (PS/2), it ran a new operating system, OS/2, co-developed by IBM and Microsoft. This greatly confused the customers. Its lasting legacy would be VGA graphics (Video Graphics Array).

Unlike Apple, which was losing money thanks to its proprietary operating system, Redmond-based Microsoft (not a Silicon Valley company) was booming, thanks to an operating system (MS-DOS) that worked on so many computers. Microsoft went from 40 employees and $7.5 million in revenues in 1980 to $140 million in revenues and 910 employees in 1985. In 1987 Microsoft's stock hit $90, catapulting its main owner, Bill Gates, who was just 31, onto a list of billionaires.

While Apple languished and IBM blundered, some startup computer manufacturers boomed. Michael Dell was still a student at University of Texas at Austin when in 1984 in his dormitory room he founded PCs Limited, later renamed Dell Computer. He decided to specialize in custom PC-compatible computers. This relieved the customer of the tedious and risky business of assembling components to customize the machine. Dell also wanted to deal directly with the customer, initially by mail order only. It was a return to the business model of the early hobbyists. Dell's revenues rose exponentially. Dell's success relied on an automated supply-chain system that removed the need for inventories: its PCs were "made to order." Dell's success mirrored Compaq's success in the early 1980s: both owed their low prices more to a distribution strategy than to a technological breakthrough.

Gateway 2000 was another company that was created by a young hobbyist, built to order, and sold directly to customers. It was formed in a South Dakota barn by Ted Waitt. In 1987, it introduced its first PC. In 1991 it was ranked the fastest growing company in the US. Dell was the heir to a glorious dynasty of Texas electronic businesses that started with Texas Instruments and continued with Tandy and Compaq.

All of them would soon have to battle on another front. In April 1985, Japanese manufacturer Toshiba launched its T1100, one of the earliest IBM-compatible laptops (the project of Atsutoshi Nishida). That machine set the standard in terms of features: internal rechargeable batteries, an LCD (Liquid Crystal Display) screen and a floppy-disk drive. HP had already debuted its first laptop, HP-110, in 1984, which was also IBM-compatible (running MS-DOS on the Intel 8086) but Toshiba took the idea to a new level.

Therefore there were several business models for the personal computer industry:

- Lock customers with a proprietary operating system (IBM and Apple);
- Copy the de-facto standard and get to market fast (Compaq); compete with Unix workstations (AT&T);
- Copy the de-facto standard and make to order "just-in-time" (Dell);
- Produce not just desktop PCs but also portable "laptops" (Toshiba), and;
- Focus on a cross-platform software platform (Microsoft).

Networks

As personal computers became more powerful and easier to use, the client-server architecture became a serious alternative to the monolithic mainframe. In a client-server architecture, the software application was split into a client portion, which ran on a personal computer, and a server portion, which ran on a more powerful computer. Many clients (MS-DOS PCs or Macintosh machines) were connected to the server. A Unix minicomputer was much easier to connect to than an IBM mainframe. The server hosted the database. By distributing software away from centralized mainframes and onto networked personal computers, companies created more flexible environments and saved money. Mainframes were rapidly abandoned. Software companies built fortunes by porting "legacy systems" (applications created for the mainframe) to minicomputers. Thousands of mainframe programmers of the Cobol generation lost their jobs to software engineers of the C-language and Basic generation (Basic having become the language of choice on personal computers).

In 1984 Oracle's executive Umang Gupta founded Gupta (one of Oracle's earliest engineers) started Gupta Technologies to port client-server relational database technology (named SQLBase) to the personal computer.

Computer networks began to proliferate, both within a corporation and among corporations (due to the Internet). A router is a computer-based device for routing and forwarding data to the computers of a network. Judy Estrin, a pupil of Vint Cerf at Stanford and a former Zilog engineer, had already started a company to sell routers, Bridge Communications in 1981 in Mountain View.

Stanford took the lead again. In 1981 Stanford had a team working on a project to connect all its mainframes, minis, LISP machines, and Altos. William Yeager designed the software (on a PDP-11) and ubiquitous student Andy Bechtolsheim designed the hardware. Leonard Bosack was a support engineer who worked on the network router that allowed the computer network under his management (at the Computer Science lab) to share data with another network (at the Business School). In 1984 he and his wife Sandy Lerner (manager of the other lab) started Cisco in Atherton to commercialize the Advanced Gateway Server. It was a revised version of the Stanford router. Their product was developed in their garage and first sold in 1986 through word of mouth. They had correctly guessed that connecting networks to networks would become more important as more corporations needed to connect geographically distributed offices, each having its own network.

Other networking companies also launched. In 1983 Bruce Smith, a former executive at a satellite communications company on the East Coast, founded Network Equipment Technologies (NET) in Redwood City to provide high-end multiplexers to large companies. In 1985 two Xerox PARC engineers, Ronald Schmidt and Andrew Ludwick, started SynOptics in Santa Clara to develop Ethernet products. In 1985 Washington-based bar owner Jim Kimsey founded Quantum Computer Services that introduced a new business model. He provided dedicated online services for personal computers (initially only Commodore models). One could use a personal computer to connect to a bigger computer where other applications could be found (such as videogames). In 1988 Quantum would add service for Apple and PC-compatible computers, and rename itself America Online (AOL).

In 1986 there were already 30 million personal computers in the US. Yet very few of them were "online" (capable of connecting to a service run on a remote computer) because modems were slow and expensive. In 1987 US Robotics of Chicago unveiled a 9600-baud modem, but it cost $1,000.

In 1985 the first domain name of the Internet, Symbolics.com, was registered.

For decades most directors of Information Technology (or Electronic Data Processing, as it was more commonly called) had reported to chief financial officers, the reason being that a computer was a massive investment and it was typically not trivial to justify the investment to the company's management. The personal computer and office productivity software put a computer and an application on every desk. This had two effects. First of all, a lot of information technology did not require the approval of the chief financial officer because it was as cheap as buying a desk or a typewriter. Secondly, the proliferation of such software and hardware, coupled to the chaotic rapidly evolving nature of the computer industry, created the need for someone to keep track of what I.T. tools the company's productivity depended on. The role of the person in charge of data processing changed: instead of being simply the liaison between various departments and the massive mainframe computer, it became the czar in charge of deciding which hardware and which software should be used across the company. In 1986 Business Week magazine published an article titled "Management's Newest Star: Meet the Chief Information Officer" that launched the trend. The success of the client-server model was indirectly due to the growing power of the CIO and to the main duty of such figure: to bring order within the company. The client-server model centralized again power, like it was in the old days of the mainframe, but did so in a highly distributed world. The CIO became much more important than a manager of EDP had always been, because it soon became apparent that the company's productivity depended in large part on the client-server strategy.

Far away from Silicon Valley, Martin Cooper's 1973 prototype of a cellular phone finally became a commercial product when Motorola introduced the DynaTAC in 1984, a phone capable of making wireless phone calls over a network deployed by Bell Labs in 1983, the Advanced Mobile Phone System (AMPS). Just like computers in their infancy, this was not a product that ordinary families could afford, but its ubiquity in movies and on television fired up the imagination of millions of potential consumers.

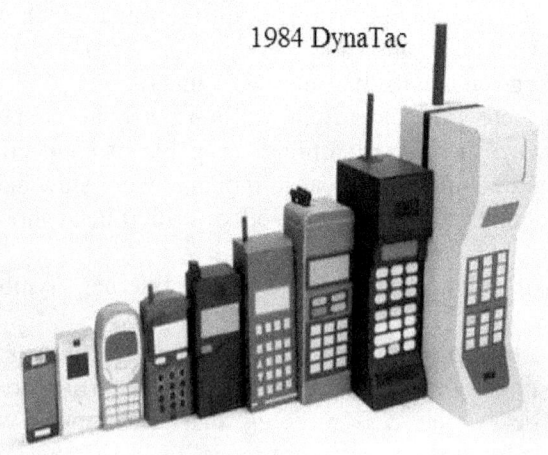

The DyntaTAC

The most important event of the era, however, was one that few noticed, especially since it came from a government agency. In 1985 Michael Marcus, an engineer working for the Federal Communications Commission (FCC) of the USA, the agency in charge of regulating telecommunications, had the idea of liberalizing the use of three useless bands of wireless spectrum: 900MHz, 2.4GHz and 5.8GHz. These came to be known as the "garbage bands". The US government basically allowed anybody to use those bands without the need for a licence, something that existed only for the old ham-radio channels. Little did Marcus know that he had just started a major revolution, the Wi-Fi revolution.

Cisco's Old Offices (2010)

Storage

Meanwhile, the saga of storage devices that had started with Alan Shugart's floppy disc continued to spawn new ideas and companies. In 1984 SUN had unveiled the Network File System (NFS), designed by Bill Joy and managed by Bob Lyon. It had a software component that allowed computers to access data storage over a Unix network. When DEC, HP, IBM, and eventually AT&T adopted NFS, it became an industry standard for distributing data storage over a Unix computer network.

Following Novell's NetWare for networks of personal computers (1983) and SUN's NFS for networks of UNIX workstations (1984), computer networks saw the birth of the first machines dedicated to data storage and shared by many computers. 3Com's 3Server (1985) conceived data storage devices as a new type of computer appliance that could be shared by all the computers of an Ethernet local area network. In 1988 3Com and Microsoft introduced a software for OS/2 called LAN Manager and IBM followed suit with its own LAN Server.

Middleware for local area networks such as NFS enabled new architectures for storing data. Auspex, founded in 1987 in Santa Clara by Adaptec's boss Larry Boucher, introduced the first data storage appliances for a computer network. Among the young engineers hired by Boucher were MIPS' file-system expert David Hitz and Chinese-born Berkeley and Stanford engineering alumnus James Lau.

Auspex's dedicated NFS server for the UNIX market popularized the concept of the data storage server for a computer network, the "network attached storage" (NAS) appliance.

The Threat from Japan

The Bay Area was beginning to have the larger share of computer-related innovations. In the mid 1980s, only a handful of events compared with the boom of Silicon Valley. A few came from Japan, which was going through its own technological boom. In 1984 Sony and Philips introduced the CD-ROM for data and music storage. In 1984 Fujio Masuoka at Toshiba invented flash memory, a cheaper kind of EEPROM. This caused a significant revolution in the design of storage. Since the invention of "Williams tubes", computer architectures had split memory into a small, fast, short-term unit of DRAM and a larger, slow, long-term storage drive. The common forms of storage were hard-disk drives and floppy-disk drives, i.e. units that contained spinning disks and movable read-write heads. Flash memories required solid-state drives: drives with no drive motor (and, in general, no significant mechanical parts). The most popular technology of flash memory, NAND, represented a serious threat to EEPROMs that were used for configuration data.

In 1983 Nintendo, which so far had mostly copied other people's games (1978's "Block Fever" was a clone of Atari's "Breakout" and 1979's "Space Fever" was a clone of "Space Invaders"), launched the Family Computer, a videogame console designed by Masayuki Uemura. They renamed it the Nintendo Entertainment System two years later in the US, where it single-handedly resurrected the videogame console.

Changing of the Guard

In the fast-moving Bay Area, a new generation was taking over and the old one was rapidly being buried. In 1987 National Semiconductor acquired Fairchild from Schlumberger, which had acquired it in 1979 with the whole of Fairchild Camera and Instrument. In the same year ComputerLand (that in 1985 was valued at $1.4 billion) was purchased for a modest sum by a private equity firm. Zilog had long succumbed to Exxon and the managers of its historical Z80 era had already quit.

SUN was causing another revolution. Between 1986 and 1987, its revenues almost tripled. By the end of 1988, it would pass DEC in market shares of workstations (SUN 38.3%, DEC 23.1%, Apollo 16.7%, Hewlett-Packard 10.6%). SUN ended up eroding DEC's supremacy in the academic and then in the engineering market, which had traditionally been the bedrock of DEC's success.

Their business ideologies were, in fact, opposite. DEC still belonged to the era of vertically integrated manufacturers that produced in-house virtually all the hardware and software components of the computer. SUN, by contrast, pioneered a manufacturing industry that relied on third parties to provide all the components. The DEC generation believed that a company needed to personally make the key components of its products. The SUN generation believed that such key components ought to be delegated to specialty shops in Silicon Valley (and, eventually, around the world). In-house development was unlikely to match the same "best of breed" quality across the board guaranteed by a portfolio of specialized companies. SUN's departments were only in charge of designing, coordinating, assembling, and selling. The complexity of creating a product had shifted from a network of internal laboratories to a network of external suppliers. What had changed was the pace of technological innovation. The small startup SUN had been able to introduce more products in its first five years in its market segment than a multi-billion dollar corporation like DEC. The DEC generation relied on proprietary components to keep the competition at bay. The SUN generation relied on the frenzied pace of product releases, knowing that each product was easy for the competition to clone but difficult to clone in time before a new product would make it obsolete. In the end, the SUN model greatly increased its revenues per employee. It also reduced its exposure to the risk of capital-intensive operations.

The SUN model would create a huge secondary economy in Silicon Valley of hyperspecialized companies that would never become household names despite achieving considerable revenues. Apple also adopted the SUN model, whereas HP managed to fare better than DEC even with the old model of vertical in-house integration. In 1987 SUN seemed to renege on its own "open-architecture" ideology when it switched from off-the-shelf hardware and software to its own RISC microprocessor, SPARC, and its own operating system, Solaris. However, it was still outsourcing the production of its components.

SUN's Headquarters at the Agnews Development Center (2010)

Cyberculture

In the 1980s, the media and the intelligentsia were fascinated by the possibilities of the "cyberspace," the invisible medium/dimension of data. Thanks to networks, data now traveled through a space and lived a life of its own. William Gibson invented a whole new genre of science fiction with his novel "Neuromancer" (1984); he popularized the term "cyberspace." In 1983 Bruce Bethke had written the story "Cyberpunk," which introduced another term in the genre: the punk that roams cyberspace. The media had been creating a mythology of hackers, of software engineers who could manipulate programs and data. The media had also been speculating on the possibilities of Artificial Intelligence. All these threads resonated with a society that was haunted by the fear of a nuclear holocaust and an alienated urban life.

In January 1986 a "computer virus" nicknamed "Brain" started spreading among IBM PCs. Every time a user copied something from an infected floppy disc, the user also involuntarily copied the virus on the PC, which then replicated itself on any other floppy disc used by that machine. Computers had become vulnerable to contagious diseases just like living beings.

The virus had been created in faraway Pakistan by the owners of Lahore's computer shop Brain (Basit Farooq Alvi and Amjad Farooq Alvi). The original personal-computer virus "Elk Cloner" had done relatively little damage because it was confined to the Apple II world, but the widespread adoption of the IBM PC standard had created a whole new world of opportunities for digital contagion.

The 1980s had witnessed a rapid rise in the status of the software engineer. No longer a nameless cog in vast corporate bureaucracies, the software engineer had emerged from the personal computer revolution as the cyberspace equivalent of the medieval knight-errant. Steven Levy's book "Hackers - Heroes of the Computer Revolution" (1984) glorified them. The decade would end with Hans Moravec's "Mind Children" (1988), that quipped "Robots will eventually succeed us: humans clearly face extinction" and with Fereidoun "FM-2030" Esfandiary's futuristic vision "Are You a Transhuman?" (1989), while the following decade would open with Ray Kurzweil's book "Age of Intelligent Machines" (1990), predicting the coming of machines smarter than humans, what Vernor Vinge had called "the singularity".

Ray Kurzweil

Suddenly, the future of humankind was in the hands of this obscure new worker, the hacker. In 1981 Wau Holland formed a club of sociopolitically-aware Berlin hackers, the Chaos Computer Club (CCC). In 1984 this club started organizing a conference for hackers in Hamburg, the Chaos Communication Congress (C3) while publishing the magazine Die Datenschleuder. In 1984 David Ruderman and Eric Corley (aka Emmanuel Goldstein) founded the hacker magazine 2600 in New York. Another early society of hackers was Cult of the Dead Cow (cDc Communications), founded in 1984 in Lubbock (Texas) with the motto "Global Domination Through Media Saturation", that spawned the hacker conference HoHoCon in 1990, modeled after the first hacker conference in the USA, the Summercon held in St Louis in 1987. Another influential magazine was Hack-Tic, established in 1989 in the Netherlands and modeled after C3's Die Datenschleuder.

Synthetic Biology

Syntetic biology, which offered the prospect of creating genes, proteins, and even living creatures, started to arise. In May 1985 Robert

Sinsheimer organized a meeting of biologists in Santa Cruz (south of the Bay Area) to discuss the feasibility of sequencing the entire human genome. In a few months Leroy Hood 's team at the California Institute of Technology in Pasadena refined an automated method to sequence DNA, i.e. the first automated DNA sequencer, which made it possible (not just theoretical) to sequence the entire human genome. Lloyd Smith was the main developer of the machine thanks to his background in both engineering and chemistry. Within one year that sequencer was launched on the market by Sam Eletr's Applied Biosystems in Foster City, which also provided an automated protein synthesizer, protein sequencer and DNA synthesizer (these were easier technologies to develop). This gave Applied Biosystems a virtual monopoly in DNA synthesis for several years. Leroy Hood's team included a young Mike Hunkapiller, who was also one of the first employees of Applied Biosystems.

A brand new discipline was born when in 1984 Steven Benner at the University of Florida created a gene encoding an enzyme, the first artificially designed gene of any kind. Synthetic biology is to biology what mechanical engineering is to physics: its goal is to build biological systems that do not exist in nature. In 1988 Benner organized the conference "Redesigning the Molecules of Life', the first major conference on synthetic biology.

Meanwhile a third company joined Alza and Genentech among the successes of the Bay Area's pharmaceutical industry. A 29-years old employee of the venture capital firm Menlo Ventures, Michael Riordan, founded Oligogen (later renamed Gilead Sciences) in August 1987 in Foster City, a company that, after a number of acquisitions, would experience exponential growth thanks to a focus on antiviral drugs to treat chronic and global diseases such as AIDS, hepatitis C and the flu (Tamiflu for the flue, Viread for AIDS, Sovaldi for hepatitis C), becoming the biggest biotech company in the world.

The Anthropology of High-Tech Individualism

Only a fraction of the high-tech workforce was born and raised in the Bay Area. The others were, by definition, "strangers." Some of them had come to study, and therefore could count on a network of friends from college. Many of them had come for work while in their 20s or 30s. Their social life was not easy in a region where individualism was pushed to the extreme. People lived alone most of the day: commuting by car (one person per car) because public transportation was inefficient, working in a cubicle, living in apartments. The housemate was often a social choice, not an economic one: it was a chance to occasionally talk to somebody. Companies encouraged employees to mingle by throwing company parties and the likes. Some companies (notably SUN) even organized their workplace to mirror a college campus.

The connections tended to be very weak. Friendship tended to be rather superficial. Most people's "friends" were just random acquaintances who would not hesitate to "flake out" on an appointment.

The poverty of social life was, however, offset by the broad range of summer and winter activities that quickly became a feature of the regional psyche. The geography blessed the Bay Area with proximity to the skiing area of Lake Tahoe, the beaches of the Pacific coast, the forests and waterfalls of Yosemite, the desert of Death Valley, and the mountains of the Sierra Nevada. Furthermore, this part of California enjoyed six months of virtually no rain, a strong motivation to spend weekends outdoors. During the week, people who lived in the ubiquitous apartment complexes could enjoy the annexed amenities, from the swimming pool to the gym.

The ethnic Babel, the appeal of the outdoors, and the apartment life caused a decline of quintessential American entertainment such as bowling, billiard, baseball, and fishing/hunting.

Social events were monopolized by work-related issues. High culture was virtually inexistent, completely subcontracted to San Francisco and Berkeley. Restaurants, not politics, made news.

Silicon Valley engineers were also the users of the technology invented there. The region posted a higher percentage of users of computer technology than any other region of the world. An emblem of this recursive lifestyle was Fry's, the first electronic superstore that opened in 1985 in Sunnyvale selling everything from cables to computers. The technology manufactured there had therefore a direct influence on shaping the lifestyle of this heterogeneous workforce. In fact, it was a unifying factor. High-tech (not the church or the government) provided an identity to the community. An endemic problem in Silicon Valley was the turnover of engineers, who could easily switch jobs overnight, and who were generally more interested in short-term financial success than in long-term career advancement within a large organization. At the same time, the volatility of the job market in Silicon Valley was even higher than in other parts of the US. The lifespan of a company was totally unpredictable. A sense of insecurity was inherent in the lives of these highly paid professionals. At the same time, it was a lot easier to land a high-tech job in Silicon Valley than anywhere else on the globe just because of statistics (the sheer number of high-tech companies). A sense of arrogance was therefore also inherent in the lives of this population. Sometimes the psychological relationship was upside down: the company had to be grateful that an engineer worked for it (whereas in the rest of the world it was usually the worker who was grateful to the company).

Insecurity and arrogance coexisted in the same mind, with wild swings from one to the other depending on the company's performance.

The typical career consisted in parasiting on a company's success until that success began to taper off, and then jump onto another company's bandwagon. It was a career path of quantum jumps. It also implicitly required a process of lifelong training in order to avoid obsolescence. It wasn't just instability: it was accelerated and self-propelled instability.

Culture and Society

The main event of those years in the cultural life of San Francisco was probably the WELL. Started in 1985 by Stewart Brand of the Whole Earth fame, and modeled after Murray Turoff's EIES, the "Whole Earth Lectronic Link" (or "WELL") provided a virtual community of computer users, structured in bulletin boards for online discussions. Brand had just invented social networking. Its impact on the "alternative" lifestyle was significant. It was the first time that a computer-based system had such an impact on a computer-illiterate public.

On the WELL people freely exchanged knowledge without expecting to be paid for it. It was a miniature "sharing" economy. In 1969 the physicist Gerard O'Neill at Princeton University had envisioned a human colony in outer space. The WELL implemented O'Neill's space colony not in outer space but in what William Gibson had just nicknamed "cyberspace". In 1987 Howard Rheingold coined the term "virtual community". Among the most followed members of the WELL was John Perry Barlow, an alumnus of Timothy Leary's acid trips in New York who had written lyrics for the Grateful Dead.

Howard Rheingold working on his Time Machine
in his Mill Valley studio

Stewart Brand's nonprofit Point Foundation (the umbrella for the various Whole Earth projects) and the Homebrew Computer Club organized the first large-scale meeting of computer hackers, in November

1984 at Fort Cronkhite, in the Marin Headlands just north of San Francisco. 150 hackers attended, including Steve Wozniak and Bill Atkinson from Apple, Lee Felsenstein from Osborne, Richard Greenblatt from the MIT, Richard Stallman from GNU, hypertext pioneer Ted Nelson.

Cyberspace continued the metaphor of consciousness expansion, fifth dimension, mystical experience and transpersonal communion of the hippies replacing drugs as the vehicle with computer networks.

One decade after Daniel Bell's "The Coming of Post-industrial Society" (1973), the new rising knowledge-based society was being hijacked by the counterculture of the Bay Area and began shaping not a new political order but a new economic and social order. In particular, this new order privileged networks over hierarchies.

In 1984 Ken Goffman, then better known as R.U. Sirius, started the underground magazine High Frontiers, billed as "the Space Age Newspaper of Psychedelics, Science, Human Potential, Irreverence & Modern Art", making yet another connection between the counterculture of the Bay Area and the emerging high-tech scene (in fact, it would change its name to Reality Hackers before becoming Mondo 2000).

In 1984 British-born broadcasting veteran Harry Marks and graphic designer Richard Wurman organized in Monterey (two hours south of San Francisco) the first Technology Entertainment and Design (TED) conference, which would become an annual series starting in 1990.

In 1986 Judy Malloy published the computer-mediated hyper-novel "Uncle Roger" on the WELL. In 1983 Christina Augello had founded the Exit Theatre, that was becoming a reference point for the performance scene.

Stewart Brand, Creator of the Whole Earth Catalog (2010)

The Whole Earth Catalog had provided the first link between the art crowd of San Francisco and the high-tech crowd of Silicon Valley. During the 1980s the links multiplied: in 1981, Trudy Myrrh Reagan organized in San Francisco the first YLEM meeting of artists working with new technologies; in 1984, Roger Malina, an astronomer at UC Berkeley, established Leonardo in San Francisco to foster the integration of art and science; in 1984, Marcia Chamberlain at San Jose State University organized the first CADRE conference.

Science was never quite predictable in the Bay Area. In 1984 the "Search For Extraterrestrial Intelligence" or SETI Institute, a non-profit organization founded by Thomas Pierson and Jill Tarter and supported by NASA and later by private philanthropists, opened its doors in Silicon Valley. It implemented what NASA Ames' "Project Cyclops" had recommended in 1971 under the leadership of HP's director of research, Bernard Oliver.

In January 1985 Kevin Kelly launched the magazine "Whole Earth Review," the successor to Stewart Brand's "Whole Earth Catalog," except that it was now an opinion journal. It introduced virtual reality, the Internet, and artificial intelligence to the masses of Silicon Valley hackers. Its articles embodied the idealistic and futuristic aspects of software development in the Bay Area.

The marriage of academia, corporate world and military-industrial complex was becoming even more promiscuous now that the Bay Area was strategic. For example, in 1987 in Berkeley former SRI's strategist Peter Schwartz, now working for an oil corporation, cofounded the consulting firm Global Business Network with SRI's marketing analyst Jay Ogilvy, and hired Stewart Brand of the WELL, who was already consulting for the same oil corporation. This quickly became one of the most influential "think tanks" in the USA, specializing in the kind of "scenario planning" pioneered by Herman Kahn at the Hudson Institute.

Driven by college radio stations and alternative magazines, music for young people underwent a major transformation. Despite the limitations of the instruments, the musical avantgarde (for example, Negativland, Naut Humon, Constance Demby and Robert Rich) was experimenting with techniques once reserved to the research centers. Rock music, ranging from avant-metal band Faith No More to avant-folk ensemble American Music Club, displayed a preference for destabilizing genres.

The Mission District continued to be a center of street art. In 1984 Patricia Rodriguez of Las Mujeres Muralistas fame and and Ray Patlan (a Vietnam War veteran and Chicago muralist who in 1970 had helped jumpstart the Pilsen community center Casa Aztlan for Mexican immigrants and who had moved to SF in 1975) launched the PLACA project that gathered more than 30 artists to protest the USA's involvement in the civil wars of Central America. This was the beginning of Balmy Alley, between 24th Street and Garfield Square, soon to boast the highest concentration of agit-prop murals in the state.

In 1986 Larry Harvey started the first "Burning Man" event on Baker Beach in San Francisco. By simply burning a sculpture, he started one of the most influential grass-roots festivals of the age. In a sense it represented a fusion of the psychedelic and of the hobbyist cultures of the Bay Area. In a few years Burning Man moved to a desert, and attracted thousands of independent artists willing to burn their art after displaying it. Somehow, that phenomenon mirrored the whole Silicon Valley experience (and, not coincidentally, would become extremely popular among Silicon Valley "nerds" who otherwise had no interest in art). "Burning Man," born out of a counterculture that reacted against what Silicon Valley represented, was an appropriate metaphor for what Silicon Valley represented.

Startups: Fabless Manufacturing, Networking, Mobility, and Nanotech (1987-90)

Outsourcing the Fab

By the late 1980s software (both system and application) had trouble keeping up with the progress in hardware. Hardware indirectly enabled a lot of functions that software was not exploiting yet. So while in April 1989 Intel introduced the 80486, containing 1.2 million transistors and performing 20 million instructions per second, IBM was right to ignore (yet again) the new microprocessor. Meanwhile its competitors Compaq, Olivetti, and Zenith rushed to introduce 486-based computers.

However, the real news for Silicon Valley's semiconductor industry was not technological but logistical. In 1985 the government of Taiwan hired Chinese-born Texas Instruments' vice-president Morris Chang to run the Industrial Technology Research Institute (ITRI). Chang promoted the outsourcing of semiconductor manufacturing by US companies to Taiwanese companies. In 1987 he personally founded the Taiwan Semiconductor Manufacturing Corporation (TSMC). Taiwanese companies were able to slash costs, mainly because of cheap labor.

This led to the establishment in Silicon Valley of "fab-less" semiconductor companies, i.e. hardware companies that did not own a fabrication lab but instead used TSMC for the actual manufacturing process. The model was pioneered by Chips and Technologies and Xilinx, and particularly by their executives Gordon Campbell and Bernard Vonderschmitt. Cirrus Logic, founded in 1981 by Indian-born MIT alumnus Suhas Patil, and Adaptec, founded in 1981 by Laurence Boucher, were other early fab-less chip "manufacturers" in the valley.

The fabless phenomenon became a form of inter-firm cooperation in disguise. Whenever a Silicon Valley manufacturer outsourced a project to a Taiwanese fab, it directly improved the Taiwanese plant both by injecting capital and by the project's new requirements. This indirectly constituted a favor to the competitor who would outsource next to the same plant. As long as this meant that the shared Taiwanese plant was going to be always better at serving one's needs, it was accepted that it would also be better at serving the competition's needs. It was like living in a polyandrous relationship in which it was accepted to share the same wife as long as that wife became better and better at being a housewife for all the husbands.

The Software Industry

Since CSC's IPO of 1963, very few software companies had gone public. The first software company to "go public" after CSC had been Cullinet in 1978, and Cullinet had also been the first software company to be valued at over a billion dollars. In 1971 the Nasdaq had opened to raise capital specifically for small high-tech firms, but it had remained a niche stock market. Software, however, ended up benefiting from a change enacted in 1978 by the USA that allowed pension funds to invest in venture capital funds. It wasn't that venture capitalists fell in love with software companies but simple statistics: the amount that venture capital firms managed in 1977 was $2.5 billion; in 1983 it had skyrocketed to $12 billion. The US economy had suffered a decade of high inflation and stagnation following the 1973 OPEC crisis. It had come out of the tunnel in 1983, which turned out to be the best year for IPOs since 1969. There was also pressure on investors to diversify because the US economy was transitioning out of the auto, steel, oil and aircraft economy that had dominated the country for almost a century. In 1950 the USA had produced about two-thirds of all the cars manufactured in the world, and 47% of the world's steel, but by 1980 Japan was threatening US supremacy in both cars and steel (the US share of car production had fallen to 21%, the US share of steel production was down to 14%). High-tech startups benefited from all these factors, simply because there was so much money and so much enthusiasm. The existence of the Nasdaq had certainly helped steer some of the available money towards young, small, software startups. Computer Associates had gone public in 1981. Lotus had been one of the beneficiaries of the 1983 boom. That year there were, in fact, 173 IPOs in the high-tech industry of the USA. For the first time in the history of computers, in 1983 investors had moved away from hardware and towards software. The feeling was that hardware had little left to say after IBM had standardized the world of both small and large computers, and after the rapid rise of Japan in the semiconductors industry. In 1984 stock prices of high-tech companies had fallen across the board, but the momentum remained and in 1986 several software companies (Microsoft, Oracle, Adobe) went public. In 1985 Lotus replaced Cullinet as the largest software company in the USA (by sales). In 1990 Microsoft would cross the $1 billion mark in revenues and, thus, overtake Lotus. By 1990 software was receiving (17.4%) twice as much venture capital money as hardware and biotech, just before "the dotcom boom". Improved access to public equity finance helped the young and small high-tech companies succeed in fields dominated by large well-established corporations. The latter started losing market share to the newcomers in the 1980s and would continue to bleed throughout the 1990s.

The late 1980s witnessed a flurry of new computer models to replace the old text-only systems with graphical environments, and to add more power and more memory. The main beneficiaries were the software companies, whose power kept increasing.

However, no West Coast company could compete with the giants of the East Coast. IBM remained by far the largest software company in the world: only 13% of IBM's 1989 revenues came from software, but that corresponded to $8 billion. IBM's total revenues of $62 billion constituted about a third of the world's total revenues for hardware and software. The first software company to reach one billion dollar in sales was Computer Associates in 1989, based in New York and still mainly focused on applications for mainframe computers. Massachusetts-based Lotus, which had sold over four million copies of 1-2-3 by 1988, now trailed behind Oracle, with sales of $692 million in 1990. In January 1990, Microsoft released Office for Windows, which integrated Word, Powerpoint, and Excel. The days of Lotus's domination in the application business were numbered.

Data Management in the Bay Area

At the turn of the decade the largest software company in the Bay Area was Oracle. Its relational database management system had become the de-facto international standard after IBM had involuntarily legitimized SQL in the mid 1980s. The difference between IBM and Oracle is that Oracle had targeted minicomputers and notably Unix. In 1982, before IBM introduced the DB2, Oracle had 24 employees, a customer base of 75 companies, and revenues of $2.5 million. In 1987 revenues had reached the $100 million mark. In 1989 they skyrocketed to $584 million, and then they almost doubled in one year, just short of a billion dollars for the fiscal year ending in May 1990. This was one case in which a much bigger competitor had helped, not killed, the independent by legitimizing its (better) technology. Seattle-based Microsoft was slightly ahead of Oracle with revenues of $804 millions in 1989.

The other database manufacturers of the Bay Area were also booming. In 1988 Sybase became the darling of the stock market by introducing a client/server relational database, SQL Server, and signing a deal with Microsoft to port SQL Server to Windows (the joint project would lead to Microsoft's own namesake product). In 1989 Phil White took over at Informix and turned it around in a dramatic way. By 1993 it would become one of the Bay Area's most valuable companies.

Two other database companies thrived. First, in April 1988 Michael Pliner (former founder of networking company Sytek) started Verity, basically a spin-off from Advanced Decision Systems and largely staffed with MIT alumni such as Clifford Reid, to capitalize on ADS's text retrieval system for topic-based queries. Topic, initially designed for the Strategic Air Command of the Air Force by David Glazer and Phil Nelson, was one of the first commercial "search engines." Second, Legato, founded in September 1988 in Mountain View by Bob Lyon and Russell Sandberg (the SUN engineers who had helped Bill Joy create NFS), introduced a device to improve the performance of SUN's NFS. Yet it would soon become a leader in the more strategic field of cross-platform automatic data backup and recovery.

The increasing importance of sharing data across applications on a variety of software platforms in real time spawned a new industry of "middleware". In 1987 Indian-born Boston-based Vivek Ranadive founded Teknekron Software Systems (which in 1997 would evolve into TIBCO and relocate to Palo Alto) to market an "Information Bus" capable of shuttling mission-critical data between software programs. It rapidly digitized Wall Street's transactions.

At the hardware level, SanDisk, founded in 1988 by two EEPROM experts from Intel, Israeli-born Eli Harari and Indian-born Sanjay Mehrotra, was soon to become a significant competitor of Asian leaders Toshiba and Samsung in the strategic field of flash memory cards.

Xerox's Inventions at Work

Xerox PARC's inventions continued to spread through Silicon Valley, but mostly at other companies. In January 1990, Adobe released Photoshop for the Macintosh, thus completing the desktop-publishing revolution. Photoshop, actually developed by Thomas Knoll, a student at the University of Michigan, allowed ordinary computer users to do things that were difficult even for a professional printer. IBM itself introduced the Interleaf desktop-publishing software for its personal computers.

Operating systems made some headway. In 1988 a Los Angeles-based company, Elixir, ported the Xerox Star windowing GUI to the IBM PC and to MS-DOS, but it was too little too late to compete with the Macintosh. Smalltalk, the first object-oriented environment, had never been marketed by its inventor, Xerox. Los Angeles-based Digitalk had already developed in 1983 a version of Smalltalk for the IBM PC, the first commercial release of Smalltalk. In 1989 Adele Goldberg, who had taken over management of Smalltalk at Xerox PARC from Alan Kay, founded ParcPlace in Mountain View to market a version of Smalltalk for Unix, Windows, and Macintosh platforms. Both companies (that eventually merged) were trying to capitalize on the appeal of Smalltalk's elegant software development environment and graphical user interface, but Smalltalk was an interpreted language and therefore very slow. Last but not least, it was not endorsed by any major company.

Documentum, based in Pleasanton and founded in January 1990 by Howard Shao of Xerox PARC and John Newton of Ingres, was incubated by Xerox's own venture-capital arm, Xerox Technology Ventures, to consolidate PARC's efforts in document management software.

In 1988 Alan Cooper (of Digital Research and General Ledger fame) sold Microsoft a visual form generator ("Ruby") that, combined with Microsoft's BASIC programming language, would become Visual Basic. The spirit was pure PARC: a friendly environment to develop business applications on personal computers. It also introduced a new way for people to augment a system by seamlessly integrating third-party software code ("widgets") into the system.

Meanwhile, PARC's other great invention, ethernet, had spawned an industry of its own, and the demand for "broadband" was increasing dramatically. Sensing an opportunity, Indian-born inventor Vinod Bhardwaj founded Sunnyvale-based Kalpana in 1987 that in 1990 introduced the first Ethernet switch. A "switch" is a device that connects the computers of a Local Area network (LAN). The switch optimizes the traffic of data packets, thereby reducing bandwidth usage and increasing the overall bandwidth of the network. Another early player in that market was Crescendo Communications, founded in 1990 by Italian-born former Olivetti executives Luca Cafiero and Mario Mazzola.

Software for Manufacturing

The market for enterprise resource planning (ERP) software had been expanding rapidly. Corporations could run their entire business, from procurement to sales, via one monolithic system. SAP dominated that market. In the US the leader was JD Edwards. Both their platforms ran on mainframes. That industry came to the Bay Area in 1987, when David Duffield founded PeopleSoft in the East Bay. PeopleSoft started with the idea of taking the human-resource management system developed for the mainframe by Duffield's previous company, Integral Systems (that he had founded in 1972 in New Jersey but relocated in 1976 to Walnut Creek, near Berkeley), and port it to the client-server architecture. The product rapidly overtook the mainframe-based competition, generating revenues of $1.9 million in 1989 and $6.1 million in 1990. PeopleSoft went on to overtake JD Edwards and eventually absorb it.

Meanwhile, a new sector of software for manufacturing was being invented in Detroit. In 1982 General Motors began to plan a new car, the Saturn. Meanwhile GM had hired Wharton Professor Morris Cohen to improve its factories. Cohen's proposals went into the new Saturn factory, and basically amounted to linking all GM dealers with the factory's mainframe via satellite. Cohen had modeled GM's business as a series of "supply chains," each one representing a stream of "resources" (such as raw materials and third-party components) towards a finished product that is delivered to the end customer. By doing that, the Saturn factory had built the first supply chain management (SCM) system, integrating suppliers, factory and customers. A company named Intellection (later renamed i2) was founded in Dallas in 1988 by two former Texas

Instruments employees, Indian-born Sanjiv Sidhu and Myanmar-born Ken Sharma, to create an independent SCM software package (called Rhythm). Needless to say, the border between ERP and SCM was blurred at best.

Locally in the Bay Area, there were many companies serving the needs of the semiconductor industry. For example, Rasna Corporation, founded in November 1987 in San Jose by George Henry and other engineers of IBM's Almaden Research Center (plus Keith Krach, founder of the robotics division of General Motors), sold computer-aided engineering tools for the semiconductor industry. Their compnay was eventually purchased by Parametric Technology of Boston, which had just purchased CAD pioneers Evans & Sutherland.

3D Printing

Silicon Valley also missed the train on one of the most important innovations in manufacturing: 3D printing. There were multiple inventors, because "additive manufacturing" can be implemented in many different ways. In 1967 Wyn Swainson, still a student in Denmark, applied for a patent titled "Method of Producing a 3D Figure by Holography" that was probably the first kind of 3D printing. He completed his studies in chemistry at UC Berkeley, obtained a patent in 1971, and opened a company called Formigraphic in Bolinas, north of San Francisco. In 1974 Formigraphic (later renamed Omtec Replication) demonstrated the printing of a 3D object. Charles Hull filed a patent in 1984 for "stereolithography" or SLA, a laser-based process that works with liquid resins (he was still working for a company called UVP in Los Angeles). In 1986 Carl Deckard at the University of Texas invented Selective Laser Sintering (SLS) that applied the laser to the ancient technology of sintering and could print a wide range of materials: plastics, ceramic, metal, etc; but Deckard's idea had been preceded in 1979 by a similar invention by Ross Housholder in Las Vegas. In 1987 Michael Feygin in Los Angeles invented Laminated Object Manufacturing (LOM), also known as "paper 3D printing" because it uses paper. In 1988 Frank Arcella at Westinghouse in Pittsburgh invented Laser Additive Manufacturing (LAM) for making metal parts, a technique that used a high-power laser and titanium powder. Fused Filament Fabrication (FFF) or Fused Deposition Modeling (FDM) was developed by Scott Crump in Minnesota in 1989, who instead used a filament of molten plastic. As it is often the case with US inventions, some foreigners had come first. In 1980 Hideo Kodama of Nagoya Municipal Industrial Research Institute in Japan had already published the general idea of 3D Printing. Alain LeMehaute working at General Electric in France had filed an SLA patent a few weeks before Charles Hull for the same technology. In 1984 Yoji Marutani of the Osaka Prefectural Industrial Research Institute (OPIRI) invented his own version of stereolithography; and in 1986 patents for 3D printing were filed by

Takashi Morihara of Fujitsu in Japan and Itzchak Pomerantz of Cubital in Israel. Hull introduced his first commercial 3D printer, called SLA-1, in 1988 with his Los Angeles-based company 3D Systems. Crump founded Stratasys in 1989 and shipped his first 3D printer, called 3D Modeler, in 1991 (FFF was patented by Stratesys, FDM is very similar but more open). In 1989 Deckard founded Nova Automation, later renamed Desk Top Manufacturing (DTM) that manufactured the first SLS printer in 1990, the Mod A. Feygin started selling LOM printers in 1991 under the company name Helisys, later renamed Cubic.

3D Scanning was the complementary technology to 3D printing and it was also born at about the same time. LIDAR (the name was born as a combination of "light" and "radar", but now it stands for "Light Detection and Ranging") is a radar device that uses light instead of sound. In 1960 NASA began experiments on a device projecting lasers and then capturing the signal that bounces off objects. In 1972 the first satellites of the Global Positioning System (GPS) were launched, and the lidar started being used to rapidly capture shapes of landscapes and to construct three-dimensional models. In 1977 Michel Clerget, Francois Germain and Jiri Kryze at the national French laboratory IRIA (later renamed INRIA) invented the laser-based 3D scanner. In 1989 Jeremy Dunn built the first lidar "gun" for the police that helps detect drivers violating the speed limit. The first commercial product was a head scanner introduced in 1987 by David and Lloyd Addleman's Cyberware Laboratories of Monterey (south of the Bay Area). The lidar basically offered the best of two worlds: a cameras is an optical system, that, like the eye, sees the shape and size of objects but doesn't see well in the dark or in bad weather; the radar, on the other hand, can detect objects and how far away they are, but cannot provide information about their shape and size.

Unix and Internet

While Microsoft's operating systems were spreading from computer to computer, Unix continued to stumble. Unix had been stuck in a time warp of sorts after AT&T and SUN had taken separate roads with incompatible implementations. Just when peace was being agreed upon by AT&T and SUN, the war resumed in 1988 on another front. IBM, DEC, Hewlett-Packard and others formed the Open Software Foundation (OSF) to enact an open Unix standard, clearly a preemptive strike against the blossoming AT&T/SUN alliance.

Elsewhere in the US during the late 1980s, the trend towards networking continued at all levels. In 1988 Bellcore, the descendant of the glorious Bell Labs (that AT&T had to abandon when the government broke it up in 1984), invented "Digital Subscriber Line" (DSL). It was a communications technology that provided broadband on a regular phone line. Price permitting, this allowed every household in the world to use their existing phone line to establish a high-speed connection with a computer. This enabled the transmission of bulky files, such as the ones produced by scanning a document or by a digital camera.

The Internet was still exclusive. In order to access it, a user needed an account (a login name and password) at a university or research laboratory or government agency. With few exceptions the user interface was Unix, so the Internet user needed to be fluent in Unix commands. The old UUCP protocol was still the main way to provide access to Usenet and e-mail. UUCP was the invisible "language" spoken by the nodes of the Internet as they transferred and forwarded data.

The public internet started with the early internet service providers (ISPs). Rick Adams, a system administrator at the Center for Seismic Studies in Virginia, pioneered the idea of providing those UUCP-based services commercially to companies in 1987 when he founded Uunet, the first independent ISP. Initially it simply provided access to Usenet and e-mail, but in 1990 it also launched its AlterNet that made the Internet even easier to access. Uunet's customers were mainly companies that needed to do research on the Internet. At the same time in 1989 Barry Shein in Boston started the ambitiously named "The World," another pioneering ISP. Every small business willing to purchase a modem could get on the Internet. There was precious little for ordinary households on the Internet other than e-mail, but every household could do the same. In 1989 CompuServe, Ohio's pioneer of "dial-up" time-sharing services, connected its proprietary e-mail service to the Internet. This allowed its customers to exchange e-mail with Internet users. CompuServe was pushing information to their customers, providing some support for special-interest discussion groups and offering a chat system.

Cheap computer models with built-in modems began to appear.

The main addition to the Internet was perhaps the one developed by Jarkko Oikarinen in Finland and debuted in 1988: Internet Relay Chat, basically an Internet version of "Relay", developed by Jeff Kell in Tennessee in 1985 for the academic network Bitnet. That was the birth of real-time text transmission over the Internet, i.e. of instant messaging and online chat.

Fighting computer viruses became big business. The vast majority was propagated by simply copying files from one disk to another, but several were already spreading over networks. In 1987 John McAfee founded in Santa Clara one of the earliest companies specializing in anti-virus software. In 1988 Eva Chen founded Trend Micro in Taiwan and Tjark Auerbach founded Avira in Germany. In 1991 Symantec released Norton Anti-Virus.

With public networks came the first dangers. In 1988, "Morris," the first Internet "worm," unleashed by graduate student Robert Morris at

Cornell University, infected most of the Internet, an omen of the dangers of networking.

As computer networks mushroomed, it became economically unfeasible to provide every terminal user with expensive computers such as Unix workstations. In 1984 MIT had created the specifications for a "thin client," i.e. a very simple machine to connect to a network. Simply called "X," it created an industry of "X terminals." They also came to be associated with graphics because the X protocol mandated a graphical user interface (GUI) on the terminal and enabled the transmission and remote display of high-resolution images. These X terminals were therefore capable of displaying graphics generated on a server, and basically constituted a cheaper alternative to Unix workstations such as SUN. Network Computing Devices was founded in 1987 in Mountain View by Doug Klein and others, including a young Martin Eberhard, who had worked at San Jose's ASCII terminal maker Wyse Technology. It was soon run by Judy Estrin, a pupil of Vint Cerf at Stanford and the founder of Bridge Communications, to sell X terminals.

However, the Internet was still mainly a tool for research labs and government agencies. In 1988 the first implementation of the Integrated Services for Digital Network (ISDN), an international communications standard enacted by the International Telegraph and Telephone Consultative Committee (CCITT), heralded the age of digital transmissions of voice, video, data over traditional telephone networks and telephone copper wires.

In 1990 DARPA transferred control over the Internet to the National Science Foundation. Note that commercial activities were still banned on the Internet itself, although common on several private networks such as CompuServe (Ohio), Prodigy (formed in 1984 in New York state by CBS, IBM and Sears), GEnie (a General Electric spin-off of 1985 based in Maryland), Quantum Link (launched in 1985 in Virginia and later renamed America OnLine) and Delphi (founded by Wes Kussmaul in Boston in 1983). Email, electronic bulletin boards and online news were already the norm for many users of the Internet and for many customers of those private for-pay networks.

Meanwhile, collaborative software platforms called "groupware" (a term coined by Peter and Trudy Johnson-Lenz in 1978) became popular in the 1990s. Ray Ozzie and other former students of the University of Illinois's CERL, who had grown up with the online community PLATO Notes, ported Notes to the personal computer with funding from Lotus. The result in 1990 was Lotus Notes, a system for interconnected personal-computer users to share a project. Because it allowed people at the bottom of the organization to interact directly, without the mediation of the management, it was the precursor of social networking.

By 1986 the GPS had matured into a reliable technology and the US government was ready to allow commercial use of it. That year Ed Tuck, a Los Angeles-based telecom veteran who was also an aviator, came up with the idea of a hand-held device to connect ordinary people with the GPS. He founded Magellan with Don Rea of Omicron Labs. Using the gallium-arsenide chip made by Oregon startup TriQuint Semiconductor, an Intel 8086 processor and a digital ASIC by VLSI Logic, in 1989 they produced the first commercial navigation device: the Magellan NAV 1000. Their GPS devices were used in 1991 during the invasion of Iraq, which became the first widely-publicized success story of the GPS. Magellan was followed by Garmin in 1991.

While little of this was done in the Bay Area, someone in Silicon Valley understood what it all meant. Mark Weiser at Xerox PARC coined the term "ubiquitous computing" in 1988, prophesizing that the world was just beginning to enter a new era of computing, not personal computing but ubiquitous computing.

Laptops and Videogames

Two off-shoots of the personal computer were becoming increasingly significant in terms of revenues, and both were dominated by Japanese companies.

First, laptops were becoming important, especially to travelling business users. After Toshiba had revolutionized the field, there had also been rapid progress in creating smaller mobile computers with the power of a personal computer. In 1988 Compaq introduced its first laptop PC with VGA graphics, the Compaq SLT/286. In 1989 NEC released the UltraLite, an even lighter laptop (but still based on the older 8086 processor). Finally, in September 1989 Apple released the first Macintosh portable.

Laptops appealed to individuals who needed to work in different locations on the same data. Instead of having to connect to a mainframe whenever they needed to enter or access a record, the "mobile" workers were enabled by the laptop to carry that record with them. Initially the laptop was a success mainly with the sales force but it soon spread through the hierarchies and even became a status symbol for the executive management itself. In 1990 the number of mobile personal computers sold in the US skyrocketed to more than one million (versus eight million desktops).

Second, the leadership for videogame consoles had decisively shifted to Japan. In 1988 Sega introduced the Mega Drive/Genesis and in 1990 Nintendo introduced the Super Nintendo Entertainment System, both destined to sell tens of millions of units. No video console introduced in the US in those years would even remotely compete with the Japanese numbers.

However, a new concept was being born in the Bay Area that would have wide-ranging consequences. SimCity was a simulation game, first released in 1989 and created by game designer Will Wright for Jeff Braun's Maxis in Emeryville (near Oakland). It was different in that there was no winning and no losing, no enemy and no weapons. A player simply created a city from scratch.

The "Wintel" personal computer (Windows operating system, Intel microprocessor) was becoming a serious game platform thanks to a generation of VGA-compatible graphics cards. In 1990 Texas' family-run Origin released an epochal game, Chris Roberts' Wing Commander, whose almost three-dimensional graphics represented a quantum leap forward for the industry. The belief that games running on personal computers could not compete with games running on consoles was shattered forever.

Biotech

The futuristic industries of the Bay Area, biotech and nanotech, were still growing slowly.

In 1990 Swiss pharmaceutical giant La Roche acquired a majority stake in Genentech, whichhad become the largest biotech company in the world with revenues of about $400 million. The takeover legitimized the whole industry.

The history of genetics is largely a Boston enterprise, centered on the MIT. In 1980 David Botstein founded Genomics with his paper about "linkage mapping", the process of linking a gene to a disease. The problem at the time was gene sequencing, an expensive and slow process. The technique used at the time, chromosome walking, would require years of work to achieve significant results. Polygenic diseases (diseases due to more than one gene) require association mapping in population, which is even more time consuming.

The first major success in linkage mapping probably came in 1990, when UC Berkeley's Mary-Claire King identified the gene linked with increased risk for breast cancer, BRCA1. This indirectly led to a controversy that shaped the biotech business for 20 years. In 1994 Myriad Genetics, a Utah company, sequenced the gene and patented it. In the next two decades almost 2000 genes were patented until, in 2013, the Supreme Court ruled that companies cannot patent DNA that occurs in nature. The faster sequencing techniques made it possible to identify many more genes that cause diseases. By 2001 the number of such known genes was about 1,300.

The government entered the picture of the bioscience in a grand way. In October 1988 the National Institutes of Health, in collaboration with the Department of Energy, established the Office for Human Genome Research. It was later renamed the National Human Genome Research Institute (NHGRI). James Watson, one of the co-discoverers of the structure of DNA, was its first director. The US and other nations (eventually Britain, China, Japan, Germany, France, Canada and New Zealand) launched the International Human Genome Project with the mission to determine the sequence of the human DNA and to map the approximately 25,000 genes of the human genome. The Human Genome Project was mostly an MIT project.

Nanotech

The term "nanotechnology" (originally introduced by Japanese scientist Norio Taniguchi in 1974) had been popularized by Eric Drexler 's book "Engines of Creation - The Coming Era of Nanotechnology" (1986). Drexler also founded the Foresight Institute in Menlo Park with Christine Peterson.

"Nano" referred to technology that operates at the atomic and molecular scale, 100 nanometers or smaller. Materials are built from atoms. The configuration of the atoms can produce materials with completely different properties, like coal versus diamond, or sand versus silicon. Molecular manufacturing would open a new era for the fabrication of materials. This vision was originally propounded by theoretical physicist Richard Feynman in 1959.

Progress in nanotechnology was enabled by the invention of the Scanning Tunneling Microscope (STM) in 1981 that allowed scientists to work on individual atoms, and by the invention of the Atomic Force Microscope in 1986. In 1989 Don Eigler at IBM's San Jose Almaden labs carried out a spectacular manipulation of atoms that resulted in the atoms forming the three letters "IBM."

The problem with nanotechnology was, of course, that its tools were extremely expensive. The electron synchrotron nicknamed "Advanced Light Source" in construction at the Lawrence Berkeley Lab (completed in 1993) was designed to generate laser-like beams 10,000 times brighter than the brightest light ever produced on Earth. It was the ideal tool for exploring the structure of materials, for observing the nucleus of biological cells and for building subatomic microstructures; but even that wasn't "nano" enough.

The Culture of Risk

While all of this was going on, the Bay Area contributed relatively little to groundbreaking technological innovation. It was mostly incremental evolution.

The real innovation was on another dimension. Silicon Valley did not depend anymore on the military industry, and its financial independence had created a new business model that questioned the old world order in many ways. Funding from the military had helped create a very stable (hardware) industry that, a few decades later, had spawned a new, highly unstable industry of small software companies. Behind it there was a new attitude towards risk that somehow may have been part of the regional psyche since the days of the Far West, but was also due to the nature of the old semiconductor business.

Building chips had always been a tricky business. As chips got smaller and faster, that business began to border on magic. By the late 1980s, companies such as Intel had to build a completely new plant in order to create a new generation of semiconductors, and each new plant easily cost in the neighborhood of $1 billion. The smaller the chips were, the higher their demand for capital. At the same time these products had a very short lifespan, in most cases less than two years. During their lifetime these products were also subject to price wars that reduced their return on investment.

The rule of thumb in the 1980s was that 25% of the new electronics firms failed within a few years. Nonetheless, semiconductor components (memory chips, programmable logic, micro-processors, custom-made circuits) constituted the heart of the most successful appliances ever, from calculators to videogames. It was worth the risk.

Investors learned that it was a statistical game: invest in several startups, and only a few would survive, but those would make a lot of money for a short period of time. Any company that stayed in the business learned to live with high risk, aware that they could be gold mines today and broke in two years.

That culture of risk remained after its very creators had succumbed to it. The culture reincarnated in the software industry of the late 1980s. The creation of wealth continued and now depended on the venture capital available locally rather than on the defense industry. Many of the new investors were former startup founders themselves. They recycled their money in the same environment in which they had made it. They had been raised in that culture of risk.

And it was more than a culture. It was a whole infrastructure designed to promote, assist, and reward risk-takers in new technologies. That infrastructure consisted not only of laboratories, plants, and offices, but also of corporate lawyers, marketing agencies, and, of course, venture capitalists. Coupled with the continuous flow of international students from the local universities, this world represented an entire ecosystem at the service of a risk-taking culture.

Law firms, for example, specialized not only in incorporating startups and documenting the early funding process, but also in protecting intellectual property. No other region in the world boasted attorneys that were more efficient and skilled in protecting a company's intellectual property. This hidden economy of corporate lawyers pre-dated the boom of the 1980s. It certainly helped that California law always displayed a bias towards the small company. This was probably the legacy of having had to fight the East-Coast conglomerates in the old days when the West Coast did not have any large conglomerate. The task of defending California businesses was left to the state, and the state enacted laws to that extent. Even more important might be the laws that did not exist here: the best-known example was probably the lack of a law forbidding employees of a firm to migrate to a competing firm. Other states had such laws because the local conglomerates lobbied for them in the old days to protect their dominant status.

By then Silicon Valley represented a significant demographic change for the US: a shift in political and economic power from the old industrial and financial capitals of the Northeast and Midwest towards a new pole of industry and finance based on the West Coast.

This had even wider geopolitical implications: the biggest competitor of California was Japan, not Western Europe. The old "Atlantic" economy, whose industrial and financial centers stretched from the East Coast and Midwest of the US to Western Europe, was being replaced by a new "Pacific" economy, whose industrial and financial centers stretched from the Far East to California and Texas. It wasn't just the technology that had moved to the Pacific, it was also the capital. The venture capitalists based in Menlo Park and San Francisco accounted for a rapidly growing share of the world's venture capital. In fact, the semiconductor industry, which was slowing down, would have dragged the Bay Area down with it if it weren't for the large amounts of capital available to a completely new industry, the software industry.

There was really no compelling reason for a software company to open business in the Silicon Valley. After all, Microsoft was based in Seattle, and Apple's computers supported many fewer third-party developers than Microsoft. IBM, still the largest hardware, software and consulting company in the world, was based far away. The reason that a new industry boomed in Silicon Valley was, ultimately, that there was a lot of money around. The universities and companies of the region had attracted bright, highly educated brains from all over the US and the world. The combination of capital and brains replaced a declining industry with a booming one.

As a consequence, the symbiosis between venture capital and educational centers (Stanford, Berkeley, UCSF, and also San Jose State University, which churned out software engineers by the hundreds) had become an addiction.

The downside, of course, was the temptation to generate a profit as quickly as possible. The great investor of the 1950s and 1960s, the US military, thought and planned long-term. It had no interest in return on investment. The new investors of the 1980s had a short-term view of business. Investors began to promote corporate strategies that were focused not on innovation but on return on investment. This fear became national when Japan's MITI funded ambitious long-term projects that no Silicon Valley startup could possibly match because no investor would invest in long-term prospects.

However, the short-term approach helped translate well with the market for products. The Silicon Valley startup was usually "visionary" but grounded in the reality of technological feasibility and of market readiness. Furthermore, the Darwinian system of small startups as a whole was more likely to find a solution to a problem than, say, a large bureaucratic company. Progress was incremental, but was rapid.

So the venture capital firms had created a ghost industry that evolved in parallel to the technological one. This ghost industry was focused on making money typically through one of two ways: the IPO (the startup goes public for a value much higher than the capitalist's investment) or an acquisition (a large company, often based outside the Bay Area, buys the startup for a price much higher than the capitalist's investment).

Venture capital firms did not incubate healthy, long-lasting businesses as much as they incubated their own prospects for profit. This ghost economy was purely concerned with IPOs and acquisitions, independently of the intrinsic (social, scientific, human) value of a startup's technology. It was as much a gamble to make money as stock gambling at Wall Street, except that the multiplicator could potentially be much bigger.

Considering the voracious nature of the whole process of IPOs and acquisitions, it is quite amazing that, at the end of the day, Silicon Valley as a whole did generate real, groundbreaking products that triggered social changes all over the world.

The precarious lives of startups also created a culture of employment promiscuity. Engineers became accustomed to the idea that they may have to change jobs many times in their career. Each new job was a bet on the chances of a company. This culture created a further order of flexibility in that people were also more willing to change jobs on their own. A new startup could easily find the right brains to develop a new technology, whereas elsewhere in the world people were less prepared to switch jobs.

It helped that so many Silicon Valley residents were immigrants (from other states or from other nations). They were not afraid to move to a new environment and start a new life. The goal in Europe and on the East Coast was the career: ascend the ladders of the company's hierarchy. This was hard to conceive in Silicon Valley, where a company's (business) life expectancy was much lower than its employee's (biological) life expectancy. The fact that people living in Europe and on the East Coast were, instead, more reluctant to change jobs was, in fact, an important factor in determining the evolution of their economies. Silicon Valley's dream was a linear progression from engineer in a startup to founder of a startup to investor in a startup. This dream encouraged people to take chances working for a startup, to take chances creating startups, and to take chances investing in startups. It was a self-fulfilling prophecy and a self-sustaining metabolic cycle.

Now that venture capitalists employed or were themselves technology specialists, their role had changed in a subtle way. A venture capitalist had always had a vested interest in helping the company he had funded. But the technology-savvy venture capitalist, totally immersed in the community of innovators and with strong ties to the academia, could do more. She had to become a knowledge broker, helping shape companies and their businesses through her network of contacts. Venture-capital firms had become more and more active in guiding if not running the business of their portfolio companies, going from whom to hire for the executive team to which companies to choose as partners.

Part of this passion for startups was also the legacy of the anti-establishment (and therefore anti-corporate) sentiment of the 1960s. Software, in particular, appealed to the long-haired alternative type of kid, being novel, invisible and creative. It was at about this time that Silicon Valley witnessed the rise of a cult of personality that went beyond mere admiration. Jobs, Ellison, Noyce, and McNealy became more than founders or leaders; they became myths and prophets. The Fairchild founders had not been folk legends at all. The HP founders had been respected, but not over-hyped. They had been role models for a selected number of people who knew their responsible and dignified role in running the company.

On the other hand, the leaders of Apple, Oracle, Intel, and SUN acquired a semi-divine status in Silicon Valley. These mythical figures fought epic battles, typically against Bill Gates, Silicon Valley's public enemy number one. The local media chronicled their fantastic odysseys. Their charisma replaced the charisma of the engineers who had truly invented their technologies (the likes of Kirby, Faggin, Wozniak, and Bechtolsheim).

This phenomenon had a net effect on the ambitious youth of Silicon Valley. The trend had been shifting away from inventing a product to starting a company, with the emphasis on the business plan rather than on the technological breakthrough.

One of the most influential figures of the era, Robert Noyce, cofounder of Fairchild and Intel, and coinventor of the integrated circuit, nicknamed "the Mayor of Silicon Valley", died in June 1990. That event, metaphorically, marked the end of the era of hardware and the beginning of the era of software. The following year something truly monumental was going to happen that would change the world forever.

Culture and Society

None of this could have happened if the Bay Area had not continued attracting brainpower from all over the world. The old model of lifetime employment in a large, safe company still prevailed on the East Coast, in Western Europe, and in Japan. The West Coast, instead, spearheaded the preference for the small, dynamic company. Even if it didn't offer benefits, required one to work on weekends, and was likely to go bankrupt, the startup offered a big upside through equity. Silicon Valley's agile, dynamic and brutal Darwinian system won over all the other technology centers in the US and Europe. Silicon Valley came to embody the old myth of the "the land of opportunity," and therefore became an even bigger attractor for young educated people. Between 1970 and 1990 the population of San Jose alone almost doubled, from 445,779 to 782,248 people. In 1989 San Jose passed San Francisco in population. The San Francisco Bay Area was now officially a misnomer.

While it was attracting engineers, the Bay Area continued to attract artists and musicians who thrived on diversity. The collective of chamber, electronic, ethnic music that revolved around Lights In A Fat City and Trance Mission, or the iconoclastic collective of Thinking Fellers Union Local 282 were emblematic of what the Usenet had labeled "alt-rock." Visual artists formed the multidisciplinary gallery Luggage Store (properly the 509 Cultural Center) in 1987. This followed the Lab, which was also founded by interdisciplinary artists (in 1984), which in turn followed the Capp Street Project, founded in 1983 by Ann Hatch to promote avantgarde installations.

Michael Gosney launched the "Digital Be-in" in January 1989 in San Francisco, an event mixing technology and art that transferred the ideals of the counterculture to the digital age.

The strand of anti-technological spirituality was still proceeding in parallel with the monumental achievements of the high-tech industry: the two behaved like entangled Siamese twins. The human-potential movement that had mutated into the new-age movement was still quite popular in the Bay Area. In August 1987, psychedelic painter Jose Arguelles organized the Harmonic Convergence (1987) in Sedona (Arizona) to celebrate what he believed to be a planetary alignment correlated with the Mayan calendar. Believers rushed to power centers, or vortexes, were the phenomenon would be maximized. One vortex was Mount Shasta, located 400 kilometers north of San Francisco.

Mark Jury's documentary "Dances Sacred and Profane" (1987) popularized "body modification", pioneered by the likes of Roland Loomis, aka Fakir Musafar, who liked to hang himself in the air via hooks pierced into his chest, thereby resurrecting the Native American practice of O-Kee-Pa during their Sun Dance festival while simultaneously inventing the subgenre of performance art called "flesh hook suspension" and jumpstarting the "modern primitive" movement. Promptly, Vale Hamanaka (aka V Vale) and Andrea Juno paid tribute to the booming art of body piercing and tattooing in their book "Modern Primitives" (1989).

Another quasi-religious movement was born in Los Angeles. The "extropian" movement believed in the power of science and technology to yield immortality. Its members practiced cryogenics to preserve their brain after death. The term "extropy" was coined by Tom Bell, juxtaposing it to "entropy". Max More, an Oxford philosopher, had helped set up the first cryonic service in Europe (later renamed Alcor). Relocating to Los Angeles, in 1988 More founded the magazine "Extropy", subtitled "journal of transhumanist thought" and founded the "Extropy Institute", which in 1991 had its own online forum. The extropian movement had strong anti-government libertarian/anarchic political views, predicting a technocratic society in which the power would shift to the people. By the time Wired published the influential article "Meet The Extropians" in 1994, the extropian movement included members and sympathyzers such as Hans Moravec, Ralph Merkle, Nick Szabo, Hal Finney, as well as co-founders Tom Bell (aka Tom Morrow) and Perry Metzger. Merkle would go on to become a leader in nanotechnology, Szabo and Finney would pioneer Bitcoin, Metzger would launch the cryptography mailing list, and Moravec would lead the "singularity" movement.

In 1990 Burning Man came into its own. The first effigy had been built and burned by Larry Harvey and Jerry James in 1986 at one of Suicide Club alumna (and old-school hippy) Mary Grauberger's summer solstice beach parties on Baker Beach in San Francisco, but it was in 1990 that Kevin Evans and John Law decided to transplant the event to the Black Rock Desert in northern Nevada (simply because the San Francisco police had shut down the traditional one at Baker Beach). Law and Evans had been members of the Suicide Club. The Suicide Club had disbanded in 1983 when visionary Gary Warren died, but the group had reorganized in 1986 as the Cacophony Society, inspired by the Dada cultural movement. Carrie Galbraith was leading the "zone trips" of the Cacophony Society, inspired by Andrei Tarkovsky's film "Stalker" (1979), and in 1988 artists such as Kevin Evans had started joining the society. This was a less secret, more inclusive and public society that indulged in what would later be called "flash mobs". Jerry James was a humble carpenter and the other two were jobless and penniless. That september about 70 people attended the first real Burning Man, which originally had simply been planned as a "zone trip". The number went up to 200 in 1991 and 500 in 1992. By 1996 more than 10,000 people flocked to the desert. Many, if not all, of the activists around the original Burning Man had apprenticed at Survival Research Laboratories. Burning Man was where the hippy, punk, machine art, Briarpatch and many other cultures met and merged.

From the 1960s through the 1980s in San Francisco the philosophy of the counterculture had largely been one of "public deeds", not mere theory.

John Law arguing with Piero Scaruffi on the rooftop of Oakland's highest building

From those days the Bay Area assumed a physiognomy that wouldn't change for a while. Passed by San Jose, San Francisco was no longer the biggest city of the Bay Area, but remained a major financial center and virtually its only cultural center.

In terms of music, art and culture, Berkeley was its eastern appendix, with UC Berkeley still producing a lively counterculture. During the 1980s UC Berkeley was a unique center for alternative music, boasting three of the largest record stores in the world within the space of three blocks. It also had non-stop, improvised collective drumming in the lower Sproul Plaza. Next to it, Oakland was still a poor crime-ridden city. The East Bay between Oakland and San Jose was home to large immigrant communities from the Indian subcontinent and from Latin America.

Silicon Valley from San Jose to Mountain View was a breathtaking industrial area with few equals in the world. Virtually any non-residential street was lined with multi-story office buildings, a veritable "who's who" of the high-tech industry.

North of Mountain View was the Peninsula, which included Stanford University. The human landscape around Stanford was quite different from the one emanating from Berkeley. It was less culturally extravagant and more business-oriented. The Peninsula contained some of the wealthiest communities in the world: Atherton, Woodside, Portola Valley, Menlo Park, Los Altos Hills, and Palo Alto itself (originally an industrial and student area, but which turned into an expensive town by the boom). An impressive amount of private capital was held in this area. The I-101 corridor was still industrial, especially between Redwood City and the San Francisco airport. It included Oracle and Genentech, but towards the hills the Peninsula was the habitat of new and old multimillionaires.

Surfers: The World-Wide Web, Netscape, Yahoo, Multimedia, and Bioinformatics (1990-95)

The World-Wide Web

The 1990s opened with one of the most influential inventions of all times: the Web. The British engineer Tim Berners-Lee of CERN, Geneva's multinational high-energy physics laboratory (funded by multiple European governments) and the largest Internet node in Europe, realized that applying the hypertext paradigm to the Internet would create a worldwide network beyond the imagination of the original visionaries of hypertext. He set out to define a HyperText Markup Language (HTML) to write hypertext documents linking each other. Berners-Lee implemented the server on a NeXT computer, and wrote the first client, a "browser" that he named "World-Wide Web." The server transferred ("served") webpages to the client according to a simple protocol, HTTP (HyperText Transfer Protocol). The browser was inspired by DynaText, developed in 1990 by Electronic Book Technologies. It had been founded in Rhode Island by original hypertext visionary Andries van Dam and some of his collaborators at Brown University, notably Steven DeRose (who had done most of the design of DynaText).

HTML was nothing more than a language to "publish" a document. There had been many before. The HTML code tells the browser how to display the content of the page. Since its Version 6 of 1975 (the first one to be released outside Bell Labs), the Unix operating system had included a widely used text-formatting system, "nroff." Since 1986, the scientific community had used LaTex (developed by Leslie Lamport at the SRI International) to produce technical papers. A world standard for these "mark up" languages had been defined in October 1986, the Standard Generalized Markup Language (SGML). HTML was, in fact, a more primitive relative of these languages. The real innovation was the "link" that, when the user clicked on it with the mouse, instructed the browser to jump from the current page to another page, hosted on the same or another computer (via the HTTP). This simple idea dramatically changed the user experience on the Internet. A major quantum leap in the high-tech industry had come from a government-funded laboratory.

The Web was disclosed to the whole Internet world in August 1991. In December 1991, physicist Paul Kunz set up the first World-Wide Web server in the US at the Stanford Linear Accelerator Center (SLAC). In April 1992 there was already another browser, Enwise, written for Unix by four Finnish students at the Helsinki University of Technology. The first major browser in the US was ViolaWWW, completed by Taiwanese-born student Pei-Yuan Wei at UC Berkeley in December 1992. It was a project inspired by the look and feel of Apple's Hypercard. These two were notable for being graphical browsers.

At just about the same time in December 1991, the US government got involved. It passed the High-Performance Computing and Communication Act, originally proposed by Senator Al Gore. Gore envisioned a "National Information Infrastructure" that would create a vast network of public and private information systems to deliver potentially all the information of the nation to potentially all the citizens of the nation. This law funded a number of research projects around the US, and in particular it funded the project for a graphical browser at the National Center for Supercomputing Applications of the University of Illinois. The employees in charge of it were Marc Andreessen and Eric Bina. Their goal was to create a user-friendly browser with a graphical user interface. They completed their Mosaic web browser in 1993. The project existed because in 1985 the National Science Foundation had set up four (then five) "supercomputing centers", the main one being at the University of Illinois because the original proposal had come from its professor Larry Smarr. The center's first hit had also been related to the Internet: the first (and free) Telnet for the Macintosh and the Windows personal computers (1986), allowing anyone with a modem to access the Internet from home. In retrospect, the Mosaic browser was simply a smarter Telnet for the newly invented World-wide Web.

Mosaic's graphical user interface made all the difference. It also made it easier to display documents containing both texts and images. Originally developed for UNIX, it was soon ported to Windows, turning any PC into a client for the World-wide Web. The National Center for Supercomputing Applications released Mosaic in November 1993. Within six months more than one million people were using Mosaic to access the World-wide Web. Andreessen found a job in Silicon Valley. There he met Silicon Graphics' founder Jim Clark who encouraged him to commercialize Mosaic.

In April 1994 the duo opened Mosaic Communications Corporation, later renamed Netscape Communications, in Mountain View. In October 1994 Mosaic Netscape was available for download. In 1995 about 90% of World-wide Web users were browsing with Netscape's Navigator. Netscape went public in August 1995 even before earning money. By the end of its first trading day, the company was worth $2.7 billion and Clark had become overnight half a billionaire.

In 1994 Berners-Lee introduced the Uniform Resource Locator (URL) to express the hierarchy of domain names of the Internet into World-wide Web names (e.g., www.stanford.edu). The most popular domain was ".com," which became known as "dot com." It was originally meant to identify commercial activities, as opposed to ".edu" (for educational institutions), ".gov" (for government agencies) and ".org" (for non-profit organizations). The craze that followed Netscape's IPO became known as the "dot-com craze."

Netscape did more than simply start a new gold rush. It made the Web easy to navigate for anybody, as long as they knew how to type on a keyboard and they could find a computer connected to the Internet. It leveled the playing field so that the illiterate computer user could browse the Web the same way that a pro did. Thanks to Netscape's browser, the shapeless and non-intuitive cluster of digital information that had accrued on the Internet became intelligible and meaningful to everybody. This in turn prompted more and more people to add content to the Web. It now became clear that one boom had enabled the other one: the personal computer boom of the 1980s had placed a computer in millions of households, and that now constituted the vast public of the Web. A key factor was that the Netscape browser was free for individuals and non-profit organizations. Netscape also "protected" the Internet from monopolies that would have loved to hijack it. Its browser used open standards and indirectly forced much larger corporations to adopt those same standards, thus avoiding the kind of wars that still plagued the world of operating systems.

Netscape's Old Offices (2010)

Searching the Web

Meanwhile the World-wide Web had created another kind of application. Already in 1990, before anyone had heard of the Web, some students in Montreal had created a "search engine" named "Archie" to find sites on the Internet, which in those days were accessed via FTP (File Transfer Protocol).

Before the Web took hold, the most popular way to catalog and transmit documents over the Internet was Gopher, created by Mark McCahill at the University of Minnesota and also debuted in 1991. Immediately, two applications were born to search Gopher catalogs: Veronica (in Nevada) and Jughead (in Utah). EINet's Galaxy, launched in January 1994 in Texas, was the first catalog of websites. WebCrawler, created by Brian Pinkerton at the University of Washington and launched in April 1994, was the first search engine for the web, a website that indexed and then searched the texts it found on the web. At about the same time Michael Mauldin at Carnegie Mellon University started the project Lycos to catalog pages of the web, which went live in July. By 1999 Lycos, one of the first dotcom to post profits from advertising, had become the most visited website in the world. For the record, Mauldin also developed an Artificial Intelligence-based chatterbots, Julia, who in 1997 mutated into Sylvie and in 2000 into Verbot.

In 1993 the Web had clearly won over Gopher. A catalog of websites was casually circulating at Stanford University. In January 1995, the authors of that catalog, Stanford's students Jerry Yang (originally from Taiwan) and David Filo, launched Yahoo! (Yet Another Hierarchical Officious Oracle!), which was simply a website dedicated to cataloging all the existing websites in some predefined categories.

The Internet grew geometrically. In October 1994 the Internet already consisted of 3,864,000 hosts. It had increased in size by 61% in one year. The need for search tools was becoming obvious. Tools like Yahoo! greatly increased the usefulness of the Web: instead of knowing only the few websites run by friends, one could now find out about websites run by complete strangers.

The Internet was affecting culture and the public. It was writer Jean Armour Polly who coined the phrase "Surfing the Internet" (1992). Surfing soon became an activity for a growing population of Internet users. Some did it for entertainment and some did it for work/study. The Internet had existed for a long time. It took the Web to turn it into a major attraction. And, thanks to the Web, applications that had been around for more than a decade became widely popular (notably e-mail).

Email had created a powerful alternative to "snail" mail. A new technology would soon provide a powerful alternative to the telephone. The origins of instant messaging for personal computers go back at least to the CompuServe CB Simulator of 1980 and Q-Link, the original America OnLine chat system (acquired from PlayNET, that had operated it since

1984, basically a version for Commodore machines of the old Unix "talk" command). However, it was only with Tribal Voice, founded in December 1994 in Colorado by John McAfee (of antivirus software's fame) and later relocated to Scotts Valley, ICQ, introduced by the Israeli company Mirabilis in November 1996, and AOL Instant Messenger, launched by AOL in May 1997, that instant messaging reached the masses and became a viable alternative to a phone call.

Microsoft responded in 1999 with the text chat service MSN Messenger, that made "texting" popular with teenagers.

In theory, Netscape allowed anyone to see any website. In practice, however, most people used services like America OnLine to access the Internet. AOL provided a simple way to connect a home computer to the Internet: the customer would receive a floppy disc in the mail with all the software needed to perform the magic. The price to pay was freedom. The customers of AOL would typically only see what AOL wanted them to see, i.e. an AOL-sanctioned subset of the World-wide Web. Most people were content to visit the AOL pages and rarely ventured outside the AOL world.

The Net Economy

For decades the Internet had been used only for research and entertainment (if e-mail and Usenet groups can be defined as "entertainment"). Commercial activity was de facto banned from the Internet, which was viewed as a scientific tool and not as a shopping mall. It was still funded by a military agency and not for the use of consumers. Somehow the advent of the Web led to relax that ethical rule, and the most shameless commercial activities began to surface (initially just individuals who took advantage of the network to buy/sell items). The impact on society was colossal.

Technically speaking, commerce on the Internet had always been illegal. However, most corporations maintained an Internet node and did so for business purposes. However, it was still illegal to blatantly market and sell products or services on the Internet (with the exception of the Usenet, because UUCP was administered separately). The Internet's backbone (the NSFnet) was run by the National Science Foundation (NSF). In 1992 the US government allowed commercial networks to link to the NSFnet, despite protests from the academia. The result was that in a few years the commercial networks made the NSFnet look expensive and obsolete. In 1995 the government finally decided to relieve the NSF of the responsibility for the backbone, therefore de facto legalizing commerce over the entire Internet.

The World-wide Web did not create e-business. Electronic commerce had existed before the Internet (notably, Electronic Data Interchange), and e-commerce had existed the Internet before the WWW. For example, in

1991 William Porter, who already owned a stock-brokerage firm in Palo Alto, founded E*trade to offer online electronic trading via AOL and CompuServe. But the WWW basically provided a friendlier (and free) user interface, which encouraged many more businesses to go online.

The first online stock brokerage, E*Trade, was launched in 1992 from Palo Alto by William Porter and Bernard Newcomb via America Online and Compuserve, offering brokerage services directly to individual investors.In 1994 the first online bank opened, First Virtual, designed by two email experts such as Nathaniel Borenstein (author of the MIME standard) and Marshall Rose (author of the POP3 protocol). First Virtual also introduced the first online payment service, rivaled by CyberCash in Virginia, also launched in 1994.

In 1996 Douglas Jackson in Florida debuted a digital currency on the Web, E-gold, that by 2009 would count 5 million users before being shut down by the US government (it also became a safe haven for money launderers).

The venture capital world of Silicon Valley was ready for it. A number of founders of successful companies of the Bay Area had retired and had become venture capitalists themselves, so called "angels." Hans Severiens knew many of them and proposed that they joined forces. So in 1994 the "Band of Angels" was born. In the true spirit of Silicon Valley it wasn't just a scheme to pool money together. The primary goal was to pool knowledge together, not money. They met every month. They led the way.

Collaboration among venture capitalists had always been a trademark of Silicon Valley, and probably one of the reasons for its success. Frequently sharing a history in the valley's high-tech industry, venture capitalists and angels formed a highly interconnected network of firms. Successful entrepreneurs became successful because of that network, and were expected to join the network after they had become successful. Since venture-capital firms frequently invested with other firms in the same startup, they depended on each other's well being. Since they invested in multiple companies at the same time, their main interest was not in a particular startup but in the broader picture. In a sense, the venture-capital world of Silicon Valley did not invest in a company but in Silicon Valley as a whole.

Last but not least, venture capital firms in Silicon Valley exhibited a high degree of technological competence, either directly through their partners or indirectly through their consultants. Here venture capitalists nurtured startups, shaping their management structure and providing advice at every stage of development. They relied on informal networks of high-tech specialists and knowledge workers. Venture capital had not grown much since the heydays of the microprocessor. It was about $3 billion in 1983. It was about $4 billion in 1994. Then it skyrocketed to $7.64 billion in 1995.

Netscape's dazzling IPO in August 1995 was a dividing line in the history of Silicon Valley just like the 1956 foundation of Shockley Transistor and the 1971 Intel microprocessor. Internet companies multiplied and many of them received shocking amounts of funding. It had never been so easy for a startup to go public. The dot-com craze had reinvented yet again the landscape of the Bay Area. This time the repercussions on Wall Street were direct and immediate. The new Silicon Valley propelled the technology-heavy stock index Nasdaq to the stars, creating wealth all over the world.

A software industry that was not glamorous but was becoming increasingly strategic had to do with Internet security. In particular, Midwestern entrepreneur Kevin O'Connor invested in Internet Security Systems, founded in 1994 by Georgia Institute of Technology's student Christopher Klaus. The company would be purchased by IBM in 2006 for $1.3 billion.

Not everybody was trying to make money out of the Internet. In 1993 three students at the University of California in Santa Cruz (Rob Lord, Jeff Patterson and Jon Luini) launched IUMA (Internet Underground Music Association), a platform for independent musicians to publish their works and share them with the audience.

An early Yahoo Screenshot (1994)

Multimedia, Networking and Mobility

Progress in desktop publishing continued at an ever more rapid pace. Apple's most impressive product of those years was perhaps QuickTime, introduced in December 1991. It allowed developers to incorporate video and sound in Macintosh documents. In 1992 Macromedia was born in San

Francisco from the merger of Authorware, which sold a graphical programming environment, and MacroMind, whose Director was a multimedia-authoring environment. Director turned its users into "directors" of a film: it was a novel metaphor for building applications, mainly useful for creating the software of stand-alone kiosks. In 1993 Adobe Systems introduced the file format PDF (or Portable Document Format) to create and view professional-quality documents, and the free Acrobat reader for it.

After original founder John Walker relocated to Switzerland, in 1992 Carol Bartz from SUN revitalized Autodesk and became one of the first women of power in Silicon Valley. In 1990 Autodesk had released 3D Studio, a 3D modeling, rendering and animation tool designed by Tom Hudson that would be used for films such as "Johnny Mnemonic" (1996) as well as best-selling videogames such as "Tomb Raider" (1996), the "Lara Croft" series and "World of Warcraft" (2004). By 1994 Autodesk had become the sixth-largest personal computer software company in the world. Bartz was credited as having coined the "3F" philosophy: "fail fast-forward", i.e. risk failure but recognize it when it happens and move on quickly (a concept later popularized by Marissa Mayer).

The boom of graphic applications led to a demand for better graphic processors. Santa Clara-based Nvidia was a fabless semiconductor company founded in 1993 by Jen-Hsun Huang, previously at LSI Logic and AMD, and two SUN engineers (Chris Malachowsky and Curtis Priem) to design graphic chipsets for personal computers. In 1995 Nvidia debuted the NV1, the first commercial graphics processor that integrated 3D rendering, video acceleration and GUI acceleration; but the timing was unfortunately: just a few months after the NV1 started shipping Microsoft released its DirectX specifications.

Founded in 1989 in Fremont by Dado Banatao (who had pioneered fabless manufacturing with Chips and Technologies), S3 Graphics introduced in 1991 the first graphics accelerator card, the 86C911, in 1994 the Trio64 chipsets that became a hit in the high-end OEM market, and in 1995 the Virtual Reality Graphics Engine (ViRGE), a low-cost graphics chipset that was a 2D/3D hybrid.

Rambus was founded in 1990 by Mike Farmwald and Stanford professor Mark Horowitz to commercialize a new DRAM architecture to deal with the rapidly increasing graphic and video applications, requiring high data transfer rates to display high-resolution images.

Communications were also driving rapid progress. Cisco had entered the Ethernet switch business by acquiring Crescendo Communications in 1993, Kalpana in 1994 and Grand Junction in 1995. By 1997 Ethernet switching was producing more than $500 million in annual revenues for Cisco. Cisco then acquired Statacom in 1996 and Ardent in 1997 to enter the ATM market (Asynchronous Traffic Mode, a purely hardware alternative to fast Ethernet).

C-Cube, started in August 1988 in Milpitas by Weitek's Edmund Sun and Alexandre Balkanski, had already begun making chips for video compression technology (MPEG codecs).

Early cloud services were developd too. In 1990 Marc Porat at Apple started a project code-named Paradigm that aimed to build an innovative hand-held mobile device. In May 1990 Porat and two Apple software engineers, Bill Atkinson and Andy Hertzfeld, decided to start a company to develop the idea, General Magic. Their vision was now more ambitious: they wanted to put the power of a real computer into the hands of a casual mobile user. At the time this was technologically impossible, so they thought of creating a "cloud" of services running on interconnected devices: by roaming the cloud, even a simple, weak device could muster the computing power of a real computer. They came up with the Telescript programming language to write applications for hand-held device (a "personal intelligent communicator") that would physically and opportunistically spread onto remote computers but eventually deliver back a result to the user of the hand-held device. Telecom and IT (Information Technology) giants such as Sony, Motorola, Matsushita, Philips and AT&T invested in the idea. Commercially, it was a spectacular flop, but a new paradigm had indeed been introduced: "cloud computing."

EO, launched in 1991 by French-born C-Cube's executive Alain Rossmann to manufacture a personal digital assistant that was also a cellular telephone using GO's PenPoint operating system that recognized handwritten commands (basically, the hardware "arm" of GO).

Meanwhile Apple invested in developing a pen-based tablet computer with software for handwritten recognition, eventually released in 1993 as the Newton platform. Newton was another flop, but launched the vogue for small, mobile personal digital assistants (PDAs) in Silicon Valley (a decade after the Psion). Incidentally, it was running the ARM processor from Britain. Newton failed but indirectly it helped ARM survive by targeting small devices. In 1991 HP too had entered that market with the Jaguar. Apple therefore was a late comer, but its MessagePad (the first device based on Newton) came with a stylus and handwriting recognition. More importantly, it looked "cool."

Digital pictures and printing started to overtake the chemical photo variety. In 1990, Los Angeles-based Dycam, probably the first company founded (in 1988) to link electronic photography and computers, introduced the world's first digital camera, Model 1. It was capable of storing pictures as digital files on an internal one-megabyte RAM chip and of downloading them to a PC. The Kodak DCS100 arrived half a year later. It had taken 15 years from invention to commercialization because Kodak's engineer Steven Sasson had invented the digital camera already way back in 1975. In 1991 the Nikon D1 set the standard for digital single-lens reflex cameras. Meanwhile in 1990 Kodak had launched the Photo CD, a box to convert negatives or slides to image files on a CD, but it used a proprietary format instead of Jpeg. The first camera that could download images into a personal computer (via the serial port) was the Apple QuickTake 100 (introduced in February 1994), that could store up to 32 images at a resolution of 320x240 pixels on a flash memory. However, it was the Kodak DC40 (March 1995) that made the concept popular worldwide. In May 1994 Epson introduced the Stylus Color, the world's first color inkjet printer that allowed households to print their own digital photos. Early digital cameras used an analog process to convert the image into a set of pixels (a process originally invented at Bell Labs in 1969 by Willard Boyle and George Smith for computer data storage). Image sensors made of CMOS technology, the same technology used to make computer processors and computer memories, were invented in 1993 by Eric Fossum at NASA's Jet Propulsion Laboratory in southern California. Yet these Active Pixels Sensors (APS) would not become popular until the 2000s.

In a rare instance of cross-industry collaboration, IBM, Intel, Microsoft, Compaq, DEC, and others joined together to define a Universal Serial Bus (USB) for personal computers, eventually introduced in 1996. It would make it a lot easier to connect peripherals to computers, and it would enable gadgets such as digital cameras to be treated like computer peripherals. By 2009 more than three billion devices would have a USB port.

Meanwhile, Finland was the leader in the field of mobile (cellular) phones. In 1982, a European consortium of national telecommunications agencies, notably France Telecom and Deutsche Bundespost, had joined together to create a common standard for mobile phone communications, the Groupe Special Mobile (GSM). They had envisioned that every mobile phone would be equipped with an integrated circuit, called a SIM (Subscriber Identity Module) card, to contain information about the user, so that the information would be independent of the mobile phone and therefore portable across phones (an idea that had been pioneered in 1972 by the German mobile phone system B-Netz). The first SIM card was made in 1991 in German by Giesecke & Devrient for the Finnish wireless network operator Radiolinja, the one that launch the first GSM service (now renamed Global System for Mobile Communications), heralding the second generation (2G) of mobile telephony (digital instead of analogic). Meanwhile, Qualcomm in San Diego was developing a different technology, CDMA, launched in 1992, but adopted only in North America (and eventually sold to Japan's Kyocera). GSM and CDMA made Bell Labs' AMPS obsolete.

In 1993 Nokia introduced a feature to send text messages to other cell phones, the Short Message Service (SMS).

British computer scientist Neil Papworth is credited with having sent the first message, thereby creating the popular acronym "LOL" in December 1992, but he sent it from a computer, not from a mobile phone (phones didn't have a full keyboard yet).

Despite the fact that there were already 34 million cell-phone subscribers in the US in 1995, the field was virtually non-existent in Silicon Valley.

Qualcomm was computerizing the low-power mobile communications at the time when the emphasis was still on high-power land lines, which were getting faster and faster thanks to fiber-optics. Its founders, in 1985, were Andrea Viterbi and Irwin Jacobs, who had studied at the MIT with Claude Shannon. Viterbi was the main mind behind the Code Division Multiple Access (CDMA), a system to maximize capacity in a medium (the air) where the wireless spectrum was a limited resource. Qualcomm understood that collapsing chip costs made computing a resource less precious than the wireless spectrum and therefore used computing to maximize what can be done with and in the wireless spectrum. (In 2012 Qualcomm's market capitalization would surpass Intel's)

Cell-phone technology truly came to the Bay Area in 1992, when Martin Cooper (Motorola's prophet of cellular phones) established ArrayComm in San Jose to improve the capacity and coverage of cellular systems. While not particularly successful, ArrayComm would train and spread alumni in the region.

Smartphones to access the internet were in the making. Redwood City-based Unwired Planet (later renamed Phone.com and Openwave) pioneered mobile Internet browser software technolony called a "microbrowser. It developed Handheld Device Markup Language (HDML), basically an HTML for handheld devices. While most companies in the mobile-phone business were busy adopting the "push" paradigm of SMS, Openwave adopted its own "pull" paradigm. One year later Openwave and three giants of mobile communications (Ericsson, Motorola and Nokia) would turn HDML into WML (Wireless Markup Language), the international standard for cell phones to access the Internet.

Speech-recognition technology would turn out to be crucial for the user interfaces of mobile devices, and one of the main research centers was the old SRI International. Michael Cohen led a team that developed the technology used in the Air Travel Information System (ATIS), a project originally funded by the DARPA, a technology that combined two in-house backgrounds, one in voice recognition and one in natural language processing. In 1994 Cohen quit and founded Nuance in Menlo Park that would become one of the leaders in the sector (Nuance would be licensed by Siri for the Apple iPhone and Cohen would be hired by Google in 2004).

Thad Starner, a student at the the MIT Media Laboratory, started wearing a self-made custom computer device in 1993. He would eventually graduate with a thesis titled "Wearable Computing and Contextual Awareness". At roughly the same time Daniel Siewiorek at Carnegie Mellon University designed wearable computing devices, mainly for the military, such as the VuMan3.

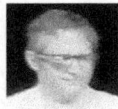

Thad Starner

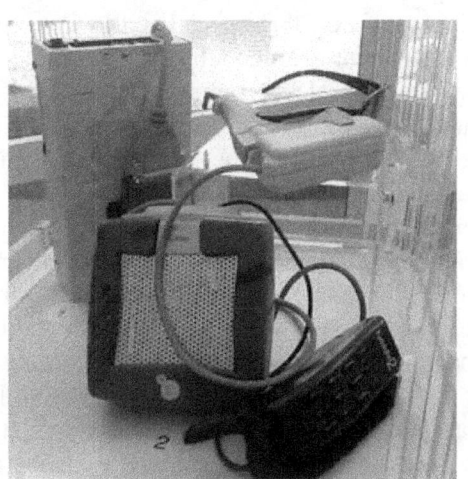

MIT's Lizzy 1 (1993)

Daniel Siewiorek demonstrating a 1993 VuMan3

A precursor of wearable computing was the "active badge" developed in 1990 at Olivetti's German labs, a badge that broadcast a person's location.

In 1994 Steve Mann, a student at the MIT Media Lab, started experimenting with wearable devices, which years later would make him the hero of the documentary "Cyberman" (2001). In 1998 he built the first smartwatch, a watch that ran Linux. In 1997 Carnegie Mellon Univ, the MIT and Georgia Tech organized the first IEEE International Symposium on Wearable Computers.

In 1994 DARPA and the US Army had funded a project code-named "Land Warrior" to redesign the clothing of the infantry soldier. This was originally assigned to Hughes Aircraft Company and other giant defense contractors but in 1999 it was wisely transferred to Exponent, a Palo Alto-based engineering firm with roots in Stanford University, originally called Failure Analysis Associates, that specialized in investigating aviation and space disasters. Exponent would deliver a wearable computer, a head-mounted display and wireless communications. (In 2001 the contract would be granted to a consortium of giant corporations under General Dynamics that would lead to the program's dismissal after a huge hemorrage of taxpayers' money).

Meanwhile, "augmented reality" was implementing the "ultimate display" that Ivan Sutherland had described in his paper "A Head-Mounted Three-Dimensional Display" (1968). Augmented reality referred to systems capable of displaying virtual objects in a real environment in real time. They became fashionable again after Robert Zemeckis' film "Who Framed Roger Rabbit?" (1988). The first successful systems included Michael Bajura's medical data display application at the University of North Carolina at Chapel Hill (1992), Louis Rosenberg's Virtual Fixtures at a military laboratory in Ohio (1992), Steven Feiner's KARMA (Knowledge-based Augmented Reality for Maintenance Assistance) at Columbia University (1992), and Tom Caudell's manufacturing application at Boeing (1992), Caudell being credited with coining the expression "augmented reality". See-through head-mounted displays already existed, for example those made by Hughes Electronics. In 1993 Paul Milgram's group at the University of Toronto built ARGOS (Augmented Reality through Graphic Overlays on Stereovideo). During the 1990s research focused on the problem of calibrating see-through head-mounted displays so that the real world and the virtual world could be synchronized. Then came augmented-reality conferencing system (that allowed users to see each other as well as virtual objects) such as Dieter Schmalstieg's Studierstube at Vienna University of Technology (1996) and Jun Rekimoto's Transvision at Sony in Japan (1996). In 1999 Hirokazu Kato in Japan developed ARToolKit, an open-source software for the creation of augmented-reality applications.

Contributions to wearable and virtual reality also came from the world of videogames, such as Nintendo's Virtual Boy console (1995) Nintendo had released in 1989 its Power Glove, a wearable three-dimensional input device. The history of virtual reality intersects with the history of videogames. For a while Britain, where Roy Trubshaw had pioneered the idea, was the leader in the field of MUDs with games such as "MIST" (1986) and "AberMUD" (1989), followed by Denmark with "DikuMUD" (1991); but their virtual worlds were text-based, not graphical. In 1990 "GemStone III" was launched in Missouri, a graphical MUD that would spread on CompuServe, Prodigy and America OnLine (AOL).

There was an excitement in the virtual-reality community comparable to the excitement in the personal-computer community a decade earlier. In 1990 Mark Bolas and others founded Fakespace in Mountain View, a spin-off of NASA's Ames Research Center, to build devices for virtual reality. In 1990 Brenda Laurel and NASA veteran Scott Fisher, both alumni of the Atari Systems Research Laboratory, founded Telepresence Research. 1990 also saw the first sales of the virtual-reality system developed by W Industries (founded by former IBM scientist Jonathan Walden in 1985 in Britain and later renamed Virtuality), targeting the research labs of big corporations. In 1991 Ben Delaney started the magazine "CyberEdge Journal" and Brenda Laurel published "Computers as Theatre" (1991). Virtual Research Systems, founded in 1991 in Sunnyvale by Bruce Bassett, began selling a cheap "Flight Helmet", based on the old design of NASA's VIVED. In 1993 the IEEE organized the first academic conference on virtual reality: the Virtual Reality Annual International Symposium (VRAIS), held in Seattle. In 1994 Linda Jacobson published "Garage Virtual Reality", a survey of the independent 3D-graphics scene. Brett Leonard directed the film "The Lawnmower Man" (1992) and Robert Longo directed "Johnny Mnemonic" (1995). Sega demonstrated (but never released) the Sega VR in 1993. In 1995 Future Vision Technologies, a spinoff of the University of Illinois at Urbana-Champaign, developed a head-mounted display for the consumer market, the Stuntmaster, and in the same year a company based in Sacramento marketed the iGlasses goggles. They all had the same problems: a true stereo display made of two high-resolution color LCD screens coupled with motion tracking was too expensive and caused serious motion sickness. Unfortunately, the excitement vastly exceeded the reality of the technology.

Nonetheless, virtual-reality platforms such as EON Reality, founded in 1998 in Sweden by Mats Johansson, Dan Lejerskar and Mikael Jacobsson, would soon begin to appear.

Virtual Boy

IBM versus Microsoft

Microsoft continued to dominate the operating-system market. In May 1990, Windows 3.0 finally had the success that had eluded previous versions of Windows. The difference was that Windows now boasted a vast portfolio of well-tested applications, starting with Microsoft's own Word, Excel, and Powerpoint. Windows 3.0 gained widespread third-party support. When 3.1 was released in April 1992, three million copies were sold in just two months. When Windows 95 was released in August 1995, the frenzy was even bigger. In 1991, Microsoft had revenues of $1,843,432,000 and 8,226 employees. Bill Gates was becoming one of the richest men in the country. More importantly, millions of computer users were abandoning the text commands of MS-DOS for the overlapping windows, the pull-down menus and the mouse clicks of Windows.

The holy alliance between IBM and Microsoft that had turned Microsoft into a software powerhouse came abruptly to an end in 1990. Microsoft realized that Windows 3.0 was a much more successful product than OS/2 could ever become. It was available on a lot more platforms, it was sold pre-loaded by a lot of computer manufacturers, and it boasted a fast-growing catalog of third-party applications. On the other hand, OS/2 was sponsored only by IBM and it was much more expensive. Microsoft decided to part ways and continue to focus on Windows. IBM had lost its grip on the computer industry: for the year 1992 it reported a loss of $4.96 billion, the highest in the history of the US up to that point. In January 1993, as one stock kept rising while the other one kept plunging, Microsoft's market value ($26.78 billion) passed IBM's ($26.76 billion), though IBM still employed many more people and still had revenues of $64 billion. The market just didn't believe that IBM's business model had a future.

Digitalk and ParcPlace had introduced commercial versions of the object environment Smalltalk and had created a small but devoted following for it. In 1991 IBM launched its own Smalltalk-based project that in 1995 yielded the object-oriented environment VisualAge. Apple, in turn, had started Pink, a project to design an object-oriented operating system written in the object-oriented version of C, the C++ programming language. In 1992 IBM and Apple banded together and formed Taligent in Cupertino with the goal to complete Pink and port it to both platforms. The whole plan was widely viewed as an anti-Microsoft move, now that Microsoft was a common enemy. Again the project failed, but it yielded at least one intriguing idea: the "People, Places and Things" metaphor that provided procedures for these three categories to interact at a high level of conceptualization.

In fact, the deluge of Windows could not be stopped: Microsoft became the largest software company in the world with annual sales in 1994 of over $4 billion. It even began to draw the attention of the US government, which feared a monopoly in software. The US government forced Microsoft to be less "evil" towards the competition, but it was only the beginning of a series of lawsuits and investigations into Microsoft practices both in the US and in Europe.

The rise of Microsoft and the decline (and sometimes demise) of the traditional giants of IT came at a price: the shrinking research lab. When the IT and telecom worlds were ruled by the likes of IBM and AT&T, the research laboratories were huge and their ambitions were huge. Those labs invented the transistor, the Internet, the programming language, the operating system, the hard disk, the relational database, and Unix. Microsoft's research laboratories invented nothing. AT&T's descendants (the regional Bell companies and the new telecom companies) invented nothing. IBM and AT&T did not need to acquire other companies: their products came from their research labs (the likes of Rolm and Lotus contributed relatively minor product lines to IBM). Microsoft and later Google bought their most famous products from startups. Their cash did not buy them great research teams: it bought them great intellectual-property lawyers who filed patents for countless trivial features of their products, a tactic meant to discourage competitors from venturing into the same areas of development. The Microsoft era was the era of the business plan: companies relied on a business plan, not on technological innovation, in order to achieve domination. No wonder that they did not produce anything comparable with the transistor or the many inventions of IBM.

In Silicon Valley, in particular, the rate at which companies were created and destroyed was one practical explanation for why the old-fashioned research lab became less and less viable. It was basically inherent to the Silicon Valley model of frenzied growth that no single company could afford to have a long-term plan, and especially one that was not focused on any one product. Life expectancy was very low. And the only way to prolong your life was, in fact, to live by the day. It was the law of the wilderness transferred from the lawless towns of the Far West to the high-tech industry. That was, ultimately, the lesson learned from the experience of Xerox PARC.

Free Unix

While the great Unix wars were still going on, in 1991 a Finnish student, Linus Torvalds, a believer in the philosophy of Stallman's Free Software Foundations, developed a new Unix kernel, called Linux. He equipped it with GNU tools (at the time GNU did not offer a kernel yet). In this way Torvalds had accomplished what Stallman had advocated: a free and open-source version of Unix. However, initially the only support came from independents, certainly not from the big corporations who were fighting the Unix wars. In 1994 Marc Ewing, a graduate from Carnegie Mellon, completed his Red Hat Linux and started Red Hat in North Carolina. Novell's engineer Bryan Sparks in Utah founded Caldera, with funding from Novell's former boss Ray Noorda, to distribute a high-end version of Linux. In January 1993 Novell itself bought all the rights to the Unix source code from AT&T for $150 million.

Storage

EMC, founded in 1979 near Boston in Massachusetts by Richard Egan and Roger Marino, had begun as a humble maker of memory boards for workstations (the first one in 1981 for the Prime workstation) then it soon invented storage business. Before EMC the external storage of a computer came with the computer. EMC started selling external computer storage independently in 1989, and the following year it launched its best-selling product, Symmetrix, the first "storage array" for computer mainframes sold by an independent company (IBM was selling its own 3390 disk subsystem). EMC would become the fastest growing high-tech company in the nation with the best performing stock of the decade.

One company tried to compete with storage specialists such as the East-Coast giant EMC and the Japanese colossus Hitachi. Network Appliance was an Auspex spin-off founded in 1992 in Sunnyvale by David Hitz and James Lau. They introduced a lower-cost and more scalable "network attached storage" (NAS) appliance of the kind pioneered by 3Com. Data storage over Ethernet was a simple concept but also a gold mine, that allowed NetApp to double revenues every year throughout the 1990s. Theirs was a Copernican revolution: instead of using (expensive) custom hardware to run a general-purpose operating system as fast as possible, they used standard hardware running proprietary software that did only one thing: store and retrieve data.

One of the first consumer products to use flash memory as storage was the Psion MC 400 of 1989. In 1991 SanDisk created an affordable flash-based solidstate drive. Up to that point the flash memory had been mostly used inside the computer, not for removal storage. In 1995 Toshiba replaced the floppy disk with a NAND-type flash memory, the SmartMedia card, while Intel introduced a different NAND format, the MiniCard, backed by Fujitsu and Sharp. Flash memory would become ubiquitous in digital cameras and other consumer electronics, but soon the winning format would be CompactFlash, unveiled by SanDisk in 1994 and adoped by Canon and Nikon for their digital cameras and camcorders.

Enterprise Resource Planning (ERP)

ERP and supply chain management (SCM) were ripe for growth in the Bay Area. PeopleSoft added a financial module in 1992, pushing revenues up to $575 million in 1994. Next it added a manufacturing module in 1995, after acquiring the supply chain management system developed by Red Pepper Software, pushing revenues to $816 million in 1997. It was one of the most sensational success stories of the client-server era. Red Pepper had been founded in 1993 in San Mateo by Monte Zweben, a former scientist at NASA's Ames Research Center, where he had developed an artificial intelligence-based scheduling system for NASA's Kennedy Space Center.

In 1993 former Oracle sales executive Thomas Siebel started Siebel to market a software application for sales force automation, the first step towards customer relationship management (CRM).

Meanwhile, in 1992, SAP had launched R/3, moving its ERP system from the mainframe to a three-tiered client-server architecture and to a relational database. It was an immediate success. In 1994 SAP's revenues increased 66% and then 47% the following year to $1.9 billion, three times what they had been in 1991.

In 1994 Japan's Denso invented the QR Code (Quick Response Code), an alternative to the barcode with greater storage capacity, the first major innovation in identifying manufacturing parts since 1974 (when the first item was sold by a store using a scanner to read a barcode using the Universal Product Code invented by IBM).

Another software invention that came from Germany was the multi-dimensional array data model, originally conceived by Peter Baumann in 1994, an extension of the relational data model (with query language that was an extension of SQL). This technology, organizing data in multi-dimensional arrays instead of one-dimensional sets, would introduce a more powerful way to handle data such as images.

Competing Economic Models

In 1991 the US computer industry posted its first "trade deficit:" more computer technology was imported than exported (in dollar value). The dynamics of the various regions were wildly different. In the US, the computer industry was constantly changing, with large companies disappearing overnight and new giants emerging almost as quickly. In Europe, on the other hand, the computer market was dominated by old bloated companies: Nixdorf in Germany, Bull in France, ICL in Britain, and Olivetti in Italy.

The Europeans had generally been more eager to jump on the bandwagon of "open systems," despite the fact that their revenues largely depended on proprietary custom design, notably in operating systems. Their business model typically emphasized the one-stop shopping experience for their customers, and those customers were typically very large businesses (notably banks).

Europeans preferred to sell "solutions" rather than individual pieces of hardware and software, a solution being a tailored combination of hardware and software. For many years these components had been made in house. It was basically a scaled-down and nationalistic version of the IBM business model. They could successfully compete against IBM because of two factors: political protection from national governments, and national non-English languages (in an age in which only a tiny minority of Europeans understood English). They all employed hardware and software from the US, but they made a point of changing the name and the interface to turn it into a proprietary product. Their products could be very creative. Olivetti, in particular, had developed a Unix-like real-time operating system, Multi-functional Operating System (MOS), designed by Alessandro Osnaghi and initially implemented at their Cupertino labs. They mostly endorsed Unix (as an alternative to IBM), and joined the Open Systems Foundation and similar standardizing alliances. An OSF laboratory was opened at Grenoble in France.

However, the large computer manufacturers of Europe had started on a decline that would rapidly lead to disaster. In 1982 Bull had been nationalized by the French government. In 1990 German conglomerate giant Siemens acquired Nixdorf, the Japanese conglomerate Fujitsu acquired 80% of ICL, and Olivetti struggled to survive (it would capitulate in the mid 1990s). The transition to open systems turned out to be a form of mass suicide.

Europe did not fare much better in the realm of software: only SAP began a worldwide power, dominating the ERP sector even in the US. Japan managed to become a powerhouse of hardware but failed to make a dent in software.

However, it was not clear from what the US computer industry derived its advantage. After all, the World-wide Web was "invented" at CERN by a pan-European team, and Finland was the first country to implement a GSM network. If one had to name a region that was forward-looking, it wouldn't be Silicon Valley but Switzerland, the world's most energy-efficient economy, that had pioneered both "greentech" (renewable energy, "green" buildings, waste management, sustainable transportation) and biotech since the late 1980s. Nonetheless, only a specialist in Swiss affairs could name a Swiss company, and even that specialist would probably not be able to name a single Swiss invention of the era.

The overall economic model clearly played a role. The German economic model favored gradual innovation and long-term planning (the kind of thinking that was useful, say, in metallurgy). In contrast, the US model favored disruptive innovation in real time (besides favoring overconsumption and overborrowing). Silicon Valley was the ultimate implementation of the US philosophy.

At the same time, the Silicon Valley model was not just unbridled capitalism as often depicted elsewhere. For example, in 1993 leaders from government, business, academia, and the community established the Joint Venture Silicon Valley Network. They sponsored the Economic Development Roundtable (later renamed Silicon Valley Economic Development Alliance) and other initiatives to make the region as business-friendly as possible, while another spin-off, Smart Valley, helped schools, local government and community centers get on the Internet.

Intel benefited from the booming market for personal computers, and in 1992 became the world's largest semiconductor company, ahead of NEC and Toshiba. Its revenues had doubled in five years, reaching $8 billion. It was taking its revenge against the Japanese that almost bankrupted it a few years earlier.

In 1991 the US computer industry posted its first trade deficit, but it was not good news for Europe or for Japan. Unseen to most, it was good news for the still very poor countries of India and China.

Biotech

Because of the success of Genentech, the biotech industry was expanding in the Bay Area, albeit at a modest pace. In 1990 Michael West from the University of Texas' Southwestern Medical Center in Dallas started Geron with funding from oil-industry tycoon Miller Quarles. He wanted a "cure" against aging (in other words, immortality). In 1992 the company relocated to Menlo Park where West had found more venture capital. In 1998 its scientists, led by Calvin Harley, would isolate human embryonic stem cells (but never get any closer to marketing immortality). In 1992 Calgene, a spin-off of UC Davis, near Sacramento, created the "Flavr Savr" tomato, the first Genetically Manufactured Food (GMF) to be sold in stores (in 1994). The Flavr Savr tomato caused a new bubble in biotech. In 1996 there was another spike in biotech IPOs, with 53 companies raising almost $1.5 billion.

The science of biotech itself, however, was progressing rapidly. To start with, the Human Genome Project was finally underway. In 1992 the saga of Craig Venter began. Venter, raised in the San Francisco peninsula, had joined the National Institutes of Health in 1984 in Maryland, at the time still run by James Watson as a traditional biomedical center. In 1992 Venter, frustrated that the center wouldn't move faster towards automation of genetic processing, quit his job and the Human Genome Project to set up The Institute for Genomic Research (TIGR) a few kilometers away, in Rockville. It was funded by venture capitalist Wallace Steinberg of New Jersey with $70 million over seven years and staffed with many of Venter's old coworkers at the NIH. Meanwhile, Steinberg hired William Haseltine, who had pioneered research on AIDS at Harvard University since the 1970s in collaboration with Robert Gallo of the National Cancer Institute (who a few years later would discover the cause of AIDS, HIV). Steinberg put Haseltine in charge of a new company named Human Genome Sciences (HGS), the business plan being that Venter's TIGR would create a database of genetic information and Haseltine's HGS would sell it to pharmaceutical companies.

This was a bold plan because until then no biomedical company had ever made a profit by simply selling information. It corresponded to a vision of future medicine as "bioinformatics." In 1993 HGS sold its genetic database to SmithKline Beecham for $125 million. In 1995 Robert Fleischmann of TIGR used research by Nobel laureate Hamilton Smith of Johns Hopkins University in nearby Baltimore to sequence ("map") the genome of a free-living organism, the bacterium Haemophilus Influenzae, responsible for ear infections. This success triggered a series of genome sequencing projects around the US.

The ability to modify a complex genome with precision remained one of the goals of synthetic biology. In 1994 Srinivasan Chandrasegaran's team at the Johns Hopkins Bloomberg School of Public Health invented a technique for editing genomes, called Zinc Finger Nuclease (ZFN), that opened the doors to gene therapy. In 1995 Edward Lanphier founded Sangamo BioSciences in Richmond (north of Berkeley) to commercialize their technology.

Other researchers were working hard at products too. Stephen Fodor was doing research at the Affymax Research Institute, a pharmaceutical company founded in 1988 by Alza's Zaffaroni in Palo Alto, on fabricating DNA chips using the same manufacturing techniques used to make semiconductors. Meanwhile, Peter Schultz was a pioneer in combinatorial chemistry at the Lawrence Berkeley Lab. They both wanted to overcome the slow pace at which genetic testing was carried out and find a method for simultaneously testing thousands of molecules. In 1991 Fodor succeeded in creating a "DNA chip" using photolithography. With help from Zaffaroni, the duo started Affymetrix in Santa Clara in 1992 to produce "gene-chips" (microarrays), the biological equivalent of electronic chips, by printing a huge number of DNA molecules on a silicon wafer.

Affymetrix introduced the first DNA chip in 1994, the GeneChip. Pat Brown and Mark Schena at Stanford University worked on a different method (a robotic method) and in 1995 introduced the term "DNA microarray". Edwin Southern at Oxford University (and the founder of Oxford Gene Technology in 1995) was working on a technique based on inkjet printing, and so did Alan Blanchard at the University of Washington, who in 1996 invented the technique adopted by Agilent. Nimblegen Systems adopted an improved version of Affymetrix's technique. Illumina adopted the method invented by David Walt at Tufts University in 1998. They all wanted to leverage techniques originally developed for silicon semiconductors and used them to instead improve the speed at which DNA tests could be performed. Their microarrays made it possible to simultaneously test thousands of molecules.

Along the same lines in 1992 South African-born geneticist Sydney Brenner (a pupil of Francis Crick at Cambridge University who had just moved to the Scripps Institute in San Diego) joined Applied Biosystems' founder Sam Eletr to start Lynx Therapeutics in Hayward. The company developed a massively parallel method for simultaneous interrogation of multiple DNA samples in a single test.

After the Human Genome Project had enumerated all human genes, the next step would be to understand what those genes mean. Molecular Applications Group, founded in 1993 in Palo Alto by Stanford's biologists Michael Levitt and Christopher Lee, applied the techniques of data-mining software to genetic information in order to help biotech companies figure out the function of a protein from its DNA.

The business potential of human-genome science was obvious from the beginning to pharmaceutical companies: knowing how the genome works would allow medicine to understand which ones cause which diseases, and possibly how to cure them.

The first "genomic" startup to have an IPO in November 1993 was the invention of a New York venture-capital firm. In 1991 a group had acquired a St Louis-based biotech startup, Invitron, founded by scientist Randall Scott. Then they had transformed it into Incyte Pharmaceuticals, a Palo Alto startup. In 1994 Incyte launched a service for personal genomics, LifeSeq. It was accessible by yearly subscription for several million dollars and basically contained two databases: a catalog of genes of the genome, and a catalog of where each was expressed and what its probable function was. LifeSeq had actually been constructed for Incyte by consulting biotech firm Pangea Systems. It was founded in 1991 in Oakland by Dexter Smith and Joel Bellenson, a scientist who had worked at Stanford on an early DNA synthesizer. Pangea later (1997) introduced a search engine for genetic databases, and eventually (December 1999) put it online as DoubleTwist.

In 1995 Greg Schuler at the National Center for Biotechnology Information designed a way to automatically refine the GenBank into a new database, UniGene.

Some progress was made to solve aging. In 1993 Cynthia Kenyon, a pupil of Brenner at Cambridge University now at UCSF, discovered that a single-gene mutation could double the lifespan of the roundworm Caenorhabditis Elegans. This finding stimulated research in the molecular biology of aging.

A few years later (1999) Leonard Guarente at the MIT would discover a gene that increases the lifespan of yeast, and the family of these genes, "sirtuin", became known as "the anti-aging gene". In 1999 Guarente and Cynthia Kenyon founded Elixir Pharmaceuticals to make anti-aging products.

The media focused on biotechnology for pharmaceutical applications ("red biotech") and for genetically-modified food ("green biotech"). But there was also a third application: biotechnology to produce biochemicals, biomaterials and biofuels from renewable resources ("white biotech").

This latter technology was based on fermentation and biocatalysis. It typically required "bioreactors" fueled with tailored micro-organisms (e.g. yeast, fungi and bacteria) to convert crops or other organic materials into sugars and then into useful chemicals. The "products" of white biotech ranged from sophisticated ingredients for red and green biotech to bulk chemicals such as biofuels. The promise was to replace the synthetic, petroleum-based materials that had become popular in the 20th century with biodegradable materials. These would also require less energy to manufacture and create less waste when disposed.

Biologists such as Chris Sommerville at Stanford University and Yves Poirier at the University of Lausanne in Switzerland carried out pioneering experiments to prove the feasibility of environmentally friendly (biodegradable) plastics, a line of research picked up by Kenneth Gruys at food giant Monsanto in St Louis. In 1992 the Bio/Environmentally Degradable Polymer Society was established in Ontario (Canada).

Robotic surgery was pioneered by Computer Motion, founded in 1989 in Goleta (southern California) by Yulun Wang. They developed a voice-activated robotic system for endoscopic surgery called AESOP that in 1993 became the first robot approved in the USA for surgery. A few years later, in 1999, Intuitive Surgical (founded in 1995 in Sunnyvale by Frederic Moll as Integrated Surgical Systems) introduced the DaVinci Surgical System, a commercial version of work done at SRI Intl in the 1980s, the Green Telepresence Surgery system.

French Anderson carried out the first human gene therapy in 1990 at the National Institutes of Health (NIH). The news helped generate enthusiasm for the new technology. Within a decade there would be, worldwide, more than 400 clinical trials to test gene therapy. (Alas, Anderson became more famous as a glaring example of miscarriage of justice, spending several years in jail for a crime that he did not commit).

Affymetrix's Offices (2010)

Greentech

Another nascent industry had to do with energy: fuel cells. Their promise was to open an era of environmentally clean power plants. In 1991 United Technologies Corporation, a large East-Coast defense contractor, became the first company to market a fuel-cell system, mainly used by NASA in the Space Shuttle. Meanwhile, research on lithium batteries at the Lawrence Berkeley Lab spawned the startup PolyPlus Battery, which opened offices in Berkeley in 1991.

The Anthropology of the Digital Frontier

Ironically, all the technological changes had not changed the nature of society all that much. Society in Silicon Valley still embedded the "frontier" model: most individuals were single and male. Most immigrants were male, whether coming illegally from Mexico to clean swimming pools or legally from India to write software. The main difference from the old days of the frontier was that they, at some point, would bring their wives with them (as opposed to patronizing brothels). The national immigrants (coming from other states of the US) were mostly male (and almost exclusively male in the engineering and executive jobs). Graduates from San Jose State University in the late 1990s were still only 18% female. Women, however, did not just stay home: more and more women studied business, law, and marketing, all professions that could potentially lead to highly paid jobs. The "saloon," too, had changed dramatically: the new saloon was itinerant, located at the home or in a bar where a party was being thrown, and the party was often meant as a business opportunity (an event to find a new job, not an event to find a wife).

Spare time was still chronically limited, with many people working weekends and even holidays. The standard package granted only two weeks of vacation, and immigrants (whether from other countries or other states) used them mostly to visit family back home. The real vacation often came in the form of a "sabbatical" of six or twelve months. It was difficult to take a few days off during a product's lifecycle. It was easier to just take six months and be replaced by someone else during that period.

At the same time there was increased pressure to know the world, because business was increasingly international. And the world was increasingly the countries touched by the Pacific Ocean, not the Atlantic Ocean.

After many venture capitalists moved to Menlo Park in the 1980s and Palo Alto in the 1990s, San Francisco lost its role as the financial center of the Bay Area. It resumed its old role as the entertainment hub for the frontier. Silicon Valley engineers and entrepreneurs moved to San Francisco for, essentially, the nightlife. Compared with the sterilized and structured lifestyle of Silicon Valley, where people's main forms of entertainment were the gym and the movie theater (or, at home, the videogame and the video) and everything closed at 10PM, San Francisco promised a "wild" lifestyle.

However, Palo Alto itself was rapidly becoming an ideal concentration of restaurants, cafes and stores, most of them lining up on University Avenue (the continuation of Stanford's Palm Drive). It had lost its "student town" charm and become one of the most expensive places to live. The nearby Stanford Shopping Center was becoming the most celebrated shopping experience in the whole Bay Area.

Mountain View, which historically had no fewer influential startups, proceeded to create something similar to University Avenue in its "intellectual" heart, Castro Street. It was originally lined with bookstores, via a seven-block renovation project that ended in 1990. Mountain View had just inaugurated in 1986 its outdoor 22,000-seat Shoreline Amphitheatre, a major venue for music concerts.

Culture and Society

The marriage of the World-wide Web and of the utopian WELL culture recast old debates about personal freedom into the new distributed (and government-operated) digital medium. Notably, the Electronic Frontier

Foundation was formed in San Francisco in July 1990 by three people: Lotus founder Mitch Kapor; John Perry Barlow (a former lyricist for the Grateful Dead now turned libertarian activist); and by Usenet and GNU veteran (as well as former Suicide Club member) John Gilmore, to defend civil liberties on the Internet (he had become rich as one of the early employees of SUN). It evoked the myth of the hippy commune settled in a rural world. It was created in response to "Operation Sundevil" launched in 1990 by the FBI to arrest hackers involved in credit card and calling card fraud. It was the first major operation of its kind, since the authorities had rarely bothered to investigate (let alone prosecute) the "phreakers". In 1996 John Perry Barlow would also publish the "A Declaration of the Independence of Cyberspace".

The cyberlibertarian movement got its manifesto in 1994, when Esther Dyson, the daughter of the famous physicist Freeman Dyson, who had joined the Global Business Network in 1988, published "The Magna Carta for the Knowledge Age", co-written with George Gilder (author of "Microcosm - The Quantum Revolution In Economics And Technology" in 1989), Hewlett-Packard's physicist George Keyworth, and Alvin Toffler (author of "Future Shock" in 1970 and "The Third Wave" in 1980). That Magna Carta caused quite a stir among those who thought of cyberspace as potentially a space for the counterculture. Despite its title, the manifesto directly or indirectly supported the big corporations lobbying the government for maximum deregulation, something that hardly justified their claim that cyberspace belonged to the people. Many saw it as an attempt to steal cyberspace from the people and hand it over to big telecom corporations eager to reshape cyberspace to their economic advantage, just what the conservative politicians were advocating. Two years later (in 1996) the USA adopted a landmark Telecommunications Act, that boosted the online activities of the telecom giants. The debate around the new digital technologies yielded books such as Howard Rheingold's "Virtual Community" (1993), Kevin Kelly's "Out of Control" (1994), Nicholas Negroponte's "Being Digital" (1995) and, a little later, "The Long Boom" (1999) by Peter Schwartz, Peter Leyden and Joel Hyatt.

Kevin Kelly

In 1993 Kevin Kelly, the publisher of the "Whole Earth Review", joined the magazine "Wired", where he continued to deal with the interaction of technology, culture and society. Wired's founder, Louis Rossetto had run Electric Word in Amsterdam and founded Wired in San Francisco with his employee Jane Metcalfe, and using funds provided by the Global Business Network and by Nicholas Negroponte of the MIT Media Lab.

Incidentally, its online emanation, the commercial web magazine HotWired, launched one year later with a new form of advertising, the "banner", that would soon spread around the web turning websites into billboards. Wired had been preceded by a far more radical publication, Mondo 2000, started in 1989 by Ken Goffman and Alison Kennedy in Berkeley, a glossy magazine devoted to underground cyberculture that dealt with both the technology of the Internet age and the "smart drugs" of the rave age.

Mondo 2000 and Wired were instrumental in moving technology to the lifestyle of young college-educated people. They served, and helped grow, the hacker culture created in the 1980s. Hacker conferences multiplied, notably Defcon, started in Las Vegas in 1993 by Jeff Moss, and HOPE (Hackers on Planet Earth), founded in New York in 1994 by the hacker magazine 2600.

Echo, an online community founded in 1990 by Stacy Horn in New York's Greenwich Village, was the East Coast equivalent of the WELL, but with a much higher rate of female participation. In 1995 a former SUN marketing executive, Dan Pelson, launched the online magazine Word, and hired Jaime Levy as creative director, one of the few people who had experience in digital publishing, having produced a floppy disk magazine, Electronic Hollywood (1990) and having started a salon, CyberSlacker (1994), for programmers and animators at her East Village loft. Levy, gathering a cast of creators met on New York's online community Echo, turned Word into a futuristic website devoted to multimedia storytelling: audio, animated graphics, video streaming, the interactive social game Sissyfight (2000), and even (in 1998) the chatbot Fred The Webmate (styled after Joe Weizenbaum's artificial intelligence Eliza of 1966 by Japanese-born art director Yoshi Sodeoka). The Word was one of the earliest online magazines and arguably the most experimental. (When The Word shut down in 2000, it revealed the fundamental problem of Internet-based culture: the original tools used to create its multimedia contents rapidly disappeared and the magazine's issues are virtually impossible to recreate, unlike, say, the Dead Sea Scrolls that we can still read 2,000 years later). In 1998 one of these online magazines, The Drudge Report, run by Matt Drudge from his Florida home, would make history by breaking the Monica Lewinsky scandal to the public before printed magazines.

The 1990s were the age of the raves, all-night dance parties often held illegally in abandoned warehouses. The longest economic expansion in the history of the US helped fuel the decade-long party. The music scene expanded dramatically yielding not pop stars but all sorts of alternative concepts: prog-rock trio Primus, folk-rock combo Red House Painters, acid-rock project Subarachnoid Space, stoner-rockers Sleep, the surreal electroacoustic act of the Thessalonians and electronic/digital composer Pamela Z.

The visual arts were also expanding dramatically, fueled by a growing art market. A new generation of art galleries emerged in the early 1990s, such as the Catharine Clark Gallery (established in 1991), and the Yerba Buena Center for the Arts was inaugurated. San Francisco continued to specialize in creating subcultural movements (as opposed to high-brow art and music). The 1990s witnessed a boom in mural and graffiti art, notably Ricardo "Rigo 23" Gouveia, Margaret Kilgallen, Barry McGee ("Twist") and Ruby "Reminisce" Neri. The Clarion Alley Mural Project (CAMP) was established in October 1992 by local residents. Students from the San Francisco Art Institute originated the "Mission School," an art movement centered in the Mission district that was inspired more by street art than by museum art. They often built their artworks with found objects. Chris Johanson emerged from this crowd. In 1990 even the San Francisco main dump began a program of artists in residence, mainly an idea of pioneering environmental artist Jo Hanson. Harrell Fletcher and Jon Rubin, both students at the College of Arts and Crafts, opened a "gallery" in Oakland where they created art installations about the neighborhood using neighborhood residents. In 1995 Amy Franceschini founded the artist collective Futurefarmers to promote participatory art projects.

In 1992 a group of San Francisco street artists (Aaron Noble, MichaelO'Connor, Sebastiana Pastor, Rigo 92, Mary Snyder, Aracely Soriano) started painting murals in Clarion Alley, between Mission and Valencia streets and between 17th and 18th Streets, the beginning of what came to be known as the Clarion Alley Mural Project (CAMP).

Mark Pauline's Survival Research Labs had raised an entire generation of machine artists, several of whom were responsible for the apocalyptic sculptures of Burning Man. Kal Spelletich, founder of the influential machine art collective Seemen in Austin, moved to San Francisco in 1989 and joined SRL. The 1990s opened with the robotic opera "Trigram" (1991) by Chico MacMurtrie and a few years later (in 1994) Marc Thorpe organized the first "Robot Wars" at Fort Mason in which remote-controlled cybernetic gladiators battled to death like in medieval tournaments. Meanwhile, Death Guild, a 1993 club modeled after London's legendary Slimelight by David "DJ Decay" King, defined the look of the gothic/industrial scene.

Piero Scaruffi, Dan Kottke, Kal Spelletich and John Law at the
Stanford coffee house in 2015

San Francisco was also becoming the hub of one of the most vibrant
design schools in the world, thanks to designers such as the four Michaels:
Michael Vanderbyl, Michael Manwaring, Michael Cronin and Michael
Mabry. While the first graphic designer to embrace the Macintosh was
April Greiman in Los Angeles, San Francisco was the base of Rudy
Vanderlans, who started Emigre (the first major magazine that used the
Mac), and of John Hersey, another pioneer of computer-based graphic
design.

The environmental movement was still vibrant, sometimes bordering
on guerrilla warfare. In 1992 a small crowd of bicyclists staged an event
called "Commute Clot" that began a tradition of invading the streets of San
Francisco on the last friday of every month. It spread to many cities of the
world, better known as "critical mass biking".

However, the Bay Area that had witnessed the hippies and the punks
was falling into the hands of high-tech nerds. As its universities graduated
thousands of software and hardware engineers every year, thousands more
immigrated into the area. The age witnessed another wave of immigration
of youth from all over the world, just like 30 years earlier. But, unlike in
1966, this time the drivers were not "peace and love" but vanity and greed.

The metropolitan area of the Bay Area expanded dramatically in all
directions, but especially southward and eastward. Its population was
cosmopolitan and young. Agriculture had definitely been wiped out. The
demographic change made the Bay Area even more tolerant and open-
minded. In 1993, the political science professor Condoleezza Rice became
Stanford University's youngest, first female, and first non-white provost.

Condoleezza Rice

iBoomers: Google, Hotmail, Java, the Dotcoms, High-speed Internet, and Greentech (1995-98)

Searching the Internet

Netscape's billion-dollar IPO started the "dot-com bubble" of the late 1990s. Visionaries all over the world envisioned the Internet as a vehicle that would revolutionize business. The Internet would reduce the importance of the "brick and mortar" company (for example, of the physical store) and create new ways for companies to market/sell their products online. Consumers could shop online from a vast worldwide catalog.

Sensing a lethal threat, in August 1996 Microsoft, which so far had contributed nothing to the Internet, introduced Internet Explorer 3.0, which many judged superior to Netscape's Navigator, until then the popular favorite (boasting an 85% market share), and gave it away for free with its operating system. Many observers interpreted this as a strategy to kill Netscape (whose browser was not available for free) while it was still small. Microsoft's move not only fatally wounded Netscape (eventually bought out by America OnLine for $4.2 billion), but de facto preempted any other company from developing a browser for the Windows operating system. Internet Explorer had been quickly packaged by recycling code from the commercial version of Mosaic marketed by Spyglass (the business arm of the University of Illinois). Microsoft also acquired in January 1996 the tool developed by Boston's Vermeer Technologies for building websites, FrontPage.

Eventually (in 1998) the government would force Microsoft to unbundle Internet Explorer from the Windows operating system, but it would be too late to save Netscape.

Search engines were still at the forefront of the Internet revolution. The Bay Area quickly generated startups in that field. In February 1995, Steve Kirsch launched the search engine Infoseek, based in Sunnyvale. It pioneered "cost-per-impression" and "cost-per-click" advertising. Yet the company's main claim to fame might be that it raised Yanhong Li, the engineer who in 1999 moved to China and co-founded the Chinese search engine Baidu.

At Stanford six students, notably computer scientist Graham Spencer and political scientist Joe Kraus, started the project Architext in February 1993. It changed its name to Excite when it launched in December 1995. Excite was notable for being started by a team without a product. The six kids founded the company before deciding what to do with it. The initial investors, Geoff Yang and Vinod Khosla, were instrumental in turning Spencer's tool for searching text archives into a search engine for the Web, an idea that had not occurred to the founders. Thanks to a deal with Netscape, Excite went on to become the number-two search engine and the fourth most visited website in the world. They became the poster children of venture capitalists' often repeated (but rarely applied) motto that it is wiser to fund a great team than a great idea.

DEC had opened a research center in Palo Alto. The center created an internal search engine called AltaVista, made available to the Web in October 1995. AltaVista boasted a more sophisticated technology than previous search engines, notably Louis Monier's crawler (the software that roams the Web looking for documents) and it allowed users to input natural-language queries. In 1997 it even introduced automatic language translation, Babel Fish, based on the old Systran system. DEC was the only one of the computing giants to enter the search business: Microsoft ignored the field, as did IBM and AT&T.

David Patterson and others at UC Berkeley had obtained DARPA funding for a project called Network of Workstations (NOW) that envisioned a supercomputer built out of networked personal computers and workstations (a forefather of cluster computing). That architecture was used by Eric Brewer and his graduate student Paul Gauthier to create the fastest search engine yet, Inktomi, and spin off a namesake company. HotBot, launched in May 1996, was based on Inktomi's technology and quickly overtook AltaVista as the number-one search engine.

None of the early players figured out how to make money with searches. Their main asset was traffic (the millions of Internet users who accessed the webpage of the search engine), but none of these startups figured out how to turn traffic into profits. They morphed into general-purpose portals, the Web equivalent of a shopping mall.

Yahoo!, meanwhile, was happy to use other people's search technology: first Open Text (a spin-off of the University of Waterloo in Canada), then AltaVista, and then Inktomi. Yahoo! went public in April 1996. In the first hour of trading its value reached $1 billion. Not bad for a company that so far had revenues of $1.4 million and had lost $643,000.

An alternative approach to indexing the Web was pursued by the Open Directory Project (originally Gnuhoo), a public index of websites launched in June 1998 by SUN's employees Rich Skrenta (the inventor of the first personal computer virus) and Bob Truel. It was a collaborative effort by thousands of volunteer editors, initially modeled after the old Usenet. ODP was acquired by Netscape in October 1998. It surpassed Yahoo!'s directory sometime in 2000.

Search the web using Google!

10 results ▾   Google Search   I'm feeling lucky

Index contains ~25 million pages (soon to be much bigger)

About Google!

Stanford Search Linux Search

Get Google! updates monthly!

your e-mail   Subscribe   Archive

Copyright ©1997-8 Stanford University

An Early Google Screenshot (1998)

Google was founded in 1998 by two Stanford students, Larry Page and Russian-born Sergey Brin. They launched a new search engine running on Linux; it was an offshoot of a research project begun in 1996. The amount of information available on the Web was already causing information overload, and the issue was how to find the information that was really relevant. Google ranked webpages according to how "popular" they were on the Web (i.e. how many webpages linked to them). Google went against the trend of providing ever more sophisticated graphical user interfaces: the Google user interface was just text (and very little text). In 1999 Google had eight employees. Their first "angel" investor (before the company even existed) was Andy Bechtolsheim of SUN. Then (in June 1999) they obtained $25 million from Sequoia Capital and Kleiner-Perkins.

Outside the Bay Area, the most significant player was perhaps InfoSpace, founded in March 1996 by former Microsoft employee Naveen Jain, who built an online "yellow pages" service, also offering "chat rooms" where users could exchange live text messages.

These companies did not invent search technology. Search technology had existed for a while. Verity was the main vendor of tools for searching text archives. However, companies like Verity, that had pioneered the field and were getting rich by selling text search to the corporate world, were too busy maintaining their legacy applications to think about making a Web version of their tools. There was still a huge divide between software companies working in the old off-line world and the software companies working in the new on-line world. The former did not quite understand the Web yet and, in fact, would never catch up. The wheel had to be reinvented by young inexperienced kids because the older, experienced, skilled, and competent experts were stuck in a time warp.

The concept of the "chat room" had been pioneered on the Web by at least Bianca's Smut Shack, started in February 1994 in Chicago by David Thau and Chris Miller.

Social networking was born in April 1995 when Cornell University's students Stephan Paternot and Todd Krizelman launched theGlobe.com, an online community that expanded the old concept of the Usenet. In November 1998 theGlobe.com went public. On its first trading day the price of its stock closed at 606% the initial share price, setting an all-time record for IPOs.

Another application that would become popular on the Internet was born in Israel: in 1996 ICQ debuted. Invented by Arik Vardi, it would become the first instant messaging program to spread worldwide.

The Garage where Google Started (2010)

Creating a Webpage

Creating a website and finding a place that would host it was still a bit too complicated for the masses, but it got a lot easier and even free in 1995 when David Bohnett and John Rezner launched GeoCities in Los Angeles (the original name was BHI, Beverly Hills Internet). GeoCities basically created a web within the Web. The GeoCities web was structured in six virtual neighborhoods. Users (known as "homesteaders") could choose a neighborhood and an address within that neighborhood. GeoCities automatically created a webpage for each homesteader and provided an easy way for the homesteader to customize it. In October 1997 Geocities reached the milestone of one million users. In August 1998 it went public. By the end of the year it had become the third-most visited website on the Web after AOL and Yahoo. In January 1999 Yahoo purchased GeoCities for $3.57 billion.

Two Williams College classmates, Bo Peabody and Brett Hershey, and an economics professor, Dick Sabot, launched the website Tripod in 1994 out of their office in northwestern Massachusetts Tripod, like Geocities, became popular as a place where Internet users could easily create webpages, but its most lasting invention would be the "pop-up" ad, "invented" by Ethan Zuckerman in 1998.

Social networking was born in April 1995 when Cornell University's students Stephan Paternot and Todd Krizelman launched theGlobe.com, an online community that expanded the old concept of the Usenet. In November 1998 theGlobe.com went public. On its first trading day the price of its stock closed at 606% the initial share price, setting an all-time record for IPOs.

Getting Online

The explosion of interest for the Internet meant, first and foremost, an explosion of ISPs (internet service providers). The government helped the commercial boom of the Internet in yet another way. In 1994 the National Science Foundation commissioned four private companies to build four public Internet access points to replace the government-run Internet backbone: WorldCom in Washington, Pacific Bell in San Francisco, Sprint in New Jersey, and Ameritech in Chicago. Then other telecom giants entered the market with their own Internet services, which they often subcontracted to smaller companies. By 1995 there were more than 100 commercial ISPs in the US. The user had to pay a monthly fee and was sometimes also charged by the hour. Some ISPs simply gave users remote access to a Unix "shell" running on the ISP's server. Services based on SLIP (Serial Line Internet Protocol), the first protocol (1988) devised for relaying Internet Protocol packets over "dial-up" lines, and later PPP (Point-to-Point Protocol) implied that the user was given a modem and had to dial a phone number (sometimes a long-distance number) to reach the ISP.

In 1995 the leading ISPs were: Uunet (yearly revenue of almost $100 million), which targeted companies (not individuals) willing to pay $1,000 a month for Internet service; Netcom (just over $50 million), which skyrocketed from zero to 400,000 subscribers in its first year thanks to a simpler pricing scheme (a flat fee for 400 hours) targeting the consumer market; and PSINet. Also in 1995 telecom giant AT&T unveiled its ISP service, called WorldNet, which copied Netcom's flat-rate model. In April

1996 Pacific Bell, a regional telephone company, began offering Internet access to most of the four metropolitan areas of California (Bay Area, Los Angeles, Sacramento, San Diego).

The number of ISPs in the nation passed 3,000 at the beginning of 1997, and about 1,000 more were born in the next six months. By the year 2000, Uunet, the first and still the largest ISP, running 500,000 kilometers of fiber and cable, owned about 30% of the Internet's infrastructure. Dial-up pioneer CompuServe (acquired by AOL in 1997) was a distant second. Metricom, founded in Los Gatos (south of Cupertino) in 1985, pioneered the business of a wireless ISP in 1994 when it launched Ricochet Networks and offered service to Cupertino households. By 1996 it was covering the whole Bay Area.

At the other end of the dial-up connection, companies like Ascend Communications of Alameda (near Oakland) made fortunes by selling equipment to manage dial-up lines (acquired in 1999 by Lucent for $20 billion).

The one piece of equipment that almost everybody needed was the modem. US Robotics was an example of a company that never bent to the standards (its modems used proprietary protocols) and managed to become the leader in its sector. In 1997 3Com purchased US Robotics for $6.6 billion.

Browser-based Computing

Unless one worked for a university or research laboratory, an individual's e-mail was run by her or his ISP. When a user subscribed to the service, the ISP gave the user one or more e-mail addresses. The user had to install software on the home computer that periodically downloaded email messages. Starting with Soren Vejrum's WWWMail (launched in Denmark in February 1995), several attempts had been made at providing an email service that could be accessed from a browser.

Hotmail was the first big winner. In July 1996, two former Apple hardware engineers, Sabeer Bhatia and Jack Smith, funded by venture capitalist Tim Draper of Draper Fisher Jurvetson, launched Hotmail. It liberated the Internet user from the slavery of the ISP. Hotmail was a website. Hotmail users checked their e-mail on the Web, regardless of where they were. E-mail had just become location-independent. Even better: e-mail "traveled" with the user, because it could be accessed anywhere there was a web browser. Its model was so easy to understand that Hotmail signed up more than 8.5 million subscribers by December 1997, in just 18 months. It helped that Hotmail was free. Microsoft bought Hotmail in December 1997 (for about $400 million).

Another secondary business created by the emergence of the browser had to do with a browser's "plug-ins." A plug-in was a piece of software written by someone else that was incorporated into the browser to add a functionality that was not present in the original browser. One could add and remove plug-ins at will, thus customizing the browser. Macromedia released two of the most popular and innovative plug-ins for Netscape's browser Navigator: Shockwave in 1995, an evolution of Director to display videos; and Flash Player in 1996, an evolution of the animation tool FutureSplash acquired from Jonathan Gay's FutureWave. Flash would quickly become the world standard for embedding multimedia files into HTML pages (in other words, for displaying videos within webpages). Most plug-ins were made available for free.

In 1995 SUN launched Java, originally developed by James Gosling. It was both an elegant object-oriented programming language and a virtual machine. The advantage of a virtual machine is that any application written for it runs on any physical machine on which the virtual machine has been ported. Java basically recycled the concepts made popular among older software engineers by Smalltalk. Language-wise, the nearest relative of Java was NeXT's Objective-C. Java, however, specifically targeted the new world of the Internet, for no other reason than portability of applications. SUN gave away Java for free and Netscape soon introduced a feature to process webpages that contained "applets" written in Java.

The promise of Java as the Esperanto of the Internet was such that venture-capital firm Kleiner-Perkins hastily created a $100 million fund to invest in Java startups. Supported by a growing number of companies, notably IBM and Oracle, Java indeed became the language of choice for Internet applications. The more the Internet grew, the more Java grew. Eventually it started threatening the decade-old supremacy of the C language.

A web server is a software tool that transfers ("serves") pages of the World Wide Web to clients via the Hypertext Transfer Protocol (HTTP). It is the foundation of a Web-based application. The browser wars between Netscape and Microsoft also extended to the web server in 1995 when Microsoft introduced a free add-on to its NT operating system, Internet Information Server. It competed against Netscape's web server that cost $5,000. WebLogic, formed in 1995 in San Francisco, launched an application server for the Java 2 Enterprise Edition (J2EE). It was acquired in 1998 by San Jose-based BEA, founded by Chinese-born former SUN manager Alfred Chuang. Another pioneering Java application server was delivered by Steve Jobs's NeXT in 1995: WebObjects. It was also an object-oriented rapid application development environment.

The Original Offices of Hotmail (2010)

Building Bricks

Many of the tools required by Internet-based applications were available for free. In 1995 in Oregon a veteran of the Smalltalk environment, Ward Cunningham, who had his own software consulting business, created WikiWikiWeb, the first "wiki." It was an online manual (of reusable software programming methods) maintained in a collaborative manner on the Internet. Soon there would be "wikis" for everything. A wiki is an online knowledge-base that is created, edited, and maintained by a community of users. Any member of the community is allowed to change the content of any webpage of the knowledge-base from within an ordinary browser. The knowledge-base (in this case the manual) has no single author. It continuously evolves as more knowledge is provided by the users.

Meanwhile, a community of Unix developers launched the Apache server in 1996 as open-source software. The project extended and refined the web server implemented by Robert McCool at the government-funded National Center for Supercomputing Applications of the University of Illinois at Urbana-Champaign. Apache made it possible for anybody to start a website on their own home or office computer, thus increasing the amount of content and the number of applications that reached the Web.

In 1997 the World Wide Web Consortium (W3C), founded in October 1994 at MIT by Tim Berners-Lee as the international standards organization for the World-wide Web, introduced the XML standard for exchanging documents on the Web, thereby recasting EDI (Electronic Data Interchange) for the age of the Web.

In 1998 a struggling Netscape that was being strangled by the free Microsoft browser and the free Apache server decided to license the code of its browser for free as open source so that anybody could use it to build a better browser. Thus began the project "Mozilla." It was a desperate survival strategy.

In 1998 Adam Stiles (based in the Los Angeles area) introduced a new web-browser called SimulBrowse (later renamed NetCaptor) that allowed users to open multiple webpages at the same time, i.e. the first browser with "tabs". Opera followed suit in 1999 and Mozilla would include tabs in 2002 in the very first release of its Phoenix browser (later renamed Firefox).

Hotmail's Exponential Growth

Hotmail grew its user base faster than any media company in history and so in an instructive case study.

The founders were both hardware engineers, not software engineers. This was a case in which the idea came from a user viewpoint, not from a technology viewpoint. They needed a way to bypass the company's firewall and figured out how to do it. Many software engineers could have done the same because they knew the Web technology well enough but simply did not come up with the idea because they personally didn't need it. Being hardware engineers helped Hotmail's founder deliver a sturdy no-nonsense "product." Software engineers are artists who proceed by trial and error, and are not terribly concerned if their product has bugs (one can always fix the bugs later). Hardware engineers cannot afford bugs: every time a mistake is made, the cost is huge. Therefore Hotmail's founders naturally delivered something that was ready to be used by millions of people. About 100,000 people signed up for Hotmail in the first three months. Most new software needs a lot of tweaking before it gets it right: theirs didn't need any tweaking. Hotmail was a case in which the cultures of hardware and software converged and leveraged each other.

Hotmail, like Yahoo, was also another story that proved the unprecedented power of the Internet to spread news by word of mouth. Email, the very nature of Hotmail's business, was also the most powerful grass-roots tool ever to spread information. Hotmail's founders did two things to further improve its efficiency. First, they added a tagline to every email that invited the recipient to join Hotmail. Second, they gave each and every user an email address that contained "hotmail.com" so that each recipient would know (even without reading the tagline) that Hotmail existed. Both were useful for "branding"; but neither would have worked if Hotmail had not been useful and usable. Users spread the gospel that there was a simpler, better and cheaper way to do email.

Hotmail's concept (Web-based email, or "webmail") was a very easy concept to copy. In fact, it was copied. It was copied by many and by several companies that were much larger. Hotmail, however, proved how difficult it was to catch up. Precisely because the Internet medium was so unique in rapidly multiplying users, it created a de-facto standard even before the industry could do so. Once it became a de-facto standard, a startup (such as Hotmail) enjoyed a huge advantage even over much larger companies (such as Microsoft). The advantage was such that the larger company would have to invest millions in R&D and marketing for several years to match the startup. Indirectly this also ended up discouraging large companies from trying to catch up with successful startups: much cheaper to just buy them for outrageous prices. Rocketmail became Hotmail's main competitor after being a partner (they build Hotmail's directory of registered users) and being funded by the same venture capitalist. Eventually, Yahoo bought Rocketmail (in 1997) the same way Microsoft had bought Hotmail.

Finally, Hotmail bet on advertising as a viable source of revenues. Hotmail failed to prove that concept (it was never profitable) but represented one more step towards proving it. Hotmail's founders realized that email was even more powerful than Yahoo to generate "click-throughs" (actual visits to the advertised website). Indirectly, Internet start-ups realized that advertising (and marketing in general) had become such a key component of the capitalist society. One could almost claim that more creativity was going into marketing a product than in designing it. That industry had been consistently looking for innovative advertising vehicles: the newspaper, the nickelodeon, the radio and the television. The Internet boom took place at precisely the time when advertising was booming too. Cable television revenues had an 82% growth rate in 1994-95. The Web was also capable of delivering interactive advertising. And its advertising led straight to the store (through a mouse click, i.e. a "click-through").

Ads were perceived by the masses as a negative feature. Many startups failed because they were perceived to be too "commercial" once their web-based services started displaying too many ads. It was a tricky balance. On the one hand, startups needed the revenues from ads that were proportional to the number of people visiting their websites. But on the other hand, ads were making their websites less attractive and therefore reducing the number of visitors. Websites without any ads were more likely to earn the trust of the Internet public than websites with ads. However, the Internet public was not willing to turn that "trust" into financial support: websites that tried to charge a fee for each visit were even less likely to survive than websites that displayed ads. The Internet public was an odd beast: it wanted information without advertising, but it was not willing to pay for that information in any other manner. The good news for Internet startups is that the costs of operation were very low (Hotmail had 15 engineers when it was bought by Microsoft for $400 million).

Internet startups that followed the "free service" model indirectly adopted the view that their real product was the user base. A car manufacturer makes a car and makes money by selling the car. Many websites offered a web-based service that was only an excuse to create a large user base, and then they made money by selling advertising to corporations interested in selling whatever products/services to that user base; or upselling a different kind of service to that user base.

The Net Economy: 1995

Dotcom companies soon appeared in every sector of society; electronic commerce spread quickly.

Amazon.com: In 1995 Jeff Bezos, a former Wall Street investment banker who had relocated to Seattle, launched Amazon.com as the "world's largest bookstore," except that it was not a bookstore but a website. Amazon was the quintessential declaration of war to the "brick and mortar" store.

Craigslist.com: It was launched in 1995 by Craig Newmark from his San Francisco residence, provided a regional advertising platform (initially only for the Bay Area) that quickly made newspaper classified obsolete (since it was free and reached more people). It became a cult phenomenon, spreading by word of mouth. Newmark refused investments and offers to sell.

Craig Newmark of Craiglist (2010)
(Photo: Stephanie Canciello, Unali Artists)

Xing Technology: Based in southern California, it developed the first live audio and video delivery system over the Internet, StreamWorks, i.e. a system to play an audio or video file while it is downloaded from the Internet. Xing was acquired by RealNetworks in 1999.

Progressive Networks (later renamed RealNetworks): Formed in Seattle by ex-Microsoft executive Rob Glaser in 1995, it introduced the RealAudio "streaming" audio software. These two companies enabled live broadcasts on the Internet. In 1993 a concert by rock band Severe Tire Damage at the legendary high-tech laboratory of Xerox PARC was streamed live around the world, the first Internet live broadcast of music. In 1995 the online magazine The Word routinely streamed live content, and also in 1995 the television channel ESPN SportsZone used RealNetworks to stream live a baseball game. Live streaming went truly mainstream in 1996 when Marc Scarpa streamed the Tibetan Freedom Concert from San Francisco's Golden Gate Park, and the term "webcast" became commonplace. In 1998 RealNetworks, Netscape and Columbia University finalized the Real Time Streaming Protocol (RTSP), a protocol that, unlike the "stateless" HTTP, had "state" and was therefore better suited to live streaming.

Viaweb (Yahoo Stores): In 1995 New York-based computer scientists Paul Graham and Robert Morris (famous for having created the "Morris worm" in 1988 when he was still a student at Cornell University) started Viaweb (sold to Yahoo in 1998). It was a website to create online stores which made it easier for many people to get into e-commerce. It was also one of the first Web-based applications: it ran on a server and was controlled by the user by clicking on the links of a webpage displayed on a browser. Viaweb was similar to what had been done with X-terminals to run X-Windows (the browser being the equivalent of the X terminal).

eBay: In 1995 French-born Armenian-Iranian and former General Magic's engineer Pierre Omidyar founded AuctionWeb (renamed eBay in 1997), a website to auction items. The idea was that strangers would buy from strangers whom they never met and with no direct contact. By the end of 1998 eBay's auctions totaled $740 million.

The online dating system Match.com was launched in 1995 in Los Altos by Gary Kremen, one of the pioneers of Internet-based classified advertising with his company Electric Classifieds (1993)

Other companies ventured into Internet telephone, security, and website development tools. In 1995 the Israeli company VocalTec released the first commercial Internet phone software, i.e. a system capable of dispatching telephone calls over the Internet. In 1995 Kevin O'Connor, with the money he made at Internet Security Systems, started Internet Advertising Network (IAN), which later acquired and retained the name of the DoubleClick system of New York's Internet ad agency Poppe Tyson, largely the creation of Tom Wharton. Indian-born Samir Arora, who had managed Hypercard at Apple, founded NetObjects in 1995 in Redwood

City to develop tools for people to build their own websites (at the time not an easy matter).

In 1995 only 15% of Internet users in the US were women. Yet two New York media executives saw that the number was growing and that women were not served adequately by the new male-dominated medium. Candice Carpenter (Time Warner) and (Doubleday) Nancy Evans founded the female-oriented portal iVillage in June 1995.

In 1995 corporate lawyer Stacy Stern, Stanford law and economics student Tim Stanley, and German-born Stanford student Martin Roscheisen created FindLaw, a portal for law-related information, the first time that case law was made easily accessible to the US public.

Some also started thinking about the possibility of combining Internet and the television. In July 1995 former Apple and General Magic employee Steve Perlman (a hobbyist who had studied liberal arts) founded Artemis Research, later renamed WebTV. He wanted to build a set-top box based on custom hardware and software which would allow a television set attached to a telephone line to plug into an Internet service using a dial-up modem and to browse the Web via a thin client. The goal was to turn the World-wide Web into a home appliance. The WebTV set-top box (introduced in September 1996 by Sony and Philips) was not very successful but it pioneered the idea of accessing the Web via a consumer electronics device instead of a workstation or personal computer. In 1997 WebTV was acquired by Microsoft.

Internet IPOs escalated rapidly during the decade. AOL had gone public in 1992. UUNet and Netscape went public in 1995; Lycos, Excite, Yahoo!, CompuServe, Infoseek and E*Trade in 1996; Amazon in 1997. There had been ten Internet IPOs in 1995 but there were already 40 in 1998, and there would be 272 in 1999. In 1999 "dotcom" startups would receive more than 40% of venture capital investment.

The dotcom boom also boosted the stock of e-learning, a field pioneered by Stanford in the 1960s. However, very few of the startups of the era survived, notably Saba, founded in 1997 in Redwood Shores by Oracle's executive Bobby Yazdani.

At this point the "users" of a dotcom service were typically technology-savvy professionals, especially those raised on Unix. At the time not everybody was connected to the Internet, not everybody had access to high-speed lines, and not everybody understood what the World-Wide Web was. In 1996 there were 14 million households in the US with Internet access, almost all of them on dial-up lines. Even in 1998, when the number of users in the US had skyrocketed to 75 million, the vast majority still used dial-up services. Ordinary people were still reluctant to use email, let alone sophisticated ecommerce websites. Many households were just beginning to get familiarized with computers.

Craigslist's Office (2010)

The Net Economy: 1996-97

Significant innovations for the Web were push technology and subscription models. In February 1996 Pointcast, founded by Christopher Hassett, started a fad for "push" technology with its software that gathered information from the Web and then displayed it on a personal computer, which amounted to basically the opposite of surfing (a software agent sending information to the user instead of the user searching the Web). Marimba, a spin-off of SUN's Java group founded in 1996 in Mountain View by Arthur van Hoff and Jonathan Payne and headed by Kim Polese (at the time a rare female CEO of a high-tech startup), offered subscription-based software distribution so that one could automatically get updates to its applications.

The movie industry was helped by an early Web subscription-model business named Netflix. In August 1997 Reed Hastings, who had been selling tools for programmers with his first startup Pure Software, founded Netflix in Scotts Valley (between San Jose and Santa Cruz). He wanted to rent videos (initially on DVD) via the Internet. DVD rentals were a direct strike against movie theaters, one of the pillars of social life in the 20th century. Netflix upped the ante by removing even the DVD store and allowing movie buffs to simply order movies online. The movie still required a physical device, the DVD, but was delivered at home.

The world was being mapped and made available. In 1997 Jim Gray of Microsoft, working with Aerial Images of North Carolina, created the web-based mapping service TerraServer that also offered satellite images from the United States Geological Survey (USGS) and Russia's space agency Sovinformsputnik. In 1996 Chicago-based GeoSystems Global launched the web-based mapping service MapQuest that also provided address matching. In 1996 Jim Clark of Silicon Graphics fame founded Healtheon (originally Healthscape) to create software for the health-care system (to "map" treatment data).

In October 1996 Microsoft launched Expedia, an online travel agency (that would become the largest travel agency in the world in the 2010s).

eBay's Campus (2010)

A few companies even ventured into early social networking. In 1997 Stanford University's engineering students Al Lieb and Selina Tobaccowala founded Evite, a free website to manage invitations. A milestone for web-based social networking software was SixDegrees.com, launched in 1997 by New York's corporate lawyer Andrew Weinreich and named after the hypothesis that all human beings are linked by at most six connections. A user could link to friends and family and reach people beyond the first level of connection. At the peak it had one million registered users.

The world of finance was affected too. Online stock brokerage moved to the Web with E*Trade, launched in 1992 in Palo Alto by William Porter and Bernard Newcomb. Internet banking (a bank with no physical branch) was pioneered by ING Direct, founded in 1996 in Canada by Arkadi Kuhlmann.

The Net Economy: 1998-99

As the technology became more reliable, the applications became more sophisticated too, spreading to broadcasting, books, and groceries.

In 1998 UC Berkeley Professor Abhay Parekh founded FastForward Networks to provide radio and television broadcasting over the Web (FastForward's first customer was RealNetworks when it set up its Real Broadcast Network).

NuvoMedia was founded that same year in Palo Alto by Martin Eberhard (one of the founders of Network Computing Devices) and Marc Tarpenning, introduced the Rocket eBook. It was a paperback-sized handheld device to read digital books downloaded from online bookstores ("ebooks"). Another e-book reader was introduced at the same time by rival SoftBook Press, founded by Amiga's videogame guru James Sachs and by publishing industry executive Tom Pomeroy in 1996 in Menlo Park. The two startups were eventually purchased by Rupert Murdoch's media conglomerate.

Webvan, born in 1999 to deliver groceries purchased online (initially only in San Francisco), raised $375 million in 18 months and at one point it was worth $1.2 billion (the archetype of the "unicorn"). Kozmo in New York, started in 1998, was even more ambitious, planning to deliver all sorts of goods within one hour: it raised $280 million.

Internet banking was pioneered by ING Direct (1996, Canada), Everbank (1998, Florida) and Ally Bank (2001, Utah).

At the moment that companies started doing business on the Web, it became important to have reliable services to display webpages in real time. Akamai, founded in 1998 by MIT mathematician Thomson Leighton and his student, Israeli-born Technion alumnus Daniel Lewin, replicated content to servers located around the world in order to minimize the time it took to deliver it to the end users.

The New Nature of Innovation

The semiconductor boom had largely been the making of one legendary company. Fairchild Semiconductor gave birth to more than 50 semiconductor startups. The vast majority of Silicon Valley engineers working in semiconductors during the 1960s had worked at Fairchild at one time or another. The history of the semiconductor industry in Silicon Valley is the Fairchild genealogical tree. The semiconductor boom largely consisted in the refinement of one technology. It was a very vertical kind of technological development.

The age of Apple, Cisco, SUN, and Oracle was different. This boom was more diversified. The inventions of Apple, Cisco, SUN, and Oracle had little in common. Furthermore, neither of them gave rise to a significant genealogical tree. Compared with Fairchild Semiconductor, relatively few startups were created by former Apple, Cisco, SUN, or Oracle engineers, and fewer survived or stayed independent (Salesforce.com is one of the rare few). No major company of the size of Intel emerged from any of these. What each of them created was a chain of suppliers. There was a vertical economy that relied on them but the boom was becoming more horizontal.

The dotcom age was completely horizontal. The dotcom boom was wildly diversified. It wasn't just the refinement of a technology, but the application of a technology to many different applications in wildly different fields. The dozens of dotcoms were exploring a vast landscape. Some dotcoms refined previous ideas (for example, search or social networking), but most of them did not refine a previous application at all: they were the first to implement that application on the Web. If someone else had preceded them, there was no relationship between the two sets of engineers (it was not a Fairchild-Intel kind of relationship). The Internet resettled Silicon Valley in a new landscape, and the dotcom boom was mostly about exploring this new landscape and finding gold mines in it.

One reason that dotcoms did not bother to refine previous dotcoms' inventions (the way semiconductor startups had done in the 1970s) was that there were so many opportunities. Why compete with an existing dotcom? Another reason that dotcoms did not bother to refine previous dotcoms' inventions was outsourcing: the job of refinement was best left to India.

Network Neutrality

The dotcom boom owed a lot to a fundamental principle of the Internet, never encoded in a law but tacitly accepted by the whole community. The network had to be company-neutral and application-agnostic. The network was simply a highway that anybody could use. There was no VIP lane. No matter how large and powerful a corporation was, it had to use for its ecommerce activities the very same network that the poorest student was using to set up her personal website. The Internet had been conceived to be as general as possible and with no particular application in mind.

The dotcom boom was a boom of applications, not of platforms. The innovation went into the applications. The platform was roughly still the same as in the 1980s if not the 1970s.

The application boom was driven by the neutrality of the Internet. First of all, that neutrality protected the small Internet startup from the "brick and mortar" corporation. Everybody could get a fair chance in the marketplace, a fact that was not true in the "brick and mortar" economy where large businesses could use a plethora of tactics to hurt smaller newcomers.

Secondly, the network allowed the producer (the creator of a Web-based service) to offer its "product" directly to the consumer (the user). There was no need for an intermediary anymore. In the traditional economy users shopped for the products that an intermediary had decided to deliver to the store. It was not the user who decided which products would show up at the store: it was a chain of intermediaries starting from the product planning division all the way down to the store owner. The Internet removed the whole chain. People were creating applications on the Web, and users were deciding which ones became successful.

In the "brick and mortar" economy a corporation decided which product to sell and then proceeded to publicize it. In the "net" economy, instead, it was the user who decided which "product" (website) to use. The marketing for that product, its website, was the "buzz" created within the community of users. There was no advertisment publicizing a website, no salesman selling it door to door, and no store displaying it on its window.

Getting Online Part II

Internet dial-up services were multiplying, but dial-up access was slow. Two technologies appeared at the end of the 1990s to remedy the problem. The US government made another important decision for the future of the Internet in 1996. The "Telecommunications Act" allowed cable television providers to offer Internet services. Milo Medin, a former NASA scientist, and tycoon William Randolph Hearst III started At Home Network (@Home), technically a joint venture between TCI (the largest cable operator in the US) and the venture capital firm Kleiner Perkins Caufield & Byers. Their mission was to deliver Internet broadband to a million homes by the first quarter of 1997. Tthe high-speed cable ISP was born! In 1997 US West launched the first commercial DSL (Digital Subscriber Line) service in Phoenix. Cable Internet used the cables laid down for cable television. DSL used the ordinary telephone lines. Neither was widely available at the time.

The obvious beneficiaries of the age of networking were the companies that specialized in networking hardware. By the mid-1990s the three Silicon Valley giants Cisco, 3Com, and Bay Networks (formed by the merger of SynOptics and Billerica, acquired in 1998 by Northern Telecom) had achieved $1 billion in revenues. Indian-born Pradeep Sindhu, a former semiconductor scientist at Xerox PARC, founded Juniper Networks in 1996 in Sunnyvale to manufacture high-end routers in direct competition with Cisco. When it went public in 1999, its IPO was one of the most successful in history, turning it overnight into a $4.9 billion company.

The astronomical growth of Internet communications also created demand for high-speed fiber-optic cables to connect not only research centers but also millions of ordinary homes.

Fiber optics are made of thin glass wires. Optical switches convert the digital signals into light pulses. The light pulses are transmitted over these optical cables instead of the copper wires of the traditional telephone lines.

A fiber-optic cable has a much broader bandwidth than a copper cable. Therefore optical fibers can be used to transmit large amounts of data over large distances.

The story of fiber optics goes back many decades, but applications were not feasible until more progress in both optical fibers and laser technology (the only light source capable of high-speed modulation) took place in the 1960s and 1970s. Seven months after Theodore Maiman's demonstration of the first laser (the ruby laser), a team at Bell Labs (Ali Javan, William Bennett and Donald Herriott) demonstrated the first continuous-wave laser. Robert Hall at General Electric created the first semiconductor diode laser already in 1962, but it was not a practical one. Only in 1970 did someone invent a semiconductor diode laser capable of emitting continuously and at room temperature (Zhores Alferov in Russia, followed by Bell Labs), and only in 1975 did a company begin commercialization of the technology (Laser Diode Labs, a spinoff of RCA Labs). By the following year Bell Labs was demonstrating laser diodes with a long life. Throughout the 1960s fiber optics communication was promoted mainly by Charles Kao at Stanford, but its feasibility had to wait until 1970 when the first practical optical fiber was developed by glass maker Corning Glass Works. In 1975 Manfred Boerner at Telefunken Labs in Germany demonstrated the first fiber-optical data transmission. Commercial applications had to wait for optical fiber amplifiers, which came of age with pump laser diodes. The age of fiber optics truly began in 1988 with the first transatlantic cable to use optical fibers, the TAT-8 (a collaboration among AT&T, France Telecom and British Telecom), the eighth transatlantic communications cable, capable of carrying 40,000 telephone simultaneous conversations (as opposed to the 138 conversations of the 1966 transatlantic cable).

The boom for optical cables began in 1996, when the US government enacted the Telecommunications Act that deregulated the telecom market. This created ferocious competition among local and global telecom companies at the same time that the pundits predicted an exponential rise in broadband need due to the advent of the Web.

It is not a coincidence that the capacity of optical cables almost doubled every six months starting in 1992 until in 2001 it achieved a bit rate of 10 terabit per second. Lucent, a 1995 spin-off of AT&T (including Bell Labs), that between 1997 and 1999 had spent a fortune to acquire some 30 startups, and Canadian giant Nortel, which had deployed the world's first commercial fiber-optic link in 1980, dominated the market. In 1999 Lucent introduced the all-optical LambdaRouter, the first optical network switch, advertised as 16 times faster than electronic switches of the time. In 1999 Nortel and Lucent together owned more than 50% of the $12.3 billion market, a market that had just grown by 56% from 1998.

There was big money even in acquisitions. In 1999 Cisco acquired Cerent of Petaluma (north of San Francisco, formed in 1996 with funding from Vinod Khosla) for $7.4 billion, and became the third power. Meanwhile Nortel bought Xros of Sunnyvale in 2000 for $3.25 billion. In 1988, the Southern Pacific Railroad began installing fiber-optic cable along its lines and in 1995 it spawned Qwest, headquartered in Denver, Colorado. By 1999 it had revenues of $3.92 billion. Aerie Networks of Denver raised $100 million of venture capital in its first two years (1999-2000). Sycamore Networks, located in Massachusetts, was worth $29.1 billion in September 2000.

Silicon Valley became one of the hotbeds of optical technology. A spin-off of Optivision founded in 1997 in San Jose by Indian-born Rohit Sharma, ONI Systems was one of the first to go public. Then came the deluge: Kestrel Solutions of Mountain View; Lightera Networks of Cupertino; Calient of San Jose; Mayan Networks of Mountain View; Amber Networks of Fremont; Zaffire of San Jose; Luminous Networks of Cupertino; Luxn of Sunnyvale and others.

The world was suddenly awash in fiber-optic cables. This overcapacity, not mandated by governments but simply the result of business miscalculations, dramatically lowered the cost of broadcasting information, thereby increasing the motivation to broadcast information. The fiber-optic rush created on the Internet the equivalent of the freeway system created by the US government in the 1950s. It did so rapidly and at no cost to the taxpayer. The cost was political: the vast fiber-optic infrastructure did more than connect the nation electronically: it connected the nation to India too, thus accelerating the process of outsourcing IT jobs to India.

Something else was brewing amid all the startup frenzy, but mostly elsewhere. In 1988 Mark Weiser had proposed the vision of a future in which computers will be integrated into everyday objects ("ubiquitous computing") and these objects are connected with each other. This became known as the "Internet of Things" after 1998 when two experts in RFID at the Massachusetts Institute of Technology, David Brock and Sanjay Sarma, figured out a way to track products through the supply chain with an RFID tag linking to an online database. Neil Gershenfeld published the book "When Things Start to Think" (1999) and later (2001) established the MIT's Center for Bits and Atoms (2001).

In 1996 Japan's Sony had introduced the chip FeliCa for RFID technology. The foundations had been laid down. Silicon Valley had pioneered RFID applications with Identronix, but little had come out of it.

A Brief History of the Open-source Movement

The World-wide Web was a major boost to the open-source movement. Open-source software was born as a reaction by the "counterculture" to the big corporations and investment firms that had started changing the software industry in the 1980s. Until 1970 there had been basically no software industry. In the 1980s software emerged as both a "mission-critical product", for which corporations were willing to pay a lot of money and a "consumer good" that millions of computer users were willing to purchase. The software engineers who embarked in open-source projects were idealists who disliked the commercial success of software. In the 1980s it was not easy to share and distribute software. It was mainly done on Unix machines connected via the Internet. The "social media" of the Unix world were the "newsgroups" of the Usenet invented in 1980. For example, the most influential "scripting" language of the Unix world, Perl, was released by its creator Larry Wall in 1987 on the comp.sources.misc newsgroup. In 1991 Guido van Rossum, based in Holland, released Python, soon to become a very famous programming language, on the alt.sources newsgroup. Another example of free software that became very popular before the age of the World-wide Web was the X Window System, developed in 1984 at the MIT by Jim Gettys and Bob Scheifler. It was the most popular windowing system on Unix machines at the time when Apple and Microsoft where beginning to make the "windows-mouse" paradigm popular. At that time Richard Stallman launched the GNU Project and founded the Free Software Foundation. The first GNU was released in 1989 and contained a complete set of software development tools that were completely free for anybody. The first famous GNU success was Linus Torvalds' Linux, a variant of the Unix operating system, that was released in 1991 and became a GNU item in 1992. Much of the impulse towards free software came from UC Berkeley, where in 1977 Bill Joy had created the version of Unix called BSD (Berkeley Software Distribution). That version of Unix became very popular on the workstations of the 1980s. As part of BSD, in 1979 Eric Allman created the program "delivermail" that became "sendmail" and that managed most of the email traffic on the Internet throughout the 1980s. Much of the free software was developed by students. In 1992 William and Lynne Jolitz created a version of BSD called 386BSD that was completely free. They named it that way because they wanted a Unix for the personal computers that ran the Intel microprocessor 80386, small cheap computers that were faster than the traditional (and much more expensive) DEC machines that ran BSD Unix. Later their 386BSD would evolve into FreeBSD, NetBSD, and OpenBSD, all of them available for free. What had become as a leftist insurrection against capitalism was mutating into an academic practice. A former Berkeley student, Brian Behlendorf, was one of the software engineers who wrote the Apache HTTP Server in 1995. They were known as the "Apache Group" that later became the Apache Software Foundation. The Apache software was extremely important for the success of the World-wide Web. Incidentally, when he was not working on software,

Behlendorf was helping the Burning Man festival. In 2006 the same Behlendorf would be invited to speak at the World Economic Forum in Davos. His story was typical of how people in the Bay Area could mix counterculture, art, business and technology. In 1998 Netscape created Mozilla, the open source version of its Internet software. Jamie Zawinski was one of the leaders of that project. The term "open source" was probably invented in 1998 by nanotech guru Christine Peterson, co-founder of the Foresight Institute in Palo Alto. The first conference on free software, the "Freeware Summit" organized in 1998 in Palo Alto by the publisher Tim O'Reilly. was quickly nicknamed the "Open Source Summit". Participants included Linus Torvalds, Guido van Rossum, Brian Behlendorf, Jamie Zawinski, and Eric Raymond (who had written an influential article titled "The Cathedral and the Bazaar" in 1997). By now the beneficial effects of open-source software were becoming obvious: collaboration was increasing the ability of the community as a whole to innovate. It was the spirit of collaboration of the San Francisco counterculture transported into the world of computers. The only thing that was missing, in order to cement the open-source community, was a central catalog of all the available free software. SourceForge was founded for that purpose in 1999 by VA Linux (later VA Research and VA Software), a Sunnyvale-based maker of Linux personal computers founded by Larry Augustin and James Vera.

Cyberculture and Cybersociety

The Internet was also beginning to be used for cultural purposes. The online magazine Salon was founded in 1995 in San Francisco by David Talbot, a former editor for the San Francisco Examiner. In April 1999 Salon would purchase the glorious WELL. Slate was founded in 1996 in Seattle by Michael Kinsley, initially under the ownership of Microsoft. Slate and Salon basically transferred the print magazine to the Web, while The Word was trying a completely new format, specifically adapted for the Web.

The term "blog" came to be associated with websites run by an individual who published content on a more or less regular basis, the Web equivalent of a television talk show or of a newspaper column. In 1998 Bob Somerby, an op-ed writer for the Baltimore Sun, started "The Daily Howler," the first major political blog. In 1998 Piero Scaruffi, formerly the manager of Olivetti's Artificial Intelligence Center in Cupertino, launched his own website Scaruffi.com to publish articles on music, cinema, politics, etc. In September 1997 Michigan's computer-science student Rob Malda launched Slashdot, a website catering to an audience of the open-source hobbyists ("news for nerds") that provided an index of stories published by other websites or magazines, the first news aggregator.

Anthropologists were excited about the convergence of the virtual communities enabled by cyberspace and the technology of virtual reality that had matured since the pioneering years. In 1994, Ron Britvich in southern California created WebWorld, later renamed AlphaWorld and then again renamed Active Worlds. In it people could communicate, travel, and build. Bruce Damer was a former member of the Elixir team in LA. Inspired by the hippie communes of the 1960s, they had purchased a ranch in the Santa Cruz Mountains south of Silicon Valley, established the Contact Consortium in 1994. In 1996 the ranch yielded three-dimensional virtual-reality environments such as a virtual town (Sherwood Forest) and a virtual university (The U).

A virtual-reality project that would have an impact throughout the country was the "CAVE". The Electronic Visualization Lab at the University of Illinois Chicago created a "Cave Automatic Virtual Environment", a surround-screen and surround-sound virtual-reality environment in which graphics was projected from behind the walls of a room. The walls themselves are basically just very large screens, and ditto the floor. Many universities would build a Cave system in the next decade.

In 1994 Ron Britvich in southern California created WebWorld, later renamed AlphaWorld, in which people could communicate, travel and build; and in Silicon Valley a former hippy named Bruce Damer opened the Contact Consortium that in 1996 launched 3D virtual-reality environments such as a virtual town and a virtual university. At that time (about 1996) a new kind of "massively multiplayer game" appeared, the MMORPG. The genre was invented in 1996 by the Korean game "Baramue Nara" ("Baram" in the USA), followed by "Meridian 59" (1996), developed by brothers Andrew and Chris Kirmse in Virginia, and "Ultima Online" in 1997, developed by Electronic Arts' game designer Richard Garriott who also coined the term MMORPG. The emphasis here was on having many players at the same time, which indirectly laid the foundations for the software of virtual-reality.

The Anthropology of Transience

Silicon Valley's real (non-virtual) society was characterized by transience at all levels. People were coming and going. Companies were being started and closed. This society of transience created a landscape with no monuments. Not even rich people cared for building monuments. In a place that had no great buildings, a company's sign might become a landmark. Buildings were to be destroyed so nobody felt the need to start a building meant to last forever like all civilizations had done before.

This "flatness" of the world created a strange contradiction: there was no visible sign of Silicon Valley's grandeur. The greatness of Silicon Valley was defined by products designed in corporate rooms and built in laboratories that were hidden from the public. People could read about what made Silicon Valley great but there was no exterior manifestation to prove it. The office buildings of Intel, Hewlett-Packard, Oracle, and Apple were almost incognito. Dubai was erecting one skyscraper after the other, and Shanghai would soon begin to do the same. The Roman and the British empires had left countless public buildings to celebrate their triumphs. Silicon Valley, by contrast, didn't even have a landmark of the kind that any midsize city in the US could boast of (like Seattle's Space Needle or St Louis' Arch). A tour of Silicon Valley's historical buildings was a tour of garages and offices. Silicon Valley was "inside," not "outside."

It is not that these rich individuals and companies were reluctant to spend their money. They did spend. In the 1990s Silicon Valley contributed more than one billion dollars to charitable causes. However, the typical contribution was in the form of philanthropy. A company or an individual was more likely to spend a fortune in a "project" (whether helping the poor in Africa or helping a local organization) than in a building. It was all part of the mindset of transience: a project does not depend on a physical location.

Civic life was, in fact, often shaped by philanthropy rather than planned by government. Silicon Valley's very beginning had been shaped by an act of philanthropy and not by an act planned by the government: Stanford University.

Bubble Deals

The business model that became ubiquitous among dotcom startups was about becoming popular and cool, not necessarily making money. The dotcom startup was after market share, not profits. In other words, the competition was about getting as many users as possible, typically by providing a service for free, hoping that eventually the large number of users would also bring in revenues. Therefore the typical dotcoms were operating at a net loss. Very few actually had a plan on how to make money. Most of them envisioned a day when they could charge a fee for their services, but the trend was obviously in the opposite direction, with more and more companies waiving fees for their online services. Netscape, for example, made Navigator available for free in January 1998. A different avenue to profitability was taken by the dotcoms that began to sell advertising space on their websites, notably Geocities in May 1997.

In the second half of the 1990s there were more than 100 venture capital firms at work in the Bay Area. The five most prominent were Accel (founded in Palo Alto in 1983 by Jim Swartz and Arthur Patterson, both former partners of Jay Adler 's firm in New York), Kleiner Perkins Caufield & Byers, Crosspoint Ventures, Sequoia Capital, and Hambrecht & Quist. In 1998 Taiwanese computer manufacturer Acer opened Acer Technology Ventures to invest in Silicon Valley startups. Venture capitalists were becoming popular heroes too, notably John Doerr, a former Intel salesman. At Kleiner-Perkins he had invested in SUN, Compaq, Lotus, Genentech, Netscape, Amazon, and Google.

The new wave of software companies had further changed the demographics of Silicon Valley with a significant injection of brains from Asia. By 1998 Chinese and Indian engineers ran about 25% of Silicon Valley's high-tech businesses, accounting for $16.8 billion in sales and 58,000 jobs. But the bubble was getting frothy. In November 1998 Netscape surrendered and was purchased by America OnLine (AOL). It was a bad omen for the dotcoms.

Other Boomers: The Y2K Bug, Wi-Fi, Personal Digital Assistants, and DNA Mapping (1995-98)

The Y2K Bug

At the same time that the dotcoms were booming, another factor contributed to a dramatic increase in software revenues: the Y2K phenomenon.

"Y2K" was an abbreviation for "Year 2000." The vast majority of business software for large computers had been written in the 1960s and 1970s, and then ported to new generations of computers. Because of the limitations of storage at the time, and because, quite frankly, very few people expected those applications to last that long, most businesses could run only until 1999. Their applications had no way to represent a date beyond 1999 (the commonly used two-digit abbreviation of the year, for example "55" instead of "1955," would turn the year 2000 into the year 1900).

Panic spread when the corporate world realized what that meant. As the world entered a new century, unpredictable glitches could bring down the world economy and cause all sorts of disasters. Virtually all the business software in the world had to be rewritten, or at least analyzed to make sure there was no "Y2K bug." At one point, the Gartner Group estimated the cost of fixing the Y2K bug at $600 billion.

This was a boon for software companies that serviced legacy applications. So much code needed to be rewritten that, globally, one of the main beneficiaries of the Y2K panic was India. Since 1991 it had begun liberalizing its protectionist economy, and it boasted a large and cheap English-speaking IT workforce. US companies had to outsource millions of codes to Indian companies. India's National Association of Software and Service Companies (Nasscom) estimated that India's software exports in 1998-99 reached $2.65 billion, growing at a yearly rate of over 50%. Y2K-related projects accounted for $560 million or about 20% of the total.

The Y2K economy fueled the software industry at the same time that the Internet was doing it, thus generating an economic bubble on top of another bubble. The mayhem was so loud that very few people realized that the year 2000 was the last year of the 20th century, not the first year of the 21st century. That honor belonged to the year 2001: for the age of the computer anything with a zero at the end ought to be a beginning, not an end. The second millennium of the Christian calendar lasted only 999 years (the first millennium had been from year 1 to 1000, i.e. 1000 years).

A 1999 article by international consultant Peter de Jager in the reputable magazine Scientific American concluded: "I believe that severe disruptions will occur and that they will last perhaps about a month." Highly educated people stockpiled food and water, and some decided to spend the last day of the year in bunkers. The apocalypse would come, but it would come a few weeks later, in March 2000, and it would have little to do with the way computers represent dates.

Software Tools

Meanwhile, the proliferation of software startups in Silicon Valley was not limited to the Internet and the Y2K bug. In 1998 Stanford's scientist Mendel Rosenblum (an assistant to John Hennessy on multiprocessor projects) was working on SimOS, a project to create a software simulator of hardware platforms. Such software would be able to run the operating systems written for those hardware platforms. Rosenblum and others founded VMware to pursue that mission. In May 1999 they introduced VMware Workstation, which was not a workstation but a SimOS-like software environment (a "virtual machine"). It allowed a Unix machine to run the Windows operating system (and therefore all of its applications). Eventually they would broaden the idea to allow one physical computer to run multiple operating systems simultaneously. Server virtualization had already been popular in the mainframe era, but Rosenblum was the first one to implement it on smaller computers.

Red Hat had become the darling of the Linux world. In 1998 it merged with Sunnyvale-based Cygnus Solutions, founded in 1989 by John Gilmore and Michael Tiemann to provide tools for Linux. When Red Hat finally went public in August 1999, it achieved one of the biggest first-day gains in the history of Wall Street. Meanwhile, in 1999 Marc Fleury started the Georgia-based JBoss project for a Java-based application server (JBoss would be acquired by Red Hat in 2006).

The Internet and Y2K booms on top of the pre-existing software boom increased the need for software development environments. One of the paradigms that took hold was Rapid Application Development (RAD), originally championed by James Martin at IBM in 1991 but fitting very well the frantic world of Silicon Valley. Instead of developing an application top-down, RAD calls for the immediate creation of a working prototype followed by a series of incremental improvements (in a sense, similar to what Nature does). Delphi, released by Borland in 1995, was an early example of a development environment for RAD. Java also called for a new type of development environment. Visual Cafe, released by Symantec in 1997, was an early example. There had been and there continued to be a proliferation of software tools to overcome the dearth of software engineers and the pressure to deliver ever faster.

In those years, supply chain management was brought to the Bay Area. Agile Software, founded in 1995 in San Jose by Bryan Stolle, sold a suite to help firms manage bills of materials (BOMs). Ariba was started in 1996 in Sunnyvale by Keith Krach (a GM veteran) and by Paul Hegarty (NeXT's vice-president of engineering); it automated the procurement process. Both pioneered business-to-business (B2B) commerce over the Internet. Supply chain management was as hot as ERP. Sales of i2's Rhythm went from $26 million in 1995 to $65 million in 1996, and in 1999 i2 would boast a 13% share of the $3.9 billion supply-chain software market. ERP was already well established in the Bay Area thanks to PeopleSoft and Oracle, although the German companies continued to dominate. In 1997 the total revenues for the ERP software market was $7.2 billion, with SAP, Baan, Oracle, J.D. Edwards, and PeopleSoft accounting for 62% of it.

The Computer Market at the Turn of the Century

For the time being the evolution of computers was largely independent of the dotcoms.

34 million households owned a computer in 1996 in the US.

In 1997 IBM's revenues were $68 billion, but now a big chunk of them came from technical support to its aging mainframes, a business that employed 160,000 people. In 1997 IBM introduced a new generation of mainframes based on Intel microprocessors, the Netfinity series. In 1995 IBM purchased Lotus Development, one of the many moves that realigned IBM towards the world of personal computers.

Compaq was the rising star. In 1994 it had overtaken IBM in personal-computer sales. In 1997, the year it shipped 10 million personal computers and laptops, Compaq's revenues skyrocketed to $24.6 billion. Compared with Dell and Gateway, Compaq was most successful with corporate customers. In the second half of the 1990s it moved aggressively to capture that market from IBM. In 1997 Compaq acquired Tandem Computers and their line of fault-tolerant servers, a move that gave Compaq more credibility in mission-critical business applications. In 1998 Compaq acquired Digital Equipment Company (DEC), which had been struggling to adjust to the new world of personal computers. DEC was certainly in trouble: despite reducing its workforce (in 1997 it employed 50,000 people, down from a peak of 130,000), DEC still employed about 65% more people than Compaq to generate about 50% lower revenues. However, DEC's products included both high-end servers (priced at $1 million and up) and low-end servers (priced under $100,000), plus workstations. More importantly, 45% of its revenues came now from services: DEC's technical and customer support was a worldwide army of 25,000 people. That was exactly what Compaq needed to take on its rival IBM.

Dell got an edge in PCs and Toshiba built one in laptops. In 1996 Dell began selling its computers via its website. The website used NeXT's just released WebObjects technology. It allowed consumers and businesses to order directly, and even to customize the configuration of their PC. By spring 1999 Dell had erased the US sales gap with Compaq (Compaq 16.8%, Dell 16.4%), although Compaq continued to sell more units abroad. The market for laptop computers was dominated by Toshiba, which in 1997 enjoyed a market share of 20.4%. Toshiba also introduced the first DVD player in 1996.

Compared with the fortunes of IBM, Compaq, Dell, and Toshiba, the two Silicon Valley giants, Hewlett-Packard and Apple, had a mixed record. Since 1995 HP had become one of the most successful personal-computer manufacturers. It owned more than 50% of the market for printers in that market. And it looked very aggressive: in 1994 it had partnered with Intel to develop a 64-bit processor (code-named "Merced") that promised to be a dramatic departure from Intel's x86 architecture. However, when it was eventually released in 2001 with the official name of Titanium, it was a flop because in the meantime Intel had released a faster x86-based processor, the Pentium. As for Apple, which had allied with IBM and Motorola in 1994 to use their PowerPC microprocessor for a new line of high-end Macintoshes, in 1996 it purchased NeXT, and with it the Unix-based NextStep operating system and the WebObjects technology, a Java-based application server for rapid object-oriented software development of Web-based applications. Steve Jobs was therefore back at Apple. In 1997 Apple followed Dell in using WebObjects to create a website (the "Apple Store") to sell customized machines directly to the end customer. However, Apple was bleeding. It couldn't compete with the DOS/Windows-based computers and in 1999 it laid off 2,700 of 11,000 employees.

Steve Jobs used the experience in design that he had gained at NeXT, as well as the skills of Jonathon Ive (appointed Apple's top industrial designer in 1997), to create the sexy iMac that debuted in 1998 and that, selling two million units in its first year, began the resurrection of the company. It was the beginning of the "i" series of products, that in 1999 continued with the iMovie, a video-editing software for the generic user.

34 million households owned a computer in 1996 in the USA.

A Wireless Future

The new semiconductor companies often targeted emerging niche markets. In 1994 wireless pioneer Proxim had introduced a product to let ordinary computers exchange data via the ether, which truly inaugurated the era of office wireless networks. In May 1998 John Hennessy (of MIPS fame) and Teresa Meng of Stanford University opened in Santa Clara a startup named Atheros that specialized in chipsets aimed at wireless local area networks, later known as "Wi-Fi networks".

The story of Wi-Fi had begun in 1985, when the US government had made the so-called "garbage bands" (900MHz, 2.4GHz and 5.8GHz) available to anybody. In 1988 Victor Hayes of NCR (a company that was considering connecting wireless cash registers) and Bruce Tuch of Bell Labs had begun working on a wireless standard similar (in purpose) to the one devised for the Ethernet. This standard-defining committee, that came to be called 802.11, took almost a decade to complete its research, but eventually in 1997 the specifications were published. In this case it was a government decision (not a technological invention) and it was cooperation (not competition) that created the vast market of Wi-Fi devices.

As wireless LANs moved to the home, this would turn out to be a lucrative market. Marvell was started in 1995 in Santa Clara by Indonesian-born Sehat Sutardjia, his Chinese-born wife Weili Dai and his brother Pantas. It was a fabless maker of semiconductors used in data storage and mostly serving Asian companies. Marvell too would rapidly jump onto the wireless bandwagon.

Gadgets

This was also the age of the gadgets propelled by digital technology but decoupled from the computer industry.

In the arena of videogames, in 1995 Sony introduced the Playstation, one of the most popular platforms of all times. In 1998 sales of videogame consoles in the US alone amounted to $6.2 billion, which dwarfed the sales of videogame software on personal computers ($1.8 billion). The situation had reversed itself one more time, and now the videogame console was rapidly gaining, thanks to a combination of lower prices and much improved performance.

Progress in graphics video, animation, and audio continued at a rapid pace. In 1995 the Moving Picture Experts Group (MPEG) of the International Organization for Standardization (ISO) published the "mp3" standard (more properly, MPEG-1 Layer 3) for digital audio and video compression, largely the 1989 thesis of German student Karlheinz Brandenburg. Mp3 had been designed to compress video and audio into the bit-rate of a CD. While Mp3 proved inadequate for videos, it became a very popular format for digital music. In March 1998 Korean-based Saehan Information Systems released the MPMan F10, the first portable Mp3 player, capable of storing nine songs.

Digital media companies proliferated around San Francisco's South of Market (SoMA) district, an area previously known mostly for night-clubs and abandoned warehouses that was now nicknamed "Multimedia Gulch." More than 35,000 people worked in the multimedia sector in San Francisco in 1999. Many of them were self-employed or worked for small companies: there were almost 1,000 multimedia businesses. The Multimedia Gulch briefly transplanted Silicon Valley's model to the "city."

Ironically, the company that had pioneered 3D graphics in the Bay Area was the exception to the general euphoria. Silicon Graphics' spectacular growth peaked in 1995: its market capitalization reached $7 billion in 1995 and revenues were $2.2 billion. However, the company began a rapid decline as it seemed to live in a different world where the Internet did not exist. It mostly specialized in visual effects for Hollywood.

A successful movie, John Lasseter 's "Toy Story" (that premiered in November 1995), made history for being the first feature-length computer-animated film. Lasseter, a former Walt Disney animator, worked at Lucasfilm under Ed Catmull at a groundbreaking computer-animated short, "The Adventures of Andre and Wally B" (1984), for which they used even a Cray supercomputer. When Jobs purchased Lucasfilms in 1986 and turned it into Pixar, Lasseter was given the power and freedom to invest in that technology, but it took almost a decade to come out with a full-length film. This followed the short animated films made by Pacific Data Images (PDI) since the mid-1980s and was followed by their first feature films: "Antz" (1998), "Shrek" (2001) and "Madagascar" (2005). Personal computers, instead, had to live with humbler features. For example, in 1997 RealNetworks introduced RealVideo to play videos on a computer, but it still used a proprietary format.

Gadgets started to infringe on TV. Introduced in the Bay Area in 1998, TiVo, developed by former Silicon Graphics executives Jim Barton and Mike Ramsay, was a digital video recorder capable of digitizing and compressing analog video signal from a television set and of storing it onto a computer's hard-disk. (The company had originally been founded in 1997 as Teleworld). At that point the tv viewer was able to do with television programs what a computer user could do with data, except that it completely changed the experience of watching television because it gave viewers control over "when" they watched television programs. A TiVo user could watch a program at any time, as many times as she wanted, and could fastforward through commercials and pause during a live program. This receiver, that sat on top of the television set and looked like a VCR, could store up to 40 hours of programming, and it could be programmed to record an entire season of a television series. It was a relatively simple idea but it changed forever the definition of "live event" and ended the age in which all viewers were synchronized on the same program."

A hyped event of 1996 in Silicon Valley was the release of a hand-held pen-based computer called Palm Pilot. It was a computer with no keyboard, whose user interface was simply a screen on which the user could write in natural language. The founder of Palm, Jeff Hawkins, had studied automated hand-written text recognition at UC Berkeley. It was the first pen-based user interface to gain wide acceptance. In 1998 the Palm Pilot had almost 80% of the market for palm-sized computers, and in 1999 it would enjoy four consecutive quarters of triple-digit revenue growth. Palm had already been purchased by US Robotics in 1995, which then merged with 3Com in June 1997.

Jeff Hawkins, Founder of Palm Computing (2010)

The most sensational high-tech product introduced abroad in 1996 was probably Nokia's 9000 Communicator, which invented the category of "smart phones." Palm had tried to create a "personal digital assistant" (PDA) starting with a computer. Finnish conglomerate Nokia, the world leader in mobile phones, started with a mobile phone, adding computer capabilities based on an Intel 386 processor running Berkeley Softworks' GEOS operating environment on top of DOS. In 1994 IBM had done something similar with its short-lived Simon. The Nokia 9000 ran over GSM, the IBM Simon ran over Bell Labs' AMPS.

In 1997 Psion, the British company that had invented the personal digital assistant, adopted the ARM processor in its Series 5 in conjunction with a brand new operating system that was later renamed Symbian, a joint venture with Ericsson, Nokia, Panasonic, and Motorola.

One of the most daring gadgets introduced in the mid-1990s was a by-product of the feud between Microsoft and Oracle. In 1996 Oracle introduced a disk-less desktop computer, the network computer. Larry

Ellison preached a world in which data did not have to reside in the house or the office of the user, but could reside on the Internet. Ellison envisioned a future in which the computing power was on the Internet and the user's machine was simply a tool to access that computing power. Indirectly, this was also a world in which desktop computers had no need for Microsoft's operating systems. The net computer was the counterpart to General Magic's hand-held device, and yet another premonition of "cloud computing." Alas, it also became another embarrassing Silicon Valley flop.

Until then connecting devices to computer had involved different cables for different kinds of devices. In 1996 an Intel team led by the Indian-born scientist Ajay Bhatt introduced the specifications for USB (Universal Serial Bus), a method that would soon greatly simplify the lives of consumers worldwide and dramatically increase the number of devices that can be connected to a computer.

In 1998 Sony launched its own removable flash-memory card format, the Memory Stick, and "memory stick" would remain the affectionate term for all removable flash-memory units that one could carry in the pocket. In 1999 SanDisk, Matsushita and Toshiba unveiled yet another standard for NAND flash memories: the Secure Digital (SD) format. The SD card would displace CompactFlash as the most popular flash-memory format for consumer electronics the way that CompactFlash had displaced SmartMedia in the previous decade.

A major revolution was taking place in hard disks, a revolution that would soon allow small cheap computers to store large images and videos. In 1997 IBM introduced the first hard disk that used the GMR effect for its read-out heads. The Giant Magnetoresistive (GMR) effect had been discovered in 1988 by Albert Fert and Peter Gruenberg. Stuart Parkin at IBM's Almaden Research Center applied it to data storage and created the "spin valve" that was used in the Deskstar 16GP Titan. This new technique would rapidly improve the storage of extremely densely-packed information. Within a decade Hitachi (having bought IBM's business) would release the Deskstar 7K1000, the first hard-disk drive capable of storing one terabytes of data.

3D Printing

The inkjet printer had been popularized in the 1980s by Hewlett-Packard and Canon. A more complex kind of inkjet technology, called 3DP (also known as "powder and inkjet" and "Z printing") was developed at the MIT in 1993 by Michael Cima and Emanuel Sachs for printing objects, not pages. But Silicon Valley was still indifferent to 3D printing technology and 3DP was implemented far from the Bay Area: in 1996

South Carolina's Z Corp introduced the first 3D printer based on the MIT technology, the Z402, and in 2000 Z Corp would introduce the first multicolor 3D printer, the Z402C; and in 1997 Sanders Prototype (later Solidscape) of New Hampshire introduced the ModelMaker wax printer based on the MIT inkjet technology. In 1997 Los Angeles-based Soligen used the inkjet technology of the MIT for printing cast-metal parts and renamed it Direct Shell Production Casting (or DSPC). Another system for building metal parts, also based on MIT's 3DP inkjet technology, was ProMetal, introduced in 1999 by ExtrudeHone of Pittsburgh (later renamed Ex One). Another technique that uses a laser beam to fuse together powders, called Selective Laser Melting (SLM), was invented in 1995 at the Fraunhofer Institute in Germany. Electro Optical Systems (EOS) of Germany, that in 1991 had introduced one of the first stereolithography machines and in 1994 had introduced one of the first SLS systems in the world, turned SLM into its Eosint M250. Frank Arcella set up his company AeroMet (actually a subsidiary of MTS) only in 1997 to commercialize LAM printers. In 1996 Direct Metal Deposition (DMD), the technique invented at MIT for metal parts, mutated into Laser Engineered Net Shaping (LENS) at the Sandia National Laboratories in New Mexico. Invented by Dave Keicher, it was commercialized by Optomec in 1998.

Silicon Valley was too busy with the dotcom boom to pay attention to 3D printing.

GPUs

Personal computer graphics of the 16-bit, 2D generation was dominated for a while by the Canadian company Array Technology Inc (ATI), manufacturers of 1987's EGA Wonder and 1988's VGA Wonder. They had been founded in 1985 by three Hong Kong immigrants (Kwok Yuan Ho, Lee Lau and Benny Lau).

Computer games ran on DOS because it was impossible to achieve high performance on Windows. The first major improvement came with the introduction of 32-bit operating systems, and not so much 1991's System 7 for the Apple Macintosh, that initially charmed few developers, but Windows 95, introduced by Microsoft in 1995. The second important factor was the drop in DRAM price: in 1995 Intel introduced the low-cost 430FX chipset that supported Extended data out DRAM. Regular DRAM was becoming as fast as the expensive Video DRAM (or VRAM). Finally, standards became to emerge. In 1992 Silicon Graphics released an API for both 2D and 3D graphics, OpenGL (an evolution of their proprietary IRIS Graphical Library), that was meant for their traditional Unix market but became a standard for PC gaming in 1996 when Texas-based game developer id Software, that had revolutionized PC gaming with 1993's "Doom", ported its stylish 3D game "Quake" to Windows using OpenGL. In 1996 Microsoft released its own API, Direct3D (an evolution of the technology developed by British company RenderMorphics, founded in 1992 by Servan Keondjian and Doug Rabson). For a while, however, the winner was neither Direct3D nor OpenGL: Brian Hook of 3Dfx Interactive, a company founded in 1994 in San Jose by three former Silicon Graphics employees (Ross Smith, Gary Tarolli and Scott Sellers), wrote Glide API in 1995. Glide versions of Activision's "MechWarrior 2" (1996) and id Software's "Quake II" (1997) were among the hits that legitimized Glide as the ruling standard of the late 1990s.

The net result of these developments was a boom in 3D graphic cards for personal computers, aiming at the mainstream consumer. The first consumer 3D-graphics accelerator cards came to the market in 1996: 3Dfx Interactive (founded in 1994 in San Jose by former employees of Silicon Graphics) introduced Voodoo1, the accelerator that truly left behind the world of 2D graphics; Array Technology (a Canadian company acquired in 2006 by Advanced Micro Devices) launched its 3D RAGE; and Rendition, founded in 1993 in Mountain View, introduced the V1000 chipset based on a RISC architecture. Brian Hook at 3Dfx wrote the Glide API that would become the dominant 3D graphics API for videogame designers. While this trio competed for supremacy, the boost in speed generated a boom in videogames (with "video" truly meaning "video"). Then in 1999 Nvidia's GeForce 256 virtually defined the modern "graphics processing unit" (GPU), 2000's GeForce 2 GigaTexel Shader (GTS) hit 1 gigatexel/second (1 billion filtered textured pixels per second, a texel or texture pixel being the fundamental unit of texture space), and 2001's GeForce 3 (released three months after NVIDIA acquired 3dfx) would introduce pixel shading, the technology for 21st century videogames.

Biotech

In biotech the state-of-the-art moved fast. The Human Genome Project had been slow to get started, like all big projects, but at last in April 1996 human DNA sequencing began in earnest at several universities funded by the National Institute of Health. Most of these research centers were using the sequencing machines of Applied Biosystems, acquired (in February 1993) by East-coast pharmaceutical colossus Perkin-Elmer. Also in 1996, Sydney Brenner (Francis Crick's successor at Cambridge University, now at the Scripps Institute in San Diego) founded the Molecular Sciences Institute in Berkeley, and the year that Monsanto, a multinational corporation, acquired Calgene.

For the media 1996 was the year of cloning. A team assembled by Ian Wilmut at the Roslin Institute in Britain cloned "Dolly" the sheep, the first time that a mammal had been cloned in a lab from adult cells. The experiment was centered on the ideas of Keith Campbell, who in 1995 had already succeeded in cloning a pair of lambs, albeit from embryonic cells. In May 1999 Geron of Menlo Park bought the rights on Roslin's nuclear-transfer technology for $25 million.

PE Biosystems, the new name of Applied Biosystems after being acquired by Perkin-Elmer, had become a wealthy company with revenues of $871 million by 1998. It sold sequencing machines to the centers of the Human Genome Project. The company's new President, Michael Hunkapiller, a former assistant of Leroy Hood at CalTech, boldly attacked his academic customers by deciding to launch a private project to decode the human genome before the Human Genome Project. Basically, he was convinced that the result depended on his machines, not on the army of biologists of the research centers (and that private industry is more efficient than government bureaucracies). He hired a man who shared his passion for automated genetic processing, Craig Venter of Maryland's Institute for Genomic Research, where the first sequencing ("mapping") of a living being's genome had been carried out in 1995. Venter had fallen out with Haseltine after their mutual investor Steinberg had died in 1997, since Venter was more interested in the science and Haseltine in creating a multibillion-dollar pharmaceutical conglomerate.

In May 1998 Michael Hunkapiller and Venter set up a new company, Celera Genomics, which soon relocated to the Bay Area (Alameda, near Oakland). Technically, both Biosystems of Foster City and Celera Genomics of Alameda were owned by Applera, a spin-off of Perkin-Elmer's Life Sciences Division which in 2000 also became the official new name of Perkin-Elmer. However, in 2006 Applera renamed itself Applied Biosystems and spun off Celera Genomics. It was a confusing business story that still left two tightly related companies, one engaged in building machines and the other one in using those machines to sequence DNA. The main investor in both was Cuban-born businessman Tony White, the head of their parent company (which used to be called Perkin-Elmer) who had brokered the deal between Venter and Hunkapiller. Celera Genomics filled a staff of distinguished scholars, including Nobel laureate Hamilton Smith, and bought 300 of Applied Biosystems' most advanced machines to create the world's largest automated factory for mapping DNA.

A new method to sequence DNA ("sequencing by synthesis technology") was devised in 1997 at Cambridge University by Shankar Balasubramanian and David Klenerman, who in 1998 founded Solexa in Hayward 9acquired in 2007 by Illumina).

The Israeli-born computer scientist Victor Markowitz, who had developed a data management system for genome databases at the Lawrence Berkeley Labs, founded the bioinformatics company Gene

Logic in Berkeley in 1997 to market a database management system for gene expression data to biotech companies.

In 1997 the Department of Energy established the Joint Genome Institute (JGI) in an industrial park in Walnut Creek (northeast of Berkeley) to coordinate the three main biological laboratories involved in genomics: Lawrence Berkeley Labs, Lawrence Livermore Labs and Los Alamos (located in New Mexico). In 2010 JGI would hire Victor Markowitz of Gene Logic as chief information officer.

The local universities were central to biotech's development. In the 1990s Stanford held 124 biotech patents, SRI International had 50, and the University of California as a whole had 321 (mainly at Berkeley and San Francisco). Some private companies had many patents too: Genentech 335, Incyte 322, Alza 238, Syntex 168, Chiron 167. Genentech's former employees had opened more than thirty Bay Area-based startups. South San Francisco, where the Genentech campus was located, had become a major R&D center for biomedicine. For example, Exelixis and Cytokinesis had been started in 1997 a few blocks from Genentech) Investment in biotech companies peaked at $1 billion in the year 2000, up from $668 million in 1999. Between 1995 and 2000 $3 billion in venture capital had created 71 startups. At the beginning of 2000 the Bay Area's 90 publicly-traded biotech companies reached a market capitalization of $82 billion. Meanwhile, in 1998 James Thomson at University of Wisconsin and John Gearhart at Johns Hopkins University reported that they had grown human embryonic stem cells.

As biotech boomed, nanotechnology finally began to take off in the second half of the 1990s. One important startup was NeoPhotonics, founded in 1997 by Timothy Jenks and specializing in photonic integrated circuits.

A merge of biotech and nanotech (Micro-Electro-Mechanical Systems or MEMS) took place in 1996 with the founding of Cepheid in Sunnyvale by former Syntex executive Thomas Gutshall, Bill McMillan (who had invented a rapid automated analysis system at Syntex), MEMS pioneer Kurt Petersen (of Transensory fame), and Greg Kovacs of Stanford's Center for Integrated Systems. Their goal was to build machines that perform rapid molecular testing, typically to detect infectious disease and cancer, i.e. to provide DNA test results when and where they are needed.

Culture and Society

San Francisco's counterculture reacted again in its own idiosyncratic manner to the capitalistic culture of Silicon Valley. Since Silicon Valley had adopted the religion of ever faster and cheaper products, in 1996, Stewart Brand of Whole Earth fame and Danny Hillis, who had designed the supercomputer Connection Machine at MIT, established the "Long

Now Foundation" to promote slower and better thinking, long-term thinking.

Underground subversive, so called "guerrilla", art staged a significant coup in 1997 when Brian Goggin, coming out of the Burning Man culture, took over the dilapidated Hugo Hotel on 6th and Howard streets and started hanging home-built furniture provided by about 100 volunteers from the hotel's walls. ("Defenestration" would be razed in 2014, after the disorderly invasion of Silicon Valley and consequent gentrification of the city).

"The planetary display for the 10,000 year clock of the Long Now Foundation (2014)"

Meanwhile, pop and dance musicians such as Dan Nakamura, Matmos, Kit Clayton, Kid 606, Blectum From Blechdom and Irr. App. (Ext.) were pushing the envelope of digital music, showing what could be done with a simple laptop, while the psychedelic tradition survived in Devendra Banhart.

During the 1990s the population of the Bay Area grew by 13%. The San Francisco- Oakland- San Jose metropolitan region had seven million people in 2000, making it the fifth largest metropolitan area in the US.

The Anthropology of the Untouchables

In the 1990s the median income in Santa Clara County was almost twice the median income in the US, but within the Valley the income gap kept increasing. There were at least three classes with widely different income levels.

The common laborers (such as the security guards who worked night shifts, the cleaning people, and the clerks of the gas stations) had a low income. It was difficult for them to afford the cost of living of the Bay Area. Many of them resided in the East or South Bay, where rent was cheaper, and many of them lived in old-fashioned familiar nuclei. They were not very visible: you had to take one of the freeways into the Bay Area very early in the morning to see them commute to work from distant places.

Then there was the huge mass of engineers, who could afford a nice car and a nice apartment. However, the cost of living was such that many of them shared a house or an apartment with someone else. Those who bought a house most likely bought a town home in a subdivision. Each subdivision provided long lines (or circles) of identical homes with minimal separation from each other. These were the most visible inhabitants of the valley, stuck in traffic during rush hours.

The upper class consisted of the rich: either hereditary rich or beneficiaries of the computer boom. Their company was acquired, their company's stock had skyrocketed, or they were just highly paid executives. This third class was much larger than in any other part of the world. Entire areas of Atherton, Woodside, Portola Valley, and Los Gatos were carpeted with multimillion-dollar homes.

And yet the lower class was dreaming of sending its children to school so that they would become engineers, and the engineering class was dreaming of becoming millionaires, so both castes happily accepted their subordinate roles.

Finally, there was the old generation who bought a home in the 1960s and lived a much more relaxed life in single-family detached houses, most of them with a swimming pool and a large backyard. They paid very little for their house before the computer boom. During the 1990s, as they began to retire, many of them sold their homes to the younger generation of the computer boom. This generation of ordinary middle-class families quietly faded away, enjoying the profits from their investment in real estate but rapidly obsolete in the digital age.

Survivors: Paypal, Wikipedia, and Genomics (1999-2002)

The Bubble Bursts

The party was wild. The dotcom boom was driving all sorts of indicators through the roof.

Between 1998 and 1999 venture-capital investments in Silicon Valley firms increased more than 90% from $3.2 billion to $6.1 billion. In 1999 there were 457 IPOs in the US. The vast majority of the companies that went public were high-tech startups and about 100 were directly related to the Internet. An impressive number were based in Silicon Valley. In 2000 the number of public companies in Silicon Valley reached 417. In 2000 venture-capital investment in the US peaked at $99.72 billion or 1% of GDP, mostly going to software (17.4%), telecommunications (15.4%), networking (10.0%) and media (9.1%). By the end of 1999, the US had 250 billionaires, and thousands of new millionaires had been created in just one year. Microsoft was worth $450 billion, the most valued company in the world, even if it was still many times smaller than General Motors. Bill Gates was the world's richest man with a fortune of $85 billion.

One of the worst deals ever in the history of Silicon Valley took place in January 1999, when @Home acquired a struggling Excite for $6.7 billion. It was at the time the largest Internet-related merger yet. Later that year Excite refused to buy for less than one million dollars the technology of a new search engine developed by two Stanford students, Google.

A symbolic event took place in January 2000 when America Online (AOL), the pioneer of dial-up Internet access, acquired Time Warner, the world's largest media company. A humble startup of the "net economy" had just bought a much larger company of the old "brick and mortar" economy. At one point or another in the early months of 2000s, Microsoft, Cisco, and Intel all passed the $400 billion mark by market valuation, and the only company of the old economy that could compete with them was General Electric.

Then came the financial crash of March 2000. The dotcom bubble burst even faster than it had expanded. Within 30 months (between March 2000 and October 2002) the technology-heavy Nasdaq lost 78% of its value, erasing $4.2 trillion of wealth. The losses in Silicon Valley were astronomical. In 2001 there were only 76 IPOs.

There were multiple causes for the crash, i.e. for the inflated values of dotcom stocks. One was certainly the gullible and inexperienced "day traders" who enthusiastically purchased worthless stocks. Another one was the incompetent or dishonest Wall Street analysts who created ad-hoc reports to justify the aberrations of those worthless stocks. A final boost may have come from the US central bank, the Fed, which pumped more money into the system in late 1999 so that people had cash and wouldn't need to stockpile more for a Y2K Armageddon.

If this were not enough, the large IT companies based on the East Coast were probably hurt more by the end of the Y2K panic than by the dotcom crash. The first of January of 2000 came and went without any apocalypse. The Y2K paranoia was rapidly forgotten, as if it had never existed. The last day of December of 1999 would remain the best day ever to fly, because planes were empty: people were so afraid that airplanes would crash all over the world. Unfortunately, the Y2K paranoia had created an easily predictable "boom and bust" situation. Billions of dollars had been spent in acquiring new hardware and software before 1999, but all of this, by definition, came to an end one minute after midnight. It was one of the few cases in which a "bust" was widely advertised before it happened.

There was no question that the dotcom bubble had gone out of control, but the drop in IT investment after the Y2K scare exacerbated the problem.

The direct impact of the stock-market crash was on jobs. Half of all dotcoms shut down. The other half had to restructure themselves to live in a new age where growth was proportional to (not independent of) profits. They needed to make money, and, failing real revenues, the only solution was to cut costs.

Silicon Valley learned how to trim costs in the early 2000s. On top of the layoffs due to cost cutting, there were three additional problems. First of all, the number of software engineers coming out of universities had massively increased to keep up with demand: but now there were no jobs for these young graduates. Secondly, Silicon Valley companies had begun outsourcing jobs to India: 62% of India's exports of software in 2000 went to the US. Thirdly, the US government had just bent to the demands of the IT industry to increase the number of visas for foreign IT workers, causing a flood of immigrants: 32% of Silicon Valley's high-skilled workers were foreign-born in 2000, and mostly from Asia. These combined factors caused the first massive decline in employment in the Bay Area since the end of the Gold Rush era.

The 2001 recession was significant because California, and the Bay Area in particular, had been largely immune from recessions since the Great Depression. Recessions in California tended to be milder, while recoveries were faster and stronger. In 2001 the opposite happened: California fared a lot worse than the rest of the nation.

Out of the Ruins

The Nasdaq crash did not mean that the Internet was already dying. On the contrary, in 2000 it was estimated that 460 million people in the world were connected to the Internet and that 10 billion e-mail messages a day were exchanged over the Internet. In 2001 alone 42 million users traded $9.3 billion worth of goods on eBay. For the first time, even a small business in a remote town could reach a market of millions of people. To mention just one emblematic statistic, Merrill Lynch reported that trades by institutional clients over its e-commerce platforms amounted to $1.9 trillion in 2000. According to the US Census Bureau, the grand total of e-commerce was just short of one trillion dollars in 2000. 94% of e-commerce was B2B (Business to Business, basically the Internet-based version of the decade-old Electronic Data Interchange) and not yet B2C. Retail e-sales (B2C, Business to Consumer) were only $29 billion in 2000, but in the following years they would increase rapidly, with a double-digit year-over-year growth rate.

Some of the most innovative ideas for the Web emerged out of the Bay Area right in the middle of the crisis. In February 1999 Marc Benioff founded Saleforce.com to move business applications to the Internet, pioneering "cloud" computing (you don't need to own a computer in order to run a software application). SalesForce launched the "software-as-a-service" (SaaS) revolution: corporations were no longer required to purchase, install and run business software in house, but they could instead pay for it only when using it. This would become a trillion-dollar market within less than two decades.

eHow.com was founded in March 1999 to provide a practical encyclopedia to solve problems in all sorts of fields via articles written by experts in those fields. Friendster, launched in 2002 in Morgan Hill, south of San Jose, by Jonathan Abrams, allowed people to create "social networks." Blogger.com, founded in August 1999 by Evan Williams and Meg Hourihan, enabled ordinary Internet users to create their own "blogs," or personal journals. Dave Winer, a blogger whose blog Scripting News (1997) was influential in Silicon Valley, pioneered audioblogging with "Radio Userland" (2000).

Even music search was affected. Tim Westergren, an alumnus of Stanford's Center for Computer Research in Music and Acoustics (CCRMA), had devised a search engine for music called Savage Beast and had launched the Music Genome Project out of his Menlo Park home to archive songs based on their musical genes and calculate musical proximity (the algorithm was largely the work of co-founder Will Glaser): the search engine simply looked for songs whose genome was similar to a given song. In January 2000 that project website evolved into Pandora, an Internet-based streaming radio simulator that "broadcast" music based on the listener's preference: given a song, Pandora produced a customized radio program of similar songs.

Tim Westergren of Pandora

The smartphone application Shazam, designed by Stanford alumnus Avery Wang and launched in 2002 in Britain as "2580", allowed users to identify songs.

When in 2000 Yahoo opted for Google's search engine, Inktomi read the ink on the wall (that Google was going to wipe out the competition) and decided to invest in a new field: streaming media. Inktomi paid $1.3 billion for FastForward Networks, which specialized in large-scale delivery of radio and television broadcasting over the Web in the wake of Seattle's RealNetworks. In December 2001 Listen.com launched Rhapsody, a service that provided streaming on-demand access to a library of digital music (RealNetworks acquired Listen.com in August 2003).

Relatively few businesses were accepting credit cards for transactions on the Internet. Billpoint, founded in 1998 in Redwood City by Jason May and Jay Shen, tried to change that by offering a simple method to transfer money between individuals. It was used for purchases on websites such as Excite@Home and eBay, and it was acquired in 1999 by eBay that re-launched it in 2000, but a more formidable enemy was going to dominate that sector.

Virtual Money

The late boom bought dreams of virtual money. German-born Peter Thiel, founder in 1987 of the conservative student magazine Stanford Review and a successful currency trader, funded Confinity in December 1998 in Palo Alto with two editors of the Stanford Review, Luke Nosek and Ken Howery. The company was the brainchild of cryptography expert Max Levchin. He was a Ukrainian Jew from Chicago who brought with him a group of University of Illinois alumni, including Russel Simmons and Jeremy Stoppelman (all indirect beneficiaries of the National Center for Supercomputing Applications' Mosaic project). Their goal was to develop a system for Palm Pilot users to send ("beam") money to other Palm Pilot users, i.e. to make payments without using cash, cheques, or credit cards.

The first entities to be impressed by Confinity were European: Nokia and Deutsche Bank used Confinity software to "beam" from a Palm Pilot their $3 million investment in the company to Thiel. Meanwhile, X.com had been founded also in Palo Alto by South African-born Elon Musk in March 1999 after he had sold his first company Zip2 (its software powered websites for news media companies). X.com offered online banking services including a way to email money.

In 2000 Confinity and X.com merged to form PayPal. Confinity's original concept evolved into a web-based service to send money over the Internet to an e-mail address, therefore bypassing banks and even borders. Thiel's utopian vision of a universal currency was embedded in much anti-government rhetoric that reflected the traditional anti-establishment mood of the Bay Area from a right-wing perspective.

However, ironically, PayPal quickly had to devote most of its efforts to fight fraud. For example, to make sure that the user was a human being and not a program, Dave Gausebeck and Levchin resurrected a technique invented by AltaVista in 1997. Their display blurred and distorted characters and asked the users to enter them on the keyboard. Basically it was a reverse Turing test (a machine that tries to figure out if it is talking to a human), which became popularly known as CAPTCHA (Completely Automated Public Turing test to tell Computers and Humans Apart).

PayPal's success was immediate. It beat all its competitors that had preceded it in trying to help consumers sell and buy over the Internet. Paypal was another case, like Netscape before it, of the public choosing a standard before either government or corporations could do so. In October 2001 PayPal already boasted 12 million registered users. Its IPO in early 2002 netted $1.2 billion dollars. The establishment, however, struck back: both banks and local governments tried in every legal way to derail PayPal. Eventually, PayPal found that the only way to survive was to sell itself to eBay in July 2002, for $1.5 billion.

PayPal was an impressive nest of talents, and extremely young ones among its 200 employees. Levchin was 26 at the IPO, Musk was 31, and Thiel was the oldest at 35. Half of those 200 would quit by 2006 and found or staff new startups. In December 2002 Reid Hoffman of PayPal launched LinkedIn in Mountain View, the main business-oriented social networking site. In 2002 PayPal's co-founder Elon Musk founded Space Explorations Technology or SpaceX to develop space transportation (in December 2010 his Falcon 9 would become the first private spaceship to orbit Earth). Roelof Botha became a partner at Sequoia Capital, and Thiel started his own venture-capital fund, Clarium Capital. In the following years former PayPal employees would start Yelp (Jeremy Stoppelman and Russel Simmons in 2004), YouTube (Chad Hurley, Steven Chen and Jawed Karim in 2005), Slide (Max Levchin in 2005), and Halcyon Molecular (Luke Nosek in 2009).

It was not just a mafia (as the "Paypal Mafia" was widely known in Silicon Valley), but a self-sustaining and cooperative group because it included venture capitalists, entrepreneurs, managers, and engineers. PayPal was neither the only one, nor the most advanced, method of online payment. For example, Pay By Touch, founded in 2002 in San Francisco by John Rogers, allowed users to pay with a swipe of their finger on a biometric sensor.

By 2015 the companies founded by former PayPal employees would be worth more than $60 billion (in order of valuation: Tesla, LinkedIn, Palantir, SpaceX, Yelp, YouTube, Yammer), a staggering amount given that there were only about 200 PayPal employees. No other corporation after Fairchild had created such a lucrative family tree. As Conner Forrest wrote, "PayPal's success rate relative to billion-dollar companies is 350 times that of Google."

The Old Offices of Paypal (2010)

Monetizing the Web

In June 2000 Google had achieved the feat of indexing one billion pages, a world record. Google's technology was clearly superior in many ways to the technology of the other web-search contenders. In January

2001 Google hired Wayne Rosing, a Silicon Valley veteran who had overseen the Lisa at Apple and Java at SUN. In February Google completed its first acquisition (an archive of the old Usenet, dating back to 1995) to create an extra application (Google Groups). It was the same tactic used in the past by Microsoft to create its portfolio of applications. Venture capitalists John Doerr of Kleiner-Perkins and Michael Moritz of Sequoia Capital became more involved in steering the business of the company, which eventually led to hiring another Silicon Valley veteran, Eric Schmidt (Zilog, Xerox PARC, SUN), as chairman. In 2002 Google got the support of AOL, the new owner of Netscape and a rival of Microsoft.

Eric Schmidt of Google

The Faustian deal for Google's rapid success was AdWords, a pay-per-click advertising system, by far its main source of revenues. Google had started selling "sponsored links" in 2000, a practice already followed by their rivals. This was a manual process involving a salesperson and it mainly targeted large corporations. AdWords, instead, introduced in 2002, was mostly automated and, because it slashed the price of posting an advert on the Web, it targeted medium and small businesses that had been reluctant to advertise on the Web.

The days of a commercial-free Web were not only over: Google defacto turned the Web into an advertising tool that incidentally also contained information. The business model was the ultimate in cynicism. Millions of website editors spread all over the world added content to the Web on a daily basis, and Google used that colossal amount of free content as a vehicle to sell advertising services to businesses. Web surfers used Google to search for information, but Google "used" them to create the audience that justified the amount it charged for advertising. Both the producers of content and the consumers of content were getting no money out of this splendid business model. Intermediaries had always made money in business, but this case was different. Google was an intermediary of sorts in the flow of content from producer to consumer and was making money even though there was no money transaction between producer and consumer. The money was coming from an external entity that wanted to sell its products to the consumer. Every time someone added a webpage to the Web it made Google more powerful. Unlike traditional intermediaries, which made money by charging a fee per each transaction, Google never charged the user anything for searching. Yahoo and Excite had already understood the power of this business plan but Google was the one that implemented it to perfection.

Except for the few headline stories, the new Silicon Valley startup was very different from the exuberant ones of the 1990s. The term "ramen profitable" was coined by venture capitalist Paul Graham to refer to a startup that makes enough money to pay the bills while the founders aim for a big score.

Google's Campus, formerly the Silicon Graphics' Offices (2010)

Winners and Losers

Many of the established Silicon Valley companies did well through the recession. For example, Oracle in 2000 abandoned the client-server architecture in favor of the browser-based architecture and in the first quarter of 2001 posted growing revenues of $2.3 billion. Siebel at that time owned almost 50% of the customer relationship management (CRM) market in 1999 and minted money.

Advanced Micro Devices (AMD) beat Intel to a historical milestone. In February 2000 its microprocessor Athlon broke the 1000 megahertz (1 gigahertz) barrier. Intel's Pentium III (running at the same speed) came out a few months later. However, 2001 decimated the sector. Revenues for the semiconductor industry plunged more than 30% in 2001, with Intel alone declining 21% from $33.7 billion in 2000 to $26.5 billion.

British chip manufacturer ARM had been selling embeddable RISC chips since 1991, and in 1998 its technology was mature enough that it was licensed by Qualcomm for its cell-phone technology. By 2001 ARM dominated the market for embedded RISC chips, particularly for cell-phone applications. Only Intel, IBM, AMD and Taiwan-based fabless VIA owned a license for Intel's x86 technology, while ARM had made it very easy for anyone to license its technology. Besides the merits of its chip, its business model was friendlier to manufacturers interested in developing their own custom processors. It was no surprise that dozens of other companies had done so.

Palm was in troubled waters: by the end of 2001 its revenues had collapsed 44%.

Progress in smartphones was accelerating. In 2001 Nokia introduced the smartphone 5510 that featured a QWERTY keyboard, SMS, a digital music player, a game console, a calculator and FM radio. In March 2002 the Canadian company Research In Motion (a spin-off of the University of Waterloo) introduced the "smart phone" BlackBerry 5810. It was a hand-held device with a real keyboard that allowed users to check e-mail, make phone calls, send text messages, and browse the Web. The telephone had just been turned into a wireless email terminal, and email had become a mobile service. Silicon Valley took notice and in October 2002 Danger, founded by former WebTV's employee Andy Rubin in Palo Alto, released the mobile phone Hiptop, later renamed T-Mobile Sidekick.

However, Silicon Valley scarcely cared when Ericsson, Nokia, Toshiba, IBM and Intel joined together to form the Bluetooth Special Interest Group to promote the short-range wireless technology invented by Ericsson that would become the standard for the headphones of mobile phones and for many other devices. In 2000 Ericsson introduced the first mobile phone with built-in Bluetooth, the T36.

In July 1999 Hewlett-Packard appointed Carly Fiorina as CEO: she became the first female CEO of a company listed in the Dow Jones

Industrial Average, another tribute to the Bay Area's propensity to encourage diversity. In May 2002 Hewlett-Packard acquired Compaq, becoming the largest manufacturer of servers, the second largest computer company in the world after IBM, and the only serious contender for Dell in the personal-computer market. It looked like after the breathtaking ups and downs of the personal-computer market, the company that was still standing was one of the older generation. Because Compaq had purchased DEC, HP now contained a division that contained a division that was the old rival DEC. Symbolically, this represented the end of the war between Silicon Valley and Boston. At the peak of that war nobody would have imagined that some day DEC would end up being just a small division within a Silicon Valley company. And DEC had been the very originator of the "Route 128" boom in the Boston area.

The other surviving giant of the old generation, IBM, had pretty much left the personal-computer market, but dominated software services. In 2000 software and services accounted for 50% of IBM's business. The history of computer manufacturing looked like a vast graveyard of distinguished names, from Univac to DEC to Compaq.

Meanwhile, a new discipline was being born, or, at least, named. In 1999 a panel on "Big Data" was held at the Visualization Conference in San Francisco, featuring, among others, presentations by Steve Bryson and David Kenwright.

Corporate-tech

Web-based commerce was there to stay and some of the obscure winners of those years were companies that could see beyond the temporary debacle. In particular, e-commerce, being entirely software-driven, lent itself to better analytics. During the following decade a huge number of startups would try to capitalize on this fact, continuing a trend towards retail sales optimization that had been going on in Corporate America ever since. DemandTec, founded in 1999 in San Mateo by Stanford's professor of supply chain management Hau Lee and economist Mike Neal, became one of the leaders in analytical software tools for retailers, or Consumer Demand Management (CDM) software. Such products performed a behind-the-scene scientific study of shoppers' behavior on the Web to help e-retailers with their pricing and marketing strategies. This was also one of the early applications of "cloud computing" (software that sits on the Web, invisible to the user) coupled with large-scale data management.

Consumer Multimedia

A sector that showed promise was the whole consumer multimedia business. Photography had gone digital thanks to ever-cheaper digital cameras. Music had gone digital, especially when free software allowed music fans to "rip" CDs into mp3 files. And digital formats for videos were beginning to spread. Consumers needed two things: applications to display and play these digital files, and storage to save them. In 1999 IBM released a 37.5-gigabyte hard-disk drive, at the time the world's largest. In November 2000 Seagate Technology, which had been purchased for $3 billion by Veritas Software, based in Mountain View and specialized in storage management software, smashed that record with the Barracuda 180-gigabyte hard drive. 3PAR was founded in 1999 in Fremont by former SUN executive Jeffrey Price and Indian-born former SUN chief architect Ashok Singhal to deliver shared storage devices. It utilized allocation strategies of "just-enough" and "just-in-time" for increased efficiency.

In 1995 the Israeli company M-Systems, founded in 1989 by Dov Moran, had introduced the first flash-memory drive, and in 1999 it introduced the first USB flash drive, marketed as "a hard disk on a keychain". That was the birth of flash-based solid-state drives, an alternative (with no movable parts) to the electromechanical hard-disk drives (with movable parts, including a spinning disk) that was going to revolutionize the industry. M-Systems was acquired by Milpitas-based flash-memory pioneer SanDisk in 2006.

Meanwhile, in 2000 Microsoft demonstrated the Windows Media Player to play both music and videos under Windows. In January 2001 Apple responded with its iTunes software (available also on Windows in 2003). iTunes was simply a repackaging of a product acquired by Apple in 2000, the digital jukebox SoundJam MP, which had been developed in 1998 by two former Apple engineers, Jeff Robbin and Bill Kincaid, whose project at Apple had ironically been terminated in 1996 when Apple had bought Steve Jobs' NeXT. In October 2001 Apple chose a completely different route from the past: it launched a consumer device, the iPod (designed by Tony Fadell), to play music files. It was basically a "walkman" for mp3s with a five-gigabyte internal hard-disk (a market created in 1998 by South Korea's SaeHan with the world's first MP3 player, the MPMan, and until then dominated by Singapore's Creative Technology with its digital music players Nomad). Apple also defied common wisdom by launching a chain of fashionable Apple Stores, an idea perhaps modeled on what Olivetti did in the 1950s (Olivetti stores such as the one opened on New York's Fifth Avenue in 1954 and especially the one in Venice's St Mark Square of 1959 were created by celebrated architects, the latter by Carlo Scarpa).

The Apple Store in Palo Alto

The history of P2P, one of the big innovations of the era, was mostly based outside the Bay Area. Shawn Fanning, a student at Boston Northeastern University, came up with the idea of a Web-based service to distribute mp3 files, i.e. music, over the Internet. His Napster went online in June 1999. It allowed consumers all over the world to share music files, thus circumventing the entire music industry. The music industry reacted with a lawsuit that eventually shut down Napster in July 2001. It was too late to stop the avalanche, though. Napster inspired a new generation of similar Web-based services, except that the new generation improved Napster's model by using Peer-to-Peer (P2P) architectures.

A P2P service basically facilitates the transfer of files between two computers, but does not physically store the file in between the two computers. Kazaa, for example, was developed in Estonia by Ahti Heinla, Priit Kasesalu and Jaan Tallinn, and introduced in March 2001 by the Dutch company Consumer Empowerment. In July 2001 San Francisco resident Bram Cohen unveiled the P2P file sharing protocol BitTorrent, soon to become the most popular service of this kind. It was faster than previous P2P services because it downloaded a file from many different sources at the same time (if multiple copies were available on multiple servers). These whiz kids became heroes of the counterculture for defying the music industry.

In 2000 the former Yahoo scientist Jim McCoy started Evil Geniuses for a Better Tomorrow to provide a P2P platform, MojoNation, inspired by videogames. The Mojo model came out of the debate on "Agoric computing": how to exploit concepts of free-market economics to solve problems in large-scale computation. In fact, the "mojo" was a cybercurrency, even though it was used to provide balanced and secure computation for a network. EGBT also pioneered a new model of P2P. In

2001 SUN would introduce a similar open-source project, XTA (Juxtapose). In 2001 a Jim McCoy associate, Bram Cohen, created BitTorrent, while another EGBT alumnus, Zooko Wilcox-O'Hearn, turned MojoNation into Mnet.

Napster and BitTorrent relied on a central server. However, Justin Frankel's and Tom Pepper's Gnutella (2000) was conceived in Arizona but it relied on a peer-to-peer network. Another decentralized network was Freenet, originally organized in London a few months later by Irish-born Ian Clarke in 2000. Four employees of Microsoft published "The Darknet and the Future of Content Distribution" (2002), acknowledging the increasing power of inscrutable password-protected networks within the Internet. Anonymous peer-to-peer networks started using the Onion Router (TOR), the outcome of a military research project launched in 1995. One of the original scientists, Paul Syverson, helped Roger Dingledine and Nick Mathewson develop the onion router TOR that became operational in 2002. Such dark nets would become very popular with political dissidents in places where the Internet was massively censored, e.g. in Syria before the civil war (but also by child pornographers, drug dealers, counterfeiters and terrorists). The Freenet itself would become a dark net in 2008.

Gaming was also undergoing a dramatic transformation. In 1996 the San Francisco Chronicle's website had introduced "Dreadnot," a game built around a fictional mystery that took place around real locations in San Francisco. It featured real people and used phone numbers, voice mailboxes, email addresses, and other websites (in other words, an interactive multiplatform narrative). It was the first "alternate reality game" and it was free. A few years later in nearby Redwood City the team of game designers of Electronic Arts began working on "Majestic," that eventually debuted in July 2001, the first "alternate reality game" for sale. In keeping with the theme of the genre, it was credited to two fictional game designers, Brian Cale and Mike Griffin. These games involved the real life of the players, and therefore Electronic Arts marketed it with the motto "It plays you." The game that launched the genre on a planetary scale was Microsoft's "The Beast," that debuted a few weeks before "Majestic." It was the brainchild of Jordan Weisman.

Unbeknownst to Silicon Valley, a major revolution was taking place in the Far East. Among the pioneers of smartwatch technology had been Seiko's Data 2000 watch (1983), the first in a line of smartwatches that would last for decades, Casio had been making smartwatches since at least the VDB-1000 (1991). Computerized watches became serious business at the turn of the decade with Samsung's SPH-WP10 (1999), the world's first watch phone, which would be followed by several other models over the years, Casio's WMP-1 (2000), the world's first watch capable of playing MP3 files, Casio's WQV (2000), the world's first watch to include a camera, followed by Casio's GWS-900 G-Shock (2004), the world's first watch capable of mobile payment. In the USA interest for smartwatches had always been tepid, with half-hearted experiments such as IBM's Watchpad (2001), jointly developed by IBM and Citizen Watch and running Linux, and later Microsoft's SPOT (2004).

Wireless

Intel, Siemens, Motorola and Philips had formed an alliance for wireless networking called HomeRF, that was also supported by AT&T, but in 1999 Richard van Nee of Lucent and Mark Webster of Harris Semiconductor (later renamed Intersil) debuted their 802.11b standard, operating in the 2.4GHz band. The consortium including these two companies as well as 3Com and Nokia formed the Wireless Ethernet Compatibility Alliance that competed with HomeRF. In 1999 Lucent delivered the world's first 802.11b card to Apple and Apple incorporated it into its iBook laptop. In 2000 IBM debuted 802.11b on its notebooks, Intel switched to Wi-Fi in 2001 and in 2002 the group changed name to "Wi-Fi Alliance". The final blow to HomeRF came in 2001 when the coffee-house chain Starbucks chose Wi-Fi for its stores. Apple and IBM had understood that Wi-Fi would soon become a household term, allowing millions of home computers to communicate with the modem that connected them to the Internet.

Radio Frequency Identification (RFID), a wireless technology that used radio waves to track items, had been invented in the 1970s but largely forgotten. In 1998 MIT professors David Brock and Sanjay Sarma developed Internet-based UHF RFID that made it feasible for top retailers such as Wal-mart (that had pioneered bar coding in the 1980s) to deploy RFID technology extensively (typically for inventory purposes within supply chain management). Wal-mart eventually mandated RFID to all its suppliers by 2005. Among the early manufacturers of RFID products was Alien Technology, founded in 1999 in Morgan Hill (south of San Jose) by Stephen Smith, a professor of electrical engineering at UC Berkeley.

RFID found another application in contact-less credit cards (or "blink technology"). These were credit cards with an embedded RFID microchip that didn't need to be swiped but simply waved. The idea was pioneered by the Upass card, based on Mifare technology, which was introduced in Korea in 1996, while in Hong Kong it was the Octopus card, based on the Felica standard, in 1997, both to pay for public transportation, and by oil company Mobil's Speedpass keychain in 1997 for gasoline pumps.

The leaders were in Europe and in Japan. The European market was dominated by Mifare, developed in 1994 in Austria by Mikron (Mifare meaning "MIkron Fare Collection System") and acquired by Dutch conglomerate Philips in 1998, while Sony's FeliCa, introduced in 1996, ruled in Japan. Both were proprietary technologies because they had been introduced before the international standard was decided.

Encryption for digital communications had been born in the Bay Area (PKI, in 1976) but owed its improvement to Israeli scientists. Adi Shamir (who had invented the crucial RSA algorithm for PKI) proposed a simpler form of encryption in 1984: Identity-Based Encryption (IBE), in which the public key is some unique information about the identity of the sender (typically, the person's email address). The first practical implementation of IBE was the work of Stanford's Israeli-born Computer Science professor Dan Boneh in 2001. Two of his students, Rishi Kacker and Matt Pauker, started Voltage in 2002 in Palo Alto (or, better, in Stanford's dormitory) to develop security software for corporate customers.

Meanwhile, the Europeans and the Japanese kept improving the mobile device that used to be a voice communication device. In 1999 Japan's Kyocera introduced the first mobile phone that contained a video recorder and player, the VP-210 Visual Phone, the first phone that could make videos. In 1999 Finland's Benefon introduced the first mobile phone that contained a GPS unit, the first phone that knew its location: the Esc. But the GPS boom started in earnest in 2000 when the USA removed the military secret from the GPS system and provided full commercial access to the satellites. In November 2000 Japan's Sharp introduced the first mobile phone that contained a digital camera, the J-SH04 (five months earlier Samsung in North Korea had already released the camera phone SCH-V200, but its camera was not truly integrated with the telephone function).

Wikipedia

The website that would have the biggest impact on society, Wikipedia, originated in the Midwest. Chicago-based day trader Jimmy Wales had co-founded in 1996 Bomis, a website of pornographic content for a male audience. At the same time he was preaching the vision of a free encyclopedia and, using Bomis as his venture capitalist, he had hired Ohio State University's philosopher Larry Sanger as the editor-in-chief of this Nupedia, which debuted in March 2000. The concept was aligned with Richard Stallman's Free Software Foundation, except that it was not about software but about world knowledge.

Next came the wiki. In January 2001 Sanger decided to add a "wiki" feature to let contributors enter their texts. Wikis had become popular in company's intranets as ways to share knowledge, basically replacing the old concept of "groupware." This method proved a lot more efficient than the traditional process of peer review, and therefore "Wikipedia" (as Sanger named it) was already surpassing Nupedia in popularity when Bomis decided to pull the plug. Wales realized that Wikipedia was the way to go, abolished Nupedia, and opened Wikipedia to everybody. Formally established in 2003 as a non-profit foundation based in San Francisco, Wikipedia became a free, multilingual encyclopedia edited collaboratively by the Internet community. Within a few years it would contain more information that the Encyclopedia Britannica ever dreamed of collecting. It was another example of how utopian ideals percolated into the Internet world.

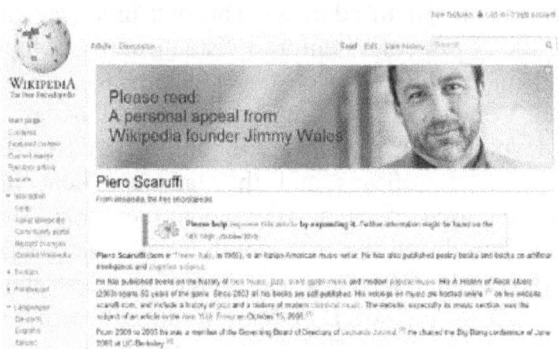

A Wikipedia Screenshot (2010)

Larry Sanger left to join the Digital Universe Foundation based in Scotts Valley. It was founded in 2002 by Utah-based entrepreneur Joe Firmage, a former Novell executive, and by German-born astrophysicist Bernard Haisch. Its mission was to create a more reliable web-based encyclopedia, Digital Universe (originally called OneCosmos).

The "copyleft movement" was a new intellectual trend shaped on the Web. It rejected the praxis of big media corporations who retained all rights and thus stifled creativity. Larry Lessig, a law professor at Stanford Law School, founded the Creative Commons in 2001 in San Francisco to promote sharing and diffusing creative works through less binding licenses than the traditional "all rights reserved" copyright. Lessig went on to found at Stanford in 2008 the Center for Internet and Society (CIS) "to improve Internet privacy practices."

In the second half of the 1990s the Zapatistas, a small rebel group in Mexico, had staged a publicity coup by using a network of alternative media to publicize their political agenda on the Internet. Following their lead, in late 1999 political activists spread around the world started the Indymedia project to provide and distribute alternative coverage of the protests against the World Trade Organization that were taking place in Seattle. Indymedia used software originally developed by hackers in Sydney that allowed individuals to update the website in real time. In 2001 violent anti-G8 protests erupted in the Italian city of Genoa, and Indymedia played an even bigger role in disseminating agit-prop news.

Indymedia would die out after Facebook and other social media began providing more professional platforms.

In 1996 Brewster Kahle, the founder of Alexa (and previously the first man to get married at the Burning Man Festival in 1992), began to archive the World-wide Web. In 2001 he launched the Internet Archive that initially simply allowed the public to browse the archived pages, but rapidly expanded to offering free digital copies of texts, images, films, etc.

Uploading

The key difference between this generation of the Web's users and the previous generation was not so much in the number of people who were browsing it but in the number of people who were uploading content to it.

Digital content had been around for decades. The vast majority of archives in the developed world had already been converted to databases. Large amounts of text had been scanned and digitized. New text was almost all in digital form. No other appliance since the ice box had disappeared so rapidly from households like the typewriter did in the 1990s. The telex had been replaced by e-mail. Newspapers and magazines had converted to digital composition. And now an increasing number of individuals were producing digital texts at an exponential pace, whether students writing their essays for school or adults writing letters to friends. Digital cameras and digital recorders were flooding personal computers with digital images and sounds. Napster-like services were popularizing the idea that a song is a file.

All this digital material was available, but it had been largely kept private on someone's home or work computer. The browser and the search engine, by definition, had encouraged people to "download" information from the Web, not to "upload" information to it. Wikipedia, blogs, P2P tools, social networking sites and soon YouTube and Flickr heralded an era in which the rate of uploading was going to almost match the rate of downloading. In fact, uploading was becoming a form of entertainment in itself. The 1990s had been the age of democratizing the Internet. The 2000s witnessed the democratization of the "uploading": more and more individuals began to upload their digital content to the Web in what became one of the most sensational processes of collective knowledge creation in the history of humankind.

In this scenario the business model of America OnLine was terribly outdated. Warner, originally a film production company, had merged in 1990 with publisher Time. Then Time Warner had entered the cable television business by acquiring Ted Turner's TBS in 1996. The media conglomerate now owned films, tv shows and articles. Then in 2000 America OnLine (AOL) purchased Time Warner and AOL Time Warner was born, the first media conglomerate of the Internet age that was making everything from cinema to email. The idea was to couple content and online distribution. It failed because AOL was rapidly losing its grip on the World-wide web as the era of dial-up access was being replaced by the era of Digital Service Lines (DSL) and cable broadband. There was no need anymore for AOL's dial-up service (that came with the limitation of being able to see only the part of the World-wide Web that AOL owned).

Biotech

Unfortunately the dotcom crash also affected the biotech industry. Funding for biotech startups collapsed after reaching a peak of $33 billion in 2000. It didn't help that Bill Haseltine 's Human Genome Sciences, one of the most hyped startups on the East Coast, turned out to be an embarrassing bluff. It raised a huge amount of money before the dotcom crash, but it did not introduce any pharmaceutical product. In 1999 a teenager, Jesse Gelsinger, died during a clinical trial of gene therapy at the University of Pennsylvania. This tragic event killed gene therapy for two decades. Luckily, philanthropy offset the retreat of the venture capitalists. In 2000 Victoria Hale, a former Genentech scientist, started the first non-profit pharmaceutical company, the Institute for OneWorld Health, in San Francisco. In 2000 the Bill and Melinda Gates Foundation became the world's largest foundation, and specifically addressed biotechnology.

Biofuels too (not only medicines) began to attract capital. In 2002 Codexis was founded as a spin-off from drug developer Maxygen. Amyris Biotechnologies, founded in 2003 by some Berkeley scientists including Jay Keasling and Kinkead Reiling, raised over $120 million in venture capital in a few years due to the Institute for OneWorld Health. Solazyme, based in South San Francisco and founded in 2003 by Jonathan Wolfson and Harrison Dillon, specialized in fuel derived from algae.

In 2000 the government-funded Human Genome Project and the privately funded Celera made peace and jointly announced that they had succeeded in decoding the entire human genome.

After the publication of the draft (in 2004) laboratories all over the world proceeded to sequence the genome of several other organisms. By comparing the human genome with the genome of other organisms, scientists figured out what the human genome is, and the picture was wildly different from what expected. It turns out that the human genome contains only 21,000 genes, but thousands of non-coding RNA genes and millions of regulatory elements. The transposons, that were assumed to be just "junk", turn out to be crucial for spreading new genetic "ideas", i.e. for enabling evolution, and evolution mostly works on the regulatory elements (very little has changed in the genes themselves over millions of years).

Enumerating the genes of human DNA enabled a new discipline: genomics, the study of genes. In particular, biologists were interested in finding out which genes cause which diseases, and how to create a predictive medicine or just how to develop smarter diagnoses. In other words, Celera and the HGP had produced billions of bits of information, but the next task was to interpret that information and apply it to understanding human diseases. This implied that someone had to scavenge that mass of information looking for useful bits. Silicon Genetics was founded in 2000 in Redwood City by Australian-born mathematician Andrew Conway of Stanford's Biochemistry Department to focus on "expression software," software tools to investigate gene expression.

DoubleTwist, Human Genome Sciences and Invitron were examples of companies that revised their business plan accordingly. They were biomedical companies trying to sell not pharmaceutical drugs but information and analysis. That was the bioinformatic side of the biotech business. Then there was the genomic side of the business, which analyzed a specific person's genome against that mass of annotated information.

An important step towards personal genomics was the establishment in October 2002 of the International HapMap Consortium. It was a collaboration among research centers (Canada, China, Japan, Nigeria, Britain, and four in the US, including UCSF) to create a "haplotype map" of the human genome. This map was about SNPs (Single-Nucleotide Polymorphisms). SNP means that a nucleotide of the DNA can have different values in different individuals of the same species. The 10 million or so SNPs that exist in human populations explain why some people are more likely to develop a certain disease than others.

In 2003 MIT's Tom Knight envisioned a catalog of standardized "biobricks" (biological parts) that synthetic biologists could use to create living organisms. His model clearly mirrored the way the personal-computer industry got started, with hobbyists ordering kits from catalogs advertised in magazines and then assembling the computer in their garage.

In 2002 Jeffrey Trent of the National Human Genome Research Institute, established the non-profit Translational Genomics Research Institute in Arizona.

The sequencing of the human genome made the database of Palo Alto-based pioneer Incyte partially irrelevant, but Incyte continued to acquire biotech startups and in 2000 launched an online version of Lifeseq that offered information about a gene's functions at a more affordable price. DoubleTwist, instead, in 2002 succumbed to the double whammy of the dotcom crash and the sequencing of the human genome.

The media seized on the announcement (in October 2001) by Advanced Cell Technology (ACT) that it had cloned the world's first human embryo, causing the ire of right-wing President George W Bush who opposed human cloning on religious grounds. ACT was a spin-off of the University of Massachusetts founded by James Robl whose lab there had been the first to clone calves from somatic cells. The team included

Jose Cibelli, a pupil of Robl who had experimented with nuclear transfer to rejuvenate cells, Robert Lanza, who was working on clones of endangered species, and even Michael West of Geron fame (who had joined ACT in 1998). Their goal was actually to generate embryonic stem cells that were needed for controversial medical research.

Meanwhile, an important milestone was achieved by synthetic biology. In July 2002 Eckard Wimmer 's team at University of New York at Stony Brook created the first synthetic virus by cloning the polio virus from its chemical code that they had simply downloaded from the Web.

The next step in biotech automation after the DNA chip/microarray was the "lab on the chip". Since the 1960s there had been a lot of progress in "micro-electro-mechanical systems" (MEMS). These devices were already around before the invention of the microprocessor. In 1964 Harvey Nathanson at Westinghouse made the first MEMS, and the first success story of MEMS was the "thermal inkjet" technology that Canon and Hewlett Packard pioneered in the late 1970s, followed in 1993 by Analog Devices' micro-accelerometer (widely used in many industries today, for example in airbags). Initially MEMS simply exploited the fabrication technologies of the semiconductor industry, but in 1999 Lucent introduced the all-optical router and triggered the boom of optical MEMs of the 2000s. But the enabling technology was "microfluidics", the ability to make millions of microchannels ("micro" in the sense that they measured micrometers in diameter) that handle very tiny quantities of fluids. This was the result of a US military program: the Defense Advanced Research Projects Agency (DARPA) wanted a system to quickly detect biological and chemical weapons and so in 1997 created a program called "Microflumes" to fund research in microfluidics. In 1978 James Angell at Stanford had already been working on "micromachines" and one of his students, Stephen Terry, in 1979 had unveiled what can be considered as the first "lab on a chip", a device for separating, identifying and analyzing the components of a gas (originally, it was commissioned by NASA and meant to analyze the atmosphere of Mars. But progress in MEMS and in microfluidics led to today's "lab-on-a-chip" products. In 1999 Hewlett-Packard's spinoff Agilent introduced the first commercial "lab-on-a-chip" product, the 2100 Bioanalyzer. Even more important was the Agilent 5100 of 2004. These constituted the vanguard of systems that enabled biotech startups to conduct analysis of thousands of DNA and protein samples per day. After the success of the Human Genome Project, the goal shifted to putting the whole human genome on a microarray. In 2002 Wilhelm Ansorge at the European Molecular Biology Laboratory (EMBL) in Germany succeeded.

The pharmaceutical industry kept growing in the area around South San Francisco, fueled in no small part by Stanford's School of Medicine.

For example, in 2002 Israeli-born professor Daria Mochly-Rosen started KAI Pharmaceuticals.

Plexicon, founded in December 2000 in Berkeley by Croatian-born Israel biochemist Joseph Schlessinger and Korean-born structural biologist Sung-Hou Kim was one of the many "drug discovery" startups, i.e. companies that were not focused on one specific biotech experiment but on discovering a new method of accelerating drug discovery in general.

In 2000 UC Berkeley chemist Henry Rapoport and others founded Aduro Biotech (later renamed Oncologic) to treat cancer, one of the first startups to marry nanotechnology and biotechnology.

Neurotech

There was also renewed interest in artificial intelligence, a field that had markedly declined since the heydays of the 1980s. However, the action came mostly from futurists and intellectuals rather than from practitioners, and the funding came from philanthropists rather than the academia or the government. The Singularity Institute for Artificial Intelligence (SIAI), devoted to super-human intelligence, was founded in 2000 in San Francisco by Eliezer Yudkowsky, while in 2002 Jeff Hawkins (of Palm Computing fame) founded the Redwood Neuroscience Institute in Menlo Park.

The Stanford Artificial Intelligence Laboratory was quietly experimenting with robots and in 2005 would win the "Grand Challenge," a race of driver-less cars funded by the DARPA in the Nevada desert, with its Stanley, a modified Volkswagen Touareg.

Greentech

Times of economic crisis had always been good for imagining completely new business sectors. An emerging theme in Silicon Valley was energy, especially after the 2001 terrorist attacks that highlighted how vulnerable the US was to the whims of oil-producing countries. In 2001, KR Sridhar, an alumnus of India's prestigious National Institute of Technology who had worked on NASA's Mars mission, founded Ion America (renamed Bloom Energy in 2006) in Sunnyvale to develop fuel-cell technology to generate environmentally-friendly electricity. Within a few years it had raised $400 million in venture capital money. Its fuel cells (eventually unveiled in February 2010) were based on beach sand. Each unit cost between $700,000 and $800,000. Google and eBay were among the early adopters of these fuel-cell power generators. Fuel cells opened up the possibility of liberating individuals from the slavery of power plants and transmission grids.

Founded in 2002 in San Jose by Stanford engineering student Brian Sager and by Martin Roscheisen of FindLaw fame, NanoSolar (the first solar energy company based in Silicon Valley) collaborated with Stanford University and Lawrence Berkeley National Laboratories. They developed an ink capable of converting sunlight into electricity; it became the foundation for its family of flexible, low-cost and light-weight solar cells.

Bloom Energy's Offices (2010)

Nanotech

Nanotechnology, on the other hand, seemed to benefit from the dotcom crash, as venture capitalists looked elsewhere to invest their money. The US government enacted a National Nanotechnology Initiative in 2001, which helped fuel the sector. New startups in Silicon Valley included Nanosys, founded in 2001 to produce "architected" materials, and Innovalight, founded in 2002 and specializing in solar cell technology. Venture capitalists saw opportunities in the convergence of biotech, infotech, and nanotech. However, the nano hype mainly resulted in books and organizations with pompous titles, such as "Kinematic Self-Replicating Machines" (2004) by Robert Freitas and Ralph Merkle.

In the old tradition of government intervention to boost high-tech investments, in 1999 the Central Intelligence Agency (CIA) set up an odd not-for-profit venture-capital firm in Menlo Park, called In-Q-Tel. It would invest in leading-edge technologies such as nanotech and biotech. One of their investments in Silicon Valley was in Keyhole, founded in 2001 by Brian McClendon and John Hanke. It developed a geospatial data visualization tool (software to display three-dimensional representations of satellite images).

Creative Destruction

By the year 2000 something monumental had happened in the USA, despite the "dotcom crash". The high-tech economy of computers, biotech and telecommunications had passed in size the industries that had dominated manufacturing for almost a century: auto, oil, steel and aircraft. In fact, by 2000 the semiconductors industry had become the largest manufacturing industry in the USA. The USA was no longer the leading country in autos and steel, but it was in hardware, software and biotech. In these fields a revolution within the revolution had taken place: small young companies (such as Compaq, Dell, Cisco, SUN, Gateway, EMC, Apple, and Microsoft) had successfully eroded the market shares of the big older companies (such as IBM, HP and Cullinet) that had dominated in the previous decades.

Many of the dominant high-tech companies of the 1970s and 1980s had actually disappeared, notably DEC. Something similar had happened within the semiconductors industry when Intel went past the old dominant players, Texas Instruments and Motorola.

Pundits misquoted Schumpeter's "creative destruction" (1942), when in fact Schumpeter never praised the small startups (he thought that the big companies were "the most powerful engine of economic progress"). The "creative destruction" of the high-tech industry was almost the antithesis of Schumpeter's "creative destruction": it destroyed the very "engine of economic progress" while creating a bigger engine. Schumpeter had not foreseen that a proliferation of small dynamic firms could provide more momentum to progress than a group of large multinationals, and even displace the latter.

Innovation transformed into an erotic fetish. Richard Florida's book "The Rise of the Creative Class" (2002) created the myth of Silicon Valley. Clayton Christensen's "The Innovator's Dilemma" (1997) had turned Joseph Schumpeter's concept of "creative destruction" into "disruptive technologies" to explain Silicon Valley's boom. The word "innovation" spread from US publishing houses to the most remote corners of the world, becoming a quasi-religious mantra that was supposed to solve all problems.

Bionics

The Bay Area's passion for creating a society as inclusive as possible had always made it a friendly place for disabled people, particularly around the Berkeley campus. In 2000 DARPA decided to fund a project at UC Berkeley's Robotics and Human Engineering Laboratory. It built technology capable of mobilizing paralyzed people. These "exoskeletons," named BLEEXes (Berkeley Lower Extremity Exoskeletons), were lightweight battery-powered artificial legs that helped a disabled person not only to walk but also to carry a heavy load. The first BLEEX was introduced in 2003. In 2005 the director of that laboratory, Homayoon

Kazerooni, founded a company, Berkeley ExoWorks (later renamed Berkeley Bionics), to commercialize the devices. In 2010 Berkeley Bionics would introduce eSuit, a computer-controlled suit to make paraplegics walk. Berkeley Bionics would be later renamed one more time, to Ekso Bionics, and in 2012 Homayoon Kazerooni would found another startup of the same kind, Suitx.

This opened the era of "wearables" that had been pioneered at the MIT by the likes of Thad Starner and Steve Mann at the MIT Media Lab, although most of the progress took place in Europe. In 1998 Sundaresan Jayaraman's team at Georgia Tech developed the first version of the "Wearable Motherboard", a smart shirt. In 2000 a collaboration between Phillips Electronics and Levi Strauss resulted in the first commercially-available wearable electronic garments, the ICD+ jacket, incorporating GSM cellular communications and MP3 music player. In 1998 Finland's Clothing+ (aka Mikko Malmivaara) developed a heart-rate sensing shirt and in 2000 Reima commercialized Clothing+'s "Smart Shout", a body belt for hands-free mobile phone communications. In 2000 SoftSwitch (England) introduced a fabric-control keypad to incorporate audio communications and heating systems into jackets for winter sports. In 2002 an MIT Media Lab alumna, artist Maggie Orth, founded International Fashion Machines (IFM) to make digital interactive textiles.

The Anthropology of E-socializing

Email became pervasive in the 1990s. Email and the Web came rapidly to be used not only for business but also for personal matters, fun, and family. High-tech tools were not social in themselves but the people who produced them and used them daily discovered their "social" value. They soon came to be used as social tools too to replace the lacking social life of Silicon Valley; to create networks of soccer players, hikers, music listeners, etc. This "discovery" that high-tech tools were valuable for building social networks would have widespread implications. It also meant that individuals came to be progressively more and more often plugged into the network.

Email developed a new mindset of interaction with the community: it allowed people to delay a response, to filter incoming messages, to assign priorities. Of course, this had already been made possible by answering machines; but email was written and was stored on the computer. Email also allowed a message to have multiple recipients, which led to the creation of mailing lists. In other words, email increased control over personal communications.

Electronic socializing also helped remove some of the ethnic barriers that still existed. After all, in 1997 more than 80% of newborn babies had parents of the same ethnic group. For a region with such a large percentage of foreign-born people, it was surprising that the ethnic background still mattered so much. The advent of e-socializing removed some of the formalities that one expected from friends.

High-tech also fostered mobility of information at the expense of mobility of bodies. Telecommuting became more common, if not widespread. Telecommuters lived and worked in the same place: the home office. And they worked when inspired. They had no work hours, as long as they delivered their task by the deadline. Teleconferencing and telecommuting further reduced personal interactions. Co-workers became invisible although present 24 hours a day. On one hand, high-tech tools made one reachable anywhere any time. On the other hand, it also estranged one from the community.

Silicon Valley's engineers were the first users of their technologies. But the opposite was also true: Silicon Valley's engineers could also be the last users of technologies developed in other regions. For example, the rate of adoption of cellular phones was a lot slower than in Europe.

One reason why the virtual community was so successful was that the physical community was so unsuccessful. Silicon Valley was a sprawling expanse of low-rise buildings but did not have an identity as a community (other than the identity of not having an identity). San Jose, in particular, had become one of the richest cities in the nation. It was, however, not a city, but just an aggregate of nondescript neighborhoods that had grown independently over the years. In true Silicon Valley fashion, the city decided to create a downtown area overnight that would introduce a flavor of European lifestyle. It spent almost one billion dollars to create a large shopping, dining, and entertainment complex strategically located at the border with Santa Clara and Cupertino. In 2002 Santana Row opened for business. It was totally artificial.

The Myth

Throughout the 1990s, thanks to the dotcom boom and to the favorable global political environment (the Cold War had ended in 1991 with a complete conversion of the communist world to capitalism), there was much discussion about how to export Silicon Valley's model to other regions of the world, notably Singapore, India, and China. Nobody found quite the right formula, although they all took inspiration from many aspects of Silicon Valley.

In the US itself there were different opinions on how to foster innovation. For example, in 2000 Microsoft's former research head, Nathan Myhrvold, founded Intellectual Ventures, a secretive enterprise with a business model to purchase as many patents as possible in just about every imaginable field. But the emphasis was more on filing patents than on incubating viable companies. Owning a huge portfolio of patents is mainly a legal business, involving armies of intellectual-property attorneys, and it can be lucrative because any other company trying to develop a product in the same sector will have to buy the related patents. Of course, this "patent farming" business hampers rather than fosters innovation because many smaller companies will never even think of venturing into a field for which a billion-dollar venture fund owns a patent. Regardless of the philanthropic merits of encouraging inventors from all over the world, Silicon Valley looked down on this kind of approach: it was artificial and it did not create a real integrated networked economy.

This business was so lucrative that soon other "patent trolls" would appear, notably VirnetX, that sued Microsoft in 2010 and Apple in 2012, founded in 2006 near Santa Cruz by Kendall Larsen, and Virginia-based Straight Path IP, that sued Sony, LG, Toshiba, Apple and Verizon within one year of being founded in 2013. These "non-practicing entities" used questionable tactics to extort licensing fees from rich corporations using ambiguous patents as their legal weapons. Apple wrote: "Smartflash makes no products, has no employees, creates no jobs, has no US presence, and is exploiting our patent system to seek royalties for technology Apple invented." This was actually the one case that had some merit (Smartflash was founded by British inventor Patrick Racz, who had really invented the technology he was defending), but the description of the patent troll well reflected the perception in Silicon Valley about these lawyer-dominated companies (or non-companies). The fact that it was legal to be a "patent troll" did not diminish the fact that it was amoral. Raping women used to be legal in prehistoric time, and so was slavery not long ago. That doesn't mean it was moral. It simply means that governments took a long time to enact appropriate laws to punish those practicing rape or slavery. Straight Path's website claimed "Straight Path, its executives, directors, and employees operate with the highest levels of personal and professional integrity." Not many were impressed by the "personal integrity" of patent trolls.

Microsoft's co-founder Paul Allen had pioneered this approach in 1992 when he had established the Palo Alto-based Interval Research Corporation. It was a technology incubator that made no products but filed a lot of patents that were used 18 years later to sue just about every major company in the Web business.

Downsizers: Facebook, YouTube, Web 2.0, and Tesla (2003-06)

Distributed and Small

The early 2000s were an age of downsizing. Silicon Valley companies had to learn the art of cost cutting. Startups had to learn the art of actually developing a product and selling it. Once again, the beneficiary was India. Creating a lab in India (where software engineers earned a fraction of Silicon Valley engineers) was a relatively painless way to dramatically cut costs. By 2005 more than 50% of all jobs outsourced by Silicon Valley companies went to India.

The Rise of the Smartphone

Computing devices had been getting smaller since the first Eniac was unveiled. That trend had never really stopped. It just proceeded by discontinuous jumps: the minicomputer was a significant downsizing from the mainframe, and so was the personal computer from the minicomputer. The laptop/notebook, however, was just a variation on the personal computer, the only major difference being the screen. In 2005 sales of notebook computers accounted for 53% of the computer market: the traditional desktop computer was on the way out. IBM pulled out of the market for desktop computers. There was a clear trend towards a portable computing device, but the laptop per se did not truly represent a quantum leap forward, just a way to stretch the personal-computer technology to serve that trend.

At the same time sales, of smart phones were booming too, but there was a lesson to be learned. In 2004 Motorola introduced the mobile phone Razr, an elegant-looking device that by July 2006 had been bought by over 50 million people, propelling Motorola to second position after Nokia. Yet sales started dropping dramatically in 2006. Motorola learned the hard way an important rule of the cell phone market: phones went in and out of fashion very quickly. There was room for more players, and Silicon Valley had largely been on the sidelines until then.

Ironically, the mobile smartphone of the 2000s rediscovered the three-line navigation menu button (known as the "hamburger icon") that the Xerox Star personal workstation had used in 1981 (because of graphical limitations).

A humbler form of wearable computing was born in April 2003 with the Nokia HDW-2, the first Bluetooth headset for mass consumption.

No Silicon Valley company (or, fot that matter, US company) was part of the consortium formed in 2004 to develop and promote Near Field Communication (NFC), basically the smartphone equivalent of the old RFID. This was a method to allow smartphones to exchange data by simply pointing at each other at close range. The founders were Nokia, Philips and Sony. It would take seven years for Silicon Valley to catch up (when Google would introduce the technology in its NFS-enabled smartphones).

The Dotcoms

The positive note for the dotcoms was that the Web was spreading like a virus all over the world. By 2006 Google had indexed more than eight billion pages, coming from the 100 million websites registered on the Web. In March 2006, the English version of Wikipedia passed one million articles. The Internet was being accessed by 1.25 billion people in the world. The dotcom bubble had not been completely senseless: one just had to figure out how to capitalize on that massive audience.

By 2005 Yahoo!, Google, America OnLine (AOL) and MSN (Microsoft's Network) were the four big Internet "portals," with a combined audience of over one billion people. Never in history had such a large audience existed. Never in history had Silicon Valley companies controlled such a large audience (most of that billion used Google and Yahoo!). There were only two threats to the Internet: spam (undesired marketing emails) and viruses (malicious software that spread via email or downloads and harmed computers).

Free Software

The desktop computer was still dominant device, and the Windows operating system was still the dominant platform, but there was grumbling, especially about the costs and the new (and often unpopular) releases of the WIMP camp.

Ubuntu, a free and user-friendly variant of the Linux operating system for personal computers, was first released in Britain in 2004 by South African entrepreneur Mark Shuttleworth and quickly became popular in the open-source community. It was a descendant of Debian, invented in 1996 by a German student of Purdue University (in Indiana), Ian Murdock. One could run free applications such as the VLC player, develop in 2001 by students at the École Centrale of Paris, and a full Microsoft-compatible office productivity suite, SUN's open-source project Open Office, lunched in 2000 (that would evolve in LibreOffice was purchased by Oracle in 2010). Within a few years Ubuntu would become a popular alternative to

Windows, used to run Wikipedia and to provide cloud services for Netflix, Uber, Lyft, Dropbox, Paypal, Snapchat, Pinterest, Reddit, and Instagram. It would be even used in 2013 on China's Tianhe-2 supercomputer.

In July 2003 AOL spun off Mozilla. It was originally founded by Netscape to foster third-party development on the browser under a free open-source license. It quickly built a reputation as a new browser. The first chair of the Mozilla Foundation was Lotus' founder Mitch Kapor. The lesson learned by Netscape through Mozilla was that the open-source model works, but it is a Darwinian process, and, just like in nature, it works very slowly. The Mozilla community hated Microsoft's Internet Explorer and therefore loved the Netscape browser. Unfortunately, this meant that dozens of people added features to Mozilla to the point that it became famously fat and slow.

Mozilla needed a re-birth. This came in 2002 when a new batch of developers (mainly Stanford students Blake Ross, who had started working on Mozilla at the age of 14, and Dave Hyatt) produced a "lighter" version of the Mozilla browser. It was eventually named Firefox. Firefox was indeed a state-of-the-art browser that could match IE (whose team Microsoft had just disbanded anyway in 2001). Yet precious time had been lost. In 2003 Microsoft's Internet Explorer (IE) owned 95% of the browser market. The market share of Apple's Safari was negligible, but Apple made its WebKit rendering engine open source in 2005, a fact that would have far-fetched consequences a few years later in the age of the smartphones.

The End of Moore's Law

Intel capitalized on the popularity of the Web with a new generation of microprocessors. Wi-Fi became a household name after Intel introduced the Centrino for laptops in March 2003 (largely the vision of Indian-born Anand Chandrasekher). From that point on a laptop would be associated with wireless Internet as much as with mobility.

In 2004 the first Wi-Fi-certified cell phones reached the market. These were portable devices that provided both Wi-Fi and cellular communications. In other words they merged the worlds of email (and web-browsing) and phone conversation (and text messaging). The Nokia's Symbian-based 9500 Communicator and Motorola's Windows-based MPx were the vanguard of this generation. Both were equipped with a QWERTY keyboard, and the MPx also incorporated a 1.3 megapixel camera (which by this point had become a fairly standard feature on high-end phones).

Mobile television, already available in South Korea since 2005, spread worldwide in a few years, finding millions of customers in Asia, Africa, and Latin America. Ironically, the West lagged behind, and in 2010 mobile TV was still a rarity in the US. But even in this case Silicon Valley was actually at the vanguard: the leading mobile TV chip maker, Telegent Systems, a fabless company founded in 2004 by LSI Logic's inventor Samuel Sheng, was based in Sunnyvale.

In reality, Moore's Law started failing in 2005, when Intel and AMD introduced their first "dual-core" processors. The problem was the heat generated by denser and denser circuits. In 2001 Patrick Gelsinger, an Intel engineer, had extrapolated the trends and showed that computer chips were heading for temperatures as hot as nuclear reactors. Intel's solution was to put multiple cores on the same chip. The original microprocessor was basically a computer on a chip. A multi-core processor was the equivalent of putting many computers on one chip. Moore's Law appeared to continue to hold because the consumer cared about the chip, not about how the chip was configured. The clock speed was actually reaching a plateau, but transistors were becoming cheaper and more power-efficient, thanks to progress in lithography at the foundries.

For the record, AMD beat Intel to market with its Opteron dual-core microprocessor in April 2005. Intel's first dual-core microprocessor, the Pentium D, came out in May. Within one year Intel already had a quad-core processor, and soon the single-core processor would become an ancient relic.

Google and its Inventions

Google's growth had been particularly stunning, dwarfing even the excesses of the dotcom bubble. In 2003 Google had 10,000 servers working nonstop to index the Web (14 times more servers than employees). In 2002 Google acquired Blogger and in 2004 they acquired Keyhole (a CIA-funded startup), the source for their application Google Earth. More than a search engine, Google was expanding in all directions, becoming a global knowledge provider. In early 2004 Google handled about 85% of all search requests on the Web. In fact, a new verb was coined in the English language: to "google" something (search for something on the Web). Google's IPO in August 2004 turned Google's founders, Sergey Brin and Larry Page, into billionaires. In 2004 an ever more ambitious Google launched a project to digitize all the books ever printed.

In 2004 Google hired German-born natural-language expert Franz-Josef Och, whose machine-translation system at the University of Southern California had been selected by DARPA. In 2005 Google introduced its own automatic-translation system to translate webpages written in foreign languages. In October 2004 Google acquired Danish-born Australian-based Berkeley alumnus Lars Rasmussen 's company Where2 and its mapping software; and in 2005 Google introduced Google Maps. MapQuest, the pioneering Web-based mapping service acquired by AOL in 2000, lost to Google Maps because the latter allowed third-party developers to add information to the map and use the map in their own software. The time-consuming process of scaling a web application was more easily done by "exploiting" the Internet community of software developers.

Much was being said of Google's ethics that allowed employees vast freedom to be creative. However, almost all of Google's business was driven by acquisition of other people's ideas. Gmail, developed internally by former Intel employee Paul Buchheit and launched by invitation only in April 2004, was not much more than Google's version of Hotmail. What made it popular was the hype caused by the "invitation-only" theatrics, plus the large amount of storage space offered. The only clear difference over Hotmail was that Gmail offered a gigabyte of storage versus Hotmail's two megabytes, i.e. 500 times more memory. Google Checkout, introduced in June 2006, was a poor man's version of PayPal. Google Streetview, introduced in 2007, was quote similar to Vederi's ScoutTool (StreetBrowser), launched in 2000. So Vederi sued.

Google's Android operating system for smartphones, acquired in 2005 from the namesake startup and introduced in 2007, was widely believed (not only by Steve Jobs) to be a diligent but uninspired imitation of the iPhone's operating system. The "semantic" improvement to the Google search engine of 2009 was due to the Orion search engine, developed in Australia by Israeli-born Ori Allon an acquired in 2006.

Google replicated Microsoft's model. Its own research labs were incredibly inept at inventing anything original, despite the huge amount of cash poured into them. That cash mostly bought them patents on countless trivial features of their products, a tactic meant to prevent innovation by the competition. What drove Google's astronomical growth was (just like in Microsoft's case) the business strategy, not the inventions.

Google's real innovation was in the field of advertising. In June 2003 Google introduced AdSense, designed by Paul Buchheit right after Google acquired the technology from Applied Semantics (which had been founded in 1998 by Caltech graduates Gilad Elbaz and Adam Weissman in Los Angeles).. It was a vast technological improvement over AdWords: content-targeted advertising. AdSense was capable of "understanding" the topic of a webpage and therefore automatically assign to it the relevant ads among all the ads provided by paid advertisers. By systematically monitoring the behavior of its search engine's users, Google had invented (or, at least, perfected) an automated system with three aims: first, for advertisers to create more effective ads; second, for Google itself to display more relevant ads; and third, for users to view the most relevant ads. The traditional ad in a newspaper had mostly been a one-sided decision, based on what an advertiser wanted to print and how much it was willing to pay, mediated by one of the newspaper's salespeople. In Google's world the ad became a computer-mediated deal among three entities: the advertiser, Google's AdSense and the user. Basically, AdSense created an infinite feedback loop that allowed advertisers to continuously improve their adverts, and at the same time promoted a race among advertisers to develop the "fittest" ad in a sort of Darwinian process. If previous progress in search-based advertising had lowered the barrier from large corporations to small businesses, AdSense enabled any content provider (from established news media to the smallest website on a rock star run by a teenage fan) to monetize its content. Of course, this also led to an alienating process in which very serious texts were being used to publicize trivial products (famously AdSense associated ads about plastic bags with the news of a murderer who had stuffed its victim's body parts in a plastic bag). The new landscape for advertisers was the whole behavior of the user, that Google monitored as much as possible through the user's searches. Thus, for example, someone dying of cancer and desperately searching the Web for medicines and devices would automatically be turned by AdSense into a golden business opportunity for any company advertising those medicines and those medical devices.

Yahoo! had lost part of its sheen, but still generated yearly revenues of $1.6 billion in 2003 (up from $953 million in 2002), with an astronomical yearly growth and market value. In 2003 it acquired Overture/GoTo, nurtured by Los Angeles-based incubator Idealab, and introduced the "pay per click" business model for advertisers instead of the traditional "per view" model. GoTo had also introduced the idea of letting advertisers bid to show up higher in the results of a search (the "pay-for-placement" model).. In 2006 revenues would reach $6.4 billion. Note that these dotcom companies were mainly selling ads. The initial dotcom business plan of simply becoming popular had eventually worked out: all you needed was a large audience, and then the advertisers would flock to your website. What was missing in the 1990s was the advertisers.

Social Networking

Initially, instead, the idea behind the dotcoms had been to transfer commerce to the Web; hence e-commerce. This was a more than viable business, but, in hindsight, it lacked imagination. It soon proved to be viable mostly for the already established "brick and mortar" corporations.

It took a while for the dotcoms to imagine what one could "sell" to one billion people spread all over the world: social networking. For the first time in history it was possible for one billion strangers to assemble, organize themselves, discuss issues, and act together.

Social networking was another practical implementation of Metcalfe's law, that the value of a network of users increases exponentially with each new user.

Friendster had already been imitated by a few websites, notably tribe.net, founded in 2003 in San Francisco by Mark Pincus, Paul Martino and Valerie Syme.

The first truly successful social-networking site was MySpace. It was launched in 2003 in Los Angeles and purchased in July 2005 for $580 million by Rupert Murdoch's News Corp.

In February 2004 Harvard student Mark Zuckerberg launched the social-networking service Facebook. It soon spread from college to college. Weeks later Zuckerberg and friends relocated to Silicon Valley and obtained funding from Peter Thiel of PayPal. Somehow this one took off the way that previous ones had not. Facebook started growing at a ridiculously fast pace, having signed up 100 million users by August 2008 on its way to becoming the second website by traffic after Google by the end of the decade.

In 2005 Gina Bianchini and Netscape's founder Marc Andreessen launched Ning, a meta social-networking software. It allowed people to create and customize their own social networks. Inktomi's founders Brian Totty and Paul Gauthier formed Ludic Labs in San Mateo in 2006, a venture devoted to social media software for consumers and businesses that launched offerfoundry.com, talkfilter.com and diddit.com.

Three factors contributed to the birth of "podcasting". First, the adoption in 1995 of the mp3 standard for audio files. Second, in 1999 Netscape launched RSS (Rich Site Summary, but mostly known as "Really Simple Syndication"), a system that allowed users to subscribe to the articles published on a blog. Developed by Dan Libby and Ramanathan Guha (a former A.I. scientist and Apple engineer), it incorporated Dave Winer's own system of syndication. Third, in 2001 Apple introduced the iPod, in theory a music player but de facto a general-purpose platform to play digital audio files. The iPod wasn't necessary (and, in fact, initially it didn't even play mp3 files), but it popularized the idea of the digital audio file that one can download on a personal device. Podcasting is "audioblogging" in the age of the mp3 and RSS: mp3 audio files distributed via RSS. It was pioneered by Kevin Marks in 2003 in Britain, and by serial Internet entrepreneur and reality-show producer Adam Curry in 2004 in the Netherlands. In 2005 Evan Williams (of Blogger fame) and Noah Glass launched the podcasting platform Odeo.

Last but not least, in 2006 Jack Dorsey created the social-networking service Twitter (initially just as a component of Evan Williams' Odeo), where people could post short live updates of what was going on in their life. A "tweet" was limited to 140 characters. That limit reflected the way people wanted to communicate in the age of smart phones: very brief messages. Twitter soon became popular for current events the way CNN had become popular during the first Gulf War. In 2004 an MIT scientist, Tad Hirsch, had developed TxTMob, a platform that enabled individuals to send anonymous text messages to large groups of people. This had been designed for political activists just like Indymedia, except that it was even more oriented towards the "mob". One of Twitter's developers was Evan Henshaw-Plath, who was precisely one of those political activists with a background in Indymedia and TxtMob, and he took TXTMob as the foundation for Twitter's technology.

The Unix (and in particular Linux) world had been the first example of a social networking platform. It was used to refine the platform itself. Facebook and the likes simply adopted the concept and transferred to it the sphere of private life.

Facebook's sociological impact was colossal. For example, Facebook offered a "Like" button for people to applaud a friend's statement or picture, but did not offer a "Dislike" button. Facebook was creating a society in which it was not only rude but even physically impossible to be negative. The profile picture of the Facebook user was supposed to be a smiling face. The whole Facebook society was just one big collective smile. The Web's libertarian society was turning into a global exercise in faking happiness. After all, the French historian Alexis de Tocqueville had warned in 1840 (in his study "Democracy in America") that absolute freedom would make people lonely and desperate. In a sense, social networking universes like Facebook were testing the possibility of introducing a metalevel of behavioral control to limit the absolute freedom enabled by the Web.

Google, eBay, Facebook and Twitter shared one feature that made them such incredible success stories was: simplicity. Initially, they all had a humble, text-only "look and feel" in the age of graphic design, banners, chat rooms, etc. All that Twitter had needed to change the world was 140 characters.

In Asia the most successful of these sites was still Friendster.

By this time instant messaging had become very popular but there were countless different providers, each of their own protocol. Meebo, founded in 2005 in Mountain View by Sandy Jen, Elaine Wherry and Seth Sternberg was an instant-messaging service that integrated all the most popular instant-messaging services such as AIM, Windows Live Messenger, MySpaceIM, Google Talk, ICQ and Yahoo Messenger. (Meebo was acquired by Google in 2012).

The story of "crowdfunding" began in New York: in 2001 Brian Camelio launched artistShare, the first music crowdfunding site. In 2005 Kiva, founded by Matt Flannery and Jessica Jackley in San Francisco, made waves with a new form of idealistic capitalism, "microlending" (typically for small businesses in third-world countries).

Facebook's Original Building (2010)

Your Life Online

In November 2005 a group of former Paypal employees, all still in their twenties, got together to launch a new website, YouTube. The founders were Steve Chen (a Taiwanese-born software engineer), Chad Hurley (an art designer) and Jawed Karim (a German-born Stanford student working part-time). Based in San Mateo, they were funded by Roelof Botha of Sequoia Capital, another PayPal alumnus. The concept sounded innocent enough. It was just a way for ordinary people with an ordinary digital videocamera to upload their videos to the Web. It turned out to be the perfect Internet video application. By July 2006 more than 65,000 new videos were being uploaded every day, and more than 100 million videos were viewed by users worldwide every day. In October Google bought YouTube for $1.65 billion.

YouTube did more than simply help people distribute their videos worldwide: it ushered in the age of "streaming" media. "Streaming" means to watch a video or to listen to a recording in real time directly from its Web location as opposed to downloading it from the Web on one's computer. YouTube's videos were "streamed" to the browser of the viewer. YouTube did not invent streaming, but it demonstrated its power over cable television, movie theaters, and any previous form of broadcasting videos to the masses.

Another idea that matured in the 2000s was Internet-based telephony. Skype was founded in Europe in 2003 by Niklas Zennstroem and Janus Friis to market a system invented by Kazaa's founders Ahti Heinla, Priit Kasesalu, and Jaan Tallinn. Internet users were now able to make free phone calls to any other Internet user, as long as both parties had a microphone and a loudspeaker in their computer. The lesson learned in this case was that telephony over the Internet was a major innovation for ordinary consumers, not companies, but ordinary consumers could not afford suitable computers until the 2000s. Skype was not charging anything for the service, so, again, the business model was just to become very popular all over the world.

Microsoft would purchase Skype in 2012, thus de facto ending the era of its MSN Messenger.

Another service that matured at this time was Internet-based music streaming. This had been pioneered by Listen.com, founded in 1999 in San Francisco by Silicon Graphics veteran Rob Reid, but became Rhapsody, charging a flat monthly fee for streaming music, with the 2001 acquisition of the streaming engine of TuneTo.com. In 2005 David Hyman launched MOG in Berkeley, and in 2006 Daniel Marhely launched Deezer in France.

Expanding the concept of the female-oriented portal iVillage, Indian-born former Apple scientist and NetObjects founder Samir Arora set up Glam Media in 2003 in Brisbane, near South San Francisco, staffing it with the old NetObjects team. They initially focused on the fashion/lifestyle website Glam.com targeting the female audience.

Yelp, founded in 2004 in San Francisco by "Paypal mafia" members Jeremy Stoppelman and Russel Simmons, joined Amazon and social media in letting customers recommend, judge and rate products and services, i.e. do the marketing that really matters. Yelp embodied the new philosophy of crowd-marketing that would come to be called "Likeonomics". Sites like Yelp would rapidly displace CRM as the most effective way to market a product/service.

Online dating website Match had been one of the early success stories of the dotcoms. eHarmony, launched in 2000 in Los Angeles by psychologist Neil Warren, was the second online dating website to spread worldwide. OK Cupid, launched in 2004 as SparkMatch by Harvard University students, was acquired in 2011 by Match, and the same company that owned Match (IAC) would create Tinder in 2012 in Los Angeles.

YouTube's Old Offices (2010)

E-commerce

The net economy was, however, recovering from the dotcom burst. For example, Amazon lost a staggering $2.8 billion between 1995 and 2001. Its first profit was posted at the end of 2001, and it was a mere $5 million. But in 2005 it posted revenues of $8.5 billion and a hefty profit, placing it inside the exclusive club of the "Fortune 500." In 2006 its revenues would top $10.7 billion. In 2007 sales would increase a stunning 34.5% over the previous year. eBay's revenues for 2006 reached $6 billion. Netflix's revenues were up 48% from the previous year, just short of one billion dollars, and it had almost six million subscribers.

It took a while before the business world understood the benefits of selling online: it makes it easier to track customer's behavior and fine-tune your marketing to attract more customers or to attract more advertisers. The amount of data generated world-wide had been increasing exponentially for years, and those data were mostly ending up on the Internet. Enerprise software was ridiculously inadequate to dealing with that avalanche of data. A new kind of applications, spearheaded by Splunk, launched by serial entrepreneurs Rob Das and Erik Swan in 2002 in San Francisco, filled that niche: analyze customer behavior in real time and churn out business metrics data.

Digital Entertainment

A lesson was creeping underneath the massive amount of music downloaded both legally and illegally from the Internet. In 2003 the file-sharing system Rapidshare was founded in Germany, the file-sharing system TorrentSpy went live in the US, and a BitTorrent-based website named "The Pirate Bay" opened in Sweden. In 2005 Megaupload was founded in Hong Kong. In 2006 Mediafire was founded in the US. These websites allowed people to upload the music that they had ripped from CDs, and allowed the entire Internet population to download them for free. The "fraud" was so extensive that in 2006 the music industry in the US (represented by the RIAA) filed a lawsuit against Russian-based Internet download service AllOfMP3.com for $1.65 trillion. Needless to say, it proved impossible to stop half a billion people from using free services that were so easy to use. Music downloading became a pervasive phenomenon.

Apple's iTunes store, opened in April 2003, was the legal way to go for those who were afraid of the law, and by the end of 2006 a hefty 48% of Apple's revenues was coming from sales of the iPod, one of the most successful devices in history. Digital videos came next, although the sheer size of the video files discouraged many from storing them on their home computers.

The lesson to be learned was twofold. One lesson was for the media company: it was virtually impossible to enforce copyrights on digital files. The other lesson was for the consumer: it was wishful thinking that one could digitize a huge library of songs and films because that would require just too much storage. A different system was needed, namely streaming.

The phenomenon of digital music downloading was another premonition of an important change in computing. From the viewpoint of the "downloader," the whole Web was becoming just one huge repository of music. Its geographical location was irrelevant. It was in the "cloud" created by multiple distributed servers around the world.

The situation was quite different in the field of books. In the late 1990s, companies such as SoftBook Press and NuvoMedia had pioneered the concept of the e-book reader. Microsoft and Amazon had introduced software to read ebooks on personal computers (Amazon simply purchased the technology in 2005 from the French company Mobipocket that had introduced it in 2000). That was at the time when there were virtually no ebooks to read. This changed in 2002 when two major publishers, Random House and HarperCollins, started selling digital versions of their titles. Amazon became and remained the main selling point for ebooks, but "ebookstores" began to appear elsewhere too, notably BooksOnBoard in Austin (Texas) that opened in 2006. In October 2004, Amazon had hired two former Apple and Palm executives, Gregg Zehr (hardware) and Thomas Ryan (software), who in turn hired mostly Apple and Palm engineers, and had started a company in Cupertino called Lab126 to develop a proprietary $400 hand-held e-book reader, the Kindle. It was eventually introduced in November 2007. The Kindle was not just a software application but a custom device for reading books. That device, conceptually a descendant of the Palm Pilot, was the device that tilted the balance towards the ebook.

The company that democratized video was instead based in San Francisco: Pure Digital Technologies, originally founded in 2001 by Jonathan Kaplan to make disposable digital cameras. In May 2006 it launched the Flip video camera, sold in popular department stores at an affordable price. Designed for direct conversion to digital media and particularly for Internet video sharing, it helped countless unskilled users of the Internet become amateur filmmakers. In just 18 months PDT sold 1.5 million of its one-button camcorders and became the leader of that market. The lesson to be learned here was that the smartphone was going to threaten the existence of entire lines of products, well beyond voice communication.

The Bay Area had a mixed record in the field of photography, with only the Flip gaining ephemeral momentum for a few years. Lytro was founded by Stanford's computational mathematician Ren Ng in 2006 and based in Mountain View. It aimed at designing more than a cheaper better camera: it went for the light-field cameras, a camera capable of capturing much more information and therefore of creating a much richer digital representation of the scene. The most obvious benefit was to be able to refocus the image after having taken the picture. The technology had been originally invented at the MIT Media Lab in 1992 by John Wang and Edward Adelson. Yet it was Mark Levoy's team at Stanford University that perfected it made it fit for the consumer market.

Woodman Labs (later renamed GoPro), founded in 2003 in San Mateo by Nick Woodman would become one of the success stories of the 2010s. It introduced a wrist-worn camera, the GoPro Hero, that let users snap photos on 35mm color film. This rapidly evolved into the Digital Hero (2006) and finally into the HD HERO (2009) that offered audio and high-definition video.

In 2002 the United States government found five DRAM manufacturers guilty of manipulating the market: Samsung, Hynix (spun off by Hyundai in 2001), Infineon (spun off by Siemens in 1999), Elpida (a 2000 joint venture among NEC, Mitsubishi and Hitachi), and Micron (founded in Idaho in 1978 by former Mostek engineers to make DRAM chips). In reality the price for memory had been collapsing after the dotcom bust and, despite a spike in 2002, it continued to do so. In 1980 a gigabyte of memory cost several million dollars; in 2001 that price had plunged to about $1,000, and within a few years it would fall below $100, thus enabling high-resolution digital photography and video.

The Aging Internet

The dramatic success in the 2000s of the new business models of Netflix (videos), YouTube (videos), Apple (music), Facebook (news), Google (news) and Twitter (news) was beginning to bring out a fundamental problem of the Internet. All these services depended on the ability to distribute content over the Internet Protocol (IP). In other words, the Internet was increasingly being used as a media distribution network (in other words, to access data). Unfortunately, it had been designed to be a (host-to-host) communications network.

The Internet was becoming simultaneously the world's greatest distribution network and one of the world's worst distribution networks.

Nobody was proposing to dump the Internet yet, but it was obvious that the system needed to be tweaked. In particular, the router had to be reinvented. In 2006 Xerox PARC came up with Content Centric Networking (CCN), a project under the direction of Van Jacobson of Cisco and the Lawrence Livermore Laboratory. CCN was an idea already pioneered by Ted Nelson in 1979 and developed by Dan Cheriton at Stanford in 1999. It aimed at redesigning the Internet around data access.

An even more powerful kind of criticism was leveled at the Web: it did not contain enough "semantic" information about its own data. According to Danny Hillis of the Connection Machine fame, it contained information, not knowledge, and what was needed now was a knowledge web.

In July 2005 in San Francisco he established Metaweb, a company that proceeded to develop what in March 2007 became Freebase, an open, free and collaborative knowledge base. For all practical purposes it worked just like Wikipedia, except that its output was a set of structured data, or, better, "meta-data". In July 2010 Metaweb would be acquired by Google.

The program of rewriting the Internet as a safe and anonymous network was continued by MaidSafe, invented in 2006 in Britain by David Irvine. MAID (Massive Array of Independent Disks) SAFE (Secure Access For Everyone) removed the central servers and the central databases from the Internet, and instead added lots of encryption to protect the data. The goal was to build "a safe Internet". Irvine used concepts of volunteer-computing to decentralize the Internet: the storage came from hard-disk space "donated" by volunteers on the Internet connected via peer-to-peer protocols. Data stored on MaidSafe were broken down into tiny chunks, heavily encrypted, and then randomly distributed around the world. Only the owner had the power to reassemble and decrypt these chunks. The transactions were not stored anywhere: there are literally no traces left of any operation performed with MaidSafe. MaidSafe's network was based on SafeNet: a super-secure platform that aimed at "decentralizing" all the services available on the Internet, such as messaging, email, social networks, data storage, video conferencing, etc. SafeNet rewrote the Internet without any need for servers and databases. A user could log into any computer of the network and the computer would instantly become "her" computer, showing her data, her applications and her profile. When she logged out, no trace of her work was left behind.

Serving the Old Economy

Some sectors, like business software and Oracle, had little to learn from the dotcom revolution. In the 2000s Oracle represented an old-fashioned business model, the one that targeted "brick and mortar" companies. However, the Web had not slowed down the growth of software demand by the traditional companies that manufactured real products: it had increased it. They all needed to offer online shops backed by the fastest and most reliable database servers.

The escalating transaction volumes for e-business were good news for Oracle. Oracle was the undisputed leader in providing database management solutions, but these companies also demanded ERP systems and CRM systems. Oracle proceeded to acquire two Bay Area companies that had been successful in those fields: PeopleSoft (2004) and Siebel (2005). Now Oracle could literally connect the plant of a company to its corner offices and even to its traveling salesmen. In 2005 the total revenues of ERP software were $25.5 billion, with SAP making $10.5 billion and Oracle $5.1 billion. Oracle's founder and CEO, Larry Ellison, was estimated to be worth $18.7 billion in 2004, one of the richest people in the world.

A new generation of database management software to improve tasks for data analytics by employing Teradata's "shared nothing architecture" emerged with Vertica, founded in 2005 by Michael Stonebraker of Ingres fame (and acquired by HP in 2011), Greenplum, founded by Scott Yara and Luke Lonergan in 2003 in San Mateo (and acquired in 2010 by EMC), whose Bizgres shipped in 2005, and ParAccel (San Diego, 2005). At the same time, the database management appliance pioneered by Teradata spawned the generation of Boston's Netezza (founded in 1999 as Intelligent Data Engines by Foster Hinshaw and acquired by IBM in 2010), that launched its first "data warehouse appliance" in 2003.

High-density flash memory drives of the kind invented by M-Systems (acquired in 2006 by SanDisk) were improving and replacing hard drives in high-performance servers. The new star in this market was, however, not a Silicon Valley company but Fusion-io, founded by David Flynn in 2006 in Utah.

Oracle's Campus (2010)

Robots and Avatars

Recovering from the dotcom crash, Silicon Valley was more awash with futuristic ideas than ever before.

In 2005 Yan-Tak "Andrew" Ng at Stanford launched the STAIR (Stanford Artificial Intelligence Robot) project to build robots for home and office automation by integrating decade-old research in several different fields.

In 2006 early Google architect Scott Hassan founded Willow Garage to manufacture robots for domestic use.

Willow Garage in Menlo Park

Willow Garage would spawn a new generation of robotic companies: Savioke, OSRF, Suitable Technologies, hiDof, Unbounded Robotics (later Fetch Robotics), Simbe, as well as Industrial Perception and Redwood Robotics (both later acquired by Google). Willow Garage's PR2 robot of 2010 (mostly designed by Eric Berger), as well as the Robot Operating System (ROS), laid the foundations for the robotic developments of the following decade. Willow Garage contributed to the rise of open-source robotics also via the Point Cloud Library (PCL) for three-dimensional perception, spun off by Willow Garage in 2011 and based on original work by Radu Rusu in Germany before he joined Willow Garage; and the Open Source Robotics Foundation, opened in 2012 in Mountain View by a Willow Garage team (Brian Gerkey, Tully Foote, Nate Koenig, Steffi Paepcke) with ROS' architect Morgan Quigley from Stanford. The Open Source Computer Vision Library (OpenCV) had been started at Intel in 1999 by Gary Bradski. Another influential startup was Meka Robotics, an MIT spin-off founded in 2006 by Aaron Edsinger and Jeff Weber, but soon relocated to San Francisco (and acquired in 2013 by Google), that built robotic limbs providing a high degree of dexterity.

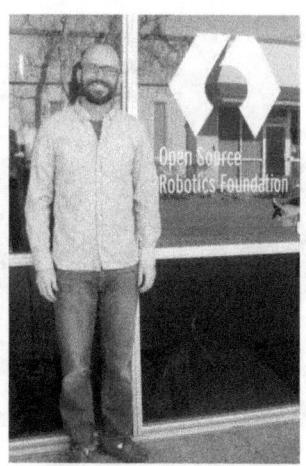

Morgan Quigley at the Open Source Robotics Foundation

The old school of industrial robots that preexisted Willow Garage was well represented by Precise Automation, founded in 2004 in Fremont by Brian Carlisle and Bruce Shimano (the founders of Adept).

The field of Artificial Intelligence came out of its long winter when in 2006 Geoffrey Hinton at the University of Toronto introduced a new technique for neural networks, "deep belief networks", thereby launching a new branch of Artificial Intelligence: "deep learning". Thanks to the contributions of scientists such as Yann LeCun and Yeshua Bengio (all of them on the East Coast), deep learning staged dramatic progress in very few years. If one doesn't count the various search engines (namely Xerox PARC-spinoff Outride, Stanford spinoff Kaltix, Brazil-based Akwan, and Australian-based Orion), in 2006 Google made its first move in the world of A.I. by acquiring Neven Vision, founded by the German scientist Hartmut Neven and specializing in face and object recognition. Google would go on to use it to tag images on the Internet and in 2010 it would introduce a mobile application to search for images, Google Goggles.

The emphasis on virtual worlds had a positive effect on the US videogame industry. After losing the leadership to Japan in the mid-1980s, the US recovered it in the 2000s because Japanese videogames were not as "immersive" as the ones made by their US competitors. For example, the simulation game "The Sims," created by SimCity's creator Will Wright for Maxis in February 2000, had become the best-selling PC game of all times within two years of its release. With the exception of Nintendo, which successfully introduced the Wii home console in 2006, Japanese game manufacturers were losing market shares for the first time ever. The Wii popularized hand-held motion-sensitive controllers, which led to a new generation of videogame consoles controlled by gestures and spoken commands.

However, the next big thing in videogames was online virtual worlds in which users created "second-life" avatars and interacted with each other. In 1999 Philip Rosedale had founded Linden Lab to develop virtual-reality hardware. In 2003 Linden Lab launched "Second Life," a virtual world accessible via the Internet in which a user could adopt a new identity and live a second life. Hotelli Kultakala (later renamed as Habbo Hotel), launched in August 2000 by Aapo Kyrola and Sampo Karjalainen in Finland, and Go-Gaia (later renamed Gaia Online), launched in February 2003 by Derek Liu in San Jose, were among the pioneers. In 2003 Will Harvey (from Stanford) and Jeffrey Ventrella (from the MIT Media lab) launched another virtual world, There.com, in San Mateo. One year later, in 2004, Eric Ries and Will Harvey founded IMVU in Mountain View, an early attempt to merge social networking and virtual reality. They all became extremely popular, involving millions of users spread all over the world. In February 2006 Alyssa Picariello even established a website to chronicle life in Gaia Online: the Gaiapedia.

Gamers are correct in claiming that the videogame community came first, as Korean game "Baramue Nara" or "Baram" (1996) and "Ultima Online" (1997), developed by Electronic Arts' game designer Richard Garriott (who also coined the term MMORPG), predated Second Life. And massively multiplayer games such as "EVE Online", introduced in 2003 by Simon & Schuster Interactive (a MMORPG that could be used by tens of thousands of players at the same time) and "World of Warcraft" (WoW), launched in 2004 by Blizzard Entertainment (still the largest MMORPG in the world in 2015), basically transposed the concept of Second Life back to the gaming market.

MMORPGs kept improving. EVE Online, introduced in 2003 by Simon & Schuster Interactive could have tens of thousands of players at the same time. "World of Warcraft", launched in 2004 by Blizzard Entertainment, would become the most popular MMORPG.

Mobile Payment

The "electronic wallet" was another application of the smartphone. Nokia pioneered the combination of smartphone and RFID with the Nokia 5140 in 2004. That was the first GSM phone integrated with RFID reading capability. The Japanese used mainly Sony's FeliCa chip for their electronic wallets (by the end of 2009 Sony had shipped more than 400 million FeliCa chips). In 2004 Sony and Philips Semiconductors, the semiconductor arm of Philips (spun off in 2006 as NXP) developed Near Field Communication (NFC) and Nokia joined them in founding the NFC Forum. Like RFID, NFC was a wireless technology for short-range communications between electronic devices. The main advantage was that it was cheaper and easier to implement, and therefore should foster mobile payments using a smartphone. NFC chips allowed for two-way communication instead of only one way. In 2007 Nokia unveiled the first fully integrated NFC phone, the Nokia 6131 NFC, while Sony and NXP were still holding on to their proprietary standards FeliCa and Mifare. At the same time in 2004 Wal-Mart began forcing RFID on its suppliers, a fact that contributed to the boom of interest in RFID. This is when the Bay Area entered the fray. Blaze Mobile, founded by telecom veteran Michelle Fisher in Berkeley, invented the NFC payment sticker in 2006.

Those were also the days when "fintech" became a reality. Wesabe, launched at the end of 2006 by Jason Knight and Marc Hedlund in San Francisco, was a web-based finance management tool, one of many web-based competitors of market leader Quicken, a crowded field that, in 2006, also included Nikhil Roy's Houston-based SpendView (later renamed Rudder) and Connecticut-based Geezeo. In 2007 Shashank Pandit and Ashwin Bharambe founded Buxfer in Mountain View. They all succumbed to Mint, a similar service launched in 2007 by Aaron Patzer in Mountain View and acquired by Intuit two years later.

Nonetheless, it was in Africa that mobile payment took off in earnest. Given the poor financial infrastructure but the broad availability of cellular phones, people spontaneously started "trading" airtime credit as a replacement for monetary transactions. In 2004 Mozambique's cellular-service provider Mcel institutionalized the practice by introducing a full-fledged airtime credit swapping service. This service allowed users to remove money from monetary transactions throughout Mozambique. Using a similar principle, Safaricom, de facto an East African subsidiary of British multinational Vodafone, introduced a money transfer system in Kenya called M-Pesa through which mobile phone users could "store" money on their phone and "text" money to others (via traditional SMS technology). M-Pesa remained the largest mobile payment system in the world well into the 2010s. By 2012 Africa was awash in popular mobile payment services: EcoCash in Zimbabwe (2011), mKesh in Mozambique (2011), Easywallet in Nigeria (2012), as well as several Mpesa spinoffs.

Wearables

Wearables, while still a tiny "novelty" market, continued to stage progress. In 2004 German chipmaker Infineon introduced a smart jacket with a mobile phone and an MP3 player. In 2003 Susumu Tachi at the University of Tokyo started working on "transparent clothes" using a trick called "retro-reflective projection" (thanks to a built-in camera in the back of the "cloak of invisibility"). In 2003 Burton introduced the Amp Jacket, a snowboarding jacket incorporating an iPod. In 2004 Los Angeles-based Vivometrics launched its smart shirt "LifeShirt". Adidas demonstrated its "self-adapting" shoes and North Face unveiled a "self-heating" jacket. In

2006 Eleksen (England) launched a wireless fabric keyboard. In 2006 Sensatex (Maryland), borrowing technology from Georgia Tech that was funded by DARPA for the 21st Century Land Warrior program, debuted its SmartShirt a shirt with fiber-optic wires seamlessly knit into the clothing and even fully washable. This smartshirt monitored the person's movement, heart rate, and respiration rate in real time.

Engineering the Future

The Web was only a decade old but high-profile critics were already complaining that it was inadequate. Berners-Lee in person had written an article in 2001 explaining the need for a "Semantic Web" in which a webpage would be able to declare the meaning of its content. In 2004 the first "Web 2.0" conference was held in San Francisco to promote the idea that the Web had to become an open platform for application development, with such development increasingly decentralized and delegated to the users themselves. The term had originally been coined in 1999 by San Francisco-based writer Darcy DiNucci. In the beginning of the Web one could only be either a producer or a consumer of webpages. The user of a browser was a passive viewer of webpages. Web 2.0 aimed for "active" viewers of webpages. A Web 2.0 webpage is a collaborative effort in which the viewers of the page can modify it and can interact with each other. Wikipedia was an example of a Web 2.0 application; and Google's search indirectly too, since it relied on a "page ranking" algorithm that was based on what was linked by millions of webpages all over the world.

The first widely publicized example of Web 2.0 was Flickr, a photo-sharing service that allowed users to "tag" photos (both their own and other people's), founded in February 2004 by game industry veterans Caterina Fake (based in San Francisco) and Stewart Butterfield (based in Vancouver). Unlike Ofoto and Snapfish, whose websites were just ways to encourage people to print photos, Flickr understood that in the age of ubiquitous camera phones and social networking the real value was in sharing photos across the community. Soon people started taking pictures precisely for the purpose of posting them on Flickr, pictures that they would not otherwise have taken.

Yahoo! was the first major dotcom to invest in Web 2.0. It acquired Flickr in March 2005 and introduced in June its own My Web service, which allowed webpage viewers to tag and share bookmarks. Then in December it bought the most popular website for social bookmarking and tagging, Del.icio.us (originally started by Wall Street financial analyst Joshua Schachter in 2003). Basically, Yahoo! wanted to present itself as a "social search" that was fine-tuned by humans as they browsed the web, as opposed to Google's impersonal algorithmic search.

The technical underpinning of Web 2.0 consisted of free tools such as Ajax (Asynchronous JavaScript and XML), a concept invented in 2003 by

Greg Aldridge in Indiana (but the term was coined only in 2005 by San Francisco-based writer Jesse James Garrett). Ajax was a platform for website developers to create interactive web-based applications (essentially HTML, XML and JavaScript).

In a nutshell, the goal was simple: to allow the viewer to make changes to a webpage on a browser without reloading the whole page. This, obviously, had been done before: JavaScript, among other tools, had been available in Netscape's browser since 1996, and web-based applications were already pervasive during the first dotcom boom but most of them went out of business quickly. Amazon allowed users to post reviews of books since the very beginning. However, Web 2.0 had a more ambitious vision: that the Web could be viewed as a platform for creating applications, a platform that would eventually replace the individual computer. The Web 2.0 was another example of a software revolution enabled by open-source software. The reason that so many startups emerged in this space is that the cost of starting one was minimal.

Blogging started to democratize too. Matt Mullenweg in San Francisco introduced in 2003 a new popular platform for people to create their own website or blog: Wordpress. The reason it spread like wildfire is that it was maintained as "open source" by a growing community of volunteers. In June 2003 Mark Fletcher, already the founder of ONElist (acquired by Yahoo! in 2000), launched Bloglines, the first Web-based news aggregator.

Digg, founded in November 2004 by serial entrepreneur Jay Adelson in San Francisco, pioneered the idea of letting visitors vote stories up or down (i.e., "digging" or "burying"), thus bridging the world of news aggregators and social networking.

By 2012 Digg, initially a darling of the Internet, was worth very little, due to both a more complicated user interface and to the emergence of powerful competitors with very similar concepts for people to share news. San Francisco-based Redditt had been founded in Boston in June 2005 by Steve Huffman and Alexis Ohanian, two graduates from the University of Virginia, one year before Digg. 2012 is the year when its traffic passed Digg's and Reddit kept growing. It was just easier for people to submit a bunch of stories quickly to Reddit than to Digg. Because of its own algorithm, Digg had become a sort of elitist club in which about 25% of the stories that went popular were submitted by the same few dozen of people. Reddit was powered by a more democratic algorithm that, indirectly, distributed "glory" among all its users, including beginners. Digg then started posting "sponsored links" prominently, which definitely turned off the troops. Reddit, meanwhile, in 2008 introduced "subreddits" (categories). One particularly popular subreddit, dating from May 2009, was IAmA ("I Am A") where users can post "AMAs" (for "Ask Me Anything"), a way for users to interact. It was used by many celebrities.

TechCrunch was founded in June 2005 by Michael Arrington out of his home in Atherton to publish high-tech news and gossip about Internet startups.

That inherent lack of semantics was actually good news for a new batch of startups that saw that limitation as a business opportunity: as the amount of data increased, the need to understand those data would also increase exponentially.

Paypal's co-founder Peter Thiel, Alex Karp and others founded in 2004 in Palo Alto (with funding from the CIA) Palantir Technologies to make data-mining software for the government and financial companies.

In New York in 2007 former DoubleClick's founder Dwight Merriman and fellow DoubleClick alumni Kevin Ryan and Eliot Horowitz founded 10gen (later renamed MongoDB) for mining of unstructured data such as text, video and audio files.

Yahoo!'s Campus (2010)

Biotech

Biotechnology was becoming mainstream and synthetic biology was the new frontier, though its goal was not clear. Yet the businessmen behind it envisioned the possibility of building new living species (initially just bacteria) that would perform useful industrial or domestic functions. It would exist just as electronics had led to devices that performed useful industrial and domestic functions (the word "military" was carefully omitted). Scientists in synthetic biology was actually not very interested in cloning existing species: why not use existing species then? They were interested in modifying existing organisms to create organisms that do not exist in nature. Genetic engineering is about replacing one gene, whereas synthetic biology is about replacing entire genomes to generate "reprogrammed organisms" whose functions are different from the original ones (because the DNA instructions have changed).

Synthetic biology exploited the power of microbes to catalyze a sequence of biological reactions that transform a chemical compound into another compound. In 2004 MIT's scientist Drew Endy, who had just co-founded a public repository called "the Registry of Standard Biological Parts", organized the first synthetic biology conference and started the first company to commercialize synthetic biology, Codon Devices. In 2005 Endy published an influential article in Nature titled "Foundations for engineering biology". In 2006 Jay Keasling inaugurated the world's first synthetic biology department at the Lawrence Berkeley Laboratory. UCSF too became a major center of biological research. In 2003 Christopher Voigt founded a lab to program cells like robots to perform complex tasks, and in 2005 UCSF opened an Institute for Human Genetics. In 2006 Chris Voigt's team at UC Berkeley engineered a bacterium to target cancer cells in the human body. In 2007 Craig Venter's team in Maryland carried out a full-genome transplant: they transplanted the genome of a bacterium (Mycoplasma Mycoides) into the cytoplasm of a different bacterium (Mycoplasma Capricolum).

One example of synthetic biology that captured the attention of the media in April 2005 was the announcement that Keasling at Amyris had successfully converted yeast into a chemical factory by mixing bacteria, yeast, and wormwood genes. This "factory" was capable of turning simple sugar into artemisinic acid, the preliminary step to making an extremely expensive anti-malarian drug, artemisin. Artemisinin was commonly extracted from a plant but science was now able to manufacture the anti-malarian drug in the laboratory, pretty much at will. (The world would, however, have to wait until 2013 for French multinational Sanofi to introduce a commercial pill, designed by Keasling's Amyris). The goal of synthetic biology was now to create "designer microbes" by selecting genes based on which protein they encode and the path they follow. Some day, synthetic biology could even replace industrial chemistry, which relies on a sequence of chemical reactions to manufacture materials.

Venter's saga continued. After disagreements with Celera's main investor Tony White, in January 2002 Venter left Celera taking Hamilton Smith with him. In 2003 they synthesized the genome of a virus (just eleven genes) which, unlike the artificial polio virus at Stony Brook, truly behaved like a virus. With a keen sixth sense for money and publicity, in September 2004 Venter started his own non-profit institute in both Maryland and California (San Diego) to conduct research in synthetic biology and biofuels. In particular, he worked on building the genome of a bacterium from scratch and on inserting the genome of one bacterium into another. Bacteria are the simplest living organisms, made of just one cell.

In 2007 Venter's team carried out a full-genome transplant: they transplanted the genome of a bacterium (Mycoplasma Mycoides) into the cytoplasm of a different bacterium (Mycoplasma Capricolum).

The first international conference of Synthetic Biology was held in 2004 at the MIT.

Bioinformatics continued to thrive. Two former Silicon Genetics executives, Saeid Akhtari and Ilya Kupershmidt, started NextBio in Cupertino in 2004 to create a platform to perform data mining on public and private genomic data.

In 2003 the biochemist Joseph DeRisi at UCSF used a microarray (a gene chip) to identify the coronavirus causing SARS (Severe Acute Respiratory Syndrome), a method that inaugurated a new way to to identify pathogens (by analyzing DNA).

In 2004 the first commercial microarrays with the whole human genome became available from Affymetrix (whose GeneChip was still dominating the market for microarrays), Agilent (that still relied on the technique based on inkjet printing), Applied Biosystems and Illumina (all based in California, the first three in the Bay Area). Technically speaking, the first company to offer a whole-human-genome microarray was probably Wisconsin-based NimbleGen Systems in 2003. Then the battle began for lower prices and better "annotation" of the genes (in 2009 Arrayit, founded in 1993 as TeleChem International in Sunnyvale by Rene Schena and Todd Martinsky, would introduce the H25K).

US citizens were spending billions of dollars in blood tests. Theranos, founded in 2003 in Palo Alto by Stanford dropout Elizabeth Holmes, offered a cheaper, simpler and faster way to test blood: no needle, just a few drops of blood. The company would skyrocket to stardom and Holmes would be known as the world's youngest female self-made millionaire, while boasting one the weirdest boards of directors ever seen in Silicon Valley, which at one point would include two former secretaries of state (Henry Kissinger and George Shultz), two former senators (Sam Nunn and Bill Frist), a former secretary of defense (William Perry) and even a retired admiral.

In 1998 James Thomson at the University of Wisconsin had isolated human embryonic stem cells. This discovery made it possible for scientists to generate all the building blocks of our body in a laboratory, because stem cells are the cells that can become any other cell in the body. Scientists could see a near future in which medicine would be able to grow replacement tissues (for example, to replace burned skin) and body organs. Regenerative medicine suddenly became a reality. Several companies were born all over the world: Cellectis (France, 1999), Mesoblast (Australia, 2004), Capricor Therapeutics (Los Angeles, 2005), Pharmicell (Germany,

2006), etc. In 2004 the state of California launched a California Institute for Regenerative Medicine. Research in the USA was slowed down by ethical considerations until 2007 when Shinya Yamanaka at Kyoto University in Japan created embryonic stem cells in his laboratory (his technology was immediately licensed by Cellectis).

Nanotech

Nanotechnology was still a mystery. While returns were low and nano startups routinely switched to more traditional manufacturing processes, during both 2006 and 2007 venture-capital firms invested more than $700 million in nanotechnology startups.

A promising avenue was to wed "nano" and "green," a mission particularly nurtured in Berkeley. NanoSolar engineers formed the core of Solexant, founded in 2006 in San Jose by Indian-born chemist Damoder Reddy and by Paul Alivisatos, Professor of Chemistry and Materials Science at UC Berkeley. Alivisatos was also the director (since 2009) of the Lawrence Berkeley Laboratory to manufacture printable thin-film "quantum dot" photovoltaic cells using a technology developed at the Lawrence Berkeley Laboratory. This was held to be the next generation of solar technology: flexible, low-cost, and high-yield.

Other solar research was promising too. Michael Crommie, a scientist at the Materials Sciences Division at the Lawrence Berkeley Laboratory and a professor of physics at UC Berkeley, was working on solar cells the size of a single molecule. Canadian nanotechnology specialists Ted Sargent of the University of Toronto developed a "quantum film" capable of a light-capturing efficiency of 90%, as opposed to 25% for the CMOS image sensors employed in digital cameras. In October 2006 he founded InVisage in Menlo Park to make quantum film for camera phones.

The biggest news in the world of nanotech came from England: in 2004 Andre Geim and Konstantin Novoselov at the University of Manchester isolated graphene, a one-atom thick layer of pure carbon, a material that is the lightest material known and, at the same time, the strongest material known (200 times stronger than steel), the best conductor of heat at room temperature and the best known conductor of electricity (capable of carrying electricity at a speed of 1 million meters per second).

Greentech

Skyrocketing oil prices and concerns about climate change opened a whole new range of opportunities for an environmentally friendly energy generation, nicknamed "greentech" or "cleantech." Of the traditional kinds of renewable energy (wind power, solar power, biomass, hydropower, biofuels) solar and biofuel emerged as the most promising. At the same time, the US started investing in fuel-cell companies in 2005 with the goal of fostering commercial fuel-cell vehicles by 2020. By 2008 it had spent $1 billion. California embarked on a project to set up a chain of stations to refuel hydrogen-driven vehicles (despite the fact that the state had only 179 fuel-cell vehicles in service in 2007).

Silicon Valley entrepreneurs and investors delved into projects to produce clean, reliable, and affordable energy. A startup that focused on renewable fuels was LS9, founded in 2005 in South San Francisco to create alkanes (a constituent of gasoline) from sugar by Harvard Professor George Church and Chris Somerville, the director of UC Berkeley's Energy Biosciences Institute; it was financed by Vinod Khosla and Boston-based Flagship Ventures.

Cars were another interesting sector. After selling their e-book company NuvoMedia, in 2003 Martin Eberhard and Marc Tarpenning founded Tesla Motors in Palo Alto to build electrical cars. In 2006 they introduced the Tesla Roadster, the first production automobile to use lithium-ion battery cells.

The Tesla Roadster (2010)

In 2004 SUN's co-founder Vinod Khosla, who had joined venture capital firm Kleiner Perkins Caufield & Byers, founded Khosla Ventures to invest in green-technology companies. One year later another SUN co-founder, Bill Joy, replaced him at Kleiner Perkins Caufield & Byers to invest in green technology.

Another legendary "serial entrepreneur" of Silicon Valley, Marc Porat of General Magic fame, turned to building materials for the "green" economy and founded three startups to develop materials for reducing energy consumption and carbon emission: Serious Materials (2002) in Sunnyvale for eco-friendly materials; CalStar Cement (2007), a spin-off of the University of Missouri based in the East Bay (Newark) that manufactured eco-friendly bricks; and Zeta Communities (2007) in San Francisco for pre-assembled homes that operate at net-zero energy.

Meanwhile, UC Berkeley and the Lawrence Berkeley Laboratory launched a joint "Helios Project" for artificial photosynthesis, i.e. to convert sunlight into fuel.

Sebastian Thrun at Stanford built the robotic car that in 2005 won a "race" sponsored by the Pentagon in a California desert. Thrun was then hired by Google to work on autonomous vehicles that, in following years, would be seen driving over California highways with only one person in the car: the passenger.

In 2006 Elon Musk (of Paypal, Tesla and SpaceX fame) co-founded with his cousins Peter and Lyndon Rive what would become California's main provider of residential solar power: Solar City, based in San Mateo.

Solar City

Culture and Society

The arts mirrored progress in the high-tech industry. The 2000s were the decade of interactive digital art, practiced by the likes of Camille Utterback and Ken Goldberg. Andy Cunningham and Beau Takahara formed Zero1 in San Jose to promote the marriage of art and technology. In 2004 Michael Sturtz, who in 1999 had founded the alternative art school The Crucible in Berkeley, began staging spectacular fire-themed shows, including operas and ballets. In 2005 the Letterman Digital Arts Center opened in San Francisco to house Lucasfilm's lab. The first Zer01 Festival for "art and technology in the digital age" was held in San Jose in 2006, sponsored by San Jose State University's CADRE. Stephanie Syjuco's counterfeit sculptures, Lee Walton's web happenings, and Amy Balkin's ecological projects referenced the issues of the era. In 2006 San Mateo held the first "Maker Faire". In 2006 Josette Melchor and Peter Hirshberg formed the Gray Area Art Foundation. In 2000 Fecalface.com was launched to support the alternative art scene (later also a physical gallery, the Fecal Face Dot Gallery). The Adobe Books Backroom Gallery, another epicenter of new art, opened in 2001. The Mission School's mission of mural paintings and found-object sculpture was being continued by Andrew Schoultz and Sirron Norris. Also Dave Warnke focused on stickers and hand-painted posters, Sandro "Misk" Tchikovani specialized in three-dimensional letters, and Damon Soule explored mixed media on found wood.

It was widely believed (although poorly documented) that San Francisco boasted the highest per capita consumption of books. In 1999 Jack Boulware and Jane Ganahl started a literary festival called Litstock that later mutated into Litquake.

Hacker parties had always been popular in Silicon Valley but during the 2000s they reached new height, both in terms of size and enthusiasm. In May 2005 a group of high-tech geeks convened at the Hillsborough house of David Weekly, a Stanford graduate who was working on his startup (later incorporated as PBwiki). That was the first "SuperHappyDevHouse", a concept that soon became popular in Silicon Valley: a casual meeting in a casual environment of creative engineers to work in the same building on their pet projects. Unlike the many networking events, the goal was not necessarily to publicize one's idea nor to meet other people: it was to go home having written some actual software or at least come up with ideas for some software. Unlike hacker competitions, it was not about showing one's dexterity at coding. And, unlike the raves of San Francisco, it was not a wild party of drinking and drugs; quite the opposite in fact. It was a way to create a more stimulating environment than the cubicles of an office, and, in fact, more similar to the dormitory of a university campus. (The idea would spread internationally within a few years). The ambition was to emulate the success of the Homebrew Computer Club of the 1970s, although the similarity was mostly superficial.

In 2002 Bram Cohen and Len Sassaman founded the CodeCon conference for hackers at the DNA Lounge in San Francisco. This would become an annual event and spread all over the world.

The Bay Area, already home to the Search For Extraterrestrial Intelligence Institute (or SETI Institute), became the birthplace of another project aimed at discovering life in the universe, and one that, yet again, resurrected the social-utopian spirit of the Bay Area: SETI@Home, launched in 1999 by UC Berkeley astronomers, which harnessed the power of millions of home computers provided by volunteers and distributed around the globe (5 million in 2014) with the goal of trying to detect radio transmissions from extraterrestrial civilizations picked up by a telescope based in Puerto Rico.

More importantly, this was the first major example of "volunteer computing", in which the "crowd" was providing a computational power bigger than any supercomputer could provide. In 2000 Vijay Pande at Stanford launched Folding@Home, a project of volunteer computing for research on how proteins "fold". Most of these projects of volunteer computing used the Berkeley Open Infrastructure for Network Computing (BOINC), developed since 2002 by David Anderson for SETI@Home.

In 2000 the computer scientist Bill Joy, one of SUN's founders, had written an article titled "The Future doesn't need us" warning against the threat posed by robotics, genetics and nanotech. Meanwhile, Jaron Lanier was ranting against the "digital Maoism" of Silicon Valley. The very founders of the high-tech world started a debate about the pros and cons of the new technology.

The Anthropology of Pan-Ethnic Materialism

The cultural diversity of the Bay Area continued to ablate religious certainties. A person's loyalty to her religious group was undermined by the proximity of so many other religious groups (in the workplace, at shared homes, in sport activities). This led to an increasingly higher degree of flexibility in choosing one's faith. The new-age movement, with its syncretic non-dogmatic view of spirituality, had left its own influence on the region, even though its message was now being interpreted in a more materialistic manner. For many people religion was to be shaped by how one wanted to behave. For example, greed and promiscuity were definitely "in" for the vast majority of independently religious people. Religious axioms that constrained one's lifestyle were not particularly popular. Religious practices that were perceived as beneficial to one's mind and body were. Thus Zen retreats and yoga classes were popular even among people who did not believe in Buddhism.

Santa Clara Valley had traditionally been a Catholic region. It had become a unique experiment within the Catholic world: a Catholic region with sizeable minorities of other religious groups that were not poor segregated immigrants (as was the case in Italy or France), but who lived on equal footing with the original Catholic families. Both the percentage and the level of integration were unique among Catholic regions.

The time and attention usually devoted to religious functions were translated to the high-tech world. The public rituals of religion were replaced by public rituals of lectures and high-tech symposia. The mass in a church was replaced by a business or technology forum. The technology being produced downplayed the cultural differences. People tended to recognize themselves more strongly as workers of a company than as members of a religious or ethnic group.

Re-inflating Cities

Those who had predicted the demise of Silicon Valley had completely missed the point. In 2005 Silicon Valley accounted for 14% of the world's venture capital. San Jose's population of 912,332 had just passed San Francisco and San Jose had become the tenth largest city in the US. The Bay Area as a whole was the largest high-tech center in the world with 386,000 high-tech jobs in 2006.

Sharks: the iPhone, Cloud Computing, Location-based Services, Social Games, and Personal Genomics (2007-10)

The Decline of the Computer

The late 2000s were the age of streaming media, smart phones, and cloud computing; all trends pointed towards the demise of the "computer" as it had been known for 50 years.

In 2007 Utah-based Move Networks, founded in 2000 by Novell's cofounder and Netware's architect Drew Major (and acquired in 2011 by EchoStar), introduced "adaptive streaming" for HTTP that provided a way to broadcast television on the Internet (HTTP being the same protocol that serves webpages to a browser). This technology represented an alternative to the prevailing RTSP protocol for live video over the Internet. Adaptive streaming customized the delivery of content in real time, based on the network's current capacity to handle data. Using the same principles, Microsoft (2008), Netflix (2008), Apple (2009) and Adobe (2010) quickly introduced their own HTTP-based streaming technologies. In 2011 the world adopted a standard called MPEG-DASH (Dynamic Adaptive Streaming over HTTP) for live streaming multimedia content (such as the content streamed by YouTube and Netflix) over the Internet. By 2016 about 50% of Internet traffic would be flowing over MPEG-DASH.

Music and file sharing were at the bleeding edge. In 2008 digital music downloads grew by 25%, to $3.7 billion (including 1.4 billion songs). This accounted for 20% of all music sales, but the music industry estimated that over 40 billion songs were illegally file-shared, which meant that 95% of the market for digital music downloads was underground. In 2009, file-sharing services ranked among the Internet's most popular websites: Rapidshare was 26th and Mediafire was 63rd. In 2009 BitTorrent accounted for at least 20% of all Internet traffic. The numbers were so large that it was hard to believe all these people were criminally motivated. It was instead an important signal that people like to download files instead of buying physical objects. Movies, on the other hand, were encoded in very large files: it was more effective to "stream" them than to download them. Here, too, the public was sending the message that the physical object was becoming redundant.

As images, music, and videos proliferated (at increasingly higher resolutions), the demand for storage became prohibitive. At the same time that the demand for remote downloads increased, network bandwidth was increasing rapidly. It then became sensible to think of keeping the files on the Internet instead of downloading them on the home computer. In the past the main reason to download them before viewing them had just been that the network was "slow." Once the network became fast enough, using a home computer to store multimedia files became redundant, and consumers started playing them directly from the Internet. For example, Netflix (that had become the main movie rental-by-mail service) launched its streaming feature in January 2007. In just two years its catalog grew to more than 12,000 titles (movies and television episodes). In March 2010 YouTube broadcast the Indian Premier League of cricket live worldwide, the first major sport competition to be broadcast live on the Internet.

Smart phones that allowed browsing the Web and exchanging e-mail had become very popular, notably the BlackBerry and the Razr, but the brutally competitive field was not for the faint of heart. In June 2007 Apple, which after the iPod had become the master of fashionable devices, introduced the iPhone. It immediately captured the imagination of the younger generation thanks to sleek design (courtesy, as usual, of Jonathon Ive's glass and metal minimalism), a multitouch user interface, a (touch) QWERTY keyboard, the Safari browser, an email client, Google Maps, 3.5-inch widescreen display to watch videos, a 2-megapixel camera coupled with a photo management application, Wi-Fi, an MP3 player, and a real operating system that turned it into a computer (a platform for software applications, not just a gadget). Last but not least, it was backed by telecom giant AT&T. Never mind that it lacked stereo Bluetooth support, 3G compatibility. copy and paste, and it came with a stingy memory. In 2008 Apple also introduced the "App Store," where independent software developers could sell their applications for the iPhone. By April 2010 there would be more than 180,000 "apps" and by October 2013 there would be more than one million. Apple had created in the digital age a new industry that was the equivalent of the cottage industry, an industry of independents who worked from their own homes.

In 2007 Google began freely distributing Android. It was a Linux-based open-source operating system for mobile phones that had originally been developed by a Palo Alto stealth startup named Android and founded by Andy Rubin and others. Google also created the Android Marketplace to compete with the App Store (by April 2010 it had 38,000 applications for Android-based devices). Motorola was the first company (in late 2009) to deliver an Android-based smart phone, the Droid, and reaped the benefits: it shipped 2.3 million units in the first quarter of 2010, thus resurrecting itself after the collapse of the Razr. In 2010 Taiwanese cell-phone manufacturer HTC entered the Android market with its Indredible phone, and so did Samsung with its Galaxy S. Every Android manufacturer had little control on its future, though, because the success of its device depended on Google's whims and on the whims of the carrier (Verizon, AT&T and Spring being the main ones).

At the beginning of 2010, Research In Motion was estimated to have 42% of the market, followed by Apple with 25%, Microsoft with 15% and Android-based devices with 9%. Android sales in the first three months of 2010 accounted for 28% of all smart phone sales, ahead of iPhone's 21% but still behind BlackBerry's 36%. This would change more rapidly than anybody predicted.

The loser was Palm, which released its Pre at the same time as Apple released the iPhone. It didn't have the charisma to compete with Google and Apple, and in April 2010 was sold to HP. In March 2008 John Doerr of Kleiner Perkins launched a $100 million venture-capital fund, the iFund, for iPhone applications, crediting the iPhone as an invention more important than the personal computer because it knew who the user was and where s/he was.

Apple's iOS was a hit because of its multi-touch technology, but that was hardly an Apple invention. Touch-screen technology had come from Europe, and it had been in Britain (at Xerox's EuroPARC) that sixteen years earlier (in 1991) Pierre Wellner had designed his multi-touch "Digital Desk" with multi-finger and pinching motions. Then a student Wayne Westerman at the University of Delaware and his professor John Elias had founded (in 1998) Fingerworks to commercialize a technology to help people with finger injuries use a computer. Fingerworks had gone on to sell a full line of multi-touch products, notably the iGesture Pad in 2003. Apple had acquired Fingerworks' multi-touch technology in 2005. The iOS, unveiled in January 2007 (although it was not named that way until March 2008), was a Unix-like operating system that incorporated that technology: one-finger swipe to scroll horizontally, a finger tap to select an object, A reverse two-finger pinch (an "unpinch") to enlarge an image, etc. Incidentally, in 2001 Paul Dietz and Darren Leigh at Mitsubishi Electric Research Labs (MERL) in Boston had even developed a multi-touch interface that could even recognize which person is touching where ("DiamondTouch").

It was easy to predict that soon more users would access the Internet from mobile devices than from desktop computers (and probably many of them would be unaware of being on the Internet). In 2009, almost 90% of households in the US owned a cell phone. Yet the average time of voice minutes per call (1.81 minutes) was lower than in 2008, despite the fact that millions of households were disconnecting their land phone lines. At the beginning, voice conversation was the only application for cell phones. Then came text messaging, Web browsing, navigation and so forth.

Text messaging, in particular, proved to resonate with the psychology of the digital age. It was less time-consuming and disruptive than a voice call, even if it took longer to type a message than to say it. Voice communication was rapidly becoming an afterthought, while a myriad of applications (most of which had nothing to do with telephone conversations) were becoming the real reason to purchase a "phone." The purpose of a cell phone was more data than voice. Handset design was less and less "cheek-friendly," more and more palm-friendly, because people were not supposed to "hear" but to "see" with their cell phone. In 2010 the cell phones from Nokia (that were truly meant to be telephones) were to the Apple and Android smart phones what typewriters were in the age of the personal computer.

Phones were penetrating other key devices. In 2008 Chrysler pioneered the router system that installed the Internet even in cars (by connecting a cellular device to a wireless local-area network). At the end of 2009 there were already 970,000 cars equipped with Internet access.

Responding to the pressure, in 2010 Apple launched a very thin and light laptop, the second-generation MacBook Air. Samsung responded in 2012 with the Series 9 notebooks, Lenovo in 2015 with the ultra-light Lenovo LaVie, and HP in 2016 with the HP Spectre 13, billed as "the world's thinnest laptop".

In May 2010, a symbolic event took place when Apple's market capitalization ($227 billion) passed Microsoft's ($226 billion). In August 2011 Apple passed ExxonMobil to become the most valuable company in the world based on market capitalization.

Apple's Infinity Loop and Headquarters (2010)

Towards Computing as a Utility

At the same time the traditional computer was attacked by the paradigm of "cloud computing." This was Internet-based computing in which the computers are hidden from the users and computing power is delivered on demand, when needed, just like electricity is delivered to homes when and in the amount needed.

A classic example was Spotify, a service launched in 2008 by Swedish serial entrepreneur Daniel Ek that allowed subscribers to stream music. Napster had figured out a way that Internet users could simply gift each other music (alas, this was deemed illegal). Apple's iTunes had created the virtual music store, from which customers could buy (and download) their music. Spotify did not sell music, and its subscriber did not pay to "own" the music: they paid to listen to it. The music remained on the cloud, owned by the music companies or by the musician. Spotify did not require any hardware to play music, just a regular computer or smartphone (all of which were by now capable of playing the most popular music formats).

Public cloud storage had been legitimized in 2006 when Amazon had introduced its Simple Storage Service, or S3, service that anyone could use. Box, founded near Seattle in 2005 by Aaron Levie and Dylan Smith but soon relocated to Silicon Valley (Los Altos), decided to use its own servers (not Amazon's) and to target the corporate world. Dropbox, founded in 2007 by MIT students, created a friendlier service based on S3.

Cloud computing was typically built on "virtual" infrastructures provided by "hypervisors," or virtual-machine monitors, that allowed multiple operating systems to run concurrently on a single computer, enabling any application to run anywhere at any time.

The pioneer and leader of virtualization had been Vmware. Its 2008 revenues increased 42% to $1.9 billion, and new hypervisors were offered by Oracle (VM, introduced in 2007 and based on open-source Xen technology), Microsoft (Hyper-V, introduced in 2008), and Red Hat (Enterprise Virtualization, introduced in 2009). The virtual-machine monitor Xen was developed in 2003 at the University of Cambridge by Ian Pratt's team and acquired by Florida-based Citrix Systems in October 2007. In August 2010 Hewlett-Packard acquired 3PAR, specialized in data storage for cloud computing shared by multiple companies ("utility storage").

There were only four companies selling the kind of storage required by cloud computing: IBM, Hitachi, 3PAR, and EMC. EMC was based in Boston, but in 2003 had acquired three Silicon Valley success stories: Documentum, Legato, and VMware.

EMC represented yet another business in which Silicon Valley had largely failed to lead. Founded in 1979 by Richard Egan and Roger Marino to make memory boards for minicomputers, in 1990 EMC had introduced a data storage platform for mainframe computers, Symmetrix (designed by the Israeli-born engineer Moshe Yanai). It was the right time: the explosion of data that came with the Internet created a demand that only data storage systems like Symmetrix could satisfy.

The next step after virtualizing the operating system and the databases was to virtualize the network, which was precisely the mission of Palo Alto-based Nicira Networks, a 2007 spin-off of a joint Stanford-Berkeley project around the dissertation of Stanford student Martin Casado supervised by British-born Stanford professor Nick McKeown and UC Berkeley professor Scott Shenker.

In 2011 Oracle acquired Montana-based RightNow Technologies, a provider of cloud-based Customer Relationship Management (CRM) applications to compete directly with SalesForce. Locally, similar services were offered on the cloud by Pleasanton-based Workday, the new company of PeopleSoft's founder Dave Duffield (started in 2005).

Virtualization allowed a "farm" of computing power to create a virtual machine for a customer, no matter where the customer was located. A computing environment (made of disparate software and hardware components) could be dynamically configured to represent several different machines, each assigned to a different customer. This "multi-tenant system" was conceptually similar to a power plant: it supplied computing power over the Internet to multiple customers the way a power plant supplied electricity over the electric grid to multiple customers.

For decades, software and hardware manufacturers had relied on business plans that envisioned selling the very same system to multiple customers who were using it to perform identical tasks. Ubiquitous and cheap broadband was fostering an era in which a "computing utility" could provide that service (hardware and software) to all those customers over the Internet, with no need for those customers to purchase any of the components (just pay a monthly fee).

Knowledge production was becoming centralized the way energy production had become centralized with the invention of the electrical grid (spreading the power created by a power plant) and the way food production had become centralized 5000 years earlier after the invention of the irrigation network. Each "network" had created a new kind of economy, society and, ultimately, civilization.

Social networking too was destined to become a "utility" of sorts for businesses. The idea of collaboration software over the Web had been pioneered by startups such as Jive Software, founded in 2001 by two students from the University of Iowa, Matt Tucker and Bill Lynch, and originally based in New York. In the age of Facebook it was renamed "enterprise social network service" and embraced by startups such as Yammer, originally developed in 2007 by Adam Pisoni and David Sacks (a Paypal alumnus) at Geni in San Francisco, and spawned off in

September 2008 (and bought by Microsoft in 2012). This platform hinted at the first major revolution in ERP since SAP's glorious R3.

Google versus Microsoft

The 1990s had been the decade of Microsoft. Microsoft owned the operating system, and it owned the most popular applications. Microsoft's success relied on the concept of the personal computer: one user, one application, one computer. Web-based computing represented the first serious challenge to Microsoft's business model. Due to increased bandwidth and more sophisticated Internet software, it had become possible to create applications that ran on websites and that users could access via their Web browser. It was basically a client-server architecture, except that the "server" was potentially the entire Internet, and the client was potentially the entire human population.

Cloud computing was on-demand Web-based computing. The concept was pioneered by startups such as Saleforce.com. In February 2007, Google targeted Microsoft's core business when it disclosed a humbler version of cloud computing, Google Docs. That suite could be accessed by any computer via a Web browser, and included a word-processor and a spreadsheet program (both acquired from independent companies, respectively Upstartle and 2Web Technologies). One could already imagine the end of the era of the operating system, as the Web replaced the need for one. A computer only needed a browser to access the Web, where all other resources and applications were located.

Microsoft was still dominant and powerful. In 2008 Microsoft Windows owned almost 90% of the operating system market for personal computers, while Google owned almost 70% of the Internet search market. The future, though, seemed to be on Google's side. In April 2010, Microsoft's IE commanded 59.9% of the browser market, followed by Firefox with 24.5% and Google's own Chrome (first released in September 2008 and based on Apple's WebKit)) with 6.7% That was a steep decline from the days when IE was ubiquitous.

On the other hand, Google's revenues depended almost entirely on third-party advertising. The "war" between Google and Microsoft was well publicized, but the war between Google and Yahoo! was probably more serious for Google's immediate future. In 2007 Google paid $3.1 billion for DoubleClick, the New York-based company that dominated "display advertising." This was the method favored by Yahoo! when Google was piling up millions with its keyword ads. As the quality of browsers and computers improved, Yahoo!'s glamorous ads became more and more popular, and they were served by DoubleClick. By acquiring it, Google struck at the heart of Yahoo!'s business. And now Google had all the pieces to create an "advertising operating system." In 2009 Yahoo! owned

17% of the market for display ads, followed by Microsoft at 11% and AOL at 7%.

Google's strategy became even more aggressive in 2010 when it launched into an acquisition spree. Notably, it purchased BumpTop, the three-dimensional GUI developed since 2006 by University of Toronto's student Anand Agarwala, and Plink, a visual search engine developed by two Oxford University's students, Mark Cummins and James Philbin. Chrome OS was first released in November 2009. It was a variant of the Linux-based operating system Ubuntu that was developed in Britain by Mark Shuttleworth's Canonical. At the same time, the products that Google engineers truly invented and that the company widely hyped, such as the social networking platform Buzz and the groupware Wave, were embarrassing failures.

Google's technology was consistently inferior to what the Silicon Valley landscape was producing. For example, Superfish, started in 2006 in Palo Alto by Israeli-born semiconductor-industry veteran Adi Pinhas and A.I. guru Michael Chertok, launched in 2010 a visual search tool that, unlike Google Goggles, was able to recognize pictures regardless of perspective, lighting, distance and so forth.

The effect of Google's domination of the search-engine market was the same as the effect of Microsoft's domination of the personal-computer operating-system market: to stifle innovation. Google had built its reputation on returning webpages based on their "relevance." Now it was mostly returning commercial websites that had little relevance to the search string, and the ubiquitous Wikipedia (for which one was better off just searching within Wikipedia itself). A very relevant article written by a scholar was very unlikely to show up in the first page of results. The "irrelevance" of Google's searches was mainly driving an entire economy based on advertising products and services. And, of course, the fact that the Web was being littered with the ubiquitous "Google Adwords" hardly represented a welcome change. Most of the text and images that flooded a user's screen constituted commercial ads (in ever more creative and invasive fashions). Due to the proliferation of Google AdWords, the Web was becoming not only unsearchable but also unreadable.

Alas, Google had a virtual monopoly on web search: any search engine that was truly committed to "relevance" had scarce chances of success against Google, just like any operating system for personal computers against Microsoft.

Powerset, a natural language search engine developed in San Francisco by Lorenzo Thione and others, went live in 2008 and was almost immediately acquired by Microsoft; Cuil, founded in Menlo Park by two former employees of Google, Russell Power and Anna Patterson as well as Patterson's husband Tom Costello, went live in 2008 and shut down in 2010.

The line-up of winners in the cloud world was small. In 2009 Microsoft was still the largest software company in the world with revenues of $50 billion, while Google's revenues were "only" $22.8 billion. Google had already passed IBM's software revenues ($22 billion), Oracle ($17.5 billion) and SAP ($15.3 billion, and the most troubled of all of these). By comparison, the wildly popular Facebook only made an estimated $550 million in 2009. At one point in March 2010 Microsoft was the second largest company in the US, with a market capitalization of $256 billion, following oil producer Exxon ($315 billion) and followed by a fast-growing Apple ($205 billion) that had passed the retail giant Walmart ($205 billion). Google's market capitalization was $184 billion.

Those numbers sent two messages, both adverse to Microsoft. The personal computer was being attacked simultaneously on two fronts, by the smart phone and by web-based computing. In April 2010 Apple further weakened the personal computer when it introduced the tablet computer iPad, which sold one million units in less than one month.

Another battlefront was television. In 2010 Google debuted an open platform for television sets that was the home-video equivalent of its mobile-phone platform Android. It was another attempt to marry content and hardware, something that only Apple had successfully achieved so far but with a proprietary platform. Not being a maker of hardware, Google chose again to offer an open platform. The first hardware partner to sign up was Japanese conglomerate Sony. Sony had a history of championing networked television. An early adopter of WebTV, Sony had introduced already in 2000 a product called AirBoard, a tablet computer that let users watch television, surf the Internet, view photos and wirelessly control several gadgets. Sony wasn't interested as much in TV-based web surfing (the feature provided by the alliance with Google) as in video and music streaming, i.e. selling its content (not just a piece of hardware) to the consumers. Sony owned a vast library of films and music. Google did not make any hardware and did not own any content. Google had become a giant by simply facilitating the connection between the hardware and the content, but now it was debatable who owned the future: the company that laid the cable connecting a device to some content or the companies making the device and providing the content?

The wild card in this scenario was Facebook. It began the year 2009 with 150 million users and grew by about one million users a day, the fastest product ever to reach that many users in just five years. In 2010 it was approaching half a billion registered users. In June it was being valued at $23 billion, despite not being profitable yet. In May 2007 Facebook had announced an open platform for third parties to develop applications. This amounted to a Copernican revolution: applications were no longer written for an operating system but for a social network. This event spawned a new industry of widget makers for the Facebook platform, notably

RockYou (originally RockMySpace), founded in Redwood City in 2006 by Lance Tokuda and Jia Shen. However, Facebook was also being widely criticized for its ever-changing privacy policies after having contributed to distribute all over the world sensitive personal information of millions of people. It had basically become the premier stalking tool in the world.

The price paid by users of social networking platforms was a massive dissemination of private information. By the late 2000s there was so much information available on the Web about individuals that it was natural to put together a person's lifestyle just by browsing her name. A new kind of application, social network aggregators, was soon born to help that process. In 2006 a group of Stanford students based in Mountain View, including Harrison Tang, came up with such an idea and developed Spokeo. In October 2007 in Mountain View former Google employees including Paul Buchheit (the creator of Gmail and AdSense) and Bret Taylor (the creator of Google Maps) launched FriendFeed, capable of integrating in real time information posted on social media. In July 2009 it was acquired by Facebook.

Facebook indirectly also set a new (low) standard for creating a startup. In the fall of 2007 B. J. Fogg, an experimental psychologist who was running the Persuasive Technology Lab at Stanford, instructed his students to create Facebook applications with the only goal of having as many people as possible use them in as short a period of time as possible. The students were forced to create no-frills applications whose main asset was that they were easy to use and spread around. That class alone created a number of millionaires because many of those applications became hits on the Facebook ecosystem. These Stanford CS student authors went on to join successful companies. They had just hit on a new formula to create a successful product: just make it easy to use and spread virally. You can always refine it later.

In April 2012 Facebook paid $1billion for tiny San Francisco-based startup Instagram, a mobile photo-sharing service for the iPhone that had been introduced in October 2010 by Kevin Systrom (formerly at Google) and Brazilian-born Mike Krieger, both Stanford graduates.

Google basically used Internet technology to steal advertising from media: it was not a tech company but an advertising agency. Facebook, targeting a young audience that gets bored quickly, was a talent scout, constantly trying to ride the next "flavor of the day": Instagram, What's App, ...

Another social networking platform for photo sharing and messaging, specifically designed for the iPhone (and later mobile devices in general) was Path, launched in November 2010 in San Francisco by Shawn Fanning of Napster fame and by former Facebook executive Dave Morin (and acquired by South Korea's Kakao in 2015). What initially distinguished Path from Facebook was that it limited the number of friends to 50.

Location was becoming important again. Craigslist had been the last major Web-based service to address the geographic community, while almost every other major service addressed the virtual community of the whole Web. The trend was reversed by the end of the decade. In 2010 Facebook belatedly added Places, a location-based service. It was similar to Foursquare, founded in 2007 in New York by Dennis Crowley and Naveen Selvadurai, and Gowalla, launched in 2009 from Austin, Texas by Josh Williams and Scott Raymond. These services basically let friends equipped with mobile devices know each other's location. Meanwhile, Google rolled out Realtime Search that performed location-based filtering of status updates, for example to find out what is going on in a town. In 2011 Google tried to acquire discount-coupon site Groupon, launched in November 2008 in Chicago by Andrew Mason. Groupon brokered deals between consumers and local stores. Maybe it was not "Google versus Microsoft" after all, but "Google versus Facebook."

Incidentally, in 2010 eBay acquired shopping engine Milo, founded in 2008 in Philadelphia by Jack Abraham. Milo kept track of which goods were available in neighborhood stores.

Because of Google and Facebook, the way people used the Internet had changed dramatically since the day that Marc Andreessen had created the Netscape browser. Nonetheless, the browser had not changed much since those days. Microsoft's Internet Explorer, Mozilla's Firefox, Google's Chrome, and Apple's Safari had simply copied the concept, the look and the buttons of the original, barely introducing collateral features.

A startup that tried to "upgrade" the browser to the age of Facebook was Mountain View-based RockMelt, founded in November 2008 by Eric Vishria and Tim Howes, both former employees of networking company Opsware before it was acquired by Hewlett-Packard. It also marked Marc Andreessen's returns to his roots, since he was the main financial backer of RockMelt. RockMelt represented the typical paradigm shift that periodically shook Silicon Valley. In this case the victim was Facebook. Instead of having the Facebook user look at the Internet through the filter of his Facebook page and his friends' Facebook pages, RockMelt allowed the user to view the Facebook world and many other popular services (e.g., real-time news) as an extension of the browser.

The other thing that had not changed much since the invention of the Web was the search engine. While Google dominated the field, its search engine was largely agnostic about the contemporary boom of social networks. The emergence of "social search" technology was well represented by Blekko, founded in Redwood Shores in June 2007 by Rich Skrenta. He was the high-school hacker who had created the first personal-computer virus in 1982; the SUN guru who had created the Open Directory Project; and the entrepreneur who had created Topix. It was basically a hybrid approach that mixed the traditional machine-powered search engine with the human-powered wiki. Nor was Facebook a dogma in its space. In March 2010 former Google employee Ben Silbermann launched the image bookmarking system Pinterest out of Palo Alto. Within two years it was second only to Facebook and Twitter among social networking platform. The key difference was that it organized networks of people around shared interests not social connections.

For the record, in 2007 independent consultant Chris Messina (cofounder of the idealistic Citizen Agency) invented the Twitter hashtag, a way to group conversations on Twitter. It became even more useful in 2008 after Twitter acquired the search tool Summize (a two-year old Washington-based startup founded by Eric Jensen, Abdur Chowdhury and Ajaipal Virdy).

The first browser to integrate social networking and media services had actually been Redwood City-based Flock, launched in 2005 by Bart Decrem and Geoffrey Arone.

Facebook was also coming under attack because of its loose security policies. Furthermore, Facebook content was exclusive to the Facebook website, and there was a deliberate attempt by Facebook to isolate the Facebook user from the rest of the Internet world. While dissatisfaction was pervasive, the people who dared to take on Facebook were almost always technology enthusiasts based outside the Bay Area. In 2004 Chicago-based developer Michael Chisari, started Appleseed, the first open source social networking engine. In 2007 Belgium-based developer Laurent Eschenauer announced OneSocialWeb. This one was based on XMPP, the technology behind Instant Messaging. David Tosh and Ben Werdmuller, two researchers at the University of Edinburgh in Britain, founded Elgg in 2004. The most hyped by the media of this generation of open-source social networks was Diaspora, developed by four New York University students.

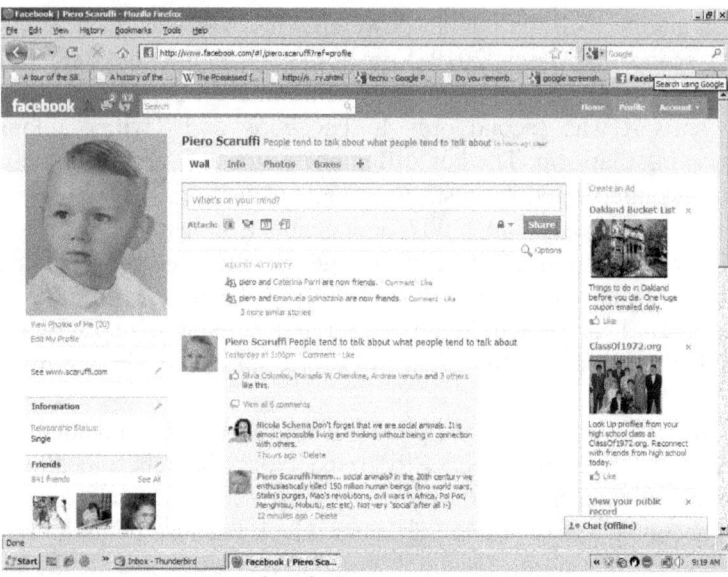

A Facebook Screenshot (2010)

In 2007 Justin Kan, a recent graduate in Physics and Philosophy from Yale University, started streaming his life nonstop 24/7 over the Internet via a webcam attached to his head, thus implementing what many dystopian films and novels had predicted. His live video broadcast on Justin.tv lasted for eight months. Then, with help from Emmett Shear and others, he turned Justin.tv into a public channel for anyone to "lifecast". Given the success of the idea for sports and games, in 2011 those channels spawned a separate, San Francisco-based company: Twitch.tv , founded by Shear and Justin.tv's product designer Kyle Vogt (and acquired by Amazon in 2014).

Live video-streaming platforms multiplied after the success of Twitch. Periscope was founded by Kayvon Beykpour and Joe Bernstein in San Francisco in 2014, and Twitter acquired them in 2015. At the same time in 2015 Meerkat, founded in 2012 in San Francisco by Ben Rubin and Itai Danino, launched its platform for Twitter users to instantly stream their lives over smartphones.

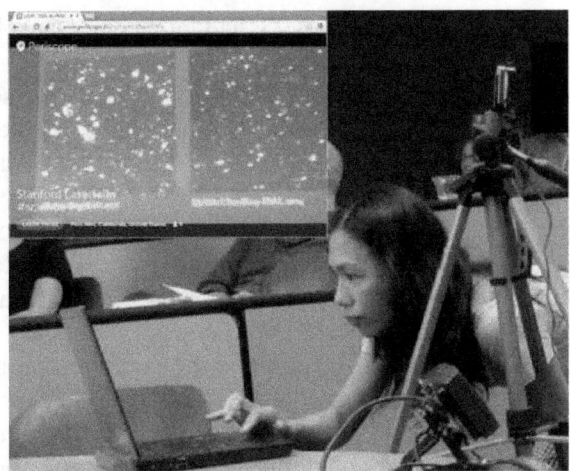

Our friend Wu Bin broadcasting a Stanford L.A.S.E.R. live with Periscope

This generation of live-streaming apps had been enabled by new 3G and 4G cell phone networks. Precursors included Redwood City-based Qik (founded by Ramu Sunkara, Bhaskar Roy and Nikolay Abkairov in 2006), that launched in 2008 and was acquired by Skype in 2011; Israeli-based Flixwagon, founded by Sarig Reichert, which also launched in the same year; and Britain-based Next2Friends, founded in 2007 by Roy Shelton and Anthony Nystrom, which also launched in 2008. For the record, live video streaming over the Internet had been inaugurated in 1995 in Holland by Jacques Mattheij (using a Silicon Graphics workstation), way before Silicon Valley even thought of it. "Life-streaming" had been born in 1996 at Pennsylvania's Dickinson College when 19-year old student Jennifer Ringley had installed a webcam in her dorm room and started uploading black-and-white images photos of herself to JenniCam.org to track her daily life.

The Bay Area Giants

The other giants of Silicon Valley were left scrambling for an exit strategy during these times of upheaval. In 2008, Hewlett-Packard purchased Texas-based giant Electronic Data Systems (EDS) in a shift towards services, and in 2009 Xerox followed suit by purchasing Affiliated Computer Services. HP also purchased Palm, now a struggling smart-phone maker (April 2010). The value of Palm was twofold: an operating system designed for cloud computing; and an application development environment based on a drag-and-drop metaphor. This was also a last-ditch attempt to enter the market for mobile operating systems that was rapidly becoming a duel between Apple (iOS) and Google

(Android). After all, Palm's WebOS had pioneered the phone software platform based on Web technology.

In 2006 HP had finally passed Dell in worldwide personal-computer shipments (16.5% market share versus Dell's 16.3%), while Gateway had disappeared, having been bought in 2007 by Acer of Taiwan: for the first time a Silicon Valley company ruled the personal-computer market.

However, the glory of becoming the biggest personal-computer maker in the world did not mean much at a time when Apple's tablet was crippling personal-computer sales, and in August 2011 HP announced that it was going to spin off (i.e. exit) its personal computer business. This came at the same time when HP dumped the recently acquired Palm (and its WebOS mobile platform introduced in January 2009) and at the same time that HP acquired British database application company Autonomy. Autonomy and EDS represented the future of HP, not personal digital assistants and personal computers.

In 2010 a new player emerged in the battle for the mobile operating system, and, while it was not based in the Bay Area, it relied on technology developed by a Bay Area startup. Long ridiculed for its lack of design style and for its long list of flops (the Bob desktop metaphor, the Spot wristwatch, the Tablet PC, the Ultimate TV, the Zune music player, the Kin smartphone), Microsoft (partnering with Nokia) finally got it right with the mobile operating system Windows Phone: it was derived from the Danger technology that they had acquired from the same man who sold Android to Google, i.e. Andy Rubin.

Oracle, instead, still aiming mainly at the corporate world, acquired middleware experts BEA in 2008 and decided to enter the hardware market by purchasing a struggling SUN in 2009.

Cloud computing started to take hold even in corporate settings. In 2009 Cisco partnered with Massachusetts-based EMC, the largest provider of networked storage in the world, to found Acadia and convert the old data-centers of the corporate world to cloud computing. In the same year Cisco introduced its first line of servers, the Unified Computing System. It competed directly with HP and IBM while upping the ante by integrating VMware's virtualization software (that now allowed to move applications from one server to another at the click of a mouse). At the beginning of 2010 Cisco posted its best quarter ever, with sales of $10.4 billion. Intel was largely immune to the turmoil: in 2010 it posted record sales again.

In March 2009 AMD spun off its manufacturing unit to create GlobalFoundries. Within a year it became the world's second largest silicon-chip foundry company after Taiwan's TSMC.

However, the next battleground for chips would be in the mobile space. British chip manufacturer ARM still dominated cellular-phone applications which required all-day battery life. Third-generation cellular phones were being integrated with video, music, and gaming and this triggered a boom in chips for mobile devices. Ironically, both Intel and AMD had exited that market in June 2006. Intel had sold its ARM-based technology to Marvell, and AMD had sold its MIPS-based technology to Raza Microelectronics. In 2010 Intel reentered the market with both an in-house project (Moorestown) and the acquisition of German-based Infineon. ARM chips were already powering devices such as Sony television sets, the Amazon e-reader Kindle, and hotel keycard locks, and analysts foresaw a future in which thousands of small devices would need ARM chips to interact among themselves and to retrieve information from the Internet. In 2009 ARM was a $0.5 billion corporation versus Intel's $35 billion, but the trend was towards ARM's small low-power chips. Intel took action in November 2010: for the first time it accepted to manufacture someone else's chips (San Jose-based fab-less Achronix, a competitor of XIlinx and Altera in the high-end accelerating chip market). Intel also entered the market traditionally dominated by Taiwanese and Chinese factories. It was unlikely this was due to a desire to enter the brutal market of contract manufacturing and more likely a desire to learn new markets. And, when in September 2011 Microsoft announced that the Windows operating system would for the first time also run on the ARM platform, Intel signed a deal with Google to use Intel chips in Android phones. Intel had been incapable of adapting to ARM's licensing business model.

The boom of smartphones also benefited makers of Wi-Fi chips, such as Atheros and Marvell: 56 million Wi-Fi-enabled cellular phones shipped in 2008 (a 52% increase over the previous year). More than 54 million smartphones were sold in the first quarter of 2010, an increase of 56% over the previous year.

It was not unusual for Silicon Valley to be late on innovation, but this was embarrassing for a region named after silicon. All the big providers of chips for smartphones (San Diego-based Qualcomm, Texas Instruments, Korea-based Samsung, Irvine-based Broadcom) except for Marvel were based outside the Bay Area. Even Apple's iPhone used a chip manufactured by Samsung. Ditto for all the providers of wireless telecommunications networks: Verizon (started in 1983 as Bell Atlantic) was based in Philadelphia (and in 2015 it acquired AOL and in 2016 Yahoo), AT&T was based in New Jersey, Sprint was based in Kansas (although its origins were in the Bay Area), T-Mobile was the subsidiary of Deutsche Telekom, and Clearwire was founded in 2003 in Seattle.

Intel's Headquarters (2010)

Beyond Moore's Law

A bigger problem lay ahead for the semiconductor industry in general. In ultimate analysis a lot of computer technology's accelerating progress was due to its fundamental component: the transistor. Transistors were expensive in the 1960s. In 1982 they were already cheap enough that $1 could buy a few thousand of them. Twenty years later in 2002 the same dollar bill could by more than two million of them. Thirty years later in 2013 the same dollar bill could buy 20 million transistors.

The semiconductor industry was very aware that Moore's law was rapidly coming to and end. As transistor gets smaller, it gets harder to make them. For the first time in 50 years there was a real chance that the price of transistor would stall or even increase. The industry began experimenting with new materials, such as carbon nanotubes and graphene, and even with quantum computing.

Social Games

Virtual worlds were booming. The audience for pioneering virtual worlds such as Gaia Online and Habbo had passed five million monthly active users. The next front was the social network. Launched in May 2008 and only accessible as an application on Facebook, the virtual world YoVille passed five million monthly active users in March 2009. By allowing people to create "second-life" avatars and interact with each other, YoVille de facto created a new concept: a virtual social network within the real social network. The success of YoVille spawned a generation of browser-based "social games" running on Facebook. YoVille itself was acquired in July 2008 by Zynga, founded in July 2007 in San Francisco by serial entrepreneur Mark Pincus. In June 2009 Zynga released FarmVille, a shameless clone of the Facebook-based social game Farm Town that was introduced by Florida-based Slashkey a few months earlier. In 2010 FarmVille had become the most popular Facebook game, boasting more than 50 million users. Zynga also introduced Mafia Wars (2009), a shameless copy of another pioneering social game, David Maestri's Mob Wars, that had debuted on Facebook in January 2008 (Maestri was still an employee at Freewebs). Six months after the release of Playfish's Restaurant City from Britain, Zynga released Cafe World.

Competitors soon started retaliating by copying Zynga's games too. While Zynga kept churning out clones of popular games, the founder of Freewebs (now renamed Webs), Shervin Pishevar, opened Social Gaming Network (SGN) in January 2008 in Palo Alto to develop original social games for the Facebook platform. Whatever the strategy, the Bay Area was becoming again the epicenter for videogame evolution. By 2010 Apple was promoting the iPhone itself as a gaming platform, further eroding Nintendo's console-based empire.

Videogames were still selling strongly. Activision was setting one record after the other, selling 4.7 million copies of "Call of Duty - Modern Warfare 2" on its first day in 2009 and 5.6 million copies of "Call of Duty - Black Ops" on its first day in 2010 (grossing more than $650 million worldwide during the first five days of sales). In December 2010 Activision's Cataclysm sold 3.3 million copies in the first 24 hours.

Note that the "Call of Duty" games were developed by Infinity Ward in southern California (Encino) using the id Tech 3 engine developed in Texas by PC game pioneer John Romero and others at Id Software. The technological breakthroughs were coming from somewhere else.

Videogames had become a huge industry, a phenomenal economic success. However, the state of the videogame craft was not all that advanced if one considered that videogames still relied on the original idea: create something that stimulates interest via the two primal impulses (kill and make money, given that sex was off limits) and make it as addictive as possible so people will come back for the sequel. Zynga's "FarmVille" was an addictive game exploiting the pulse to get rich, and hits like "Call of Duty" were addictive by exploiting the pulse to kill. Not exactly high art. In August 2008 San Francisco-based game designer Jonathan Blow released "Braid", a videogame for Microsoft's Xbox. The concept was completely different. Blow focused on his own aesthetic values, on sophisticated scripting and subtle psychology. Blow conceived the videogame as an art (not "art" as in "craft" but "art" as in "Michelangelo" and "Van Gogh"). He then invested the profits into producing an even more "artistic" game, "The Witness", introduced in March 2012.

The very notion of how to play a videogame was changing. OnLive was launched in March 2009 in Palo Alto by Apple alumnus and WebTV's founder Steve Perlman after seven years of work in stealth mode. OnLive, which went live in June 2010, was out to kill the videogame console by providing videogames on demand to any computer. The videogames were hosted on the "cloud" of the Internet instead of requiring the user to purchase them on physical cassettes. This was advertised as "5G wireless": 2G (1992) marked the transition from analog to digital voice; 3G (2001) enabled Internet browsing; 4G provided basic video streaming; and 5G was meant to provide high-definition video streaming.

OnLive didn't succeed, but Perlman continued the experiment within his incubator Rearden, eventually spawning Artemis in 2014 (co-founded by Pearlman and his Italian-born chief scientist Antonio Forenza) just when mobile video began to account for more than 50% of all mobile data. The big service providers were trying to increase capacity by adding more antennas (i.e. by shrinking the size of the wireless cells) but there was a physical limit due to signal interference, and Perlman was instead focusing on exploiting that very interference to achieve fiber-optic speed in cellular communications. A humbler approach came from Kumu Networks, a 2012 spinoff of Stanford University based in Santa Clara, whose device could work both as a radio receiver and a radio transmitter at the same time, thus doubling the capacity of a radio channel, i.e. of the existing wireless spectrum.

In 2010 the first blockbuster of iPhone videogaming took off. Angry Birds, developed by Finnish game developer Rovio Mobile, founded in 2003 by three students from Helsinki University of Technology (Niklas Hed, Jarno Vakevainen and Kim Dikert). Introduced in December 2009, it sold over 12 million copies in just one year.

User Experience

As 3D motion-control and motion-sensing products started to become affordable and therefore popular (e.g., Microsoft's Kinect, a motion sensing input device introduced in 2010 for the Xbox videogame console, based on technology originally developed by PrimeSense in Israel), the idea was copied in the Bay Area by a new generation of startups, notably San Francisco-based Leap Motion, founded in 2010 as OcuSpec by David Holz and Michael Buckwald. Leap Motion introduced motion-controlled input devices that, unlike Microsoft's ruling Kinect, reacted to natural gestures to manipulate objects on the screen. In 2013 Hewlett Packard was the first major manufacturer to embed that user interface in its computers.

Meanwhile, Apple acquired PrimeSense, the company that developed Kinect, and Google acquired gesture-recognition startup Flutter, also founded in San Francisco in 2010 (by Navneet Dalal and Mehul Nariyawala).

Second Life spawned a new generation of virtual worlds: Google launched the short-lived Lively world in 2008, and Meez debuted its "nations" in 2009 in San Francisco.

The most significant improvement in human-computer interface of the time (as far as related to smartphones and tablets) was the Swype keyboard, originally developed for the Windows Mobile operating system by Seattle's Swype, founded in 2003 by Cliff Kushler (co-inventor with Dale Grover and Martin King of the T9 predictive text system used on cell phones of the 2000s) and by Randy Marsden (developer of the Windows Mobile touch-screen keyboard). Swype was capable of guessing the intended word when the user slides his finger on a touch-screen from the first letter to the last letter of the word. First introduced by Samsung in late 2009 and acquired by Nuance in 2011, Swype spread like wildfire on Android devices. In 2010 SwiftKey, started in London in 2008 by Jon Reynolds and Ben Medlock and acquired in 2016 by Microsoft, debuted a system capable of predicting the next word the user intends to type. These were all part of a trend to improve the speed of typing on ridiculously small devices. As the keyboards got smaller and smaller, the speed of the skilled typist had been lost. People were writing more but much slower than the older generations. This opened opportunities for a deluge of startups to offer systems to speed up typing.

In 2010 Steve Jobs of Apple largely decreed the demise of Adobe's multimedia platform Flash when he hailed HMTL5 as the standard of the future for video on the Web (and one year later Adobe itself adopted HTML5 instead of Flash on mobile devices). HTML5 had been formally introduced in 2008 by the Web Hypertext Application Technology Working Group (WHATWG), a group formed by Apple, Mozilla and Opera Software (a Norwegian maker of Web browsers since 1997).

Improvements in "user experience" had a split-personality kind of effect. On one hand they were truly improving the life of the user, while on the other hand they were turning that improved experience into an increasingly lucrative opportunity for the business world. The proliferation of sensors, location-based applications and social media (continuously capturing information about the user) was leading to increasingly more sophisticated, personalized (and intrusive) personal assistants, capable of "anticipating" the user's behavior and the user's needs.

3D Printing

Silicon Valley was still silent in the field that was promising the biggest industrial revolution since the invention of the computer: 3D printing. SLS, the technology pioneered by Carl Deckard's DTM, became a feasible technology in 2006 when EOS in Germany introduced two SLS models, the Formiga P100 and the Eosint P730. And 3D printing in general benefited from innovations such as "polyjet printing", the ability to combine different materials in the same printed part, a technique introduced in 2008 by Objet Geometries of Israel. Up to this point, the leadership had come from small companies and independent inventors, not from the universities. The only exception had been the MIT, with its 3D inkjet technology. This changed in 2005 when Adrian Bowyer at the University of Bath launched an open-source project, RepRap, to develop a self-replicating 3D printer. Bowyer made history in 2008 when his Darwin machine built a copy of itself (RepRap self-replicated!), but, even more importantly, this 2008 machine, that was based on FDM, was the first low-cost 3D printer. If the Macintosh had created publishing for the desktop, RepRap created 3D printing for the desktop. Because everything in RepRap was open source, Bowyer had just started the open-source movement for 3D printing. In 2009 MakerBot, a descendant of RepRap founded in New York by Bre Pettis, Adam Mayer and Zach Smith launched a website called Thingiverse where hobbyists could share for free their 3D models, and Philips' spinoff Shapeways (also based in New York) launched an online market for 3D models. In 2009 BitsFromBytes in Britain launched the RapMan, a "Do-It-Yourself" kit for hobbyists to build their own 3D printer at home. A few months later MakerBot of New York launched an even more popular kit. These were the first RepRap-based 3D printers to be commercially available, although they were just kits that you had to assemble at home. Ironically, the futuristic project to create a machine that can print parts to make other machines did not succeed but the project to spread the technology of 3D printing and make it more affordable started a revolution. RepRap "democratized" 3D printing. None of this transpired in Silicon Valley.

Cyber-currency

In 2009 a person disguised under the moniker Satoshi Nakamoto introduced the digital currency Bitcoin. This became the first successful currency not to be printed by a government. From an engineering point of view, its main achievement was that the system was capable of creating copies that could not be copied. Bitcoin seemed to prove again the theorem that major progress in peer-to-peer technology only came from independents. The previous proof had come from Napster. Bitcoin was the latest in a long genealogy of "dark nets".

A mathematical model for "cryptocurrencies" (currencies that are not controlled by a central government but by cryptographic means) was first described in 1998 by Wei Dai on the "cypherpunk" forum (a forum founded in 1992 in Santa Cruz by Timothy May, an early employee at

Intel). Wei Dai's idea was simple: let everybody have a record of every transaction, so that no one can cheat the others; an anonymous and distributed system instead of a governmental and centralized system. In other words, shifting the power to a P2P network instead of a central government. Wei Dai had been inspired by Tim May's "The Crypto Anarchist Manifesto" that inaugurated that forum. Wei Dai wrote: "I am fascinated by Tim May's crypto-anarchy. Unlike the communities traditionally associated with the word "anarchy", in a crypto-anarchy the government is not temporarily destroyed but permanently forbidden and permanently unnecessary."

At the same time Nick Szabo (based in Seattle and sometimes confused with a former mayor of Cupertino) wrote his proposal for a currency called "bit gold" with a more sophisticated way to prevent people from double spending a cybercurrency. His model was actually eerily reminiscent of videogames and fantasy movies in which masters assign difficult tasks to novices in order for them to become masters. In 1997 Szabo, an expert in law, described how cryptocurrencies could be used to implement "smart contracts" on the Internet. The "difficult tasks" were a variation on the "proof of work" method employed by anti-spam software since the 1992 to fight email spammers. One such "proof of work" method was Hashcash, originally proposed in 1997 by the British hacker Adam Back. In the 2000s this would evolve into the family of "secure hash algorithms", standards published by the US government, of which SHA-256 (introduced in 2001) would become the most famous.

Bitcoin's distributed blockchain mechanism was making central authorities of trust obsolete. Trust had always been guaranteed by something like the national bank or the title company. Blockchain created trust through an algorithm. Its potential applications extended way beyond digital currencies. Any form of peer-to-peer contract (whether selling a house or renting a car) could be made safer through blockchain. Indirectly, blockchain was raising the issue of what the function of government can be in the digital era, when computer algorithms can maintain "order" with no need for a police force. Decentralization had always meant chaos, but blockchain was a system based on decentralization that actually guaranteed order; and, unlike government databases, it was virtually invulnerable to hacking.

The extropian Hal Finney became the first person to ever receive a bitcoin. Bitcoin had its roots in four unorthodox alternative movements: P2P networking, the extropian movement, the cyberpunk movement, and "dark nets".

The success of peer-to-peer models generated a lot of enthusiasm in the digital counterculture. Ori Brafman's "Starfish And The Spider" (2007) and Yochai Benkler's "The Wealth of Networks" (2007) publicized the notion of "decentralized autonomous organizations" (DAOs) and Michel Bauwens publishe the "Peer-to-peer Manifesto" (2008).

Other mysterious figures appear throughout the chronicles of early bitcoin, like Dave Kleiman, based in Florida, a paraplegic and a computer security expert who died a horrible death, alone and poor, in 2013, and his long-distance friend, Craig Wright, another computer security expert but based in Australia and with a PhD in theology, who in 2016 confessed to be the real Satoshi Nakamoto but then recanted for fear of the authorities. These two had just co-written a paper together, "Overwriting Hard Drive Data" (2008), but that was about the possibility (or, better, impossibility) of recovering data after they are written over, and the third author of that paper, Shyaam Sundhar of Symantec in Washington, distanced himself from any bitcoin project.

Mobile Payment

Some startups understood that mobile users carry a computer with them, not just a phone. In fact, they even carry a GPS that knows their location.

Bling Nation, founded in 2007 in Palo Alto by Argentinian serial entrepreneur Wenceslao Casares and Venezuelan economist Meyer Malka, developed a sticker for smartphones (or any other device) with an embedded NFC chip to charge purchases to a Paypal account.

In 2009 Jack Dorsey (of Twitter fame) founded Square and designed a "reader" that allowed anybody with a mobile phone to make a payment and anybody with a mobile phone (and a Square-provided "cash register") to accept it (no cash, no credit cards, no RFID, no receipt).

The Empire

Looking at the numbers, Silicon Valley had never been healthier than it was in 2008, before the big worldwide financial crisis struck. It had 261 public companies and countless startups. eBay was selling $60 billion worth of goods in 2007, a figure higher than the GDP of 120 countries of the world. In 2007 venture capitalists invested $7.6 billion in Silicon Valley and an additional $2.5 billion in the rest of the Bay Area. The Bay Area boasted the world's highest concentration of venture capitalists. Silicon Valley's share of venture-capital investment in the US reached 37.5% at the end of 2009 (compared, for example, with New York's 9.2%). Silicon Valley had 2.4 million people (less than 1% of the US's population) generating more than 2% of the US's GDP, with a GDP per person of $83,000.

The rest of the Bay Area was equally stunning: by 2009 the Lawrence Berkeley Labs alone boasted 11 Nobel Prize winners, more than India or China, and UC Berkeley boasted 20. So the tiny town of Berkeley alone had 31, more than any country in the world except the US, Britain, Germany, and France. Add Stanford's 16 and UCSF's 3 for a grand total of 50 in a region of about 19,000 square kilometers, smaller than Belize or Slovenia. In 2006 the Bay Area received three Nobel prizes out of nine: one each to Stanford, Berkeley, and UCSF. In the last 20 years the winners included: Richard Taylor of Stanford University (1990), Martin Perl of Stanford University (1995), Douglas Osheroff of Stanford University (1996), Steven Chu of Stanford University (1997), Robert Laughlin of Stanford University (1998), and George Smoot of the Lawrence Berkeley Labs (2006) for Physics; William Sharpe of Stanford University (1990), Gary Becker of Stanford University (1992), John Harsanyi of UC Berkeley (1994), Myron Scholes of Stanford University (1997), Daniel McFadden of UC Berkeley (2000), Joseph Stiglitz of Stanford University (2001), George Akerlof of UC Berkeley (2001), and Oliver Williamson of UC Berkeley (2009) for Economics; Sydney Brenner (2002), the founder of the Molecular Sciences Institute in Berkeley, Andrew Fire of Stanford University (2006), and Elizabeth Blackburn of UCSF (2009) for Medicine; Roger Kornberg of Stanford University (2006) for Chemistry.

Another Nobel prize in Physics came in 2011: Saul Perlmutter of Lawrence Berkeley Lab. And then Brian Kobilka of Stanford in Chemistry in 2012. And then in 2013 Michael Levitt for Chemistry (Stanford), Randy Schekman for Medicine (Berkeley) and Thomas Sudhof for Medicine (Stanford).

The Bay Area was more than a region: it was an economic empire. The number of jobs that had been outsourced to countries like India probably exceeded the number of jobs created in Silicon Valley itself. And the relationship with the rest of the world was as deep as it could be. A study by Duke University found that 52.4% of Silicon Valley's high-tech companies launched between 1995 and 2005 had been founded by at least one immigrant. This phenomenon was probably a first in history. At the same time investors flocked from all over the world. For example, in 2008 Taiwanese conglomerate Quanta invested into two Silicon Valley's "fabless" startups: Tilera (founded in October 2004 by Anant Agarwal) and Canesta (founded in April 1999 by Cyrus Bamji, Abbas Rafii, and Nazim Kareemi).

Neurotech

In neurotech the new approach was based on computational power. In practice, the cumbersome, slow and expensive computers of the 1960s had forced computer scientists to focus on models, whereas now the small, fast and cheap processors of the 2010s were encouraging computer scientists to use brute force. The availability of colossal amounts of information on the Web made this change of strategy even more appealing. For example,

Stanford's professor Andrew Ng led a team at Google that wired 16 thousand processors to create a neural net capable of learning from Youtube videos. The new approach contained little that was conceptually new, just a lot more computing power. The "deep belief networks" at the core of the "deep learning" of these systems was an evolution of the old "neural network" of the 1980s and it had mostly been done by Geoffrey Hinton at the University of Toronto.

Diffbot, the first startup to be funded in 2008 by Stanford's on-campus venture capital fund StartX, used artificial intelligence to analyze and catalog the whole World Wide Web.

The sensation in robotics was coming from Boston. In 2012 Rethink Robotics, founded in 2008 by one of the most celebrated robot scientists in the world, Rodney Brooks, introduced Baxter, a low-cost programmable industrial robot that promised to make robots affordable for small companies.

In 2007 the Stanford Artificial Intelligence Laboratory unveiled "Switchyard", better known as the Robot Operating System (ROS), a toolkit for developers of robot applications, later expanded at nearby Willow Garage.

Progress in Artificial Intelligence was also coming from an idea originally advanced by Carver Mead at the California Institute of Technology (Caltech) in 1990: build processors that look like the brain. In 2008 Dharmendra Modha at IBM's Almaden Labs launched a project to build such a "neuromorphic" processor, i.e. made of chips that operate like neurons.

Google's broadly publicized "driverless car" was a project begun by Sebastian Thrun at the Stanford Artificial Intelligence Laboratory, the descendant of Thrun's robotic vehicle Stanley (2005).

In 2007 Velodyne, founded in 1983 by David Hall in Morgan Hill (south of San Jose) to make hi-fi stereo equipment, introduced the commercial lidar that was adopted by Google in 2010 for its project of a driverless car.

The leader in computer vision chips for object-detection was Mobileye, founded in 1999 in Israel by Hebrew University's computer scientist Amnon Shashua with Ziv Aviram, that had introduced the first chip in 2004. In 2009 Andras Ferencz, who studied Computer Vision at UC Berkeley with Jitendra Malik and then worked at Xerox PARC, joined Mobileye and by 2016 their chips would already be tested on cars by Audi, BMW, General Motors, Ford and Tesla.

Google's self-driving car

More prosaic applications were needed in the age of smart phones, cloud computing and social networking. SRI International's Artificial Intelligence Center, that had already spawned Nuance in the 1990s, spawned Siri in the new century. Adam Cheyer was the leader of a software project (code-named CALO/PAL and sponsored by DARPA in 2003) to develop a personal assistant capable of learning and self-improving. Founded in 2007 by Cheyer with Dag Kittlaus (a telecom executive from Norway) and Tom Gruber (an alumnus of Stanford's Artificial Intelligence Lab who had worked on collaborative knowledge management), Siri launched a virtual personal assistant for mobile devices that was acquired by Apple in 2010.

In 2007 Adam Cheyer also co-founded San Fracisco-based Genetic Finance (later renamed Sentient Technologies) with two former coworkers, Antoine Blondeau and Babak Hodjat, from San Jose-based Dejima, where he worked briefly in 2002-3 in between his first and second stints at SRI. Sentient worked on machine learning algorithms, initially for financial applications, and in 2016 would become the most funded A.I. startup in the world.

New Zealand-born Oxford-educated physicist Sean Gourley and Bob Goodson (Yelp's first employee and a YouNoodle co-founder) started Quid in San Francisco in September 2010. Quid developed a global intelligence platform for tackling large unstructured data sets (initially about high-tech innovation, i.e. about Silicon Valley startups).

The groundbreaking technologies feeding the social-networking frenzy kept coming from other regions, though. For example, face-recognition came to the masses via Face.com, launched in May 2010 by an Israeli company founded by Moti Shniberg, who had previously founded the pattern-recognition firm ImageID in 1998, and by Gil Hirsch. They turned their technology into a smartphone application (KLiK) and a Facebook application (Photo Finder), both real-time facial recognition programs capable of automatically identifying friends in photos (Face.com was acquired by Facebook in 2012).

Virtual Reality

The Bay Area had pioneered virtual reality but then pretty much lost interest in it. It was now sitting on the side while major developments were bringing the technology to the general audience: mass market immersive-reality devices such as Sony's head-mounted display HMZ-T1, introduced in November 2011; mass-market tracking devices such as the Microsoft Kinect, launched in November 2010 and originally conceived to allow gamers to interact with the Xbox 360 game console via gestures; and mass-market lenticular printing (that creates the illusion of three dimensions or the effect of a changing image as it is viewed from different angles) by companies such as Futuredisplay, founded in 2003 in South Korea.

The open-source project OpenSim, compatible with Second Life's software, was launched in 2007 by Darren Guard in Britain, to help developers create virtual worlds.

Biotech

Biotech, just like infotech, was moving towards the individual, which in its case meant personal genomics for predictive medicine. Navigenics was founded in Foster City in November 2007 by cancer specialist David Agus and Dietrich Stephan of the Translational Genomics Research Institute to provide genetic testing for predisposition to a variety of diseases. It was still an expensive service but the rapid cost reduction in DNA chips and the knowledge derived from the Human Genome Project helped bring it closer and closer to the masses. New biotech startups included iZumi Bio, founded to develop products based on stem-cell research (2007) and iPierian, founded to develop products based on cellular reprogramming (2007). In 2009 Swiss pharmaceutical giant LaRoche purchased Genentech for $46.8 billion.

The cost of a personal genetic test-kit was $3 billion in 2003, and there was only one (the Human Genome Project). In 2009 the cost had decreased to $48,000. It was made by San Diego-based startup Illumina, originally formed in 1998 by venture-capital firm CW Group to commercialize a system developed at Tufts University, that in 2007 had acquired Solexa's gene sequencing technology. Complete Genomics was founded in March 2006 in Mountain View. It announced a genome-sequencing service for under $5,000.

The genesis of this company spoke loud about the mature state of the industry. One of the founders was serial entrepreneur Clifford Reid, co-founder of Sunnyvale-based information-retrieval startup Verity in 1988 and of San Mateo-based digital video communications company Eloquent in 1996. The other founder was Serbian-born biologist Radoje Drmanac, who had participated in the Human Genome Project since 1991 and had later (1994) co-founded Sunnyvale-based biotech startup Hyseq. By the end of 2009 only about 100 human genomes had ever been sequenced. Complete Genomics planned to sequence 5,000 human genomes in 2010, 50,000 genomes in 2011 and 1 million genomes by 2014.

In 2007 a milestone was achieved by Knome, a startup just founded in Boston by Harvard professor George Church, when it introduced the first commercially available human genome sequencing.

Human-genome sequencing firms were proliferating, each using a different technique and each focusing on different data. 23andme, founded in April 2006 in Mountain View by former Affymetrix executive Linda Avey and by Sergey Brin's wife Anne Wojcicki, analyzed parts of the human genome to derive useful medical information. Its kits were priced under $500 by 2010. Halcyon Molecular, founded by Michael and William Andregg in Arizona in 2003 and relocated to Mountain View in 2008, hired PayPal's Luke Nosek in September 2009 and set a goal to sequence individual genomes in a few minutes and for less than $100. In 2007 the Bay Area boasted about 700 biomedical companies.

Synapse, founded in 2008 at Stanford University by a team of entrepreneurs and software engineers, boasted one of the largest repositories of human molecular profiles. As these tools were landing into doctor's offices, it became important to link a patient's genomic data with traditional non-genomic data such as the patient's medical history and lifestyle to provide a comprehensive health assessment. Swedish biologist Hossein Fakhrai-Rad, whose previous startup, ParAllele Bioscience, was acquired by Affymetrix in 2005, founded Genophen (later renamed BaseHealth) along with Finnish software engineer Karim Pourak in 2009 in Redwood City.

Laboratories around the world needed synthetic DNA in order to carry out experiments. There was an obvious need for more efficient and rapid ways to make DNA. In 2009 in Boston George Church and Drew Endy founded Gen9 to mass-produce custom-designed genes, in particular by using silicon chips.

However, the promises of the Human Genome Project were still largely unrealized. In particular, the thesis that genes cause diseases had sent biologists hunting for the common variants in the genome of individuals who are affected by the same health problems. Ten years later, the "common variant" strategy was being attacked by an increasing number of scientists, throwing into disarray the whole industry of personal genomics.

Meanwhile, life was being made in the lab. In 2007 Venter's team carried out a full-genome transplant: they transplanted the genome of a bacterium (Mycoplasma Mycoides) into the cytoplasm of a different bacterium (Mycoplasma Capricolum). Venter's new venture heralded the birth of synthetic biology as a business. In May 2010 Hamilton Smith's team at the Craig Venter Institute in Maryland achieved another milestone in synthetic biology by building a bacterium's DNA from scratch in the lab. He then transplanted it into the cell of a host bacterium of a different species, where the artificial DNA took control of the host cell and started replicating. The resulting living being behaved like the species made of synthetic DNA. It was the first time that a living cell was being regulated entirely by artificially manufactured DNA. They had just managed to reprogram a living being. That living being's parent was a computer. This event opened the doors to an industry that would design custom bacteria on a computer and then build them in the lab.

Eventually, one could envision a day when individuals would be able to program a living organism on a handheld device connected to the lab and order the living organism on the fly. This vision was becoming possible in reality because all the economic factors were converging. It was becoming increasingly easier to sequence ("map") the DNA of an organism, a fact that resulted in ever larger databases of genomes of existing organisms. It was becoming increasingly cheaper to synthesize ("build") DNA molecules. Both processes were a lot faster than they used to be, due to their rapid computerization. The only tool that was missing for a broader availability of life synthesis was a tool to edit the DNA sequences. The other tool that a wary humankind would have liked to see was the equivalent of the "undo" feature of computers. The media frenzy around this event resembled the media frenzy of the 1950s when computers were labeled as "electronic brains" that would eventually take over the world. Now it was bacteria which were bound to take over the world. Venter's next target was algae. Bacteria are single-cell organisms.

So are algae. Algae can be used to make biofuels, because they can make carbon dioxide into fuels by photosynthesis.

"Biohacking" was around the corner. In 2005 Rob Carlson In 2005 a young biologist, Rob Carlson , left Sydney Brenner's non-profit research laboratory Molecular Sciences Institute in Berkeley and continued his biological experiments at home, and founded his own garage startup, Biodesic. In 2008 Jason Bobe and Mac Cowell founded the DIYbio organization on the East Coast. In 2009 four talented young New Yorkers (molecular biologist Ellen Jorgensen, bioengineer Oliver Medvedik, freelance journalist Daniel Grushkin and interdisciplinary artist Nurit Bar-Shai) established the nonprofit organization Genspace to promote biohacking, and the following year opened a shared and public biotech laboratory. In 2009 Angela Kaczmarczyk and others founded the Boston Open Science Lab (BossLab). Silicon Valley responded with BioCurious, another volunteer-run non-profit organization. It was established in 2010 in Sunnyvale by a group of young independent biologists (Eri Gentry, Raymond McCauley, Tito Jankowski, Joseph Jackson, Josh Perfetto, Kristina Hathaway). These hackerspaces for biotech marked the rise of a community of worldwide hobbyists taking advantage of public-domain databases of genetic parts. In 2010 UCLA organized a symposium titled "Outlaw Biology?" at which biohacker Meredith Patterson delivered the speech "A Biopunk Manifesto". Rob Carlson published a book titled "Biology is Technology" (2010), that became the motto of this movement.

In 2010 two of BioCurious' founders, Tito Jankowski and Josh Perfetto, founded OpenPCR in San Francisco to manufacture a machine that could bring biotech to the desktop, basically a copy machine for DNA. Most genetic applications (such as DNA detection and sequencing) required a machine to perform Polymerase Chain Reactions (PCRs), i.e. to amplify sections of DNA. OpenPCR dramatically lowered the price of these PCR "printers" and made them affordable for individuals.

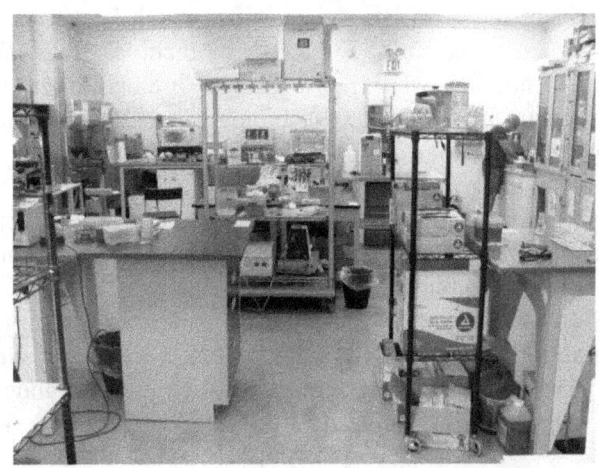

BioCurious in Sunnyvale

In 2010 Austen Heinz founded Cambrian Genomics in San Francisco to manufacture the first "laser printer for living beings", a machine capable of rapidly and accurately producing DNA. (Heinz committed suicide in 2015 at the age of 31). Arcturus BioCloud, founded in 2014 in San Francisco, made it even easier: it aimed to be a virtual bio-foundry for rapid prototyping microorganisms using the cloud to communicate with its users.

Drew Endy at Stanford University was working on creating a catalog of "biobricks" that synthetic biologists could use to create living organisms. His model clearly mirrored the way the personal-computer industry got started, with hobbyists ordering kits from catalogs advertised in magazines and then assembling the computer in their garage.

Drew Endy at Stanford

In 2003 researchers from MIT, Harvard, and UCSF had unveiled the MIT Registry of Standard Biological Parts, which later folded into iGEM, the International Genetically Engineered Machine. Both iGEM and the BioBricks Foundation were Drew Endy's brainchildren. By 2014 the repository would contain 20,000 biological parts (biobricks). "Open-source" biotech was starting a global grassroots revolution in synthetic biology. Every year the iGEM Jamboree, first held in 2004 in Boston, gathered young bioengineers from all over the world to create new life forms, mostly microbes for useful applications. There would be 2,500 competitors from 32 countries in 2014.

The Personal Genome Project was an interesting merger of crowd-sourcing and biotech ideas. Originally launched in 2005 by George Church at Harvard University, its goal was to advance the discipline of "personal genomics" by enrolling thousands of volunteers willing to have their complete genomes and medical records published on the Internet, so that researchers all over the world could study them and find correlations among genes, environment and diseases. By 2015 the project would count on more than 16,000 volunteers.

In 2012 a Stanford bioengineering team led by Markus Covert produced the first complete computer model of a free-living organism, the bacterium Mycoplasma genitalium.

Complete Genomics' Headquarters (2010)

Greentech

On the greentech front, in 2008 solar technology accounted for almost 40% of worldwide private investments in greentech, followed by biofuels at 11%. In the US, venture capitalists invested a grand total of $4 billion into "green-tech" startups in 2008, which was almost 40% of all investments in high-tech in the US. Solar-energy company Solyndra was started in May 2005 in Fremont (East Bay) by Chris Gronet, formerly an executive at Applied Materials that manufactured equipment for the semiconductor industry. By 2009 Solyndra had $820 million in venture funding and more than a billion dollars in product orders. In March 2009, the Department of Energy helped Solyndra build a 500-megawatt factory for cylindrical solar cells at the cost of $733 million; but then Solyndra went bankrupt in September 2011 leaving behind mostly doubts about the whole industry. In 2007 Google's founders established Google.org, the non-profit arm of Google, to fund greentech startups. In 2008 they invested in eSolar, a Pasadena-based manufacturer of solar thermal plants, and in AltaRock Energy, a Sausalito-based firm tapping geothermal energy.

Siluria was founded in 2008 in Menlo Park by MIT professor Angela Belcher, who developed a method to reprogram the DNA of viruses so that they create inorganic materials. They applied the method to produce gasoline from natural gas.

Solar startups multiplied after President Obama's blessing. Twin Creeks Technologies, founded in 2008 in San Jose by veterans of the semiconductor industry such as Indian-born Siva Sivaram and Venkatesan Murali; and Cogenra Solar (originally called SkyWatch Energy), a spin-off of semiconductor manufacturer Applied Materials led by Gilad Almogy, started in 2009 in Mountain View and was funded by Vinod Khosla.

Innovation, as often in the past, was not really coming from Silicon Valley, though. The big news in greentech came from Boston-based 1366 Technologies (founded by MIT professor Ely Sachs in 2007), that developed a more accurate way to cast the silicon wafers for solar cells so that solar cells can be produced at lower costs. This company was leapfrogging Silicon Valley startups using a typical Silicon Valley model: partnership with the DARPA to bring the technology to maturity and then application to a commodity product.

A different kind of "greentech" was represented by the companies that aimed at serving the "green" market. Simbol Materials, founded in 2008 in Pleasanton by Luka Erceg and Scott Conley, hired geochemists from the Lawrence Livermore National Laboratory and bought technology from that lab to produce lithium from geothermal brines (the best source of renewable energy).

More interesting were the many attempts at fundamentally changing the way people behave. For example, in 2008 Simon Saba founded his own company in San Jose to design and manufacture a mass-market sport electric car. He envisioned the Saba as a Tesla for ordinary families.

The potential for linking infotech and greentech did not go unnoticed. German giant SAP had pioneered the field with software to perform carbon accounting, energy auditing, safety management and resource planning, soon followed by archrival Oracle. Anticipating legislation about climate change (that would penalize the emission of greenhouse gases) a few Bay Area startups entered the space of software for energy and emission management to help companies control their "carbon footprint." Hara was founded in 2008 by SAP's executive Amit Chatterjee and run by Oracle alumni. In January 2009 Tom Siebel, the founder of Siebel Systems who had become a passionate advocate of net-zero energy homes, launched C3 with a board that comprised former secretary of state Condoleezza Rice and Shankar Sastry, the dean of engineering at UC Berkeley. UC Berkeley had nurtured the science of energy conservation. One of its scientists, Charlie Huizenga, had founded already in 2005 Adura Technologies, whose software aimed at monitoring and optimizing the lighting of a building.

Solyndra's Offices (2010)

Cold Fusion

In 1985 the US, the Soviet Union, Japan, and the European Union had launched a joint project to build the International Thermonuclear Experimental Reactor (ITER). The hope was that it would lead to a power plant fueled by fusion. ITER had been designed according to the Soviet tomahawk reactor invented by Soviet physicists Igor Tamm and Andrei Sakharov.

The holy grail of nuclear fusion, however, was "cold fusion," i.e. fusion that does not require the high temperatures generated by such an expensive reactor. In March 1989 Stanley Pons, a chemist at the University of Utah, and Martin Fleischmann from the University of Southampton in Britain had announced that they had achieved "cold fusion," i.e. nuclear fusion at room temperature (about 20 degrees Celsius). Within a few months the scientific community had come to consider it a bluff, which discredited the entire field. Meanwhile, ignored by the media, in 1989 New Zealand electrochemist Michael McKubre had just begun to study cold fusion at SRI International. For about two decades the field had virtually been silenced by mainstream science. By the end of the 2000s interest had returned, as cold fusion would solve the problem of energy forever. Construction of ITER, mostly funded by the European Union, finally began in 2008 in southern France after India, mainland China, and South Korea had joined the original quartet. At the same time mainstream science began to accept the results on "cold fusion" that Michael McKubre's lab had achieved.

Meanwhile, hot fusion remained the scientifically proven way to go. The Livermore Labs were entrusted in 1997 with the National Ignition Facility (NIF). The project required high-power lasers to trigger nuclear fusion in the hydrogen fuel. The term "ignition" refers to the point when more energy is generated than is consumed by the plant. The Lawrence Livermore National Laboratory basically planned to simulate the nuclear fusion of a star (more than 100 million degrees Celsius, hotter than the center of the sun) with the world's most powerful laser.

Lasers

One of the great scientific endeavors of the 2000s was a joint project among CalTech, MIT, and Stanford to detect gravitational waves: the Laser Interferometer Gravitational-Wave Observatory (LIGO). The most expensive project ever funded by the National Science Foundation (NSF), LIGO became operational in August 2002 in two observatories located 3,000 kilometers apart (Louisiana and Washington state). The experiment required the most precise measurement ever. Capitalizing on laser amplification studied by Robert Byer 's team at Stanford, Ueda Kenichi in Japan developed transparent ceramic laser for high-energy applications that, in turn, led to Northrop Grumman's announcement in 2009 that it had created a 100-kilowatt laser, an impressive achievement for a discipline that in 1984 could only produce two-milliwatt lasers. This combination of high precision and high energy was unprecedented in history. Livermore Labs' researchers realized that the technology could also serve the purpose of the National Ignition Facility (NIF).

Lasers were also employed at the Lawrence Berkeley Labs to create a new generation of "miniature" particle accelerators. In 2006 Wim Leemans' team accelerated electrons to a billion electronvolts (1GeV) in a distance of centimeters rather than hundreds of meters. The next project was the Berkeley Lab Laser Accelerator (BELLA), in which a laser would produce one-quadrillion watts (one billion million watts) for a millisecond, enough to accelerate electrons to an energy of 10 GeV in a distance of just one meter.

Meanwhile, SLAC inaugurated the Linac Coherent Light Source (LCLS), that in April 2009 produced the world's brightest X-ray laser (X-rays being much higher-frequency radiations than microwaves). It was now technically possible to pinpoint a biological cell, and, generally speaking, explore matter at the molecular scale.

The Community: Coworking Spaces, Incubators and Accelerators

If Silicon Valley had always failed to create a community of engineers, the boom of the startup model led to the creation of a community of aspiring startup founders. The idea of the incubator was pioneered by Bill Gross, a Caltech graduate who had founded a few companies around its campus and who founded Idealab in 1996, again in Pasadena. Y Combinator was started in 2005 by Paul Graham in Mountain View, and went on to become the most famous of incubators thanks to the success of its 2008 alumnus Airbnb. By 2015 it had launched more than 800 startups and the value of its portfolio exceeded $80 billion (as a comparison, Intel's valuation at the time was $140 billion). The philosophy behind the two incubators was critical. Idealab depended on its team's ideas, nurtured them internally and finally spun them off as independent businesses: the founders of Idealab's startups were really "co-founders". Y Combinator, instead, looked for ideas and talents in the outside world and simply mentored them. Y Combinator came to be known as an "accelerator": it accelerated the time to market great ideas. Y Combinator also made it easier for startups based outside Silicon Valley to move their operations to Silicon Valley. Indirectly, it motivated thousands of engineers to move to Silicon Valley.

Y Combinator

Plug and Play Tech Center, founded in 2006 in Sunnyvale by Iranian serial entrepreneur Saeed Amidi, specialized in the international connection: in 2015 about 40% of its 400 startups hailed from abroad. Its first success story was Renaud Laplanche's and Joaquin Delgado's LendingClub, which would go on to post the largest IPO for a US tech company in 2014. Rocket Internet, founded in 2007 in Berlin by brothers Marc, Oliver and Alexander Samwer, invented the mass-market version of the accelerator: they specialized in launching startups that copied other people's successful ideas. Meanwhile, the idea of a co-working space had been pioneered in London by the Hub, opened in 2005 by Jonathan Robinson and others. This was a space that provided office facilities and a think-tank to people interested in starting high-tech ventures, people who wanted to save money on infrastructure but also and mainly to share their experience and meet other creative people. The idea was transported to San Francisco by Citizen Space, the office space rented by Chris Messina and Tara Hunt in 2006 where aspiring startup founders could share their experiences. At one point the biggest "hackerspace" in the city was Sandbox Suites, opened in 2007 by Roman Gelfer and Sasha Vasilyuk. Across the Bay in Oakland the premiere community space for high-tech was Tech Liminal, founded in 2009 by Anca Mosoiu, which was followed in 2011 by Sudo Room, founded by 23 people including Jenny Ryan and Marc Juul. More typical of the hacker counterculture were the Metalab, founded in 2006 in Vienna by Paul Bohm and Philipp Tiefenbacher, and Noisebridge, established in 2007 in San Francisco by Jacob Appelbaum of the Tor project and Mitch Altman (a veteran of Jaron Lanier's virtual-reality startup VPL Research) after they attended a C3 hacker conference in Germany.

Mitch Altman at Noisebridge

Accelerators with coworking spaces popped up everywhere, notably Brandery, founded in 2010 in Ohio, and Techstars, founded in 2006 in Boulder (Colorado) by David Cohen, Brad Feld, David Brown, and Jared Polis, that became a franchise incubator with branches in all the main cities, helping corporations set up their own incubator program (an incubator of incubators).. But the epicenter remained the Bay Area, where they multiplied rapidly: Parisoma, opened in 2008 in San Francisco by French veterans; AngelPad, founded in 2010 in San Francisco by former Google executive Thomas Korte; 500 Startups, launched in 2010 in Mountain View by former Paypal executive Dave McClure; Matter.vc, founded in 2012 in San Francisco (with a five-month acceleration program, one of the most extensive in the business); Upwest Labs, opened in 2012 in Palo Alto by Israeli veterans Shuly Galili and Gil Ben-Artzy; Founders Space, opened in 2014 in San Francisco by videogame industry veterans Steve Hoffman and Naomi Kokubo; Alchemist, an incubator for B2B startups, founded by Stanford professor Ravi Belani in 2012 in San Francisco, an emanation of the city's Harvard Club; as well as incubators specifically targeting a nationality, notably the ones for Chinese startups such as Innospring, founded in 2012 in Santa Clara by Chinese-born angel investor Eugene Zhang, and Hanhai zPark, founded in 2013 by Victor Wang and other investors in San Jose. Among coworking spaces some of the most popular ones were Hacker Dojo, opened by David Weekly and others in 2009 in Mountain View; RocketSpace, founded in 2011 in San Francisco by Duncan Logan; and the GroundFloor in Santa Clara, opened in 2012 by brothers Max and Peter Bloom.

Founders Space

There were infinite variations on the theme of the incubator/accelerator. Blackbox was a "live and work" house in Atherton, opened in 2010 by the Syrian-born Fadi Bishara, that specialized in international startups and investors. NFX Guild, founded in 2015 in Palo Alto, did not accept applications: the startups were selected by a team of "scouts", and mostly targeted an Israeli audience. Expa, founded in 2013 in San Francisco, by Uber's co-founder Garrett Camp, called itself a "startup studio". R/GA, founded in 2013 in New York, focused on the Internet of Things. In 2015 Google launched its own Launchpad Accelerator.

The other model that had taken hold since 2011 was the "company builder". In 2011 angel investor Nova Spivack, who in 2000 had helped SRI Intl set up the incubator nVention to commercialize SRI's research and in 2001 had set up his own incubator Lucid Ventures, coined the expression "venture production studio". The concept had been pioneered in Los Angeles by Bill Gross' IdeaLab. A company builder was a think tank capable of raising money, providing staff resources, writing business plans, obtaining intellectual-property rights, specifying MVPs (minimum viable products), hiring business managers, and, last but not least, publicizing the startup. The model worked so well that it soon spawned imitators in several other cities. Twitter's co-founders Ev Williams and Biz Stone were the brains behind Obvious Corp, that opened in San Francisco in 2006. New York gave birth to two of the most influential company builders: in 2006 Kevin Ryan and Dwight Merriman (both former DoubleClick executives) set up AlleyCorp, and in 2007 John Borthwick, Billy Chasen and Andy Weissman started Betaworks. In 2010 Eric Lefkofsky (a Groupon co-founder), Brad Keywell and Andrew Mason founded Lightbank in Chicago. In 2011 Mike Jones (a former CEO of Myspace) teamed up with Peter Pham and others to launch Science in Los Angeles. Company builders in the Bay Area were almost all based in San Francisco: Michael Birch and his wife Xochi Birch started Monkey Inferno in 2011; PayPal's co-founder Max Levchin started HVF (Hard Valuable Fun) in 2011; Snapfish co-founder Raj Kapoor started Cofounder.co in 2012; Iranian-born serial entrepreneur Shervin Pishevar started Sherpa Ventures in 2013.

Meanwhile, someone came up with the ultimate idea of combining entrepreneur training and collaborative workspaces, basically inventing the university for startup creation. In 2009 serial entrepreneur Adeo Ressi launched the Founder's Institute, originally based in Palo Alto, a "university" for startup founders in which the goal was to launch a company by the end of a four-month program and payment was by tuition and equity. It would expand to more than 70 cities by 2015. Similar "institutes" were soon created in many other parts of the world: TechHub, founded in 2010 in London by Elizabeth Varley and Mike Butcher; General Assembly, founded in 2011 in New York by Jake Schwartz, Adam Pritzker, Matthew Brimer, and Brad Hargreaves; Galvanize, founded in 2012 in Denver by Lawrence Mandes, Chris Onan, Jim Deters; etc. They had precious few success stories, but thousands of enthusiastic applicants.

Makers Movement

From ham-radio amateurs to the Homebrew Computer Club, the Bay Area had always been a hotbed of the Do-It-Yourself (DIY) culture. Make magazine, founded in 2005 by Dale Dougherty of the Tim O'Reilly publishing house (one hour north of San Francisco), spawned the Maker Faire of 2006 in San Mateo, a conference that would rapidly spread around the world. Tech Shop, founded in 2006 by Jim Newton and Ridge McGhee in Menlo Park, pioneered the concept of the shared workshop offering its members not only classes but also tools and equipment. The incubator for makers was Hacker Dojo in Mountain View, following the example of PCH Innovation, that had opened in Ireland in 1996 by Liam Casey.

Makers could sell their products on websites such as Etsy (founded in 2005 in New York by Robert Kalin).

The most important "makers" in Silicon Valley remained the software engineers. For them Tom Preston-Werner, a former Powerset engineer, started GitHub in 2008 in San Francisco, that was a sort of social networking platform for open-source software developers. While not glamorous like Facebook, Twitter and Pinterest, by 2015 it would count on 1.2 million users. The importance of the open-source movement for the startup ecosystem was colossal. Free software lowered the threshold for kids to start their own projects. The more complex a piece of software, the higher the cost to start a company in that field. Without open-source software, only big corporations would have been able to start a project in those fields. The reward for the individual who donated a piece of software was personal glory and a sense of achievement. The Bay Area created a whole culture that encouraged engineers to contribute to the open-source repositories. That culture, in turn, enabled a boom of startups. Basically, the open-source world went from being about tools to being about networking and finally to being a real culture. Eventually students began to appreciate that their contributions to the community could count as academic credentials. And, at the other end of the spectrum, big corporations could view this huge population of GitHub contributors as a business opportunity as long as they could be turned into enthusiastic adopters of a platform. Give it to the open-source community, and see what they can do with it.

Fintech

The financial world moved decisively online during the Great Recession. The demand of small businesses that could not borrow money was met by non-bank lenders such as OnDeck (New York, 2007), Kabbage (Atlanta, 2009) and Funding Circle (London, 2010).

Another alternative form of lending was devised by two companies founded in 2006 in San Francisco: peer-to-peer (social) lending. Prosper, founded by Chris Larsen, and LendingClub, founded by former Oracle executive Renaud Laplanche, provided marketplaces for lending that matched those who wanted to borrow money with people who wanted to lend money. Their platforms marked the marriage of fintech, P2P and the sharing economy The concept had been pioneered by Zopa in London the year before. Initially peer-to-peer lending was geographically confined but Virginia-based Zidisha, founded in 2009 by Julia Kurnia as a nonprofit, showed how one could also link lenders and borrowers in different countries.

Automated financial advisory was legitimized by the success of Betterment, founded in 2008 in New York by Jon Stein, and Personal Capital, founded in 2009 in Redwood City by EverBank's co-founder Rob Foregger, Paypal's former CEO Bill Harris and digital security expert Louie Gasparini. It was perhaps the most obvious case of automation in the financial world because all financial advisors were already using algorithms. Creating an algorithm-based financial advisor simply required access to those algorithms.

Culture and Society

The debate on "net neutrality" erupted in 2007, following a case in which the largest Internet provider in the country was caught discriminating against some Internet traffic. Since its inception, the utopia behind the Internet had been that Internet providers and governments should not discriminate economically against any data traveling on the Internet; they should not charge more for better service, should not decide who gets faster or slower speed, etc. That was precisely what Comcast, the largest cable-television and Internet provider after the 2002 acquisition of AT&T Broadband, was caught doing in 2007. The concept of net neutrality was particularly dear to the children of the Bay Area counterculture. Not surprisingly, the debate ended up pitting the telecom superpowers of the East Coast, namely Verizon (Philadelphia), AT&T (New Jersey) and Comcast (originally founded as American Cable Systems in Tupelo, Mississippi, in 1963 by Ralph Roberts but relocated in 1969 to Philadelphia), against the Silicon Valley superpowers (Google, Yahoo, Twitter and Facebook among others). In 2015 the government would rule that the Internet was a public utility, like phone service, and forbade providing faster service to anybody.

The future was more mysterious than ever, even though these technologies diverged in so many directions. The debate about the future permeated many Bay Area circles, mostly centered around oracles of the future ("futurists"). Taking inspiration from the private International Space University (ISU), founded by MIT professors in 1987, in 2009 OCR inventor Ray Kurzweil and ISU's founder Peter Diamandis started the Singularity University, located at Moffett Field. It basically bestowed academic credentials upon futurists. Sometimes the futurists' rhetoric was oddly reminiscent of the post-hippie new-age spirituality of the 1970s, except that now it was focused on achieving immortality (scientists at the Singularity University speculated that in the future immortality could be achieved by downloading one's consciousness onto a computer).

Ray Kurzweil at Singularity University

In 2007 writers Gary Wolf and Kevin Kelly of Wired magazine introduced the term "quantified self". The concept caught up quickly and in 2011 the first international conference was held in Mountain View. The "quantified self" movement started from the premise that our lives continuously produce data. We can physically record those data by wearing sensors connected to computers. These data can then be used to document a person's life: self-tracking and self-monitoring.

The Seasteading Institute, founded in 2008 in Sunnyvale by Patri Friedman, envisioned cities floating in the middle of the ocean as utopian libertarian communities to experiment with alternative social systems.

The arts reacted seemingly by discarding the whole notion of a future, by embracing in fact a playful tone even when they confronted tragic themes. Al Farrow used guns and bullets to sculpt his "Cathedral" (2007). In 2010 Scott Sona Snibbe, one of the many Bay Area practitioners of immersive interactive art, turned one of his interactive software artworks, Gravilux, into an application for the iPhone and iPad. It was downloadable for free from the iTunes store: within weeks it became a worldwide success. At the intersection of art and science in 2001 neuroscientist Semir Zeki had founded the Institute of Neuroesthetics in Berkeley, and in 2008 Piero Scaruffi started the Leonardo Art Science Evenings (LASERs) in San Francisco, that within eight years would spread to more than ten universities worldwide. In 2010 Patricia Maloney launched the online art magazine Art Practical, out of the California College of the Arts in San Francisco.

Berkeley's passion for "including" disabled people culminated in 2010 with the inauguration of the Ed Roberts campus, a place not only devoted to people with disabilities but designed (by architect William Leddy) to make sure that anyone (anyone) could use it, even blind people without arms or legs.

Skyrocketing real-estate costs in San Francisco were sending more and more artists across the bay to Oakland. Oakland had long been famous mainly for crime. In 2007 it still had the third highest murder rate in California with 120 murders (one every three days). In 2012 it was still the 7th deadliest city in the USA. This, of course, simply reflected the widespread poverty and neglect: between 2007 and 2012 more than 10,000 homes were foreclosed. Secondly, Oakland had become the state's capital of "weeds" (marijuana) or, at least, was at the forefront of the campaign to legalize cannabis. An entire district was nicknamed "Oaksterdam", a reference to Amsterdam, the European city where marijuana was virtually legal. In 2004 Oakland voters approved "Measure Z", which officially made marijuana-related "investigation, citation and arrest" a low priority for the city's cops. In 2007 Richard Lee even founded the Oaksterdam University, a non-profit organization teaching how to grow (medical) marijuana. There were shops where anyone, paying a small fee, could get a prescription to buy marijuana. It didn't look like the ideal place for engineers, and, in fact, Oakland's only major success story of the high-tech community was Pandora. In 2013 venture capitalists poured $7 billion into San Francisco's two thousand high-tech companies providing 50,000 jobs. In the same year venture capitalists poured slightly over half a billion into Oakland's 350 high-tech companies, providing not even 6,000 jobs (10% of which worked at Pandora). However, the cost of office space was about half in Oakland than in San Francisco. But the arts thrived and Oakland was increasingly on the map for major art shows. In 2006 eight art galleries located in the Northgate and Temescal (north Oakland) neighborhoods of Oakland (21 Grand, 33 Grand, Auto 3321, Boontling Gallery, Buzz Gallery, Ego Park, Front Gallery, and Rock Paper Scissors Collective) joined together to launch "The Art Murmur", a free art walk open to everybody held on the first Friday of every month. The demographic shift underway was easy to detect: between 1990 and 2011 the black community went from 43% of the population to 26%. Landlords were evicting black families (typically lower-income families) to rent to higher-income families. In 1994 California voters passed Proposition 184 (better known as the "three-strikes" law), mandating life sentences for those convicted of three violent felonies; and in 1996 Bill Clinton signed a law authorizing landlords to evict tenants suspected of any crime. The combined effect of these two laws was to decimate the black community.

A side-effect was to open neighborhood to the artists who were fleeing the high rent prices of San Francisco.

An important ideological change was taking place inside the Bay Area's universities about using new digital media to export knowledge to the rest of the world. For example, Khan Academy was launched in 2006 by Salman Khan to make a free K-12 education available through short instructional videos on YouTube. Copying that idea in 2011, Stanford professors Peter Norvig and Sebastian Thrun created free courseware on the Web that could be accessed by students worldwide. In 2011 Sebastian Thrun quit Stanford to start the online university Udacity that would educate tens of thousands of students worldwide for free. Also in 2011 two Stanford researchers, Andrew Ng and Daphne Koller, whose free Web-based courseware had already been used by more than 100,000 students, launched their own startup, Coursera, aiming at providing interactive courses from Stanford, UC Berkeley, the University of Michigan, the University of Pennsylvania and Princeton University in all sorts of disciplines.

SlideShare, launched in 2006 in San Francisco by software engineer Jonathan Boutelle and UC Berkeley neuroscientist Rashmi Sinha (and acquired by LinkedIn in 2012) allowed anybody to upload slide presentations on any subject, rapidly creating the largest repository of knowledge after Wikipedia. By the end of 2013 there were more than 10 million presentations available on SlideShare viewed 3 billion times a month.

By 2015 Udacity had 1.6 million users and Coursera 12 million. A similar revolution was taking place in primary and secondary education (the so called "K-12" in the USA). Edmodo, founded by Nic Borg and Jeff O'Hara in 2008 in San Mateo, would be used by more than 50 million people worldwide in 2015. Udemy, started by Eren Bali in 2010, offered an online marketplace where anyone could upload and sell a class. Schoology, founded in 2009 in New York by three students of St Louis' Washington University (Jeremy Friedman, Ryan Hwang and Tim Trinidad), provided a cloud-based platform for teachers to share their educational material with other teachers and for third parties to write applications. By 2015 it boasted 12 million users in more than 130 countries. This movement represented the first real change in public education in decades, since early Internet-based educational software such as WebCT (developed in 1996 at the University of British Columbia by Murray Goldberg) and CourseInfo (developed in 1997 by Daniel Cane and Stephen Gilfus at Cornell University). Education was one field where technology was still roughly the same as at the time of the first eLearning systems of the 1970s, simply with tablets replacing terminals. At the same time, education had become ever more expensive, coming to constitute almost more than 7% of the country's GDP (more than one trillion dollars in 2015). It helped that in 2009 the governors of several states had come together to define a cross-country standard for education the Common Core Standards Initiative, thereby creating a much bigger market for any educational platform.

Meanwhile, the ever-shifting demographics of the Bay Area were experiencing another major make-up. This time, they were Muslims. Most of them came from the Indian subcontinent and chose Fremont as their new hometown. In October 2006, an Afghan woman wearing the Muslim head scarf was killed in a brazen daylight shooting. That tragic incident put Muslims on the social map of the Bay Area. The Zaytuna Institute, the first Muslim liberal arts institution in the US, had been founded by Shaykh Hamza in 1996 in Berkeley. The first Bay Area Muslim Film Festival had been held in March 2004 in Berkeley. The Muslim population of the Bay Area was estimated at 250,000 in 2008.

The success of Paypal, Facebook and the likes had transformed Palo Alto from a student town to a startup town. Mountain View, the first beneficiary of the dotcom since the days of Netscape and Yahoo and now the heartland of Google, was on its way to become another exclusive community. Silicon Valley had expanded north (to Oracle's Redwood City and to Genentech's South San Francisco) but not quite north to the intellectual hubs of Berkeley and San Francisco that, despite nurturing several startups, never quite experienced the same ebullient business creativity, as if to prove that a startup needs irresponsible thinking more than it needs worldly erudition.

However, Silicon Valley was paying an increasingly high psychological price for its lifestyle. Nowhere else in the world could one see so many people driving alone in their car to work and back home (or just to the mall/gym/whatever). Nowhere else in the world could one find such a widespread use of cubicles in office buildings, so that each person has her/his personal space. And probably in no other urban center was the single-family detached home so popular as in California. An increasing number of people lived by themselves, drove alone to the office, worked alone in a cubicle, ate their lunch alone... All of these used to be not only social but even crowded activities. From the beginning the suburban environment within which Silicon Valley prospered seemed to be designed to provide some kind of "isolation". Not quite "loneliness", but certainly a degree of separation that reinforced the North American tendency towards individualism and bottom-up organization. Socialization was happening through the institutions created by that bottom-up approach, such as the ancient Gold Rush practice of meeting in saloons (nowadays bats and restaurants) or at the rodeo (now a gym). As Silicon Valley sociologist said in a private conversation while we were discussing this issue, "There must be a reason if eating is so important here". People had never been so far from family and never had so superficial friendships. No surprise then that social media became so popular in Silicon Valley: their function was, fundamentally, to keep people isolated while connecting them.

Peter Norvig at Singularity University (2012)

The Anthropology of the Age of Self-awareness

The 2000s were the decade when Silicon Valley was obsessed with itself. The Tech Museum of Innovation opened in 1998 in San Jose, and the Computer History Museum opened in 2003 in Mountain View. Silicon Valley had always been a bit surprised of being a world-famous phenomenon. The Stanford Silicon Valley Archives reopened in 1999 at the Green Library and began amassing donations of documents from companies and individuals. As many of its original founders were reaching the age of the memoir, Silicon Valley was becoming a self-celebratory phenomenon.

In fact, some began to argue that Silicon Valley was, ultimately, the history of single individuals, or, better, titans: David Packard, Robert Noyce, Steve Jobs, Bill Joy, Larry Ellison, Marc Andreessen, Larry Page, Mark Zuckerberg, Peter Thiel, Elon Musk, etc. The cult of personality had never been high in a place that traditionally abhorred the rich and powerful, but things were obviously changing, as manifested by a flurry of hagiographies: Mike Wilson's "The Difference Between God and Larry Ellison" (2003), Stewart Gillmor's "Fred Terman at Stanford" (2004),

Leslie Berlin's Robert Noyce's biography "The Man Behind the Microchip" (2006), Michael Malone's Hewlett and Packard biography "Bill & Dave" (2007), Joel Shurkin's William Shockley biography "Broken Genius" (2008), and continuing with Walter Isaacson's best-selling biography of Steve Jobs (2011), Michael Lewis' Jim Clark biography "The New New Thing" (2014), etc. And if this phenomenon sounded a little bit like the mythology of the Far West, it is because it was, indeed, rather similar.

In another act of self-celebration, in 2006 Julie Newdoll of YLEM gave a commission to sculptor Jim Pallas, who specialized in plywood hitch-hikers. She wanted sculptures of six founding fathers of Silicon Valley (DeForest, Hewlett, Packard, Shockley, Terman and Noyce) to be dispatched around the US equipped with tracking devices.

This society saturated with high-tech was still humane. A few events were emblematic of the anti-technological reaction that was more pervasive than ever despite the appearances. First was the growing popularity of the outdoors. A store like REI, founded in 1938 in Seattle by a group of mountaineers, became a conglomerate due to its success in the Bay Area, where it maintained eight locations. It specialized in sporting goods, notably for hiking, climbing, and biking. The Bay Area had always been obsessed with fitness (and the gym had become ubiquitous) but this went beyond fitness. Silicon Valley engineers used their spare time to train for the epic hikes of Yosemite and the High Sierra, as well as for marathons, bike races, and triathlons, no matter how unprepared they were.

Nonetheless, those were also the days of the hackathons, the ultimate passtime for fanatic engineers. The word "hackathon" was used at the JavaOne conference of June 1999 in which software engineers were invited to collaborate and compete in creating some software applications, but the term became popular after Andrew Hyde of TechStars organized the first Startup Weekend in 2007 in Colorado. David Weekly had already started in 2005 in Silicon Valley the event SuperHappyDevHouse (SHDH), from which the working space Hacker Dojo was born. Then the hackathon, sometimes lasting 48 hours, became a favorite hobby of thousands of Silicon Valley engineers. In 2011 in San Francisco Greg Gopman hosted a hackathon called AngelHack, that would quickly spread all over the world.

HackerDojo

The "Burning Man" festival had moved to an isolated corner of the Black Rock desert in Nevada where it had completely lost its "counterculture" status. It was now one of the most advertised and expensive events of the year. But it was a futuristic, urban experiment. During Labor Day weekend in September, tens of thousands of people, mostly from the Bay Area, set up a tent city, lived in it, and were stimulated to be creative and spontaneous. Then they simply "undid" it all, leaving no traces behind. Burning Man had become famous for its fantastical and participatory art installations (that were meant to be burned at the end of the festival) and for its picturesque costumes and body art of the crowd. But it was becoming more interesting as a self-organized community. Burning Man had originally been studied as a semi-religious ritual of purification and communion by the high-tech generation, but now it was also studied as a city powered by solar energy and motorized by biodiesel. It was decorated with the arts instead of billboards, and cleaned by the citizens themselves. By comparison, the European equivalent was the "Love Parade," which was really just a big party of music, alcohol, and drugs.

And then there was the end of the world. The cycles of the Maya calendar end with the year 2012. This and other coincidences led to the formation of theories about some kind of impending apocalypse that became a favorite topic of discussion among engineers who had never cared about Maya history (and, alas, probably didn't really know who the Maya were).

Growing awareness of the role of technology in shaping society was mirrored by growing moral anxiety. In October 2011 a new class of corporation was created in California, the "benefit corporations", which are corporations whose charters specifically mandate the pursue of ethical and environmental goals instead of giving priority to maximizing the financial return to shareholders.

While these phenomena could be viewed as reactions to the materialism of high-tech business, they were also emblematic of a shift towards more superficial hobbies. Knowledge-driven hobbies had been replaced by skills-driven hobbies: salsa dancing, mountain biking, snowboarding, marathon running, etc. This shift translated into a rapid collapse of the independent bookstores, several of which were vestiges of the counterculture of the 1960s. It wasn't just the online bookstore that killed them: it was also a rapidly declining audience for high-brow culture. In 2001 Printers Inc. in Palo Alto closed. Kepler's in Menlo Park closed in 2005 but was saved by a grass-roots campaign. In 2006, both Cody's in Berkeley and A Clean and Well Lighted Place in Cupertino had to shut down.

In reality, there were increasingly big differences between the various poles of the Bay Area. Long work hours and maddeningly slow traffic were progressively isolating Silicon Valley from the rest of the Bay. Silicon Valley was a region of low-rise residential buildings and town-home parks organized in geometric neighborhood that were largely self-sufficient. Therefore the need to visit other parts of the Bay was minimal. The distances between Silicon Valley and the artistic world of San Francisco, and the political world of Berkeley, and the scientific world of Stanford had increased dramatically. No wonder that Silicon Valley was (in)famous for no cultural variety: everybody read the same book, watched the same movie and sang the same song. Its inhabitants were too isolated from culture. Silicon Valley was giving a new meaning to the word "provincial".

For a long time the engineering world had been fundamentally male. The 21st century began with an increasing number of women joining the ranks of engineers. There was also significant progress in promoting women to executive jobs. Young female executives included Sheryl Sandberg (1969), chief operating officer of Facebook, and Marissa Mayer (1975), a vice-president at Google and soon the CEO of Yahoo. However, there still was no female equivalent to Hewlett, Packard, Gordon Moore, Steve Jobs, Bill Joy, Larry Ellison, Marc Andreessen, Larry Page, Mark Zuckerberg, Elon Musk, Peter Thiel, etc. The people who fueled the boom of Silicon Valley were all men; and almost all white. So much for the much vaunted diversity of Silicon Valley.

A typical event at the Computer History Museum (2015): no more than 5% of
the audience is female, and there isn't a single African-American

This society was still very transient. In 1992 unemployment in Silicon
Valley had reached 7.4%. In 2000 it had declined to 1.7%. One year later it
had increased to 5.9%. By 2007 it was down again. It was not the same
people who left and came. Those who left probably never came back. It
was terribly difficult to resettle in the Bay Area after one left it, both in
terms of real estate (home prices tended to skyrocket during a recovery due
to a chronic shortage of housing) and in terms of employment (easy for a
recent immigrant or fresh graduate to take a risky job, difficult for
someone who already had a career somewhere else). Silicon Valley was
the one region of the world whose identity was not defined by the people
who lived in it, because they changed all the time.

However, perhaps the most unique aspect of culture and society in the
San Francisco Bay Area was that there was absolutely no building
reflecting the booming economic, technological and political power.
Rarely had human civilization been so invisible. There was no
breathtaking skyscraper, no imposing monument, no avantgarde city
landmark: Silicon Valley and the rest of the Bay did not invest a single
penny in advertising its own success. In March 2012 the New York Times
estimated that all fine arts museums of San Francisco combined ranked
13th in the nation for investments in new acquisitions, even behind the
Princeton Art Museum, with a total that was less than 10% of what the
Metropolitan Museum of New York alone spent.

The Gift Economy

At the end of the Great Recession of 2008, economists were beginning
to understand one important factor among the causes of the chronic
unemployment in the US: free community content. In 2006 YouTube only
had 60 employees, but they were managing 100 million videos. YouTube's
employees were not making the videos: millions of people around the
world were donating them to YouTube. If a Hollywood studio had decided
to create 100 million videos, it would have had to hire hundreds of
thousands of people to act them, direct them, produce them, edit them, and
upload them. In 2004, Craigslist only had ten employees moderating more
than a million advertisements posted every month. A newspaper handling
the same amount of advertisements would have to hire hundreds of editors.
In 2005 Flickr only had nine employees, but they were managing a
repository of millions of pictures. Those pictures were taken around the
world, edited, uploaded, documented and even organized by millions of
users. A magazine that decided to create a similar repository of pictures
would have to hire thousands of photographers, tour guides and editors. In
2005 Skype only had 200 employees, but they were providing telephone

service to more than 50 million registered users. Any telecom in the world that provided a comparable service employed tens of thousands of technicians, operators, accountants, etc. One of the fundamental discoveries of the "net economy" had been that users of the Web around the world are happy to contribute content for free to websites willing to accept it.

This phenomenon obviously displaced workers who used to be paid to create that very content. This phenomenon was not creating joblessness but merely unemployment: it was creating unpaid jobs. Millions of people worked (some of them for many hours a day) to create and upload content to other people's businesses (such as Wikipedia, Facebook, Twitter, Flickr and YouTube). They were working, but they were not employed. They worked for free, out of their own will. Not even slaves did that. Indirectly, the Web had created a broad new class of knowledge workers: volunteer amateur editors. Their net effect was to displace the existing knowledge workers, such as photographers, journalists, actors, directors, researchers, writers, librarians, musicians, as well as all the engineers and clerical staff who provided services for them.

When thousands of knowledge workers lose their job, i.e. when their purchasing power collapses, inevitably this has a repercussion on the entire economy and creates further ripples of unemployment. Every time someone adds a line to Wikipedia, a professional knowledge worker becomes less indispensable and more disposable. Every time someone adds a picture to Flickr, a video to YouTube, news on Twitter, a notice on Facebook, or an ad on Craigslist, the job of a professional becomes more vulnerable. In the past each wave of technological innovation had come with a wave of new jobs that replaced the old ones.

Society had to train millions of users of word processors to take the place of million of typists. Companies had to churn out computers instead of typewriters, a process that involved hiring more (not fewer) people. In fact, each wave of technological progress typically created new opportunities for knowledge workers, and this class therefore expanded rapidly, creating more (not less) employment (and higher incomes). The expansion was still happening: there ware now millions of people making videos instead of just a few thousands, and there ware now millions of people taking pictures and millions posting news. The difference was that this time they didn't ask to be paid: they were doing it for free.

Therefore businesses could operate with a minimal staff: the old knowledge workers were replaced by free labor. Therefore the number of knowledge workers was still increasing (and even exponentially), but the number of those who were paid for their work was shrinking dramatically.

It was an illusion that YouTube was run by only a handful of employees. YouTube "employed" millions of "employees." It just so happened that 99% of them were happy to work (provide content) for free.

Therefore there was no need anymore to actually hire people to create content. Protectionists were complaining that developing countries were "dumping" cheap products on the US market that caused US companies to go out of business. Protectionists were inveighing against "unfair trade." But the real enemy of employment was free labor. Nothing kills jobs faster and more permanently than free labor. That is a form of competition that was coming from inside the US society, an accidental by-product of technological progress.

This accidental by-product was actually the dream of socialist utopians. The net economy had created production tools that were available for free to everybody. That was precisely Marx's definition of socialism: the collective ownership of the means of production. This accidental by-product was also the dream of the hippie utopians of the San Francisco Bay Area. In the 1970s Stewart Brand of the WELL had imagined precisely such a virtual community of people engaged in the free production and exchange of knowledge goods: a community of people investing their time and sharing their content for free. The utopian society of Marx and Brand had materialized as a "gift economy" (a term coined in 1985 by Lewis Hyde and applied to the net economy in 1998 by Richard Barbrook) in which a few businesses provided the means of production to a mass of millions of volunteer amateur editors.

The free labor of these many worker ants allowed a very small number of queens to get extremely rich while causing millions of middle-class families to lose their income.

The irony is that they were often the same people. The very person who uploads a picture, a text or a video for free is the person who will (directly or indirectly) need to look for another (often less remunerative) job as a (direct or indirect) consequence of that act of free labor.

The Internet had indeed democratized society. Everybody could now start their own business. At the same time the Internet had increased the value of knowledge, another step in the progress of human civilization from survival-based goods to knowledge-based goods. The problem was that the Internet had also democratized knowledge production: everybody could now provide content, and they were willing to do it for free.

The net economy was, in fact, rapidly evolving towards an economy of one-man operations. There were now Web-based tools available to build, run, and monetize a business that only required limited technical skills and no more than a few days of work. One person alone could create an assembly line entirely on the Web to produce a mass-market product/service (in the same category as YouTube, Flickr and Craigslist). That assembly line did not employ any worker other than the founders who assembled it. Once the one-person business was up and running, its success mainly depended on how many people were willing to contribute content for free, i.e. how much free labor you could harvest on the

Internet. One could foresee a future when a startup would require even fewer founders. If successful (i.e., if it ever managed to attract millions of amateur content providers), it would employ even fewer people, and only those very few would benefit financially from its success.

In the age of smartphones and email there was another victim: physical proximity was no longer a necessity for a startup. There was no need to be based, say, in Palo Alto, where the cost of living was so high. The time had come for geographically distributed startups. For example, StackOverflow was founded in 2008 by Jeff Atwood in Berkeley and Joel Spolsky in New York, and employed people in different states.

These startups of the "gift economy" were annoyed by the pressures of investors. Therefore it came as no surprise that in April 2010 Jared Cosulich and Adam Abrons founded Irrational Design with the explicit goal of not seeking venture capital. The "business plan" of the startup was to be creative, with no specific product in mind. Venture capitalists were perceived as hijacking the minds of the founders to focus on a lucrative product. Irrational Design was emblematic of a generation that aimed for precisely the opposite: let the minds of the founders invent at will, with no regard for market response or potential acquisitions.

In July 2002 eBay paid $1.5 billion for PayPal, a tiny unprofitable online payment service. In October 2006 Google paid $1.65 billion for YouTube, a video uploading site that had no revenue.

The traditional economy had tended to concentrate wealth in the hands of a few large companies that had run giant empires of hundreds of thousands of employees around the world. The gift economy was rapidly concentrating wealth in the hands of a few individuals who ran giant empires of tens of millions of unpaid amateurs.

Twitter's Offices (2010)

The New Labor

Websites like Etsy, founded in 2005 in New York, and eLance, founded in 1999 in Boston by Beerud Sheth, were allowing anybody to become a self-employed businessman. As jobs disappeared due to automation, the population of "entrepreneurs" was destined to skyrocket.

As Venkatesh Rao argued in his article "Entrepreneurs Are The New Labor" (2012), the number of startup founders was destined to increase exponentially but they could no longer be viewed as the old-fashioned entrepreneurs: in reality they were becoming the modern equivalent of specialized work. Artisans, craftsmen. The startup had become the modern form of apprenticeship: startup founders learn how the modern, lean company works. When a bigger company buys them out, they are de facto "hired" and transition from apprenticeship to full-fledged work. Large companies will increasingly be aggregations of startups, they will increasingly rely on a workforce of entrepreneurs.

The Assembly Line Model of Startup Funding

The first boom of Silicon Valley's venture capital world took place in the mid-1980s when large semiconductor companies needed money to build "fabs" (short for "fabrication plants"). A fab is an extremely expensive project that requires hundreds of millions of dollars. The age of one-man startups, though, did not require such massive investments. The returns (as a percentage) could be even higher with a much smaller investment. Unlike fabs, that need an accurate plan of implementation, Web-based startups could adjust their functions in real time based on user's feedback. So all one needed to start a company was just a good idea and a rudimentary website. Instagram, a company of 16 people, had 130 million customers when it was bought by Facebook in 2012.

At the end of the 2000s it was getting so easy and cheap to start a company that the business of funding companies was beginning to resemble an assembly line. When car manufacturing became cheap enough, Ford built an assembly line and launched the first mass-market car. Something similar was happening in Silicon Valley in 2010 in the business of manufacturing startups. Sometimes angels would invest without even having met the founders in person.

This logic was being pushed to the extreme limit by a new generation of angel investors who were sometimes barely in their 30s. The Google, Facebook, and PayPal success stories, plus all the startups that they acquired (Google acquired more than 40 companies in 2010 alone), had created plenty of very young millionaires and even some billionaires. They could comfortably retire, but it was "cool" to become angel investors and help other young founders get started and get rich. These new angels were "kids" compared with the veterans of 3000 Sand Hill Road. Yet many of these kids felt that they could more accurately guess the future of the world and jumped into the game passionately. Needless to say, these kids tended to fund startups that were started by kids even younger than them.

The mindset of both investors and founders was very different from the mindset of investors and founders of the 1980s. The credentials of a founder were often based on popularity, not on a professional business plan. In fact, these new investors "hated" the Wall Street type of founder. They loved, on the other hand, the "cool" kid. The successful founder was someone who could create "buzz" on the Internet about his or her idea, even if he or she had no clue how to monetize that idea. It was, in a sense, the psychology of the high school transplanted into the world of finance. The intellectual idealism of the early Internet was being replaced by the subculture of high-school gangs (albeit one that abhorred drugs and violence).

The new angels, in turn, were not professionals educated by Stanford or Harvard in the subtleties of economics; they were former "cool" kids. They invested based on their instinct, trying to guess who would become the next cool kid. To some extent the venture capital business had always been a statistical game: you invest in ten startups hoping that just one makes it big. But it had always been backed by some (economic) science. It was now becoming pure gambling. The psychology required from an angel investor was more and more similar to the psychology of the gambler who spent the day in front of a slot machine in Las Vegas casinos. The inception of this new kind of venture capitalism was commonly taken to be 2005, when Paul Graham started Y Combinator in Mountain View and incubated eight seed-stage startups.

Another significant change in the way startups are funded took place when the "crowd-funding" website Kickstarter launched (in 2008 in San Francisco by day trader Perry Chen, online music store editor Yancey Strickler and web-designer Charles Adler). The concept had been pioneered by Brian Camelio's New York-based music company ArtistShare: raise money among ordinary people to fund a (music) event. Kickstarter transferred the concept into the world of the Bay Area startups with amazing success: by July 2012 Kickstarter had funded more than 62,000 projects that had raised more than 200 million dollars. Kickstarter got further help from the government when the JOBS Act was enacted in April 2012: it made it legal for smaller investors to fund a company and with fewer restrictions.

Kickstarter's main rival was Indiegogo, founded in 2008 by Wall Street analyst Danae Ringelmann with Slava Rubin and Eric Schell in New York. Another formidable rival would emerge from San Diego in 2010, GoFundMe.

Last but not least, the early adopters too were of a different kind than for previous generations of products. The early adopter of an Intel product or of an Oracle product was a multinational corporation. The early adopter of an Apple gadget was a professional with a good salary, and typically a technology-savvy one. Now the early adopter of a website (say, a social networking platform) was, instead, just a kid himself. The early adopter was not paying anything to use the "product" (the social networking platform). Therefore the profile of the early adopters was, for the first time ever, disconnected from their financial status and instead related to how much spare time they had and were willing to spend on the Internet. The early adopters were typically very young. These "kids" created the "buzz." They established the credentials of a new platform. The adult audience followed the trend set by a very young audience.

The Big-Brother Web

Google, Facebook, and other cloud companies justified their new features on the basis of providing "better services," but in reality they were providing better services mainly to marketers. The multinational marketers (such as WPP Group) were now in control of the Web. They drove the new features of the most popular websites. For that reason Google and Facebook were improving the "services" of tracking what people do on the Internet. In theory, this vast database of individual behavioral patterns was meant to provide a personalized experience on the Internet. In practice, its motivation was economic. Marketers were willing to pay more for advertising on platforms that tracked individual behavior. For the marketers it meant the difference between a shot in the dark and targeted advertisement. Targeted ads were obviously much more valuable. Google's and Facebook's founders kept swearing that there was no "Big Brother" in the future of their worlds, but a sort of Big Brother was precisely the ultimate outcome of their business plan.

One major event created even more anxiety. In August 2010 Google signed a deal with Verizon that basically terminated the "net neutrality" principle. The Internet had been born as a noncommercial platform. Therefore it had been easy to enforce a principle that every piece of data, no matter how powerful its "owner," should move at the same speed through the vast network of nodes that physically implement the Internet. That principle was never codified in a law, but it had been respected even during the dotcom boom, allowing, for example, Amazon to grow at the expense of the traditional bookstore chains and Netflix to hurt the business of the traditional movie theater chains. The Google-Verizon deal represented a major departure because it specifically stated that the age of wireless access to the Internet was different in nature. Since the future of the Internet was obviously to be wireless, this was not a hypothetical scenario: it was a promise.

The Changing Nature of Innovation

Significant changes were occurring in the very focus of innovation. Technological innovation was no longer what it used to be, especially for the software industry. Silicon Valley had become the testbed for extremely complex system engineering (rather than the testbed for new ideas). The real value was to be found not in the products themselves (their features and their looks) but in the complexity that surrounded and enabled their success. Oracle (the distributed ERP system), Apple (especially iTunes), Google (billions of simultaneous searches and videos), HP and Vmware (the cloud), and Facebook (billions of simultaneous posts) were ultimately engaged in solving very complex problems of scale. The customer paid for a product (and sometimes didn't even pay for it) but in reality the customer was buying an infrastructure. For example, Google's great innovation in its early years was the search engine, but the rest of Google's history was largely a history of acquiring or copying other people's ideas: the real contribution by Google consisted in turning rudimentary platforms (such as Android and Maps) into formidable robust distributed platforms.

The big Silicon Valley companies (notably Google and Oracle) were now growing through acquisition. They specialized in turning around not businesses but platforms. They had become extremely efficient reengineering factories.

The hardware industry was prospering but knowing that physical limits were going to be reached soon. In particular, it was getting more and more difficult to achieve faster speeds without generating unmanageable heat. Increasing the clock speed of a chip also increases its consumption which also increases the heat it generates. The stopgap solution had been to squeeze multiple processors on the same chip, but that was becoming impractical too. There was a general feeling that the age of the CMOS transistor was about to come to an end. For some the solution was to move away from transistors. Stan Williams at Hewlett-Packard was working on "memristors" based on titanium dioxide. Transistors are "volatile", i.e. they must be continually powered in order to preserve information, whereas "memristors" would be a nonvolatile technology, that only needs to be powered when "reading" or "writing" information (changing its state or checking its state).

Memristors had been theoretically discussed by Leon Chua at UC Berkeley in 1971, but only in 2008 did Williams prove their existence because memristance is easier to detect at nanoscale. A memristor is neither a resistor nor a capacitor nor an inductor. It is a fourth fundamental circuit element with properties that cannot be achieved by any combination of the other three. Memristors could provide an alternative to D-RAM and eliminate the need of "booting" a computer (a process that basically consists in copying information from a magnetic disk to the computer's memory every time the computer is switched on).

At Stanford University the Robust Systems Group led by Subhasish Mitra was researching nanocircuits: the smaller the circuit the smaller its demand for power and the heat it generates. In 2013 Mitra's group demonstrated the first carbon nanotube computer, the CNT.

The change here reflected the new dynamics of the computer industry. In the past change had been driven by the demands of bureaucratic, military or space applications, i.e. by government demand, and to some extent by the needs of corporate America. Now change was driven by the insatiable appetite of consumer electronics.

Another concept that had not changed in decades was the one underlying magnetic data storage. In 2011 Andreas Heinrich's team at IBM's Almaden Research Center reduced from about one million to 12 the number of atoms required to store a bit of data. In practice, this meant the feasibility of magnetic memories 100 times denser than the most popular hard disks and memory chips.

Quantum computing was, instead, still largely ignored in Silicon Valley. The idea of using the odd features of Quantum Physics to create supercomputers dated from 1982, when one of the greatest physicists, Richard Feynman, speculated that a computer could store information by exploiting precisely the principles of quantum superposition (that a particle can be in two states at the same time) using "qubits" (quantum bits) instead of binary bits. In 1994 Peter Shor at Bell Labs proved an important theorem: that a quantum computer would outperform a classic computer in a category of difficult mathematical problems. In 1997 British physicist Colin Williams and Xerox PARC's Scott Clearwater published "Explorations in Quantum Computing", a book that actually described how a quantum computer could be built. Vancouver's D-Wave, founded in 1999 by quantum physicists Geordie Rose and (Russian-born) Alexandre Zagoskin of the University of British Columbia, aimed at doing precisely that. In February 2007 D-Wave finally demonstrated its Orion prototype at the Computer History Museum in Mountain View. In 2009 Yale's professor Steven Girvin unveiled a macroscopic quantum processor (quantum processors were supposed to be very microscopic). In May 2011 D-Wave announced the sale of its first commercial quantum computer (purchased by Lockheed for the Quantum Computing Center that it established with the University of Southern California in Los Angeles), although purists debated whether it qualified as a real "quantum" computer.

The Electronic Empire

The world economy was hit hard in September 2008 by a financial crisis that started in the US, due to reckless banking speculation. The crisis was mostly a Wall Street problem, but it dragged down the entire economy. However, high-tech companies in the Bay Area did relatively well, most of them reemerging after two years unscathed. The dotcom crash had been useful to teach them how to trim costs quickly in the face of an economic downturn.

Silicon Valley had traditionally been indifferent to national and especially internationally events. Even the various wars that the US fought (World War I, World War II, Korea, Vietnam, the first and second Iraqi wars, Afghanistan) were perceived as distant echoes and, quite frankly, as business opportunities. This happened despite the strong anti-war sentiment of San Francisco and Berkeley, yet another contradiction in the ideological dynamics of the Bay Area. This was true because of the relative isolation of California, but also because for a long time Silicon Valley's core business did not need anybody else. Silicon is the second most abundant chemical element of the Earth's crust after oxygen.

The entire industry of semiconductors had a colossal advantage over other industries: its primary element was cheap and widely available. There was no need for wars in the Gulf War and no wild spikes in prices like for gold. Software had an even smaller resource footprint: a software engineer just needed two fingers to type on a keyboard. Until the 1990s, Silicon Valley saw the rest of the world either as a market or as an outsourcing facility.

The age of the cell phone, of the videogame, of the digital camera, and of the digital music player, instead, relied on another material, tantalum, which was far less abundant. Tantalum was obtained from coltan (columbite-tantalite) and one country held the largest reserves of coltan: the Democratic Republic of Congo. That nation also held another record: the bloodiest civil war since 1998. Reports started circulating that the civil war was funded by the smuggling of coltan towards the Western companies that needed it for their consumer electronics products. At the same time stories also appeared of the terrible work conditions in the Chinese factories of Shenzhen, where hundreds of thousands of low-paid workers assembled electronic devices for US manufacturers (notably Apple).

Meanwhile, lithium batteries, widely used in mobile electronic devices, obviously relied on lithium being available and cheap. Yet about 50% of the world's reserves of lithium were based in Bolivia, which had just elected a socialist president with an anti-US agenda. China had become the biggest producer of "rare earths" (vital to cell phones, laptops and greentech) and pressure was mounting to reopen the Californian mines that used to dominate the world markets. The 50 million tons of electronic waste generated worldwide each year were mostly sent for disposal to developing countries where valuable metals were converted into scrap metal for resale at the cost of human lives and environmental disasters.

At the same time California was going through very turbulent financial times for the first time in its history. It had one of the highest unemployment rates in the country, slow growth, and a chronic budget deficit. Silicon Valley had risen (from the 1940s to the 1990s) in a state that was booming. Now it was embedded in a state that was failing. Putting it all together, Silicon Valley was no longer insulated from global politics as it had been for decades.

It was not a coincidence that in 2010 two of its most popular executives, Meg Whitman and Carly Fiorina, entered the national political scene. Even more relevant was the role of Silicon Valley technology which influenced world events. In 2009, Iranian youth took to the streets using Twitter to coordinate and assemble protests against their rigged national elections. In 2010, students armed with cell phones and social networking software overthrew the Tunisian dictator. Later in 2011, a webpage created by Google executive Wael Ghonim indirectly started the mass demonstrations against the regime in Egypt. In response to the events, the Egyptian government took down the Internet within its borders. A few days later Google launched a special service to allow the protesters in Egypt to send Twitter messages by dialing a phone number and leaving a voice mail: the purpose was not to help Twitter (a competitor) make money but to help the protesters win the revolution. Silicon Valley was becoming a political player largely independent of any government.

Google vs Apple vs Facebook vs...

During the 2000s, Google largely represented the battle between the Web-based world against the desktop-based world of Microsoft. Google won this ideological battle, as even Microsoft was beginning to move towards cloud-based applications. Yet Google made little money out of it. Mostly it was the big virtualization platforms that were benefiting from this epochal switch in computing platforms. Google and Facebook were growing thanks to business plans that relied almost exclusively on selling advertising. They both offered a free service (in Google's case, many free services) based on content (text, images, videos, posts) provided for free by millions of "volunteers" (the public of the Web). Both companies made money by selling advertising space to companies eager to publicize their products to the viewers of all that content. Neither Google nor Facebook was creating any content. They were just being parasites off of other people's content. Neither had found a way to make money other than through advertising techniques. From a strategic point of view there was a difference between the two though.

Google's search engine had been invincible for a few years, but by the end of the decade it was increasingly weaker than other kinds of businesses. It was becoming apparent to Google's own management that the switching cost for a user to adopt one of the newer (and perhaps better) search engines was virtually zero. The network effect of a search engine is low by definition (a network effect is how much the value of the product depends on the number of users using it). On the contrary, Facebook enjoyed both high switching costs that kept users from leaving and so its network effect was very high (the more people that used it, the more valuable it was). It was no surprise then that in 2011 Google announced Google+, its second attempt at establishing a viable social-networking platform (after the embarrassing Buzz). By then Facebook had passed 750 million users.

At the same time Google invested in the smartphone market. In July 2008 Apple had launched the App Store for iOS applications (an iOS device was an iPhone, iPod Touch or iPad). By July 2011, the App Store had 425,000 apps (uploaded by thousands of third party developers), downloaded 15 billion times, on 200 million iOS devices. By then Google's equivalent, the Android Market, had 250,000 applications, downloaded 6 billion times, on 135 million Android devices; and it was growing faster. Google was activating new Android devices at the rate of 550,000 per day. By the end of 2011 Android smartphones owned 46.3% of the market and Apple iPhones owned 30%, leaving RIM (14.9%) and Microsoft (4.6%) way behind: there was now one area in which Silicon Valley alone beat the rest of the world.

Google's management, probably aware that Google's successes tended to be the ones acquired from others as opposed to the ones developed internally, launched Google Ventures, the venture-capital arm of the company. Basically, it was beginning to make sense for Google to invest its huge cash reserves into other companies rather than into Google's own R&D. Google was trying yet another revolutionary business model: to become an incubator of startups (infotech, biotech and cleantech). As an incubator, it offered a much more powerful infrastructure than a venture capitalist could, starting with office space at its Googleplex and computing power in its gargantuan server farm. Google even offered a huge bonus ($10,000 in 2011) to any employee who suggested a startup resulting in an actual investment.

Three major development platforms were competing for world domination: the Facebook Platform (launched in 2007), the iPhone App Store (in 2008) and the Android platform (2007).

The company that was rapidly losing its sheen was Yahoo! Its advertising business remained strong but Yahoo! had done the opposite of Google: invested in creating content, even hiring journalists and bloggers. Yahoo! had basically moved towards becoming a media company at a time when Google and Facebook had been moving towards the more cynical model of purely exploiting the content created by their users. In a sense, Yahoo! still believed in quality at a time when Google and Facebook were proving that quality did not matter anymore and that advertising revenues depended almost exclusively on quantity. To make matters worse, Yahoo! had not contrived a way to have its users disclose personal information the way Google and Facebook had, which meant that Google and Facebook (happy to violate as much privacy as tolerated by the law) could offer targeted advertising to their advertising customers.

Yahoo alumni seemed to be more creative than the company itself. In 2009 two Yahoo executives, Brian Acton and Jan Koum, founded WhatsApp in Santa Clara to provide instant messaging over the Internet Protocol for smartphones (Android, BlackBerry, iPhone, etc). While Facebook and Google were not paying attention, WhatsApp did to SMS what Skype had done to the old telephone service: it turned it into a computer application. By the end of 2009 Whatsapp already had one million users; but that was just the beginning of its meteoric rise: one year later they were ten million, and by the end of 2012 Whatsapp had passed the 200 million users mark. WhatsApp became extremely popular because it provided the easiest way to send a text message to people all over the world, with no advertisements and no gimmicks. In 2014 Facebook acquired WhatsApp for a huge amount of money. By then WhatsApp had 450 million users and was growing faster than Twitter, but had always refused the advertisement-based model of all the major dotcoms and was therefore making very little money.

Another front in the multiple wars that Google was fighting was the intellectual-property front. In November 2010, a consortium including Microsoft, Apple, Oracle, and EMC paid $450 million for 882 networking-software patents owned by Novell, or about $510,000 per patent.

The purpose became clear a few days later: Apple had levied multiple lawsuits against Android-based smartphone manufacturers like HTC and Samsung, accusing them of "copying" the iPhone, and now HTC was in a position to sue Apple using some of the patents purchased by Google.

During the second decade of the century Silicon Valley was devastated by such patent wars. Google, Apple, Oracle and others filed patents by the thousands (and bought even more) and then filed lawsuits against each other. A patent was becoming a weapon of mass destruction: the richest corporations could file patents about the most trivial of ideas and use it to prevent competitors from implementing entire families of products. The main losers were the small companies and the startups: they did not have an army of attorneys to file patents and did not have an army of attorneys to fight the big corporations in court. We will never know how many inventors were on the brink of creating revolutionary products and either gave up, were forced to give up or were acquired by bigger companies. The process of filing a patent was considered ridiculous by the very corporations that indulged in it, but there was no chance of changing it: those same corporations hired an army of lobbyists in Washington to counter any attempt to rectify a clearly flawed process. A patent is a license to sue. It rarely represents a true innovation. In most cases it represents the exact opposite: an impediment to innovation, and even a blunt threat to anyone who dares innovate. Companies that had limited cash were forced to spend much of it fighting lawsuits instead of spending it to fund research and development. In other words: more and more money was being spent to fund lawyers than to fund research.

They were not interested in Novell's technology, but simply in protecting themselves from potential lawsuits. In June 2011 a consortium that included Microsoft, Apple, Ericsson, Sony, EMC, and Research In Motion purchased the 6,000 patents for wireless communication owned by bankrupt telecom company Nortel. They paid $4.5 billion, or $750,000 for each patent. Microsoft now co-owned the Nortel patents for voice services and the Novell patents for Linux, while Apple co-owned the Nortel patents for manufacturing and semiconductors and Oracle owned the patents for Java (acquired from SUN). Google's Android service was left naked and subject to lawsuits. In August 2011 Google paid $12.5 billion for Motorola's smartphone business in order to acquire its 24,500 patents, which was about $510,00 per Motorola patent. The purpose became clear a few days later: Apple had levied multiple lawsuits against Android-based smartphone manufacturers like HTC and Samsung, accusing them of "copying" the iPhone, and now HTC was in a position to sue Apple using some of the patents purchased by Google.

The Rest of the World

India's Silicon Valley

The history of India's involvement with computers started with the five Indian Institutes of Technology (IITs), established in Kharagpur (1950), Mumbai (1958), Chennai (1959), Kanpur (1959) and Delhi (1961), and supported by five different countries from both the democratic and communist worlds (Kanpur was the USA-affiliated one). Meanwhile, the Indian families that could afford it were sending their children to graduate in Britain and in the USA. The Indian-born historian Peter James Marshall at Cambridge encouraged Indian students to become entrepreneurs not academics because he saw that as the most pressing need for post-independence India. The main destination in the USA was the MIT and the Indian graduates from the MIT mostly remained in the USA, but they created a network that provided the first link between the high-tech industry of the USA and India. In 1972 MIT-graduate Narendra Patni founded the software enterprise Data Conversion (later renamed Patni Computer Systems) with offices both in Boston (USA) and Pune (India). In 1981 some of Patni's engineers (mostly from the MIT too) founded Infosys in Pune. Meanwhile, the government had decided to install high-speed satellite communications in Bangalore, the site of the Indian Institute of Science (founded in 1909 thanks to steel industry magnate Jamsetji Tata). Because of that decision, in 1985 Texas Instruments opened a software laboratory in Bangalore. Within a few years Infosys and Wipro too moved their operations to Bangalore.

Bangalore had several advantages over other cities. To start with, it was a center of the defense industry (Bharat Electronics, Hindustan Aeronautics, the National Aeronautics Laboratory, the Aeronautical Defence Establishment, the Electronics and Radar Development Establishment) as well as the home of several strategic industries (the Indian Telephone Industries, the Gas Turbine Research Establishment, and the Central Power Research Institute, Hindustan Machine Tools). In 1988 a private venture capital company had already been established, the Technology Development and Information Company of India (TDICI). Soon the city opened several industrial parks, including Electronics City and the Peenya Industrial Estate (the largest in India).

In 1986 Patni obtained the first contract from a USA company (Data General) for offsourcing software to India. By 1990 India could already boast 3 million scientists and engineers graduating from 80 universities, and more than 200 research institutes specializing in electronics. Meanwhile, in 1991 India liberalized its protectionist economy, that had long been influenced by anti-capitalist precepts. During the 1990s Infosys enjoyed double-digit growth rates. By 2010 it would become one of the largest software companies in the world, with over 100,000 employees. However, Infosys well represented the problem, not the solution: by 2010 this industrial colossus had been granted only twelve patents in the USA Microsoft had fewer employees, but had passed the 5,000 patent mark already in 2006.

High-tech spread from Pune and Bangalore to other cities; notably in 1998 Hyderabad opened the Cyber Towers, nicknamed "Cyberabad", the first phase of the Hyderabad Information Technology and Engineering Consultancy (HITEC) project.

In general, graduates from the IIT lacked the counterculture spirit that was pervasive in the Bay Area, the passion for nonconformist behavior (and ideas), the curiosity about nontechnical topics (literature, philosophy, visual arts, history, etc), the push to innovate rather than just execute orders. Many graduates from the IIT did extremely well around the world (and notably in Silicon Valley) but many more became simple hired hands in the software industry, and the vast majority held humble (if well-paid) jobs back in India contributing little in terms of imagination. Most of them were trained to be not intellectuals but skilled craftsmen; not the successors to the great philosophers of India but the successors to their grandparents' world of religious sculptors and shoemakers.

The Asian Miracle

East Asia is a more complex story.

Asian economies managed to progress from starvation in the 1960s to the top tier of development and wealth. In 1981 East Asia still had the highest poverty rate in the world, higher than Africa. In 2011 two of the top three economies in the world were from East Asia, and very soon they might have three out of four including the number one.

There is no single cultural/political explanation for the Asian miracle because the countries of Asia spanned a broad spectrum of philosophies (Confucian, Shinto, Buddhist, Hindu, Muslim) and of political systems: fascism (South Korea, Singapore, Taiwan, Thailand), communism (mainland China), socialism (India), democracy (Japan, Hong Kong).

There were actually two Asian miracles. The first Asian miracle was low-tech and largely based on cheap labor and loose business regulations. The first Asia miracle relied on a simple business plan: do what the West does but do it cheaper and possibly better. This became an art in itself. It also caused the rapid Westernization of all US allies in Asia (that until World War II had largely held on to their traditions). The second Asian miracle was high-tech and based on improving Western high technology. By this time Asia had become very Westernized and, in particular, democracy had become widespread.

The first Asian miracle was largely the consequence of the Cold War between the USA and the Soviet Union. The USA helped the Asian (and

Western European) economies develop in order to create stable and strong defenses against the communist world. The USA encouraged trade with its oversea allies, and tolerated that they competed unfairly with US-based manufacturers by keeping their currencies very low.

Government intervention was crucial to the development of these economies: they all boomed under the supervision of a benevolent dictatorship that nurtured and guided the private sector.

Most of the political leaders of the first boom came not from the aristocracy but from the very poor class. These leaders were interested in copying Western industrial methods but ignored Western economic theory: they used common sense and traditional values. They nonetheless became enlightened leaders who somehow made mostly good choices to turn their starving countries into economic tigers. They in fact greatly improved the economies of their respective countries.

All the early boomers lacked natural resources. In order to pay for them, they had to focus on exporting. The big open market was the USA. Therefore it was natural that they focused on exporting to the USA. The USA also provided the military protection that helped these countries focus only on the economy. Security was guaranteed and paid for by the USA. What these early boomers had in common was not a cultural or political background but that they were all allies of the USA during the Cold War.

The first "Asian tigers" were Japan, South Korea, Taiwan, Singapore and Hong Kong. They embodied different philosophies (Shinto, Buddhist, Confucian) and came from different histories: Japan was already westernized, Taiwan partially (as a Japanese colony), Korea never was, Hong Kong and Singapore were British colonies The role of the state varied from ubiquitous (Japan) to totalitarian (Singapore, South Korea, Taiwan) to indifferent (Hong Kong). The governments were run by people who were mostly of humble origins and uneducated. A widespread figure was the "benevolent dictator", whose main goal was not his own wealth or a dynasty but the good of the country. East Asian countries lacked natural resources. To pay for imports, they exported cheap goods to the USA. They developed a knack for understanding Western consumer behavior and social trends. The USA de facto paid for their development . The geopolitics of the Cold War (need to contain the Soviet Union) de facto drove the early Asian boom. What they had in common is not cultural or political background but that they were allies of the USA during the Cold War. In these countries technological progress remained largely in the hands of large national conglomerates. Singapore, however, established a unique model: it favored foreign investment by multinationals over nurturing national conglomerates. They ignored Western economic theories and used common sense and traditional values. They also ignored social and economies ideologies of the Third World. Centralized economies enabled long-term planning and short-term decisions. The government rewarded with favors the companies that achieved world-class results. Asian people demanded economic growth before democratic growth. These were not "nice" places to live in: they were overcrowded and poor for a long time. Nor did they benefit from high education: relatively few people were able to obtain a computer-science degree (or a science degree in general) unless they were able to pay for an education abroad.

The second Asian miracle was largely the consequence of the end of the Cold War. The collapse of the Soviet Union and of its communist block turned the whole world into one colossal capitalist market. The Asian countries applied their learned skills on a larger scale to a larger market. Globalization favored Asian products over the more expensive products from Western Europe and the USA. However, by now Asia had learned sophisticated industrial and business methods, and was not restricted to cheap goods. Its factories had developed into high-tech factories by serving US manufacturers, but the know-how could now be recycled internally to create factories that served Asian manufacturers. Therefore Asia found itself capable of competing with the West in the much more lucrative high-tech field.

This second Asian miracle introduced two colossal players. Mainland China simply followed the path of Western imitation that had been tested by the old "tigers". India, however, could also sell a widespread knowledge of the English language and Western-style universities that graduated scores of mathematically-inclined students, two factors which created an opportunity for the service industry. Again, the natural customer was the USA, in this case the booming computer and Internet industry. The USA, again, provided the military protection that helped these economies grow in a world largely at peace. West of Pakistan, Asia was relatively at peace. The real trouble was in the Middle East and East-Central Asia, i.e. in the Islamic world. The USA and its Western allies of NATO were busy maintaining some kind of order there, which also provided for safe trade routes. Even mainland China, that quickly became the USA's main rival on the world stage, relied on trade routes from Africa and the Middle East that were guarded by the mighty military of the USA.

The second generation of "Asian tigers" (in the 1990s) includes China, India, Thailand and Malaysia. Again, they came from different philosophies: Confucian, Hindu, Buddhist, Muslim. The role of the state was significant in that liberal reforms reduced the power of the state (especially in China and India). Their government was mostly run by well-educated technocrats.

Of the two Asian colossi, China probably had the better infrastructure. India had the disadvantage of poor transportation and electricity infrastructure. That, combined with restrictive labor laws, discouraged the kind of labor-intensive sectors that were booming in its eastern neighbors. While Taiwan, Singapore, South Korea, etc, China capitalized on cheap labor to capture offsourced jobs from the USA, India capitalized on English-speaking, college-educated and cheap engineers to capture offsourced jobs from the USA. The USA lost blue-collar (low-paying low-skills) jobs to East Asia and ended up losing white-collar (high-paying high-skilled) jobs to India.

A popular joke is that in China the conglomerates succeeded because of the government, whereas in India the conglomerates succeeded despite the government. Indian conglomerates had to aim for self-sufficiency. Jindal produced steel and power through backward integration from its own captive coal and iron-ore mines. Gautam Adani bought port and coal mines, built a power plant and a railway. Unlike China's labor-intensive exports, India became an exporter of capital-intensive items that require skilled workers

Asia's High-Tech Industry

In the second half of the 20the century the only country that competed with the USA in terms of mass-scale innovation that changed the daily lives of billions of people was Japan: the transistor radio (1954), the quartz wristwatch (1967), the pocket calculator (1970), the color photocopier (1973), the portable music player (1979), the compact disc (1982), the camcorder (1982), the digital synthesizer (1983), the third-generation videogame console (1983), the digital camera (1988), the plasma TV set (1992), the DVD player (1996), the hybrid car (1997), mobile access to the Internet (1999), the Blu-ray disc (2003), the laser television set (2008). However, Japanese innovation mostly came from conglomerates that were very old: Mitsubishi (1870), Seiko (1881), Yamaha (1887), Nintendo (1889), Fujitsu (1934), Canon (1937), Toyota (1937), Sony (1946), NTT (1952), etc.

With the exception of the media hub in Tokyo (mostly devoted to pop culture), there was no major industrial cluster in Japan that could compare with Silicon Valley. Tokyo's "high-tech" regions were the traditional industrial hub that grow around big companies, like Aichi, the location of Toyota's main plant and of many Toyota suppliers, Hiroshima, Sendai, Yonezawa. Later a sort of Silicon Valley emerged in Fukuoka, in the far south of Japan (Kyushu island) thanks to a cluster of universities (Kyushu University, Kyushu Institute of Technology, Kitakyushu University, the Institute of Systems & Information Technologies) and mostly for the semiconductor industry.

South Korea followed a similar path to high-tech innovation. Like Japan it relied mainly on well-established companies like Samsung (1938). Like Japan the environment was hostile to foreign companies. Like Japan there was little interaction between universities and industry, with professors more similar to government bureaucrats than to incubators of ideas or coaches of entrepreneurs.

However, South Korea also had two regions that looked a bit like Silicon Valley. In 1973 South Korea established the Korea Advanced Institute of Science and Technology at Daedeok, south of Seoul. This area began to attract R&D labs and eventually to spin off startups. It therefore came to be known as "Daedeok Valley" and officially as Daedeok Science Town. The software industry, instead, assembled around Teheran Road in Seoul (between Gangnam Station and Samseong Station), nicknamed "Teheran Valley", a three-km stretch that probably got the majority of South Korean venture-capital investment during the dotcom boom.

In terms of process, however, Taiwan was the real story. In 1973 Taiwan established the Industrial Technological Research Institute (ITRI) to develop technologies that could be turned into goods for foreign markets, an institute that would spawn dozens of semiconductor firms (starting with UMC in 1980 and TSMC in 1987), and then the pioneer of Asian state-founded high-tech parks, the Hsinchu Science-based Industrial Park, established in 1980 about 88 kms from Taipei near four universities. In 20 years more than 100 companies were formed by graduates of those universities. Taiwan was also the place where venture capital took off in Asia and was also the first place that implemented the feedback loop between university and corporate R&D typical of Boston and Silicon Valley. TSMC launched the independent silicon-chip foundry, that turned Taiwan into Silicon Valley's main destination for outsourcing chip manufacturing, and which in turn helped create a vibrant chip-design industry with companies such as MediaTek (1997) and NovaTek (1997).

Neither Japan nor Korea nor Taiwan attracted highly educated immigrants from elsewhere like Silicon Valley did. The only Asian country to do so was Singapore. It is not a coincidence that Singapore was also the country that invested the most in attracting foreign businesses (and their know-how). Singapore too developed an advanced venture-capital industry and fostered interaction between its universities and the private industry.

Neither of these countries created a vibrant software industry like Silicon Valley.

China was a late-comer and capitalized on its neighbors' many experiments, avoiding Japan's model because it simply did not have the kind of old established manufacturing and financial giants that Japan had. The idea of a "Chinese Silicon Valley" came to nuclear scientist Chunxian Chen of the Academy of Sciences after a 1979 trip to California. Back home in 1980 he tried unsuccessfully to start a privately-funded Advanced Technology Service Association just outside Beijing. However, the Academy took up his idea and began to play the role of incubator for high-tech startups, one of which would become Lenovo, most of them based along the ten-km Zhongguancun Street. The idea appealed to both staff and students of the two leading universities of Beijing, Peking University and Tsinghua University, who needed to make more money than the tiny government salaries and subsidies. Finally, in 1988 the government gave its blessing and the whole region came to be called Zhongguancun Science Park. In little over than a decade massive government incentives created thousands of new companies, the vast majority in software and telecommunications.

In 2008 the USA entered the Great Recession while Asia was still booming. Nonetheless in 2010 Asians overcome Hispanics as the largest group of immigrants to the USA. That is Asia's single biggest failure: people were still leaving the continent by the hundreds of thousands even at a time when Asia looked like a land of opportunities and the USA was widely considered on the way out as a world power. One had to wonder what it would take to reverse the tide if the biggest economic crisis in 70 years didn't do it.

The Importance of Process and of Evolution

The most important event in the modern history of Asian industry, however, may predate all of this. In 1953 Taiichi Ohno invented "lean manufacturing" (or "just-in-time" manufacturing) at Japan's Toyota. That was one of the factors that turned Toyota into a giant success story (and eventually into the largest car manufacturer in the world). More importantly, it created the mindset that the process is often more important than the product. When (in 1987) ITRI's president Morris Chang launched Taiwan's Semiconductor Manufacturing Company (TSMC), the first independent silicon-chip foundry in the world, to serve the "fabless" companies of the USA, he simply applied that mindset to the computer industry and realized that one could decouple the design and the manufacturing. That does not mean that only the design is creative: the design would not lead to a mass-market product (and possibly to no product at all) without a highly efficient manufacturing process that lowers the cost and improves quality.

From the point of view of the Asian suppliers, what was really revolutionary (and not just evolutionary) was the process, not the product. The fabless process and the offshore customer-service process were the real breakthroughs, not the new laptop model or the new operating system. Without significant progress in Asia in the industrial process many great success stories of Silicon Valley products may have not happened at all. The world viewed from Silicon Valley was a world centered on the place where a product was designed and marketed. The world viewed from Japan, Taiwan and Korea was a world centered on the industrial centers that could manufacture products based on whatever design, faster, cheaper and better. The world viewed from India was a world centered on the army of software engineers that could deliver software based on whatever needs, faster, cheaper and better. From the Asian viewpoint, it was the increasing evolutionary efficiency of the "builders" that allowed Silicon Valley to create "revolutionary" products and new markets. For example, despite being a relatively small economy and boasting virtually no invention that ordinary people can name, Taiwan rapidly became the fourth country in the world for patent filing (after the USA, Japan and Germany); and Japan rapidly became the country with the highest percentage of GDP spent in R&D.

That "evolution" stemmed from a mindset driven by incremental progress, the equivalent of new releases of an operating system, each one enabling a whole new range of features (and prices) for the next product to capture the headlines.

From the viewpoint of Asia, ideas for "revolutionary" products are actually easy. What is difficult is "making" those products, not imagining them.

Furthermore, it is debatable which region and system has yielded more "revolutionary" products. The argument that small companies and Silicon Valley rule is an opinion, not a fact. The perception is that in Japan innovation was driven only by big companies. That perception is true. What is not true is the perception that the source of innovation was significantly different in the USA. It is easy to forget that Silicon Valley has invented very little: most of the things that changed the high-tech world (from the transistor to the disk drive) were invented by big companies (like AT&T and IBM), and many of the really revolurionary ones (the computer, the Internet, the World Wide Web) were invented by government labs. Blaming Japan for relying too much on big companies and big government means not knowing what Silicon Valley actually does, which is not to invent the computer nor the Internet nor the transistor nor the smartphone. In fact, the rigid bureaucratic big-company system of Japan has invented a lot more than Silicon Valley. And it has arguably created more wealth for ordinary people, turning a poor country into one of the richest countries in the world.

The Western Contribution to the Success of Asia's High-tech Industry

Part of the success of Asia was obviously made in Silicon Valley: the fiber-optics boom of the 1990s helped collapse the cost of a leased telecom line between California and Bangalore, and then the Voice Over IP technology of the early 2000s made it irrelevant. Without this simple improvement in the cost of communications India's software industry would not have picked up the way it did. The dotcom boom introduced dozens of online services that eliminated the distance factor and therefore helped remote firms compete with local firms. Even the passion for industry standards that has always been a peculiarity of the USA ended up favoring those abroad who wanted to create critical mass for their services of outsourcing.

The government of the USA has indirectly been proactive in creating opportunities for Asian firms. When Bell Labs invented the transistor, it was under government pressure that its owner AT&T decided to license transistor technology at a low price to anybody who wanted it, including the company that later became Sony. It was under government pressure that IBM decided to "unbundle" the software applications from its mainframe computers, thereby spawning a software boom worldwide. It was the government that created and funded the Arpanet, that went on to become (as Internet) the backbone of the global outsourcing movement.

The biggest gift of the West to Asia was perhaps the revolution in management that had started in earnest in the 1920s but got a phenomenal boost in the 1990s with the collapse of the communist world and the boom of free trade. The USA boasted the most advanced class of business administrators in the world in terms of maximizing profits (at least short term), and their discipline almost inevitably took them to outsource both manufacturing and services. One of the tools that they used was also a Western invention: ERP software to manage complex sophisticated distributed supply chains.

And, of course, it was the USA and its allies that had taught Asia to speak English: India, Hong Kong and Singapore had been British colonies, and Taiwan, South Korea and Japan had been militarily occupied by the USA in one fashion or another. The language turned out to be an important factor in leapfrogging ahead of the Europeans.

Another, less obvious, reason why it was so easy for Asian companies to do business with Silicon Valley is that Silicon Valley (and the high-tech industry in general) was in reality being less innovative than it appeared to be to consumers: both software and hardware (consumer) products tended to follow a predictable evolutionary path that it was easy for suppliers to anticipate with the required building blocks and services.

Of course, we don't mean that Asia was just a lucky beneficiary of some Western policies. These various forms of indirect "help" from the West would not have worked without native factors that were already in place. In brief, those successful regions of Asia had traditionally valued higher education (and now also and especially in engineering and science), enjoyed enlightened state planning (that, for example, placed emphasis on electronics while Europe was still focused on cars and appliances), boasted world-class work ethos (that guaranteed quality and reliability) and were largely non ideological (they didn't view capitalism as evil, like large segments of the European public, and did not harbor religious/ethnic hostilities towards Westerners).

The Missing Ingredients in Asia

However, nothing like Silicon Valley has emerged in East Asia. One simple reason for this is that it is not only startup founders who have to be visionary in order to achieve technological breakthroughs: venture capitalists have to be visionary too. In Singapore, for example, they are government bureaucrats. Asia has a tradition of keeping the money in the hands of trusted (and prudent) bureaucrats. The USA has a tradition of letting the (reckless) successul self-made man be the one who funds the next big thing.

However, that cannot be the whole story. For example, Japan never created a vibrant software industry. But it would be unfair to blame it only on the economic and political system: very few startups in Silicon Valley were founded by Japanese immigrants, despite the fact that the number of Japanese engineers working in Silicon Valley has always been significant. Compare with the incredible percentage of Indian and Chinese immigrants who started companies. And this despite the fact that Japanese education is routinely ranked higher than Indian and Chinese education.

It might look surprising that a country like Singapore, that appears to be a lot more "modern" than the San Francisco Bay Area, contributed less to technological innovation than Silicon Valley. Singapore is a model of urban design and management. Silicon Valley is decades (if not a century) behind Singapore, meaning that it would probably take a century for Silicon Valley to catch up with Singapore's infrastructure projects, not to mention to match Singapore's architectural wonders (compared with Silicon Valley's none). It's not only the subway and the quality of roads that are superior in Singapore: Singaporean citizens are far more "high-tech" than their peers in Silicon Valley. Singaporeans had cell phones when these were still a rarity in Silicon Valley. Silicon Valley still has to match the Internet speed that Singaporeans have been enjoying for years. People in Silicon Valley got the first taste of mobile payment a decade after it became commonplace in Singapore. And yet, as hard as it may have tried, Singapore produced no Apple, no Oracle, no Google and no Facebook. The reason might be the very concept of what high-tech is. In Silicon Valley people need just a cubicle to work (and a car to get there, given the stone-age public transportation). They are perfectly happy living in a culturally poor place of ugly buildings and restaurant chains. In Singapore people expect a town that is comfortable; a nice place to live in. High-tech is a means to an end just like concrete and plastic. It is part of the urban fabric. It is one of the elements that contribute to making Singapore a model of urban design and management. In Silicon Valley people are willing and even excited to be worked to death like slaves for the privilege of being part of the high-tech world that designs the tools of tomorrow (and for a tiny chance of becoming the next billionaire). In Singapore there is nothing particularly prestigious about working in high tech: the prestige is in using it to do something that is relevant to society. Silicon Valley assumes that one can change the world just by releasing a new device or a new website that will spread virally. Singapore assumes that one can change the world by adopting whichever the best available tools are at the moment, and it is largely irrelevant who invented them; just like it's irrelevant who makes the blue jeans or the shoes that became popular after independence.

The single most visible advantage that Silicon Valley had over the rest of the world is immigration. The exodus of brains from India and China did not stop during their boom years. No matter how many billionaires were created by the booming high-tech industry in China, there were still thousands of Chinese students willing to work as salaried employees in Silicon Valley rather than return to China's land of opportunities.

In 2013 more than 350,000 Chinese returned home after graduating abroad, which was 17 times more than the number for 2003, but in 2013 more than one million Chinese were studying abroad, 11 times more than in 2003.

China's High-tech Industry

The story of China's software industry borders on the incredible because it was born so late in time that it basically coincided with the "dotcom boom" in the USA. Whereas in the USA the World-wide Web represented yet another generation of software, in China it pretty much represented the first one. Chinese software was born online.

China's software industry first emerged out of the primitive enterpreneurial culture fostered in the provinces bordering Hong Kong. This was the heroic era. Several of the pioneering programmers (some of them self-taught) became legendary like the heroes of China's martial arts.

Kau Pak Kwan, hailed as "China's first programmer" (or, better, the first one to become rich and famous), who in 1989 had created the the first Chinese wordprocessor (later renamed WPS) while working for Hong Kong-based PC clone manufacturer JinShan, founded Kingsoft and developed an entire Microsoft-compatible office automation suite. (Kingsoft in 2012 even introduced its own browser, Liebao).

Ufida (later renamed Yonyou), founded in 1988 in Beijing by two veterans of the Ministry of Finance, Wenjing Wang and Qipiang Su, developed Chinese accounting software and then became China's reigning ERP company. Its main domestic rival was Kingdee, founded in 1991 by Shaochun "Robert" Xu, a former software engineer in a government agency.

Neusoft was founded in 1991 by Jiren Liu, one of the earliest Chinese graduates in computer science. The company was an offshoot of the pioneering software lab that he had established in 1988 at Shenyang's Northeastern University. In 1996 Neusoft became the first software company listed in the Chinese stock market.

The hardware industry had gotten an earlier start. In 1984 Chuanzhi Liu of the Chinese Academy of Sciences had founded in Beijing a privately-run but state-owned company, Legend (later Lenovo), to sell IBM's personal computers in China. In 1997 Lenovo passed IBM to become China's main vendor of personal computers.

Huawei was founded in 1988 in Shenzhen by Zhengfei Ren, a former telecommunication engineer for the Chinese army, to make cheap copies of Western private branch exchange (PBX) switches for rural towns, and by 2012 it had overtaken Sweden's Ericsson to become the world's biggest telecom-equipment maker.

Another telecom giant, Zhongxing Semiconductor (later renamed ZTE) was founded in 1985 also in Shenzhen (that borders with Hong Kong) by the Chinese aerospace ministry, and by 2010 it became the world leader in the CDMA market. Both companies were helped (if not outright established) by the Chinese government.

Meanwhile, a geographic shift had taken place thanks to the government's 1988 decision to establish the Zhongguancun Science Park outside Beijing: the center of mass shifted from the south towards Beijing. The other tectonic shift was the introduction of the Internet: in 1994 the Chinese government allowed Spring to connect China to the Internet (on a very slow data line). These events led to the second generation of software heroes.

In 1991 Zhidong Wang, who had already created the first Chinese-language platform for personal computers, founded Suntendy Electronic Technology and Research (later renamed Stone Rich Sight or SRS) to develop a Chinese version of the Windows operating system (RichWin, launched in 1993). His partner was a legendary self-taught computer scientist of the National Research Institute, Yanchou Yan, who had designed China's first computer systems and developed a Chinese-language version of Microsoft DOS. In 1998 venture capitalists encouraged the merger of his company with Sinanet, a platform developed in 1995 by three Taiwanese-born Stanford graduate students (Hurst Lin, Jack Hong and Ben Tsiang) to post news from Taiwan on the Internet using Chinese characters. Thus Sina was born. The power of the Internet was demonstrated to the Chinese public in 1999 when the USA accidentally bombed the Chinese embassy in Belgrade: government propaganda paled in comparison with the deluge of both live news and outraged opinions posted on Sina's website. Thanks to that crisis, Sina became the largest Internet portal in China. For the record the previous bump in traffic (when Sina was still called SRS) had come from China's participation in the 1997 qualifying games for the soccer world-cup. In 2009 Sina launched Weibo, China's Twitter equivalent.

Its main competitor, Sohu, launched in 1996 as Internet Technologies China (ITC), was an offshoot of Boston's MIT where its founder Charles Zhang had created a Chinese search engine. That soon became China's most popular search engine.

In 1998 Yueqiao Bao, who had become famous for developing the MSDOS-compatible operating system PTDOS (originally created in 1992 while working in a rubber factory and later renamed UCDOS), founded OurGame, China's premiere online gaming platform.

William Ding, a former Sybase engineer, founded Netease in 1997 and created the first bilingual email system.

Jiangmin Wang became rich and famous thanks to the antivirus company he had founded in 1996, Jiangmin Science and Technology (also known as New Science & Technology).

In the 1990s the southern city of Shenzhen became the epicenter of the Shanzhai phenomenon: illegal replicas of Western electronic products, and, in particular, mobile phones. At one point Shanzhai shops may have manufactured as much as 20% of the world's mobile phones. The creativity of these amateur engineers was impressive. For example, phones with two SIM cards were common in Shenzhen (and sold all over the world) way before Nokia's spinoff Benefon released the Benefon Twin in 2000.

In 1998 Shenzhen University's graduates Huateng Ma and Zhidong Zhang founded Tencent (originally called Tengxun) to develop the instant messaging platform Open ICQ or QQ. By 2010 Tencent had become the world's third-largest Internet company by market capitalization.

Tencent's original OICQ

In 1995 Jack Ma, an English teacher of Hangzhou with no computing training started China Yellowpages, one of China's earliest dotcoms, and in 1999 he founded the portal Alibaba, that in 2003 launched a consumer-to-consumer marketplace, Taobao, borrowing ideas from both eBay and Amazon. In 2014 Alibaba's IPO set a new world record.

In 2000 Robin Li and Eric Xu realized that there was an opportunity for a Chinese search engine and founded Baidu in Beijing. The opportunity was both political and social: the Chinese government was keeping a tight control over Western search engines and those search engines were not designed for Chinese characters. The main brain behind Baidu was Li, who in 1996, while working for a Boston-area aggregator of financial data, invented a page-ranking algorithm for search engines that would later inspire the Google founders, and who had then joined Infoseek in Silicon Valley. Baidu quickly became the second search engine in the world by number of users, and expanded to provide a sort of Wikipedia for the (highly censored) Chinese nation. And Li became one of the richest people in China.

Baidu's founder was influential in injecting the Silicon Valley style into the old-fashioned business world of Beijing. Baidu would remain a symbol of casual office environment, flat organization, no honorific titles, no formal dressing and so forth (even a "no smoking" policy in a country notorious for chain smokers). The median age at Baidu would still be a record-setting 25.8 in 2015 when Baidu would have grown to 50,000 employees. Ditto for Sina and Sohu, also founded by returnees. This generation of "returnees", who founded the early Internet startups in China, created a virtual link with the startups of the USA even without formal business affiliations.

Between 1988 and 2003 high-tech ventures in Beijing's Zhongguancun grew from 527 to more than 12,000.

Success stories kept multiplying throughout the decade. For example, Qihoo 360, founded by Zhou Hongyi and Qi Xiangdong in 2005 in Beijing, counted on half a billion users of its antivirus software by 2016.

Instead the semiconductor foundry Semiconductor Manufacturing International Corporation (SMIC) was founded in Shanghai's Zhangjiang High-Tech Park in 2000 by former TSMC and former Texas Instruments executive Richard Chang. By 2013 it had become the fifth largest in the world after Taiwan's TSMC, Silicon Valley's Globalfoundries (formerly AMD), Taiwan's UMC and Samsung.

Joseph Chen, a Stanford and MIT graduate, started Renren (originally called Xiaonei), China's Facebook equivalent, in 2005 in Beijing. In 2011 Tencent released the social networking platform Weixin/WeChat for smartphones. WeChat became a hybrid of Facebook and Skype, providing free voice and text messaging as well as social interaction à la Facebook, and greatly reducing the appeal of QQ and RenRen. This became one of the greatest success stories of the Internet Age: by 2014 WeChat had almost 500 million monthly active users. Tencent managed to dominate both age groups. QQ targeted the younger generation and made money with games, especially second-life games. Wechat targeted older users, especially professionals. By 2015 WeChat was also becoming the Chinese equivalent of Paypal, providing online banking and payment.

WeChat

Founded at the end of 2005 in Beijing by Jinbo Yao, 58.com, better known as Wuba, was the Chinese clone of Craigslist.

Companies that pioneered online shopping in China included: Dangdang, founded in 1999 in Beijing by Peggy Yu and Li Guoqing; Joyo, spawned off by Kingsoft in 2000 and acquired in 2004 by Amazon; and Alibaba's Taobao.

Then in 2004 Qiangdong "Richard" Liu launched the online website Jingdong Mall, later renamed 360Buy.com and later renamed again JD.com, from Beijing's Zhongguancun to sell an increasingly broader range of goods and to deliver them via a fleet of motorcycles. The delivery part was not negligible: China did not have anything like FedEx and UPS. In 2007 JD.com emulated Amazon by creating its own logistics network that enabled it to deliver goods in less than 12 hours in many cities.

China was even more successful in developing an international greentech industry. Zhengrong Shi was raised and trained in Australia, at the University of New South Wales, where Martin Green had pioneered silicon solar cells. After working for Pacific Solar, a spin-off of Green's laboratory, in 2001 he moved to Wuxi, near Shanghai, and founded Suntech, at a time when China's total solar capacity was two megawatts. Suntech opened its first solar-panel factory in 2002. By 2009 China's solar panels accounted for about 50% of world shipments. In 2016 China would produce 4,000 megawatts of solar energy, and five of the ten largest solar-panel manufacturers in the world would be based in China.

The 2010s saw the globalization of China's high-tech industry, particularly with the success of WeChat and Alibaba.

At this point the Internet industry was dominated by three big companies, collectively known as the "BAT" (Baidu Alibaba Tencent).

The heroes of the past were being replaced by sophisticated teams. For example, Xiaomi, which in 2014 passed Samsung to become the leader of China's mobile phone market (and third globally behind Apple and

Samsung), had been founded in 2010 (just four years earlier) by a team comprising: Kingsoft veteran (and soon to be billionaire) Jun Lei, former Kingsoft engineer Wanqiang Li, former Motorola executive Guangping Zhou, former Google and Microsoft executive Bin Lin, former Microsoft executive Jiangji Wong, Google engineer Feng Hong, Chuan Wang, founder of two hardware companies, and De Liu, founding director of the Industrial Design Department at Beijing University of Technology. Xiaomi introduced its first phone in August 2011 and used only the Internet to market it and sell it (mainly the Twitter-like platform Weibo). The big leap forward came with the Redmi model in 2013. Chinese companies were now being designed to be global players from the start.

Note that China had succeeded where Japan, Taiwan and South Korea had failed. Neither of these original "tigers" managed to create a vibrant software industry comparable to the one experiencing exponential growth in the USA. China, a late comer whose software industry was born during the Internet era, managed to create just that kind of software industry in a very short period of time.

There were several factors that made China's companies unique. First of all, they could not rely on advertising as the sole source of revenue like Yahoo, Google and many others did in the USA. Chinese portals needed to "move goods", and get a cut on the transaction. Secondly, those goods had to be cheap: these companies had to specialize in selling cheap goods to cheap people. Thirdly, they had to create a degree of trust between user and provider that was much higher than anything needed in the USA where mail catalogs have been the norm for more than a century. In particular, Chinese companies needed to provide real customer service. Customer service in the Microsoft era had decline to a "you are on your own" level: go online and see if anyone has found a solution for your problem. Chinese companies, instead, were striving to provide excellent customer support. Compare the dedicated customer support provided by Taobao, WeChat and Xiaomi with the non-existent customer support provided by their Silicon Valley counterparts eBay, Facebook and Apple.

There was a fundamental difference between the Chinese model and the Silicon valley model. The typical startup in Silicon Valley started out by catering to a relatively small section of society, i.e. to the people or corporations that were willing to spend money on untested ideas/products/services: tech-savvy and high-income individuals or Fortune 500 corporations. The privileged individuals who belonged to this section of society could use their mobile phones to improve their lives in a plethora of ways. The rest of the world had to wait until these ideas/products/services had been tested and had generated a profit (sometimes when competitors from abroad had already started offering clones for much less). Many tech companies served that tiny minority that could afford their services. That minority de facto subsidized the Silicon

Valley startups and corporations that were working on the next big (expensive) thing, The Chinese model, instead, was the exact opposite. The Chinese startup tended to target the lower middle class first. If Apple embodied the "higher-income-consumer-first" business model, Xiaomi embodied the "mass-market-first" business model; ditto for Uber versus Didi Dache. (India's Flipkart and Snapdeal were following the Chinese model).

By the same token, the Chinese Internet companies were more likely to invest in O2O ("online to offline") than their Western counterparts. Delivery was cheap in China, and the overworked Chinese consumers, armed with smartphones, could easily afford the price of home delivery. China also had a more fragmented business world of "mom and pop" stores. Solving the issue of "multipoint to multipoint" logistics was not terribly expensive in China compared with the Western countries.

China launched the Internet+ initiative in 2014 to bring online the countless small businesses who still weren't. An entire street of Beijing's Zhongguancun district (now affectionately known as "Z-Park") was renamed Innoway in 2014. A traditional hub of bookstores, it was turned into a hub of startup incubators, each disguised as a coffeehouse. Garage Cafe had already opened in 2011. Z-Park, home to success stories such as Baidu, Lenovo, JD and Xiaomi, incubated 13,000 new startups in 2014 alone, bringing the total to about 20,000 for a combined revenue of $500 billion. Other Chinese cities followed suit, especially those, like Hangzhou, that were blessed with a top-notch university. This high-tech corridor, running from Beijing to Shenzhen, began to replace the old centers of export-led manufacturing, the Pearl River Delta and the Yangtze River Delta.

In 2015 there were more than 500 million smartphone users in China. In 2014 Chinese smartphone users downloaded 185 billion apps (mostly gaming and shopping), 59% of all downloads worldwide.

Venture capital too was growing rapidly in China. In 2014 it grew more than 300% to $15.5 billion. Up until the mid 2010s there had been little motivation for Chinese startup to succeed in the USA because they had access to plenty of capital in China, because of the fast growing e-economy in China, and because of the high valuations for tech startups in China compared with Silicon Valley. In any case, venture capitalism was a young science in China. The Chuang Yeban, the Chinese equivalent of the NASDAQ index, had been inaugurated only in 2007. Before 2007 high-tech companies were de facto owned by the government. It was still a young science because venture capitalists were de facto discouraged from investing abroad: the government limited currency exports. Investments abroad were mainly carried out by large companies, most notably Lenovo's acquisitions of IBM and Motorola business, but also Alibaba invested in Tango, Lyft, Shoprunner, search engine Quixey and mobile gaming publisher Kabam; while Tencent invested in Snapchat and design website Fab, and LeTV invested in Atieva, a designer of electrical cars.

Despite the similarities between Zhongguancun and the Bay Area, the culture shock couldn't be bigger when it came to the investors. Chinese venture capitalists liked what had already been successful: they invested in the copycats. Chinese venture capitalists liked what sold in China, which could be replicated only in immature markets. China's evaluations were astronomical, fueled by investors who had made money in other industries and who did not understand the technology.

The main drawback to Internet applications in China was the very slow speed of Internet connections (China ranked (82nd in the world at the end of 2014, according to Akamai), but slow Internet speeds in China were blamed on the "Great Firewall of China", the vast apparatus of censorship put in place by the government of mainland China mainly to fight (quote) "Western hostile forces", and not on technological backwardness. The Great Firewall of China, introduced in 2003 after five years of work (officially known as the "Golden Shield Project"), was blocking or at least limiting just about every Western social media (Facebook, Twitter, etc), the most popular Western search engines (such as Google), and many portals of general knowledge (from YouTube to Slideshare), not to mention millions of ordinary websites (such as Piero Scaruffi's www.scaruffi.com), thus depriving the Chinese population of valuable sources of information.

China was also the only country in the world that was successful at creating a domestic clone of whatever succeeded in the USA: Baidu instead of Google, Renren instead of Facebook, WeChat for chatting, Weibo instead of Twitter, Alibaba's Taobao instead of Amazon and Ebay, Didi Kuaidi instead of Uber, YouKu instead of YouTube, LeTV (founded by Yueting Jia) instead of Netflix, MoMo instead of OK Cupid, Tmtpost instead of the Huffington Post, and so on. Viewed from the outside this seemed like a grotesque show of copycats, and even the Chinese joked that the main high-tech business in China was C2C ("Copy to China"), but it had created bigger software companies than Europe or the rest of Asia ever dreamed of.

Innoway in Beijing's Zhongguancun

A Timeline Of Asia's High-Tech Industry

1949: Japan's MITI is established as an architect of industrial policy

1954: Sony's transistor radio

1954: Fujitsu enters the computer market

1958: The USA forces Taiwan's regime to abandon plans to recover the mainland and focus on economic development

1959: Hitachi builds its first transistor computer

1961: Shigeru Sahashi becomes director of the Enterprises Bureau at Japan's MITI

1964: South Korea launches plan to improve exports

1965: Chinese physicist Kuo-ting Li becomes Minister of Economy in Taiwan ("the father of Taiwan's economic miracle")

Dec 1966: Taiwan's Ministry of Economy establishes an "Export Processing Zone" (EPZ) in Kaohsiung, whose tenant companies enjoy privileges but must export all their output

1967: Sony introduces the Video Rover, the first portable videotape recording system (the first "portapak")

1968: Singapore's plan to woe foreign multinationals

1968: Japan's Epson introduces the first digital printer, the EP-101

1969: Texas Instruments, National and Fairchild open plants in Singapore

1969: Shih Ming and Andrew Chiu found Taiwan's first semiconductor company, Unitron

1969: Japan's Seiko introduces the world's first commercial quartz wristwatch

1969: India's Tata appoints Faqir Chand Kohli in charge of computer services

1970: Japan's Sharp and Canon introduce the first pocket calculators

1971: Unitron's engineer Stan Shih designs Taiwan's first desktop calculator

1971: Busicom introduces the LE-120A Handy, the world's first pocket calculator

1972: Indian-born MIT-graduate Narendra Patni founds Data Conversion (later Patni) in the USA with back-office operations in Pune

1973: Taiwan establishes the Industrial Technological Research Institute (ITRI) to develop technologies that can be turned into goods for foreign markets

1974: Tata obtains a software contract from Burroughs, the first major software project offsources by the USA to India

1973: Japan's Canon introduces the first color photocopier

1973: Ichiro Kato's team at Waseda University in Japan unveils the first full-scale anthropomorphic robot in the world, Wabot-1

1973: South Korea establishes the Korea Advanced Institute of Science and Technology at Daeduk

1974: Tai-Ming "Terry" Gou founds the plastic factory Foxconn in Taiwan

1974: Japan's Hitachi produces its first IBM-compatible mainframe computer

1975: Azim Premji's Mumbai-based Wipro starts selling the first computer made in India

1976: Stan Shih and his wife Carolyn Yeh found the calculator maker Multitech (later Acer) in Taiwan

1977: 57 foreign firms, including IBM, dclose down their Indian plants rather than meet Indian demands for some degree of Indian ownership

1978: Deng launches economic reforms in mainland China

1978: Karnataka State's agency Keonics establishes Electronics City in Bangalore, India

1979: Mainland China sets up a Special Economic Zone (SEZ) in Shenzhen to experiment with foreign investment and export manufacturing

1979: Japan's Sony introduces the portable music player Walkman

1980: Japan's Sony introduces the double-sided, double-density 3.5" floppy disk

1980: Japan's Yamaha releases the first digital synthesizer

1980: Wipro, to fill a gap after IBM left India, hires Sridhar Mitta who sets up offices in Bangalore to make computers

1980: Taiwan's ITRI spawn the first startup, UMC

1980: The USA grants mainland China most-favored-nation status, i.e. access to US investors, technology and market

Dec 1980: Taiwan's minister Kuo-ting Li establishes the Hsinchu Science Park

1980: The largest semiconductor manufacturers in the world are: Texas Instruments, National, Motorola, Philips (Europe), Intel, NEC (Japan), Fairchild, Hitachi (Japan) and Toshiba (Japan).

1981: Taiwan's Multitech (later Acer) introduces its own computer, the Micro-Professor MPF-I

1981: Infosys is founded in Pune, India, by Patni employee Narayana Murthy

1981: Japan's Sony introduces the video camera Betacam, the first camcorder

1982: Japan's Sony introduces the compact disc

1982: The first biotech drug, Humulin, is approved for sale

1983: Japan's Sony releases the first consumer camcorder

1983: Japan's Nintendo launches the videogame console Nintendo Entertainment System

Dec 1983: Taiwan's Multitech (Acer) introduces one of the earliest IBM-compatible personal computers

1983: Japan's Seiko introduces the Data 2000 watch, the world's first smartwatch

1984: Stan Shih of Taiwan's Multitech (Acer) founds the research firm Suntek in Silicon Valley

1984: Fujio Masuoka at Japan's Toshiba invents flash memory

1984: Japanese firms introduce the 256K DRAM chips

1984: Liu Chuanzhi of the Chinese Academy of Sciences founds a privately-run but state-owned company, Legend (later Lenovo), to sell IBM's personal computers in China

1985: Taiwan hires US-based semiconductor-industry executive Morris Chang to run the ITRI

1985 Texas Instruments opens a software laboratory in Bangalore, India

1986: Taiwan's Acer, leveraging its supply-chain optimization strategy, releases the world's second computer based on Intel's 386 microprocessor (one month after Compaq)

1986: The Japanese government founds the Advanced Telecommunications Research Institute International (ATR)

1986: (Leroy Hood inventes the automated gene sequencer)

1987: ITRI's president Morris Chang founds Taiwan's Semiconductor Manufacturing Company (TSMC), the first independent silicon-chip foundry in the world, to serve the "fabless" companies of the USA

1987: Ren Zhengfei founds the telcom-equipment maker Huawei in mainland China

1987: The largest semiconductor manufacturers in the world are Japan's NEC, Japan's Toshiba and Japan's Hitachi

1988: Foxconn opens a pioneering factory in China's experimental city Shenzhen

1988: China sets up the Zhongguancun Science Park outside Beijing

1988: Japan's Fujitsu introduces the world's first fully digital consumer camera

1988: Barry Lam founds Quanta Computer in Taiwan

1989: Singapore's Creative Technology introduces the Sound Blaster card for personal computers

1990: China's Lenovo introduces its first homemade computer when the market is dominated by IBM, HP and Compaq

1991: Wipro wins a software contract from a US customer that interacts via the Internet

1993: American Express outsources the management of its credit-card business to its Indian office led by Raman Roy, the first major project of business-process outsourcing to India

1991: The Indian government sets up the Software Technology Parks of India (STPI) to promote software exports and opens the first park in the Electronics City of Bangalore

1991: Japan's Sony releases the first commercial lithium-ion battery

1992: Japan's Fujitsu introduces the world's first mass-produced plasma display

1992: South Korea's Samsung becomes the largest producer of memory chips in the world

1993: Japan's Fujistsu introduces the fastest supercomputer in the world, the Numerical Wind Tunnel

1994: Japan's Sony introduces the PlayStation

1994: Alpha and Frank Wu found the contract manufacturer AmTran Technology in Taiwan

1996: Japan's Toshiba introduces the first DVD player

1996: Japan's Sony introduces the chip FeliCa for RFID technology

1997: The Octopus card in Hong Kong pioneers contact-less credit cards

1997: Japan's Toyota introduces the Prius, the first mass-produced hybrid vehicle

1997: Lenovo passes IBM to become China's main vendor of personal computers

1997: Japan's Panasonic introduces the first flat panel television set

1997: Cher Wang, the richest woman in Taiwan, founds HTC

1998: South Korea's SaeHan Information Systems introduces the first mass-produced mp3 player, the "MPMan"

1998: Tencent is founded in China by Huateng Ma and Zhidong Chang to develop the instant messaging platform Open ICQ or QQ

1998: A merger creates China's Sina and China's Tencent is founded

1999: Jack Ma founds Alibaba in China

1999: Singapore's Creative Technology introduces the Nomad line of digital audio players

1999: Japan's NTT DoCoMo ("Do Communications over the Mobile network" introduces the "i-mode" service that allows mobile phones to access a broad range of Internet services

1999: Alibaba is founded in China by Jack Ma, an English teacher with no computing experience

1999: Lucent Technologies announces the first optical network switch

1999: Apple incorporates the first Wi-Fi card (made by Lucent) into a computer

1999: South Korea's Samsung introduces the SPH-WP10, the world's first watch phone

2000: Japan's Casio introduces the WMP-1, the world's first watch capable of playing MP3 files, and the WQV, the world's first watch to include a camera

2000: Robin Li and Eric Xu launch the search engine Baidu in China

2000: Japan's Sharp introduces the J-SH04, the first mobile phone with a built-in camera

2000: Japan's Honda introduces the humanoid robot ASIMO

2000: Almost 50% of Japanese who access the Internet do so via a cell phone

2000: The foundry Semiconductor Manufacturing International Corporation (SMIC) is founded in Shanghai's Zhangjiang High-Tech Park

2001: South Korea's Hyundai spins off its electronics division as Hynix

2002: South Korea's Samsung is the second semiconductor manufacturer in the world after Intel, and Japan's Toshiba is third, passing Texas Instruments

2002: There are more than 2,000 startups in Seoul's Teheran Valley, and 69% of them are in IT

2002: China's Suntech, founded by Zhengrong Shi, opens its factory of solar

2002: Vizio is established in the USA to sell AmTran's television sets

2003: Between 1988 and 2003 high-tech ventures in Beijing's Zhongguancun grew from 527 to more than 12,000

2003: Sony introduces the first Blu-ray disc player

2003: Hitachi and Mitsubishi create the joint venture Renesas Technology specializing in microcontrollers (embedded chips)

2003: Asia produces about 40% of the world's IT goods and consumes about 20% of them

2003: Japan accounts for 21% of all patents awarded worldwide

2004: South Korea's Samsung is the world's largest OLED (Organic Light-Emitting Diode) manufacturer, producing 40% of the OLED displays made in the world

2004: Japan's Epson introduces the mirrorless camera

2004: Japan's Casio introduces the GWS-900 G-Shock, the world's first watch capable of mobile payment

2005: Taiwan's companies produce 80% of all personal digital assistants, 70% of all notebooks and 60% of all flat-panel monitors

2005: Lenovo acquires IBM's personal computer business

2005: Joseph Chen founds Renren in China

2006: Between 1993 to 2006 the number of new science and engineering PhDs increased by 24% in the USA, by 189% in South Korea, and by more than 1,000% in mainland China

2007: The world's largest vendors of personal computers are HP, Dell, Taiwan's Acer, China's Lenovo and Japan's Toshiba

2007: Japan's Hitachi releases the Deskstar 7K1000, the first 1 TB hard disk drive

Aug 2007: Taiwan's Acer acquires its US rival Gateway

2008: Japan's Sony unveils the world's first OLED tv set, the XEL-1, the world's thinnest tv set at just 3 mm

2009: Asia employs 1.5 million workers in the computer industry while the USA employs only 166,000

2009: Vizio, whose products are made by Taiwanese company AmTran, becomes the main tv-set brand in the USA

2009: Chinese solar panels account for about 50% of total shipments

2009: South Korea's Samsung announces mass production of 512 Mbit phase-change memory

2009: Taiwan's Foxconn (Hon Hai Precision Industry), becomes the world's largest manufacturer of electronics with revenues that dwarf Apple's and Intel's, employing 800,000 people

2009: India's Infosys sets up the largest corporate university in the world at Mysore

2009: China's Sina launches Weibo

2010: China's Tencent is the world's third-largest Internet company by market capitalization

2010: Xiaomi is founded in China

2010: Renesas acquires NEC's semiconductor division, becoming the world's largest manufacturer of microcontrollers (embedded chips) and the world's fourth largest semiconductor company

2010: Taiwan's Quanta Computer is the largest manufacturer of notebook computers in the world

2010: South Korea's Samsung introduces the smartphone Galaxy S

2010: Taiwan's HTC introduces the world's first 4G smartphone, the EVO

2010: Japan's Sony demonstrates a rollable OLED display

2011: Tencent releases the social networking platform Weixin/Wechat

2011: Tencent releases the social networking platform Weixin/WeChat for smartphones

2012: China's Huawei overtakes Sweden's Ericsson to become the world's biggest telcom-equipment maker

2012: Taiwan's Acer introduces the world's thinnest notebook, the Aspire S5

2012: China's Huawei overtakes Sweden's Ericsson to become the world's biggest telcom-equipment maker

2012: South Korea's Samsung sells twice as many smartphones as Apple and five times more than Nokia

2012: South Korea's Hynix merges with SK Group to form the world's second-largest memory chipmaker after Samsung

2012: The Tokyo Institute of Technology creates a robot that learns functions it was not programmed to do (based on Osamu Hasegawa's technology)

2013: South Korea's Samsung introduces the world's first mobile phone with flexible display, the Galaxy Round

2013: China's Tianhe-2 is the fastest supercomputer in the world

2014: China's Xiaomi is third behind Apple and Samsung in the mobile phone market

2014: China's Xiaomi doubles its revenues in just one year

2014: China's Alibaba sets a new world record with its IPO

2015: Japan's Sharp introduces the in-cell type touch display that combines LCD and touch sensor.

2016: China's Sunway TaihuLight is the fastest supercomputer in the world

Silicon Valleys in Time

If a historian specializing in technological evolution had examined the world a century ago, s/he would have never bet her money on a primitive, underpopulated and underdeveloped region like the San Francisco Bay Area. She might have picked a place in the USA (most likely Boston, New York or Philadelphia), but more likely a place in Western Europe, probably somewhere between Oxford and Cambridge. With 20/20 hindsight everybody has a theory about why it all happened in "Silicon Valley" (that for our purpose is really the broader Bay Area) but most of those theories are easily disproven if one studies other regions of the world: the same conditions existed somewhere else and to an even greater degree.

One needs to spend more time analyzing the previous cases of economic, technological and cultural boom. Three obvious candidates are Athens in the 5th century BC, Firenze (Florence) of the Renaissance and the electrical Berlin of a century ago. There was little that made Athens truly special. Other cities might have succeeded better than Athens, particularly the ones on the coast of what is today Turkey that were the cradle of Greek civilization. However, Athens was probably the nicest place to live: the attitude of its citizens was different, somewhat eccentric for those times. Eventually it was that attitude that led to the invention of democracy and capitalism. I would argue that it was also that the real protagonist of Athens' renaissance was that attitude (harder to pinpoint than the wars and political upheavals that historians describe in detail).

It may have been easier to predict Firenze's (Florence's) ascent given that the city had been getting richer since at least the 12th century. However, who would have bet on a city state within a peninsula (Italy) that was mostly famous for endemic warfare? And if you had to pick an Italian city-state why not Venezia (Venice) that was creating a little empire (not surrounded by dozens of city-states like Florence was in Tuscany) and that constituted a crucial link between the superpower (Constantinople) and Western Europe? Again, what stands out is the attitude of the Florentines: if you liked adventure and innovation, it was nicer to live in Florence than in greedy, narrow-minded Florence, and eventually Florence did produce more liberal regimes and enlightened dictators instead of Venice's faceless dogi.

The "electrical Berlin" of the early 20th century came out of a black hole: Germany did not even exist 30 years earlier. Germany was the last place in Europe that was still politically divided in tiny medieval-style states the late 19th century. When Germany got unified, the spirit of unification certainly fueled nationalistic pride but, again, there was hardly anything special about German science and technology up to that point (there was indeed something special about German philosophy and German poetry, but one can argue it actually went against progress). What was unique about Berlin at that time was the enthusiasm of its population: the attitude, again, was indeed unique. In all three places it was the attitude (the spirit) of the population that was markedly different from the norm. In all three places that attitude rewarded the independent in ways that were not the norm, and it instituted a stronger degree of meritocracy than elsewhere.

The same might be true also for the San Francisco Bay Area. The great universities, the mass immigration and the venture capital (knowledge, labor and money) came later. What was already there was the spirit of the Frontier, the spirit of the eccentric independent explorer that later would become the hobbyist and the hacker.

Silicon Valleys in Space

There have been many attempts to recreate Silicon Valley in other countries. It was worth examining the ones in Western Europe that at the time led the world in universities, immigrants and capital.

France created Sophia Antipolis, a technology park in Southern France. First of all, it was created by the French government with a socialist-style centralized plan. The region has become a magnet for foreign IT companies that want a foothold into Europe, but hardly the creator of domestic startups that the Bay Area is in the USA. There are a few factors that make a huge difference: there is social pressure to join big corporations, not to start small companies; if you do open your own company, failure is terminal; very few foreign talents have been (permanently) attracted to the area; on the contrary many of the French talents trained there have emigrated to the USA where they did start the kind of company that they would not start in France. Note that, by all accounts, the quality of life in southern France matches if not surpasses the quality of life in California.

The Munich metropolitan area in southern Germany has become another high-tech hub. In this case the German government did not quite plan a Silicon Valley per se: it was the defense industry that brought advanced manufacturing to the area in ways not too different from how the defense industry bootstrapped Silicon Valley's high-tech industry. The advanced manufacturing that led to the success of companies like BMW transformed an essentially rural community in Bavaria into a high-tech hub. Here there are also excellent educational institutions: the Fraunhofer Institute and the Max Planck institute, that provide world-class public education. The quality of life is quite high by European standards (and the weather is much better than in most of Germany). The socialist underpinning here is represented by the fact that the main "venture capitalist" has been Bayern Kapital (an arm of the state government). The region has indeed spawned a varied fauna of infotech, biotech and cleantech startups just like in Silicon Valley. The region has also avoided the brain-drain that consumes most of Western Europe: relatively few German entrepreneurs and engineers have moved to the USA. However, this region too has failed to attract significant numbers of foreign talents.

Four factors made Germany completely different from the Bay Area. First of all, Germany's fundamental problem was the high cost of its labor (about ten times the cost of labor in China in 2010). Therefore the whole nation was engaged in a collective distributed project to devise ever more efficient ways to manufacture goods. Therefore both universities and corporations focused their research on innovating the manufacturing process, rather than innovating the products made through those processes. The German system is biased towards perfecting existing technology rather than creating new technology. RWTH Aachen spent billions of euros to create a technology park that specializes in just manufacturing techniques. Stanford's technology park was never meant for just one specific application of technology. Secondly, the relationship between industry and academia has always been different in Germany than in the USA. German corporations fund academic research that is very specific to their needs, whereas universities in the USA receive money that is generically for research. This means that the transfer of know-how from academia to industry is much smoother and faster in Germany than in the USA, but at the same time the students are raised to become workers and then managers in the existing corporations rather than start new creative businesses. Thirdly, Germany's big success story could also be a curse: Germany achieved an impressive degree of distribution of high education, spreading world-class research institutes all over its territory (the Max Planck Institute had 80 locations in 2010, the Fraunhofer Society had 60), but this also means that most of the bright scientists, engineers and entrepreneurs don't need to move to another city, as they can find a top-notch technological centers right where they live. Silicon Valley was mainly built by immigrants (from both other states of the USA and from abroad). It was one place where everybody converged to do high-tech because most of the rest of the country did not have the conditions that are favorable to the high-tech industry. Germany provides them almost to dozens of regions, therefore none of them can become the equivalent of Silicon Valley. Finally (and this is true for all of continental Europe), German industry has to deal with a strong anti-technological and anti-capitalist sentiment that was created over the decades by an alliance of socialists, environmentalists, hippies, philosophers, psychologists and so forth.

So far the main success stories of Europe have come from these regions: SAP (Heidelberg), ARM (Cambridge) and Nokia (Oulu). The European region that came closest to resembling Silicon Valley (although at a much smaller scale) was Oulu in northern Finland, where more than a thousand startups were born in the 2000s, most of them in wireless technology, but also in biotech, cleantech and nanotech.

Israel was, actually, the country with the highest venture capital per person in the entire world ($170 compared with $75 in the USA in 2010). Its startups focused on the military, communications, agricultural and water technology that were essential for the country's survival. Many of these startups were acquired by Silicon Valley companies. None of these startups managed to grow to the point of becoming an international player.

The Selfies (2011-16)

The Saga of Apple

In July 2011 Apple had more cash and securities ($76 billion) than the cash reserves of the government of the US (which was facing a temporary liquidity crunch due to debt ceiling debates). Google was on a buying spree (basically an admission of inferior technology) while Apple rarely bought anything from others (an impressive demonstration of technological superiority). Apple had always been a strange company, a distant second to Microsoft in operating systems for personal computers, but possibly better respected than Microsoft (certainly so in Silicon Valley), as if Microsoft's rise was mere luck while Apple's survival was pure genius.

Meanwhile, Apple continued to refine its MacOS to the point that Microsoft's Windows look positively troglodytic to the Apple base. The iPod and the iPhone increased Apple's reputation in designing wildly appealing products, even though neither fully dominated its market (there were lots of digital music players, and Google's Android was growing a lot faster than Apple's iOS). The MacOS and iOS had, however, an incredible following worldwide, unmatched by any other desktop and mobile software platform. And, last but not least, Apple ruled the handheld tablet market with the iPad (almost 70% of the marked in mid-2011). Apple had never embraced social computing (just like it had been slow to embrace the Internet to start with) and it was late in cloud computing (the iCloud was announced in June 2011).

Yet there was a general feeling that Apple did things only when it was capable of stunning the world. No other company could afford to be so late to the market and still be expected to make a splash.

The philosophical difference between Google and Apple was even wider than between Google and Microsoft: Apple still conceived the Web as a side-effect of computing, not as the world inside which computing happens, whereas Google (whose slogan was "nothing but the Web") was pushing the vision of the Web as "the" computing platform.

The difference in business models was even more profound: Google was making (mostly buying and distributing) relatively trivial technology and letting people use it for free (with the advertisers footing the bill), de facto turning the Web into a giant advertising billboard. Meanwhile, Apple was expecting people to pay a premium for its devices and services, just like any other traditional, quality-branded good.

In fact, one of Apple's great and unlikely success stories was its retail stores: the "Apple store" was popular worldwide, making Apple of the most valuable brands in the world. In July 2011, revenues from its retail stores were $3.5 billion, up from $2.6 billion the previous year (2011 was a terrible year for the whole Western economies). Apple was planning to open 40 new stores in the following six months, mostly abroad.

Google was trying to make computing more or less free, while Apple was trying to make computing as fashionable as cosmetics and apparel. Apple had tried this before, when its closed platform Macintosh had competed with Microsoft's open platform Windows. Now it was the relatively closed iPod, iPhone and iPad versus Google's Android platform. In many ways the iPod, the iPhone and the iPad marked a regress in computing. They were computers, but limited to a few functions (that they did very well). For the sake of making those functions as mobile as the transistor radio (the first great mass-market portable electronic device) Apple reduced the power of the computer. In theory application developers could add their own applications to the iPhone, but in practice Apple had veto rights over which applications were allowed (so much for freedom of choice and the free market).

Apple's success was frequently viewed as the work of one man, Steve Jobs; but Jobs had to retire in August 2011 for health reasons.

When Steve Jobs, the ultimate icon and mythological figure of Silicon Valley, died in October 2011 (one day after the official Apple release of the intelligent assistant Siri), his legacy was the legacy of the whole of Silicon Valley: a new discipline that, borrowing other people's inventions, was not solely about the functionalities of a product and was not solely about the "look and feel" of a product, but was very much about the way that the human mind and the human body should interact with technology. It was a discipline born at the confluence of the utopian counterculture of the Sixties, the tech hobbyist culture of the 1970s and the corporate culture of Wall Street; and it was about creating a new species, a machine-augmented Homo Sapiens (Home Sapiens Plus?). Just like Silicon Valley as a whole, Jobs had mostly copied other people's ideas, but turned them into existential issues. Jobs elevated to a sophisticated art the idea that producer and consumer should engage in one and the same game: exhibitionism; and then congratulate each other, and even worship each other like fraternal deities.

It was telling that very few people noticed the death, also in Palo Alto, and just six months later, of Jack Tramiel, the founder of Commodore, the first company to sell a million units of a personal computer and whose Commodore 64 sold four times the sales of the Apple II.

Flowers and apples in front of Steve Jobs' home the day after he died

The Age of the Smartphone App

The importance of the "app store" was skyrocketing by the day, just like the availability of applications had favored Windows on the desktop, except that this time around Microsoft was on the losing end. In 2013 Microsoft announced the acquisition of Nokia's mobile business within two years the two companies introduced state-of-the-art smartphones such as the Nokia Lumia 1020, equipped with a camera worthy of professional digital cameras, and the Nokia Icon, whose user interface was as advanced (if not more advanced) than the Android's and the iPhone's ones. Unfortunately, Nokia's smartphones were running Windows Phone, and Windows still did not have the same apps available to Android and iPhone. No matter how technologically advanced, Nokia's smartphones were doomed to be outsiders.

In 2013 worldwide sales of smartphones passed the one billion mark, posting a 38.4% increase from the previous year, with Samsung accounting for 31.3% of the units, followed by Apple with 15.3%.

While apps continue to proliferate in all possible fields, the biggest success stories had to do with extending the social network enabled by smartphones.

Tencent had been founded in China in 1998 by Huateng Ma and Zhidong Zhang to develop the PC-based instant messaging platform Open ICQ or QQ. In 2009 the Chinese government had blocked access to Facebook, and soon Twitter and Youtube were banned too (as well as millions of other websites including www.scaruffi.com). In January 2011 Tencent released the social networking platform Weixin/Wechat, designed by Allen Zhang, which simply integrated the features of all those social networking platforms, and also provided a sort of digital walkie-talkie (verbal instant messaging, very popular in a nation whose complex language is not friendly to texting). Within three years it had 300 million users, growing faster than Facebook.

Tango, founded in 2009 in Mountain View by Eric Setton and Israeli serial entrepreneur Uri Raz, provided a voice and video messaging mobile platform for all smartphones, competing with Apple's proprietary Facetime. The app went viral so quickly that Tango already had one million users after just ten days of launching (Tango later added entertainment, gaming and ecommerce and became a "unicorn" after Alibaba invested in it in 2014).

Snapchat was started by Stanford students Reggie Brown and Evan Spiegel in 2011 for smartphone users to share photos and videos. In the age when the public was increasingly concerned about privacy, Snapchat pledged to delete every messages from its servers within a few seconds.

This was, after all, the age of the "selfie", the self-portrait photograph posted on social media for all your friends to see how cute and cool you are.

WhatsApp and Snapchat (and Weixin/ WeChat in China) competed for the same market, but were fundamentally different business models. WhatsApp allowed users to send and receive texts, voice, pictures, audio and video. WhatsApp charged a tiny yearly subscription to its users. WhatsApp was only available on phones, not on computers. WhatsApp served a wide range of age groups. WhatsApp had no advertisements. Snapchat was also available on Apple and Android devices. Snapchat had some advertisement but was absolutely free. Snapchat deleted from the memory of the device videos and photos within 10 seconds of sending them. Snapachat was the perfect tool for "selfie" maniacs and therefore had an audience mainly of young people.

The company that had perhaps the biggest trouble adjusting to the new world was Yahoo! In 2012 it hired Marissa Mayer from Google, the rare case of a major CEO coming from the ranks and files of a high-tech company. She launched into an acquisition spree of her own, purchasing 16 startups in her first year at the helm of the company. The biggest purchase (2013) was blogging platform Tumblr, founded in New York in 2007 by Marco Arment and David Karp (who was barely 20). This was not the first attempt by Yahoo! to enter the blogging sphere. Yahoo! had already purchased the most famous blogging site of 1999, Geocities, only to cause its rapid demise. Just like then, Yahoo! was more interested in Tumblr's customer base of 105 million bloggers than in contributing to progress in this technology. And, just like in the age of Geocities, it was still not clear how these platforms were supposed to make money. Most of the other acquisitions were for mobile applications and services, like the gaming platform PlayerScale and the video platform Qwiki. Among them was London-based "whiz kid" Nick D'Aloisio's news aggregator Summly (originally called Trimit and developed for iOS in 2011, when he was still

15), based on Artificial Intelligence software coming from SRI International. Just like with Google, this was also a way to hire top software engineers (the so-called "acqui-hire" method).

The mother of all applications was the "personal assistant", or, better, the voice-controlled contextual search tool. Apple had introduced Siri with the iPhone 4S of 2011 after merging a personal-assistant technology acquired from Siri with the speech-recognition technology acquired from Nuance.

During the year 2012 Apple's Siri was joined by a number of competitors: Samsung's S-Voice, launched in May 2012 for its Galaxy S3 smartphone; LG Quick Voice, launched in June 2012 for its Optimus Vu smartphone, and, last but not least, GoogleNow, launched in July 2012 on Samsung's Galaxy Nexus smartphone. In 2014 Amazon released Alexa, developed by the same Amazon's Lab126 in Sunnyvale that made the Kindle. Microsoft followed suit in 2014 with its Cortana. In 2014 Apple's iOs8 introduced the "Hey Siri" feature that enabled any app to summon Siri; and in 2015 Uber introduced a similar feature to summon Uber from any other app.

The new generation of intelligent assistants included Kasisto (2013), an SRI International spin-off just like Siri, and Digital Genius, designed by London-based Russian-born Dmitry Aksenov, as well as some specializing in scheduling meetings, such as Clara (2013), founded by Maran Nelson and Michael Akilian in San Francisco, and X.ai (2014), founded by Dennis Mortensen in New York. In 2015 Facebook launched its own virtual assistant, M.

However, these "assistants" were still a far cry from a real "contextual and predictive technology".

Social apps for the mobile world continued to multiply. Flipagram, founded in 2013 in Los Angeles (by Raffi Baghoomian, Brian C. Dilley, Joshua Feldman, Farhad Mohit), and funded by Michael Moritz and John Doerr (who famously invested together in Google), offered an app that allowed users to quickly produce short video clips combining photos, videos, text and music. In 2014 Fyusion, founded in 2013 in San Francisco by Willow Garage alumni Radu Rusu, Stefan Holzer and Stephen Miller, debuted the mobile photo app Fyuse that pushed social media beyond panoramic snapshots and towards immersive 3D photography.

The age of the selfie quickly turned into the age of the short video. Snapchat passed 6 billion daily video views in 2015, just three years after the introduction of its video service. By then Facebook boasted 8 billion daily video views. In 2015 Google acquired Fly Labs, founded by Tim Novikoff in 2012 in New York, creator of immensely popular video-editing apps for the iPhone. Cinematique, founded by Randy Ross in 2012 in New York, provided a platform for making interactive online videos. In 2014 Shutterstock, an online marketplace for trading stock images launched in 2003 in New York by Jon Oringer, debuted an in-browser video-editing tool, Sequence. In 2016 Moviefone's founder Andrew Jarecki launched a video editing app for the iOS, KnowMe.

Bitmovin, founded in 2013 in Palo Alto by one of the DASH creators, Christian Timmerer of the Alpen-Adria Universitaet Klagenfurt in Austria, delivered high-performance MPEG-DASH players for HTML5 and Flash on smartphones as well as computers.

New creative kinds of collaboration tools were introduced in the 2010s, notably: TinySpeck (later renamed Slack), founded in 2013 in San Francisco by Stewart Butterfield of Flickr fame with Serguei Mourachov, Eric Costello and Cal Henderson; and HipChat, founded in 2010 in San Francisco by Chris Rivers, Garret Heaton and Pete Curley, and acquired by Australian company Atlassian in 2012. Slack was tapping into a transformation of the main decades-old form of interpersonal digital communication: email. Email had been attacked on one side by chat applications, that provided a much simpler way to carry out instant bidirectional communication than traditional email. Email itself had become less of a person-to-person communication tool and more of a machine-to-person communicaton tool and a campaign-to-the-masses communication tool, as many emails were generated by machines (not only marketing but also receipts, social-media notifications, bank statements, etc) and many emails were crafted for an audience by a Mailchimp user (Mailchimp having become the main email marketing platform, originally founded in 2001 in Georgia by Ben Chestnut). Google too had contributed in giving email a bad reputation among younger people by unnecessarily overloading Gmail (the most popular email application) with features and icons that sounded confusing, complicated and old-fashioned to kids used to one-click communications. Slack was one of the tools that became popular because, indirectly, reduced email communications (in this case within a group).

In 2013 Quip (founded in San Francisco by former Facebook technologist Bret Taylor and by former Google engineer Kevin Gibbs) launched a mobile office application.

In 2016 Vivaldi, founded in 2013 by Opera's co-founder Jon von Tetzchner and Tatsuki Tomita, launched a browser for "power users" with old-fashioned features like keyboard shortcuts and command lines. Vivaldi came out of an open-source culture: it used Google's Blink engine (the rendering engine of Google's Chromium), developed in 2013 jointly by Google, Opera, Intel and others. Almost simultaneously Google instead moved to kill the browser by unveiling the Gboard keyboard, a keyboard with a button to summon a search without having to open a browser.

The dark side of the Internet came to light in 2011, when a researcher discovered that spyware developed by Carrier IQ (a company founded as Core Mobility in 2005 in Sunnyvale by former Apple engineer Konstantin Othmer) was recording detailed user behavior on smartphones sold by AT&T, Sprint, T-Mobile, Apple and Samsung, which accounted for the majority (only two major manufacturers, Nokia and Research in Motion, never used this spyware). This followed a 2010 lawsuit, in which Skyhook Wireless sued Google for patent infringement, that indirectly revealed to the public a vast and secret three-year project by Google (from 2007 until the lawsuit) to collect WiFi signals using StreetView vehicles (hence renamed "Wi-Spy vehicles" by the hacker community). Skyhook Wireless, founded by Ted Morgan in 2003 in Boston, had become the world leader in "location intelligence", i.e. the leading source of information about Wi-Fi locations. That information provides a more accurate and battery-friendly way to pinpoint a mobile user's location than GPS or cell tower triangulation, the user's location being in turn very valuable for advertisers and therefore meaning big money for search engines. Google had a vested interest in improving its knowledge and tracking of the exact location at any time of users of Android smartphones. Skyhook was candidly admitting on its website that "Wi-Fi is far more than a network connection - it's a location source." In other words, Wi-Fi had become a way to track where a mobile user was.

In 1975 the FBI had funded the development of fingerprint scanners but it took decades for the technology to reach the consumer market. In 2011 Motorola became the first company to offer a fingerprint scanner in a smartphone (its Atrix). The fingerprint scanner used by Motorola in Atrix 4G was made by Authentec, which was acquired by Apple in 2012. Sure enough in 2013 Apple added a fingerprint scanner to the iPhone. A few months later HTC used the technology developed since 2010 by Validity (founded in 2000 in San Jose and acquired by Synaptics in 2013) for its One Max. China's Xiaomi introduced its fingerprint scanner in 2015.

Gaming

The world of gaming was shaken in 2012 when Ouya, founded in San Francisco by Julie Uhrman, announced an Android-powered open-source gaming console. Unlike other platforms, that charged game developers, Ouya promised no licensing fees, no retail fees and no publishing fees. While less powerful than the best-selling consoles of the time (like Microsoft's Xbox 360 and Sony's PlayStation 3), Ouya was promising a whole new world of games, not confined to the big developers. In July 2013 Ouya raised more than $2.5 million in just 8 hours on Kickstarter.

In 2012-13 the big videogame console producers introduced a new generation: Microsoft's Xbox One, Sony's PlayStation 4, Nintendo's Wii U. None of these was based in Silicon Valley. However, two of them

(Xbox and PlayStation) were powered by general-purpose processors made in Silicon Valley (by AMD) instead of the custom chips of previous generations. Furthermore, one reason why nobody in Silicon Valley was trying to compete with the giants of consoles was that mobile devices were rapidly becoming a major platform for gaming.

Gaming engines such as Denmark-based Unity (David Helgason and Nicholas Francis) and Palo Alto-based Corona (Walter Luh, 2008) were making life easier for designers.

Silicon Valley was not innovating in mobile game design but it was acquiring. In 2015 Activision Blizzard paid a fortune for one of the most successful mobile games yet, "Candy Crush Saga", launched in 2012 and already downloaded by more than 500 million people (mostly women) on smartphones and Facebook. King had been founded in 2003 in Sweden by Riccardo Zacconi and others, a spin-off of Melvyn Morris' online dating website uDate.com (after it was acquired by Texas-based Match.com).

3D open-world gaming had been pioneered by games such as Yu Suzuki's "Shenmue" (1999) for Sega and "Grand Theft Auto III" (2001) by DMA Design in Britain. Markus Persson's "Minecraft" (2011) in Sweden became the most powerful game of that genre, registering its 100 millionth user in 2014.

Virtual and Augmented Reality

The head-mounted displays of the early days of virtual reality had been heavy and cumbersome, and required cables running to a supercomputer. In 2013 Google Glass, manufactured by Foxconn, captured the headlines: it coupled that kind of display with a "wearable" computer and provided the kind of functionalities offered by Internet-enabled consumer electronics. Thad Starner, one of the pioneers of wearable computing, was the mastermind behind Glass, a project largely implemented by Greg Priest-Dorman at Georgia Tech. Google Glass, which was basically a wearable smartphone, failed because it was socially disruptive, eventually killed by social stigma. Autodesk adapted the concept of the Google Glass to the CAD market and created Autodesk Virtual Reality (AVR) Glass, introduced in 2014. Google Glass failed just like its closest competitor, Atheer, founded in 2011 in Mountain View by Lebanese-born entrepreneur Soulaiman Itani and Allen Yang, whose glasses offered a wider 65-degree field of view (as opposed to Google Glass' 12 degrees) but required a physical cable to an Android smartphone.

Greg Priest-Dorman

The vanguard in this field was perhaps Lumus, founded in 2000 in Israel by Yaakov Amitai, that in 2012 introduced see-through wearable displays.

Virtual Reality had failed in the 1990s, but between 1995 and 2015 three factors changed the conditions for adoption: 1. the cost of LCD screens had declined (thanks mainly to Hitachi's In Plane Switching design and Samsung's Multi-domain design) so that in 2007 for the first time LCD TV sets surpassed CRT TV sets in worldwide sales; 2. the cost of 3D motion capture had declined (Microsoft Kinect had come out in 2010); and, last but not least, 3. movies such as "The Matrix" (1999), a Hollywood remake of Rainer Fassbinder's "World on a Wire" (1973), had popularized the idea of life in a simulated world and had therefore inspired a new generation to live inside virtual worlds.

In 2014 Facebook acquired Oculus, a manufacturer of virtual reality headsets for games founded in 2012 in Irvine by Palmer Luckey and Jack McCauley, and originally funded through a Kickstarter campaign.

Oculus' cofounder Jack McCauley

Jaunt VR, founded in 2013 in Palo Alto, introduced a 360-degree camera that allowed users to create a virtual-reality video. In 2015 Matterport (founded in 2010 in Mountain View by Matt Bell and by David Gausebeck, the engineer who designed the first commercial CAPTCHA security system at PayPal) introduced a $4,500 camera to turn interior spaces into virtual worlds. Lucid VR, founded by Han Jin and Adam Rowell in Fremont in 2014 with the aim of becoming the GoPro of virtual reality, introduced the LucidCam, a stereoscopic 180-degree 3D camera.

Lucid VR's cofounder Han Jin

360 degree cameras soon flooded the market. In 2015 the big camera brands introduced their models, such as Ricoh's Theta, Kodak's SP360, Lytro's Immerge, as well as the Jump built by Google and GoPro (marketed as Odyssey in 2016), and (in 2016) Nokia's Ozo. In 2016 two French independents responded with the Orah 41 by VideoStitch (founded in 2012 by Nicolas Burtey in France), and the 360cam by Giroptic (also founded in France in 2008 by Richard Ollier).

The alternative to these cameras was the light-field technology that could create a 3D representation similar to a hologram. Refocus Imaging (later Lytro), founded in 2006 in Mountain View by Ren Ng, introduced the first light-field camera for consumers in 2012.

In 2016 GoPro indeed entered the virtual-reality market with an "end-to-end platform": the six-camera Omni VR coupled with the LiveVR wireless streaming tool and the GoPro VR video channel, plus partnerships with 100+ developers.

In 2015 Samsung Gear VR, powered by Oculus and strapped to a Samsung Galaxy (Android) phone, further lowered the threshold to play with virtual-reality games, but Google already offered a cheap virtual-reality viewer, Cardboard (developed by David Coz and Damien Henry in Google's Paris office), that used the smartphone as a screen.

The Gear VR became "the" Christmas toy of 2015, but all the user could really do was to move her head around. At the end of 2015 Taiwan's HTC introduced its own virtual-reality gadget, Vive, powered by Valve (Valve being a successful creator of videogames founded in 1996 in Seattle by former Microsoft employees Gabe Newell and Mike Harrington), which, thanks to its tracking features, offered room-size virtual reality (but required a powerful computer); and China's LeTV announced its Cool 1, that was basically a clone of Google's CardBoard. Smartphone-based virtual reality was being enabled by Google's Project Tango (2014), that packaged an Android smartphone, a developer kit and advanced 3D sensors to track motion and build a visual map using 3D scanning. The first smartphone to use Google's Tango technology was Lenovo's Phab2Pro, introduced in 2016.

By 2016 the viewers could be divided in three groups:

- Tethered to computer, small range of movement: Facebook Oculus
- Tethered to computer, large range of movement: HTC Vive
- Attached to a smartphone: Samsung Gear VR, Google Cardboard

In 2016 Intel announced its stand-alone headset (neither computer nor smartphone required), Project Alloy .

The leader in music and video gadgets, Apple, had not yet introduced its own virtual-reality product but was actively acquiring related technologies: in 2013 it acquired the Israeli company PrimeSense, most famous for designing the motion-detection technology of Microsoft's Kinect in 2010; in 2015 it acquired the German company Metaio, a Volkswagen spin-off specializing in augmented reality; in 2015 it acquired the Swiss company FaceShift, a spinoff from Lausanne's Polytechnique Federale, whose technology captured the user's facial expressions in real time and created an animated avatar; and in 2016 it acquired Ogmento (later renamed Flyby Media), founded in 2010 in New York by Cole Van Nice and Oriel Bergig.

Meanwhile, NextVR, founded by filmmaker DJ Roller and David Cole in 2009 in Los Angeles promised live VR experience for live broadcast.

In 2015 Apple acquired Swiss-based Faceshift, a spinoff from Lausanne's Polytechnique Federale, whose technology was capable of capturing the user's facial expressions in real time and creating animated avatars of the user.

In 2013 graphics-processing specialist Nvidia demonstrated a head-mounted display that used light fields. A near-eye light field display was also being developed by Florida-based startup Magic Leap, founded by Rony Abovitz

Virtual Reality required a new generation of user interfaces, beyond voice and touch. Portland's OnTheGo, founded in 2012 by Ryan Fink, introduced a purely software system to track a user's gestures, a gesture-recognition system that could work on any Android-based smart glass with a standard camera. (It was acquired by Atheer in 2015).

Augmented Reality systems allowed the user to mix virtual and reality objects. Meta, founded in 2012 in Redwood City by Meron Gribetz, introduced the first augmented reality system in 2014, see-through glasses that allowed wearers to move and manipulate 3D content using hand gestures.

Coincidentally, Google shut down Glass the very same week of 2015 in which Microsoft announced HoloLens, a cordless, self-contained smart-glasses headset with an embedded Windows computer, whose user interface replaced the mouse with the gaze of the user and the mouse click with a motion of her finger. It allowed the user to walk around three-dimensional virtual objects and employed gaze, gesture and voice to modify them. To carry out the same functions, Oculus' Rift needed to be supplemented with gesture recognition (Leap Motion or Kinect) and stereoscopic cameras; and Rift was plugged into a host computer, whereas HoloLens was stand-alone. Microsoft leveraged technology acquired from Osterhout Design Group, a company founded in 1999 in San Francisco by Ralph Osterhout that introduced its first consumer glasses in 2015. If Facebook/Oculus targeted the gaming community, Microsoft aimed at the enterprise, viewing the HoloLens as a productivity tool.

However, what truly made augmented reality popular was a mobile game introduced by Niantic and Nintendo in 2016: Pokermon Go. Niantic, founded in 2010 in San Francisco by John Hanke and initially incubated within Google, had already tested the market for augmented-reality mobile games with Ingress in 2012. Pokermon Go became a worldwide phenomenon: within one month of its introduction, it was downloaded more than 100 million times.

A number of startups wanted to give virtual reality a social life, improving over the original Second Life model. In 2013 David Gudmundson, Eric Romo and Gavan Wilhite launched Altspace in Redwood City. In the same year Second Life's original inventor Philip Rosedale started High Fidelity in San Francisco.

The media were mostly emphasizing the devices to "consume" virtual reality (either for fun or for work), not the tools that helped designers to create their own virtual world. The main platforms for virtual-reality creators were sold by veterans of the gaming world who had been offering engines to create 3D games for a decade or more: Unreal Engine 4 (North Carolina, 1998), Razer OSVR or Open Source Virtual Reality (San Diego, 1998), EON Reality (Sweden, 1998), Worldviz (Santa Barbara, 2002), Unity 5 (San Francisco, 2005), as well as Autodesk's Stingray (2015), built around the Bitsquid technology that Autodesk acquired in 2014.

Virtual Reality was one of the factors triggering a revolution in human-machine interfaces. Israeli-based Lumus offered a see-through display for augmented reality. Survios, founded in Los Angeles in 2013, an offshoot of the University of Southern California's Mixed Reality Lab, offered an immersive headset à la Oculus that was also capable of tracking the user's physical movements à la Kinect. Various versions of "optical touch" turned every object into an input device. Zhen Liu, a Chinese-born graduate from Harbin's Institute of Technology, introduced in 2013 in Singapore Touchjet Pond, that turned every surface into a touch-screen. Israeli-based Lumio turned any surface into a keyboard by tracking the movement of the fingers on a projection. Measuring neural activity became more affordable and led to wearables that could determine one's state of mind, from South Korea's SOSO (tested in schools to determine children's concentration) to Israel's ElMindA.

Wearable Computing

In 2011 Los Altos-based WIMM Labs (founded in 2009 by former Intel executive Dave Mooring and acquired in 2013 by Google) introduced the Android-based Wimm One smartwatch. 2012 and 2013 saw the debut of mass-market smartwatches such as the Samsung Galaxy Gear and the Sony SmartWatch, both powered by Android, and the Pebble smartwatch, running its own operating system but capable of communicating with both Android and iOS apps. The latter, introduced by Palo Alto-based Eric Migicovsky's garage startup, set a new record ($10 million) in Kickstarter funding. A similar feat was achieved later that year by Laurent LePen's Omate for its TrueSmart smartwatch (LePen was based in China but the company was based in Mountain View). In 2014 Google introduced the Android Wear platform. The first smartwatches based on Wear were Motorola's Moto 360 (2014), Sony's Smartwatch 3 (2014), LG's G Watch (2014) and Samsung's Gear Live (2014). Apple introduced its Apple Watch in April 2015, and this quickly became the bestselling smartwatch in the world.

Wearable devices posed a challenge to high-tech companies because they involved issues more related to fashion than to technology. Hence San Francisco-based Fitbit, founded in 2007 by James Park and Eric Friedman, maker of the Tracker, partnered with Tory Burch, a boutique specializing in women's designer apparel, Google partnered with industrial designer Isabelle Olsson for Google Glass, and Intel partnered with retail chain Opening Ceremony, founded in 2002 in New York by fashion specialists and Berkeley-graduates Carol Lim and Humberto Leon. Apple hired Angela Ahrendts, former chief executive of iconic luxury British retailer Burberry.

In 2016 Snapchat introduced its Spectacles, that were simply a more limited version of Google Glass (10 seconds videos only) but much cheaper and with a more ordinary look, almost the counterbalance to Google Glass' alien-futuristic look.

Scientific progress too was introducing new variables. For example, in September 2010 a team led by Ali Javey from UC Berkeley unveiled an "electronic skin", a flexible and touch-sensitive film of superconductive nanowire transistors.

Fitbit had a virtually infinite number of competitors, from Misfit, founded in 2011 in San Francisco by Sonny Vu and Sridhar Iyengar, to Moov, founded in 2014 in Mountain View by Meng Li, Nikola Hu, Tony Yuan (offering a wearable band and a voice app to coach users).

In 2016 SRI International spun off Superflex, headed by Rich Mahoney, focusing on "wearable robotics" for helping the disabled and the elderly, DARPA's "Warrior Web" program to enhance soldier performance).

In 2016 Berkeley-based BioBeats launched an app that took data from several existing wearables and used machine-learning algorithms to deliver advice to the user's smartphone. The machine-learning algorithm acted as a coach dedicated to maximize the user's health.

Naked founded in 2015 in San Francisco by Farhad Farahbakhshian, developed a "home body scanner", a 3D scanner that looked like a mirror and provided data about the body.

Ubiquitous Computing

The 2000s were bringing back the hardware. The biggest revolution of the 2000s may not have been the Internet (which has been hijacked by the likes of Google and Facebook to become an advertising platform) but the sensor revolution. Thanks to progress in micro-electronics, batteries and wireless connectivity, sensors had become orders of magnitude cheaper and thickly networked. Sensors were opening virtually infinite horizons to a new generation of applications. Wearable computing, self-driving cars, embedded nanotechnology, robots and so forth were the "real thing". By comparison, social media were simply entertainment, that are replacing late-night clubs and bars. There was a reason that they were called "social" and not "industrial"...

Bendable Gadgets

The flat panel display was slowly being replaced by the flexible display. In 1974 Xerox PARC had invented the "electronic paper": Nicholas Sheridon produced the "Gyricon", the first flexible e-paper display. But real progress began only after the introduction of the organic light-emitting diode (OLED), invented in 1987 by Hong Kong-born Ching Tang at Eastman Kodak. In 2006 Philips had introduced the first rollable display, and in 2008 Nokia had demonstrated a flexible OLED display for mobile phones (the Morph). Also in 2008 German-based Plastic Logic (founded in 2000 by Henning Sirringhaus at Cambridge University to make plastic electronics) had announced a bendable display, although it was never released. In 2010 Japan's Sony had demonstrated a rollable OLED display. After so many promises, the bendable display became a reality in 2013 when South Korea's Samsung first demonstrated an

AMOLED bendable color screen and then introduced the world's first mobile phone with flexible display, the Galaxy Round. Also in 2013 Intel, Plastic Logic and Queen's University in Canada built the tablet computer PaperTab with a plastic flexible display. In 2016 South Korea's LG demonstrated an OLED bendable color screen that could be rolled up like a piece of paper, and Polyera, founded by Phil Inagaki in 2005 at Princeton University to develop flexible transistors, introduced the Wove bendable smartwatch.

3D Printing

The 2010s saw some consolidation in the field of 3D printers: Stratasys acquired Objet in 2011 and MakerBot in 2013; and 3D Systems, that had already acquired DTM in 2001, acquired BitsFromBytes in 2010 and Z Corp in 2012.

The decade finally witnessed the long-overdue boom of 3D printing technology. The field had certainly been hampered by the multitude of patents. Until 2009 it was difficult for anyone, except the original companies, to make 3D printers. After the open-source RepRap started, several startups launched kits so that individuals could create their own RepRap 3D printer in the garage. When a major Stratasys patent related to the FDM technique expired in 2009, FDM went open-source, and hundreds of FDM machines flooded the market. Patents for SLA and SLS technologies expired in 2014, and caused a similar gold rush in 3D printing. Finally, the Bay Area started paying attention. In 2013 WobbleWorks, founded in 2010 in San Jose by MIT Media Lab's alumnus Peter Dilworth and Maxwell Bogue, launched the 3Doodler, a 3D printing pen based on FDM that allowed users to create objects in mid-air. In 2013 Formlabs (an MIT-spinoff founded by Maxim Lobovsky, Natan Linder and David Cranor) introduced a stereolithography 3D printer for the desktop. In 2014 New Matter, started in Los Angeles by Caltech scientist Steve Schell under the aegis of incubator Idealab (i.e. serial entrepreneur Bill Gross) and funded on IndieGoGo, introduced a 3D printer for the home and school market, the MOD-t (another FDM printer). In 2015 Carbon3D, a spinoff of the University of North Carolina that had relocated to Redwood City, unveiled a 3D printing process named Continuous Liquid Interface Production (CLIP), a kind of liquid-based stereolithography (SLA), that improved the printing speed. Around the world the number of startups multiplied rapidly. In 2016 Hewlett Packard entered the fray with its Multi Jet Fusion, that used technology invented by Loughborough University in Britain.

3D printing was "democratizing" product manufacturing, but the world still needed to democratize product design. Two Autodesk alumni, Evi Meyer and Erik Sapir, founded uMake in 2014 in San Francisco to offer a mobile alternative to Autodesk's 3D-design tools. In 2015 Autodesk added a cloud-based service for makers to design 3D objects, coupled with a venture fund to invest in the boldest ideas. In 2015 Rita Wong in San Francisco launched Valsfer, a social-networking platform to connect designers and manufacturers.

When 3D printing met wearable technology, a whole new horizon of applications opened up. In 2010 Dutch fashion designer Iris van Herpen pioneered 3D-printed fashion. Until 2014 the idea was mainly exploited by provocative artists such as New York-based Chinese-born artist Xuedi Chen, who 3D-printed "disappearing" lingerie (that revelead more and more of her naked body as she was active online), and Dutch designer Borre Akkersdijk, who 3D-printed garments with embedded electronics. In 2012 Wisconsin-based student Bryan Cera had even 3D-printed a wearable cell phone that could be worn like a glove. In 2014 New York-based architect Francis Bitonti 3D-printed a nylon gown based on the Fibonacci series (and in 2015 even designed a digital jewelry collection). 2015 saw an avalanche of new applications. Christophe Guberan, Carlo Clopath and Skylar Tibbits from the MIT 3D printed a "reactive" shoe that changes shape dynamically to provide maximum comfort. Vancouver-based Wiivv, founded by Shamil Hargovan and Louis-Victor Jadavji, launched its service of custom 3D printed insoles. New Balance 3D printed a high-performance running shoe. London designer Julian Hakes 3D-printed shoes for Olympic gold medal winner Amy Williams. Italian designer Paola Tognazzi 3D-printed garments that changed dynamically as the wearer moved. California-based Iranian-born designer Behnaz Farahi 3D-printed a "helmet" that changed shape in response to the wearer's brainwaves. Lidewij van Twillert from Delft University of Technology (Netherlands) 3D printed lingerie, and Shanghai-based Iranian-born designer Nasim Sehat 3D printed extravagant eyewear. 3D printing was reinventing the tailor in the digital age.

Big Data

The first companies to deal successfully with "big data" were probably the big two of the 2000s: Google and Facebook. It was becoming more and more apparent that their key contributions to technology were not so much the little features added here and there but the capability to manage in real time an explosive amount of data.

A Facebook team led by Avinash Lakshman and Prashant Malik developed Cassandra, leveraging technology from Amazon and Google, to solve Facebook's data management problems. Facebook gifted it to the open-source Apache community in 2008. DataStax, founded in 2010 in Santa Clara by Jonathan Ellis and Matt Pfeil, took Cassandra and turned it into a mission-critical database management system capable of competing with Oracle, the field's superpower.

A Google team led by Jeff Dean and Sanjay Ghemawat (in about 2004) developed the parallel, distributed algorithm MapReduce to provide massive scalability across a multitude of servers, a real-life problem for a company managing billions of search queries and other user interactions. In 2005 Doug Cutting, a Yahoo! engineer, and Mike Cafarella implemented a MapReduce service and a distributed file system (HDFS), collectively known since 2006 as Hadoop, for storage and processing of large datasets on clusters of servers. Hadoop was used internally by Yahoo! and eventually became another Apache open-source framework. The first startups to graft SQL onto Hadoop were Cloudera, formed in 2008 in Palo Alto by three engineers from Google, Yahoo! and Facebook (Christophe Bisciglia, Amr Awadallah and Jeff Hammerbacher) and later joined by Doug Cutting himself (Cloudera was acquired by Intel in 2014); and Hadapt, founded in 2011 in Boston by Yale students Daniel Abadi, Kamil Bajda-Pawlikowski and Justin Borgman. Other Hadoop-based startups included Qubole, founded in 2011 in Mountain View, by two Facebook engineers, Ashish Thusoo and Joydeep Sen Sarma; and Platfora, founded in 2011 in San Mateo by Ben Werther. Qubole offered a cloud-based version of Apache Hive, the project that the founders ran at Facebook (since 2007) and that was made open-source in 2008. Hive sat on top of Hadoop for providing data analysis and SQL-like query.

Meanwhile, Google developed its own "big data" service, Dremel, announced in 2010 (but used internally since 2006). The difference between Hadoop and Dremel was simple: Hadoop processed data in batch mode, Dremel did it in real time. Dremel was designed to query extremely large datasets on the fly. Following what Amazon had done with its cloud service, Google opened its BigQuery service, a commercial version of Dremel, to the public in 2012, selling storage and analytics at a price per gigabyte. Users of the service could analyze datasets using SQL-like queries. Dremel's project leader Theo Vassilakis went on to found Metanautix with a Facebook engineer, Apostolos Lerios, in 2012 in Palo Alto.

At the same time that it disclosed Dremel, Google published two more papers that shed some light on its internal technologies for handling big data. Caffeine (2009) was about building the index for the search engine. The other one (2010) was about Pregel, a "graph database" capable of fault-tolerant parallel processing of graphs; the idea being that graphs were becoming more and more pervasive and important (the Web itself is a graph and, of course, so are the relationships created by social media). MapReduce not being good enough for graph algorithms, and the existing parallel graph software not being fault tolerance, Google proceeded to create its own. Google's Pregel, largely the creature of Grzegorz Czajkowski, used the Bulk Synchronous Parallel model of distributed computation introduced by Leslie Valiant at Harvard (eventually codified in 1990). The Apache open-source community came up with their own variation on the same model, the Giraph project.

The open-source project Apache Mesos, inspired by the Borg system developed at Google by John Wilkes since 2004 to manage Google's own data centers, was conceived at UC Berkeley to manage large distributed pools of computers and was used and refined at Twitter. In 2014 in San Francisco a veteran of Twitter and Airbnb, Florian Leibert, founded Mesosphere to commercialize Mesos. Meanwhile at Google the old project Borg evolved into Omega,

Apache Spark, a project started in 2009 by Matei Zaharia at UC Berkeley, was a platform for large-scale data processing. Zaharia later founded his own company, Databricks, but the project survived and in fact grew. In 2015 IBM pledged 3,500 researchers to Apache Spark while open-sourcing its own SystemML machine-learning technology.

The old field of "business intelligence" kept mutating, or at least changing name. As "data mining" and "data analytics" became obsolete terms, a new one was coined: "data science". For example, Looker Data Sciences, founded in 2012 in Santa Cruz by Lloyd Tabb and Ben Porterfield, provided business-intelligence tool to dig into big data and make sense of them. At that point "big data" were mostly stored on high-performance data warehouses such as Amazon Redshift (2013, powered by technology acquired from ParAccel), Google BigQuery (2012), HP Vertica (built on top of Hadoop), IBM Netezza, and Teradata.

The world actually didn't have enough data, particularly from the developing world, a fact that skewed research and hampered remedies to problems. Premise, founded in 2012 in San Francisco by MetaMarkets' co-founder David Soloff and MetaMarkets' chief scientist Joe Reisinger, harnessed the power of the crowd to collect economic data around the world, provided in real-time from ordinary individuals armed with smartphones.

Beyond the Cloud

The biggest outside threat to Google and Apple was probably Amazon. On the surface the Seattle-based rival was simply a huge retailer (in 2014 carrying more than 200 million items sold by over two million third-party vendors), and mainly famous (or infamous) for destroying the business of bookstores, but deeper down Amazon was an extremely sophisticated technology company that pioneered online customer reviews and ratings, that in 2006 introduced pay-as-you-go cloud computing (later used by the likes of Instagram, Pinterest and Spotify), that in 2007 turned ebook readers into commodities, that in the 2010s turned its colossal PHX6 fulfilment center at Phoenix (Arizona) into an automated, robot-intensive facility (while making the whole supply chain available to other merchants as well), and that was rapidly moving online business towards same-day delivery and mobile shopping.

New methods for software development made it easier for startups to create distributed applications.

Introduced in 2008 and based on open-source Xen technology, Amazon's Elastic Compute Cloud (EC2) provided a self-service portal for developers to rent their own virtual private servers on which to run their own applications.

Containers were a legacy of the Unix operating system (SUN's Solaris edition of 2004, an evolution of Bill Joy's "chroot" command incorporated into Berkeley Unix in 1982). An application run within a container is isolated from the hardware platform. If it sounds like virtualization, that's because they are closely related. Containers are a faster way to implement virtual machines and a better way to optimize hardware resources. The net result for the software developer is the same: application portability across platforms. In 2008 Solomon Hykes and Sebastien Pahl founded DotCloud (later Decker) in San Francisco to provide an open-source platform based on containers that quickly built an entire community of developers. Google then legitimized the field when it introduced Kubernetes to manage clusters of containers.

The Nebula project, started in 2008 by Ray O'Brien at NASA Ames in Mountain View, evolved in 2010 into an open-source cloud platform, OpenStack, technically a joint venture with Texas-based cloud service Rackspace (a 1998 offshoot of San Antonio's Trinity University). Rackspace donated the software behind OpenStack's Swift storage service, and in 2011 acquired Anso Labs, the San Francisco-based company that maintained Nasa's Nebula cloud (and that developed the Nova computer). In 2012 some of Anso Labs' original team (including former NASA Ames scientists Chris Kemp and Devin Carlen) left RackSpace and founded Nebula in Mountain View. By 2015 more than 500 companies had joined OpenStack, basically an open-source alternative to Amazon's and VMware's cloud services.

The new generation of middleware was represented by platforms like Anypoint, introduced in 2013 by MuleSoft, a company started in 2006 in San Francisco by Ross Mason and Dave Rosenberg. It connected and integrated software as a service (SaaS) on the cloud with legacy databases and applications running on personal devices: "any application, any data source, any device, any API".

In 2015 Cisco acquired cloud-security provider OpenDNS, founded in 2006 by David Ulevitch in San Francisco (who in 2001 in Saint Louis had launched the free DNS management service EveryDNS).

Jyoti Bansal founded AppDynamics (in 2008 in San Francisco) to improve performance of cloud-based applications, which were typically heavily distributed (the startup would become a unicorn in 2015).

Notice that peer-to-peer, revitalized by the blockchain mechanism, was competing with cloud computing to introduce collectivization in cyberspace. The two models were wildly different, but both were removing the data from the individual's home computer and relocating the data somewhere else: either on a distributed network of participants or on a distributed network of corporate computers. Peer-to-peer computing had generated a lot of philosophical, sociological and political discussion by the independents who had created it and were using it. Cloud computing was less naturally analyzed and discussed, because it mostly belonged to governments and corporations, its "architects" mostly unknown.

Shopping Experience

With the proliferation of online merchants, there arose a need for simplifying the online shopping experience. For example, Wish.com launched in San Francisco by ContextLogic, a company founded in 2010 by former Google engineer Peter Szulczewski and by former Yahoo engineer Danny Zhang, was a mobile commerce platform that aimed at replicating online the shopping experience of the shopping mall.

Biotech

In 2000 the University of California had started a program called "California Institute for Quantitative Biosciences", or QB3, to help Berkeley, San Francisco and Santa Cruz researchers become entrepreneurs. The program became particularly successful in the life sciences. At the same time in 2012, pioneered at UC Berkeley by Jennifer Doudna's laboratory and at Emmanuelle Charpentier's laboratory in Sweden,, a new technique to edit genomes stole the limelight in biotechnology. Discovered as an adaptive immune system in bacteria for protection against invading viruses, CRISPR-cas9 was seen by Jennifer Doudna's group as a way to target and edit a genome. CRISPRs (Clustered Regularly Interspaced Short Palindromic Repeats) are sections of DNA that are often associated with genes that code for proteins (the genes are then called Cas, short for "CRISPR-associated"). These CRISPR-Cas systems offer a faster and cheaper way to edit genomes than the ZFN (Zinc Finger Nuclease) method, pretty much exclusively owned by Sangamo Biosciences, and the TALEN method invented in 2011 by Dan Voytas of the University of Minnesota and by Adam Bogdanove of Iowa State Univ (and owned since 2011 by the French company Cellectis and Minnesota-based Recombinetics, co-founded by Voytas). CRISPR-Cas9 startups, offering "genome-editing platforms", started popping up everywhere. The first one, in 2011, was Rachel Haurwitz's and Martin Jinek's Caribou Biosciences, a spinoff of Doudna's lab at UC Berkeley, but within a few years similar startups spread from London (CRISPR

Therapeutics, founded in 2013) to Boston (Editas Medicine, a 2013 spin-off of the Broad Institute, and Intellia Therapeutics, founded in 2014 by Caribou itself). CRISPR represented the fourth generation of genetic "cut and paste" technology after recombinant DNA, ZFN and TALEN.

The CRISPR technique made it a lot easier, faster and cheaper for scientists to change, delete and replace genes (i.e. rewrite the genomes) in any form of life, including humans. The first results, though, were limited to plant biology, and mostly came from Asia. In 2014 Gao Caixia in China created a strain of wheat that was fully resistant to powdery mildew. This experiment was followed by genetic engineering of tomatoes, soybeans, rice and potatoes. In 2015 Moritoshi Sato discovered a light-sensitive Cas9 nuclease that further improved the CRISPR technique, making it more precise and reliable. In 2015 Josiah Zayner, founder of the Open Discovery Institute in Burlingame, launched a crowdfunding campaign to fund a DIY CRISPR kit for hobbyists.

In 2013 Google funded Calico and hired Arthur Levinson, a former Genentech executive, to run it. Calico's first project was a joint venture with pharmaceutical firm AbbVie to focus on diseases that affect the elderly.

Corvus Pharmaceuticals was founded in 2014 in Burlingame by biopharmaceutical veterans Richard Miller and Joseph Buggy to make oral drugs that would help the immune system fight cancer.

This was the beginning of the age of gene therapy. Audentes Therapeutics was founded in 2012 in San Francisco (by health-care industry veterans Matt Patterson and Thomas Schuetz) to make gene-therapy products for patients who suffer from life-threatening diseases which are probably caused by genetic defects (in 2015 it also acquired Cardiogen, founded in 2014 by Louis Lange, which specifically focused on inherited cardiac arrhythmias via a technique developed in Italy by Silvia Priori).

In 2016 (according to AngelList) the Bay Area had more biotech startups than the rest of the USA combined, which basically meant about 30% of the world's startups. The history of biotech repeated the script of computer technology: the technology was invented somewhere else, and an industry dominated by European and East Coast multinationals ended up migrating to the Bay Area. The double-helical structure of DNA was discovered in Britain (by Francis Crick and James Watson), and the Human Genome Project was largely an East Coast enterprise. The big pharmaceutical companies were mostly in Europe (Novartis and Roche in Switzerland, GlaxoSmithKline and AstraZeneca in Britain, Bayer in Germany) or on the East Coast (Pfizer and Bristol-Myers Squibb in New York, and Merck, Johnson & Johnson, Wyeth, Sanofi and Organon in New Jersey). When in 1973 Stanford University's Stanley Cohen and UC San Francisco's Herbert Boyer discovered how to make "recombinant DNA"

(DNA made in a lab), the scientific community viewed it as an exciting experiment, but not many understood that it would create a whole new industry. In 1976 a young venture capitalist, Robert Swanson, convinced Herbert Boyer to form Genentech, and the rest is history: On the East Coast, the MIT began spawning Boston-based startups like Integrated Genetics, also founded in 1981. The other success story of the 1980s was Amgen in Los Angeles, founded in 1980. The pharmaceutical corporations were based around New Jersey and New York, and MIT and Harvard were world-class institutions in chemistry, engineering and biology; but nonetheless the biotech industry boomed in California. Obviously the spirit of risk-taking and "think different" was more important than money and number of scientists. Big companies were very good at marketing a biomedical product, but not very good at coming up with new ideas in a new technology. Genentech also set an important precedent: it created a new idea, but then partnered with a giant corporation to market that idea to the world. To be fair, there were many startups in the Boston area. George Church alone (the director of Harvard's Personal Genome Project) co-founded Knome, Alacris, AbVitro, Pathogenica, Veritas Genetics, Joule, Gen9, Editas, Egenesis, enEvolv, WarpDrive...

In the 1990s another Bay Area startup, Gilead Sciences, succeeded quietly thanks to a different model. Riordan switched business in 1991 to the development of antiviral drugs, realizing the enormous potential of the field. Gilead lost money until 2003, but in 1999 Roche started selling the anti-influenza drug Tamiflu (Oseltamivir), a Gilead invention, and in 2005 the US government requested emergency funding to fight an influenza pandemic and 15% of these funds were spent to buy Tamiflu. It probably helped that Gilean's board included politicians who were close to the Bush administration, and that in 2005 Gilead's former chairman Donald Rumsfeld was a minister in the US government. A second Gilead success was Tenofovir (better known as Viread), an anti-AIDS drug that the FDA approved in 2001. Gilead was blessed with relatively quick approval of its drugs by the government during that period, but there had been business genius in focusing on fighting viruses (harder than fighting bacteria) to treat chronic and global diseases (AIDS, hepatitis C and the flu). In 2009 Gilead was ranked one of the fastest growing companies by Fortune magazine, and in 2013 Gilead hit the market with another hit, Sovaldi (Sofosbuvir), for the treatment of hepatitis C, one of the most expensive drugs of all times. In 2015 Gilead was the largest biotech company, with a market value of $150 billion, larger than more established "big pharma" multinationals such as GlaxoSmithKline, AstraZeneca and Bristol-Myers Squibb.

By the 2010s biotech was one of the most funded businesses in the Bay Area, and several incubators were born. Besides QB3, there were Berkeley Biolabs (founded in 2014 by Jayaranjan Anthonypillai), IndieBio (an emanation of SOSVentures launched in 2014 in Ireland), as well as one of Bayer's CoLaborators and one of Johnson & Johnson's JLabs. The main Bay Area centers for biotech were South San Francisco (where Genentech was born in 1976), Emeryville (between Oakland and Berkeley, a natural location for UC Berkeley spinoffs), the Mission Bay district of San Francisco (where a new medical campus of UC San Francisco opened in 2003), and Silicon Valley (notably Affymetrix, the startup that invented the "DNA chip", and 23andMe, the startup that bootstrapped the genomics industry).

In the first half of 2015 the Bay Area witnessed the biggest bubble in biotech since the 1990s, with a record influx of venture capital for biotech startups. But it wasn't only the Bay Area. The biotech bubble was all over the USA. Among the star attractions of 2015 were Denali Therapeutics (San Francisco, neurodegenerative diseases), Melinta Therapeutics (New Haven, antibiotics discovery), CytomX Therapeutics (Santa Barbara, tumor-targeting antibodies), Regenexbio (Maryland, gene therapy), Dimension Therapeutics (Boston) and Voyager Therapeutics (Boston). The year 2015 was also a record year for mergers and acquisitions in biotech, just like the previous year had been a record year for IPOs (74 IPOs in one year).

The biotech boom was fueled by a simple statistical data: in the USA there were 80 million "baby boomers" about to retire over the next 20 years, presumably causing a boom in health care. There was also a general level of enthusiasm for the "miracle drugs" being developed or introduced by big pharmaceutical companies: drugs to reduce cholesterol, for cancer treatment, to improve the cognitive skills of elderly people afflicted by dementia, etc (e.g. the cholesterol-lowering drug Lipitor, introduced in 1996 by Pfizer, which in 2012 was accounting for more revenues than the GDP of Tanzania). However, biotech was a completely different business than information technology. First of all, a biotech startup needed much closer ties to the scientific community. While software was mostly about finding an app that went viral, and hardware was mostly about packing more transistors on a chip, biotech was still very much about productizing scientific discoveries. While software startups were being founded by younger and younger engineers, biotech was still such a complex business that typical startups were founded by more experienced people, and it was not unusual to see a partnership between an academic researcher and a venture capitalist. Thousands of new software apps and gadgets were launched every year, but instead very few new drugs were approved every year by the FDA, way less than 100. A biotech venture was a complex project that required skills in chemistry, biology, engineering, marketing, and even skills in dealing with the government agency that approved drugs (the FDA) and with the big pharmaceutical companies that had the power to market new drugs worldwide. Compared with software, the cost to develop a new biotech "product" was colossal. The clinical study alone could easily cost ten times more than the development of a software application, and last many years before receiving government approval. In general, the risk for the biotech industry was much higher than the risk for the computer industry. But the payback could be astronomical: a new drug could generate billions of dollars of revenues for a long time.

Personal genomics was still riding high. The Human Genome Project had cost an estimated $2.7 billion over a decade. In 2009 the cost of Illumina's genome sequencing was $48,000 and by the end of that year only about 100 human genomes had been sequenced. By 2015 the four big genome-sequencing services, namely 23andMe, Generations Network's AncestryDNA (launched in October 2007), National Geographic's Genographic Project (launched in 2005) and Family Tree DNA (that had acquired the technology from the German company DNA-Fingerprint), had already genotyped millions of people. 23andMe genotyped its first customer in November of 2007, and genotyped its millionth customer in June 2015. 23andme's service was now costing only $200. By then the gene-sequencing market was dominated by three companies: San Diego-based Illumina (that owned about 70% of the market), Silicon Valley-based Applied Biosystems (acquired in 2014 by Thermo Fisher Scientific), and 454 Corporation (founded by Jonathan Rothberg in 1999 in Connecticut and acquired by Roche in 2007).

As their machines got cheaper, the product sold to the customers also get cheaper. However, the results of those DNA tests rarely included comprehensive reports. Only a few of these "personal-genomic" startups generated reports that a health-care specialist could use to make real predictions and prescriptions. The leader in "actionable" reports was still Boston-base Knome (acquired by Utah-based Tute Genomics), that had been the first startup to introduce a commercial human genome sequencing in 2007, followed by Illumina itself, but they charged more than $10,000 for the "actionable" reports. In 2015 Maryland-based Veritas Genetics, founded in 2014 by George Church, the director of Harvard's Personal Genome Project, announced a package that included both "sequencing" and "interpretation" of the genome at an affordable price. In 2016 Las Vegas-based Sure Genomics, founded in 2014 by people who had no background in biological sciences, announced a method for its customers to perform the tests at home with a single saliva test and receive in the mail an actionable report. Helix, a 2015 San Francisco-based Illumina spinoff, was working on the first "app store" for genetic information, so that customers of a gene sequencing service could find useful "apps" to analyze their DNA report ((a model that mimics Apple's App Store). Oxford Nanopore (founded in 2005 by a professor of Chemical Biology at the University of Oxford, Hagan Bayley) also began testing the first portable gene-sequencer, called Minion, although it worked only for small genomes (e.g., the ebola virus).

The goal of genomics was, ultimately, to extend human life, i.e. longevity. In 2013 Google funded Calico (which got nicknamed "Google's longevity lab" in Silicon Valley) and hired Arthur Levinson, a former Genentech executive to run it. Levinson hired Cynthia Kenyon, the UC San Francisco biologist (who in 1993 discovered that removing a gene doubled the lifespan of worms and that injections of sugar shortened their lifespan), and Shelley Buffenstein, a specialist at the University of Texas in animals with exceptionally long lifespans.

The Human Genome Project had been a big success and had delivered a "blueprint" of how the human software works; but we are all different: there are genetic variations between person and person. Those genetic variations can make the difference between living a long and healthy life and dying at a young age of a fatal disease. The way to study "genetic variation" was to collect genetic data about as many people as possible, compare their genes, and compare genetic variations with health. For this purpose a number of universities and agencies set up programs that mixed big data, crowd-sourcing and biotech: the Personal Genome Project (launched in 2005 by George Church at Harvard), UK Biobank (launched in 2006 in Britain), the 1000Genomes project (launched in 2008 by David Altshuler of the Broad Institute in Boston), and DNA.land (launched in 2015 by Yaniv Erlich at the New York Genome Center). The crowdsourcing experiment then migrated to the West Coast, where people started talking about the "Internet of DNA" or "Internet of Living Beings". In 2013 David Haussler at the University of California in Santa Cruz partnered with David Altshuler to create to set up the Global Alliance for Genomics and Health, a peer-to-peer network of scientists and volunteers to work together on understanding genetic variations. In 2014 Google's Life Sciences division (later renamed Verily) launched Baseline, a project to provide a definition of what "healthy" means in genetic terms.

Genomics had been getting cheaper thanks to quantum leaps in laboratory automation: Affymax (later renamed Affymetrix) had introduced the first "DNA chip" in 1994 and Wilhelm Ansorge had squeezed the whole human genome on a microarray in 2002. In the mid-2010s cloud-based biotech was attempting to completely eliminate the laboratory for the customer. Transcriptic, founded by Duke University graduate Max Hodak in 2012 in Palo Alto, conducted laboratory tests using robots on behalf of customers who could be located anywhere in the world.

Meanwhile, DNA synthesis (i.e. "printing" DNA) was being revolutionized by the combined forces of miniaturization, automation and software. Scientists needed raw materials called oligonucleotides in order to perform "rapid prototyping" in polymerase chain reaction (PCR) or gene sequencing. Twist Bioscience, founded in 2013 in San Francisco by Agilent's veteran Emily Leproust, by Complete Genomics's hardware engineer Bill Banyai and by Bill Peck (who had worked at both Complete Genomics and Agilent), aimed at producing synthetic DNA on a massive scale using a silicon-based method to make oligos. In 2016 Twist acquired Israel's Genome Compiler and their technology to design genes in order to allow customers to design genes and then print DNA on demand.

Twist's cofounder Emily Leproust

These new biotechnologies were even used to create new materials. Refactored Materials (later renamed Bolt Threads), a 2009 spinoff of UC San Francisco (scientists Dan Widmaier, David Breslauer and Ethan Mirsky) manipulated bacteria to manufacture spider silk, stronger than steel but very light, that could be used for making clothes. Zymergen, founded in 2013 in Emeryville by two Amyris alumni, Jed Dean and Zach Serber, had discovered a way to insert DNA into bacteria, and to create microbes that could create new materials.

Ginkgo Bioworks, founded in 2008 in Boston by MIT's synthetic biology pioneer (and iGem co-founder) Tom Knight with other MIT alumni (Jason Kelly, Reshma Shetty, Barry Canton, and Austin Che), called itself "the world's first organism-engineering foundry". A foundry is usually a place where semiconductor chips are manufactured on behalf of companies like Intel. Ginkgo Bioworks opened a "foundry" to make living organisms: the customer sent the design, and Ginkgo delivered the organism (to make, for example, synthetic perfumes, cosmetics and foods). Both Zymergen and Ginkgo aim at becoming biotech factories for manufacturers of all sorts of consumer goods.

What was still needed was the equivalent of Computer-Aided Design (CAD) for synthetic biology. In 2010 Chris Anderson at UC Berkeley delivered Clotho, an open-source "bioCAD" platform to design organisms, and in 2014 Autodesk launched Project Cyborg, a cloud-based platform of design tools for DNA designers.

DNA is a natural substance for computing because it uses the genetic code, a code that obeys strict rules of logic. In 1994 Leonard Adleman at the University of Southern California (the same scientist who had coined the expression "computer virus" and whose student Fred Cohen had unleashed the world's first computer virus) had found a way to encode a string of data in the sequence of nucleotides and then used the chemical properties of DNA to perform a calculation. In other words, he had built a "DNA computer". In 1995 Richard Lipton at Princeton University had proved that a DNA computer could solve some mathematical problems faster than electronic computers. In fact, a few months later two of Lipton's students, Dan Boneh and Chris Dunworth, had shown that a DNA computer could break the data encryption system developed by the National Security Agency (NSA) of the USA. The first practical DNA computer was unveiled in 2002 and used for gene analysis by Olympus in Japan (a collaboration with Akira Suyama's team of the University of Tokyo), but not much progress was achieved in the following years until in 2013 Drew Endy at Stanford unveiled a biocomputer operating inside a living cell. This computer could only answer "true/false", but the question was important: it could detect a disease that could not be detected with ordinary medical equipment. A biocomputer is slow but it can operated in places where electronics cannot be deployed: anywhere inside the human body.

Another biotechnology became popular in the 2010s. Living beings are self-assembling structures. They are not built in a factory: they assemble themselves, cell by cell. DNA is an excellent "construction material" because it constructs billions of living organisms every single day. Nadrian Seeman of New York University (who had written about constructing 3D structures from DNA since the 1980s) and Paul Rothemund of CalTech (who proved that DNA can be programmed to form larger DNA structures) were the pioneers of what came to be called "DNA origami". Biologists started using DNA to "design" robots in the same way that architects use software to design objects. In 2012 two of George Church's students at Harvard University, Shawn Douglas and Ido Bachelet, developed nanorobots made of DNA with the intention that they could be programmed to target specific cells in the body, for example to seek out cancer cells and program them to self-destruct. Douglas moved to

UC San Francisco in 2012 and Bachelet to Bar-Ilan University in Israel, founding two important schools of DNA origami.

In 2012 George Church encoded his latest book into DNA. In 2013 Ewan Birney's team at the European Bioinformatics Institute encoded all 154 of Shakespeare's sonnets, an audio recording of Martin Luther King's famous speech "I Have a Dream", and a picture of their office in a string of DNA (a total of 739 kilobytes). In 2015 Sri Kosuri, a member of the Harvard team that had encoded Church's book into DNA, encoded a rock song by the band OK Go into DNA, the first music to be released on DNA. The storage ability of DNA is impressive: everything that human civilization has produced in writing (50 billion megabytes of text) can be stored in the DNA of the palm of your hand.

Scientific progress was not slowing down at all. In 2015 Chinese Scientists led by Junjiu Huang at Sun Yat-sen University in Guangzhou announced that they had genetically modified human embryos.

Neurotech

The most active company in Artificial Intelligence was, by far, Google. At the end of 2013 Google purchased Boston Dynamics, founded in 1992 in Boston by MIT professor Marc Raibert to build a new generation of robots (never actually sold to the public). It was Google's eighth acquisition of a robotics-related company, and Andy Rubin was chosen to run Google's robotics research. In 2013 Google also purchased Redwood Robotics, a joint venture formed in 2012 by SRI International, Meka Robotics and Willow Garage.

In 2014 Google acquired British-based Artificial-Intelligence company DeepMind, founded in 2011 by former game developer Demis Hassabis.

Thanks to progress in neural networks, the 2010s witnessed a resurgence of investment in Artificial Intelligence. Pretty much all the major players acquired some startup operating in this space: Amazon acquired Boston-based Kiva (2012); Yahoo acquired Mountain View-based LookFlow (2013); Google also acquired Industrial Robotics, Meka, Holomni, Bot & Dolly, DNNresearch, Schaft, a Japanese manufacturer of robots, and Boston Dynamics; Facebook acquired the Israeli company Face.com (2012), founded in 2007 by Yaniv Taigman, and used their technology to to develop the face-recognition feature DeepFace (that Facebook started rolling out in 2015) and Palo Alto-based Wet.ai (2015), that specialized in natural-language processing; Microsoft had Project Adam, Twitter acquired WhetLab in 2015, Salesforce acquired MetaMind in 2016; IBM acquired AlchemyAPI in 2015 and had the Watson project; In 2016 Intel purchased San Diego-based Nervana, founded in 2014 to make processors for deep learning, and fab-less computer vision chip-maker Movidius, founded in 2005 in San Mateo by Sean Mitchell and

David Moloney; Apple had Siri and acquired Perceptio and VocalIQ (a Cambridge University spinoff) in 2015, followed by Emotient in 2016.

In 2015 Yahoo's Flickr division introduced sophisticated auto-tagging and image-recognition features. Flicker was capable of identifying what (not only "who") was in a photograph, and then automatically categorize it. George Hinton, Yann Lecun, Andrew Ng and the other protagonists of "deep learning" became heroes or, better, prophets of the intelligent machines to come. Google hired Peter Norvig and George Hinton. Facebook hired Yann Lecun. Baidu in China hired Andrew Ng.

Silicon Valley startups included: Saffron Technology, founded in 1999 in Los Altos by Manuel Aparicio and Jim Fleming for decision support; Vicarious, founded in 2010 in San Francisco by Numenta's cofounder Dileep George to work on computer vision (one of the most secretive, backed by Peter Thiel, Mark Zuckerberg, Jeff Bezos, and Elon Musk); Wise.io, a Berkeley spin-off founded in 2012 by Joey Richards, Dan Starr, Henrik Brink, Joshua Bloom to commercialize the machine learning technology invented by Damian Eads, formerly at the Los Alamos National Laboratory; Viv Labs, founded in 2014 in San Jose by three former members of the Siri team (Adam Cheyer, Dag Kittlaus, and Chris Brigham), to work on an "intelligent" digital assistant; MetaMind, founded in 2014 in Palo Alto by Stanford graduate Richard Socher.

Petaluma-based GTFS (later renamed General Vision), founded in 1987 by Anne Menendez, introduced a 1,024-neuron chip, the NeuroMem CM1K chip, to solve pattern recognition problems.

Osaro, founded in 2015 in San Francisco by Derik Pridmore (who previously worked for Peter Thiel), worked on a form of machine learning known as deep reinforcement learning that promised to enable a robot to learn from trial-and error interactions with its environment.

MinHash, founded by Naren Chittar and Jayesh Govindarajan in 2014 in Palo Alto (and acquired in 2015 by Salesforce), developed a software to help gather online information to be used for marketing campaigns.

Google's acquisition of DNNresearch was particularly noteworthy because that startup was founded in 2012 by University of Toronto's professor Geoffrey Hinton and two of his graduate students, Alex Krizhevsky and Ilya Sutskever, the team responsible for the 2012 paper on deep learning that revolutionized the field of computer vision.

In 2015 Google gifted its deep-learning technology TensorFlow, the artificial brain behind its image search and speech recognition apps (replacing 2011's DistBelief), to the open-source world.

In 2016 SoundHound, founded in 2005 in Santa Clara by Stanford's voice-recognition expert Keyvan Mohajer, released the digital assistant Hound, whose voice-command user interface competed with Google Now, Apple Siri and the likes.

Bofen Technology, founded in Beijing by serial entrepreneur Jerry Yue (who had previously founded the ecommerce website Benlai.com), and relocated to Silicon Valley in 2016 as Brain, wanted to replace the traditional search engine with an intelligent assistant that, given the context, could find the most relevant information for the user.

More ambitious than the Silicon Valley crew was perhaps Narrative Science, founded in 2010 in Chicago by Kris Hammond, director of the University of Chicago's Artificial Intelligence Laboratory, Larry Birnbaum, and Stuart Frankel, a former DoubleClick executive. Narrative Science was the grandchild of Roger Schank's experiments in generating narratives, now trying to construct journalist-proof texts out of big data.

New York-based Wochit, founded in 2012 by two serial Israeli entrepreneurs (Dror Ginzberg and Ran Oz), created videos based on the text. In other words, you write the script and the artificial intelligence turns it into a video.

North Carolina-based Automated Insights' Wordsmith, designed by Cisco engineer Robbie Allen, was the most popular "news generator", used regularly in 2014 by the Associated Press to turn earnings reports into narratives that looked like written by professional writers.

Recognizing images was supposed to be Google's specialty but Google Goggles, introduced in 2010, had flopped (and was canceled in 2014). On the other hand, Los Angeles-based Image Searcher, founded in 2012 by Brad Folkens and Dominik Mazur, succeeded with their smartphone app CamFind. The secret was a team of hundreds in the Philippines that was frantically tagging the images submitted by users.

In 2016 Apple bought Emotient, a San Diego startup founded in 2012, that aimed to develop software for reading people's emotions based on facial expression. MetaMind, founded in 2014 in Palo Alto by Andrew Ng's student Richard Socher and acquired by Salesforce in 2016, worked on multitasking neural networks.

Deep Learning was all the rage in the 2010s after a Hinton algorithm dramatically lowered the error rate in recognizing images. Several platforms for deep learning were available as open-source software: Torch (New York University), Caffe (Pieter Abbeel's group at UC Berkeley), Theano (Univ of Montreal, Canada), Chainer (Preferred Networks, Japan), Tensor Flow (Google), etc. In 2016 two major applications of deep reinforcement learning were announced: Toyota's self-teaching cars and Google/DeepMind's AlphaGo, that beat a go/weichi master.

This was the era of the first "domestic" robots, like Luna, conceived in 2011 by RoboDynamics in Santa Monica, and Jibo, designed by Cynthia Breazeal, director of MIT Media Lab's Personal Robots group. Asia held the leadership in industrial robots: in 2014 Asia bought 139,300 industrial robots (more than half the world's total), of which 57,096 in China, 29,300 in Japan, 24,700 in Korea, compared with 26,200 in the USA. But attention was shifting to "service" robots, and in this field the Bay Area was rapidly surpassing Boston and Japan in innovation. Savioke, founded in 2013 in Sunnyvale by Willow Garage's cofounder Steve Cousins specialized in robots for customer service. Fellow Robots, founded by Marco Mascorro in Sunnyvale, was similarly focused on robots for retail assistance. Simbe, founded in 2014 in San Francisco, built a robot to check a store's shelves for items that were running out or were misplaced. Suitable Technologies, founded in Palo Alto by Willow Garage's cofounder Scott Hassan, sold a robot for videoconferencing. The robots of Unbounded Robotics (later Fetch Robotics), founded in 2014 in San Jose by Melonee Wise (an alumna of Willow Garage's PR2 project), carried out more sophisticated warehouse chores than the ones of Amazon Kiva's robots. In 2016 SoftBank announced that it was opening a store in Japan manned by its Pepper (first introduced in 2014, the result of a collaboration with France's Aldebaran that in 2008 had introduced the user-friendly Na robot). Roboterra, founded in 2014 in Sunnyvale by Yao Zhang and Yuan Zhou, targeted the educational market.

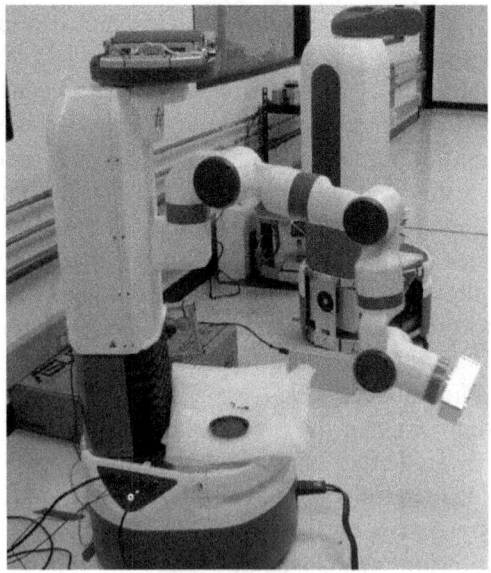

Fetch Robotics

Thanks to open-source components such as the ROS and to the collapse in sensor prices (after 2010 a Microsoft Kinect could do what an expensive laser scanner used to do), robotic startups were multiplying in the Bay Area. There had been three main poles: Willow Garage, that originated at least eight startups, SRI Intl, that originated at least four, and Otherlab, an independent research lab founded in 2009 in San Francisco by Saul Griffith and James McBride to experiment with new technologies.

The Willow Garage diaspora yielded Steve Cousins' Savioke; Scott Hassan's Suitable Technologies; Melonee Wise's Fetch Robotics; Jeff Gee's and Mirza Shah's Simbe Robotics; Radu Rusu's Open Perception; Aaron Edsinger's Redwood Robotics (acquired by Google in 2013); etc. SRI spawned Grabit and Intuitive Surgical. Otherlab incubated Kevin Albert's Pneubotics, working on metal-less "soft" robots (capable, for example, of handling food). In 2012 Kurt Konolige and Gary Bradski of Willow Garage founded Industrial Perception (IPI) in Palo Alto to build 3D-vision guided robots ("robots that can see").

While Google kept testing its self-driving car and Apple launched the top-secret "Project Titan" under Steve Zadesky, in 2015 Tesla updated the software on its electric cars with self-driving features, and in 2016 General Motors acquired Cruise Automation. This San Francisco-based startup, founded in 2013 by Kyle Vogt of Twitch.tv fame (who as an MIT student had worked on self-driving car projects) was developing a system for retrofitting cars with self-driving features. Similarly, in 2015 hacker George Hotz, who became famous in 2007 at the age of 17 for "unlocking" the iPhone and then worked at Vicarious, launched his own self-driving car startup, Comma.ai at San Francisco's "Crypto Castle", aiming to create a self-driving kit to turn existing cars into (quasi) self-driving cars. He demonstrated a prototype illegally in 2016 on a Silicon Valley highway

In 2015 Toyota invested $1 billion in the Toyota Research Institute, headed by Gill Pratt (formerly at DARPA and MIT), to conduct research on automated driving in Palo Alto and Boston.

The Sharing Economy

The "gift economy", about sharing content for free, rapidly evolved in something more lucrative and also based on the contribution of the masses: the "sharing economy", in which people make available to others under-utilized assets such as rooms and cars.

Airbnb, founded in 2008 in San Francisco by two alumni of the Rhode Island School of Design, Brian Chesky and Joe Gebbia, and by Nathan Blecharczyk, was the most famous of the bunch, offering rooms or houses for short stays in dozens of cities (600,000 rooms in 160 countries by mid 2014).

In 2007 Logan Green and John Zimmer debuted a computerized ridesharing service at Cornell University called Zimride. Relocating to San Francisco, in 2012 they launched a smartphone application called Lyft that allowed anybody to offer and order car rides. Sunil Paul launched SideCar, also in 2012, with the exact same business model (except that SideCar "matched" driver and passenger rather than simply "dispatching" a driver to a passenger).

In 2009 in the same city Travis Kalanick and Garrett Camp had launched a similar smartphone app, UberCab (later simply Uber), which initially was for limo drivers. Lyft democratized the concept and found a huge audience among ordinary people driving ordinary cars and among ordinary people going to ordinary places. In fact, the typical Lyft passenger was a social animal, ready to strike a conversation with the driver, whereas the typical Uber passenger was still viewing the driver the traditional chauffeur. By 2014 Lyft had spread to over 30 cities, and Uber had converted to Lyft's populist business plan, spreading to more than 230 cities in 50 countries and adding on average one city per week.

Startups like Airbnb and Uber turned a very physical business into a purely software business. For example, Uber combined Amazon's cloud service, Google's Maps service, Twilio's messaging service, SendGrip's email service and Braintrees' payment service and didn't own a single car, but by 2015 it became the biggest taxi company in the world. Similarly, Airbnb was the largest "hotel" chain in the world but didn't own a single hotel.

SnapGoods, founded in 2010 in New York by Ron Williams and John Goodwin, facilitated lending and borrowing household items from cameras to toasters.

The sharing economy was born during the Great Recession, when people were busy saving every penny they could, and the whole idea was ironically reminiscent of the way things worked in the old days in communist countries like the Soviet Union, when you simply flagged down cars going in your direction and offered money to be taken there.

A demonstration of how powerful the users could be in shaping a service came in 2013 when Google decided to acquire an Israeli company to replace its Google Maps service on smartphones. Freemap, founded in 2006 in Israel by Ehud Shabtai (and renamed Linqmap in 2008 when Uri Levine joined and later renamed Waze), was a community-based traffic and navigator application for smartphones that was able to provide live information about road and traffic conditions thanks to feedback from its users. Waze was inferring traffic conditions from the speed of its users, and it allowed users to report accidents and even police cars. Google Maps, the most popular mapping software of all times, was a static service, that relied on hired hands to doublecheck the accuracy of its maps. Waze was a highly dynamic service, capable of adapting to continuously changing circumstances. The difference was that Waze was driven by the users, whereas Maps was driven by a Google team.

Jack Conte (a musician, disc-jockey and filmmaker) and Sam Yarn founded Patreon in 2013 in San Francisco, a crowd-funding platform for artists and musicians where people could support their favorite "content creator". By the end of 2014 patrons were contributing $1 million per month to Patreon's artists.

Space Exploration

The field of space transportation had been galvanized by Elon Musk's widely advertised SpaceX.

Virgin Galactic, founded on 2004 in Pasadena by British billionaire Richard Branson, had been the first private company to attract media attention with a plan to develop commercial spacecraft and space tourism, but in 2014 a crash killed one of its test pilots. In November 2015 Blue Origin, founded in 2000 by Amazon's founder Jeff Bezos, became the first company to launch a rocket into space and land it gently and safely back down on Earth.

Also in 2015 Elon Musk's SpaceX successfully landed an unmanned rocket upright, something that national space agencies had failed to achieve. Within a few months SpaceX and Blue Origin demonstrated that they could return their rockets intact to Earth and reuse them. NASA's Voyager 1 spacecraft took 36 years to exit our solar system, a journey of about 0.0005 light years. The nearest star, Alpha Centauri, is 4.4 light years away. With the existing technology (the technology of using an explosion to defeat gravity) it was unlikely that human civilization would ever reach the nearest star. But in 2016 Russian billionaire Yuri Milner announced the Starshot project, headquartered on Sand Hill Road in Menlo Park (better known for the venture capitalists who fuel Silicon Valley's bubbles). Starshot aimed at launching a flock of mini-spaceships propelled by 10 million lasers spread over a square km of land. These mini-spaceships would travel at speeds much closer to the speed of light, thereby reducing the journey to Alpha Centauri to "only" 20 years. The project was assigned to former NASA Ames executive Pete Worden.

A major change in the approach to the whole field was emerging in academia, though. In 1999 Jordi Puig-Suari of California Polytechnic State University and Bob Twiggs of Stanford University had proposed the CubeSat standard, largely inspired by the standards that had allowed the personal computer industry to flourish. A CubeSat is a small satellite made of commercial off-the-shelf electronic components. The original proposal was for these "nanosats" to have a size of exactly one cubic liter. In November 2013 Orbital Sciences, based in Virginia, launched 29 satellites and Kosmotras, based in Russia, launched 32 satellites. In January 2014 Orbital Sciences sent an additional 33 satellites up to the International Space Station. Most of these satellites were CubeSat-compliant. They were built by Planet Labs, founded in 2010 in San Francisco by former NASA scientists Will Marshall, Robbie Schingler and Chris Boshuizen. Another San Francisco-based startup, Nanosatisfi, worked on affordable satellites (nicknamed "ArduSats") based on an open-source platform, again using an engineering model borrowed from the computer industry. It was founded in 2012 by four graduates of France's International Space University

(Austrian-born former CERN physicist Peter Platzer, Belgian-born Jeroen Cappaert, Canadian-born Joel Spark and Hungarian-born Reka Kovacs), three of which were also former NASA interns.

Google had spent more than $28 billion on more than 160 companies since 2001, so it wasn't really surprising that it also ventured into the sky, from Skybox Imaging, founded in 2009 in Mountain View by four Stanford graduate students (Dan Berkenstock, Wall Street financial analyst Ching-Yu Hu, aerospace engineer Julian Mann, and air force research physicist John Fenwick), that had just launched its first mini-satellite with the goal that someday users would be able to see any spot on Earth, to the New Mexico-based Titan Aerospace that made solar-powered flying drones (acquired in 2014).

The history of "home" drones was another history of how the open-source community hijacked a military technology and outsmarted the big corporations. The origin of the Unmanned Aerial Vehicles (UAVs) harks back to World War II (the OQ-2 "radioplane", designed by Walter Righter) and to the Vietnam War (the Firebee). Drones are basically remote-controlled flying robots. The "intelligence" of the drone depends on the autopilot. A rudimentary autopilot was first demonstrated in 1914 by Elmer and Zula Sperry at a conference in Paris, but the first major flight that was completely under the control of a machine took place in 1947 when a military airplane completed a transatlantic flight. Any airplane became a flying robot. The modern drone was invented by Abraham Karem, a former Israeli engineer who in 1985 built his first drone in his Los Angeles garage, which General Atomics turned into the Predator, used in 1995 over the skies of Yugoslavia. In 2002 for the first time a drone, this Predator, was used to kill someone (by the CIA during the war in Afghanistan and the target was Osama bin Laden but an innocent civilian was killed by mistake). Meanwhile, Seymour Papert's book "Mindstorms - Children, Computers, and Powerful Ideas" (1980) had exerted a huge influence on a generation of MIT students and in 1998 one of his students, Fred Martin, developed the MIT Programmable Brick, a set of hardware and software parts to build robots. Lego immediately understood the potential of this kit and marketed it as the Lego Mindstorms, a series of kits that allow children to build programmable robots. In 2007 Chris Anderson, the editor-in-chief of Wired magazine, built his first drone at home using parts from one of these Lego kits, and founded DIYDrones.com, an open-source community for drone hobbyists. Anderson met a 19-year-old wunderkid from Mexico, Jordi Munoz, who had built an autopilot using parts of a videogame remote, and in 2009 they decided to found 3D Robotics in Berkeley to make drones. This project had been preceded by open-source autopilot communities: Paparazzi started in 2003 at ENAC (France's National School of Civilian Aviation) and PX4, started in 2009 at ETH in Switzerland. In 2014 the Linux

Foundation founded a more general open-source project, called Dronecode, with founding members such as 3D Robotics and Baidu. AeroQuad and ArduCopter were open-source hardware and software projects based on Arduino for building quadcopters, projects that yielded, for example, the "universal autopilot", ArduPilot Mega (APM), which then evolved into Pixhawk. In 2016 an average amateur could already use the free DIYDrones resources to build a drone spending less than $1,000 in parts and achieve the same functionalities of the $140 million Global Hawk drone that was used by the US military over Afghanistan. To expand the potential applications of drones beyond the hobbyist market, Jonathan Downey's Airware (San Francisco, 2011) built an operating system for drones, a way to make drones programmable for use by corporations.

In 2015 Facebook built its own drone, designed by its own aerospace team, to deliver high-speed Internet connectivity to remote parts of the world.

Camera drones, such as the Chinese-made DJI Phantom and the French-made Parrot AR Drone, rapidly became common toys.

Solar energy, eletrical cars and space exploration are all fields subsidized by the US government.

From Productivity Tools to Entertainment Tools

One of the fundamental changes in the nature and spirit of Silicon Valley was the transformation from a maker of productivity tools (integrated circuits, microprocessors, personal computers, groupware, database management systems, search engines) to a maker of entertainment platforms (mainly videogames and social media).

Silicon Valley from the 1950s to the 1990s was one of the technological centers that contributed to a rapid and significant increase in industrial productivity. Its customers were the big industrial centers of the world, not only households. There was a direct chain of transmission from the innovation in Silicon Valley to the innovation at the assembly line or in millions of offices.

In the 2010s Silicon Valley innovation (at least the commercially successful one) was mainly in videogames and social media. The impact on productivity of a new Facebook timeline or of a new Zinga game was obviously not as big as the impact that the first microprocessors or the first relational databases or the first personal computers had. After all, the dotcom revolution had failed when it had tried to make money out of productivity tools sold to the usual customers (the industrial and financial powerhouses). The dotcom startups succeeded when they started targeting the spare time of ordinary people and started making money out of advertising products to those masses. The gigantic creation of wealth in Silicon Valley during the 2000s had little to do with increasing productivity.

Internet of Things

As the number of objects equipped with a communication chip increased and soon surpassed the number of people connected to the Internet, the Internet of Things (IoT) moved from the intellectual sphere to the corporate sphere.

The first appliance to be connected to the Internet was a modified Coca Cola machine at Carnegie Mellon University in 1982. In 1991 Mark Weiser had published an article in the Scientific American magazine titled "The Computer of the 21st Century" that frame the discussion around "ubiquitous computing". Paul Saffo's article "Sensors - The Next Wave of Infotech Innovation" (1997) had foretold the coming of objects capable of sensing and transmitting. In 1999 Bill Joy had included "Device to Device" (D2D) communication in his "Six Webs" framework at the Davos World Economic Forum. In 2008 Adam Dunkels (Swedish Institute of Computer Science), who in 2003 had created an open-source operating system for the Internet of Things named Contiki, organized with others the IPSO Alliance to promote the development of "smart objects" interacting via the Internet Protocol (IP).

A number of factors enabled the Internet of Things. Firstly, IPv6 was published in 2006, replacing the 25-year old IPv4 (published in 1981). IPv6 introduced a 128-bit address, allowing 2 to the 128th power (or 10 to the 38th power) Internet addresses, enough to assign an Internet address to every atom of the Earth. Secondly, hardware platforms such as Arduino, invented in 2005 by an international team based at Ivrea's Interaction Design Institute in Italy (Massimo Banzi, David Cuartielles, Tom Igoe, Gianluca Martino, David Mellis) made smart objects practical. Arduino was meant as an open-source platform for a community of makers, facilitating the transition to a world of interactive objects that could sense and control the physical world thanks to microcontroller-based kits. The first Arduino device was introduced in 2005 by SmartProjects in Italy. Most Arduino boards were based on a chip developed by Atmel in San Jose, a company (founded in 1984) specializing in microcontrollers. Thirdly, an infrastructure providing a public cloud service for machine-to-machine communication came to maturity. "Machine cloud" pioneers included Jasper Technologies, founded in 2004 in Santa Clara by Jahangir Mohammed (and acquired by Cisco in 2016), Pachube, founded in 2007 by London architect Usman Haque, and acquired in 2011 by Boston-based 8-year old cloud service LogMeIn (and renamed Xively); Axeda, founded in the Boston area in 2000 by Dale Calder and James Hansen, and acquired in 2014 by Parametric Technology (PTC), a 30-year old design-software company of the Boston area; and Spark, founded in 2008 in Minneapolis by Zach Supalla and later renamed Particle and relocated in San Francisco. Spark, for example, provided a development kit for makers and hobbyists to build smart devices and its SparkCloud to make them communicate over the Internet.

Internet of Things store in Palo Alto: b8ta

In the 2010s the prophecies of the 1990s became reality and "Machine-to-Machine" (M2M) business became a hot topic. In the attempt to forge a winning standard, major corporations formed consortia such as the Industrial Internet Consortium (AT&T, Cisco, IBM, GE, Intel) and the Open InterConnect Consortium (Broadcom, Samsung, Dell). However, the giant in this field was Qualcomm, because Qualcomm had the numbers. In 2014 more than 120 million smart home devices were shipped with embedded Qualcomm chips, and 20 million cars were equipped with Qualcom chips, and several wearable devices had chosen Qualcomm for communications. Qualcomm's "standard" was AllJoyn, whose objects could broadcast what they could do to all other nearby AllJoyn objects (via WiFi or Bluetooth).

The applications ranged from controlling home appliances to planning traffic. Connected car platforms, that allowed smarphone apps to check data such as fuel consumption and travel times, were particularly appealing in the USA: Automatic (founded in 2011 in San Francisco by Jerry Jariyasunant and Thejo Kote), Dash (founded in 2012 in New York by Brian Langel and Jamyn Edis), and Zubie (founded by Best Buy in 2012 in South Carolina and originally called GreenLight Connectivity Solutions) were among the leaders.

The most ambitious experiments were carried out in South Korea, like the Songdo International Business District, a six square kms "smart" city developed jointly with Cisco, LG CNS and ADT Caps.

In 2014 Apple introduced HomeKit to connect smart home appliances via Bluetooth and WiFi to the iPhone.

In 2015 the Wi-Fi Alliance, that included Apple, Microsoft and Intel, launched Wi-Fi Aware, a technology that allowed Aware-enabled devices to discover and communicate directly with nearby Aware-enabled devices. Once enabled, apps on one Aware devices could exchange information with apps on other Aware devices.

Rising above the chaos of standards, San Francisco-based SeeControl, founded in 2010 by Bryan Kester (and acquired by Autodesk in 2015), provided a cloud-based platform for makers to create M2M applications by connecting and managing smart sensors and devices spread around the world.

Other products for connecting (wireless) sensors to the cloud came from Libelium (Spain, 2006), one of the world's pioneers; Konekt (Chicago, 2013), that was betting on GSM instead of WiFi or Bluetooth; and Temboo (New York, 2013), that partnered with Arduino to manufacture a chip with built-in WiFi.

Chip manufacturers rushed to design boards containing all the sensors and chips needed to wirelessly connect objects. In 2014 Samsung launched the open platform ARTIK and acquired SmartThings (founded in 2012 in Palo Alto by veterans of online marketing). In 2015 Samsung acquired French startup Sigfox (founded in 2006 by Christophe Fourtet) whose goal was to build a low-cost alternative to the cellular network for connecting low-battery demand objects. In 2015 Intel introduced the Curie module, comprising a sensor hub, a microprocessor and a Bluetooth connection in a tiny space.

Bluetooth and WiFi weren't the only ways to connect objects. The Internet of Things was for low-power devices, devices that had to survive a long time with a battery. LTE (Long-Term Evolution), originally introduced in Scandinavia in 2009 by TeliaSonera, used the existing 4G wireless network. There were companies specialized in making chips for LTE communications, like Israeli-based Altair Semiconductor (acquired by Sony in 2016) and Paris-based Sequans. In 2015 two standards were proposed: Narrow Band-LTE (NB-LTE) from Intel, Ericsson and Nokia; and Narrow-Band Cellular IoT (NB-CIoT) from Huawei and Vodafone.

The Internet of Things opened up a new horizon to "smart" cities, and therefore heralded a revolution in urban planning. In 2015 Google, whose overall activities were now credited to the newly formed Alphabet, even invested in a New York-based startup to redesign urban living, Sidewalk Labs, led by Daniel Doctoroff, a former Bloomberg executive. The startup's first project was a joint venture called Intersection to bring free high-speed Wi-Fi to cities around the world like LinkNYC had done in New York.

The products on the market, however, were still modest in scope. In 2014 Google acquired Nest, founded in 2010 in Palo Alto by former Apple's designers Tony Fadell and Matt Rogers to develop "smart" home appliances (initially just a thermostat) that were capable of self-adjusting and be controlled by smartphone. August, co-founded in 2012 in San Francisco by industrial designer Yves Behar, offered a "smart lock" that could be opened either with a smart phone or over the web. Switchmate, founded in 2014 in Palo Alto by three John Hopkins graduates (Robert Romano, Daniel Peng and Ashish Dua), introduced a button controlled from a smartphone app to turn lights on and off, and potentially any other appliance activated by pressing a button. August's smartphone app, launched in 2013 in San Francisco by Jason Johnson and Yves Behar, controlled the deadbolt of a door and issued "virtual keys" to guests.

Security on Internet of Things was obviously not trivial. Some adopted a strategy similar to what doctors do to prevent infections: check for signs of intrusion and immediately isolate compromised devices before they could infect all the other devices in the network. Thus Atlanta-based Luma (founded by Paul Judge and Mike Van Bruiniss) sold a WiFi router capable of checking traffic inside the home network and detecting "infections", and Finnish-based F-Secure Sense sold a security monitor, a device sitting between the home router and connected devices to scan all traffic for "infections".

Exciting work was happening at the intersection between "open source" and home automation. Open-source hardware was coming to maturity in both Europe and the USA. Arduino Uno had no operating system so it could only run one application at a time, but it was the ideal microcontroller for "smart" objects that only did one thing. The Raspberry Pi, introduced in Britain in 2012 and originally conceived for schoolchildren by a charitable organization based around Cambridge University, was a cheap computer that fit in the space of a credit card. In 2015 TL Lim and Johnson Jeng, out of San Francisco, launched a Kickstarter campaign to fund a single-board computer called Pine64, slightly bigger than a smartphone but equipped with the most powerful ARM processor (more powerful than the most powerful laptops) and cost the equivalent of a restaurant dinner; and it is designed to work with the OpenHAB standard.

OpenHAB (Open Home Automation Bus) was designed by by Kai Kreuzer in Germany in 2010 specifically to let "smart" devices talk to each other. It was open source and written in Java. One could use it to set up a sequence of operations that involved multiple devices. OpenHAB was also compatible with ROS, the open-source Robot Operating System invented at Stanford by Andrew Ng's group and perfected at Willow Garage. ROS was the descendant of the Stanford AI Robot (STAIR) that was conceived from the very beginning with "home" robotics in mind.

Neura, founded in Israel by Triinu Magi, Ori Shaashua and Gilad Meiri and relocated to Sunnyvale in 2013, applied a bit of Artificial Intelligence to the Internet of Things so that it could not only connect "things" but also figure out what the user does with those "things" and create personalized behaviors.

The "smart city" was the ultimate target for the Internet of Things. The term was confusing because it was often used (especially in Asia) to refer to a city offering nice living, low pollution, and fast Internet: fast and ubiquitous connection for people. In the age of the IoT the term "smart city" came to refer to a city in which objects such as street lights and parking spaces were connected: fast and ubiquitous connection for things. The traditional cellular phone systems were not suited for "things" that need to be small, light and cheap: their batteries couldn't provide a lot of power. The smart city needed a networking technology for very-low-power operation, but also capable of long range transmission. The telecommunications companies that had risen during the cellular era typically thought in terms of "broadband": they wanted to provide an infrastructure that could carry large amounts of data (such as pictures and videos). Therefore they had invested in 3G, 4G, and now 5G. But these are precisely the technologies that didn't work well for connecting home and city objects. The user needed to recharge her smartphone almost every night. A long battery life was a prerequisite for the Internet of Things. Europe was ahead in developing the exact opposite: narrow-band low-power long-range radio networks. Broadband means short waves, narrow-band means long waves. The Internet of Things for "smart city" solutions needed the longest waves. Furthermore, the communication had to be secure and bi-directional. For example, Afero, founded in 2014 in Los Altos by Danger's co-founder Joe Britt, offered a Bluetooth chip for manufacturers to embed in their smart appliances and a secure platform to connect smart appliances among themselves and to the cloud. Finally, it had to be capable of tracking moving objects: mobility and localization. Europe had several well-established leaders in this kind of "ultra-narrow band" (UNB) technology with power levels that were thousands of times lower than in cellular communications: Telensa (Britain, 2005), Sigfox (France, 2009) and Actility (France, 2010). Some of their radio technologies had been developed since the 1990s. Telensa had connected LED-based street lights in several cities, and had a "smart parking" solution: magnetic sensors to detect the presence of a vehicle and to alert drivers when the parking space became available. Actility was the brain behind the LoRa Alliance, established in 2015 with Cisco, IBM, and many others.

Wireless Power Transmission

In 1902 Nikola Tesla had built the 62-meter high Wardenclyffe Tower that for 15 years terrified his neighbors in Long Island. He was convinced that it was possible to transmit electricity via the air, but he failed to prove it and the tower was demolished in 1917. Wireless power had been tested since then, but it took more than one century for the industry to catch up with his vision.

In 2007 a theoretical physicist at the MIT, Marin Soljacic, published a paper in Science magazine titled "Wireless Power Transfer via Strongly Coupled Magnetic Resonances". That paper proved that Tesla's dream was indeed feasible: electrical power can be transmitted wirelessly (60 watts of power over 2 meters) although using a different technique, magnetic resonance. He helped found WiTricity to commercialize the technology. In 2014 Intel bought a license to integrate the wireless charging feature into its Skylake processor.

At the same time, Ran Poliakine founded Powermat Technologies in 2006 in Israel. He used Tesla's idea, inductive power transfer, that, after decades of failures, had been perfected in 1991 by Andrew Green and John Boys at Auckland University in New Zealand. In 2009 Powermat introduced a device capable of charging a smartphone remotely. He then created a joint venture with the most famous brand in consumer-electronics battery, Duracell, and in 2014 their redesigned product was adopted by the coffee franchise Starbucks in 200 of their Bay Area locations. Technically speaking, the inductive technology is tightly coupled, whereas the resonance technology is loosely coupled.

Another route was followed by Energous, founded in 2012 as DVineWave in San Ramon (East Bay) by Michael Leabman, and Ossia, founded in 2008 in Seattle by Hatem Zeine: radio waves. Energous started selling its device in 2015 and in 2016 shrunk it to the size of a thumb drive. One device plugged into the USB port of a laptop, located compatible devices via Bluetooth and sent them beams in radio-frequency waves; another device (a tiny receiver chip), attached to a smartphone or wearable, converted this radio frequency into direct current. Ossia demonstrated its technology in 2013 and partnered with KDDI, Japan's second-largest wireless carrier.

In 2016 a team at the University of Washington that included Shyam Gollakota (winner in 2015 of the World Technology Award for communication technology) demonstrated a system, PoWiFi (Power Over Wi-Fi), that used traditional Wi-Fi routers.

Finally, the prototype by uBeam, founded in 2011 by University of Pennsylvania's graduate Meredith Perry, who then relocated to Los Angeles, broadcast electricity via high-pitched ultrasound beams in a manner similar to how transducers work in hi-fi speakers.

There were three competing alliances: the Wireless Power Consortium, which was behind the standard Qi (supported by Nokia, Samsung, LG, Sony, BlackBerry, and HTC), the Power Matters Alliance (the one chosen by Powermat, Duracell, AT&T, Google and WiTricity) and the Alliance for Wireless Power. In 2015 the Power Matters Alliance and the Alliance for Wireless Power merged in the AirFuel Alliance.

E-shopping

The world of online shopping had not changed much in the early 2010s after Amazon, eBay and PayPal had introduced the de-facto standards, and after Google and Yahoo had invented modern advertising.

However, startups tried to find the weakest link in the chain.

Blippar, launched in 2012 in London by Omar Tayeb and Ambarish Mitra offered an advertising platform that mixed image recognition and visual browsing. The user could simply scan an object to view information about that object.

Magic, an SMS-based assistant launched in 2015 by Mike Chen in Mountain View, delivered goods to people, thanks to an army of operators available 24 hours a day, seven days a week. This was the kind of "online-to-offline" (O2O) that was big in China. A similar product came out of Germany: GoButler, launched in 2015 by ex-Rocket Internet executives including Navid Hadzaad (Rocket Internet being a startup incubator founded in 2007 in Germany by Marc, Oliver and Alexander Samwer specializing in clones of US-based e-commerce success stories).

Instacart, founded in 2012 in San Francisico by Apoorva Mehta, Brandon Leonardo and Max Mullen, aimed for same-day grocery.

Mobile payment still had not found its king. The region where it had spread first was actually Africa, where Kenya's Safaricom had introduced M-Pesa in 2007. The country were mobile payment was rapidly becoming commonplace was China, thanks to Alipay, launched by Alibaba in 2004 to allow purchases from its own Taobao marketplace, that boomed in 2009, and then expanded to allow any purchase from any online or brick-and-mortar business. In 2007 Kevin Hartz and Alan Braverman launched Xoom in San Francisco to provide an online platform for money transfers that, unlike the traditional bank services, could make funds available immediately at the other end, anywhere in the world (initially Latin America). PayPal acquired it in 2015 (when Hartz had already left in order to found the ticket-management service Eventbrite in 2006 with his wife Julia). At the time of the acquisition Xoom was really just a replacement for the services traditionally offered by the likes of Western Union and MoneyGram (typically for remittances to developing countries such as India and Mexico). Flint, founded by Greg Goldfarb and Andrew Laszlo in

2011 in Redwood City, competed directly with Square, offering a similar credit-card payment for merchants but requiring no additional hardware because it used the mobile device's camera to scan credit cards. Paypal's mobile payment platform was Beacon, introduced in 2013, a Bluetooth-based technology that detected Beacon-enabled smartphones when customers entered a Beacon-enabled store and then automated the purchase of merchandise. Credit card giants Visa and American Express, however, sided with Stripe, founded as Slashdevslashpayments in 2010 in San Francisco by Patrick and John Collison to provide a similar platform for online and mobile payments. Apple's iBeacon (2013) was similar to Paypal's Beacon in that it used Bluetooth technology to alert devices of the presence of fellow iBeacon devices. The company then introduced Apple Pay (2014), claiming to make online payments as secure as in-store payments. The digital wallet was incorporated directly into the operating system and the smartphone included a SIM-independent secure memory chip, an NFC radio, and a fingerprint reader (the digital wallet was "physical" again). Clinkle, founded by Stanford student Lucas Duplan, launched in 2014, promising compatibility with every merchant and phone-to-phone payments.

Music streaming was still one of the biggest online businesses. In 2014 Apple bought the music streaming service just launched by Beats (the company founded by hip-hop musician Dr Dre) and in 2015 turned it into its own Spotify-like service to offset the decline in the popularity of iTunes. People, basically, were rather renting than buying music, just like they did with videos.

Fintech

Financial transactions constituted a huge market: in 2014 they generated about $600 billion in fees in the USA alone, more than twice the GDP of a country like Israel. There was a huge opportunity for automating financial services.

Branch-less banking had become commonplace by the 2010s, but lending was still a complicated process. Kreditech (founded in Germany in 2012) represented the vanguard: it provided almost instant lending to individuals based on their credit score, a purely algorithmic solution. Peer-to-peer lending, pioneered by the likes of Prosper and LendingClub, became ever more popular. A newcomer was Upstart, founded in 2012 in Palo Alto by Google veterans Dave Girouard and Anna Mongayt with a Peter Thiel alumnus, Paul Gu.

Automated financial advisory was making strides in the mainstream financial world. In 2011 Wealthfront, founded in Palo Alto by Dan Carroll and Andy Rachleff (a co-founder of Benchmark Capital), joined the ranks of the algorithm-based financial advisors, and in 2014 Charles Schwab introduced Intelligent Portfolios.

The first major success fintech story in the world of real estate was Nestio, founded in 2011 in New York to help finding residential rentals and later repackaged as a platform for residential landlords. Point, founded in 2014 in Palo Alto by Eddie Lim, tried a new concept: a home equity marketplace that allowed people to divide their homes and trade their fractional equity just like it was done with vacation rentals.

Peer-to-peer insurance networks spread both in Europe and in the USA. For example, Berlin-based Friendsurance (2010) for peer-to-peer personal and casualty insurance, London-based Guevara (2014) for peer-to-peer car insurance, and New York-based Lemonade (2015), for peer-to-peer property and casualty insurance.

Peer-to-peer payments, typically for mobile users, multiplied: Venmo, founded by Andrew Kortina and Iqram Magdon-Ismail in 2009 in New York (and acquired by PayPal in 2013); Square's own Square Cash (2013); Snapchat's Snapcash (2014), powered by Square; and Google's 2015 version of Wallet.

Venture capitalists themselves came into attack. Online collection of money from individuals to fund startups, as an an alternative to banks, angel investors and venture capitalists, was pioneered by EquityNet (founded in Arizona in 2005) that offered a social network for investors and entrepreneurs, but until 2012 investments by random individuals in businesses were not legal in the USA. Equity crowdfunding was legalized in the USA in 2012 with the "Jumpstart Our Business Startups" act. England already had Crowdcube (2011) and Seedrs (2012), and in 2011 two startups for equity crowdfunding had already opened in San Francisco: CircleU, founded by Ryan Caldbeck, and Wefunder, founded by Nick Tommarello, Mike Norman and Greg Belote.

Square's co-founder Jim McKelvey founded the most active of startup accelerators specializing in fintech, SixThirty (in 2013 in St Louis).

For the record, Israel became a major center of fintech in the 2010s thanks to its strong credentials in cybersecurity, big data and artificial intelligence. Ironically, the past investments in military applications such as computer vision, espionage and data security had turned Israel into a powerhouse for the very technologies needed by fintech. In fact, several fintech startups had their roots in 8200, the Israeli army's elite intelligence unit. By 2015 Israel had more than 400 fintech startups offering branchless services for payments, crowdfunding, lending, insurance, wealth management, fraud detection, etc. and many were already experimenting with blockchain technology. Major Western banks established research labs in Israel. For example, in 2013 Citibank opened its Citi Innovation Lab in Tel Aviv.

Blockchain Technology

Bitcoin became a world-wide phenomenon before its value crashed in 2013, and bitcoin mining became a lucrative activity in its own. Bitcoin relied on a distributed consensus system and on a "secure hash algorithm" called SHA-256, which, ironically, had been invented by the National Security Agency (NSA). This process, that basically consisted in adding records to a shared public ledger, had the fundamental property of being easy to verify but (purposefully) difficult to execute (in order to deter counterfeiting). In other words, its usefulness and safety came at a price: it was computionally very demanding. In 2013 the first ASICs (application-specific integrated circuits) for bitcoins, known as "bitcoin hash chips", became available. They specialized in "mining" SHA-256 cryptocurrencies, Soon there were farms of custom-built servers, capable of solving very complex math problems, linked to Bitcoin's network via high-speed Internet connections. Each "miner" was rewarded with some bitcoins. Avalon (China, 2012, later renamed Canaan Creative) was the first company to manufacture ASIC mining chips.

Dinner with the Avalon team

21 Inc, founded in 2013 in San Francisco by Balaji Srinivasan of Andreessen Horowitz (who also founded the bioinformatics company, Counsyl Genomics) with the motto "a bitcoin miner in every device and in every hand", introduced an embeddable bitcoin mining chip in 2013 and then the first computer with native hardware and software support for Bitcoin in 2015. In 2015 BitFury, founded in 2011 in San Francisco by veteran entrepreneurs Valery Vavilov and Valery Nebesny, introduced a "green" ASIC chip capable of delivering a minimum computing power of 100 gigahash per second.

Bitcoin mining hardware started popping up all over the world. At one point there was a farm of 45,000 special-purpose computers in northern Sweden.

In 2014 former Google engineer Mike Hearn and Gavin Andresen, a Silicon Graphics veteran and one of the original founders of the Bitcoin

Foundation in 2012, proposed an alternative platform for Bitcoin, Bitcoin XT, to fix limitations of the Bitcoin transactional system.

Bitcoin was neither the first nor the only cryptocurrency. Cryptsy, the largest "altcoin" exchange, listed dozens of them: Namecoin, Litecoin, Dogecoin, Reddcoin, Darkcoin, Bitshares, Feathercoin, Mastercoin, Devcoin, etc.

Some, like Omni/Mastercoin, introduced by JR Willett in 2013, used the same blockchain as bitcoin. Others, like Litecoin (created by former Google engineer Charles Lee in 2011, second for market capitalization in 2015), Ripple (introduced by Vancouver-based Ryan Fugger in 2012), and Primecoin/PPCoin/Peercoin (all created by an anonymous "Sunny King" between 2012 and 2013) employed different "proof of work" algorithms. Primecoin was also an example of a cryptocurrency that worked with a proof of work less demanding in computational power, more "green".

The implications of Bitcoin extended beyond the world of currencies. For example, in 2014 the Russian-born Toronto-based Bitcoin fan Vitalik Buterin launched Ethereum, superficially a platform to develop Bitcoin-like "currencies" but in reality a broader interpretation of what a digital currency is. Ethereum aimed at executing any kind of secure service as a digital contract. That was the essence of the "block chain" mechanism driving Bitcoin. Ethereum was an "app coin".

The Bitcoin blockchain offered a new method to register and transact physical and intellectual property. "Smart property" was property whose ownership was controlled via the Bitcoin blockchain; but the killer application of Bitcoin was "smart contracts" that opened up a whole new horizon of applications. A smart Contract was a program stored on the blockchain that could automatically execute the terms of a contract. With smart contracts, auto-executing code replaced the legal process of enforcing a contract. In a sense, smart contracts made the legal system redundant. Two open-source projects, Codius, invented in 2014 by Stefan Thomas and Evan Schwartz at San Francisco-based Ripple Labs, and Ethereum provided platforms for smart contracts.

Austin-based Factom, founded in 2014, was the first to provide notary services via blockchain technology.

Ethereum ignited the imagination of the counterculture. Ethereum didn't store massive data within the blockchain itself. IPFS (InterPlanetary File System), developed by Juan Benet in 2015. IPFS stored data by distributing them over the network like MaidSafe and provided an encrypted address for each piece of information. The "dark net" counterculture viewed IPFS protocol as nothing less than a potential replacement for HTTP: it could reengineer the Internet. In 2016 Ethereum consisted of three main blocks: contracts (the "decentralized logic"), IPFS (the "decentralized storage") and Whisper (a "decentralized" messaging system, still under development). Ethereum was "Turing-complete": it could implement any program. The counterculture of the Internet began to view Ethereum as the "world computer" of the future.

Fintech spread to the bitcoin world. Andrew Cook founded his Cook Investment Firm in Chile in 2011, when he was 20 years old, and in it remained the world's largest bitcoin investment fund for a while. Quickcoin, founded in 2014 in San Francisco by Nathan Lands and William Cotton, integrated a bitcoin wallet with Facebook to send bitcoins as messages. CoinBase, founded in San Francisco in 2012 by Fred Ehrsam and Brian Armstrong, offered a bitcoin marketplace and a platform for bitcoin payments. Epiphyte, founded in 2013 in San Francisco by Edan Yago, offered banking for crypto-currencies. Circle, founded by Jeremy Allaire in 2013 in Ireland, allowed users to send bitcoins to friends and family. NextBank, founded in 2015 by Dimitry Voloshinskiy, aimed to become the first all-bitcoin institution.

BitShares, founded in 2013 in Virginia by Daniel Larimer, offers financial services (including exchange and banking) on a blockchain (not bitcoin's blockchain). In 2016 CoinCloud, a trader of bitcoin for cash, installed a "bitcoin machine teller" (a BTM) in Menlo Park.

The first BTM (Menlo Park, 2016)

The blockchain was already being used for applications outside fintech. For example, Gems, launched in 2014 by Daniel Peled in Israel, used the bitcoin blockchain to implement a social messenger (therefore a "decentralized" social messenger); and Skuchain, founded in 2014 in

Mountain View by Srinivasan Sriram, applied the blockchain to the supply chain of manufacturing.

The Counterparty platform was launched in 2014 by Palo Alto-based Chris DeRose to provide a peer-to-peer financial market within the Bitcoin protocol. It enabled the creation of peer-to-peer financial applications on the Bitcoin blockchain; basically the foundations for setting up exchanges of digital currencies, smart properties, and anything else priced in bitcoins. The platform included a protocol that allowed Counterparty nodes to communicate with each other via the Bitcoin blockchain, a native currency (XCP) and wallets (both browser-based and mobile). In particular, Counterparty allowed users to create their own currencies inside the Bitcoin blockchain. Anyone could now launch their own "coin" on Counterparty.

Swarm, formed by Joel Dietz in 2014 in Palo Alto, was an incubator of Counterparty projects; a platform for launching Counterparty projects and for the initial mentorship and funding. Ethereum and Counterparty (and MaidSafe) were some of the "Bitcoin 2.0 technologies" for developing decentralized applications ("dapps").

Counterparty used the bitcoin blockchain, whereas Ethereum used a non-bitcoin blockchain.

Eris, founded in 2014 in New York by two lawyers, marketed itself as a "universal blockchain platform" because it could clone Ethereum, Bitcoin and many other blockchains. Etherparty, founded in 2015 in Los Angeles, and based on Ethereum, was cloud-based: no programming required for developing dapps.

A decentralized application was a smart contract with an unlimited number of participants. By definition, these were applications that used no server: the blockchain (distributed all over the network) served as their "backend". These applications did not use a centralized intermediary like the business applications that ran on, say, Oracle or SAP backends. They were the descendants of projects like Tor, BitTorrent and MaidSafe.

Smart contracts and dapps enabled a whole new form of organization. A contract based on laws is legally binding, but interpretation of the law is flexible, and often the outcome of a trial depends on the rhetorical skills of the defense attorney. A contract based on an algorithm (like the blockchain) is not legally binding, it is technologically-binding. Software inexorably executes the contract. The auto-executing software replaces the legal system and, to some extent, even the police. A DAO (decentralized autonomous organization) is defined by smart contracts. It is therefore an unmanned organization under the control of an incorruptible algorithm. The algorithm is, in turn, implemented in an open-source software that can be publicly audited. DAOs are autonomous; DAOs are self-enforcing; DAOs are transparent; DAOs cannot be manipulated by external agents; DAOs have no central control.

Decentralization had historically meant chaos, but the blockchain was a system based on decentralization that actually guaranteed order. Its technology was basically enforcing order through chaos. It also provided a much more secure exchange of information than government databases and corporate databases, because the security of a transaction was guaranteed by all the computers in the network.

In 2014 Susanne Tarkowski Tempelhof launched a platform to create DAOs, Bitnation, with the motto "Create your own Nation in 140 Lines of Code". A DAO provides the same services that traditional governments provide, but in a decentralized way: there is nobody in control of those services. Potentially, a DAO implementes a D.I.Y. government.

In 2016 a German startup, Slock.it, created a DAO that could act as a venture capitalist, funding startups (like Slock itself). Within a few months it collected the equivalent of $150 million on Ethereum, thereby becoming the largest crowdfunded project ever. The investors would have the power to vote on each startup that wants money.

The next step was the "Distributed Collaborative Organization", a concept introduced in 2014 by Primavera De Filippi of Harvard University and by Houman Shadab of the New York School of Law to integrate blockchain-based distributed organizations (DAOs) with the existing legal system.

In the mid-2010s, many of the bitcoin heroes moved into the "Crypto Castle", a three-story five-bedroom San Francisco house.

Semiconductors

In the age of the smartphone app people almost forgot why this region was called "Silicon" Valley. However, the semiconductor industry was still very much at the core of the valley, except that a process of consolidation was rapidly changing its shape. In 2015 Intel acquired Altera (specialized in semiconductors for communications), its biggest-ever acquisition, one year after buying LSI's networking business from Avago; and in 2015 Avago (that had been founded in 2005 over the ruins of a 44-years-old division of Hewlett-Packard and Agilent Technologies) acquired Broadcomm, besides CyOptics and Javelin (meanwhile it had acquired LSI and then sold LSI's networking business to Intel).

By then the hardware industry had embraced the multi-core chip, the only way to keep Moore's Law working. Intel's Xeon Haswell-EP of 2015 boasted 5.5 billion transistors but thanks to 18 cores. The cost per transistor had actually been rising since the Taiwan Semiconductor Manufacturing Company (TSMC) had introduced its 28-nanometer chips in 2011. In fact, in 2012 Intel started using a different kind of transistor, the "tri-gate" transistor. The rest of the world called it "FinFet" transistor. Chenming Hu had invented them at UC Berkeley in 1998, and one of his students, Yang-Kyu Choi, had founded the Nanotech lab at the Korea Advanced Institute of Science and Technology (KAIST) that was setting one record after the other in FinFet technology. In 2014 Intel started shipping the 14nm Skylake processor (400,000 times more powerful than the Intel 4004), but in 2015 Intel announced that its 10nm Cannonlake processor would be delayed to 2017. The "nanometer" scale (the separation of the transistors on the chip) was becoming impractical. The first microprocessor, the Intel 4004, had contained 2,300 transistors spaced by 10,000nm gaps. It was just getting too difficult and too expensive to operate at that scale. A Skylake transistor was made of about 100 atoms. With the same technology a 2nm transistor would be just 10 atoms wide. This was technically feasible (in fact, Yang-Kyu Choi's team at the KAIST had already built a 3nm FinFET in 2006), but extremely expensive. The cost of building a factory for microprocessors was already in the billions of dollars. In fact, in 2016 Intel's vicepresident Bill Holt openly admitted that Intel was not planning to use silicon below the 7nm threshold. Then Silicon Valley would stop being "silicon".

Consumer electronics was putting pressure on the memory industry. In particular, the price gap between hard-disk drives and solid-state drives (used mainly for NAND flash memory) kept shrinking. In 2013 Samsung announced a three-dimensional Vertical NAND (or 3D V-NAND) flash memory. In 2014 SanDisk and Toshiba opened a fabrication plant specialized in 3D VNAND in Japan, whose first product, released in 2015, was a flash chip that doubled the capacity of the densest memory chips. In 2015 Samsung unveiled the world's largest storage device, a 16-terabyte 3D NAND solid-state memory; while Intel teamed up with Micron to introduce its 3D-memory chip. 3D memory represented the first new class of memory in a quarter century. Micron and Intel joined forces to manufacture NAND flash memories back in 2005, and in 2010 Micron had acquired Swiss-Italian flash-memory maker Numonyx from Intel.

Global social networking

Facebook, which in 2013 launched the project Internet.org with Samsung, Nokia and others, planned to beam the Internet from solar-powered drones. Also in 2013, Google launched Project Loon, and originally planned to use a world-wide network of high-altitude balloons to beam the Internet to the regions that have no Internet access yet, and in 2014 it announced that it wanted to build a system of 180 satellites to beam Internet around the planet.

The proliferation of videos, of live streaming, of video calls, of video conferencing and so on was testing the limits of 4G wireless technology. The problem was postponed when in 2010 the US government accepted to double the spectrum from 500 MHz to 1 GHz by 2020 (the "national broadband plan"). In addition, Qualcomm started using the unlicensed band (the band used by things like WiFi) and turned it into LTU. This tripled the capacity of 4G wireless. But that was still not enough to match the growing demand of mobile data. Another solution consisted in simply adding more "cells" per square kilometer. Unfortunately, there was a physical limit: when cells are too close, they start interfering and become useless. In 2016 San Francisco-based Artemis introduced a new technology that used that very interference to provide more capacity, and in fact could provide a dedicated cell to each mobile device user, each device getting the full spectrum capacity. Ironically, Artemis' project was yet another by-product of military research. In 1990 DARPA and the Air Force had launched a military project called SpeakEasy that pioneered Software Defined Radio (SDR), a technology to program wireless technology at a higher level instead of programming directly on ASIC.

In 2013 NSA employee Edward Snowden revealed details of a vast government operation to spy on citizens and on foreign allies and was then granted asylum in Russia. A Palestinian hacker, Khalil Shreateh, living under Israeli occupation, became a worldwide hero when he hacked into Mark Zuckerberg's Facebook page to show how easy it was to violate someone's privacy on social media. These events encouraged Internet users to look for protection from network surveillance. Protection came in the form of "dark nets" like the TOR browser (introduced in 2008), the DuckDuckGo search engine (developed in Pennsylvania by Gabriel Weinberg in 2008), and the instant messenger Wickr with military-grade encryption (launched in 2012 in San Francisco by Nico Sell and others), tools that guaranteed worldwide anonymity to their users.

The Micro-startup

When in 2015 Microsoft acquired LiveLoop (Powerpoint groupware), Sunrise (calendar app for iPhone) and Accompli (mobile email), it added exactly 42 people to its workforce. Twitter added a grand total of 13 people from acquiring Vine (video sharing) in 2012 and Periscope (video streaming) in 2015. Facebook added 16 from acquiring Instagram in 2012 and Luma (video sharing) in 2013. Google's acquisitions in 2015 of Odysee (photo sharing) and Tilt Brush (painting in virtual reality), among others, hardly changed its headcount. One can go back to 2005, when Google acquired a nine-people startup, Android, that went on to dominate the smartphone market. By comparison YouTube, that Google acquired in 2006 when it already had 65 employees, looks like a ridiculously large deal. The moment something went viral on the Internet there were big corporations ready to buy it; but sometimes this happened even before that "something" has had a chance to go viral; in fact Twitter acquired both Periscope and Vine before they launched. (Vine had just been founded in

New York two months earlier by Dom Hofmann, Rus Yusupov, and Colin Kroll)

What the corporations were looking for was simple: talent. Google, Twitter, Facebook and Microsoft had been founded by talented people and remembered how important talent was when they started. They had neither been the first in their field nor possibly the best, but they had the talent to succeed where others did not.

Silicon Valley attributed this attitude to Google's acquisition of 45-people Applied Semantics in 2003, the deal that had coined the term "acqui-hire": that team had gone on to develop AdSense, a major source of revenues for Google.

Seattle, on the other hand, could claim that Microsoft had pioneered this model when it had acquired Groove in 2005: Microsoft had not done much with Groove's peer-to-peer collaboration software, but Groove's founder Ray Ozzie had eventually replaced Bill Gates as Microsoft's chief software architect. In other words, Microsoft had acquired Ozzie's talent, not Groove's product.

Silicon Valley could, however, respond that Microsoft acquired Danger and did nothing with it, whereas Google acquired Danger's founder Andy Rubin and its Android technology, and for a much cheaper price than Microsoft paid for Danger.

Exponential Organizations

A new buzzword was created in 2014 when Salim Ismail, a founding director of Singularity University, co-wrote with Michael Malone and Yuri van Geest "Exponential Organizations" (2014): 3D printing had gotten 400 times cheaper over just 7 years, industrial robots got 23 times cheaper over 5 years, drones got 143-times cheaper in 4 years, and sequencing the human genome got 10,000-times cheaper in 7 years.

The Investment Bubble of 2013

A staggering 88 of the 100 largest venture capital rounds of all times took place between 2007 and 2014. A huge amount of money was flowing towards Silicon Valley, largely attracted by stellar evaluation for high-tech startups. In 2014 Airbnb set a new record raising $500 million, while the even younger Lyft raised $200 million. On the East Coast, a seven-year old Dropbox raised $250 million. Silicon Valley, in fact, had not started this trend: in Texas at the end of 2008, in the middle of the worst economic recession since the Great Depression, the small HomeAway had raised $250 million. The traditional venture capital firm was increasingly joined by the hedge funds, the mutual funds and private equity firms. This phenomenon was allowing startups longer incubation periods, but it was also viewed by many as an alarm bell that a new bubble was about to burst.

This was the era of the "unicorns," or billion-dollar start-ups: Square, Stripe, Airbnb, Pinterest, Uber, Dropbox, Snapchat, Palantir, GoPro, Slack, Cloudera, Eventbrite, electronic notebook Evernote (founded by Stepan Pachikov in 2008 in Sunnyvale), Stemcentrx (a biotech company founded in 2008 in South San Francisco by Stanford scientist Scott Dylla and investment banker Brian Slingerland to treat cancer under the assumption that cancer is caused by a small population of stem cells), enterprise social media platform Sprinklr (founded in 2009 in New York by Ragy Thomas), discount shopping site Jet (founded by Marc Lore, who had sold his e-commerce company Quidsi to Amazon in 2010); etc. Most of these startups generated no cash flow, i.e. were losing money. In 2015 WhatsApp hit the one-billion user mark, but it still didn't know how to make money out of them. At the beginning of 2016 Magic Leap was valued at $4.5 billions without even having demonstrated its product.

By 2015 there were 144 unicorns with a total value of $505 billion. Utah, the state with the fastest economic growth in 2014-15, had 4 unicorns (Domo. Pluralsight, Qualtrics and InsideSales).

The unicorns were also emblematic of the decline of the Initial Public Offering (IPO). Apple had gone public in 1980 with a market valuation of $1.8 billion, Microsoft was worth less than a billion dollars at its 1986 IPO, Netscape had gone public in 1995 when it was worth $2 billion, but Twitter waited until it was worth about $25 billion and Facebook until it was worth more than $100 billion. And now many of the unicorns showed no intention of going public. Part of the reason was bureaucratic. The government had reacted to the Enron scandal, revealed in October 2001, with the Sarbanes-Oxley legislation, but that legislation, meant to protect investors and consumers, ended up being a gigantic tax on small businesses because it requires fleets of lawyers and accountants. To protect smaller investors from discrimination, the government had enacted the Regulation Fair Disclosure legislation of 2000. This mandated that all publicly traded companies should disclose information to all investors at the same time. Ironically, this made it difficult for small companies to counter hostile rumors that could devastate their stock values. Generally speaking, the regulatory system began to favor big corporations and discouraged startups from going public. Venture firms such as Marc Andreessen's explicitly stated that their goal was not to take companies public.

Until 2012 the government forced companies to go public when they reached 500 shareholders. In 2011 if a company had 500 employees and each one had been paid some shares in the company, that company was required to file for an IPO. In 2012 the government passed the JOBS Act that raised the number of maximum shareholders for a startup to 2,000.

This number made a big difference in the age of the slim IT company (in 2015 a $16 billion colossus like Facebook had only 12,000 employees) because most unicorns had only 100 or 200 employees and 10 or 20 external investors.

Management for Delight

Silicon Valley had always pioneered new forms of management. Fairchild and Intel allowed engineers to behave in a more casual manner than their counterparts on the East Coast, and Xerox PARC made it even more casual. HP pioneered a family-style approach to management. And so forth.

At the beginning of the new century new experiments characterized the biggest success stories. Larry Page debuted as CEO of Google by fighting bureaucracy, to the point that eventually middle management was wiped out; but only to retract and re-hire all those supervisors. However, Larry Page had shifted the emphasis to hiring the right people, even if that meant slowing down the pace of growth, and that principle remained in place even when the hierarchy was reintroduced.

Twitter embraced the principle that "the purpose of hierarchy is to destroy bad bureaucracy" (credited to Chris Fry). So hierarchy is good but bureaucracy is bad. That became a recurring theme. Ask people to obey a boss and they will be happy to be followers; ask them to fill a form and they will quit. So much so that Adobe removed the yearly performance evaluation, one of the most common practices in the USA, and replaced it with a year-long feedback from the boss; basically "guidance" instead of "examination".

A lot of startups also realized that the DIY (do it yourself) model is not always productive and, alas, often alienates engineers, who would rather focus on what they do best. Hence the DIFM (do it for me) model, in which the engineer expects the structure to provide everything that is needed for engineers to focus on their tasks. Even the concept of the "job description" was not always clear. Facebook hired the best and then sent them to a six-week boot camp to figure out the best way for them to contribute to the organization. Slogan: "every job is temporary". Team work was always important in Silicon Valley, but this was the age when most companies, large and small, recognized Richard Hackman's rule of thumb that "no work team should have membership in the double digits". And Bob Sutton at Stanford admonished that "one deadbeat cuts team performance by 30-40%". Combine the two rules of thumb and you get the typical engineering team of the 2010s. As for customer relationships, Intuit's Stephen Gay spoke of "Design for Delight", create an organization that "evokes positive emotion throughout the customer's journey".

Unspoken but widespread was the rule that an organization must be able to steal from others, and morally and legally justify it, while at the same time making sure, on both moral and legal grounds, that others didn't steal from itself. The history of Silicon Valley had often been the history of how a "genius" stole an idea from someone else and turned it into a runaway success (semiconductors, personal computers, database management systems, social media). Terms like "traitors" and lawsuits settled out of court are as much part of the history as the more widely publicized products.

WeChat vs Everybody Else

The truth is that, despite the ridiculous valuations, the unicorns and the million startups, the Internet world (and the world of so-called "smart" devices in general) had never been so maddeningly complicated, with thousands of "smartphone apps" on dozens of different devices. The crisis was not felt in the USA, where competition was still viewed as beneficial to the investment community (certainly not to the user, who had to use myriad applications during an average day). The crisis was not felt in China either, but for a different reason: Weixin/Wechat had largely solved the problem in just a few years since its founding. Launched in 2011 by Tencent (that originally simply offered a copy of ICQ called QQ), within 5 years Wechat had learned how to combine messaging, voice calling, video conferencing, group chatting, Facebook, Twitter, Paypal, Dropbox, and more into one simple and fast app. The original chat/messaging system designed by Xiaolong Zhang had rapidly become a universal platform for all sorts of online needs. 700 million Chinese were using it, and they were spending on average 35% of their online time on it, with little or no distinction between work and private life. Wechat had turned into a smartphone feature almost every ordinary action. For example, exchanging business cards had been reduced to beaming a QR code from one smartphone to another one. In 2016 the cash-less economy was a reality in China, where even taxi drivers and humble family restaurants accepted payment with smartphones (both Tencent's Wechat and Alibaba's Alipay) when it was still a very confusing rarity in Silicon Valley. The smartphone was a frustrating experience in the USA, where the proliferation of apps, notifications and mandatory updates was rapidly becoming more of a distraction than an attraction; whereas in China the smartphone had indeed become an indispensable limb of the body.

Culture and Society

The years of the Great Recession (2008-11) witnessed the beginning of a significant migration of high-tech companies or of their employees from Silicon Valley towards San Francisco. One reason was certainly that over the years San Francisco had invested in improving its "look and feel" (especially for young people) whereas Silicon Valley remained one of the ugliest urban landscapes in the world with virtually no aesthetic appeal for young people. San Francisco also offered the convenience of neighborhood stores and decent public transportation versus Silicon Valley's giant malls and chronically congested roads. The Great Recession of 2008-11 had greatly affected the average family, and certainly a lot of the artists and musicians who formed the backbone of San Francisco's intellectual life, while the employees of companies like Google and Facebook had been getting richer, and their purchasing power had skyrocketed.

By the end of that recession more and more Silicon Valley employees had moved to San Francisco. Companies like Google were offering free shuttle rides to their employees from San Francisco to the workplace. This, in turn, encouraged even more young, single Silicon Valley people with good salaries to move to San Francisco.

A tectonic shift in lifestyle was taking place. Silicon Valley had been born between Palo Alto (Hewlett-Packard) and Mountain View (Shockley Labs). It had then drifted steadily south (Lockheed, Intel, Apple). Then the era of software had started moving the high-tech industry north: Oracle in Redwood City; Paypal, Facebook and Google in Palo Alto; Twitter in San Francisco. This may reflect both the age group and the social class of the people involved. The hardware industry (which is, after all, a kind of manufacturing industry) was originally driven by children of the working class (Robert Noyce, Gordon Moore, Andy Grove, Steve Jobs) and they tended to be family men. Their natural habitat was in the suburbs. The early software heroes (Larry Ellison, Bill Joy) were also from working-class suburbia; but the post-Internet software industry (the generation of Larry Page and Peter Thiel), on the other hand, was mainly founded by young and single people who were often raised in the upper middle class. They wanted a city life: not "delis" and pubs, but European cheese stores and plenty of evening activities. San Francisco still had relatively underperforming schools compared with, say, Cupertino, but singles don't care for good schools: they don't have children to send to school. It was almost literally a "building" culture (Silicon Valley) versus a "coding" culture (San Francisco).

By 2013 this had become a sociopolitical issue: the free shuttle buses heading for Silicon Valley had come to symbolize the growing income inequality of the Bay. Real estate prices were skyrocketing in San Francisco while ordinary families were struggling to make ends meet. Rent rapidly became unaffordable for most people, causing an exodus of artists and musicians (and, in general, lower income individuals) towards Oakland. They were being replaced by what used to be called "yuppies": young urban professionals with little or no interest in the community.

In 2013 the community began to fight back: protesters targeted shuttle buses in well-publicized events. There was no way to stop the trend, though. San Francisco was home to more high-tech startups than ever in its history. Stopping the commuters from Silicon Valley wasn't going to make a huge difference.

The city was changing. For critics it was becoming "Silicon Valley with bad weather" (a reference to its cold foggy summers). For supporters (and speculators) it was becoming an incredible business opportunity. Silicon Valley, meanwhile, struggled to retain its charisma. It was still charismatic for millions of foreigners who knew it only from books and movies; but anyone living there had little praise for Silicon Valley's poor infrastructure and spartan buildings. Some defended Silicon Valley's plain, unsophisticated, uncultured, sober appearance as representing the spirit of the garage startups.

In 2014 San Francisco, a city with less than a million people, received 16% of all US venture investment. Venture capital was clearly moving back from Menlo Park to San Francisco. The number for Palo Alto was still impressive though (4.8%), given how small the town was.

Despite the high-tech invasion, San Francisco was increasingly a city of contradictions. San Francisco was a place in which people already lived in the future. They could hang out with their friends even when they were alone, thanks to social media. They inhabited a "sharing economy": they could book a weeklong stay in a cool apartment through Airbnb, which had disrupted the hotel industry, or hire a luxury car anywhere in the city through the mobile app Uber. However, instead of using a bullet train to travel somewhere for the weekend, they were trapped in a city with below-standard transportation. Instead of paying with their smartphone they still paid with credit cards. Their Internet connections were the slowest in the Pacific region. They proudly streamed movies at ridiculously slow speeds. They took buses that ran on diesel and, if they ever wanted to visit Berkeley across the Bay, they took a medieval-style subway called BART, and, if they ever wanted to visit Silicon Valley down south, they took a medieval-style train called Caltrain (or, worse, "express buses" that were slower than the average run-down bus of a developing country). There were neither multi-layered monorails nor magnetic-levitation trains (not to mention good-looking skyscrapers. The people who worked in the high-tech industry self-congratulated all the time about how futuristic their lives were (one reason being that they rarely took a vacation that would allow them to check how the rest of the world actually lived). Ironically, it was the people who "didn't" work in the high-tech industry who realized how "low-tech" the Bay Area was, because those were the people traveling for vacation in Asia and Europe.

The culture around the Bay Area had changed a lot in terms of sharing information. In fact, the new corporations had created a kind of police state in which employees were not allowed to say anything about their project (and often not even "what" project they worked on).

And, of course, the spreading of the high-tech industry had created a mono-culture that increasingly had no clue who Kafka or Monet were, that was wiping out decades of avantgarde music and legions of eccentric artists and performers.

It was emblematic that in 2015 only one art gallery remained at the fabled address of 77 Geary St, a multi-story building that had hosted several galleries for at least three decades. It was emblematic of the whole art scene around Union Square. Philanthropists abounded, but they were not interested in the arts. In 2012 Sergey Brin (Google), his wife Anne Wojcicki (23andMe) and Mark Zuckerberg (Facebook) joined forces with Jack Ma (Alibaba) and Russian venture capitalist Yuri Milner to establish a new international award, the Breakthrough Prize, for math and science; hardly a way to encourage young people to become artists.

A glimmer of hope came in 2015 when Silicon Valley venture capitalist Andy Rappaport and his wife, Deborah, acquired some abandoned warehouses at 1275 Minnesota Street and turned them into a new cultural center. In 2016 the San Francisco Museum of Modern Art expanded to become the largest museum of contemporary art in the Americas.

The Minnesota St Project

Burning Man had become a tourist attraction for boring nerds and rich European kids. In 2015 the city hardly noticed the centennial of the Panama-Pacific International Exposition of 1915, although two years earlier Leo Villareal had built the world's largest light sculpture. In 2011 Autodesk acquired Instructables, a portal for do-it-yourself projects founded in 2005 in San Francisco by MIT Media Lab alumni Eric Wilhelm and Saul Griffith. At the same time Autodesk launched its own artists-in-residence program, located in the renovated Pier 9 of San Francisco's port.

Autodesk Pier 9

A net beneficiary of the exodus of intellectuals and artists from San Francisco was Oakland. In 2013 a group of technology hackers, political activists, scientists, artists and writers renovated a building in Oakland, renamed it Omni Commons, and turned it into a free space for building an interdisciplinary community. Among the early tenants were the poetry publishers Timeless and Infinite Light, the hackerspace Sudo Room, the biohacker space Counter Culture Labs, and the film-making collective Black Hole. In 2014 Oakland launched its largest revitalization project since World War II, Brooklyn Basin, an entire new neighborhood by the sea (incidentally codeveloped with a Beijing-based company, Zarsion, the largest investment by China in California ever).

Increasingly, the great demented ideas were coming from other cities, not from the San Francisco Bay Area. For example, it was New York University students Sam Lavigne and Amelia Winger-Bearskin who organized the first "Stupid Hackathon" in 2014, a one-day hackathon devoted to create projects that have no value whatsoever. For example, Sam Lavigne built a Google Glass app that makes the user vomit, while Miklos Pataky and Carl Jamilkowski wrote NonAd Block, a browser extension that blocks all web content that isn't an advert. The idea spread rapidly to Europe and to San Francisco.

The Empire Continued

The influence of Silicon Valley over the rest of world was increasing, as was increasing the gap between Silicon Valley and any other region of the world. Gone were the days when Europeans looked down on Silicon Valley as a childish and doomed experiment. Gone were the days when Boston thought it could compete easily with those eccentrics of the Far

West. By 2015 the Bay Area dwarfed any other region of the world for technology and science. The top most valued companies in the world (by market evaluation) were in the Bay Area: Alphabet/Google and Apple. The Bay Area boasted the number-one companies in social media (Facebook), semiconductors (Intel) and business software (Oracle). If it declared independence, the Bay Area alone (not the whole of California) would rank 22nd in the world for GDP and third in GDP per capita. The San Francisco Bay Area would rank fifth behind the USA, Britain, Germany and France in Nobel Prize winners. In 2016 Forbes compiled a ranking of cities based on the combined net worth of their billionaires. Palo Alto came out 7th and San Francisco 10th. The other cities all had more than 8 million people. San Francisco didn't even have one million, and Palo Alto was a tiny town of only 50,000 people. In 2016 the MIT Technology Review compiled a list of the 50 most innovative companies in the world: in the top 25 there were 5 from China, 2 from Europe, 1 from Japan and 9 from the Bay Area (more in the Bay Area than in all other continents combined). In 2016 the MIT Technology Review published the list of the 50 most innovative companies in the world. In the top 25 there were 5 from China, 2 from Europe, 1 from Japan, and... 9 from the tiny Bay Area.

Russian president Vladimir Putin was widely considered to be behind the persecution (and sometimes murder) of dissident journalists in Russia. No other region of the USA was applying the "Putin doctrine" more diligently and fervently than Silicon Valley. Its billionaires had little patience for journalists analyzing their lifestyle and their speculative investments, especially when those reports revealed paranoid personalities and dubious business practices, if not outright scams. In 2016 Paypal's cofounder Peter Thiel admitted that he had spent 10 years secretly financing a lawsuit against Gawker Media, a media company guilty of exposing his homosexuality in 2007. Gawker filed bankruptcy in 2016, sending a chill through the media world: Thiel had just warned the entire industry of the financial risk displeasing a Silicon Valley billionaire. Thiel's new venture, Palantir, was a secretive arm of the CIA developing technologies to "search and analyze data" (in other words, to spy on citizens). Venture capitalist Vinod Khosla commented that journalists need "to be taught lessons". And there was no doubt in anyone's mind that all Wikipedia articles on Silicon Valley celebrities and corporations were being carefully edited by hired guns, not by independent Wikipedians. The most popular blogs of Silicon Valley (Techcrunch to name one) were as acritical of and as servile towards Silicon Valley celebrities and businesses as the Russian newspapers were of Putin. In 2011 Peter Thiel had already created controversy by launching his "20 Under 20" fellowship that pays bright students under the age of 20 a generous amount of money ($100,000) to drop out of college and go work.

Despite all the hoopla about the inclusive multi-ethnic community of Silicon Valley, the facts spoke otherwise: Silicon Valley had been and still was very much dominated by the white male culture. The technology (the transistor, the computer, the operating system, the database, the Internet, the personal computer, the World-wide Web, the smartphone) and the ideology (Fred Terman, the first startups, the venture capitalists) had been invented by Caucasian males.

By the second decade of the 21st century not much had changed: sure there were many startups founded by Asians, but the ones that defined the industry (Apple, Oracle, Netscape, Google, Facebook) were almost all founded by Caucasian males (as were Microsoft and Amazon in Seattle, and as were Texas Instruments, Motorola, Compaq, Dell and so forth in other parts of the southwest). In 2015 a whopping 85% of both Facebook and Yahoo engineers were male. At Google the number was 83%, at Apple 80%. At Twitter the percentage was even 90.

Women like Meg Whitman and Marissa Mayer made news when they were appointed to the helm of a large corporation, but they were not founders (nor inventors), and this was true in general of the high-tech industry in the world (Virginia Rometty, Marillyn Hewson, Ellen Kullman, Phebe Novakovic, Anne Mulcahy, Ursula Burns and so forth, and incidentally all of them Caucasians except Burns). Ditto for venture capital, that was mostly in the hands of big firms run by Caucasian males. In 2016 Techcrunch calculated that 67% of venture capitalists were white males, 19% were Asian males, and white and Asian females combined were only 11% (leaving 3% to all other ethnic group, males and females).

The idea of Silicon Valley as a melting pot of brains from all over the world and of both sexes was still mostly just that: an idea.

The Hyper-visionaries

The 2010s were also the age of the hyper-visionary institutions. In a sense, Stewart Brand had pioneered this idea too, when in 1996 he had established the Long Now Foundation; but the new generation of hyper-visionary thinking was much more practical and, generally, funded by billionaire philanthropists. In 2015 the Future of Life Institute was created by Jaan Tallinn (Skype cofounder), Max Tegmark (MIT mathematician) and Anthony Aguirre (UC Santa Cruz astrophysicist). Its mission was "To catalyze and support research and initiatives for safeguarding life and developing optimistic visions of the future". The advisors included astrophysicists (Stephen Hawking and Martin Rees of Cambridge University, Saul Perlmutter of UC Berkeley, Alan Guth of the MIT), biologists (Christof Koch of the Allen Institute for Brain Science, George Church of Harvard University), philosophers (Nick Bostrom of Oxford's Future of Humanity Institute), economists (Erik Brynjolfsson of the MIT), high-tech entrepreneurs (Elon Musk of Tesla and SpaceX) and Artificial

Intelligence scientists (Stuart Russell of UC Berkeley). Then in 2016 Russian billionaire Yuri Milner launched Breakthrough Starshot to build laser-propelled nano-spacecrafts into space and reach in two decades Alpha Centauri. On the board were Facebook's founder Mark Zuckerberg and astrophysicist Stephen Hawking. Milner hired Pete Worden, former NASA Ames executive, as the director of the project, and assembled a team of advisors that included UC Berkeley's astrophysicist Saul Perlmutter, Harvard's astronomer Avi Loeb, Institute for Advanced Study's mathematician Freeman Dyson, and UC Santa Barbara's astrophysicist Philip Lubin. Also in 2016 Elon Musk and Sam Altman of Y Combinator established OpenAI, a non-profit think-tank "to advance digital intelligence in the way that is most likely to benefit humanity as a whole" and hired Ilya Sutskever, research scientist at Google, as its director, as well as Greg Brockman, formerly the CTO of Strip, as its CTO. Scientific advisors included Pieter Abbeel, Yoshua Bengio, Alan Kay, Sergey Levine, and Vishal Sikka. The funding came from Amazon, Infosys, YCombinator, Peter Thiel (cofounder of PayPal), Sam Altman, Greg Brockman, Elon Musk, Reid Hoffman (co-founder of LinkedIn) and Jessica Livingston (cofounder of YCombinator).

A Birds' Eye View of Silicon Valley (2010)

Conclusions

The computer that drives your smart phone is nearly a million times cheaper, a hundred thousand times smaller, and thousands of times more powerful than a mainframe of the 1970s. In less than four decades the computing power that one can buy with the same amount of money has increased a billion times. The amount of data that one can store for $100 has also multiplied astronomically. Today a person can buy one terabyte of storage for $100   versus 28 megabytes for $115,500 in 1961 (the IBM 1301 Model 1); note that one tera is one million megas. The number of documents that one can print and mail has also increased by several orders of magnitude. The speed at which a document is transmitted has decreased from days to milliseconds, down nine orders of magnitude. The amount of free information available to the user of a computer has escalated from the documents of an office in the 1960s to billions of webpages.

Originally, computing meant speed. A computer was a machine capable of performing computations in a fraction of a second that would have required many humans working for many days. Fifty years later, this simple concept has led to a completely different understanding of what computing means. Computing power now means two things: access to an overwhelming amount of knowledge, and pervasive worldwide communication. The former has created a knowledge-based society, in which problems are solved by tapping into a vast and dynamic archive of knowledge; in a sense, the same utopia as artificial intelligence. The latter has created virtual communities. It is not obvious anymore to ordinary users how these two effects related to computing speed, the original purpose of computers, but they do.

The computer has transformed human society into a digital society, in which humans are creators, archivists, relayers, and browsers of digital data which encode world facts into Boolean algebra. It is a vastly more efficient way of encoding the world than the previous paper-based society. At the same time progress in telecommunication technology, and in particular the convergence of telecommunications and information technology, has turned the innocent phone into an all-encompassing personal assistant that is only marginally used for voice communication.

Silicon Valley is widely viewed as the symbol of this revolution.

However, computers were not invented in Silicon Valley, and Silicon Valley did not invent the transistor, integrated circuit, personal computer, Internet, World-Wide Web, the browser, the search engine, nor social networking. Silicon Valley also did not invent the phone, the cell phone, nor the smart phone. But, at one point in time or another, Silicon Valley was instrumental in making them go "viral," in perfecting a product the world wanted.

Silicon Valley's startups excelled at exploiting under-exploited inventions that came out of large East Coast and European R&D centers and somehow migrated to the Bay Area. AT&T (an East Coast company) invented semiconductor electronics and Shockley ported it to Mountain View. IBM (an East Coast company) invented data storage at its San Jose laboratories. Xerox (an East Coast company) perfected human-machine interfaces at its Palo Alto Research Center. The government invented the Internet and chose the SRI as one of the nodes. CERN (a European center) invented the World-wide Web and the first US server was assigned to the SLAC. The smartphone came from Finland. And so forth.

In fact, Silicon Valley's largest research centers were never truly "research" centers but rather "R&D" (research and development) centers. They were more oriented towards the "D" than the "R." Nothing was comparable to AT&T's Bell Labs or to IBM's Watson labs (each of which produced Nobel Prize winners, unlike, say, HP Labs or Xerox PARC). Some would argue that the "R" of Silicon Valley was done at Stanford University and UC Berkeley, but even those two research centers produced no monumental invention in the realm of high technology, nothing comparable to the transistor or to the World-Wide Web. They were much better at incubating businesses than at inventing the technology for those businesses.

The biggest of all myths must be dismissed at the onset: we must recognize that Silicon Valley invented very little. Computers were not invented in Silicon Valley. Robots were not invented here either. Silicon Valley did not invent the transistor, the integrated circuit, the personal computer, the Internet, the World-Wide Web, the browser, the search engine, social networking, nor the smart phone. Neither biotech nor greentech are from Silicon Valley. Silicon Valley was instrumental in making them go "viral." Silicon Valley has a unique (almost evil) knack for understanding the socially destabilizing potential of an invention and then making lots of money out of it; Schumpeter's "creative destruction" turned into destructive creativity. That's, ultimately, what people mean when they talk about Silicon Valley as a factory of innovation.

Don't look at Silicon Valley to guess what the next big thing in high-tech will be: it is being invented somewhere else. Silicon Valley will find a way to use it to revolutionize the lives of ordinary people or workers.

The Bay Area might also be the place that perfected the delicate balance upon which the modern capitalist state rests, the balance among government, big business and small business. Innovation in the high-tech industry has been a cooperation among big corporations (the transistor, the integrated circuit, disk storage, the database, all Japanese inventions), small companies (the microprocessor, the personal computer, the search engine, social media, biotech), and government-funded projects (the computer, the Internet, the World-wide Web, the Human Genome Project). All three groups contributed significantly to the progress of the field.

There was nothing intrinsic in the Silicon Valley model that made it work for computers in particular. Whatever it was, that model worked for high-tech in general. Silicon Valley represented a platform for perennial innovation that could be applied to other fields as well (such as biotech and greentech). It coincidentally started with "infotech," the first massively destructive industry since the electrical revolution.

The Silicon Valley model until 2000 could be summarized in three mottos: "question authority," "think different," and "change the world." Silicon Valley did not exist in a vacuum. It paralleled important sociopolitical upheavals that started in the San Francisco Bay Area and then spread all over the world, such as the free-speech movement and the hippie movement. Alternative lifestyles and utopian countercultures had always been in the genes of the Bay Area, starting with the early pioneers of the Far West. The propensity towards independence and individualism predates Silicon Valley's startups. That propensity led to the "do it yourself" philosophy of the hobbyists who started Silicon Valley. The hobbyists came first. Then came the great engineering schools, the massive government investment, the transfer of technology from academia to industry, and, at last, massive private investment. All of this would not have happened without that anti-establishment spirit which propelled the Bay Area to the front pages of newspapers worldwide during the 1960s. Many of today's protagonists of Silicon Valley are, consciously or not, part of or children of the generation that wanted to change the world. They did.

The history of the high-tech industry in the Bay Area, from Philo Farnsworth to Peter Thiel, is largely the history of a youth culture, just like the "other" history of the Bay Area, from the Gold Rush to the hippies, is a history of a youth culture. The protagonists were often extremely young, and almost invariably contributed the most significant ideas in their youth (just like rock musicians or mathematicians). One cannot separate the evolution of that youth culture and the evolution of the high-tech industry: they are each other's alter ego. In fact, the two biggest technological waves and financial bubbles were started by young people for a market of young people (personal computers and Internet, i.e. hobbyists and dotcoms). They represented the ultimate feedback loop of youth culture.

The eccentric independent is truly the protagonist of this story. Silicon Valley could not have happened in places that were not friendly towards the eccentric independent. For example, Europe was a place where employees had to wear a suit and tie in order to succeed. Therefore Europe created an upper class of people who were better at dressing up, and not necessarily the ones who were more knowledgeable, competent, and creative. In the Bay Area even billionaires wore blue jeans and t-shirts (before and after becoming billionaires). Silicon Valley could not have happened on the East Coast either, for the same reason that the hippies and the free-speech movement were not born on the East Coast: the Bay Area was permeated by a unique strand of extravagant and idiosyncratic anti-establishment sentiment and by a firm belief in changing the world. The one place that came close to replicating Silicon Valley was Route 128 near Boston, which was also the second most anti-establishment place in the nation.

However, the East Coast was similar to Europe and dissimilar from Silicon Valley in another respect: vertical instead of horizontal mobility. Europe and the East Coast encouraged employees to think of a career within a company, whereas Silicon Valley encouraged employees to think of switching jobs all the time. In Europe there was little motivation to hire someone from another company, since one could not recycle that person's skills legally, and it was even illegal to start a new business based on what one learned at a company. Hence Europe created big companies where people's main motivation was to get promote to higher and higher positions; and, typically, away from engineering. This praxis had the double effect of "detraining" engineers (as they were shuffled around in search of better-sounding titles, and typically landed non-technical positions) while limiting the flow of knowledge to the internal departments of a company, whereas in Silicon Valley engineers continuously refined their technical skills as they moved from company to company while at the same time facilitating a flow of knowledge from company to company.

Perhaps this was the ultimate reason why in Europe an engineering job was considered inferior to a marketing job or even to sales jobs, while in Silicon Valley the status symbol of being an engineer was only second to the status symbol of being an entrepreneur; and so was the salary, while in Europe marketing/sales people or even bank clerks made more money and had better prospects than engineers. Europe converted tens of thousands of bright engineering talents into mediocre bureaucrats or sales people (in a suit and tie) while Silicon Valley converted them into advisers to the board or founders of companies (in blue jeans and T-shirt).

The different cultural patterns also explain the meritocracy that has ruled in Silicon Valley with no exception since the days of the first microprocessor. It is difficult, if not impossible, to mention the heir of a major Silicon Valley entrepreneur who inherited the family business the way, say, the grandchild and the great-grandson inherited the Ford Motor Company from the original founder. Who you are matters very little in a society that was created by eccentric independents.

It certainly didn't help Europe that it relied so much on the three "Bs" (big government, big labor and big corporations) while Silicon Valley despised all three. However, the history of Silicon Valley and of computing in general shows that big government can be the greatest engine of innovation when it is driven by national interest (typically, in times of war) and that big corporations do work when they can afford to think long-term (for many years most innovation in computers came from AT&T and IBM, and in Silicon Valley they came from Xerox). Big labor was always absent from Silicon Valley, but in a sense it was volunteered by the companies themselves (the HP model).

The role of big government, big corporations, and big labor in the success of Japan and Britain is instructive. The Japanese computer industry had to start from scratch in the 1950s. The failing British computer industry had pioneered computers in the 1940s and had all the know-how necessary to match developments in the US. In both cases the government engaged in sponsoring long-term plans and in brokering strategic alliances among manufacturers, and in both cases initial research came from a government-funded laboratory. However, the outcomes were completely opposite: Japan created a vibrant computer industry within the existing conglomerates, whereas Britain's computer industry self-destroyed within two decades.

Between Japan and Silicon Valley it is debatable which region benefited more from government aid. The Japanese conglomerates were certainly nurtured and protected by the government, but their main customer was the broad market of consumers. From Sony's transistor radio to Samsung's smartphones the revenues of East Asia's high tech were coming from selling millions of units to millions of people. Silicon Valley innovation, instead, was routinely funded by the government (specifically by DARPA): the money that started Fairchild, Oracle, SUN, Netscape and many others was coming, ultimately, from contracts/grants with/from government agencies, whether NASA, CIA or (more often) DARPA.

In 1977 California had more high-tech jobs than New York and Boston combined, but both Los Angeles and the Bay Area also benefited from more defense contracts than New York and Boston combined.

When the Cold War ended and military funding began to drain, Silicon Valley found a great substitute in advertising (thereby treating technology like what it was becoming, i.e. entertainment). In retrospect, Steve Kirsch's Infoseek, that in 1995 pioneered "cost-per-impression" and "cost-per-click" advertising, might prove to be a milestone event in the history of the region, fueling a boom (of free services and products) comparable to the Gold Rush, the Oil Rush, etc.

Last but not least, the Bay Area managed to attract brains from all over the world. The competitive advantage derived from immigration was immense. Brains flocked to the Bay Area because the Bay Area was "cool." It projected the image of a dreamland for the highly educated youth of the East Coast, Europe and Asia. Because the Bay Area was underpopulated, those immigrants came to represent not an isolated minority but almost a majority, a fact that encouraged them to behave like first-class citizens and not just as hired mercenaries. The weather and money certainly mattered, but what attracted all those immigrants to the Bay Area was, ultimately, the anti-establishment spirit applied to a career. It made work feel like it wasn't work but a way to express one's self.

And, as usual, luck has its (crucial) role: had William Shockley grown up in Tennessee instead of Palo Alto, maybe he would have never dreamed of starting his company in Mountain View, and therefore neither Fairchild nor Intel nor any of the dozens of companies founded by his alumni and the alumni of his alumni would be based in the Bay Area, or in California at all. All the reasons usually advanced to explain why Silicon Valley happened where it happened neglect the fact that the mother of all "silicon" startups was based there simply because Shockley wanted to go back where he grew up

Some myths about Silicon Valley have been exaggerated and some truths have been downplayed.

Mentorship, to start with, was not as important as claimed by the mentors. It was customary that the founder of a successful company received funding to start another company. This did work in terms of profitability, because the star-appeal brought both investors and customers, but it rarely resulted in technological breakthroughs. Recycling a successful entrepreneur was just an advanced form of marketing. In practice, the vast majority of quantum leaps forward in technology were provided by young newcomers who knew very little about the preexisting business.

Another factor that has been over-emphasized is the importance that the military industry had in transferring high technology to the Bay Area. While this is certainly true, and certainly accounted for an initial transfer of engineers from other parts of the country to the Bay Area, there is very little that the military industry contributed to what today is Silicon Valley. In fact, very few startups originated from the big military contractors (if nothing else because their employees are under much stricter non-disclosure agreements) and even those few startups mostly worked for the military establishment from which they originated, a business model that dominates the technology parks around the Pentagon in Virginia, which might or might not have been a blueprint for what happened in Silicon Valley.

One factor in the evolution that is often underestimate is (as odd as it might sound) how important the shortcomings of the established industry leaders have been to foster innovation. Apple completely missed the advent of the Internet, Google completely missed the advent of social networking and Facebook will soon completely miss the "next big thing". Each of these blunders helped create a new giant and an entire new industry. If Apple had introduced a search engine in 2000, perhaps Google would never have existed, and if Google had introduced a social-networking platform in 2004, perhaps Facebook would never have existed. Each of them had the power to easily occupy the new niche... except that it failed to notice it. In most cases the founders and CEOs of Silicon Valley companies are visionaries in the narrow field in which they started, but not very skilled at noticing seismic shifts in the overall landscape.

The Bay Area was uniquely equipped with the mindset to subvert rules and embrace novelty. However, history would have been wildly different without the government's intervention. The Bay Area constitutes a prime example of technologies that moved from military to civilian use. The initial impulse to radio engineering and electronics came from the two world wars, and was largely funded by the military.

The first wave of venture capital for the high-tech industry was created by a government program. It was governments (US and Britain) that funded the development of the computer, and NASA (a government agency) was the main customer of the first integrated circuits. The Internet was invented by the government and then turned into a business by the government. Generally speaking, the federal government invested in high-risk long-term projects while venture capitalists tended to follow short-term trends. The US government was the largest venture capitalist of Silicon Valley, and the government of the US was also the most influential strategist of Silicon Valley; whereas, one could argue, venture capitalists mainly created speculative bubbles. I always joke that venture capitalists don't "act": they "react". They tend to react to a few successful startups by massively over-funding their sectors.

However, even the "bubble ideology" has a positive function in Silicon Valley: it accelerates business formation and competition.

Needless to say, it is difficult to tell which of those factors were essential to Silicon Valley becoming what it became.

There's another element to the success of Silicon Valley that is hard to quantify: the role of chance in creativity. Because of its lifestyle and values, Silicon Valley has always maximized the degree of chance. Work is often viewed as play, not duty. Fun and ideals prevail over money and status. Hence chance, hence creativity.

From this point of view the importance of the arts is often underestimated: the Bay Area was famous as a refuge for "crazy" artists way before it became known as an incubator of startups. Like every other phenomenon in the world, Silicon Valley does not exist in a vacuum.

The golden question is why Silicon Valley worked for some sectors and not for others. It failed in laser applications, although it had a head start, and it never made a dent into factory automation (despite a head start in robotics). My guess is that the individual is not enough: it takes a community of inventors. The defense industry created that community for the radio engineering and the semiconductor industry. The venture capitalists are creating it for biotech and greentech. Factory automation, however, despite the potential of causing one of the most dramatic changes in human society, was largely left to heavy industry that was not based in the Bay Area. The Defense Department created that community elsewhere. The Japanese government created it in Japan. Nobody ever created it in Silicon Valley. The whole premise of numeric control (coupling processors with sensors) remains largely alien to Silicon Valley.

There have been attempts at creating "Silicon Valleys" around the world: Malaysia's Multimedia Super Corridor, France's Sophia Antipolis, Germany's Silicon Allee (Berlin) and Bavaria, Dubai's Internet City, Bangalore's eCity, China's Zhongguancun Science Park, Russia's Skolkovo (begun in 2010), etc. The closest thing to Silicon Valley outside the US has probably been Singapore, whose GDP of $182 billion (2008) is less than half of the Bay Area's GDP of $427 billion. However, venture capitalists invested $1,370 per capita in the Bay Area (2006) versus $180 in Singapore (nonetheless ahead of New York's $107). Another close second could be Israel, a country rich with venture capitalists and high-tech companies; but Israel has been entangled in the perpetual political turmoil of the Middle East. Ditto for Jordan, a true miracle of high-tech expansion surrounded by civil wars, revolutions and counter-revolutions.

The only country that can compete with the USA in terms of mass-scale innovation that has changed the daily lives of billions of people is Japan. However, Japanese innovation has mostly come from conglomerates that are a century old. It is hard to find a Japanese company that emerged thanks to a new technology and became a major player. The whole phenomenon of venture capitalists and high-tech start-ups has virtually been inexistent in Japan.

And one simple reason is that Japanese society has little tolerance for failure, and the Japanese public has little sympathy for those who take risks. Entrepreneurs are not role models. Nonetheless, Japan boasts a spectacular degree of innovation. Innovation happens at the level of the corporate lab, of the university lab and of the government-funded research lab; but rarely at the enterpreneurial level. Stanford University receives relatively few students from Japan (certainly very few compared with those from China and India), and one simple reason is that their future will not be shaped by the model of Silicon Valley but by a model that is almost the exact opposite. Nonetheless, Japan has been a model of innovation for several decades.

Silicon Valley is improbable outside of the Bay Area. Other regions of the world may come up with their own models (like East Asia did) but replicating Silicon Valley is probably a senseless idea. As Mike Malone (one of the greatest historians of Silicon Valley) has written: "The next Silicon Valley is... Silicon Valley."

Many have written about the role of East Asian governments in the astronomical growth of their economies. Little has been written about how much those economies owe to Silicon Valley. Both the venture capitalists and the startups of Silicon Valley contributed to creating the very economic boom of East Asia that then they set out to exploit. Silicon Valley literally engineered the high-tech boom in Taiwan and mainland China as much as those governments did. Those economies have become not what they wanted to become but precisely what Silicon Valley needed: highly efficient futuristic science parks with all the tools to cheaply and quickly mass produce the sophisticated components needed by Silicon Valley companies. The same is true for India: the large software parks such as the one in Bangalore have largely been shaped by the demand of software coming from Silicon Valley, not by a government-run program for the future of software technology. Whenever such programs exist, they often embody precisely the goal to serve the demand coming from the US. The "Golden Projects" of mainland China of the 1990s, that created the high-tech infrastructure of that country, would have been pointless without a major customer. That customer was Silicon Valley.

Asians are proud to point out that in 2009 their continent employs 1.5 million workers in the computer industry while the US employs only 166,000. That is true. But they forget to add that most of those 1.5 million jobs were created by Silicon Valley. Foxconn (or, more properly, Hon Hai Precision Industry), founded in Taiwan in 1974 by Tai-Ming "Terry" Gou to manufacture plastic and that in 1988 opened a pioneering factory in China's then experimental city Shenzhen, became the world's largest manufacturer of electronics by 2009, with revenues of $62 billion. It dwarfed Apple and Intel, employing 800,000 people (more than the whole Bay Area). However, its main customers were Apple, Intel, Cisco and Hewlett-Packard, besides Sony, Microsoft and Motorola. In 2005 Taiwanese companies produced 80% of all personal digital assistants, 70% of all notebooks, and 60% of all flat-panel monitors.

This, of course, also translated into an interesting (and somewhat unnerving) social experiment: Silicon Valley was generating and investing ever larger sums of money, but creating an ever lower number of jobs. The investment and the profit were based here, but the jobs were based "there" in Asia. In fact, the Bay Area's unemployment rate in 2010 was close to 10%, one of the highest in the entire world. One could see a future when the low-level workers of the high-tech industry would start moving out of Silicon Valley towards Asia. The same was true of the other industries, from energy to biotech.

Nobody in the US government planned Silicon Valley. The president of the USA probably learned of Silicon Valley from a magazine article. The government had no direct role in creating Silicon Valley. The spirit of Silicon Valley was created by an alternative culture, by people who were thinking different, and in particular thinking of how to use technology in unorthodox ways. The San Francisco Bay Area had no advantage over many other places, like Boston, Philadelphia, London and New Jersey. These places had more brains, technology, money and powerful corporations than the Bay Area. Silicon Valley happened in a very unlikely region. What was special in that region was the way people thought. It is difficult to reproduce it in other regions. Other regions can learn a few things here and there, but they are unlikely to recreate the same phenomenon.

For more than a century the San Francisco Bay Area has been the home of people who think differently, and who come from all over the world. This area has had all sorts of unorthodox phenomena, from the ham-radio amateurs of a century ago to the "beat" poets of the 1950s, from the hippies of the 1960s to the garage kids of the 1970s who created the personal computer industry, from the artists of the 1980s who played with robots to the software engineers who turned the Internet into a social platform, from the founders of the incubators to the founders of Burning Man. I don't consider all of them "good" role models, but all of them have something in common: they like to think different, and they are not afraid of acting accordingly. Be different, believe in your idea, take the risk, and do it. If you fail, it's ok. If you don't try, it is NOT ok.

Very often (and more realistically) the expression "Silicon Valley" is used to mean "a concentration of high-tech companies". Nothing wrong with it. Japan, Singapore, Taiwan (the region of China where the Internet is open), South Korea (the half of Korea where the Internet is open) have created great high-tech industries that have given us some of the most important inventions, from digital music players to flat screens. They don't have anything that is really like Silicon Valley, but they have their own centers of innovation. Their models are sometimes very different from the Silicon Valley model. So i think that "Silicon Valley" sometimes simply means "high-tech industry". And hopefully every country will have one such region because the future belongs to the high-tech industry. The only thing that all of these regions need to have in common is the very definition of "high tech": high tech is something that becomes low tech very quickly. The personal computer that was considered a miracle of engineering just 20 years ago is today a relic that makes us laugh; ditto for my first smartphone, that was considered trendy in the mid-1990s. Today's tablet will look ridiculous in 5 years. This is high tech: high tech is what becomes low tech in just a few years. Any high-tech region has to be capable of recreating itself nonstop. To me that's what "Silicon Valley" really means around the world: a region where companies evolve and adapt to collectively remain on top of technological progress.

To decide where the next big thing in high tech will come from, i never look at the money or the big companies or at government plans. I look for "cool" places, places where i would like to live and work because i would be surrounded by a spirit of creativity. There are many places in the world where young people are creating hubs of creativity, like Berlin (the Kreuzberg and Friedrichshain districts) and Barcelona (the Gracia district) in Europe, Melbourne (the Fitzroy district) in Australia, and, before Erdogan started censoring the Internet, Istanbul (the Beyoglu district) in the Middle East. These are also the places where young college-educated people from all over the world want to live. Some of these young people will start the next big thing.

As China is rapidly emerging as an economic world power, its government has spent more than any other country in creating technology parks. I personally don't believe China (as it is now) stands any chance of creating its equivalent of Silicon Valley. I explain why to my Chinese friends by simply pointing to what China does to my website: my website is banned in China (for whatever reasons unknown to me). Obviously it is not the only one: millions of websites are banned in China. Here are some of the consequences: 1. There is an enormous amount of know-how that doesn't percolate through Chinese society (for example, my website has many resources about Silicon Valley); 2. It is impossible to raise a generation of creative kids when they can only "consume" what the government selects and mandates (that is a recipe for raising very dumb citizens); 3. On top of other reasons, this is a very strong reason why virtually no educated foreigner dreams of emigrating to China for the rest of their life the way millions of us foreigners decided to move to California. Three key factors in the success of Silicon Valley are automatically removed when a government decides to ban websites at will: know-how, creativity and immigration.

China will not create a vibrant creative society like Silicon Valley for as long as websites like Google, Facebook, Twitter and even Slideshare are banned. There is an infinite amount of knowledge that is not available to the Chinese public, including the college kids who are supposed to drive the innovation of the future. In a sense, the Chinese are not on the Internet: the Internet is the free network that the entire world uses, except for Eritrea, North Korea, Saudi Arabia, Azerbaijan, Vietnam, Iran and mainland China (Source: "2015 list of Most Censored Countries", Committee to Protect Journalists). None of these countries can raise a generation of world-class entrepreneurs to compete with Silicon Valley. As far as the high-tech industry goes, these countries can only create a local economy, mostly based on copying ideas that others have invented. Silicon Valley is a knowledge-driven economy. You cannot create a knowledge-driven economy if you ban just about every website that contains knowledge. In the long run you are much more likely to create a depression. I read and hear a lot about Chinese innovation, but i can't find Chinese innovation in the high-tech industry. Copying someone else's idea is not innovation. The Chinese have always been the best business people in the world. This is not new. What is new is that today they mostly copy foreign inventions. In the old times the Chinese were inventing them and the West was copying them. Think of paper, the printing press, even robots (automata). In the old days China was inventing, and the West was copying. Now think of computers, smartphones, search engines, social media, etc: the West is inventing, and China is copying. I don't see much innovation in China. Chinese companies (and especially very small companies, like the family-run restaurant) are world-class at understanding their market and meeting their customer's needs; and then at running their business. This has not changed since ancient times. Wherever you go in the world, whether in Malaysia or Italy or San Francisco, the Chinese community is famous for its clever and hard-working business spirit. No wonder then that the same spirit enabled Tencent, Baidu and Alibaba to be very successful. Still, i can't rank any Chinese high-tech company among the main innovators in the world.

The question that I get most often when I present these ideas is: what is the state of Silicon Valley today? Certainly, not much is left today of the original spirit. "Hobbyists" have slim chances of starting the next big thing. In the age of marketing, the entry point for starting a business and going viral is not negligible: venture capitalists tend to invest in "safe" companies and in tested management teams. There are thousands of startups, but their chance of becoming the next giant is very low.

The profile of the average person has always changed. The creative eccentric of the 20th century has been replaced by a generation of disciplined but unimaginative "nerds" who would be helpless without a navigation system and a cell phone (or just without air conditioning).

Government intervention in high-tech has been scaled down (as a percentage of the industry), with the result that there is less investment in long-term projects, and the public mood against "big government" leaves few hopes that the trend can be reversed any time soon.

Immigration laws (or, better, anti-immigration laws), economic downturns, and a chronically weak dollar have greatly reduced the number of graduate-level immigrants from other developed countries. The ones who come to study in the USA and would like to stay have a hard time obtaining a work visa. The time-consuming and humiliating procedure to obtain a green card discourages even those who do obtain a work visa. It is impressive how many of the innovators of the Bay Area were not natives of the Bay Area. Immigration has been a true engine of innovation.

At the same time, the tightly knit community of Silicon Valley has been ruined by the massive immigration of opportunists who don't have the eccentric/independent spirit, and by the outsourcing of jobs to Asia that has disenfranchised the engineer from her/his company.

In turn the two recessions of the 2000s created a culture of extreme pragmatism in the industry. The proverbial family-style management pioneered by HP has turned into a 60-hour workweek with virtually no vacation days and indiscriminate layoffs whenever needed. Both companies and employees have become opportunists instead of idealists.

Fairchild, HP Labs, Intel, Xerox PARC, Apple, and so forth had built companies not so much around a technology as around their human resources. They hired the best, and nurtured highly creative environments. Today the chances of an engineer being hired by a company may depend much more on how well her/his resume had been written by her/his "head hunter" (employment agency) than on the real skills and I.Q. of the engineer. In fact, any "headhunter" can tell you that the correlation between a person's skills and chances of being hired is very low. However, the correlation between a good-looking resume and chances of being hired is very high. Such is the way in which the labs of the 21st century are being created in Silicon Valley.

The growing power of lawyers introduced another degree of distortion in the system: the chances of being laid off by a company are becoming inversely proportional to how much one is willing to pay for an attorney. An attorney is more likely to obtain something from a company on behalf of an employee than the employee through her or his work. This is beginning to replicate the problems that Europe has with unionized labor, except that it is much more expensive to defend one's job in the Bay Area through a lawyer than to defend one's job in Europe through the unions.

To make matters worse, in 2010 rumors began to circulate that since 2005 some of the major Silicon Valley companies (Apple, Google and Intel) had engaged in a dirty scheme of not hiring each other's employees, a case that eventually ended in court in 2014. So much for Silicon Valley's vaunted job mobility. Furthermore, it was becoming common practice for companies to have their employees cede all rights on their inventions, a practice indirectly expanded by a new patent law (the "America Invents Act" of 2013) that made it harder for individuals to apply for a patent.

The academic environment offers mixed news. On one hand, it still acts as an incubator of startups. On the other hand, each college and university has greatly expanded the activities for students to the point that it has become a walled city. Students do not find the time to stick their neck outside the campus. This does not encourage interaction with other cultural environments. One can argue that such a closed system is designed to create hyper-specialists and stifle creativity.

Meanwhile, the infrastructure of Silicon Valley, and of the USA in general, risks falling behind the ones in the most advanced European countries of Asia and Europe. Gone are the days when it was Asians and Europeans who would marvel at the transportation, the technology, and the gadgets of Silicon Valley. It is now the other way around. Silicon Valley does not have anything that even remotely resembles the futuristic public transportation of Far Eastern metropolises (the magnetic levitation trains, the multi-layered monorails, the bullet trains, its clean and efficient subways). Its households have to live with one of the slowest and most expensive "high-speed" Internet services in the world (in 2012 South Korea connected every single home in the country at one gigabit per second, which was about 85 times the average speed provided to Silicon Valley homes in 2011 by the number one Internet provider, whose marketing campaing labeled it as "blazing speed"). In 2012 cellular phone coverage was poor everywhere and non-existent just a few kilometers outside urban areas. US tourists abroad marvel at what the Japanese and the Germans can do with their phones. In 2014 you could pay for gasoline with your mobile phone in Madagascar, but not in Palo Alto. The 2014 drought was enough to bring California to its knees because California (a state with 1,350 kms of coastline) never developed the desalination technology that has been known for more than 2,000 years (Aristotle explained how to do it in 320 BC). Silicon Valley produces a huge number of useless apps and gadgets, but not a single desalination plant that would actually improve the lives of ordinary families (and help farmers grow the food that those people eat).

There are other fields in which the Bay Area suffers from national diseases. Incredibly stupid immigration laws are keeping away the best brains of the world and sending away the ones who manage to graduate in the USA. And this happens at a time when countries from Canada to Chile have programs in place to attract foreign brains. At the same time, a growing wealth gap has created an educational system that disproportionally favors the children of the rich: if a student graduates from Stanford, most likely s/he is from a rich family, not necessarily a world-class student.

Unlike the other high-tech regions of the world, the (boring, nondescript) urban landscape of Silicon Valley looks like the epitome of no creativity, no originality, no personality, no style. It is difficult to find another region and time in history that witnessed an extraordinary economic boom without producing a single building worthy of becoming a historical monument.

That fact probably goes hand in hand with another blatant fact: the high-tech industry of the Bay Area has produced no Nobel Prize, unlike, say, the Bell Labs, another high-tech power-house.

There is another dimension in which Silicon Valley has changed significantly. Until the 2000s, Silicon Valley had never witnessed a case in which the leaders of a technological/business revolution where all based in Silicon Valley itself. Intel was dominant in microprocessors, but its competitors (Motorola, the Japanese) were located outside California. HP was a major personal-computer maker but its competitors were located outside California (IBM, Compaq, Dell, the Japanese and Taiwanese). Apple and Netscape were briefly dominant in their sectors (personal computers and browsers) but they were quickly defeated by the Microsoft world. Oracle faced competition from IBM (based on the East Coast) in databases and from SAP (based in Germany) in ERP.

The 2000s, instead, have witnessed an increasing concentration of power in Silicon Valley, as the companies vying for supremacy have become Google, Apple, Facebook, and Oracle. Google is becoming the monopolist of web search. Apple is becoming the reference point for hand-held communication devices. Oracle is becoming the behemoth of business software. Facebook towers over anyone else in social media (outside of China). Each of them is trying to impose not only its products but also its view of the world. Each indirectly assumes that their business models are not compatible: the others have to die. It is the first time in the history of Silicon Valley that the local giants are engaged in such a deadly struggle. This constitutes a moral rupture in the traditional "camaraderie" of Silicon Valley.

The 2010s were also the first time ever that Silicon Valley was not about "being small" but being big: Intel (the number-one semiconductor company), Oracle (number one in ERP), Apple (most valuable company in the world), Google (by far number one in web search), Facebook (by far number one in social networking), Cisco (number one in routers) and HP (number one in personal computers) were large multinational corporations, the kind that did not exist in Silicon Valley in the old days. Silicon Valley was originally about "being small". As Silicon Valley becomes a place for big corporations, the attitude towards risk-taking might change too. The whole spirit of innovation has clearly changed. More and more people move here to find a safe job with good benefits, not to challenge the status quo.

In a sense, computing technology was hijacked twice here. The first time the technology invented by corporations and governments (from the transistor to the Internet) was hijacked by independents who turned it into a global grass-roots movement with the potential to dramatically change human society. The second time the technology was hijacked by corporations and government that turned it into an advertising and surveillance medium.

Having spent a month in Dubai, this author started realizing how similar Silicon Valley has become to that city-state. Dubai is a very efficient society neatly divided in three classes: a very small group of very rich people (in this case, the natives, starting with the sheik's family), a very small group of highly-skilled and hard-working people which is responsible for running the business (mostly Westerners who spend one or two years there), and finally a large population of quasi-slaves (mostly from Islamic Asia) that perform humble tasks with very little knowledge of the bigger scheme of things. Silicon Valley has basically produced a similar three-tier society: a small group of financiers, a small intelligentsia that is responsible for inventing the business, and then a large population of quasi-slaves with regular, uneventful lives who simply implement the business without knowing much of the bigger scheme of things.

In concluding, I believe not much is left of what made Silicon Valley what it is now. Silicon Valley has become a much more conventional and crowded metropolitan area. It actually "looks" much less "modern" than other metropolitan areas. Its vast expanse of dull low-rise buildings is hardly a match for the futuristic skyscrapers of Shiodome (Tokyo), Pudong (Shanghai), Zayed Road (Dubai), or just La Defense (Paris).

However, the exuberant creativity boom of the previous decades has left a durable legacy: a culture of risk-taking coupled with a culture of early adoption of new inventions. And it is more than a culture: it is a whole infrastructure designed to promote, assist and reward risk-takers in new technologies. That infrastructure consists not only of laboratories and plants, but also of corporate lawyers, marketing agencies, employment agencies and, of course, investors. After all, the culture of "inventing" was never all that strong in the Bay Area, whereas the culture of turning an invention into a success story has always been its specialty; and it may even be stronger than ever.

The original spirit of Silicon Valley survives in one notable aspect. Nothing motivates people more than telling them that "it can't be done". Tell someone that it can't be done and the following day there will be a new startup doing just that.

It has in fact become easier than ever to start a company. The entry point is getting lower and lower. It is inevitable that sooner or later Silicon Valley will produce the Mozart of the Web, the child prodigy who will create a successful website (and therefore business) at age 8 or 10.

Silicon Valley is the engine of a world in which people are plugged into the Web because of a smartphone, search for information because of Google, socialize on the Web because of Facebook, shop on the Web because of eBay and pay on the Web because of PayPal. Soon that world will also offer biotech tools for "human life extension" and greentech devices for ubiquitous low-cost energy.

Silicon Valley is not booming anymore: it has become the very process of booming. Silicon Valley was an alternate universe. It is now gobbling up the rest of the universe.

Finally, a word about a curious historical fact. In the old days the Bay Area was famous for crazy artists and even crazier young people, best represented by the beat poets of the 1950s and the hippies of the 1960s. The Bay Area, since the times of the Gold Rush, was also a unique ethnic mix. The Bay Area also pioneered the gay and women liberation movements. However, the young people who went on to change the world with their companies and products were almost all "nerdy" male WASPs: it almost feels like the sociopolitical revolution started by the long-haired thrift-clothed multi-ethnic working-class sexually-promiscuous rebels of

Berkeley and San Francisco was hijacked by the short-haired well-dressed WASP upper-class straight male engineers of suburban Silicon Valley. The tangible legacy of the quasi-communist deeply-spiritual rebels was a work environment that was much more casual/relaxed (moccasin slippers, colorful t-shirts and khaki pants instead of suits, ties and white shirts) and less bureaucratic/feudal than on the East Coast; but the young people working and succeeding in that environment were coming from a wildly different ideological perspective, very much in favor of the dominant capitalist, materialistic, mass-consumption, white, bourgeois society that the rebels had antagonized; and the worst affront was that the hijackers were funded by the military establishment (whereas the rebels had been waving and wearing the peace sign). Silicon Valley was and still is, first and foremost, a contradiction in terms.

A Timeline of Silicon Valley

(Lines in parentheses are events that did not occur in the Bay Area but affected the development of computers)

(1885: William Burroughs develops an adding machine)

1887: The Lick Observatory is erected near San Jose, the world's first permanently occupied mountain-top observatory

(1890: Hermann Hollerith's tabulator is chosen for the national census)

1891: Leland and Jane Stanford found Stanford University near Palo Alto

(1906: Lee DeForest invents the vacuum tube)

1906: The San Francisco earthquake and fire

1909: Stanford University's President David Starr Jordan invests $500 in Lee DeForest's audion tube, the first major venture-capital investment in the region

1909: Charles Herrold in San Jose starts the first radio station in the US with regularly scheduled programming

1909: Cyril Elwell founds the Federal Telegraph Corporation (FTC) in Palo Alto to create the world's first global radio communication system

(1911: Hollerith's Tabulating Machine Company is acquired by a new company that will change name to International Business Machines or IBM in 1924)

1915: The Panama-Pacific International Exposition is held in San Francisco, for which Bernard Maybeck builds the Palace of Fine Arts in San Francisco

1916: General Motors opens a large Chevrolet automobile factory in Oakland

1917: Edwin Pridham and Peter Jensen found the electronics company Magnavox in Napa

1921: Ansel Adams publishes his first photographs of Yosemite

1925: Frederick Terman joins Stanford University to teach electronics and electrical engineering and encourages his students to start businesses in California

(1925: Burroughs introduces a portable adding machine)

(1925: AT&T and Western Electric form the Bell Labs in New York)

1927: Philo Farnsworth invents all-electronic television broadcasting while in San Francisco

(1927: Fritz Pfleumer in Germany invents the magnetic tape)

1929: The physicist Robert Oppenheimer joins UC Berkeley

1931: Ernest Lawrence designs the first successful cyclotron and founds the Lawrence Berkeley Laboratories

1933: The Navy opens a base at NAS Sunnyvale (later renamed Moffett Field)

1934: The first lesbian nightclub opens in San Francisco, "Mona's"

(1935: Germany's AEG introduces the first tape recorder)

1936: San Francisco builds the longest bridge in the world, the "Bay Bridge"

1936: Joe Finocchio opens the gay bar "Finocchio's" in San Francisco

(1936: John Lawrence, brother of Lawrence Berkeley Labs' founder, starts the Donner Laboratory to conduct research in nuclear medicine

(1937: Alan Turing describes a machine capable of performing logical reasoning, the "Turing Machine")

1937: Stanford University's Professor William Hansen teams with brothers Sigurd and Russell Varian to develop the klystron tube, used in the early radars

1937: The Golden Gate Bridge is completed in San Francisco

(1938: John Atanasoff at Iowa State College conceives the electronic digital computer)

1939: Fred Terman's students, William Hewlett and David Packard, start a company to produce their audio-oscillator

1939: Walt Disney becomes the first customer of Hewlett-Packard, purchasing their oscillator for the animation film "Fantasia"

1939: Ernest Lawrence is awarded the Nobel Prize in Physics

1939: The US government establishes the Ames Aeronautical Laboratory (later renamed Ames Research Center) at Moffett Field

1941: Stanford University's Professor Fred Terman is put in charge of the top-secret Harvard Radio Research Laboratory

1941: Glenn Seaborg and Edwin McMillan at UC Berkeley produce a new element, plutonium

1942: The US government launches the "Manhattan Project" to build a nuclear bomb under the direction of Robert Oppenheimer

1942: The health-care organization Kaiser Permanente is founded in Oakland

(1943: Tommy Flowers and others build the Colossus, the world's first programmable digital electronic computer)

(1943: Warren McCulloch and Walter Pitts describe an artificial neuron)

1944: Frank Malina founds the Jet Propulsion Laboratory (JPL)

1944: Alexander Poniatoff founds Ampex

(1944: Howard Aiken of IBM unveils the first computer programmed by punched paper tape, the Harvard Mark I)

(1945: Vannevar Bush proposes the "Memex" desk-based machine)

(1940: John Von Neumann designs a computer that holds its own instructions)

(1945: IBM establishes the Watson Scientific Computing Laboratory (later Watson Research Center) at Columbia University in New York)

1946: The Stanford Research Institute is founded

1946: Blacks constitute about 12% of Oakland's population

(1946: The first venture capital firms are founded in the U.S., American Research and Development Corporation (ARDC) by former Harvard Business School's dean Georges Doriot, J.H. Whitney & Company by John Hay Whitney, Rockefeller Brothers by Laurance Rockefeller (later renamed Venrock)

1946: John Northrop and Wendell Stanley of UC Berkeley are awarded the Nobel Prize in Chemistry

1946: Fred Terman returns to Stanford University as the dean of the engineering school and founds the Electronics Research Lab (ERL), mostly founded by the US military

(1946: The first non-military computer, ENIAC, or "Electronic Numerical Integrator and Computer," is unveiled, built by John Mauchly and Presper Eckert at the University of Pennsylvania

(1947: AT&T Bell Telephone Laboratory's engineers John Bardeen, William Shockley and Walter Brattain demonstrate the principle of amplifying an electrical current using a solid semiconducting material, i.e. the "transistor")

(1947: Norbert Wiener founds Cybernetics)

(1947: John Von Neumann describes self-reproducing automata)

1947: Ampex introduces a magnetic tape recorder

1948: The Varian brothers found Varian Associates

(1948: Claude Shannon founds Information Theory and coins the term "bit")

1949: William Giauque of UC Berkeley is awarded the Nobel Prize in Chemistry)

1950: Turing proposes a test to determine whether a machine is intelligent or not

(1950: Remington purchases Eckert-Mauchly Computer)

1951: The Stanford Industrial Park is conceived

1951: Glenn Seaborg and Edwin McMillan of UC Berkeley are awarded the Nobel Prize

(1951: The first commercial computer is delivered, the Ferranti Mark 1)

(1951: A team led by Jay Forrester at MIT builds the "Whirlwind" computer, the first real-time system and the first computer to use a video display for output)

1952: IBM opens its first West Coast laboratory in San Jose (later Almaden Research Center)

1952: Felix Bloch of Stanford University is awarded the Nobel Prize in Physics, the first for Stanford

1952: The Atomic Energy Commission establishes a Livermore Laboratory as a branch of the UC Berkeley's Radiation Laboratory

1953: Varian is the first tenant of the Stanford Industrial Park

1953: The CIA finances a project named "MkUltra" to study the effects of psychoactive drugs

1953: Electronics manufacturer Sylvania opens its Electronic Defense Lab (EDL) in Mountain View

1953: Lawrence Ferlinghetti founds a bookstore in San Francisco, "City Lights," that becomes the headquarters of alternative writers

(1954: Remington Rand introduces UNIVAC 1103, the first computer with magnetic-core RAM)

(1954: IBM introduces its first computer model, the 704)

1954: David Bohannon opens the Hillsdale Shopping Center, a suburban shopping mall

1955: The Stanford Research Institute demonstrates the ERMA computer

1956: IBM's San Jose labs invent the hard-disk drive

Mar 1956: UC Berkeley Professor Harry Huskey designs Bendix's first digital computer, the G-15

(1954: George Devol designs the first industrial robot, Unimate)

1955: The first conference on Artificial Intelligence is held at Dartmouth College, organized by John McCarthy

1955: The "Daughters of Bilitis" is founded in San Francisco, the first exclusively Lesbian organization in the US

1955: Stanford University hires Carl Djerassi

1955: Allen Ginsberg's recitation of his poem "Howl" transplants the "Beat" aesthetic to San Francisco

1955: Private investors or "angels" (including John Bryan, Bill Edwards and Reid Dennis) establish "The Group" to invest together in promising companies

(1955: Alexander Schure founds the New York Institute of Technology)

(1955: Remington Rand merges with Sperry to form Sperry Rand)

1955: Stanford University merges the Applied Electronics Laboratory and the Electronics Research Laboratory into the Systems Engineering Laboratory under the direction of Fred Terman and focusing on electronic warfare

1956: William Shockley founds the Shockley Transistor Corporation in Mountain View to produce semiconductor-based transistors to replace vacuum tubes, and hires Robert Noyce, Gordon Moore and others

1956: Charles Ginsburg of Ampex Corporation builds the first practical videotape recorder

1956: Aircraft-company Lockheed opens an electronics research laboratory in the Stanford Industrial Park and a manufacturing facility in Sunnyvale

(1956: Werner Buchholz of IBM coins the term "byte")

(Apr 1957: John Backus of IBM introduces the FORTRAN programming language, the first practical machine-independent language)

Oct 1957: Several engineers (including Robert Noyce and Gordon Moore) quit the Shockley Transistor laboratories and form Fairchild Semiconductor in Mountain View, using funding from Fairchild Camera and Instrument

(1957: ARDC invests $70,000 in Digital Equipment Corporation (DEC))

(1957: Max Mathews begins composing computer music at Bell Laboratories)

1957: Dean Watkins of Stanford's ERL founds Watkins-Johnson, one of the first venture-capital funded companies in the Santa Clara Valley

(1957: Allen Newell and Herbert Simon develop the "General Problem Solver")

(1957: Frank Rosenblatt conceives the "Perceptron," a neural computer that can learn by trial and error)

(1957: Morton Heilig invents the "Sensorama Machine," a pioneering virtual-reality environment)

(1957: Former SAGE engineer Ken Olsen founds the Digital Equipment Corporation)

1957: Rockefeller Brothers invests in Fairchild Semiconductor, the first venture-funded startup of the Bay Area

(1958: Jack Kilby at Texas Instruments invents the integrated circuit, a micro-sized silicon device containing a large number of electronic switches)

(1958: Charles Townes of Columbia theorizes about an optical laser and his student Gordon Gould builds one and names it "LASER" or "Light Amplification by the Stimulated Emission of Radiation")

1958: Draper, Gaither and Anderson is founded, the first professional venture-capital firm in California

1958: NASA opens a research center near Mountain View

1959: The first commercial Xerox plain-paper photocopier goes on sale

1959: Eveready (later renamed Energizer) introduces the alkaline battery

1959: Jean Hoerni at Fairchild Semiconductor invents the planar process that enables great precision in silicon components, and Robert Noyce at Fairchild Semiconductor designs a planar integrated circuit

1959: Dancer and mime Ron Davis founds the San Francisco Mime Troupe

1959: Arthur Kornberg of Stanford University is awarded the Nobel Prize in Medicine

1959: Emilio Segre and Owen Chamberlain of the Lawrence Berkeley Labs are awarded the Nobel Prize for the discovery of the antiproton

1959: Frank Chambers founds the venture-capital company Continental Capital

1959: GTE buys Sylvania

1959: Several Stanford students volunteer to take part in the CIA project "MkUltra" to study the effects of psychoactive drugs

(1960: William Fetter of Boeing coins the expression "computer graphics")

(1960: Digital Equipment introduces the first minicomputer, the PDP-1 (Program Data Processor), that comes with a keyboard and a monitor

(1960: Theodore Maiman of the Hughes Research Laboratory demonstrates the first working laser)

1960: Donald Glaser of the Lawrence Berkeley Labs is awarded the Nobel Prize

1960: Wayne Thiebaud at UC Davis pioneers "pop art"

1960: John McCarthy speculates that "computation may someday be organized as a public utility"

(1961: Joe Orlicky of JI Case pioneers Material Requirements Planning or MRP)

1961: Laurence Spitters founds Memorex

(1961: Max Palevsky forms Scientific Data Systems)

(1961: Charles Bachman at General Electric develops the first database management system, IDS)

(1961: Philco unveils the first head-mounted display)

(1961: Fernando Corbato at MIT creates the first working time-sharing system, CTSS or "Compatible Time Sharing System," that allowed to remotely access a computer, an IBM 7090/94)

(1961: IBM owns more than 81% of the computer market)

(1961: General Motors unveils "Unimate," the first industrial robot)

1961: Robert Hofstadter of Stanford University is awarded the Nobel Prize in Physics

1961: Melvin Calvin of the Lawrence Berkeley Labs is awarded the Nobel Prize

1961: Tommy Davis founds one of Santa Clara Valley's first venture-capital firms with Arthur Rock, Davis & Rock

1962: The San Francisco Tape Music Center for avantgarde music is established by composers Morton Subotnick and Ramon Sender

(1962: Paul Baran proposes a distributed network as the form of communication least vulnerable to a nuclear strike)

(1962: Steve Russell and others at MIT implement the computer game "Spacewar" on a PDP-1)

1962: Stanford University founds the Stanford Linear Accelerator Center (SLAC)

1962: Bill Draper and Franklin Johnson form the venture-capital firm Draper and Johnson Investment Company

1962: Michael Murphy founds the "Esalen Institute" at Big Sur to promote spiritual healing

(1962: The first commercial modem is manufactured by AT&T)

1963: Douglas Engelbart at the Stanford Research Institute builds the first prototype of the "mouse"

1963: John McCarthy moves to Stanford

1963: Syntex, a pioneer of biotechnology, moves from Mexico City to the Stanford Industrial Park

(1963: The "American Standard Code for Information Interchange" or "ASCII" is introduced

(1963: Ivan Sutherland of MIT demonstrates "Sketchpad," a computer graphics program, and the first program ever with a graphical user interface)

(1964: IBM introduces the first "mainframe" computer, the 360, and the first "operating system," the OS/360)

1964: Syntex introduces the birth-control pill

1964: Tymshare starts one of the most popular time-sharing service and creates a circuit-switched network

(1964: Robert Moog begins selling his synthesizer)

1964: Mario Savio founds the "Free Speech Movement" and leads student riots at the Berkeley campus

1964: Bill Draper and Paul Wythes form Sutter Hill Ventures

1964: MkUltra's alumnus Ken Kesey organizes the "Merry Pranksters" who travel around the country in a "Magic Bus," live in a commune in La Honda and experiment with "acid tests" (LSD)

(1964: John Kemeny and Thomas Kurtz (at Dartmouth College) invent the BASIC programming language)

(1964: American Airlines' SABRE reservation system, developed by IBM, is the first online transaction processing

1964: Former Sylvania employee Bill Perry founds computer-based electronic-intelligence company ESL

1965: Gordon Moore predicts that the processing power of computers will double every 18 months ("Moore's law")

1965: The Grateful Dead are formed in Palo Alto

Sep 1965: Ben Jacopetti inaugurates the Open Theater as a vehicle devoted to multimedia performances for the Berkeley Experimental Arts Foundation

1965: Owsley "Bear" Stanley synthesizes crystalline LSD

1965: Ed Feigenbaum implements the first "expert system," Dendral

1965: Lotfi Zadeh invents Fuzzy Logic

1965: George Hunter of the Charlatans introduces the "light show" in rock concerts

1965: Former Ampex employee Ray Dolby founds the Dolby Labs while in Britain (relocating it to San Francisco in 1976)

1965: Ron Davis of the San Francisco Mime Troupe publishes the essay "Guerrilla Theatre"

1965: The Family Dog Production organizes the first hippie festival in San Francisco

1965: Terry Riley composes "In C," music based on repetition of simple patterns ("minimalism")

(1965: The Digital Equipment Corporation unveils the first successful mini-computer, the PDP-8, which uses integrated circuits)

(1965: European computer manufacturer Olivetti introduces the first affordable programmable electronic desktop computer, the P101)

1966: Stewart Brand organizes the "Trips Festival" putting together Ken Kesey's "Acid Test," Jacopetti's Open Theater, Sender's Tape Music Center and rock bands

1966: John McCarthy opens the Stanford Artificial Intelligence Laboratory (SAIL)

1966: The first "Summer of Love" of the hippies is held in San Francisco, and a three-day "Acid Test" is held in San Francisco with the Grateful Dead performing

1966: Hewlett-Packard enters the business of general-purpose computers with the HP-2116

1966: Willie Brown organizes the Artists Liberation Front of San Francisco-based artists at the Mime Troupe's Howard Street loft

1966: The first issue of the San Francisco Oracle, an underground cooperative publication, is published

1966: Emmett Grogan and members of the Mime Troupe found the "Diggers," a group of improvising actors and activists whose stage was the streets and parks of the Haight-Ashbury and whose utopia was the creation of a Free City

1966: Huey Newton, Bobby Seale, Angela Davis and other African-American activists found the socialist-inspired and black-nationalist "Black Panther Party" at Oakland

1966: There are 2,623 computers in the US (1,967 work for the Defense Department)

1966: Donald Buchla develops a voltage-controlled synthesizer for composer Morton Subotnick, the Buchla Modular Electronic Music System

1966: The Asian Art Museum of San Francisco is inaugurated

(1967: Jack Kilby (at Texas Instruments) develops the first hand-held calculator)

1967: A "Human Be-In" is held at the Golden Gate Park in San Francisco

1967: Monterey hosts a rock festival

1968: Stewart Brand publishes the first "Whole Earth Catalog"

1968: David Evans and Ivan Sutherland form Evans & Sutherland

1968: Philip Noyce, Gordon Moore and Andy Grove found Intel ("Integrated Electronics") to build memory chips

(1968: The hypertext system FRESS created by Andries van Dam at Brown University for the IBM 360 introduces the "undo" feature)

(1968: ARDC's investment in Digital Equipment Corporation (DEC) is valued at $355 million

(1968: Computer Science Corp becomes the first software company to be listed at the New York stock market)

(1968: Dutch mathematician Edsger Dijkstra writes "GO TO Statement Considered Harmful")

(1968: Barclays Bank installs networked "automated teller machines" or ATMs)

1968: John Portman designs the Embarcadero Center in San Francisco

1968: William Hambrecht and George Quist found the investment company Hambrecht & Quist in San Francisco

1968: Frank Malina founds Leonardo ISAST in Paris, an organization devoted to art/science fusion

1968: John Bryan and Bill Edwards found the investment company Bryan & Edwards

1968: Doug Engelbart of the Stanford Research Institute demonstrates the NLS ("oN-Line System"), the first system to employ the mouse

1968: Luis Alvarez of the Lawrence Berkeley Labs is awarded the Nobel Prize

1969: Gary Starkweather of Xerox invents the laser printer

(1969: Compuserve's dial-up service)

1969: Xerox buys Scientific Data Systems (SDS)

1969: Advanced Micro Devices is founded by Jerry Sanders and other engineers from Fairchild Semiconductor

1969: The Stanford Research Institute (SRI) demonstrates Shakey the Robot

1969: Frank Oppenheimer founds the San Francisco Exploratorium as a museum of science, art and human perception

1969: Construction begins at 3000 Sand Hill Road, in Menlo Park, soon to become the headquarters of the venture-capital community

(1969: Ted Codd of IBM invents the relational database)

1969: Bell Labs unveils the Unix operating system developed by Kenneth Thompson and Dennis Ritchie

1969: The computer network Arpanet is inaugurated with four nodes, three of which are in California (UCLA, Stanford Research Institute and UC Santa Barbara)

1969: Leo Laurence in San Francisco calls for the "Homosexual Revolution"

1969: Four Stanford students found ROLM to design computers for the military

1970: Intel introduces the first commercially successful 1K DRAM chip

1970: 1970 Lee Boysel at Four Phase Systems designs the AL1, a commercial microprocessors (an 8-bit CPU)

1970: The first "San Francisco Gay Pride Parade" is held in San Francisco

1970: Gays and lesbians start moving to the "Castro" district of San Francisco in large numbers

1970: Charles Walton invents Radio Frequency Identification (RFID)

(1970: The first practical optical fiber is developed by glass maker Corning Glass Works)

(1970: Edgar Codd at IBM introduces the concept of a relational database)

1970: Five of the seven largest US semiconductor manufacturers are located in Santa Clara Valley

1970: Xerox opens the Palo Alto Research Center or PARC

1970: Alan Kay joins Xerox PARC to work on object-oriented programming

1970: Stanford's Ed Feigenbaum launches the Heuristic Programming Project for research in Artificial Intelligence

1971: Cetus, the first biotech company, is founded in Berkeley

1971: Film director George Lucas founds the film production company Lucasfilm

1971: David Noble at IBM invents the floppy disk

1971: Nolan Bushnell and Ted Dabney create the first arcade video game, "Computer Space"

1971: Ted Hoff and Federico Faggin at Intel build the first universal micro-processor, a programmable set of integrated circuits, i.e. a computer on a chip

1971: Intel unveils the first commercially available microprocessor, the 4004

1972: At least 60 semiconductor companies have been founded in Silicon Valley between 1961 and 1972, mostly by former Fairchild engineers and managers

1972: European manufacturer Olivetti establishes an Advanced Technology Centre (ATC) in Cupertino

1972: Intel introduces the 8008 microprocessor, whose eight-bit word allowed to represent 256 characters, including all ten digits, both uppercase and lowercase letters and punctuation marks

1972: Magnavox introduces the first videogame console, the "Odyssey"

1972: Nolan Bushnell invents the first videogame, "Pong," an evolution of Magnavox's Odyssey, and founds Atari

1972: Venture-capitalist company Kleiner-Perkins, founded by Austrian-born Eugene Kleiner of Fairchild Semiconductor and former Hewlett-Packard executive Tom Perkins, opens offices in Menlo Park on Sand Hill Road, followed by Don Valentine of Fairchild Semiconductor who founds Capital Management Services, later renamed Sequoia Capital

1972: Electronics writer Don Hoeffler coins the term "Silicon Valley"

(1972: A novel by David Gerrold coins the term "computer virus")

(1972: Ray Tomlinson at Bolt, Beranek and Newman invents e-mail for sending messages between computer users, and invents a system to identify the user name and the computer name separated by a "@")

(1972: IBM engineers in Mannheim, Germany, found Systemanalyse und Programmentwicklung or SAP)

1972: Bruce Buchanan leads development of the expert system "Mycin" at Stanford University

1972: European computer manufacturer Olivetti opens a research center in Cupertino (the "Advanced Technology Centre")

1973: Lynn Hershman creates the first site-specific installation, "The Dante Hotel"

1973: Efrem Lipkin, Mark Szpakowski, and Lee Felsenstein start the "Community Memory," the first public computerized bulletin board system

1973: Stanley Cohen of Stanford University and Herbert Boyer of UCSF create the first recombinant DNA organism, virtually inventing "biotechnology"

(1973: Automatic Electronic Systems of Canada introduces the "AES-90," a "word processor" that combines a CRT-screen, a floppy-disk and a microprocessor)

(1973: Vietnamese-born engineer Andre Truong Trong Thi uses the 8008 to build the computer Micral)

(1973: Japan's Sharp develops the LCD or "Liquid Crystal Display" technology)

1973: The first international connections to the Arpanet, University College of London)

1973: Intel introduces a CPU named 8088

1973: William Pereira builds the Transamerica Pyramid in San Francisco

(1973: Martin Cooper at Motorola invents the first portable, wireless or "cellular" telephone)

1973: Vinton Cerf of Stanford University coins the term "Internet"

1973: The Arpanet has 2,000 users

1973: Gary Kildall in Monterey invents the first operating system for a microprocessor, the CP/M

(1974: The barcode, invented by George Laurer at IBM, debuts)

1974: Ed Roberts invents the first personal computer, the Altair 8800

1974: Donald Chamberlin at IBM's San Jose laboratories invents SQL

1974: Xerox's PARC unveils the "Alto," the first workstation with a "mouse"

1974: Paul Flory of Stanford University is awarded the Nobel Prize in Chemistry

1974: Reid Dennis and Burton McMurtry found the investment company Institutional Venture Associates

1974: Philips acquires Magnavox

1974: Spectra-Physics builds the first bar-code scanner ever used in a store

1974: Tommy Davis launches the Mayfield Fund

1974: Vint Cerf of Stanford and others publish the Transmission Control Protocol (TCP)

1974: The Ant Farm art collective creates the installation "Cadillac Farm"

(1974: The Polish geneticist Waclaw Szybalski coins the term "synthetic biology")

1975: Xerox PARC debuts the first GUI or "Graphical User Interface"

1975: Advanced Micro Devices introduces a reverse-engineered clone of the Intel 8080 microprocessor

1975: John Chowning and Leland Smith at Stanford found a computer music lab, later renamed Center for Computer Research in Music and Acoustics (CCRMA)

(1975: Ed Catmull and Alvy Ray Smith establish the Computer Graphics Laboratory at the New York Institute of Technology)

(1975: Ed Roberts in New Mexico introduces the Altair 8800 based on an Intel microprocessor and sold as a mail-order kit)

(1975: Bill Gates and Paul Allen develop a version of BASIC for the Altair personal computer and found Microsoft)

1975: Steve Wozniak and others found the "Homebrew Computer Club"

(1975: John Holland describes genetic algorithms)

1976: Steve Wozniak and Steve Jobs form Apple Computer and build the first microcomputer in Jobs' garage in Cupertino.

1976: Stanford University researchers (Martin Hellman, Ralph Merkle and Whitfield Diffie) describe the concept of public-key cryptography

1976: Bill Joy writes the "vi" text editor for Unix

1976: William Ackerman founds Windham Hill to promote his "new age" music

1976: Burton Richter of Stanford University is awarded the Nobel Prize in Physics

1976: Biochemist Herbert Boyer and venture capitalist Robert Swanson found Genentech, the first major biotech company

(1976: Ed Catmull and Fred Parke's computer animation in a scene of the film "Futureworld" is the first to use 3D computer graphics)

1976: Institutional Venture Associates splits into two partnerships, McMurtry's Technology Venture Associates and Dennis' Institutional Venture Partners

1976: ROLM introduces a digital switch, the CBX (a computer-based PBX)

1976: Bob Metcalfe at Xerox PARC deploys the first "Ethernet" for local area networks

(1976: MOS Technology introduces the 6502 processor)

1977: Steve Jobs and Steve Wozniak develop the Apple II using the 6502 processor

1977: Bill Joy at UC Berkeley ships the first BSD version of Unix

1974: IBM's San Jose laboratories unveils the relational database system System R

1977: 27,000 people are employed in the Semiconductor industry of Silicon Valley

1977: San Francisco's city supervisor Harvey Milk becomes the first openly gay man to be elected to office in the US

1977: George Coates founds his multimedia theater group, Performance Works

1977: UC Berkeley develops the "Berkeley Software Distribution" (BSD), better known as "Berkeley Unix," a variant of the Unix operating system

1977: Larry Ellison founds the Software Development Laboratories, later renamed Oracle Corporation

1977: Atari introduces a videogame console, the 2600, based on the 6502 processor

1977: Dave Smith builds the "Prophet 5," the world's first microprocessor-based musical instrument, the first polyphonic and programmable synthesizer

(1977: Dennis Hayes of National Data Corporation invents the PC modem, a device that converts between analog and digital signals)

(1977: Ichiro Endo at Canon invents thermal inkjet printing)

(1978: The Global Positioning System or GPS is inaugurated by the USA military)

(1978: Toshihiro Nishikado creates the first blockbuster videogame, "Space Invaders")

1978: The rainbow flag debuts at the San Francisco Gay and Lesbian Freedom Day Parade

(1978: Mark Pauline founds the Survival Research Laboratories)

1978: Apple launches a project to design a personal computer with a graphical user interface

1978: Atari announces the Atari 800, designed by Jay Miner

1979: Dan Bricklin develops VisiCalc, the first spreadsheet program for personal computers

1979: Larry Michels founds the first Unix consulting company, Santa Cruz Operation (SCO)

1979: Michael Stonebraker at UC Berkeley unveils a relational database system, Ingres

1979: University of California at Berkeley launches the "Search for Extraterrestrial Radio Emissions from Nearby Developed Intelligent Populations" project or "Serendip"

1979: Lucasfilm hires Ed Catmull from the New York Institute of Technology to lead the Graphics Group of its Computer Division

1979: Kevin MacKenzie invents symbols such as :-), or "emoticons," to mimic the cues of face-to-face communication

1979: John Shoch of Xerox's PARC coins the term "worm" to describe a program that travels through a network of computers

1980: The Arpanet has 430,000 users, who exchange almost 100 million e-mail messages a year

1980: John Searle publishes the article on the "Chinese Room" that attacks Artificial Intelligence

1980: Sonya Rapoport creates the interactive audio/visual installation "Objects on my Dresser"

1980: The largest semiconductor manufacturers in the world are: Texas Instruments, National, Motorola, Philips (Europe), Intel, NEC (Japan), Fairchild, Hitachi (Japan) and Toshiba (Japan).

1980: Seagate Technology introduces the first hard-disk drive for personal computers

1980: Doug and Gary Carlston found the videogame company Broderbund

1980: Paul Berg of Stanford University is awarded the Nobel Prize in Chemistry

1980: Polish writer Czeslaw Milosz of UC Berkeley is awarded the Nobel Prize in Literature

1980: Integrated circuits incorporate 100,000 discrete components

1980: The Usenet is born, an Arpanet-based discussion system divided in "newsgroups"

1980: Apple goes public for a record $1.3 billion

1980: UC Davis researchers found biotech company Calgene

1980: John Doerr joins Kleiner, Perkins, Caufield, and Byers

1980: Ed Feigenbaum and others found IntelliGenetics (later Intellicorp), an early Artificial Intelligence and biotech startup

(1980: Sony introduces the double-sided, double-density 3.5" floppy disk that holds 875 kilobyte)

1980: Onyx launches the first microcomputer running the Unix operating system

1981: The Xerox 8010 Star Information System is the first commercial computer that uses a mouse

1980: David Patterson and Carlo Sequin launch a RISC (Reduced Instruction Set Computer) project at UC Berkeley

(1980: NESELCO introduces a touch-screen computer)

1981: John Hennessy starts a RISC project at Stanford University

1981: Ed Feigenbaum and others found Teknowledge, the first major startup to develop "expert systems"

1981: Arthur Schawlow of Stanford University is awarded the Nobel Prize in Physics

1981: Roger Malina relocates Leonardo ISAST from Paris to San Francisco

1981: Jim Clark of Stanford University and Abbey Silverstone of Xerox found Silicon Graphics in Sunnyvale to manufacture graphic workstations

(1981: The IBM PC is launched, running an operating system developed by Bill Gates' Microsoft)

1981: Andreas Bechtolsheim at Stanford University builds a workstation running Unix and networking software

1982: John Warnock and Charles Geschke of Xerox PARC develop PostScript and found Adobe to commercialize it

(1982: John Hopfield describes a new generation of neural networks)

(1982: Thomas Zimmerman of IBM Almaden builds the first commercially-available dataglove

1982: Stanford students Andy Bechtolsheim, Vinod Khosla and Scott McNealy (a former Onyx employee) and former Berkeley student Bill Joy found SUN

Microsystems, named after the "Stanford University Network," to manufacture workstations

1982: Apple's employee Trip Hawkins founds Electronic Arts to create home computer games

1982: John Walker founds Autodesk to sell computer-aided design software

1982: Gary Hendrix founds Symantec

(1982: Nastec introduces the term "Computer-Aided Software Engineering (CASE)" for its suite of software development tools)

1983: The Lotus Development Corporation, founded by Mitchell Kapor, introduces the spreadsheet program "Lotus 1-2-3" for MS-DOS developed by Jonathan Sachs

1983: Gavilan, founded by Manuel Fernandez, former CEO of Zilog, introduces the first portable computer marketed as a "laptop"

1983: Crash of the videogame console market

1983: Compaq introduces the Portable PC, compatible with the IBM PC

1983: The Transmission Control Protocol and Internet Protocol or "TCP/IP" running on Unix BSD 4.2 debuts on the Arpanet, and the Arpanet is officially renamed Internet

1983: Paul Mockapetris invents the Domain Name System for the Internet to classify Internet addresses through extensions such as .com

1983: Apple introduces the "Lisa," the first personal computer with a graphical user interface

1983: Henry Taube of Stanford University is awarded the Nobel Prize in Chemistry

1983: The Musical Instrument Digital Interface is introduced, based on an idea by Dave Smith

(1983: William Inmon builds the first data warehousing system)

1983: Gerard Debreu of UC Berkeley is awarded the Nobel Prize in Economics

(1983: Nintendo releases the Family Computer, renamed Nintendo Entertainment System in the U.S.)

1984: Cisco is founded by Leonard Bosack and Sandra Lerner

(1984: Michael Dell, a student at University of Texas at Austin, founds PCs Limited, later renamed Dell, to sell custom PC-compatible computers by mail-order only)

1984: Robert Gaskins and Dennis Austin develop "Presentation," an application to create slide presentations (later renamed "PowerPoint")

1984: The "Search For Extraterrestrial Intelligence" or SETI Institute is founded

1984: Michael McGreevy creates the first virtual-reality environment at NASA Ames

(1984: Nicholas Negroponte and Jerome Wiesner found MIT Media Lab)

(1984: General Motors builds a factory that uses Supply Chain Management software)

(1984: Wavefront introduces the first commercial 3D-graphics software)

1984: Hewlett-Packard introduces the first ink-jet printer

1984: Apple introduces the Macintosh, which revolutionizes desktop publishing

(1984: William Gibson's novel "Neuromancer" popularizes the "cyberpunks")

(1984: The CDROM is introduced by Sony and Philips)

(1984: Psion introduces the first personal digital assistant)

(1984: The CADRE laboratory ("Computers in Art, Design, Research, and Education") is established at San Jose State University

(1984: Fujio Masuoka at Toshiba invents flash memory, a cheaper kind of EEPROM)

1985: Stewart Brand creates the "Whole Earth Lectronic Link" (or "WELL"), a virtual community of computer users structured in bulletin boards for online discussions

1985: Digital Research introduces GEM (Graphical Environment Manager), a graphical-user interface for the CP/M operating system designed by former Xerox PARC employee Lee Jay Lorenzen

(1985: Microsoft releases Windows 1.0 for MS-DOS)

(1985: Commodore launches the Amiga 1000, a 16-bit home computer with advanced graphical and audio (multimedia) designed by former Atari employee Jay Miner and running a multitasking operating system and GUI designed by Carl Sassenrath)

1985: Richard Stallman founds the non-profit organization "Free Software Foundation" (FSF)

1985: Hewlett-Packard introduces the LaserJet, a printer for the home market

1985: Jobs and Wozniak leave Apple

(Jul 1985: Aldus introduces PageMaker for the Macintosh, the first system for desktop publishing)

1985: A crisis in the semiconductor industry is brought about by the dumping of cheaper Japanese products

(1985: Richard Stallman releases a free operating system, "GNU")

1985: Warren Robinett, Scott Fisher and Michael McGreevy of NASA Ames build the "Virtual Environment Workstation" for virtual-reality research, incorporating the first dataglove and the first low-cost head-mounted display

(1985: Microsoft ships the "Windows" operating system)

(1985: Jim Kimsey founds Quantum Computer Services (later renamed America Online) to provide dedicated online services for personal computers)

1985: The Arpanet is renamed Internet

1985: Jaron Lanier founds VPL Research, the first company to sell Virtual Reality products

1985: Robert Sinsheimer organizes a meeting in Santa Cruz of biologists to discuss the feasibility of sequencing the entire human genome

1986: Apple's co-founder Steve Jobs buys Lucasfilms' Pixar, that becomes an independent film studio run by Ed Catmull

1986: A book by Eric Drexler popularizes the term "nanotechnology"

(1986: Phil Katz invents the zip compression format for his program Pkzip)

(1986: A virus spread among IBM PCs, nicknamed "Brain")

1986: Larry Harvey starts the first "Burning Man" on Baker Beach in San Francisco

1986: Judy Malloy publishes the computer-mediated hyper-novel "Uncle Roger" on the WELL

1986: Renzo Piano builds the California Academy of Science in San Francisco

1986: Yuan Lee of the Lawrence Berkeley Labs is awarded the Nobel Prize

1987: Chris Langton coins the term "Artificial Life"

1987: Jerry Kaplan and others found GO Corporation to manufacture portable computers with a pen-based user interface

1987: David Duffield and Ken Morris found PeopleSoft to manufacture Enterprise Resource Planning (ERP) applications

(1987: The JPEG (Joint Photographic Experts Group) format is introduced)

(1987: Linus Technologies introduces the first pen-based computer, WriteTop)

1987: Bill Atkinson at Apple creates the hypermedia system HyperCard

1987: The largest semiconductor manufacturers in the world are Japan's NEC, Japan's Toshiba and Japan's Hitachi

(1987: Uunet becomes the first commercial Internet Service Provider, ISP)

1988: "Morris," the first digital worm, infects most of the Internet

1988: Steven Benner organizes the conference "Redesigning the Molecules of Life', the first major conference on synthetic biology

(1988: 3D Systems introduces the first 3D printer)

(1988: 1988: Digital Subscriber Line (DSL) that provides broadband on a phone line is invented by Bellcore)

1989: UC Berkeley introduces the "BSD license," one of the first open-source licenses

1989: Adobe releases Photoshop

(1989: Barry Shein founds the first Internet Service Provider, "The World," in Boston)

1990: Richard Taylor of Stanford University is awarded the Nobel Prize in Physics and William Sharpe of Stanford University is awarded the Nobel Prize in Economics

1990: Between 1970 and 1990 the population of San Jose has almost doubled, from 445,779 to 782,248

(1990: Dycam introduces the first digital camera, Model 1)

(1990: Microsoft announced that it will stop working on OS/2)

(1990: The "Human Genome Project" is launched to decipher human DNA)

1990: Michael West founds the biotech company Geron that pioneers commercial applications of regenerative medicine

(1990: Tim Berners-Lee of CERN invents the HyperText Markup Language "HTML" and demonstrates the World-Wide Web)

(1990: The first Internet search engine, "Archie," is developed in Montreal)

1990: LaRoche acquires a majority stake in Genentech

(1991: The World-Wide Web debuts on the Internet)

(1991: United Technologies Corporation becomes the first company to market a fuel-cell system)

(1991: Microsoft has revenues of $1,843,432,000 and 8,226 employees)

(1991: Finnish student Linus Torvalds introduces the Linux operating system, a variant of Unix)

(1991: Paul Lindner and Mark McCahill of the University of Minnesota release "Gopher," a software program to access the World-Wide Web)

1991: Pei-Yuan Wei introduces a "browser" for the world-wide web, Viola

1991: Apple introduces QuickTime

1992: Macromedia is founded in San Francisco

1992: Intel becomes the world's largest semiconductor manufacturer, passing all its Japanese rivals

(1992: The first text message is sent from a phone)

1992: The "Information Tapestry" project at Xerox PARC pioneers collaborative filtering

(1992: The Electronic Visualization Lab at the University of Illinois Chicago creates a "CAVE" ("Cave Automatic Virtual Environment"), a surround-screen and surround-sound virtual-reality environment (graphics projected from behind the walls that surround the user)

(1992: SAP launches R/3, moving its ERP system from mainframe to a three-tiered client-server architecture and to a relational database)

1992: Gary Becker of Stanford University is awarded the Nobel Prize in Economics

1992: Calgene creates the "Flavr Savr" tomato, the first genetically-engineered food to be sold in stores

1992: Timothy May starts the "cypherpunk" forum

(1992: Jean Armour Polly coins the phrase "Surfing the Internet")

(1992: Thomas Ray develops "Tierra," a computer simulation of ecology)

1993: Stanford University's Professor Jim Clark hires Mark Andreessen

1993: Condoleezza Rice becomes Stanford's youngest, first female and first non-white provost

1993: Thomas Siebel founds Siebel for customer relationship management (CRM) applications

1993: Steve Putz at Xerox's PARC creates the web mapping service Map Viewer

1993: The first "Other Minds Festival" for avantgarde music is held in San Francisco

1993: Broderbund introduces the videogame "Myst"

1993: Adobe Systems introduces Acrobat and the file format PDF (or Portable Document Format)

1993: Marc Andreessen develops the first browser for the World Wide Web (Mosaic)

1994: John Harsanyi of UC Berkeley is awarded the Nobel Prize in Economics

(1994: Mark Pesce introduces the "Virtual Reality Modeling Language" or VRML)

1994: The "Band of Angels" is founded by "angels" to fund Silicon Valley startups

(1994: University of North Carolina's college radio station WXYC becomes the first radio station in the world to broadcast its signal over the Internet)

1994: The search engine Architext (later Excite) debuts

1994: There are 315 public companies in Silicon Valley

1995: Stanford student Jerry Yang founds Yahoo!

1995: Salon is founded by David Talbot

1995: Steve Kirsch's Infoseek pioneers "cost-per-impression" and "cost-per-click" advertising

1995: Netscape, the company founded by Marc Andreessen, goes public even before earning money and starts the "dot.com" craze and the boom of the Nasdaq

(1995: Microsoft introduces Internet Explorer and starts the browser wars)

1995: John Lasseter's "Toy Story" is the first feature-length computer-animated film

(1995: The MP3 standard is introduced)

1995: Mario Botta builds the Modern Museum of Art in San Francisco

1995: Martin Perl of Stanford University is awarded the Nobel Prize in Physics

1995: Jacques Mattheij pioneers live video streaming over the Internet)

(1995: The Sony Playstation is introduced)

1995: Ward Cunningham creates WikiWikiWeb, the first "wiki," a manual on the internet maintained in a collaborative manner

1995: SUN launches the programming language Java

1995: Piero Scaruffi debuts his website www.scaruffi.com

1995: Craig Newmark starts craigslist.com on the Internet, a regional advertising community

(1995: Amazon.com is launched on the Web as the "world's largest bookstore," except that it is not a bookstore, it is a website)

1995: The At Home Network (@Home) is founded by William Randolph Hearst III

1996: Sabeer Bhatia launches Hotmail, a website to check email from anywhere in the world

(1996: Dell begin selling its computers via its website)

1996: Steve Jobs rejoins Apple

1996: Jeff Hawkins invents the Palm Pilot, a personal digital assistant

1996: Stewart Brand and Danny Hillis establish the "Long Now Foundation"

1996: Douglas Osheroff of Stanford University is awarded the Nobel Prize in Physics

1996: Macromedia introduces Flash

(1996: The first DVD player is introduced by Toshiba)

(1996: GeoSystems Global launches the web mapping service MapQuest that also provides address matching) Donnelley began making maps with computers in the mid-1980s to generate maps for customers. Much of that code was adapted for use on the Internet to create the MapQuest web service

(1996: The Apache HTTP Server is introduced, an open-source web server)

(1996: 1996: Monsanto acquires Calgene)

(1996: Nokia introduces the first smartphone)

1996: Sydney Brenner founds the Molecular Sciences Institute in Berkeley

1996: Brent Townshend invents the 56K modem

(1997: Andrew Weinreich creates SixDegrees.com, the first social networking website)

(1997: US West launches the first commercial DSL service in Phoenix)

1997: Reed Hastings founds Netflix to rent videos via the Internet

1997: The XML standard for exchanging documents on the World-Wide Web is introduced

(1997: Myron Scholes of Stanford University is awarded the Nobel Prize in Economics)

1997: Steven Chu of Stanford University is awarded the Nobel Prize in Physics

1997: Evite is founded by Stanford engineering students Al Lieb and Selina Tobaccowala

(1997: The total revenues for ERP software market is $7.2 billion, with SAP, Baan, Oracle, J.D. Edwards, and PeopleSoft accounting for 62% of it)

1998: Stanford's scientist Mendel Rosenblum and others found Vmware

1998: TiVo is launched in San Francisco

1998: NuvoMedia introduces the Rocket eBook, a handheld device to read ebooks

1998: Netscape makes its browser Navigator available for free in January 1998.

1998: Chinese and Indian engineers run about 25% of Silicon Valley's high-tech businesses, accounting for $16.8 billion in sales and 58,000 jobs

1998: SoftBook Press releases the first e-book reader

1998: Saul Perlmutter's team at the Lawrence Berkeley Lab discovers that the expansion of the universe is accelerating

1998: Celera, presided by Craig Venter of "The Institute for Genomic Research" (TIGR), is established to map the human genome (and later relocated to the Bay Area)

1998: Netscape launches the open-source project "Mozilla" of Internet applications

1998: Robert Laughlin of Stanford University is awarded the Nobel Prize in Physics

1998: America Online acquires Netscape

1998: Pierre Omidyar founds eBay, a website to auction items

1998: Two Stanford students, Larry Page and Russian-born Sergey Brin, launch the search engine Google

1998: Yahoo!, Amazon, Ebay and scores of Internet-related startups create overnight millionaires

1998: Peter Thiel and Max Levchin found Confinity

(1998: Jorn Barger in Ohio coins the term "weblog" for webpages that simply contain links to other webpages)

(1998: Jim Gray creates the web mapping service TerraServer that also offers satellite images)

(1998: Bob Somerby starts "The Daily Howler," the first major political blog)

(1998: Taiwanese computer manufacturer Acer opens Acer Technology Ventures to invest in Silicon Valley startups)

(1998: Steve Mann builds the first smartwatch)

1999: A panel on "Big Data" is held at the Visualization Conference in San Francisco

1999: Camille Utterback's "Text Rain" pioneers interactive digital art

1999: Between 1998 to 1999 venture capital investments in Silicon Valley firms increases more than 90% from $3.2 billion to $6.1 billion

1999: Google has 8 employees

(1999: Total revenues for supply-chain software are $3.9 billion, with i2 owning 13% of the market)

1999: Siebel owns almost 50% of the CRM market

1999: Blogger.com allows people to create their own "blogs," or personal journals

1999: Marc Benioff founds Saleforce.com to move business applications to the Internet, pioneering cloud computing

1999: Philip Rosedale founds Linden Lab to develop virtual-reality hardware

1999: The world prepares for the new millennium amidst fears of computers glitches due to the change of date (Y2K)

(1999: The recording industry sues Shawn Fanning's Napster, a website that allows people to exchange music)

(1999: A European consortium introduces the Bluetooth wireless standard invented by Ericsson)

1999: 100 new Internet companies are listed in the US stock market

1999: The US has 250 billionaires, and thousands of new millionaires are created in just one year

(1999: Microsoft is worth 450 billion dollars, the most valued company in the world, even if it is many times smaller than General Motors, and Bill Gates is the world's richest man at $85 billion)

1999: At Home acquires Excite, the largest Internet-related merger yet

2000: The NASDAQ stock market crashes, wiping out trillions of dollars of wealth

2000: Victoria Hale, a former Genentech scientist, starts the first non-profit pharmaceutical company, the Institute for OneWorld Health

2000: Venture-capital investment in the US peaks at $99.72 billion or 1% of GDP, mostly to software (17.4%), telecommunications (15.4%), networking (10.0%) and media (9.1%)

2000: 32% of Silicon Valley's high-skilled workers are foreign-born, mostly from Asia

(2000: Software and services account for 50% of IBM's business)

2000: Daniel McFadden of UC Berkeley is awarded the Nobel Prize in Economics

2000: There are 417 public companies in Silicon Valley

2000: 10 billion e-mail messages a day are exchanged over the Internet

2000: Confinity and X.com merge to form Paypal, a system to pay online

2000: The government-funded Human Genome Project and the privately-funded Celera jointly announce that they have decoded the entire human genome

(2000: Dell has the largest share of worldwide personal computer sales)

2001: Apple launches the iPod

2001: Listen.com launches Rhapsody, a service that provides streaming on-demand access to a library of digital music

2001: KR Sridhar founds Bloom Energy to develop fuel-cell technology

2001: Nanosys is founded in 2001 to develop nanotechnology

2001: Semir Zeki founds the Institute of Neuroesthetics

2001: Joseph Stiglitz of Stanford University is awarded the Nobel Prize in Economics

2001: George Akerlof of UC Berkeley is awarded the Nobel Prize in Economics

2001: Jimmy Wales founds Wikipedia, a multilingual encyclopedia that is collaboratively edited by the Internet community

2001: Hewlett-Packard acquires Compaq

2002: Ebay acquires Paypal and Paypal cofounder Elon Musk founds SpaceX to develop space transportation

2002: Bram Cohen unveils the peer-to-peer file sharing protocol BitTorrent

2002: Sydney Brenner is awarded the Nobel Prize in Medicine

2002: Codexis is founded to develop biofuels

2002: Friendster is launched by Jonathan Abrams

(2003: Skype is founded in Europe by Niklas Zennstroem and Janus Friis to offer voice over IP, a system invented by Estonian engineers)

2003: Matt Mullenweg launches a platform for people to create their own website or blog, Wordpress

2003: Linden Lab launches "Second Life," a virtual world accessible via the Internet

2003: Amyris Biotechnologies is founded to produce renewable fuels

2003: Christopher Voigt founds a lab at UCSF to program cells like robots to perform complex tasks

2003: Martin Eberhard and Marc Tarpenning found Tesla to build electrical cars

(2003: The first synthetic biology conference is held at MIT)

2004: Mark Zuckerberg founds the social networking service Facebook at Harvard University (soon relocated to Palo Alto)

2004: Mozilla releases the browser Firefox, created by Dave Hyatt and Blake Ross

(2004: Drew Endy of MIT founds Codon Devices to commercialize synthetic biology)

2004: Oracle buys PeopleSoft

2004: Google launches a project to digitize all the books ever printed

2004: UC Berkeley establishes a Center for New Media

2004: Vinod Khosla of venture capital firm Kleiner Perkins Caufield & Byers founds Khosla Ventures to invest in green-technology companies

2005: Adobe acquires Macromedia

2005: San Jose's population of 912,332 has passed San Francisco, and San Jose is now the tenth largest city in the US

2005: Andrew Ng at Stanford launches the STAIR project (Stanford Artificial Intelligence Robot)

2005: Oracle acquires Siebel

2005: Gina Bianchini founds Ning

2005: Google launches the web mapping system Google Earth that also offers three-dimensional images of terrain

2005: More than 50% of all jobs outsourced by Silicon Valley companies go to India

2005: UCSF opens the "Institute for Human Genetics"

2005: The Letterman Digital Arts Center opens in San Francisco

(2005: Sales of notebook computers account for 53% of the computer market)

2005: Yahoo!, Google, America OnLine (AOL) and MSN (Microsoft's Network) are the four big Internet portals with a combined audience of over one billion people worldwide

2005: Silicon Valley accounts for 14% of the world's venture capital

2005: 52.4% of Silicon Valley's high-tech companies launched between 1995 and 2005 have been founded by at least one immigrant

(2005: Total revenues of ERP software are $25.5 billion, with SAP making $10.5 billion and Oracle $5.1 billion)

2005: Ebay acquires Skype

2005: Solar-energy company Solyndra is founded

2005: SUN's founder Bill Joy joins venture-capital firm Kleiner Perkins Caufield & Byers to invest in green technology

2005: Former Paypal employees Chad Hurley, Steve Chen and Jawed Karim launch YouTube

(2005: Adrian Bowyer's RepRap for 3D printing)

2006: Jack Dorsey creates the social networking service Twitter

2006: The Bay Area is the largest high-tech center in the US with 386,000 high-tech jobs

2006: YouTube is bought by Google for $1.65 billion

2006: Jay Keasling inaugurates the world's first Synthetic Biology department at the Lawrence Berkeley National Laboratory

2006: Lyndon and Peter Rive found SolarCity

2006: The first Zer01 Festival is held in San Jose

2006: Roger Kornberg of Stanford University is awarded the Nobel Prize in Chemistry, Andrew Fire of Stanford University is awarded the Nobel Prize in Medicine, and George Smoot of the Lawrence Berkeley Labs is awarded the Nobel Prize in Physics

2006: Tesla Motors introduces the Tesla Roadster, the first production automobile to use lithium-ion battery cells

2006: The World-Wide Web has 100 million websites

2006: Google acquires YouTube

2006: Walt Disney acquires Pixar

2006: Scott Hassan founds Willow Garage to manufacturer robots for domestic use

2007: 48% of Apple's revenues come from sales of the iPod

(2007: Safaricom launches the mobile payment system M-Pesa in Kenya)

2007: Apple launches the iPhone

2007: Forrester Research estimates that online retail sales in the US reached $175 billion

2007: The biotech company iZumi Bio is founded to develop products based on stem-cell research

2007: The biotech company iPierian is founded to develop products based on cellular reprogramming

2007: The world's largest vendors of personal computers are HP, Dell, Taiwan's Acer, China's Lenovo and Japan's Toshiba

(2007: Knome introduces the first commercially available human genome sequencing)

2008: The Silicon Valley has 2.4 million (less than 1% of the U.S.'s population) generating more than 2% of the U.S.'s GDP, with a GDP per person of $83,000

2008: Microsoft Windows owns almost 90% of the operating system market for personal computers, while Google owns almost 70% of the Internet search market

2008: For a few months San Francisco issues marriage license to same-sex couples

2008: Venture capitalists invest $4 billion into green-tech startups in 2008, which is almost 40% of all US investments in high-tech

2008: Taiwanese conglomerate Quanta invests into Silicon Valley startups Tilera and Canesta

2008: Hewlett-Packard purchases Electronic Data Systems in a shift towards services

2008: Airbnb is founded in San Francisco

2008: There are 261 public companies in Silicon Valley

2008: 20% of smartphones in the world use an operating system made in Silicon Valley (Symbian 47%, Blackberry 20%, Windows 12%)

(2009: Satoshi Nakamoto introduces the digital currency Bitcoin)

2009: Oracle buys SUN

2009: Travis Kalanick and Garrett Camp launch the smartphone app Uber

2009: Google's market value is more than $140 billion

2009: BitTorrent accounts for at least 20% of all Internet traffic

2009: Facebook has 150 million users in January and grows by about one million users a day, the fastest product ever to reach that many users in five years

2009: President Barack Obama appoints Steve Chu, director of the Lawrence Berkeley Laboratory, to be Secretary of Energy

2009: Tesla Motors obtains a $465-million loan from the US government to build the Model S, a battery-powered sports sedan

2009: Elizabeth Blackburn of UCSF shares the Nobel prize in Medicine and Oliver Williamson of UC Berkeley shares the Nobel prize in Economics

2009: Thomas Siebel founds energy startup C3 LLC

2009: Xerox purchases Affiliated Computer Services in a shift towards services

2009: Microsoft is the largest software company in the world with revenues of $50 billion, followed by IBM with $22 billion, Oracle with $17.5 billion, SAP with $11.6 billion, Nintendo with $7.2 billion, HP with $6.2 billion, Symantec with $5.6 billion, Activision Blizzard with $4.6 billion, Electronic Arts with $4.2 billion, Computer Associates with $3.9 billion, and Adobe with $3.3 billion.

2010: Google is worth $180 billion

2010: YouTube broadcasts the Indian Premier League of cricket live worldwide

2010: Apple is worth $205 billion, third in the US after Exxon and Microsoft

2010: HP purchases Palm, a struggling smartphone maker

2010: The Lawrence Livermore National Laboratory plans to simulate the nuclear fusion of a star (more than 100 million degrees Celsius, hotter than the center of the sun) with the world's most powerful laser, called the National Ignition Facility

2010: Microsoft's IE has 59.9% of the browser market, followed by Firefox with 24.5% and Google Chrome with 6.7%

2010: Apple introduces the tablet computer iPad that sells one million units in less than one month

2010: SAP buys Sybase

2010: The smarphone market grows 55% in 2010, with 269 million units sold worldwide

2010: Craig Venter and Hamilton Smith reprogram a bacterium's DNA

2010: Facebook has 500 million users

2011: Apple's Siri

2012: Pinterest becomes the third largest social network in the USA, surpassing LinkedIn and Tagged

2012: Facebook goes public, the biggest high-tech IPO in history

2012: SpaceX launches the first commercial flight to the International Space Station

2012: Jennifer Doudna 's CRISPR-cas9 genome editing technique

2013: 92% of smartphones in the world use an operating system made in Silicon Valley (Android 75%, iOS 17%, Windows 3%, Blackberry 3%, Symbian less than 1%)

(2013: Microsoft buys Nokia's mobile-phone business)

2013: 61.5% of traffic on the Web is not human

2013: 90% of the world's data have been created in the last two years

2013: Worldwide sales of smartphones pass one billion units, while sales of personal computers decline by 9.8%

2014: Facebook has 1.3 billion members, Google owns 68% of the searches in the USA and more than 90% in Europe, Amazon owns more than 50% of the book market in the USA, LinkedIn has 300 million members, Alibaba controls 80% of e-commerce in China

2014: Facebook acquires Oculus (virtual reality)

2014: Google acquires DeepMind (artificial intelligence)

2015: There are 144 unicorns with a total value of $505 billion in the USA

2015: 224.3 million tablets are shipped in 2015, a decline of 8% from 2014

2016: Alphabet (Google) passes Apple to become the most valuable company in the world ($558 billion vs $535 billion in January)

2016: Niantic and Nintendo introduce the augmented-reality game Pokermon Go

2016: For the first time more users around the world are accessing the internet from mobile devices than from desktop computers

2016: Tesla`s Gigafactory to produce battery cell opens in Nevada

Bibliography

Note:
As a side note to this bibliography, Wikipedia turned out to be the worst possible source. Most of its articles are simply press releases from public-relationship departments, with all the omissions and distortions that they deem appropriate for their business strategies. On the other hand, vintage magazines and newspapers were an invaluable source of information and analysis. If websites like Wikipedia are going to replace the magazines and newspapers of the past, the loss to scholarship will be colossal: the most persistent marketing department (or fan) will decide what information will be available to future generations.

Too many books written about Silicon Valley rely heavily on interviews with the "protagonists" (or presumed such). Having written several "history" books, my experience is that interviews with the protagonists are not (at all) a good way to assess what truly happened. The protagonists generally hold a biased view of the events, and sometimes just don't remember well (dates, places, names).

More information, a photographic tour and biographies of many individuals mentioned in this book can be found at www.scaruffi.com

BIBLIOGRAPHY

Bardini, Thierry. Bootstrapping: Douglas Engelbart, Coevolution, and the Origins of Personal Computing. Stanford CA: Stanford University Press, 2000.

Bell, Daniel: "The Coming of Post-industrial Society" (1973)

Berlin, Leslie: "The Man Behind the Microchip"

Blank, Steve. Hidden in Plain Sight: The Secret History of Silicon Valley: website, 2009.

Campbell-Kelly, Martin & William Aspray. Computer: A History of The Information Machine, Second Edition. New York: Westview Press, 2004.

Ceruzzi, Paul E. A History of Modern Computing (2nd Edition). Cambridge: MIT Press, 2003.

Chandler, Alfred D., Jr. Inventing the Electronic Century: The Epic Story of the Consumer Electronics and Computer Science Industries. New York: Free Press, 2001.

Englisch-Lueck, Jan. Cultures@SiliconValley. Stanford: Stanford UP, 2002.

Flamm, Kenneth. Creating the Computer: Government, Industry, and High Technology. Washington, DC: Brookings, 1988.

Freiberger, Paul & Michael Swaine. Fire in the Valley: The Making of the Personal Computer, Collector's Edition. New York: McGraw Hill, 1999.

Hanson, Dirk. The New Alchemists: Silicon Valley and the Microelectronics Revolution. Boston: Little, Brown & Co., 1982.

Kaplan, David A. The Silicon Boys and their Valley of Dreams. New York: Perennial, 2000.

Katz, Barry: "Make It New - A History of Silicon Valley Design" (MIT Press, 2015)

Kenney, Martin. Understanding Silicon Valley: the Anatomy of an Entrepreneurial Region. Stanford: Stanford UP, 2000.

Lecuyer, Christophe. Making Silicon Valley: innovation and the growth of high tech, 1930-1970. Cambridge, MA: MIT Press, 2006.

Lee, Chong-Moon, William F. Miller, et al. The Silicon Valley edge: a habitat for innovation and entrepreneurship. Stanford: Stanford University Press, 2000.

Leslie, Stuart W. The Cold War and American Science: The Military-Industrial-Academic Complex at MIT and Stanford. New York: Columbia UP, 1993.

Levy, Stephen: "Hackers - Heroes of the Computer Revolution" (1984)

Lojek, Bo. History of semiconductor engineering. New York: Springer, 2006.

Markoff, John. What the Dormouse Said: How the Sixties Counterculture Shaped the Personal Computer Industry. New York: Penguin, 2005.

Morgan, Jane Electronics in the West: The First Fifty Years. Palo Alto, CA: National Press Books, 1967.

Negroponte, Nicolas: "Being Digital" (1995)

Pellow, David & Lisa Park. The Silicon Valley of Dreams: Environmental Injustice, Immigrant Workers, and the High-Tech Global Economy. New York: NYU Press, 2002.

Perry, William: "My Journey at the Nuclear Brink" (Stanford Security Studies, 2016)

Rheingold, Howard: "The Virtual Community" (1993)

Riordan, Michael & Lillian Hoddeson. Crystal Fire: The Birth of the Information Age. New York: Norton, 1997.

Roszak, Theodore: "From Satori to Silicon Valley" (Frisco Press, 1986)

Rowen, Henry, et al. "Making IT: The Rise of Asia in High Tech." Stanford: Stanford UP, 2006.

Saxenian, AnnaLee. Local and Global Networks of Immigrant Professionals in Silicon Valley. San Francisco: Public Policy Institute of California, 2002.

Saxenian, AnnaLee. Regional Advantage: Culture and Competition in Silicon Valley and Route 128. Cambridge, MA: Harvard University Press, 1994.

Schwartz, Peter et al: "The Long Boom" (1999)

Thackray, Arnold & Brock, David: "Moore's Law" (Basic Books, 2015)

Toffler, Alvin: "The Third Wave" (Morrow, 1980)

Turner, Fred. From Counterculture to Cyberculture: Stewart Brand, the Whole Earth Network, and the Rise of Digital Utopianism. Chicago: U. of Chicago Press, 2008.

Vance, Ashlee. Geek Silicon Valley: The Inside Guide to Palo Alto, Stanford, Menlo Park, Mountain View, Santa Clara, Sunnyvale, San Jose, San Francisco. Guilford, CT: Globe Pequot Press, 2007.

Wolfson, Todd: "Digital Rebellion - The Birth of the Cyber Left" (Univ of Illinois Press, 2014)

Yost, Jeffrey. The Computer Industry. Santa Barbara, CA: Greenwood Press, 2005.

Zhang, Junfu & Nikesh Patel. The Dynamics of California's Biotechnology Industry. San Francisco: Public Policy Institute of California, 2005.

Bibliography

Zook, Matthew A. The Geography of the Internet Industry: Venture Capital, Dot-Coms, and Local Knowledge. Malden, MA: Blackwell Pub., 2002.

Alphabetical Index

www.ingramcontent.com/pod-product-compliance
Lightning Source LLC
Chambersburg PA
CBHW051847170526
45168CB00001B/14